New Richmond:

A History of the Best Little Town on Earth

Phyllis Ann Waye Boone

Cathartes Press, 2016

Copyright 2016 Phyllis Ann Waye Boone

All Rights Reserved

ISBN: 978-1-944774-04-2

First e-book edition 2016, Cathartes Press

Map of New Richmond: Image courtesy of Ball State University Libraries' GIS Research and Map Collection in the Digital Media Repository; originally published in *Standard Atlas of Montgomery County of 1917*.

Contents

Contents 5
List of Photographs 9
Editorial Note 11
Dedication 13
Map 15
Chapter 1 - Historical Setting 1
    Natural Wealth of New Richmond and Coal Creek Township 1
    The Animal Kingdom 1
    Our Feathered Friends 3
    Our Early Inhabitants - Mound Builders and American Indians 4
    Pioneer Families 7
Chapter 2 - Early Business 19
    The Pioneer Village of New Richmond 19
    Assorted Business Enterprises 20
    Frame Business Buildings in New Richmond—Most of them now gone 22
    The Brick Buildings in New Richmond 23
Chapter 3 - Food Businesses in New Richmond 28
    General Stores 28
    New Richmond Grocers 39
    Meat Markets and Butchers 44
    New Richmond Frozen Food Locker Service 47
    The Bakery Business in New Richmond 47
    Drug Stores & Druggists 48
Chapter 4 - Clothing & Beauty Services 53
    New Richmond's Clothing Stores 53
    Tailors 54
    Dressmakers and Seamstresses 55
    Milliners and Their Trimmers 55
    Shoemakers & Shoe Stores 57
    Beauty Salons 58
    Barbers—Tonsorial Artists Invade the Town 60
Chapter 5 - Hospitality & Entertainment Businesses 63
    Restaurants 63
    New Richmond's Saloons 65
    Temperance Causes 69
    Hostels & Boarding Houses 71
    Hotels 71
    Pool Rooms 75
    Bookstores and Lending Libraries 76
    Bowling Alleys 76
Chapter 6 - Builders & The Housing Industry 79
    Carpenters - Builders of Our Homes 79

    Painters and Decorators 81
    Plumbers and Tinners 82
    The Tile and Brick Industry 83
    The Lumber Industry—From Sawmills to Lumberyards 88
    Hardware Merchants 91
    Furniture Stores 96
    The Village Blacksmiths 96

Chapter 7 - Farming, Husbandry, & Livestock Businesses 103
    Livery Stables and Hostlers 103
    Horses, Horse Breeders, Trainers, Races, Shows, Etc. 105
    Livestock Buyers and Shippers 109
    Draymen—Teamsters—Truckers 111
    Poultry Dealers 111
    Phillip Dewey's Deer and Elk Park 112
    Farm Implement Dealers 113
    Harness Makers and Harness Shops 114
    Threshing Machines and Rings 114
    Grist Mills and Elevators 116
    Bee Keepers 123
    The Ice Harvest 124
    The Dairy Industry 126
    Automobile Repair Shops 128
    Gas and Oil Products Agents in New Richmond 129
    New Richmond Canning Company 131
    Factories 134

Chapter 8 - Cemeteries in the New Richmond Vicinity 139
    The New Richmond Cemetery 139
    Forbes Cemetery 141
    Park Cemetery 141

Chapter 9 - Churches 142
    Methodists in Coal Creek Township 142
    The New Richmond Christian Church 151

Chapter 10 - Schools 163
    Pioneer and Log Schools of Coal Creek Township 163
    District School Buildings in Coal Creek Township 165
    J.J. Insley as School Teacher 166
    Coal Creek Township District School Histories 167

Chapter 11 - Banks and Bankers 191
    The New Richmond Bank 191
    The Corn Exchange Bank 192
    The New Richmond Building Loan Fund and Savings Association 195
    New Richmond Branch of Linden State Bank 197

Chapter 12 - New Richmond's Newspapers 199
    New Richmond *Times* 199
    New Richmond *News* 200
    New Richmond *Enterprise* 200
    The New Richmond *Record* 201
    The *Farmers Review* 203

Chapter 13 - Post Office and Rural Mail Carriers 206
    Rural Mail Carriers 208

Rural Free Delivery 209
New Richmond Rural Mail Carriers 209

Chapter 14 - Ghost Towns and Place Names of Coal Creek Township 211
Boston Store or Elmdale 211
Bristle Ridge 214
Center 217
Mount Pleasant 219
Round Hill 220
Asbury Chapel Methodist Episcopal Church 220
The Last Festival 223
Place Names and Corners 227

Chapter 15 - Government 229
The Origin of Coal Creek Township 229
Justice of the Peace in Coal Creek Township 229
Constables in the New Richmond Area 230
Notary Publics 231
Original Town of New Richmond and Additions 232
New Richmond Becomes an Incorporated Town 234
Town Officials 237
Town Hall 244
Town Marshals 245
New Richmond Jail Houses 248
Volunteer Fire Department 248
Trustees of Coal Creek Township 253

Chapter 16 - Politics 255
Early Political Meetings 255
Captain Edward T. McCrea - State Representative, 1894-1898 255
Charles Kirkpatrick - State Representative, 1902 256
Robert M. Thayer - Montgomery County Commissioner 257

Chapter 17 - Professional Life 259
Physicians of New Richmond and Coal Creek Township, With Dates They Practiced 259
The Dental Profession 278
Veterinarians 280
Undertakers 281

Chapter 18 - Entertainment and Social Organizations 283
Meharry's Grove—"The Garden Spot of Indiana" 283
Old Settler's Meetings 284
Glorious Fourth of July Celebrations 285
How Grandma and Grandpa Spent Their Evenings 286
Charivari 288
Music, Music, Music 288
Social Life in New Richmond 293
The New Richmond Comedy Company 298
Sam Bayliss' Big Sensation Show 299
Moving Picture Theaters 303
Secret Societies 305

Chapter 19 - The Horse Thief Detective Company 309
Minute Men Were Number One! 309

Chapter 20 - Noted Personalities 315
William Samuel Gaither - President, Drexel University 315

    George R. Holmes 316
    Glen Mitchell, Noted Artist..319
Chapter 21 - Transportation 323
    Pioneer Transportation 323
    Roads in Coal Creek Township 323
    The Little Yard Wide 326
    Excursions..334
    New Richmond's Depot 335
    The Automobile Comes to New Richmond..337
    Interurbans in New Richmond 345
    Aviation Fever Strikes the Town of New Richmond..348
Chapter 22 - Utilities 353
    Gasoline Arc Light Plants..353
    Electricity Comes to New Richmond 353
    New Richmond's Telephone Companies 356
    Cable Television 361
    New Richmond Water Works 361
Chapter 23 - Hollywood Comes to "Hickory, IN" 365
Sources 368
    Chapter 1 – Historical setting..368
    Chapter 2 – Buildings in New Richmond 369
    Chapter 3 – Food Businesses in New Richmond 370
    Chapter 4 – Clothing and Beauty Services 371
    Chapter 5 – Hospitality & Entertainment Businesses 372
    Chapter 6 – Builders & The Housing Industry 373
    Chapter 7 – Farming, Husbandry, & Livestock Businesses..375
    Chapter 10 – Schools...378
    Chapter 17 – Professional Life..378
    Chapter 18 – Entertainment and Social Organizations 379
    Chapter 21 – Transportation 379
Index.. 380

List of Photographs

1 - George F. Long's building 23
2 - Hollin Opera House 24
3 - George W. Washburn block 24
4 - Starr Dunn's tin shop 24
5 - AD Snyder building in 1985 (on left). Queensware display inside AD Snyder Hardware in 1902 (on right). 25
6 - Knights of Pythias building 25
7 - View of New Richmond taken from the Union Elevator - Black Bear Hotel in center of photo, livery stable across street. Upper left of photo is A.D. Snyder building. To right of this is Washburn block and Shotts' buggy factory 26
8 - Street scene looking south, taken before 1910 27
9 - Street scene looking west, taken before 1910 27
10 - Aloys Anton, tailor 30
11 - Frank Perkins' General Store 32
12 - George C. Livingston in his grocery 42
13 - John Utterback, L.P. Brown, Benjamin Rabourn, and Jefferson Waye 46
14 - Temperance Parade March 1909 70
15 - Black Bear Hotel 72
16 - New Richmond Park Shelter House 87
17 - Shotts & Cox's Carriage Repair Shop, Painting, Horse Shoeing, and General Blacksmithing. Date Unknown. 99
18 - Dick Shotts in his blacksmith shop 100
19 - Phillip Dewey's Deer and Elk Park 112
20 - Phillip Dewey's Deer and Elk Park 112
21 - Union Elevator (also known as Haywood & Detchon, Furr & Cohee, and Farm Bureau Elevators) 118
22 - Parlon Elevator (also known as New Richmond Farm Supply and Montgomery County Co-Op Elevator) 122
23 - Metal grain storage bins, New Richmond Farm Supply 122
24 - Thayer and Geiger Standard Service 131
25 - Surplus Electric Company. Photo taken in 1930s or 1940s. F.E. Drysdale sitting at desk left front; Maurice Coffman standing second from right by window. 136
26 - Round Hill Methodist Episcopal Church 146
27 - Log Church 1848 - 1873 151
28 - On right, 1888 building. Top left, 1921 building. 156
29 - Womanless Wedding – 1922 or 1923 159
30 - New Richmond Christian Church parsonage 160
31 - Walnut Grove School, District No. 1, Coal Creek Township. 168
32 - The Mug Wump School, completed October 1887 170
33 - Second brick school building, completed in 1894 171
34 - New Richmond school building with students and faculty. Photo take December 12, 1913. Note the former Christian Church building in the background. 173
35 - Center School, District No. 7, Coal Creek Township. Copy of Reuben Swank's photo, used by permission. 179
36 - Coal Creek Central School 189
37 - New Richmond Branch, Linden State Bank 197
38 - William F. Hockett 207
39 - New Richmond Post Office in 1986 207
40 - New Richmond's town hall, built 1970 244
41 - Capt. Edward T. McCrea and his Civil War rifle 256
42 - At left, "Quiatenon" - former residence of Charles Kirkpatrick. At right, old carriage house of Kirkpatrick residence. 257
43 - Dr. Stowe S. Detchon residence 269
44 - Office of Dr. Hurschell D. Kindell 271
45 - Dr. George Manners residence 273
46 - Office of Dr. D. Manners Washburn 276

47 - Dr. D. Manners Washburn residence 276
48 - Office of Dr. Charles Edward Kelsey 278
49 - Coal Creek covered bridge 283
50 - Samuel "Doc" Bayliss' Big Sensation Show Wagons. Photo taken in front of Glen Pierce's residence south of New
    Richmond near Round Hill 299
51 - Glen Mitchell as a budding artist 319
52 - Glen Mitchell in his New York studio 319
53 - New Richmond depot - Clover Leaf Railroad, circa 1924 336
54 - Edgar and Jessie (Ebrite) Jones and their EMF Studebaker, manufactured from 1909-1913 at a cost of $1,250 344
55 - Forrest Waye (at right) guarding the airplane of William Fife Jones 349
56 - Tri-County Telephone Company business office 360
57 - New Richmond water tower 363
58: Clockwise from top left: Filming a New Richmond street scene; filming Gene Hackman driving; filming a victory 367

List of Photographs

1 - George F. Long's building 23
2 - Hollin Opera House 24
3 - George W. Washburn block 24
4 - Starr Dunn's tin shop 24
5 - AD Snyder building in 1985 (on left). Queensware display inside AD Snyder Hardware in 1902 (on right). 25
6 - Knights of Pythias building 25
7 - View of New Richmond taken from the Union Elevator - Black Bear Hotel in center of photo, livery stable across street. Upper left of photo is A.D. Snyder building. To right of this is Washburn block and Shotts' buggy factory 26
8 - Street scene looking south, taken before 1910 27
9 - Street scene looking west, taken before 1910 27
10 - Aloys Anton, tailor 30
11 - Frank Perkins' General Store 32
12 - George C. Livingston in his grocery 42
13 - John Utterback, L.P. Brown, Benjamin Rabourn, and Jefferson Waye 46
14 - Temperance Parade March 1909 70
15 - Black Bear Hotel 72
16 - New Richmond Park Shelter House 87
17 - Shotts & Cox's Carriage Repair Shop, Painting, Horse Shoeing, and General Blacksmithing. Date Unknown. 99
18 - Dick Shotts in his blacksmith shop 100
19 - Phillip Dewey's Deer and Elk Park 112
20 - Phillip Dewey's Deer and Elk Park 112
21 - Union Elevator (also known as Haywood & Detchon, Furr & Cohee, and Farm Bureau Elevators) 118
22 - Parlon Elevator (also known as New Richmond Farm Supply and Montgomery County Co-Op Elevator) 122
23 - Metal grain storage bins, New Richmond Farm Supply 122
24 - Thayer and Geiger Standard Service 131
25 - Surplus Electric Company. Photo taken in 1930s or 1940s. F.E. Drysdale sitting at desk left front; Maurice Coffman standing second from right by window. 136
26 - Round Hill Methodist Episcopal Church 146
27 - Log Church 1848 - 1873 151
28 - On right, 1888 building. Top left, 1921 building. 156
29 - Womanless Wedding – 1922 or 1923 159
30 - New Richmond Christian Church parsonage 160
31 - Walnut Grove School, District No. 1, Coal Creek Township. 168
32 - The Mug Wump School, completed October 1887 170
33 - Second brick school building, completed in 1894 171
34 - New Richmond school building with students and faculty. Photo take December 12, 1913. Note the former Christian Church building in the background. 173
35 - Center School, District No. 7, Coal Creek Township. Copy of Reuben Swank's photo, used by permission. 179
36 - Coal Creek Central School 189
37 - New Richmond Branch, Linden State Bank 197
38 - William F. Hockett 207
39 - New Richmond Post Office in 1986 207
40 - New Richmond's town hall, built 1970 244
41 - Capt. Edward T. McCrea and his Civil War rifle 256
42 - At left, "Quiatenon" - former residence of Charles Kirkpatrick. At right, old carriage house of Kirkpatrick residence. 257
43 - Dr. Stowe S. Detchon residence 269
44 - Office of Dr. Hurschell D. Kindell 271
45 - Dr. George Manners residence 273
46 - Office of Dr. D. Manners Washburn 276

47 - Dr. D. Manners Washburn residence 276
48 - Office of Dr. Charles Edward Kelsey 278
49 - Coal Creek covered bridge 283
50 - Samuel "Doc" Bayliss' Big Sensation Show Wagons. Photo taken in front of Glen Pierce's residence south of New Richmond near Round Hill 299
51 - Glen Mitchell as a budding artist 319
52 - Glen Mitchell in his New York studio 319
53 - New Richmond depot - Clover Leaf Railroad, circa 1924 336
54 - Edgar and Jessie (Ebrite) Jones and their EMF Studebaker, manufactured from 1909-1913 at a cost of $1,250 344
55 - Forrest Waye (at right) guarding the airplane of William Fife Jones 349
56 - Tri-County Telephone Company business office 360
57 - New Richmond water tower 363
58: Clockwise from top left: Filming a New Richmond street scene; filming Gene Hackman driving; filming a victory 367

Editorial Note

This book has been a long time in the making.

My grandparents were lovers of history and nature. My grandmother, Phyllis Ann Waye Boone, worked on this book for a greater part of her life. My mother remembers as a teenager her mom researching and typing into the late hours. One of her memories is helping her mother type the masters for the mimeograph for the history of the New Richmond Christian Church for an anniversary homecoming celebration. This was the year my mom took typing! Another one is of going with her parents to interview Gaylord Tribby on family and town memories.

Grandma worked on this book throughout my childhood also. She had to put it on the back burner several times. Work was put on hold once due to my grandfather, Albert John Boone, Jr., being diagnosed with colon cancer. Throughout his surgery, remission, and recurrence, she sporadically worked on it. During that time, the film *Hoosiers* was being filmed in New Richmond and my grandparents were greatly involved with the crew and the pre-filming arrangements.

After my grandfather's death, my father, Roger Cain, offered to start putting her book on computer in preparation to take it to R.R. Donnelley to have printed. I remember going to Donnelley with them to talk to someone about correct formatting. While Dad was in the middle of the file conversion, Grandma was given many more copies of the New Richmond *Record*—one of the newspapers where she gleaned much of her information. They put that project on hold, as she had to revise many of her chapters.

Then work was again put on hold as her oldest daughter Bonnie was diagnosed with cancer. After surgery and treatments, more work. Her youngest daughter Cindy and her partner Dennis Bucholtz gave her a computer. Grandma started doing her revisions on that, which made it much easier to revise and edit. My aunt Bonnie was again diagnosed with cancer, and between doctor visits, Grandma faithfully worked on the history.

All but the *Hoosiers* chapter was finished when Grandma herself was diagnosed with cancer. Her goal of finishing the book helped her through the difficult days. I am privileged to be the vehicle to get her dream finished and into the public.

A childhood spent listening to her stories instilled in me an early love of history, and years of watching her at the typewriter encouraged me to pursue my own writing, which is probably why I took my Bachelor of Arts at Purdue University with a double major of History and Creative Writing.

One of my great regrets is that I didn't complete my editorial work on this book while Grandma Phyl was still living, but in the years since Phyllis Boone's death on March 2, 2001, technology has advanced enough to make it easy to self-publish a book of such localized interest.

Her accounts and painstaking lists will prove invaluable to genealogists and local historians and interest anyone whose family spent time in New Richmond.

I have done my best to leave unaltered my grandmother's narrative voice, and in most cases I have not attempted to extend the history beyond her research in 1986.

What follows is a detailed and thoroughly-researched history of New Richmond, Indiana. But it is also a personal account, filled with my family's stories from the earliest founding of the town by an ancestor on Phyllis' side, to Forrest Waye's oral history recollections, to my grandmother's own experiences of life in New Richmond—the Best Little Town on Earth.

I hope you enjoy it.

Stephanie A. Cain
Colfax, Indiana
July 30, 2016

Dedication

I dedicate this book to many people.

First to my father, Forrest Waye, whose interesting and sometimes humorous stories of New Richmond inspired me to search deeper for more information on the town of New Richmond in its early years. I was born and lived in New Richmond all of my life and wanted to record these and other stories that I found so that other people who lived there could enjoy them as much as I did. I spent most of my adult life researching this book, and the journey took me to many places.

To my mother, Vera Jane Ebrite Waye, and her ancestors who settled in and around New Richmond and Coal Creek Township.

To my three daughters Bonnie, Janice, and Cynthia, for being so patient while I was pounding on the old Underwood typewriter late into the night typing my notes.

Thanks to my granddaughter, Stephanie A. Cain, daughter Janice Cain and her husband Roger Cain, daughter Cynthia Boone, and Dennis Bucholtz for their dedication in scanning, retyping, editing, and completing this book. Their help and interest in seeing this project to its final form made me realize the importance of my life's work.

Also thanks to the Crawfordsville District Public Library staff and the elected officials and staff of the Montgomery County Courthouse for helping me with my research.

Phyllis Ann Waye Boone

Map

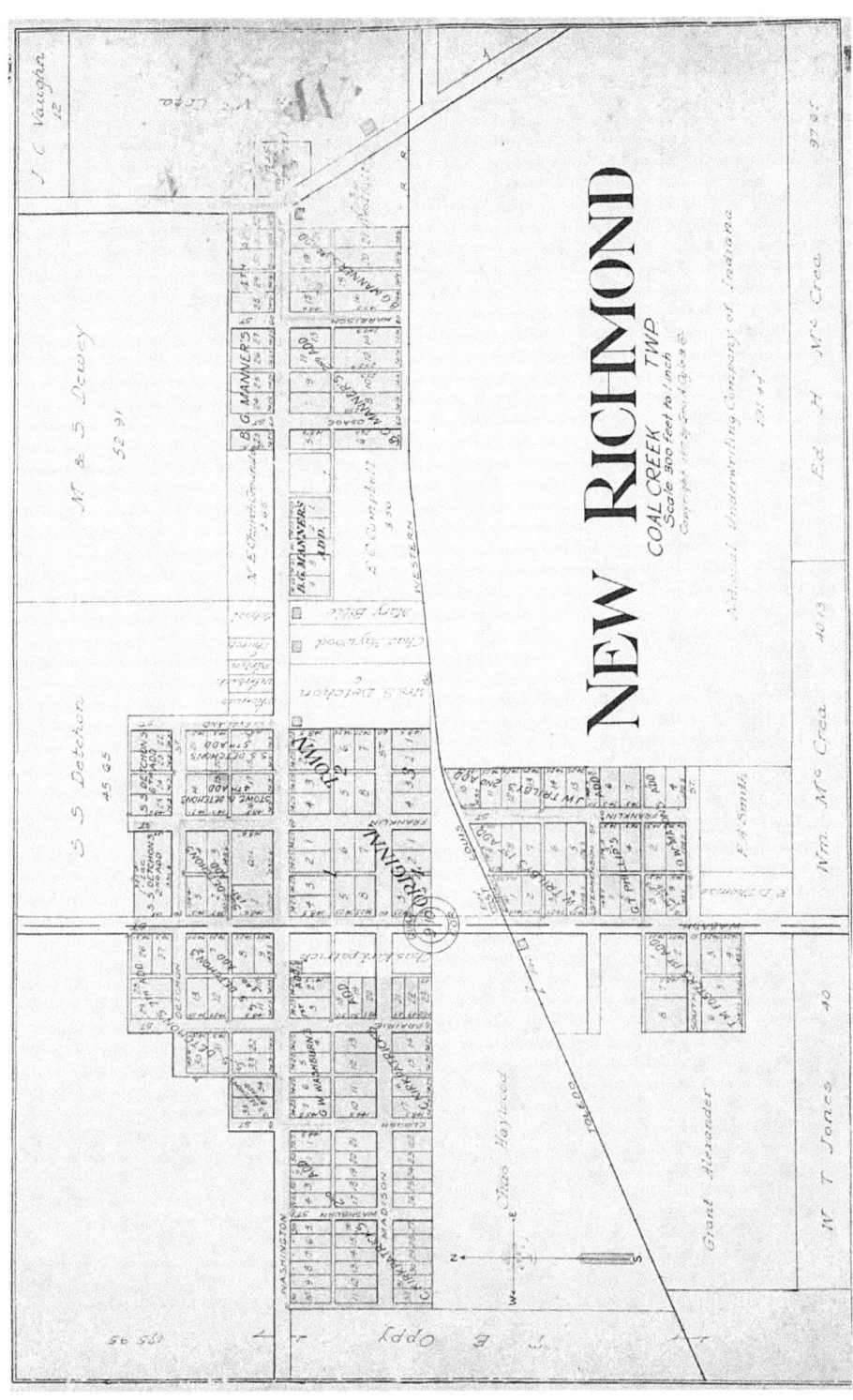

Chapter 1 - Historical Setting

Natural Wealth of New Richmond and Coal Creek Township

One year before Montgomery County was organized, the territory was surveyed. On March 22, 1822, Edward Tiffan, Surveyor General, listed the following trees in the Original Plat Book of Coal Creek Township, Montgomery County, Indiana: black oak, hickory, white oak, jack oak, elm, sassafras, walnut, and poplar. He failed to list the many native maples, the silver and hard, or sugar, variety that were still producing large quantities of maple syrup each spring. Dr. George Manners, the local physician, made maple syrup each year at his "camp" just at the south edge of New Richmond, and after his death, Jim Tribby continued to run this camp for many years. Paw-paw trees were also abundant, and paw-paws and sassafras roots were both collected and considered legal tender in New Richmond stores.

I have always felt that the timber census and sizes of the timber in Coal Creek Township and neighboring townships were underestimated in the various records, because in my recollections of the spring and summer months in New Richmond, the sound of dynamite first comes to mind. All summer long the farmers were continuously blasting out trees and stumps, clearing away more forests to make larger fields to farm. The very large logs were then loaded onto wagons—and, much later, trucks—and hauled to the nearest sawmill or to the railroad to be shipped to parts unknown. These were not little "scrub" trees either—they were huge, solid, beautiful trees. My grandmother, Fannie Patton Ebrite, said the Ebrite Farm just south of New Richmond was a solid forest from the town to the Ebrite homestead, three-fourths of a mile south. Across the road on the east side was more heavy timber. Northeast of New Richmond, Montgomery's Woods were full of very large timber. This timber stood until the 1950s or 1960s, before they started cutting it. West of New Richmond stood large tracts of timber; they too have been destroyed.

The Crawfordsville Saturday Evening *Journal* noted on February 7, 1885, "The prairie farmers are transplanting sugar and walnut trees. They grow fast and the farmers will realize a handsome reward. This should be encouraged in all localities."

The Animal Kingdom

The American Bison, or buffalo, disappeared long before the early settlers arrived, and have not returned. The once-abundant white-tailed deer, timber wolves, wildcats, lynx, marten, and coyote were hunted out very early in Montgomery County, but recently, the deer returned in large numbers. Coyotes and beavers are also becoming more common. Groundhogs, skunks (pole-cats), muskrats, and raccoon continue to survive in the area. Weasels and red foxes are not quite as abundant as they were in the early days. The men of Coal Creek Township used to hold fox hunts regularly. It has been said that the local dentist, Dr. Melvin J. Roth, was always so eager to go fox hunting that he would take off at the first mention of the word "fox," sometimes leaving his tools in the patient's mouth. As many as two hundred men, women, and children have been known to go on these hunts.

Bears frequently carried away young pigs, sheep, and other small livestock in the very early settlement of Coal Creek Township. In the winter of 1830, a black bear was discovered in the Elmdale neighborhood. The excitement disrupted school being held in a log house on the property of Edward Bennett. The whole school and community joined in the bear chase. Thomas Daisey's dogs were knocked head-over-heels by this bear. It ran up a white oak tree and was shot by George Allhands, a mile and three-quarters northeast of Elmdale. The writer for the Crawfordsville *Review* said he ate some of the bear, the first—and last—he had ever eaten (that he knew of). In March 1888, a bear had been hiding out for some time in Adam Walker's woods near Patton's Corner. It finally made its way to Parke County, after being pursued, and was shot by William Carmichal.

George Cloud was the veteran opossum hunter of New Richmond. He filled all the orders that were placed with him for those who had acquired a taste for opossum meat. He fattened half a dozen or more for Christmas dinner by feeding them pumpkins; he said, "they do well and get fat as hogs on that diet." Jefferson Waye, my grandfather, tanned possum hides and made little coin purses from them as an added source of income to his farming.

Rabbits were everywhere; the men in and around New Richmond who preferred hunting as a means of livelihood had no trouble finding "cottontails." In 1883 it was noted that "civilization with fancy guns and hunting dogs, [*sic*] couldn't even diminish the rabbits of the great Shawnee prairie." I should note that the prairie was the territory bordering New Richmond on the north; it extended east and west for several miles—as far as the eye could see.

Rabbits were hunted by large hunting parties and killed by the thousands. Butchered and traded in neighboring towns, they were also packed in barrels and sent east to big cities such as Baltimore, Boston, and New York City, in trade for oysters—a delicacy that former easterners in Montgomery County were finding it difficult to live without. Looking at the town history, one might almost believe the main purpose of the railways was to get these oysters to the new western towns. Easterners, of course, considered the western rabbits as much the same sort of delicacy. Church groups formed hunting parties into the 1920s to make money by hunting and selling rabbits to purchase oysters for their suppers. It has been reported that it took about fifteen barrels of rabbits for one gallon of oysters. The rabbits were frozen in winter and shipped in barrels on the railroad. I think New Richmond residents got the short end of the stick on this deal.

Among the reptiles in the early days were three varieties of rattlesnake: the large rattlesnake of the woods, a smaller variety, and the prairie. The copperhead, once numerous but now rare in this area, was a constant dread. Pioneer women knew how to treat snakebite—a knowledge that was put to frequent use.

The Crawfordsville papers contained several notes regarding snakes. In 1881 Samuel Beach killed seventy rattlesnakes near Pleasant Hill (Wingate). George Jones' horse was bitten by a rattlesnake, causing a badly swollen leg, in 1888. Also in 1888, Jim Alexander found in one shock of oats seven small rattlers and one large one; the young snakes each had one rattle, and the old one had twelve. Jim killed all eight. In 1889 a man living north of New Richmond was bitten by a rattlesnake and, according to the *Review*, "a quart of whiskey saved his life." One fancier of snakes who lived in Crawfordsville, Charley Beeckler, came to New Richmond to secure two rattlers for his collection. While ditching on John Stephenson's farm in 1893, William Ulsar was bitten by a small black rattlesnake and fainted into the ditch he was digging. He was lucky enough to have been found by Jim Kross, who happened to have half a pint of cold rye and soon brought him around.

In 1895 Will Stephenson was bitten by a rattlesnake while plowing Ed Coleman's farm near Round Hill, at Linden. Stephenson had taken off his shoes and was walking behind the plow when bitten on the foot; the snake did not let go until beaten off with a club. He immediately left for Linden to see a doctor. He drank a quart of whiskey, and when two doctors arrived, they began working on him; for a time it was thought he would die as his leg was swollen twice its usual size. "The whiskey saved his life and at last account he was doing well," the *Review* reported that August.

A son of Isaac Meharry was playing in a field west of New Richmond in June 1889, when he was bitten by a rattlesnake. The use of whiskey was credited with saving his life—even children were doctored with alcohol in the early days.

While plowing up part of an old virgin bluegrass pasture east of New Richmond for W.H. Montgomery, Frank Allman killed fifty rattlers. The story was printed in the Thursday, May 26, 1904, edition of the New Richmond *Review*. On the Friday before the story ran, he killed seventeen snakes; the largest had nine rattles, making it eleven years old.

In August 1906 Captain Ed T. McCrea told the story of finding a copperhead in his hay field. As he and his large force of farm help were working in the field one Thursday, someone discovered the snake, which measured four feet and seven and a half inches in length, its body as large as a man's wrist; it was quickly killed.

Among the turtles are the snapping variety, but more common are the box turtles. When farmers were laying drain tile in their fields in the 1880s, turtles were dug out by the wagonload and fed to the hogs. On Noah Insley's farm west of New Richmond, George Cloud and Jack Garret were cutting a very long ditch, and George said the turtles he threw out were "large enough to ride."

In August 1982, while driving home from Crawfordsville, I discovered a large snapping turtle at the south end of the Coal Creek bridge. The shell alone was a foot in length, the head and neck another six inches.

Ditching the fields almost depopulated the frogs and fish that were once a good source of food for early settlers. Frog legs appeared on dinner tables frequently.

OUR FEATHERED FRIENDS

When the area now known as Coal Creek Township was created, beautiful ponds, surrounded by tall, waving, prairie grass, willow trees, and cattails, were the habitat of many wild creatures. Many of the ponds were so covered with pond lilies they appeared to be covered with a heavy snow. People from Crawfordsville and other cities came to gather these lilies for wedding parties. Having to wade a little distance did not deter them.

Several different species of wild ducks and geese visited these ponds from early March to late fall, nesting undisturbed until the white man came with his guns. The writer for the Crawfordsville *Journal* always called them "quackers and honkers," and reported their arrival and departure.

The March 31, 1881, issue of the Crawfordsville Saturday Evening *Journal* tells of a large flock of geese frightening Fred Burress, who was out in his field husking "shock" corn. He jumped from his wagon into a shock of corn because the geese were headed right toward him. It aggravated him to sit inside this shock and watch them devour all the corn he had just husked. He had no gun, nor club, nor anything to get at least one of the birds for his dinner table to pay for the corn they ate. Canada Geese still visit the ponds in the New Richmond area, and several Snow Geese have also visited some of these ponds.

Sandhill Cranes were a common bird in the New Richmond area in the early history of the town. Howard Dewey, a local resident, followed the sport of riding on his horse into large flocks of Sandhills, trying to catch them by the legs. On one occasion he almost succeeded. In 1958 I came within ten feet of a Sandhill at the New Richmond Park. This was before the park was cleared of the many willow trees and other brush. The Sandhills still fly over New Richmond on their migratory flight in spring and fall, to and from Canada.

Killdeer, a familiar species and plentiful in the early years, are still seen often in the park at New Richmond and near other ponds in the area.

For many years I have witnessed the Little Green Heron wading and diving into the ponds at the park hunting for food. The biggest thrill of all was a pair of Great Blue Herons wading around the park's baseball diamond and near the back pond in September of 1981. After several steady days of rain, the ponds had overflowed and turned the ball diamond into a shallow pool. This created an ideal spot for the various water birds to hunt for food. On December 23 that same year, a Great Blue Heron flew over the grain elevator, heading for the park ponds. It may have been one of the two previously seen.

The "Jack Snipe" was once a common visitor in the Coal Creek ponds, but had dwindled in this area by the spring of 1889. Farmers had ditched their fields and ruined the natural habitat. The writer of the Crawfordsville *Review* said in the New Richmond section for March 30, 1889, "the Jack Snipe has come—so have the hunters. For every snipe there are two hundred hunters."

Because of the tall, wild prairie grass (It was rumored that the grass seed from the Shawnee prairie was taken to Kentucky after the Battle of Tippecanoe in the saddlebags of General Harrison's soldiers and became known as Kentucky Bluegrass) and the many ponds scattered about Coal Creek Township, the prairie chicken was common near New Richmond. Just parallel to the north edge of town was a little stream that created a natural nesting place for the prairie chicken. In June 1888, parties ditching for Dr. Detchon, who owned this property, set fire to the grass. After the fire was extinguished, several nests were found full of half-roasted eggs. This reduced the prairie chicken crop that year and had some effect upon the next year's crop as well. Detchon had started ditching the sloughs on his property in 1887.

The writer for the Crawfordsville *Journal* predicted on March 12, 1881, that the prairie chicken would become extinct within five years, because of extensive hunting. Despite a game law that had been passed, there were hunters killing the young chickens and hunting out of season. He also noted that the bluebird was nearly extinct, and only an occasional one was seen even that early in the history of New Richmond.

The New Richmond "nimrods" played a joke on a Crawfordsville hunter named Charley Peters and his fellow hunters. One of them said, "they gave our town a call in search of prairie chickens. Charlie, never having seen a prairie chicken [sic] the boys had a fine time, as they killed a long-legged 'thunder Pumper' and palmed it off as an old prairie hen. Charlie said it looked like a chicken—all but the legs which he thought were rather long." The American Bittern is often referred to as the thunder pumper.

Gun clubs from Crawfordsville and Lafayette came to New Richmond each hunting season, sometimes spending a week at a time, bringing their fancy breech-loading shotguns and bird dogs. They kept returning until the prairie chickens were hunted out. The game laws were no help because they were not enforced. There was a time when a sportsman would kill fifty prairie chickens, or more, in a single day. After the law had failed and the landowners realized the prairie chicken was near extinction, they posted NO SHOOTING signs on their farms. It was too late.

In July 1890, the final realization hit both farmers and hunters—there were no prairie chickens, or hens, in the New Richmond vicinity. Hunters turned to quail (Northern Bobwhite) and rabbits to fill this lack, and by 1894 the last prairie chicken had been killed. None had been seen between 1890 and 1894.

Hunters had about as much respect for the quail laws as they did for the prairie chicken laws. As early as 1889, bird lovers were concerned about this and reported that quails were being killed off in large numbers. It was predicted then that the quail would be extinct in a short time. In January of 1893, a large number of quail succumbed to the extreme temperatures. Again in February of 1895, thousands of quail died in the New Richmond area, for lack of food and drink during one of the coldest winters anyone living at the time had ever experienced.

When I first moved into my house in 1957, an ever-present sound was the "Bob White!" call of the quail in our field. As farming practices changed, the quail's habitat of tall grasses and wheat stubble was diminished. We haven't heard a quail since 1979 or 1980. Pheasants also nested on our property each year and were here as late as 1982.

Various species of birds are still numerous, including Blue Jays, Northern Cardinals, various warblers, Indigo Buntings, Baltimore Orioles, Robins, Red-winged Blackbirds, Grackles, European Starlings, Cowbirds, American Crows, Pigeons, various sparrows, Slate-colored Juncos, Brown Thrashers, Cedar Waxwings, assorted woodpeckers, Screech Owls, House Wrens, Goldfinches, Titmice, Chickadees, Meadowlarks, Horned Larks, Turkey Vultures, Red-tailed Hawks, Kestrels, Swifts, Barn and Bank Swallows, Purple Martins, Mockingbirds, and hummingbirds.

OUR EARLY INHABITANTS - MOUND BUILDERS AND AMERICAN INDIANS

The earliest inhabitants, and the culture and history of these mysterious people, may never be recorded by those who have studied anthropology and archaeology, for all the remains in Montgomery County, when discovered, were hauled off to places unknown. The study of these remains and artifacts, and the answers as to their age and possible race were never revealed to interested parties in the county.

Beckwith, in his *History of Montgomery County, Indiana*, 1881, touches very lightly on the subject by mentioning two mounds in Franklin Township, and in Madison Township he mentions the "curiosity of the situation of four knolls, or mounds, in such a way as to form a diamond. These each are about forty feet in height and the figure is longest from southeast to northwest. These mounds contain a superior quality of gravel for road building." I am no expert on Indian mounds, but the majority of the readers can probably guess what happened to parts, maybe even all, of one or two of the ancient mounds in Montgomery County, Indiana.

In the year 1892, while workmen were digging in a gravel pit on the Yountsville Pike, about two miles west of Crawfordsville, on the farm of George Britton, they found to their amazement about "a dozen skeletons lying side by side." Before they were stopped from exhuming these bodies, they had unearthed about thirty of them. Many of the skeletons were carried off by relic hunters, and there is no record as to where these were taken. No stone axes, pipes, or arrow heads, were unearthed with these bodies, so it remains a mystery as to what race or nation these remains belonged. Some thought they belonged to the American Indians who roamed over this area in the early part of the century; others thought they belonged to some early explorers who may have had their camp or village there. Another theory was that these remains were those of the Mound Builders who are known to have inhabited this country centuries ago.

On a farm a half mile north of the gravel pit, and on the south side of Sugar Creek, is a structure of earth about 80 feet long and 20 feet or more in height, which is undoubtedly the work of the Mound Builders. The writer of the article said, "all persons who have visited it pronounce it such. It may be that this earth work and the burying ground on the Britton farm were used by the same people, and that [at] an early period, a town or village was located in that vicinity."

In this same period of time a large skeleton was found by Jack Gray in another gravel pit, on the Davis farm, that measured seven feet in length. An earthen vessel containing the remains of a turtle and a raccoon was exhumed with the skeleton. Nearly two years later in another gravel pit, the remains of a "gigantic Indian buck," together with his implements of warfare, were exhumed on the farm of D.A. Myers in Walnut Township. There was other evidence pointing to the conclusion that this was another Indian graveyard.

The area surrounding New Richmond has provided collectors of Indian relics with many artifacts and evidence of very early inhabitants of some unknown race. The Mound Builders of the other townships may have had some connection to those in Coal Creek Township.

In May, 1890, Thomas Shepherd, living three miles northwest of New Richmond, discovered an Indian burial ground on his farm. Among his discoveries was a whole skeleton, and many other bones were unearthed by heavy rains. A well-preserved pipe was also found at this site. There were places where the Indians, or Mound Builders, had dug holes in the ground, carrying the earth to the top of the hill. Shepherd had never suspected the mound was a burial place before making these discoveries, but had realized the hill did have the appearance of being "made with hands."

The early settlers collected many arrowheads and other artifacts. Gaylord Tribby found on his farm an artifact in the shape of a crescent moon, which collector Ewing Mason claimed was a ceremonial fertility stone. Tribby also found many pieces of broken flint—foreign to the Coal Creek area—in his fields, as well as a large ax or hatchet. Unfortunately he gave his collections away; many such collections were passed on to future generations and have since scattered to far parts of the country. My father, Forrest Waye, saw some of these large collections in his childhood. The Indian presence was evident, but is fading away because of the loss of these private collections and the failure of nearby colleges to document and preserve the findings.

In 1899 there were reports of such articles as Indian axes being found near Number 13 School. That same year, a New Richmond resident by the name of Jim Mahan found a pipe in a gravel pit that was supposed to have belonged to "some old Indian Chief."

I have been a resident of New Richmond for over fifty years, attending the local school and associating with many residents who were natives of the town of New Richmond and Coal Creek Township when the town was in its infancy. I had never heard a word about the area being in the territory of the Mound Builders, so it came as a complete surprise when I stumbled onto articles of the discovery of an ancient Indian village site south of New Richmond.

My eyes were opened wide to some new historical thrills when I read the following headline in the Crawfordsville *Journal*, October 19, 1903, and the New Richmond *Record*, October 22, 1903: "'THE MOUND BUILDERS' Evidence of One of Their Ancient Villages in This County—Collections of Axes, Arrow Heads, and Utensils Superior to Any in the World Found on Junis H. Allen's Farm." The article did not reveal the exact location of his farm, but I knew he was a farmer residing in Coal Creek Township about three miles south of New Richmond and one mile west of Patton's Corner. The collection of axes, celts, ceremonial stones, arrow heads, and other utensils had been collected over the years by J. Lee Allen and Winton Utterback, and at almost every turn of the spade, another item was found.

In the center of the farm is a small hill; the Allens thought it was just a natural rise in the otherwise prairie land, but they began turning up relics with each planting season. They did not open the mound to any great extent, but found an ax of considerable size—supposed to have been used for hewing out trees, being much too large and unwieldy for war use. This was an almost perfect specimen and remarkably preserved. The ceremonial stone was a smooth piece of stone resembling a double-bladed ax, with two grooves cut in the blades and resembling the petrified vertebra of some monster fish. Used in human sacrificial rituals, this was the item State Geologist Mr. Blatchley was the most thrilled about. He said he believed the specimen to be the finest of the kind in the world.

Another interesting utensil was a flat piece of slate with two tapering holes of different diameters running through it. This article was believed to have been used for making deerskin thongs into bowstrings. Celts were chisel-like articles made of granite, used for scraping the pelts of animals in preparation for tanning. The tanned hides were made into clothing and moccasins. Among the arrow heads were almost every known kind and size—small ones for killing birds, medium-sized for hunting small game such as rabbits and squirrels, and the larger sizes used as weapons of war. All arrow heads were remarkably well-preserved.

In the center of the Allen farm was a small pond that the geologist believed to have been a large artificial lake the ancient tribe used as a place of worship. Blatchley believed the farm was the site of a prehistoric village. The geologist planned to obtain permission from Allen to open the mound, as he was confident that many articles of value to archaeologists would be discovered—and perhaps the remains of the ancient people might be uncovered and further studied. According to the article, the removed items were labeled and placed in the valuable collections in the State House Museum. Archaeologists all over the country speculated that the Junis Allen farm was the centuries-old site of a Mound Builders City.

A year after the first finds, a second discovery was made. A young hunter was searching along Coal Creek for duck. After following the meandering stream for several miles, he came to a place where recent high waters had washed a new channel near the base of one of the mounds in the area. An odd-looking stone attracted his attention. When he jumped down the bank, it proved to be an unusually large double-bladed stone ax. The ax fit the description of the first ax found a year earlier, and weighed nearly thirty pounds. Becoming excited about his find, the young man made a closer search of the area and was rewarded with the discovery of another perfect specimen—a heavy stone resembling what might be taken for the vertebra of some monster fish; this, too, fit the description of the ceremonial stone found the previous year. The last discovery of the hunter was a mask.

The location of this second discovery was supposed to have been the place of worship for the Mound Builders, possibly a sacrificial altar. Archaeologists believed it was customary to make death masks of the chief and his wife. If the chief died in battle, the mask was placed in a sepulcher, but if he died by sacrifice, the mask was buried with him. The discovered mask was in perfect condition, but it was uncertain which gender the mask represented. The point of execution and artistic merit were excellent, proving the state of high civilization of this ancient tribe.

When I discovered the article about the mask, the only way to express myself was with an Indian war whoop. I couldn't read the article quickly enough. Like finding an empty stocking on Christmas morning, however, the anticipation of endless gifts was soon squelched. The hunter did not reveal his name or the place where he made his discovery—and as the creek has most likely changed courses frequently since then, the location is untraceable. He also intended to sell his most valuable artifacts to a firm in New York, hoping to receive at least $500. The farm on which he made his discoveries belonged to someone else whom he said would claim the money if the location became public. Another valuable piece of Coal Creek Township history, gone for the love of the almighty dollar to parts unknown.

In the summer of 1964, one mile northeast of New Richmond on County Road 1100 North, the Mahon family began excavating some of their ground to fill some holes in the area of their house. They soon discovered they were digging up something besides soil. They first discovered a few assorted bones; when a jaw bone was turned up they realized they had found human skeletons. With careful use of a hoe they uncovered a skeleton intact from the pelvis up. Another place revealed parts of a human skeleton containing the finger bones, jaw bone, and the intact skull. The set of teeth was whole, though worn down due to a diet of roots, plants, and probably uncooked meats and fish. One skeleton was believed to be that of an Indian woman whose teeth were badly worn, possibly from chewing on the animal hides to soften them for clothing.

When the bones were discovered, the family contacted County Sheriff Demoret. A State Police officer also came to investigate; he sent the larger portions of the skeletons, as well as jaw bones and skulls, to anthropologists at Indiana University. That is the last the people of New Richmond ever heard of those artifacts. The Mahan home and two other farms are located on the top of a high ridge running from east to west, parallel to County Road 1100 North. It is possible that the road, too, was built on the burial ground, since it is situated on part of the hill.

Another area of interest is Bristle Ridge. I wouldn't rule out the possibility of the ridge containing something more than wild hog bristles beneath its surface, since it is in the vicinity of the 1903 and 1904 discoveries. Reuben Swank and Bill Lane, both former residents of the ridge, remembered playing on a huge hieroglyphic-covered boulder when they were children; on this rock was carved the head of an Indian chief. The two men later searched the area where they thought the boulder had been located, probing with metal probes, but did not rediscover the boulder for me to photograph.

One mile south of New Richmond on County Road 250 West is another high hill situated east of the road. I suspect it could be the work of human hands, although there has never been any record of skeletons being found there to this date. I have, however, been accused of making mounds out of the smallest molehills.

The east-west road through New Richmond was called the Strawtown to Covington Road; it followed an old Indian trail that the Wea, Miami, and Shawnee created on their treks to the Wabash River. The Shawnee camped and roamed about the New Richmond and Coal Creek Township area, as well as in southern Tippecanoe and Fountain Counties. The prairie that lies at the northern edge of New Richmond has been known as "Shawnee Prairie" or sometimes "Nine Mile Prairie."

Across the line in Tippecanoe County the Shawnee Indians had a large village located just west of Shawnee Mound in Jackson Township. Shawnee Mound contained Indian skeletons as well. In 1905 gravel was excavated from the mound for road-building; as the gravel bank was extended eastward, many skeletons were removed. They had been buried close together, and were the bones of very large men. One year earlier two Indian skeletons had been discovered near Shawnee Mound, during excavation for a cellar at the Jim Francis house.

Pioneer Families

Samuel Kincaid - "Father" of New Richmond

Trying to trace the history of an ancestor sometimes raises more questions than answers, and often, it becomes easier to prove a statement as incorrect, than to prove it correct. Such has been the case of Samuel Kincaid.

The 1840 census of Hamilton County, Indiana, places his birthdate between 1780 and 1790. One of the distant cousins gives Samuel's birth year as 1788. Where was he born? Until proven otherwise, we believe near Richmond, Virginia, and we are almost certain his father was Thomas Kincaid, who was born near Richmond, Virginia, December 13, 1755. Thomas served in the Revolutionary War, and in 1788, moved to Limestone, Kentucky (now Maysville), on the Ohio River. On May 17, 1804, Thomas Kincaid purchased Lot No. 109 for $7 in the town of West Union, the county seat of Adams County, Ohio. Thomas died in Winchester, in Liberty Township, in the same county, on July 3, 1819, and is buried at Winchester. The *History of Adams County, Ohio* (1900) by Evans and Stivers, gives Thomas' wife's name as Mary Patterson, born in Virginia, September 20, 1757, and died in Adams County, Ohio, March 10, 1824, and she too, is buried at Winchester. There is also some discrepancy as to his wife's name. We have found a marriage record of Thomas Kincaid to Mary Mackey on the 27th of October, 1778 in Washington County, Maryland, but no record of Thomas and a Mary Patterson.

The early Ohio tax list places Thomas Kincaid and his sons, John, Samuel, and Thomas, Jr., in Adams County, Ohio, as early as 1806. Samuel Kincaid married Pheby Vanpelt on December 8, 1808 (on the marriage record this spelling was used, but in all the land records in Montgomery and Hamilton Counties, in Indiana, the name was spelled Phebe. The most widely used spelling, however, is Phoebe). Adam Kirkpatrick performed the marriage ceremony, which took place, or at least was recorded, in the marriage records of Adams County, Ohio.

In the 1820 Census, Samuel Kincaid was living in Scott Township, Adams County, Ohio; Samuel and Phebe were both in the 26-45 age bracket, they had two males under ten years of age, and two females under ten, and one female in the 10-16 age bracket. A Mary Vanpelt was listed with the same house number as Samuel's with two grown males between sixteen and twenty-six, one female between ten and sixteen, and one female sixteen to twenty-six. Mary was the female over forty-five years of age, who was undoubtedly Phebe's mother.

The irony of the whole search is the fact that Samuel Kincaid does not appear in the 1830 Census of Montgomery County, Indiana, nor is he listed in Adams County, Ohio, that year—the most important information needed for the history of the town of New Richmond. His land records do establish his early connection with Montgomery County and Coal Creek Township, however.

The town of Crawfordsville was laid out in March 1823, and after the first courthouse in Montgomery County was completed in 1824, the odd lots that had been set aside for school purposes were being sold. One of these lots, number 37, was purchased by Samuel Kincaid for $25. Samuel moved his family to the new village and began blacksmithing.

In 1829, he moved his family once again, to Coal Creek Township. He had received land grants and entered an 80-acre tract on September 15, 1830, and another 80 acres on January 3, 1831, both in Coal Creek Township. He purchased land, improved it, and sold several acres the following years, but the most important tract was the 80 acres he purchased of William and Rebecca Forbes on March 5th, 1833, for it was on ten acres of this ground the town of New Richmond was platted on July 27, 1836. This tract was located on the west half of the northwest quarter of section ten, township twenty north, range five west. He sold most of the lots between the time the plat was made and 1839.

Samuel Kincaid erected his log cabin when he first came to Coal Creek Township on the northeast corner of Washington and Wabash Streets, north of the ground he platted. He continued blacksmithing and became the first businessman in the area of New Richmond. Samuel and Phebe Vanpelt Kincaid had the following children: Mary, or "Polly," born in 1809; James and Samuel, Jr. birthdates unknown as there is no further record of the two sons; William, born 22 January 1812; Catherine, 1813; Elizabeth "Betsy," 1816; Thomas, 12 October 1821; John, 12 March, 1824—all born in Adams County, Ohio—and the youngest child, Russell Bigelow Kincaid, was born in Coal Creek Township in the cabin mentioned above, in 1829.

William, Thomas, and John worked with their father in the blacksmith shop, and were kept busy with this work; they also helped their father clear the acreage he had purchased. Phebe and the girls occupied their time spinning and weaving, milking the cows and all the other busywork the pioneer ladies had to attend to.

Education was one of the more important goals that Samuel and Phebe Kincaid had set for their children and they all received the benefits of a common school education. Sam and Phebe could not read or write, and all their deeds and legal documents were marked with an "X". The son, William, was a trustee of Coal Creek Township in 1841 when the daughter Catherine, and her husband, Richard Dewey, gave land for school purposes.

Either Samuel Kincaid was restless and felt the need to chop down some more trees, or whatever reason he may have had, he decided to move on. He purchased a tract of land in Hamilton County, Indiana, on February 1, 1840. This deed does not give the number of acres, but he purchased from John S. Beasley, of Brown County, Ohio, a rather expensive piece of property that was subject to sale in Indianapolis, paying $640. Samuel's place of residence was listed as Montgomery County, Indiana, at this time. Samuel, Phebe and the younger children—namely, Thomas, John, Russell, Elizabeth, and Mary—were residing in Adams Township in Hamilton County, Indiana, by the time the 1840 Census was taken. William married Debby Kendall, and Catherine married Richard Dewey, and both raised their families in Coal Creek Township. William lived north of New Richmond; his farm bordered Tippecanoe County on the north, and Catherine lived east of town.

Samuel Kincaid began to divide his land holdings among his children in 1844. He then sold 160 acres, and the remaining lots of the town plat, to Allen D. Beasley the same year, severing all ties to the little village he platted. On the 9th day of October, 1845, Samuel Kincaid made his will. Perhaps he knew his time was near, because the will was probated on the 3rd day of the November Term in 1845 in Hamilton County, Indiana. The will was witnessed by George Kinnett, and Deptha (or Teptha) A. Ritchie and the usual legal formalities were recorded. The will was copied as it was recorded except for the equation signs added to separate the phrases. This document reads:

> "Now comes into Court…..Kincaid, widow of Samuel Kincaid late of Hamilton County, Indiana deceased and produces into court this following paper purporting to be the last will and testament of said deceased in the words and [?] following to wit:
> WILL—I Samuel Kincaid of Hamilton County and State of Indiana do make and publish this my last will and Testament=first I direct that my body be decently interred and that my funeral be conducted in a manner corresponding with my Estate and Situation in life and as to such worldly estate as it has pleased God to Intrust me with I dispose of the same in the manner following to wit: my son William Kincaid has received his full share and quota of my estate=Catharine Dewey has also received her full share and quota of my estate=Thomas Kincaid has received his full share and quota of my Estate=I direct that my Son John Kincaid have the west half of the Southwest quarter of Section twenty Seven (27) in Township twenty (20) North of Range three East=also that my son Russel B. Kincaid have the East half of the South west quarter of Section twenty Seven (27) in Township twenty (20) North of Range three East=John Kincaid is yet to have a Saddle and Russel B. Kincaid is to have a horse and Saddle in addition to the above=Mary Atkins my daughter=and Elizabeth Barnes my daughter are each to have in addition to what they have already received a Saddle each=I also ordain that my beloved wife hold the two ten acre fields thats now cleared and one of them now in corn and the other has been in Wheat this Season On the parcel of land allotted to John Kincaid during her lifetime free of all in Cumberances=also all the balance of my Estate I leave in the hands of my beloved wife during her lifetime then to be equally divided between my three daughters Catharine Dewey=Mary Atkins=and Elizabeth Barnes=In Witness Whereof I Samuel Kincaid the testator have hereunto set my hand and Seal this ninth day of October in the Year of Our Lord One Thousand Eight Hundred and forty five. Samuel Kincaid (his X mark)

After Samuel Kincaid's death, trying to trace the whereabouts of his widow, Phebe, left more unanswered questions. She signed, in Montgomery County, Indiana, an affidavit of consent for her youngest son Russell B. to marry Catherine Stine, on April 22, 1848. In the 1850 Census, she was living in the same household as Russell and Catherine, in Adams Township, in Hamilton County, Indiana. Phebe was 61 years of age and her birthplace was listed as New York. I never located a tombstone, or record of her death, as the State of Indiana did not keep death records this early. I strongly believe Samuel and Phebe are buried in the Boxley (or Boxleytown) cemetery in Hamilton County near their son, John, and family. The caretaker of this cemetery said the original cemetery was located nearer the creek bed and had been flooded many times. Also the creek bed had changed over the years, therefore, the newer burials were made at the site now occupied as a graveyard on a higher elevation, and the old burial sites are lost.

What happened to all of Samuel Kincaid's descendants? Three of Samuel and Phebe Vanpelt Kincaid's children left Indiana after Samuel's death. One of their descendants gave Phebe's death as 1859, but I have not located proof of this date. Only William's descendants remained in the New Richmond area. The following short sketches of his children, some only traced to the 1850 census, are listed.

Mary "Polly" Kincaid married Willis Atkins on January 16, 1844 in Hamilton County, Indiana, and they were in that county at the time of the 1850 Census with one son, Samuel R. Atkins, age 5, born in Indiana (no further record).

William Kincaid married Debby Kendall in Montgomery County, Indiana, January 18, 1831. He died November 20, 1846 at the age of 34 years leaving his young widow, and the following children: Polly Catharine, Margaret Senith, Samuel, James, Phebe Ann, Elizabeth Jane, Isabel Frances, Emily Josephine. William and most of his children and grandchildren are buried in the New Richmond Cemetery. His daughter Elizabeth Jane Kincaid married Daniel Ebrite, and they were the grandparents of Vera Ebrite who married Forrest Waye, whose descendants (of which I am one) are now residing in New Richmond.

Catherine Kincaid married Richard Dewey on September 4, 1834 in Montgomery County, Indiana. She and Richard had the following children: William, Samuel, John, Elizabeth, Phebe, Thomas H., Harriett, and Albert. The last two are buried in the New Richmond Cemetery and were their oldest children. They lived about one-half mile east of New Richmond on the old road formerly located next to the railroad track. In 1851 or 1852, Catherine and Richard and their children, along with Catherine's brothers Russell and Thomas and their families, all moved west and settled in Iowa. Thomas moved on, but the Deweys remained near El Dorado. Catherine died there on July 29, 1863 and is buried in the St. Peter's Cemetery at El Dorado. Richard and Catherine Dewey gave a parcel of land to be used for school purposes before they left Coal Creek township; the first Walnut Grove School, or District No. 1, stood on this lot. It is interesting to note the respect the children gave in naming their offspring for Samuel, Phebe, and the grandparents, Thomas and Mary Kincaid.

Elizabeth "Betsy" Kincaid married John Barnes on December 27, 1842 in Hamilton County, Indiana; they were listed on the 1850 census in that county with three daughters: Mary E., Phebe Ann, and Martha J.

Thomas Kincaid married three times; the first marriage was to Margaret Danner, in October 1843 in Tippecanoe County, Indiana. His second wife was Catherine Danner, married September 14, 1847 in Fountain County, Indiana. Catherine and Margaret were sisters. He married Elizabeth Bedford June 14, 1877 in Missouri. Thomas and his second wife Catherine, had the following children: Frederick H., Franklin, Margaret, Horace Greely, Ida, and Ella. He and the third wife had one son, Thomas, Jr. Thomas Kincaid died Sunday, October 6, 1889 at Saxton Station, Missouri, at the age of 65. He is buried in the cemetery at Saxton, now part of St. Joseph, Missouri.

John Kincaid married Loucinda Miller on March 19, 1845 in Montgomery County, Indiana. His second wife, Mary A., mother of his children, appears on the 1860 and 1870 census in Boxley, Hamilton County, Indiana. John and his third wife, Nancy E. Dowen, were married September 1874 and were listed on the 1880-1900 Census in the same town and county. The children of John Kincaid and Mary A. are: Mary Ellen, Martha J., James F., Albert, Lydia and John M., all born near Boxley in Hamilton County,

Indiana. John died October 28, 1903 at the age of 79 years, 7 months, and 16 days, and is buried in the Boxley Cemetery in Hamilton County, Indiana.

Russell Bigelow Kincaid was the only child of Samuel and Phebe born in Montgomery County, Indiana. He married Catherine Stine on April 22, 1848 in Montgomery County, Indiana, and resided in Hamilton County in 1850. Phebe, his mother, was living with Russell and his wife at the time the census was taken in Adams Township in 1850. In 1851, or 1852, Russell B. and Catherine, along with Richard and Catherine Dewey, Thomas and Catherine Kincaid, and the children, all moved west after their parent's death. Russell and Catherine adopted a daughter, Martha Ellen, and had a daughter by the name of Elizabeth Jane. Russell died February 27, 1868 at the age of 35, near West Union, Iowa, in Fayette County, and is buried in the West Union Cemetery beside his wife.

THE CAMPBELL CLAN

John B. and Elizabeth (Shipman) Campbell, natives of New Jersey, were among the earliest settlers in the New Richmond vicinity. They brought with them the following children: Jacob C., Sarah, Elisha, and William. The family had immigrated to Northumberland County, Pennsylvania, then to Ohio, and in October 1832, to Coal Creek Township, Montgomery County, Indiana. The parents moved on to Schuyler County, Illinois, where John died at the age of seventy-four, and Elizabeth at the age of eighty-three.

Their eldest son, Jacob, was born in Northumberland County, Pennsylvania, March 28, 1808, and was to become one of New Richmond's earliest, permanent settlers. He was a blacksmith by trade, and opened his shop in New Richmond in 1848. Jacob also farmed and was one of the earliest beekeepers who supplied the neighborhood with honey.

On May 23, 1833, Jacob married Mary Ann Pryor in Montgomery County, Indiana. Mary was born June 27, 1817 in Jefferson County, Indiana, and was the daughter of Nicholas and Lucinda (Wilhite) Pryor, early Coal Creek township settlers. Four of Jacob and Mary's children, namely, Lucinda, John, Robert C., and Emily, were deceased before 1881, but the other children lived to raise families, and played an important role in the early settlement of the town of New Richmond. Brief sketches of the children follow:

Mary Elizabeth Campbell, the eldest child, was born in Coal Creek Township on April 4, 1836. The home of her parents was located in the town of New Richmond, but the plat was not made until four months after her birth. On March 14, 1861, Mary E. Campbell married John M. Thomas. Thomas enlisted in Company C, 120th Indiana Volunteer Infantry on January 4, 1864. He was stationed in Lafayette where he became ill and was allowed to return home to recuperate. He returned to his company and was sent to the south, but he never completely recovered from his illness and died in Knoxville, Tennessee, August 4, 1864. He was buried in the National Cemetery at Knoxville. They had one daughter, Flora Thomas, who married Winton Alexander, son of another pioneer family of Coal Creek Township. Mary E. Thomas later married Amos "Squire" Ebrite on October 25, 1868. They had a daughter Mary Alice Ebrite who first married Charles Mitchell, and had a son Glenn. The second husband of Mary Alice Ebrite was Joseph Tortorella.

Mary Elizabeth (Campbell) Ebrite died on January 19, 1922 at the age of 85 years, 9 months and 15 days, leaving her youngest sister, Maria (or Rie) Taylor the only surviving child of Jacob and Mary Campbell. Mary E. Ebrite had lived through four American Wars—the Mexican War, Civil War, Philippine War and World War I.

Sarah J. Campbell, the second daughter of Jacob and Mary Campbell, was born May 27, 1837 in New Richmond, and died June 10, 1903 in the same town. She married Josiah Austin King and they had the following children: Lewis W., born 1858; Emma May, born April 28, 1859, died in 1935 (Mrs. William H. Hollin); Lenna L., born January 14, 1861, died 1942 (Mrs. John W. Hollin); Edward E., born 1862, died 1931; Elizabeth L. "Lizzie," born 1867, died 1890 (Mrs. Bert Page); Rose, born 1872, died 1931 (Mrs. Samuel H. Wallace); Agness, born 1874, died 1961 (Mrs. Samuel "Doc" Bayliss).

John and William Hollin established their drug and grocery store in New Richmond in the very early years of the town. They also operated the Hollin Opera House in New Richmond. Bert Page was the engineer for the McCardle Elevator in town, and Samuel (or Doc) Bayliss was a medicine showman with headquarters in New Richmond, and had a circus type show for a few years.

Elisha C. Campbell, eldest son of Jacob C. and Mary Ann Campbell, was born March 16, 1843 in New Richmond, and died December 4, 1901 from injuries he sustained from a run-away horse that was frightened by a steam engine of the Big Four railroad crossing in Lafayette. Elisha married Jennie E. Sibel January 14, 1875 in Attica, Indiana. They had three children, Frank Emmett, William Kenton, and Nellie Leona. Elisha C. Campbell served in Company B, 135th Indiana Volunteer Infantry, and for many years served as Constable in Coal Creek Township. He was a painter by trade and a broom-maker.

William Campbell was born August 5, 1847 in New Richmond and died July 23, 1901 in Corwin, Indiana, west of Romney. William first married Sarah A. Tribby, June 17, 1871. He and his second wife Ella Beal were married September 14, 1879. The record of his family is incomplete, but known children were: Nola, a son, born September 18, 1872 who was accidentally shot by a playmate and died November 4, 1886; George, Jacob, Forest, and Harley E.

William Campbell started earning a living by making brooms, then later, barbering. He then embarked in the grocery business in 1864 or 1868. He lost his building and merchandise by fire in 1874, but received aid from friends and started over. In March, 1889, he again lost everything by fire, and by October the same year, had erected a two-story frame building. His first two buildings were log structures. He had branched out into the general merchandise trade before his second building burned, and was known as the "Pioneer Store." His new building included a large hall on the second floor, and he had visions of competing with the Hollin brother's opera house, but this idea didn't succeed. Bill moved to Kirkpatrick, Indiana, in 1891, and established his new "Granger Store" in a rented room. A few years later he had erected another general store at Corwin, located west of Romney on the railroad. This was to be his final move, the place of his death, on July 23, 1901.

Artemesa Maria "Rie" Campbell was born in 1851, in New Richmond, and died June 9, 1928. She married Charles Taylor and had two sons, Fred and Winton "Wint" Taylor. Rie Campbell Taylor was the last of Jacob and Mary A. Campbell's children and had outlived them all.

The Ebrite Family

George R. Ebrite was born November 4, 1810 in Pennsylvania. On April 12, 1832 George and Mary Wright were married in Adams County, Ohio, where the Ebrite family had moved at an early date. Mary Wright was born March 25, 1809 in Ohio, and died February 13, 1882 in New Richmond, Indiana. George preceded her in death March 1, 1864. Both are buried in the old section of the New Richmond Cemetery. George R. and Mary Wright Ebrite immigrated to New Richmond, Montgomery County, Indiana, in 1839, bringing with them three children. Their youngest child, Daniel, was born in the new little village. George Ebrite was a wagon maker, carpenter, beekeeper, and farmer. He served as township trustee in Coal Creek Township, was a trustee of the New Richmond Christian Church, and did the carpentering on the first log structure erected by this congregation. The children of George and Mary Ebrite each contributed greatly to the growth of the town. They are:

Amos Ebrite, Esquire, born 5th of January 1833 in Adams County, Ohio, and died February 18, 1910, age 77 years, in New Richmond, Indiana. Amos was first married to Mary Jane Kelly on October 21, 1858. She died May 10, 1866, leaving one child, Emma Frances, who married Robert Manners. On October 25, 1868, Amos married Mary E. (Campbell) Thomas, a widow with one child, Flora Thomas. Mary was the eldest daughter of Jacob and Mary Campbell, early settlers in New Richmond. Amos and his second wife had one daughter, Mary Alice Ebrite, who married Charles Mitchell and had a son, Glenn Mitchell, an internationally known artist. Alice Ebrite's second husband was Joe Tortorella. Mary Elizabeth (Campbell) Ebrite died January 19, 1922.

Amos "Squire" Ebrite was a Justice of the Peace in New Richmond for forty years, serving from 1870 to his death in 1910. His name appears on many legal documents in the Montgomery County Courthouse and on abstracts of titles on many of the New Richmond residences. Amos also followed in his father's footsteps as a carpenter, building many of the early residences and business properties in New

Richmond. Forrest Waye remembered watching Amos Ebrite making hand-made cedar shakes for roofing. He also recalled watching Amos manufacturing slat and wire fence in his factory in New Richmond. Amos taught school in New Richmond in order to pay his way through college. He was the eldest child of George and Mary Ebrite, and outlived his brothers and sister.

Alfred Ebrite, second son of George R. and Mary (Wright) Ebrite, was born July 20, 1835 in Adams County, Ohio. Alfred never married. He served in the Civil War in Company C, 120th Infantry. Alfred returned to New Richmond after the war, and was studying medicine under the local physicians in 1870, but his health was ruined from the effects of the war, and he could not shut out the memories of the conflict. His health grew worse and he died January 9, 1886, not realizing his dream of becoming a physician. He is buried in the New Richmond Cemetery.

Catherine "Katie" Ebrite, the only daughter of George R. and Mary (Wright) Ebrite, was born March 25, 1838 in Adams County, Ohio. Katie married John M. Barcus on November 18, 1857 in the family home in New Richmond. John was a bridge contractor and was a resident of the town of New Richmond at the time of their marriage. John was the first man from New Richmond to enlist in the Civil War, enlisting in Company C, 120th Infantry, the same company as his brother-in-law Alfred Ebrite. He was mustered in March 1864. His wife Katie died a month later on April 4, 1864 at the age of 26 years, leaving a small son Paul John Barcus, who was born in 1862. Paul Barcus became a well-known Physician in Crawfordsville (see Physician section). Paul was cared for by relatives until John returned from the war and remarried. Kate Barcus was buried in the New Richmond cemetery beside her parents. Col. John Barcus died January 22, 1874 and is buried in the Masonic Cemetery in Crawfordsville.

Daniel Ebrite, born October 10, 1840, was the only child of George R. and Mary (Wright) Ebrite to be born in New Richmond, Indiana. He spent all his youth in the town, and on April 11, 1866, Daniel married Elizabeth Jane Kincaid, daughter of William and Debby (Kendall) Kincaid. Elizabeth's parents were children of the pioneer families of Coal Creek Township. William's father had platted the town of New Richmond in 1836. Daniel Ebrite carpentered several years, but preferred the life of a farmer, which he continued to his death on September 19, 1908. Elizabeth was born north of New Richmond February 4, 1841, and died November 15, 1930. Both are buried in the New Richmond cemetery.

Daniel Ebrite's obituary says, "Mr. Ebrite was a successful farmer. His father traded property which is now a part of New Richmond, and which is now in part the Detchon home, for the farm south of town in 1864. His father died shortly afterwards, when Daniel Ebrite and his mother, Mary, moved to their new home, and where he continued always to make his home until his death." This beautiful house is still standing today, one-fourth mile south of New Richmond, and is occupied by Ralph Fifer (1984). [Note: This home is now occupied by Jack and Joan Fifer, 2005]. There have been a few minor changes, but the outside of the house has not been altered, and the old well-house still remains at the back of the residence. Daniel and Elizabeth Jane (Kincaid) Ebrite's children were:

George William Ebrite, born January 18, 1867, died September 6, 1901. On September 3, 1890 Will Ebrite married Fannie Coons Patton. They had one child, a daughter, Vera Jane Ebrite, born November 5, 1894. Vera Ebrite was the last child of this family to carry the Ebrite name. She married Forrest Waye and they were the parents of Francis Waye Thayer, Phyllis Waye Boone, Gerald, Charles, Malcolm, Melvin, and Don Waye.

Jessie Lola Ebrite, born June 5, 1869, died March 12, 1958. Jessie married Edgar L. Jones April 23, 1890. They had no children. Ed and Jess Jones resided about one mile south of New Richmond. Ed was a farmer, and Jess was an avid gardener, growing all kinds of fruits and vegetables—and flowers of every variety.

Margaret Emma Ebrite, born October 10, 1879, died January 18, 1954. Emma first married George Frank Bennett and they had one daughter, Opal Jane Bennett, who married Merrill Clapp. Emma then married Fred Mason and had a son, Paul Mason.

Daniel Ebrite and all his children are buried in the New Richmond Cemetery.

The McComas Family

Arriving in New Richmond the same year, 1839, and from the same county in Ohio as the Ebrite family (Adams County), were the McComas brothers, Samuel and James. James did not remain in New Richmond, and I did not continue the search on his later residences. He and his wife, Nancy A. had the following children as taken from the 1850 census of New Richmond, Coal Creek Township: James T., William, John M., Eliza A. and Joseph—all born in New Richmond. The eldest child, James T., died at the age of seven and is buried in the New Richmond cemetery. James McComas, the father, was one of New Richmond's early blacksmiths and was born in Ohio about 1821. On September 4, 1856, James S. McComas sold lot number two in block one of the original plat of New Richmond, to Christopher J. Oppy and left the area about this time.

Samuel McComas, or "Squire" as he was known, was born in Lewis County, Kentucky, near Concord, on May 25, 1811. He resided with his parents in Kentucky until he was nine years of age when the family moved to Adams County, Ohio. Samuel married Maria Caw in Ohio, and brought his family to Montgomery County, settling in the new little village of New Richmond. His first three children, born in Ohio, were: William B., born January 13, 1833; David C., 1835; Mary A. (Polly) 1838 or 1839. Their children born in Indiana were: John T., 1841; Samuel S., 1842 (died in infancy age 4 months, 21 days, on June 23, 1842); DeLoss D., 1844; Barbara M. 1848; Charles Franklin, 1850; Samuel, 1852 (died in infancy May 2, 1853, age 1 year, 1 month 21 days); and Maria E., 1853. Samuel McComas was not to have a namesake—although two sons were named for him, both died in infancy.

Maria Caw McComas died at the age of 47 years, 10 months, 29 days, on April 20, 1859, and is buried in the New Richmond Cemetery. Samuel McComas married his second wife, Susan Pitts, on July 4, 1860, in Montgomery County, Indiana. He and Susan had seven children, namely, Arvilla (Mrs. William Dewey); Jeanette (Mrs. A. Henry Hays); Louella, not married; Robert; Hattie (Mrs. John M. Swearingen); Jemima (Mrs. Albert Wasson); and Stowe (or Stover). The two sons, Robert and Stover, were killed in a railway wreck sometime before Susan's death. Susan Pitts McComas died August 17, 1905 at her daughter's home in Indianapolis, the home of Mrs. Albert Wasson. Samuel McComas died November 16, 1897, at the age of 87 at his home on West Pike Street in Crawfordsville. His funeral was held in the New Richmond Christian Church. He and his second wife have no markers in the New Richmond Cemetery, but both are buried there. On all the census records of New Richmond, and Coal Creek Township, Samuel McComas "Squire" was listed as a farmer. What the census records fail to reveal was his other lines of work. "Squire" McComas served as Justice of the Peace in New Richmond for twenty-two consecutive years, receiving his commission about 1851. He had the distinction of becoming New Richmond's first Postmaster in 1850, and was also an auctioneer—he was paid $1.75 for crying the sale of James Kendall's estate on November 12, 1842. Samuel and his family were members of the Christian Church in New Richmond. He was listed as a member on June 2, 1877 when the congregation met to reorganize and was elected Secretary of the Board of Trustees on that date. Samuel and his first wife, Maria, deeded one-half acre of land for New Richmond's first school on June 1, 1858 for the sum of $12. There was mention of the "McComas Hotel" in New Richmond in 1880, but it is uncertain if this hotel belonged to Samuel or one of his sons. Samuel moved to Crawfordsville to retire in his old age, residing on West Pike Street, but he made it a point to visit old friends at least once a year. He was residing in Crawfordsville by December 30, 1888 when the new Christian Church was dedicated and he returned to New Richmond for the dedication of the building.

The McComas family all left New Richmond, and there are very limited records of their whereabouts. The son, William B., moved to Waynetown and he and his wife, Mary C. Hauk McComas are buried in the Masonic Cemetery at that place. He died January 26, 1900, and Mary on April 16, 1910. DeLoss, another son, was a resident of Hannibal, Missouri, in September, 1906. He brought a son, Ed, to visit his old friends in New Richmond that year. DeLoss was a railroad engineer, Ed was a brakeman, and DeLoss had two other sons who were conductors on the Western Railroad. He complimented the folks in New Richmond, saying that "she" (the town) had improved more than Crawfordsville. It was his first visit to New Richmond in 41 years.

Starr Dunn - Early Businessman

When I think of the businessmen in the town of New Richmond, the brick buildings come to mind—all of which were built between the period of 1870 to 1910—and the persons who had the buildings constructed for them.

Each brick building, except the Knights of Pythius, was constructed by men who started out in life with very little hope of such a promising future.

Among these men was Starr Dunn, who made his entry into the world under very uncertain circumstances. His natural father, a Mr. Boardman, had been murdered during a fight, the cause of which was thought to have been a labor dispute of some sort. He left his Allegheny City, Pennsylvania, home one night and did not return. His body was found later, floating in the river. His mother went into labor early, because this was such a tragic shock, and she was unable to care for the baby after his birth. The doctor who delivered him, along with his wife, took the baby home to raise, telling the mother she could visit the baby whenever she wanted. The doctor's wife became ill and went to her mother's home in Ohio, to stay until she recovered. Her mother informed her she was in no condition to raise the baby and she would take the baby and raise him. The parents of the doctor's wife were Mr. and Mrs. John Dunn. The baby was named William at birth, but when Mrs. Dunn took over the job as his mother, she renamed him Starr, because she said, he was such a shining little star. She already had a son William and thought it would be confusing with two boys in one household by the same name. It is not certain if any of this was done legally; sometimes in early days children who lost their parents simply were taken in by good neighbors and raised as their own.

Starr Dunn was born January 27, 1867 in Allegheny City, Pennsylvania, in Allegheny County. The Dunn family were residents of Zanesville, Ohio, and Starr's natural mother lost track of the baby, but finally located him when he was sixteen. She tried to persuade him to return to her home in Pennsylvania, but he refused to leave the Dunn family, the only parents he ever knew. The Dunns were quite elderly, by this time.

Starr attended the schools in Zanesville, Ohio, and he may have met his bride-to-be during school functions of some kind, because she attended the local school in Sonora, a small town near Zanesville. It was not certain just how they met, but Starr Dunn and Martha Mangold were married May 30, 1890 at Zanesville in Muskingum County, Ohio. She was the daughter of John H. and Elizabeth (Border) Mangold.

Starr went to Garret, Indiana, to learn the plumber's trade before their marriage, and had a position with the Baltimore and Ohio Railroad along the plumbing line. He and his new bride then moved to Chicago, where their first child, Stanley, was born a year later, in 1891. The second child, Ruth, was born in 1892, in her maternal grandparents' home in Ohio. The third child, Ethel, was born in 1894 in Chicago, and the fourth, Chester Starr, was born in 1897 in Chicago.

There are two different reasons given as to why this family left the "Windy City." The main reason was the employees of the railroad company were on strike, and Starr was out of a job—with four little children to feed; and the other reason was they did not feel that Chicago was a good place to bring up their children. They put an advertisement in the Sunday paper for a small town that needed a plumber. It was not certain if this was an Indianapolis newspaper, or Chicago. Starr and his wife received twenty-seven answers to their advertisement. He went to Linden, New Richmond, and Wingate to investigate the possibilities, and decided on New Richmond. Ira Stout, owner of the Black Bear Hotel, had answered the advertisement for the benefit of the New Richmond citizens, and after Dunn talked with him, his mind was made up. Ira Stout always was a good salesman—and a smooth talker.

Starr Dunn and his wife loaded up all their belongings and furniture, some of which Starr had built himself, and moved to New Richmond sometime after the birth of little Chester in 1897. They had moved into a little home, and Starr was well on his way to starting a good plumbing business, and the family was just becoming adjusted to small town life, when tragedy struck. A whole block of homes and business houses were destroyed by fire in July 1898, and unfortunately, the Dunn family lost their home and Starr's business room.

"The family was awakened late in the night by the fire," the daughter, Ethel, or "Dunny" as she was always called, related in her account of the fire, "and we were all in our night gowns. They took us all across the street to Dr. Lynn's office, and Dad had put on his trousers. Kit (daughter Ruth) ran back into the burning house and Dad ran in to get her— he burned his hands real bad then. We lost everything we owned in that fire, and Dad was ready to go right back to Chicago, but the people of New Richmond said no, they would help us get started again if he would stay. They also said they would take care of the children—and they did. Each of we children were left with some neighbors and Ira Stout provided us with a home, the house next to the Black Bear Hotel, until we could get going again. I stayed with the Kirkpatricks, Charlie and his wife, and they wanted to keep me, as they had no children of their own," but her parents would not give her up, of course. Dunny continued with her account of the fire, "I don't remember her name, but the woman who lived in, and ran the hotel—Hope—Hope Kirkpatrick, babied us children and gave us food, and looked after us. Dad eventually re-built his store and we lived above the shop then. It was a tin shop and hardware. Mom ran up and down the stairs, running the store and caring for we children. They installed a bell for the customers to summon her."

Starr Dunn had commenced to rebuild a month after the fire. In August the lumber and materials were on the grounds and brick-laying was to start soon. Dunny said he installed a water supply into this new building, and laid a water line the full length of the block to prevent such a tragedy ever happening again, but she did not say what type of pump he installed. Their house was built much later. In March 1906 the contract for Starr Dunn's "handsome new home" was let to D.W. Pierce of Round Hill. It was completed and the family moved into it on August 29th, 1906.

While they were still residing in the brick building over the shop, their last child, Mildred Elizabeth was born in 1900. Mildred was the only child of Starr and Martha Dunn's to remain in the New Richmond area. She married Gaylord Tribby and they resided on a farm south of New Richmond. Most people knew her by the name of "Punk" a nickname derived from her father who thought she was a little "Spunky" and her brother pronounced the name "Punk"—a name she carried throughout her life, Punk Tribby. Joan Oppy is the daughter of Gaylord and Mildred Dunn Tribby.

Starr Dunn and his wife never forgot the kindness and help they received from the people of New Richmond. Mrs. Dunn was always calling young children into her homes giving them cookies and candy, etc. and read stories to them. Trying to keep them out of trouble was her main concern. She baked pies and cakes, took meals to the elderly and visited with them, always trying to repay the kindness they received.

Starr Dunn and his wife were very interested in their children's education and made sure they studied, and encouraged them to finish school. They taught them the value of reading many books. In 1904, the Dunns added a small building to the east of the tin shop, and started a bookstore and lending library. This was quite successful for many years, as New Richmond did not have a library at the time. There had been an early attempt made to start a library, but it failed.

A few years later, when automobiles made their entrance into New Richmond, Starr Dunn started New Richmond's first garage. His son Stanley was very good at repairing automobiles, and helped his father. He was such a good mechanic, people with automobile trouble would go to school and take him out of his classes to fix their stalled automobiles. They interrupted him from studying until Starr and his wife decided to send him away to school so he could finish, sending him to Valparaiso. Starr then bought two Hupmobiles and started New Richmond's first taxi service from New Richmond to Wingate, and to Linden, as well as the vicinity of New Richmond. Stanley drove one of these Hupmobiles when he returned from Valparaiso.

Stanley joined the service during World War I, serving in the Regular Army Signal Corps Aviation Section, on July 25, 1917. He was commissioned Second Lieutenant in 1918 and learned to pilot a plane, a training he used after his discharge on January 8, 1919 (more about this in the Transportation chapter, Aviation and New Richmond). Starr and Martha Dunn moved to Florida in 1926 to be with their son, Stanley, when Starr's health and eyesight began to fail. He became totally blind and lived with this problem for sixteen years before his death on August 9, 1946. His wife Martha, died November 26, 1951. They both died in Florida, and were buried in Memorial Park Cemetery, St. Petersburg, Florida.

Chapter 2 - Early Business

The Pioneer Village of New Richmond

Although Samuel Kincaid set aside a fraction of his land for the little village of New Richmond in 1836, there was very little growth during the first fifty years. There were only fifty-six houses in Coal Creek Township in 1836.

Ephriam Dewey of Dilly, Oregon, wrote a letter to Edgar Walts, the editor of the New Richmond *Record*, in 1904, describing his fond memories of the town. Ephriam said, "I was born 73 years ago, two miles northeast of New Richmond on what is known as the Philip Dewey farm (Phil and Eph were brothers). Remained there until 21 years ago. Have seen New Richmond when there were only three houses there. The people that lived there then were: Sam McComas, Mr. Ebrite; and Billy Campbell. Have carried many a shovel plow on my back to get them sharpened at Billy Campbell's. There was timber on both sides of the road out to Jim Tribby's. Could have kought (sp) any of that land south of New Richmond for $2 and $3 an acre." I would like to make a few notes here: Sam McComas was the village's first postmaster; George Ebrite, a wagon maker and farmer; and he should have said Jacob Campbell, not William-Jake was the blacksmith, and father of William. Eph Dewey related his migratory pattern, saying he got married, then went to Pelly, Iowa, in 1853, then moved to Pawnee County, Nebraska, then out to Washington County, Oregon, in 1877, buying property and improving and selling it along the way west. He had a family of six sons and five daughters, and he decided that Oregon was the best state he ever lived in, making special note of the good climate for growing all varieties of fruit.

The 1850 census of Coal Creek Township verifies the names on his list, but a few more had moved in by this time. There were three blacksmiths: Jacob Campbell, James McComas, and Elisha Campbell. Physicians listed were: George Manners and John B. Johnson. Samuel McComas was listed as a farmer, but he had been appointed Postmaster before the census was taken. George Ebrite was a wagon maker and Aquilla Dillon was listed as a farmer. An early historian of New Richmond listed Dillon as the town's first grocer about this time. There were three coopers: John Rue and Henry Farley, both born in Virginia, and Charles Mills, born in North Carolina. The Christian denomination had erected its old log edifice by 1850, but it was in 1856 when the Methodists purchased a lot from Sam McComas and his wife for their first building in the village.

Broom Manufacturer

An early history of New Richmond written by William Campbell said, "The first broom manufacturer in the town was Heaman (or Herman) Detchon. The 1870 census of Coal Creek Township lists Elisha C. Campbell as a broom factory employee, but he must have been self-employed as there were no others listed in that line of work in the New Richmond area that year.

Howell Alexander reported to the correspondent of the Crawfordsville weekly *Review*, July 31, 1886, that he was cutting his broom corn and had a good yield that year. It is not known if he manufactured the brooms or just raised the crop for another person.

Daniel Ebrite, administrator of his son William's estate in 1901, listed nine dozen good brooms for sale, indicating William Ebrite was a broom manufacturer. Daniel's brother, Amos Ebrite, also manufactured brooms in New Richmond.

Assorted Business Enterprises

Weavers And Spinners

Spinning and weaving cloth was a way of life for the pioneer women and their daughters of Coal Creek Township, and proof of this statement was found while reading through the estate records of the early residents; for instance, James Kendall's wife Mary (Polly) and the daughters were spinners and weavers. The following items were sold at public auction to settle the estate after James Kendall's death on November 12, 1842 (note the fractions of cents):

> Isaac Peed, purchased one weaver's loom at $3.62-1/2; Adason Kendall-2 wevers [sic] spools, .67-1/2); Isabell Kendall-1 wool wheel, $1.06-1/4; Adason Kendall-1 spinning wheel, .18-3/4; John Shepherd-1 spinning wheel-$2.00; William Kincaid-1 pair cotton cards, .12-1/2; Milton Kendall-1 flax brake, .75; Hiram Connell-1 lot of flax, $3.87-1/2.

Several sheep were listed among the items for sale of James Kendall's estate, and the mention of cotton cards and one lot of flax (for linen) and a flax brake pretty well tells the story of the Kendall women's use of their time. There is no way of proving that Adason and Milton Kendall purchased the above items for their sisters in order to keep them in the family, but this is a strong possibility. William Kincaid married Debby Kendall and John Shepherd married Leah Kendall, both daughters of James and Polly Kendall. James Kendall may have traded some of the women's extra home-spun cloth for items needed for survival in the new wilderness.

Mary H. Campbell was said to have been the first carpet weaver residing within the town of New Richmond. The Campbell family settled in the area before the town of New Richmond was platted. Mary's son, William, made the statements, so he should have been well informed on this bit of information.

Mary, or Mollie, Stephenson was listed as a weaver in the 1903 county directory. She advertised for sale, "a Flying Shuttle Carpet Loom-in first class condition" in December, that year. Mary lived on Prairie Street in 1903, and Madison in 1907-8, but was not listed as a weaver on the last date listed.

Sugar Camps (Maple)

James Kendall's estate records listed two large sugar kettles and a keg of "shugar" [sic] in his inventory, October 29, 1842. Dr. George Manners was one of the earliest pioneers of the New Richmond community to tap his maple trees. He established a permanent building, or camp, to process maple syrup, and sugar. His grove of maple trees and camp was located at the east end of New Richmond and just across the railroad to the south. Jim Tribby continued to operate Dr. Manner's sugar camp after the doctor's death.

James Cook's sugar camp was located about one and one-half miles southeast of New Richmond. He reported making thirty-five gallons in April 1888. The following year was evidently a failure because the proprietor of the Pioneer Store said that year, "We wish someone would pass the maple syrup this way, for not one drop have we seen this year." Those who had sugar camps were preparing to work them extensively in 1890-91. Jim Tribby's sugar camp reported a good run of "water" the latter year.

Fruit Orchards

Although the fruit growers did not advertise, there were many fruit orchards in and near New Richmond. Ed and Jess Jones had an orchard containing every variety of fruit trees. Jess also planted strawberries in large quantities and traded for other items after she preserved all she and Ed could eat through the winter. Some of the better apple orchards produced well enough to have some left after the canning was completed, to be ground and pressed into cider. Capt. Tribby and Jeff Bastion, residing southeast of New Richmond, refitted their cider mill and were grinding both day and night in 1888. The name "Vinegar Hill," given to the farm located about one-half mile north of New Richmond, was in honor of an apple orchard which produced large quantities of apples, some of which were ground into cider—which later turned to vinegar.

Almost every lawn in New Richmond had apple, cherry, apricot, pear, plum, or peach trees for the family supply of fresh fruit. Charles Phillips, living northwest of town, was the champion cherry grower in 1904, picking 235 gallons. He disposed of them in the New Richmond stores "at good prices."

Sorghum Mill

Perry Coffman purchased a cane mill in 1891 and made sorghum molasses for a few years, but there is no further record of this mill.

Feather Renovator

A feather renovator set up shop in New Richmond in December 1903. There is not too much of a demand for this service today with feather beds being a thing of the past. Pillows are now tossed into the washer and dryer for renovation.

Trapper and Fur Traders

Most of the early settlers, although they were not listed as such, made a little extra cash by trapping and trading the pelts for necessary items. Frank E. Campbell was the last person in New Richmond to advertise furs for trade, listing skunks, opossum, muskrats, raccoon, minks, fox, etc. in early January 1903.

Tobacco Growers & Cigar Manufacturer

It is not too well known, but many pioneers raised rather large crops of tobacco around the New Richmond area. Once again we turn to James Kendall's estate records listing several "lots" of tobacco, in and out of the field. There were others in the township growing this crop, but I failed to make a record of each. James Kendall was one of my ancestors and I only copied his.

Dore Ammerman manufactured cigars in New Richmond around 1894-5, and perhaps a little later. Nick Washburn was said to have manufactured cigars for his cigar stores although he did not advertise as a cigar manufacturer.

Ginseng

The forests in Coal Creek Township were well supplied with the wild ginseng plant, and most of the pioneers dug the roots and bartered with the traders and storekeepers for other provisions. This herb was highly recommended for a mild tonic and stimulant. The pioneer women and children, equipped with a "sang hoe" and shoulder bag went into the deep forests to dig the roots. They took them home and washed and hung them to dry. Dealers picked the roots up from the local general store and sold them to dealers in the cities. This was one of the most valuable herbs, and the Chinese paid very high prices to the dealers.

William Kincaid's estate listed "one Sang Hoe" appraised at 12-1/2 cents—which his widow, Debby, kept. She was left with seven small children to support after his death, and this was one means of making a little extra cash, or an item to trade for other needs.

Stump Puller

James A. Bell and J.B. Hamilton advertised as "Stump Pullers" in 1904-5.

Frame Business Buildings in New Richmond—Most of them now gone

William Campbell's Pioneer Store-General Store-3 buildings, built 1868-74, 1889

In 1868 during the pioneer days of New Richmond, William Campbell built his first business house, a log structure. This building was destroyed by fire and all of the contents of the building were lost in 1874. William received aid from his friends in town and erected a new structure the same year. Again in 1889, William's pioneer store was destroyed by fire and the remains smoldered for two weeks. He was not discouraged, however, and in October the same year, William erected a new two story business room on the northwest corner of Washington and Franklin Streets. He sold the building to Douglas Bunnell in 1891. Bunnell, in turn, moved the building fifty feet to the east and established a grocery in the structure. In 1905 Bunnell remodeled the old building into a residence. This building has been razed and a small residence stands on the lot.

Hollin Brothers Drug Store-frame structure, built before 1879

The Hollin brothers purchased their first drug store from a Dr. Rainey in 1879. A Mr. Anderson was associated with the Hollin brothers at the time, and they added groceries to their stock of drugs. This building, probably a frame structure, burned to the ground in 1883. I found no record of the construction of a new building, but they were still in the drug and grocery business when they erected their new brick building in 1890.

George F. Long's Jewelry Store-built in 1886

George F. Long purchased a lot from Stowe Detchon in March of 1886. The lumber for a new business house was on the ground in April the same year, and by July the building was soon to be ready for occupancy. This little building was located on south Wabash Street in the vicinity of the tall grain elevators on the east side of the street (1984). The building was used as an office for Livingston's Livery Barn, and was razed to make room for the McCardle elevator. George Long erected a new brick building in 1890 on the northeast corner of Washington and Wabash Streets.

Frank Perkin's General Store-frame-built in 1885 or 1886

In March 1886, Frank M. Perkins moved his existing storeroom to a lot he purchased from Dr. Detchon. Perkins lost this store and most of the contents, as well as his residence, when the whole block burned on July 12, 1898. Frank then erected a new two-story brick business and residence shortly after, as he was still in the general merchandise business in 1900.

McCardle Block (Old Soldier's Home)-Frame-built in the 1880s

John McCardle, a grain merchant, erected a large frame building in the town of New Richmond in the 1880s. The building in later years was painted a bright orange, as Opal Clapp remembered it, and stood on the northwest corner of Washington and Wabash Streets. It is uncertain why it was referred to as the "Old Soldier's Home," but the building appears in an old photograph of New Richmond. It was razed in 1910 to make room for the new brick K. of P. building.

The following men had hardware stores located in this building: Blaine Archey; William Thomas; Harry O. Shelby, Snyder & Thompson, and A.D. Snyder. H.C. Johnson's Spot Cash Store was located in the building in March 1902, when a new awning was attached, and a year later a new roof was added. Hempleman's grocery was remembered by most of the New Richmond residents who were born in the 1890s and early 1900s as the occupant of this building. A butcher shop was located at the rear of Hempleman's and entry was made on the north side of the structure for this shop.

Thomas "Tommy" Patton's Hardware-Frame-built in 1888

Tommy Patton contemplated building a new hardware in 1887 and purchased the old Methodist Church property from the trustees on May 21, 1888 for $600. The property, located on south Wabash Street, contained 3/4 of an acre. Patton sold the building to the Smith brothers in 1889, who were also in the hardware business. The building was razed to make room for the brick Snyder building in 1900 or 1901. The New Richmond-Coal Creek Township Historical Museum was housed in the building from 1982 to 1987, when John Utterback bought the building.

George W. Washburn's Business—Block-Frame-built in 1888 (?)

George W. Washburn moved into the town of New Richmond in 1888 from the country. It is not known for certain when he erected his two-story business block. The building was moved to the south in 1895 to make room for the large new brick building George erected for the Corn Exchange Bank, on the southeast corner of Washington and Wabash Streets. In January, 1903, Joe Keplar sold and repaired buggies in the building, and in September the same year (1903) T.M. Shotts opened a wagon and carriage factory in the structure. The building has been remodeled into a one-story garage, owned by William Swick in 1985, and had been moved further south on Wabash Street several years ago.

Pritchard Bank Building—Frame-built about 1891

The only record of the construction of this building was in the New Richmond items of the Crawfordsville weekly *Review*, April 11, 1891, which says, "Harry Tribby is delivering lumber for the new building that is going up in our village." The first bank in town, the New Richmond Bank was organized in 1891, and L.F. Pritchard was the cashier of the bank throughout its existence. The location of the building is uncertain, but after the bank closed, the building served as a buggy and farm implement show room for Snyder & Thompson in 1897. The final chapter of this building is uncertain.

Starr Dunn's Tin Shop-Frame-built in 1898

Starr Dunn brought his family from Chicago in 1898 and established his tin shop. He had only been in business a short time when, in July the same year, his tin shop and dwelling both burned to the ground in New Richmond's big fire. The town citizens encouraged Starr to stay in New Richmond and helped him get started in business again. A month later, materials were on the ground for his new brick, fire-proof, building.

The Brick Buildings in New Richmond

George F. Long's Dry Goods, Jewelry, And Wall Paper Store-built in 1890

George Long embarked in the jewelry and watchmaking business in a small building located on south Wabash Street in New Richmond. He added dry goods and wallpaper to his merchandise and was in need of more space. In 1890 he erected a new, brick 32-by-20-foot building on the northeast corner of Washington and Wabash Streets. In 1902 his business had expanded and a 38-by-20-foot addition was made to the original structure making one room 70 feet in length. The New Richmond *Record*, a weekly newspaper, was printed upstairs in this structure. The Lane Hardware occupied this building until 1984.

1 - George F. Long's building

Hollin Brothers Drug and Grocery Store-built in 1890-brick

This is a two story brick building located on the northwest corner of Washington and Wabash Streets. It was completed on December 20, 1890, and the drugstore was doing a good business; however, an explosion of a lamp nearly burned the new structure before the fire was contained. The Hollin Opera House was located on the second floor. The Knights of Pythias, Lodge No. 288, was instituted in January, 1891, and met in their hall on the second floor of the Hollin building before erecting the K. of P. building in 1910.

2 - Hollin Opera House

Byron Alexander's Furniture and Gifts moved to this location in 1954.

George W. Washburn's Bank Building-built in 1895-brick

On May 2, 1895, the contractors Myers and Swan, were putting up a new brick building in New Richmond that was referred to as the "Bank Block." Rappert and Son did the roofing and tinning. This building is located on the southeast corner of Washington and Wabash Streets. The Corn Exchange Bank was located in the southeast room until 1910, when they moved across the street in the new K. of P. building. Other businesses that occupied this building were: Claypool & Fry's General store; Nick Washburn's Men's Clothing and Cigar Store; and Hanawalt and Son General Store, to name a few. Also occupying this building were several groceries; among them were, Campbell's; Hendrick's brothers; Shepherd's; Andrew's; Stephen's and Fiddler's.

3 - George W. Washburn block

Starr Dunn's Plumbing and Tinning Shop-built in 1898-brick

Construction of this building, located on east Washington Street, was commenced in August of 1898, just a month after Starr's frame business house burned, along with several other business houses. The building is a two-story, fireproof, brick structure. The upstairs rooms served as the Dunn family residence until 1906, when he erected a new home east of his business block. In 1904, Starr added a new building adjacent to the original structure on the east side, and established a bookstore and lending library. This room, a 20-by-30-foot structure, was built by Walter W. "Spud" Harriman, and has been razed. The Tri-County Telephone Company purchased the tin shop building in the 1970s and it now serves as a storage building. Several automobile mechanics occupied this building prior to that. Starr's son, Stanley, was the town's first mechanic and repaired automobiles in this building. The two also operated the town's first automobile taxi service from this building.

4 - Starr Dunn's tin shop

Frank M. Perkins General Store (and Residence)-built in 1898-99-brick

The Perkins building, located on east Washington Street just west of the Dunn building, was erected shortly after the big fire in 1898. Perkins also lost his original frame building and his home in this fire. The building is a two-story brick, and Frank's new brick residence was built adjacent to his business-room, having a door connecting the two. Frank carried on a general merchandise business in the building until moving to his branch store in Linden in 1904.

In 1925, the trustees of the town of New Richmond purchased the building to house the fire trucks and other fire-fighting equipment. The town hall and town jail were also located on the first floor.

The second floor was the practice room of the New Richmond Citizens Band. They also stored their equipment in this room. The Boy Scouts and the Girl Scouts met in the room over the years, and at one time during the 1940s, a community center for the youth was on the second floor.

The building was purchased by the Tri-County Telephone Company in 1981 and used for storage space.

A.D. Snyder Hardware Building-New Richmond's Sky-Scraper-built in 1901-brick

Albert Snyder's building is located on south Wabash Street and was built in 1901 at a cost of $10,000. It is 102 feet, 2 inches long and 46 feet, 6 inches, wide, and has three floors and a basement. The three main floors figure up to 13,200 square feet, and an open elevator connects all the floors (the elevator was enclosed by T.M. Layne in September of 1905). A 30-foot raised stage in the rear of the first floor was built for exhibiting stoves, ranges, and heaters. The 13-foot ceiling is of ornamental steel in a pretty design. When new, the basement contained a hot-air furnace and an independent pneumatic water system with a gasoline engine to operate the pump. The building was lighted by gasoline arc lights, nine lights being necessary for lighting the first floor. The Warner's patented shelving was made of solid oak and cost about $450, and had 150 to 200 drawers fitted with glass fronts. The shelves and drawers have since been removed from the building. This building was occupied by several hardware stores, the Mutual (or Surplus) Electric Company, Snyder's Tack and Apparel, the New Richmond-Coal Creek Township Museum (from 1982-1985), and Utterback Marketing Services (1987-present).

5 - AD Snyder building in 1985 (on left). Queensware display inside AD Snyder Hardware in 1902 (on right).

Knights of Pythias Building (K. of P.)-built in 1910-brick

The K. of P. building is located on the southwest corner of Washington and Wabash Streets in New Richmond. In October 1910, the walls of the building were nearing completion. A full force of workmen, carpenters, brick masons, and tenders were rapidly pushing with their work, hoping for the good weather to continue until they finished their part of the structure. The Corn Exchange Bank moved into the northwest corner of the building upon completion, and remained in that location until the bank closed in 1930.

6 - Knights of Pythias building

Several drug stores and restaurants were located in the room on the north, and the center room housed many grocers; Livingstone's grocery probably held the longest tenure in this room. The south room was used as a post office for many years, but at one time the room back of the bank served as a post office, with the entry made through a door on west Washington Street. Dr. Seaman had his dental office in this back room in the 1960s. The building was occupied in the 1980s by Steven's Fine Foods (restaurant) in the north room, Kunkel's Plumbing and Heating in the center room, and a storage space for Bill Snellenbarger's gas and oil supplies in the south room.

New Richmond Savings and Loan Association-Concrete block building

The New Richmond Savings and Loan Association's concrete block structure was erected by Herb and Charles Fruits. Work began in September of 1952, and the office equipment was moved into the building on October 1 the same year. The building, assets, and office equipment were sold to the Linden State Bank, and a branch bank was established in New Richmond in December of 1974.

7 - View of New Richmond taken from the Union Elevator - Black Bear Hotel in center of photo, livery stable across street. Upper left of photo is A.D. Snyder building. To right of this is Washburn block and Shotts' buggy factory

8 - Street scene looking south, taken before 1910

9 - Street scene looking west, taken before 1910

Chapter 3 - Food Businesses in New Richmond

General Stores

The Pioneer Store, William Campbell, Proprietor

William Campbell, a correspondent for the Crawfordsville weekly *Review*, was responsible for recording the events that took place in New Richmond and the vicinity in the late 1870s through 1890. His New Richmond items touched very briefly on each subject, but gave enough clues in order for me to pursue them further in the county courthouse for verification.

William's Pioneer Store was a gathering place in the town, and all the very important decisions were made in his place of business. He publicly asked the large landowners to give parcels of land in order to build the school and churches, and he continued to hint, in his column, for these same landowners to give some of their land for additions to the town. He was always speaking to the moneyed men to help finance the churches, to start a bank, or whatever the current topic for the week that needed financing may have been. The topic that disturbed him most was M-U-D. Each spring, when the snow and frozen ground began to thaw, William was very sure the citizens of the town would sink completely out of sight in the mud, and he began his annual plea for the store owners to build sidewalks. I noticed that William had made this plea several springs before he, himself, built a plank walk in front of his store. This didn't stop his complaints, though, and he made note of his new walk, then made his usual plea, followed by the comment that "wind-work was cheap, but plank costs money." The other shopkeepers promised each year to build walks, but these were empty promises.

After Dr. Stowe Detchon and Mrs. Dr. Manners started competing in the number of additions to the town of New Richmond, the topic most discussed in the Pioneer Store was what to name the streets. William and his cronies came up with such names as: Booth, Guiteau, Sullivan, Cronin, Buffalo Bill, Mrs. Gougar, Talmage, Beecher, and Elixir Streets. None of the above names were used, incidentally, but we know what the loafers were discussing in August of 1889.

The railroad construction, and the lack of consideration for the citizens of New Richmond and Coal Creek Township, caused quite a stir for many years in the local store, but William and his informers were lacking newsy items after they got the railroad running to suit them, and he wrote in his column, "If someone would get married, or killed, we would have something to write about." I have selected a few of William's choice items for readers to enjoy:

> Thirty years has made a wonderful change in this place. When we look around we see most of the old people have been laid in the cemetery. Some others moved away, and others have taken their place.

> There is a place not far from here called Vinegar Hill. We suppose the name is derived from a sour lot of people living there.

> The "Pull Back" is the name of a new order in our town. If some of our citizens gets a start and is making money too fast, it is the duty of the members to grab his coat tail and pull him back.

William Campbell has the best beer in the village-for medicinal purposes.

A P.W.D.T. Association should be started here, stands for PEOPLE WHO DON'T TALK, would be a glorious thing, etc. People who turn up noses at pool tables and will stand in the hot sun all day Sunday striking croquet balls have our deepest sympathy. Their brain lies at the wrong end of their body or would surely get sun struck.

A young man near here has been going to see his girl a number of times. The old gent and lady told the young "sparker" to marry the girl, or quit-so he quit.

The Round Hill superintendent came here, stood at the bar of one of our fancy saloons, got nine straight drinks of canned lightning, then wilted down and had to be carried to the livery stable. He was laid-out for dead, but arose the next morning with a kink in his neck and made a bee line for the saloon to finish the spree.

New Richmond is talked about in surrounding vicinities as being a place where all you do to get rich is to go. At the same time we have plenty of people here who will have a hard time to get through the winter, simply because there is no work for them. Those who think the sun, moon, and stars only circulate and revolve around this place will wake up to find out their mistake. Mark this prediction, with no factories, no nothing for a poor man to do, what will be the result? I write this to enlighten some poor people who think of moving here to spend the winter and find work. STAY AWAY, and you will not regret it."

As a youth, William Campbell had entered the business world and earned some cash making brooms, and soon embarked in the grocery trade. The book *History of Montgomery County, Indiana,* by Beckwith, gives the year he entered the grocery business as 1864, but William gives the year as 1868 in a history of New Richmond that he wrote for the Crawfordsville Weekly *Review*. The 1870 Federal census gives his occupation as a barber, but the 1874 *People's Guide of Montgomery County* lists his occupation as grocery and notion store in New Richmond. William had not been in business very long when his building and merchandise was destroyed by fire in 1874. His friends encouraged him to start over and helped him financially to do so. The 1882-83 directory lists, "William Campbell, grocery," and in 1884, '85, and 1887 the directories list, "William Campbell, Saloon and Grocery."

William became pretty successful for a small town merchant, and customers dropped into his store from the larger cities, Crawfordsville and Lafayette, on occasion. In 1886, he secured the service of a "first class shoemaker" who was to open his shop that winter. On the Fourth of July, the following summer, he was to have a balloon ascension in front of his store; the balloon was being made in his Pioneer Store for the occasion. William advertised "The Best Line of Groceries in the State, eggs, 10 cents a dozen; butter, 10 cents a pound; young chickens, 9 cents a pound, new potatoes, 75 cents per bushel, and CHIEFTAN FLOUR, made in Attica." William was to have twenty-five sacks of coffee grown in the Argentine Republic, shipped to him by Honorable B.W. Hanna, Minister to the Argentine Republic, in 1888. He advertised, "Go to Campbells and get a jug full of four-year-old cider vinegar, it is sour enough to make a pig squeal." He was asking people to settle accounts and said, "Sassafras roots is now legal tender in the vicinity and as long as the root holds out—no one will go dry." He also accepted berries, paw-paws, nuts, and other native produce from his customers for trade.

In December of 1888, William Campbell hired a "little Dutch Tailor from over the Rhine," by the name of Aloys Anton, and started a tailoring shop in connection with his grocery, boots and shoes, and notion store. The new tailor turned out new suits at a very rapid rate, and William said he could really make the sewing machine talk. He had more work than he anticipated.

William suffered a set-back in February, 1889, when his Pioneer store was the victim of another fire. He lost most of his merchandise, and the remains smoldered for about two weeks. He did not give up, but continued to conduct his business in another store room, and soon decided to rebuild. In October, the same year, he hired Buck Belt to erect a new two-story frame building. His first building was a log structure. All the rooms were spoken for in his new building before it was completed, for other business enterprises. He made plans for a big celebration to dedicate his new building. The Lafayette String Band was to furnish the music, and no one could attend unless they had a ticket, he said. E.C. Campbell, his brother, painted the new building and William was back in business. He advertised, "For overalls that wont rip-go to Campbells, [sic] cheapest in the village; tobacco, cigars, confectionary, crackers, cakes, bread, cheese, and the best coal oil in town." William received "from a distillery in Kentucky, some whiskey—for medicinal purposes—that Kentucky can feel well proud of. It is as pure as any that is made, and those desiring a liquor they can depend on should secure it—can't be beat!" I noticed that his Kentucky whiskey advertisements were placed in the New Richmond items he authored quite frequently.

10 - Aloys Anton, tailor

William Campbell had a confrontation with a gentleman living north of town and decided to sell his store. He offered for sale, "One store room; one harness shop; and a residence." He considered moving to Dayton, Ohio, where he had an offer "by which he could do well." Then he thought of erecting a mammoth store in Romney, but he settled in the new little village of Kirkpatrick and opened his new Granger Store, in April of 1891. He remained there until March of 1894, when he built a new store at Corwin, the railroad station west of Romney in Tippecanoe County.

After William moved to Kirkpatrick, his wife, Ella, moved to Chicago where she started a dress-making establishment. She was very successful and was working eight seamstresses, and received orders from as far as Indianapolis and Lafayette. William visited his wife in the "Windy City" but was still living at Corwin at the time of his death on July 23, 1901. The Simison elevator firm purchased his building at Corwin in April 1902 and dismantled it. The Campbell building was being used as Mr. Crouse's silent grog shop, an unlicensed dive, where counterfeit money was turning up, and Simison paid twice the actual worth of the building just so he could destroy the place of nuisance.

In April 1891, Douglas Bunnell purchased William's Pioneer Store in New Richmond, and sold general merchandise for a few years. He moved the building fifty feet to the east and enlarged it. The old Pioneer store building was dismantled in October 1904 to make room for a modern home. It stood on the northwest corner of Franklin and Washington Streets.

I asked the late Opal Clapp if she had ever heard of William Campbell's Pioneer Store, and she related a story her grandmother, Jane Ebrite, told about Opal's mother, Emma Ebrite. When Emma was a child, she went to his store to purchase some stick candy, and William weighed it. The candy weighed more than she had asked for, so William just bit off part of one stick and proceeded to put the rest of the stick in her sack. She informed him he could just keep the rest of that stick of candy.

Early General Store Merchants

In an early history of New Richmond by William Campbell, he says, "The first store kept in the village was kept by John Mick, he kept in the building now occupied by Mr. Worth as a residence, and is the oldest building in the town." I searched the 1830, 1840, and 1850 census records for John Mick and failed to locate him in New Richmond, nor was he listed in Montgomery County, but he may have been here between the times the census was taken.

John W. Plunkett erected a large frame business house on the southeast corner of Wabash and Washington Streets and embarked in the general merchandising business in 1867. His "general merchandise" included a barrel of well-aged Kentucky whiskey with a tin cup nearby for his customers to quench their thirst. John was charged with selling intoxicating liquors without a license in 1879. He paid his fine and made an appeal to the circuit court. This was the beginning of an ugly scandal involving a local physician and half the town—the bad half, of course. John and President Plunkett were both listed as clerks on the 1880 census, and records show John had been clerking for Wint Washburn in his store seven years later.

W.B. Walls purchased "the" general store in New Richmond and made a quick trip to Cincinnati to purchase his stock in December of 1879. In 1882 and 1883, Dayton E. Black was in general merchandise; he later studied medicine and became one of the town's leading physicians. John E. Harriman was running a general store in 1891 and 1892, but his store was listed as a department store in the directory.

In 1887, there were at least three general stores: William Campbell's Pioneer store; Jackson Smith's, which stood north of the railroad track on south Wabash Street, and Wint Washburn's. Both Smith and Washburn were agents for the local express office. W.W. Washburn started traveling for a notion house in Philadelphia with Indiana as his territory, but he continued operating his general store in New Richmond. In 1900 he had acquired a partner, Mr. Kirkpatrick, although I am not certain which Kirkpatrick was working with Wint. The two took on another partner, the same year, and the store was known for a short time only as Washburn, Kirkpatrick, and Claypool (see Claypool & Fry's general store).

William Campbell sold his Pioneer Store to Douglas Bunnell in April of 1891, and he and Thomas Morris carried on a general merchandise business for a few years. He offered his stock of goods for sale in April of 1900, and in 1905 remodeled his building into a dwelling, thus eliminating all signs of the old building.

John W. Hollin's store was listed as a general store in the 1900-01 county directory. He sold shoes and drugs, and his brother, William, conducted the grocery business (see drug and groceries section).

Other short-term general store operators were Montgomery and Zook, who were in business in May of 1891, but sold their stock to Jake Burris in October the same year. In January, 1896, Ben Warbinton opened a general merchandising business, but I have no record of the time period he left the town. A general store was being conducted by a Will Goben in April of 1896 when he sold out to a Mr. Corwin and Samuel Beach. This is the only record I found of these three gentlemen and their store.

James Carter lost two business rooms in New Richmond by fire in the big fire in July, 1898, but it is uncertain if he was running a business, or just owned the buildings.

Frank Perkins' General Store

Frank Perkins purchased from Jacob Campbell the south half of lot one, block one, in the original plat of New Richmond on August 9, 1881, and opened a general merchandise establishment. He continued in that location until March 1886, when he purchased a lot from Dr. Detchon on the north side of east Washington Street. His store was listed in the 1887 and 1890 directories of the county.

Frank purchased his stock from Lafayette warehouses. He lost his residence, most of his building, and stock of merchandise by fire when a whole row of homes and business houses were destroyed on July 12, 1898. His losses were estimated between $3500 to $5000. He and his wife, Lucy, and their four children were left homeless and with no means of livelihood except for Frank's livery stable, which was saved by heroic citizens of the town. He soon recovered, and by 1900 he was back in business, and had erected a large, two-story, brick building with a brick cottage attached to his general store. An entry between the two made easy access to his business. The residence and building are still standing on east Washington Street. The building served as the town fire department and town hall for many years.

Frank received consignments of fresh produce direct from Chicago each week consisting of celery, bananas, figs, apples, lettuce, coconuts, dates, oranges, and candies, for the holiday trade, in December of 1901. Frank was conducting a store in Linden as well as New Richmond in May of 1902. A month later, he advertised for sale $10,000 worth of stock, at cost, and all the fixtures in his store. Among the items were: ready-made clothing for men and boys, dry goods, boots, men's shoes, $2.50; ladies' shoes, $2; jewelry, toys, trunks, valises, traveling bags, groceries, crockery, calicoes, 3 cents and 4 cents per yard, granulated sugar, 21 cents lb., coffee, 10 cents lb., and coal oil, 8 cents a gallon. "Perk" failed to sell his stock, however, and continued until April of 1903 when D.M. Carson of Monticello purchased his stock. Because of illness, Carson was unable to continue the business, and sold the stock back to Perkins and moved his family to Indianapolis, the same year.

Frank continued running his store in Linden but kept his place of residence in New Richmond during this time. He had sold merchandise on time, and was asking people to settle accounts after he bought his store back from Carson, and offered all his stock at greatly reduced prices in order to recover the losses he suffered by making the trade. Frank had negotiated a trade of his store and residence property with a Minton Reed, of Mount Erie, Illinois, for a 200-acre farm in that state, but the deal fell through, and Frank was forced to file a petition for bankruptcy in June of 1904.

11 - Frank Perkins' General Store

George Washburn purchased the Perkins brick building and his residence a month later. Frank also sold his two bowling alleys at this time.

After being in business in New Richmond for 23 years, he recovered part of his merchandise and moved to his store in the Dunkle room in Linden in September the same year, where he continued to sell general merchandise until May of 1905. At that time he moved his stock of goods and his family to Meir in Grant County, Indiana. Frank Perkins was the son of Elias W. and Maggie (Kincaid) Perkins, and the great grandson of Samuel Kincaid who platted the town of New Richmond.

CLAYPOOL & FRY "THE BIG STORE"

In 1900, Melvin Luther Claypool purchased one-third interest of Washburn and Kirkpatrick's general merchandise firm in New Richmond, and the business began being conducted under the name of Washburn, Kirkpatrick, and Claypool. In September, the same year, Claypool and Harry O. Fry purchased the entire interests of Washburn and Kirkpatrick, and operated under the name of Claypool & Fry. These two gentlemen became the leading merchants in the town and spared no means in advertising.

Claypool and Fry were located in the room east of the bank, and the store extended to the room back of the bank, where the grocery department was situated. This was the old location of the bank in the Washburn brick building on the southeast corner of Washington and Wabash Streets in New Richmond.

Claypool & Fry's store carried Axminister and Brussels carpets, curtains, window shades, shoes, clothing, millinery, and groceries. In October 1902, new cloak and walking skirt departments were added to their stock.

In addition to the store was their huckster wagon. Some of the drivers were: James Moulder, in 1902, Art Claypool, 1903, Ed Mason, 1903, Nolen Snyder and Earl Waye, 1904, Darwin Layne and Robert E. Seaman, in 1905.

Claypool and Fry advertised in August of 1903: "Calico, 4-1/2 cents per yard; heavy outing, 5 cents, brown and bleached muslin, 5 cents, cotton crash, 5 cents, double fold-all wool dress goods, 33 cents per yard, walking skirts, $1 to $9, men's Prince Henry's overcoats, and Ladies-best $10.75 cloak on earth."

M.L. Claypool traded with the largest and best warehouses in Indianapolis and Chicago for his stock, spending three or four days in each city studying and buying in order to keep the stock up-to-date. In November of 1903, he advertised the latest cloak styles, "Zibeline, Mountenac, and Kersey, in colors of black, blue, brown, tan, and castor."

The "Big Store" usually placed large, full page advertisements, but one of the best was a large four-page holiday bulletin in the New Richmond Record in December of 1903. The editor said it was one of the "neatest bits of advertising ever published in that newspaper."

The following year, another department was added, competent dressmakers were secured to do all kinds of dressmaking—at reasonable prices—and customers were advised to get their orders in early before the busy season. The store advertised men's patent leather shoes, $2.50, and ladies' low-cut patent tip shoes, only $1. The millinery department offered ladies' beautiful spring hats, from $2.50 to $3.50, and children's hats, $1 to $2. In 1904 when the two proprietors considered ending their partnership, the store advertised a large dissolution sale to close out their stock, and $15,000 worth of stock was to be sold at a 25% to 50% reduction. The two decided to continue their partnership, however, and continued as one of the leading general merchandise establishments in the town. For a promotion, they purchased a little Welsh pony, Little Dixie, to give away, using the same plan the government used to allot public lands. A photograph was published in the Record, and the pony was to be on exhibition at the store each day (to win the heart of every girl and boy, no doubt) until the drawing was held. If the winner had no use for the pony, a $75 check was to be substituted. Enoch Babourn won the pony but preferred the check, and I don't know what became of Little Dixie.

Claypool and Fry put on a big millinery show to open the spring and fall season's latest fashions, and their experienced trimmers were on hand to display and style their wares. A pianist played all afternoon and evening for these shows, and refreshments of delicious fruit punch and tea cakes, or cookies, were served to their customers. In October of 1905, Miss Mertz exhibited her hats and included in the display was a lady's $50 hat made up of 49 one-dollar bills on a one-dollar wire frame. David Scott of Crawfordsville, was the pianist at this opening.

A large stock of pianos was added to the store in October of 1905. In November that same year, Claypool and Fry organized a "Corn Show" and offered a prize of a $2.50 pair of shoes to the farmer with the longest ears (of corn, of course). They also held a baby show. For another promotion, a prize was offered to the farmer who could round up the most people and bring them to New Richmond on one wagon, pulled by one team of horses. The "Big Wagon Load" was won by Jesse Pierce with 47 people on his wagon. Little Maude Miller, age 7 months, from Linden, won the baby competition, the prize being a handsome little bear-skin coat and hood. Three New Richmond bachelors judged this event, and there was no record of them being run out of town!

In November of 1905, Claypool and Fry made arrangements to sell their store to a gentleman from Rensselaer, and were to trade the store for a 240-acre farm in Newton County valued at $13,000. The deal was to be completed on December 27th, and the new owner was to take possession January 1, 1906, but because the facts were misrepresented by the other party, Claypool and Fry repudiated the contract, and continued to carry on the business. They held a large sale before the deal was cancelled in order to cut down some $7,000 worth of stock, and sold more goods during their sale than any other firm ever in the history of New Richmond. One Saturday, alone, they sold over $700 worth of goods.

The following year, the proprietors went all out on their advertising and purchasing of goods. They bought a whole carload of Kansas hard wheat flour in 50-pound bags in order to sell 30 cents under the usual price. "Kite" flour was advertised for $1.10 in March 1906, and a month later was marked down to $1. Trading stamps were given free with every 10 cent purchase at this time, and additional help was hired for the grand spring millinery opening.

The store was enjoying one of the most successful years in the business, and perhaps the proprietors thought the time was right for selling out; the "Big Store" was sold to Weymer and Dudley, of Frankfort, Indiana, in June 1906, who assumed possession as soon as the invoicing was completed.

Claypool and Fry moved their stock of pianos into the W.S. Alexander room, formerly occupied by McLain's restaurant, along with their desk, books, and accounts, until all outstanding accounts were settled. M.L. Claypool entered the piano and music business in September the same year, purchasing the stock of John A. Gilbert of Crawfordsville, and locating on east Main Street. He acquired a new partner, and the firm was known as Claypool & Lacy. Claypool moved his family to Crawfordsville soon after. Harry Fry was listed as a resident of Anderson, Indiana, in 1919.

During their stay in New Richmond, the Claypool and Fry general store employed several citizens of the town. Among the clerks employed were: Charles Claypool, grocery department, Arthur Claypool, Mime Patton, Bertha Pitts, Willard Stockton, Ruth Stanley, Jessie Kirkpatrick, Charles Westfall, John Orr, Della Clarkson, and Harriet Jones. Those employed as trimmers in the millinery department were: Grace Hopewell, Effie Jessie, Nellie Keir, Nellie Smith, Miss Mertz, and Rena Rafferty. The only dressmaker mentioned was Jennie Martin, but the store was to employ more than one, according to their announcement made at the beginning of this new department. Bookkeepers employed at Claypool and Fry were Laura Kirkpatrick and Ed Mason.

WEYMER & DUDLEY

Edward R. Weymer purchased the general merchandise stock of Claypool & Fry in June of 1906, and established his store in the same building in New Richmond, the east room of the Washburn block on the southeast corner of Washington and Wabash Streets. His establishment operated under the name of Weymer & Dudley, his infant son being the "Dudley" half of the partnership. Weyner moved his wife and infant from Kempton, Indiana, the last of June, into the rooms over the store until better accommodations were found. A month later, the family moved to the Methodist Church cottage in the east part of town. The new store proprietor presented his initial advertisement in the New Richmond *Record*, Thursday, June 28, 1906, promising to continue on much the same lines as the former owners, and stated the firm also owned stores at Kempton and Sharpsville, therefore, could offer the customers in New Richmond better prices because of buying larger volumes of merchandise. They commenced their business in New Richmond with a two-week sale, and after that sale was over, full-page advertisements were the general rule in the New Richmond Record. Items such as "men's shoes, $1.38 to $3.98; ladies' shoes, $1.38 to $2.98; men's suits $5.98 to $14.98; boys and girls shoes, 42 cents to $2.50, ladies' corsets, 86 cents to 92 cents." How about these prices, wouldn't it be nice to see such bargains again?

E.R. Weymer purchased his merchandise in Indianapolis and Cincinnati warehouses. He engaged Miss Florence Miles of Indianapolis as the head trimmer in his millinery department. Millinery departments were very big in New Richmond about this time, and he continued the tradition of the grand spring and fall openings.

Weymer and Dudley also had, in connection with the store, a huckster wagon driven by Robert E. Seaman and Jesse Pierce in the fall of 1906. These two are the only persons of which I have a record, but there may have been other drivers.

Weymer allowed the ladies of the New Richmond Christian Church to have charge of his store and gave them ten percent of all cash sales during one full day in December, the year he opened in the town. Weymer offered $.30 for eggs, and special prices for butter in trade at his store. Some of his outstanding prices in 1908 were: 50 lb. of Gold Medal Flour, $1.59; 1 can of salmon, 11 cents; Pride of Peoria Flour, $1.39; Quaker Oats, 9 cents; and coffee, 15 cents.

E.R. Weymer continued his general merchandising establishment in New Richmond until February of 1910, when he and his family moved to their farm four miles south of Frankfort. Weymer was a native of Lincoln, Illinois.

Clerks employed in the Weymer & Dudley's store were: Laura Kirkpatrick, Ruth Stanley (later Byron Alexander's mother), Charles Klopfer, and Harriett Jones. Trimmers of the millinery department mentioned were: Florence Miles, head trimmer, and Anna Hagen. Earl Waye was manager of the grocery department.

ROBERT E. SEAMAN GENERAL STORE

Robert E. Seaman purchased the merchandise of Nicholas Washburn, who was conducting a men's clothing and cigar store, in August 1908. This business establishment was situated in half of the eastern section of the Washburn block.

Seaman took possession of the store in September that year and had added groceries to his stock. He advertised "Our Daily Bread" and "Royal Flour" and was offering the highest prices paid for produce. He advertised hundreds of items during a 39 cent sale a year later, and was paying 17-1/2 cents for eggs; 13 cents for butter; 11 cents for lard, and 12 cents for chickens on the local market.

Seaman's last advertisement I found in the New Richmond *Record*, February 24, 1910, advertised Men's Clothing and Cigar Store, Robert E. Seaman, Proprietor. He later went into the real estate business.

T.F. MONTGOMERY CASH STORE

T.F. Montgomery opened up for business in the town of New Richmond on February 19, 1910 in the Washburn room next to the bank. The corner location was accessible on both Washington and Wabash Streets. Montgomery moved his stock of dry goods, notions, shoes, and gent's furnishings over from Clark's Hill, and placed them on his shelves in his new location.

A stock of groceries was added, and Earl Waye was put in charge of this department because he had held the same position in the same location for quite some time. Earl had been manager of the Weymer & Dudley's grocery department, the previous owner of the store. Montgomery added a new line of millinery for the fall opening, the same year, and also advertised phonographs, and men's suits from the Royal Tailors. In October, his business was so successful, he expanded his stock and moved his big new shoe department to the east room. This is the last information I have found concerning the T.F. Montgomery cash store.

HANAWALT AND SON

Austin Hanawalt and his son, Roy B., opened their general store in New Richmond in October, 1910, "one door west of the Post Office," his first advertisement said. They were located in the same building as the former general stores in the Washburn, or bank building, on the southeast corner of Washington and Wabash Streets. They advertised groceries, flour, tobacco, cigars, and a full line of Money-Back and Red Plume brands of canned goods, gents' furnishings—including hats, caps, underwear, and hosiery, and notions. They offered to pay the highest market prices for local produce.

A full line of sweater coats were priced from .50 to $8, and the best corduroy sheep-lined coats were only $9 in November, 1915. Palm Beach suits were from $8 to $12, in mohair or crash, and were made-to-measure. In August 1919, white and oxford shoes were advertised from $2.70 to $5.39, in assorted sizes, and they carried a full line of rubber footwear.

In April 1923, Hanawalt's store was advertising cleaning and pressing services. They cleaned and blocked hats, suits, and other wearing apparel.

Austin Hanawalt died on December 18, 1924, and his son carried on the family business until the 1930s when he accepted the position of rural mail carrier on the New Richmond route, which he continued for thirty years.

Mr. Friedman, a Crawfordsville merchant, purchased Hanawalt's stock, held a huge sale, then boxed up the remaining merchandise to sell in his store in Crawfordsville. The grocery stock was purchased by Joe Campbell, who started a grocery in the rooms formerly occupied by Hanawalt and Son.

Dry Goods Merchants

A clerk at one of the dry goods stores says that a modest young lady who desired to make a purchase yesterday, addressed the young man behind the counter, thus: "It is my desire to obtain a pair of circular elastic appendages, capable of being contracted or expanded by means of oscillating burnished steel appliances that sparkle like particles of gold-leaf, set with Alaska diamonds, and which are utilized for retaining in proper position the habiliments of the lower extremities, which innate delicacy forbids me to mention." The clerk thought a moment and said he believed she wanted a pair of garters.

John W. Plunketts Dry Goods Store

John W. Plunkett, age 28, was listed as a dry goods merchant in New Richmond on the 1870 Federal census. He later added general merchandise to his stock, and John served as the local postmaster from November 19, 1869, to October 25, 1878; therefore, the post office was located within his store.

Jackson Smith Dry Goods Store

Jackson Smith's store was listed as a general store, but in February of 1886, he sold out his entire stock of dry goods, and entered the hardware business.

William Winter Washburn Dry Goods Store

W.W. "Wint" Washburn was listed in the 1895 directory of the county as a dealer in dry goods, clothing, boots, shoes, glassware, Queens Ware, etc. George Banta clerked in his store at one time. Washburn's store was listed as a general store in earlier years, and there is more on his store in that section of New Richmond's business establishments.

Townsley and Company Dry Goods

Andrew Townsley of Crawfordsville put in a new and first class stock of dry goods in a frame business room on east Washington Street in New Richmond in March of 1898, and hired Miss Winnie Gerard as his clerk.

Andrew married Miss Pearl Dennis in Crawfordsville a short time after, and brought his seventeen-year-old bride to live in New Richmond with the John W. Hollin family until they could find a home of their own.

Townsley's dry goods store was one of the shortest-lived business firms in the town, as a disastrous fire destroyed a whole row of frame buildings, and Townsley lost all his stock and the building. The fire broke out in his dry goods store at 2 a.m. Tuesday, July 12, 1898, and was out of control before the townspeople arrived to help extinguish the flames. Townsley had $2,000 worth of insurance, but his losses exceeded that amount by $500. There is no record of his rebuilding or starting over in New Richmond.

James L. Moulder Dry Goods

The earliest record of James L. Moulder's dry goods store in New Richmond was an advertisement in the Methodist Church ladies cookbook, printed in 1912. He advertised, "Ladies and gents' furnishings, dry goods and notions" and his slogan, which some earlier residents still remember, was "Watch for the yellow bundles." One of his advertisements in 1919, though, said, "Watch for the green bundles." He must have ran out of yellow wrapping paper for his sales.

In 1915, James Moulder was an agent for Rogers Blake and Company of Chicago, a men's tailoring company, and also was an agent for the Ideal Ladies Tailoring company, a ladies' tailoring company, also of Chicago. He carried rugs and mattings for the home, as well.

New Richmond had a week-long homecoming celebration, and Moulder marked his merchandise down considerably to take advantage of the crowd that was expected. Men's overalls were only 39 cents, calico, 4-1/2 cents, ladies' parasols, $1, men's dress shirts, 89 cents, and the Warner Brothers rust-proof corsets were only 10 cents, boys' knee pants, 44 cents, and a lot of other good bargains were listed. J.L. Moulder purchased his stock in the Indianapolis wholesale houses.

A cute advertising gimmick was a beautiful silk dress pattern was to be given away "FREE!" An 8-day clock was to be placed in the store's east window, and the clock was to stop running sometime during the sale week. The person who guessed the nearest to the time the clock stopped was to receive the free pattern. In order to enter their names and the time they guessed, the customers had to buy $1 or more merchandise.

The last advertisement I have recorded on Moulder's store is July 6, 1922, but he may have been in New Richmond later. Moulder's first location was in the east room of the Long brothers brick building on the northeast corner of Washington and Wabash Streets, but later moved to the Perkins brick building.

LONG'S DRY GOODS, JEWELRY & WALL PAPER STORE

George Franklin Long, a native of St. Marys, Ohio, embarked in business in New Richmond as a jeweler and watchmaker around 1884 or 1885. He was the son of John S. and Rosetta Matson Long, who came to Montgomery County, Indiana, around 1869. George began his business venture with only fifteen dollars in cash, in a small room that later served as an office room of George Livingston's livery barn. This building stood on the east side of south Wabash Streets just north of the railroad station. The site is now occupied by the metal storage bins of the Farm Bureau elevator. George F. Long was appointed postmaster of New Richmond on December 29, 1884, and held the office until April of 1889. The post office was probably located in this small building during this period.

In early life, George aspired to be a doctor, and began studying medicine under Dr. D.M. Washburn, a New Richmond physician. He attended Indiana Medical College and was to receive his sheepskin in another six months, but lacked sufficient funds to continue his coveted vocation. He refused to accept a short time loan, and turned to the business in which he continued the rest of his life.

Within one year, George had prospered so well he had outgrown his little business room. He purchased a lot from Dr. Stowe Detchon on the north side of town, and soon had the lumber and materials on the newly acquired lot and started the construction of a new building. At the completion of the building, he made a trip to Ohio to purchase a supply of jewelry stock for his new store, and Long continued to succeed. For a small town such as New Richmond, to be so successful as to earn a living from the jewelry trade is somewhat amazing.

Long expanded his business by 1891 to include jewelry, notions, and confections. As a side-line, he served the town as a local express agent, and for a short time, was employed in the local tile factory.

On March 6, 1891, George F. Long had the distinction of establishing and publishing the town's first newspaper, the New Richmond *Times*. He sold the paper shortly after to Joseph Smith and devoted his time to the jewelry trade, realizing that running a newspaper required his full time. George F. Long was elected as the first Clerk of the town of New Richmond in 1895 when the town was incorporated, and served in that capacity until January 1906, when he refused to run again. Another first for George was introducing ice cream to New Richmond residents in May of 1887 for 5 cents a dish.

Being a very enterprising young man, Long decided to enter another field and studied optometry. He received his degree as an optician from the South Bend Optical College, a school not in existence today. Long's store advertised, "George F. Long, Jeweler and Optician—Your Eyes Tested Free—Glasses Fitted and Guaranteed."

By 1899, Long's business was known as "Long's Dry Goods, Jewelry and Wall Paper Store," and he was the local agent for Wheeler & Wilson Sewing Machines. He carried a line of Yount's Wool Blankets, from Yount's Woolen Mills of Yountsville, Indiana. For the Christmas holiday he advertised beautiful dolls, kid body, 85 cents, dressed dolls, 50 cents, Ladies' gold watch—guaranteed fifteen years, $9, ladies' Silverine watch, $5.50, Gents' watch, $5, and men's gold watch, $12.50.

George F. Long erected a 32'-by-20' brick building in 1890 on the northeast corner of Wabash and Washington Streets in New Richmond to accommodate his growing business. This building was soon outgrown, and in 1902 he erected a 38'-by-20' addition to the structure, making a room seventy feet in length by twenty feet in width. At the time of the later expansion, he had goods stocked from floor to ceiling. It is interesting to observe the cautious steps he took in expanding his buildings and his stock of merchandise. He did not start out in business until he had the cash in his hands, and worked his way up to the larger business rooms and only expanded when he had the necessary funds to pay for the buildings and merchandise. New Richmond's early businessmen did not plunge themselves into debt, and proceeded very cautiously, and by following this rule, there were very few bankruptcies.

George Long purchased his stock for the store in Indianapolis and Chicago warehouses in the later years. The trip to Ohio was more time consuming, and the two cities were fast becoming the favorite trading centers for Hoosiers.

In the summer of 1903, Long's store advertised the New Home Sewing Machine, for $17.75 with a ten-year guarantee, and table linen, 25 cents to $1 per yard. London fads in men's fashion arrived in New Richmond at this time, with embroidered monograms on handkerchiefs, neckties, etc., and Waltham Railway and Elgin watches were included in his stock that year. Blankets were from 45 cents to $1.25, and in November, thoughts were turned to corn husking equipment. Men's mittens were 5 cents a pair, or 60 cents per dozen, corn husker canton, 15 cents to 18 cents per yard, corn husking pegs, 10, 15, and 25 cents, men's underwear, best fleece-lined, from 19 to 50 cents.

Long's carried a complete line of 1847 Rogers Brothers knives, forks, and spoons in 1904, and homemade sheets from 35 cents to 65 cents; Richardson's wall paper, 30 cents per bolt and up; walking skirts, $3.50 to $10. He added a stock of millinery in April that year, and rugs and carpets, 55 cents to 65 cents; Egyptian tissue ginghams, 10 cents per yard, and Quaker collar forms, 10 cents each.

The "New Home Sewing Machine—Double Feed—Ball Bearings—Steel Needle Bar—Positive Gear Motion—Automatic Bobin Winder," etc. was $18.75 CASH, and he carried other sewing supplies. In 1906 his New Home Sewing Machine was guaranteed to run "as long as it is a machine." Two years later the sewing machine company advertised the new "drop head" and was guaranteed for "all time."

Long's store was offering to send their goods by parcel post in 1919. Their customers could order by mail or by phone. Japanese grass rugs, 9' by 12', were excellent for bedrooms, priced at $11. The New Home Midget portable sewing machine—the smallest practical shuttle machine—was only $12.50 in April of 1923.

The prices quoted in the advertisements makes interesting reading, and it makes a person stop and think about how little profit the early merchants made on their merchandise, but the cost of living was quite different then. George F. Long was always remembered by the New Richmond folks as one of the most honest merchants in the town, and was a craftsman who took great pride in his watch-making, engraving, lens grinding, and fitting eye-glasses. He suffered a stroke in his place of business and fell to the floor, dying instantly, on December 27, 1916. His brother A.D. Long continued to run the business until about 1927 or 1928, when he moved to Indianapolis and followed optometry for five years. He then moved to Bloomington and remained in that city until his death on January 2, 1952.

George F. Long's first wife, Nellie Keesee, died one week after their son Louis E. was born. He then married Mary Clough, and they had a daughter Ruby. Both of George Long's children died in infancy. George and his two wives are buried in the New Richmond cemetery.

Arthur D. Long, better known as A.D., was a native of New Richmond, born in 1873. A.D. followed in his brother George's footsteps as a skilled watchmaker, engraver, and optometrist, graduating from the same South Bend Optical College.

A.D. Long married a local girl, Sarah Florence Jones, in New Richmond in 1899. Florence was a daughter of George H. and Mary F. (Champion) Jones. They began their married life in New Richmond, where A.D. was associated with his brother, George, in the dry goods, jewelry, and wallpaper store. A.D. moved around quite a lot after that, and resided in Frankfort, Kokomo, Champaign, Illinois, South Dakota—for three years, but could not stand the cold climate or the rattlesnakes—Indianapolis, and

Bloomington, Indiana, where his death occurred. Arthur and Florence Long had six children: Carrol, Doris, George A., J. Chester, Louis, and Frances. All of the children attended the New Richmond School as teenagers and all the children graduated from high school and college.

Dr. A.D. Long was an expert engraver, and during the war engraved hundreds of identification bracelets, but the most pleasant task was engraving the high school trophies which his son Louis won. Mrs. Long's hobbies were quilting, crocheting, and embroidery. She made at least 75 quilts in her lifetime. Her death occurred September 25, 1957. Arthur and Florence Long are buried in the New Richmond cemetery.

New Richmond Grocers

Aquilla "Quill" Dillon's Grocery

New Richmond's first grocery was operated by Aquilla Dillon (also spelled Dilling). He opened his store in 1847 in an old log structure. Although he is credited as the first grocer, he was listed as a farmer on the 1850 census in Coal Creek Township. Dillon married a local girl, Sarah Ann Forbes, on November 24, 1841.

Thomas Foster's Grocery

Thomas Martin Foster, a native of North Carolina, operated a grocery in New Richmond from 1860 to 1863. The location of the early groceries are unknown.

Daniel White's Grocery

Daniel White, age 43, a native of New York, was listed as a New Richmond grocer on the 1870 census. He and his wife, Sarah L., had five children under the age of eleven at the time.

The Pioneer Store

William Campbell embarked in the grocery trade in 1864 and was listed as a grocer on the 1880 census. Six years later, it was reported his grocery business was still booming. William added notions and general merchandise to his stock of groceries later, and became one of the leading merchants in the towns' early history (more on the Pioneer Store in the general stores section).

Hollin & Anderson Grocery and Drug Store (later Hollin & Co.)

John W. Hollin and Lowell Anderson added a stock of groceries to their well-established drug business in January 1880. John's brother, William, was manager of the grocery department a few years later, and continued until his last illness (more on Hollin & Co. in the drug and general stores section).

In 1903, W.H. Hollin advertised, "Rio Coffee, 9 cents per lb., and African Java 15 cents per lb., 1 gallon Best Syrup, 35 cents, and 16 bars of Daniel Boone soap, 25 cents." In 1910 his advertisement read, "W.H. Hollin dealer in staple and fancy groceries, cigars, and tobacco." In 1922 he advertised "Ball mason jars, 1/2 gallon size, $1 per dozen, quarts, 85 cents, pints, 75 cents and tin cans, 45 cents per dozen, bulk sweet and dill pickels."

Bunnel & Morris Grocery

Douglas Bunnel and Thomas Morris were partners in the grocery business from 1891 to 1895. Bunnel purchased William Campbell's Pioneer Store for their business venture on the corner of Washington and Franklin Streets.

Montgomery & Zook

The partnership of Montgomery & Zook as New Richmond grocers only lasted from May to October of 1891. This was not even long enough for me to discover the first names of the two gentlemen, or the location of their store.

Jake Burris Grocery

Jake Burris purchased Montgomery & Zook's grocery stock in October 1891 and opened his grocery soon after. The store was listed as the Burris Brothers grocery in 1895.

Ben Warbinton Grocery

Ben Warbinton's store was referred to as a grocery in January, 1896, but he was in general merchandise as well.

H.C Johnson's "Spot Cash Store"

H.C. Johnson, of Knightstown, and brother to F.M. Johnson, a New Richmond druggist, opened his grocery about April 1, 1902 in the McCardle block just vacated by A.D. Snyder's hardware. Snyder's new brick building was just completed. Johnson carried groceries, Queens Ware, books, stationery, notions, graniteware and tin-ware. He claimed to be the "leader on low prices." He advertised items for a hot weather lunch, fine cheese, baked beans, salmon, sardines, etc. Johnson's spring chickens were 11 cents per lb.; eggs, 14 cents a dozen; side meat, 12 cents per lb; and butter, 14 cents per lb. H.C. Johnson moved to Indianapolis and was in the pottery business in 1908.

F.M. Johnson Grocery & Queens Ware Store

F.M. Johnson evidently purchased his brother's grocery and Queens Ware stock by September 1902, the same year H.C. started the grocery, because the advertisements were listed under "F.M. Johnson and Company, Grocery and Queensware," at that time.

F.M. Johnson moved his drugstore merchandise into the frame block formerly occupied by his brother's Spot Cash store and combined both businesses for a short time. Both buildings were owned by John W. McCardle. Johnson advertised Christmas goods and fine candy, the largest line of toys, books, games, Crockinole boards, building blocks, A.B.C. blocks, dolls, doll go-carts, doll heads, etc. For the boys, the usual grab-game was to be held from 10:30 a.m. to 2:00 p.m. on Christmas Day. The girls were to have a Christmas treat in the morning.

A.W. Hempleman's Grocery and Restaurant

Aleck Hempleman from West Union in Adams County, Ohio, embarked in the grocery and restaurant trade in 1903. The county directory that year lists "Grocery & Restaurant, A.W. Hempleman & Co., corner of Market and Washington Streets in New Richmond," but under the name Hempleman, the address was listed as corner of Washington and Wabash Streets. There is no street named Market in New Richmond on any map.

Aleck Hempleman placed the following notice in the New Richmond *Record*, Thursday, January 8, 1903, "If you drive to town and have a foot stone to warm before you start for home, bring it to our store. If you want a jug of hot water to keep your feet warm on your long drive home, ask us for it-you can have it." He advertised all varieties of fruits, both green and canned, and "Lover's Dreams," ten for 1 cent, and Zu-Zu, 5 cents a package. He traded with the local people for all kinds of produce—rabbits, eggs, butter, etc. He offered Broadlick's Steam Bread, 6 loaves for 25 cents, and premium tickets to be redeemed when the customer's purchases amounted to $20, for their choice of fine silverware. Hempleman's carried the famous Heinze products, and Dudley's famous coffee "that stimulates, but does not inebriate." He was paying 6 cents for rabbits in November 1903.

A.W. Hempleman advertised a barrel of salt for $6, National Light Oil, 15 cents a gallon, gasoline, 16-2/3 cents in 1904. In April, the same year, A.W. Hempleman purchased the ovens belonging to the former Grigson bakery and restaurant, made some needed repairs, converted the ovens into first-class coke fired ovens, and started furnishing local residents with "the best New Richmond baked bread ever sold in the town." He advertised, "Leave your orders for cakes, pies, crackers, or buns, at Hempleman's Per Aleck's Bread." He asked the townspeople to "come and see us bake on our new oven-everything will bear inspection and you are always welcome." In June the same year, he was delivering his bread by wagon to the outlying area, and the store was listed as A.W. Hempleman's Grocery & Restaurant. Hempleman sold his bread for the same prices as the former supplier, the fresh bread was priced at 5 cents a loaf, or 6 loaves for 25 cents-stale bread was 2 for 5 cents, and buns were baked for 60 cents per hundred. He installed a new Dunn cheese cutter for cutting cheese "in a splendid shape for the table" and offered to show people how it worked. Later he installed a new peanut roaster which amused him, and invited the citizens in to see how it worked. "Hemp" certainly knew how to entertain the good people of New Richmond, did he not?

Hempleman advertised "Per Aleck's Graham Bread" in December 1904, and engaged a new baker, Arlie Lucas from Mudlavia, to do his baking. Other bakers working in Hemp's store were Richard Sandilands and Thomas Broadlick of Kokomo. Wint Shepherd clerked for Hempleman for a while. Hempleman used many cute little slogans in his advertisements, such as:

"He who chooses wisely chooses well, then chew Per Aleck's Bread."

"A fool and his father's money are soon parted. Such is not the case when he buys "Per Aleck's Bread."

"Bull frogs have green backs-so will you if you buy your groceries at Hempleman's and keep what you save."

Hempleman's last advertisement available was in the New Richmond *Record*, Thursday, January 3, 1907. Aleck Hempleman was a resident of Terre Haute, Indiana, by April of 1909.

C.A. MCLAIN'S GROCERY AND RESTAURANT

Charles A. McLain entered the grocery and restaurant trade in New Richmond around 1903. The earliest record I found was an advertisement in the *Record*, September 10, 1903. He offered special prices on candies, nuts, and fruits for school teachers to treat the scholars at Christmas that year, and advertised oysters, direct from Baltimore, for the holidays.

In April 1905, he purchased a new soda fountain, and in June 1906, moved to a new room in order to serve his customers more conveniently. His advertisement read, "For good ice cream soda, McLains." McLain's store may have been the first, or at least one of the first, grocery with a soda fountain as an added feature in New Richmond. McLain also served baked ham and roast beef sandwiches and other short-order items for the school children at noon, and after school in the afternoon. An advertisement placed in the New Richmond Methodist Church ladies' cookbook in 1912, reads, "C.A. McLain, dealer in staple and fancy groceries, confectionery, and ice cream-also orders taken for International & Universal Suits." He also advertised cigars and tobacco products regularly.

Charles A. McLain's death occurred in 1917, and he is buried in the New Richmond cemetery. His wife, Myrtle (Herbert) McLain, and her sister, Gertrude Herbert, operated the Shadows Theatre in New Richmond for several years. Charles and Myrtle's son, Reid McLain, owned the Snowbird Custard Shop on the south side of the Fall Creek bridge on North Illinois Street in Indianapolis. He developed ice cream molds—small metal containers that produced ice cream animals, flowers, or many other designs for special occasions. At one time he had the world's largest collection of ice cream molds. Reid and his wife visited the New Richmond-Coal Creek Township Museum in 1985, and related many stories of the town's former history as he recalled his youthful days. Reid served as Colonel in the U.S. Army and was also a Big Ten football referee in former years.

Weymer & Dudley's Grocery

E.R Weymer purchased the general merchandise stock from Claypool & Fry in June 1906, and continued operating the grocery in the south room of the Washburn brick building on the southeast corner of Washington and Wabash Streets. E.R. Weymer and family moved from New Richmond in February of 1910 (see general stores, Weymer & Dudley).

George C. Livingston's Grocery

George C. Livingston operated a livery barn in New Richmond from 1900 to 1910. He sold all his rigs, horses, and equipment, and went into the restaurant business in 1910. Two years later he was the proprietor of a restaurant and grocery combination. He discontinued the restaurant, and carried on with the grocery until 1948, the last advertisement for this grocery.

George Livingston delivered groceries to the local residents as an extra service, and in 1920 he made arrangements with the local meat market owner, J.A. Bell, to have meat delivered to Livingston's customers while on his rounds. I remember Livingston's Grocery

12 - George C. Livingston in his grocery

very vividly—at the rear of the store was a large coal burning stove where the old timers gathered to swap yarns each winter evening, or played checkers. The meat counter was at the rear, and he usually had a large stalk of bananas hanging from the ceiling. Incidentally, George's daughter, Louie, found a live tarantula on the floor near the bananas one day in 1916, and speared it with her hat pin. George preserved the spider in a bottle of alcohol to show his customers. I believe I would have traded in another store for a long, long time. Cookies were stored in square tin boxes, and the wrapping paper was situated on a large roller at the rear counter for wrapping the meat or cheese. My grandmother gave my brothers and me her list of grocery items, and after we gave Livingston her list, he or one of his clerks proceeded to go to the shelves and get the items. There was no such thing as self-service in those days. The items were added on paper, then rung up on a cash register. Dema Lyons and Maude Lee both clerked for Livingston in the 1940s. Livingston died in 1950, and he is buried in the New Richmond Cemetery.

Westfall's Grocery

The only record available on Westfall's store was an advertisement in the New Richmond *Record*, August 14, 1919. Among the items listed were, "Seven Day coffee, 35 cents per lb., large cans of Carolene, or Monarch milk, 35 cents, and a box of Soap Chips, 35 cents."

Allman's Grocery

The only mention of Allman's grocery was in July 1920. J.A. Bell delivered meat from his meat market on Allman's grocery route to farmers in the vicinity.

King's Grocery

Ed King's grocery was located at the rear of the Washburn brick building on the southeast corner of Wabash and Washington. Entry to the store was made on south Wabash. This door has since been removed, and a solid wall was installed. King's slogan was, "Everything to Eat-King's Grocery." The only mention of this store was in the 1923 New Richmond High School annual, "The Jungle."

Shepherd's Plee-zing Store

Charles Shepherd advertised in 1923, "Shepherds Grocery and Meat Market-a complete line of fresh groceries, choice meats, fancy fruits and men's working clothes." From 1935 to 1937 he advertised as "Shepherd's Grocery, The Plee-zing Store."

Campbell's Grocery

Joe Campbell purchased the grocery stock from Hanawalt & Son in 1930. He then purchased the equipment and opened a grocery in the same location as Hanawalt, the east room of the Washburn block. Campbell's store was listed as, "D.J. Campbell-the Regal Store-Meats and Groceries" from September 1935 to December, 1940. A record book of the New Richmond town board shows he was still in the grocery business on January 5, 1942, as the trustees purchased supplies from his store on that date.

B.O. McNeil Grocery

Boyd O. McNeil's grocery was listed in the New Richmond Telephone Company directory printed in August 1934. This is the only record available on this store.

Stanley J. Arvin Groceries and Meats

Another short-lived grocery in New Richmond was Stanley J. Arvin's grocery and meats. He placed advertisements in the local programs for high school plays in 1939 and 1940.

Floyd's Market

Floyd Rash opened his grocery and meat market on April 5, 1941 in Long's brick building on the northeast corner of Washington and Wabash Streets. He was still in business in 1943, the last record available. Rash continued the grocery business in his store in Linden.

Hendricks Brother's Regal Store

The Hendricks Brothers opened a grocery about 1945 in the Washburn brick building on the southeast corner of Washington and Wabash Streets. They advertised, "Hendrick's Regal Store-The Thrifty Housewife's Source of Saving-groceries, meats, fruits and vegetables."

The Hendricks brothers provided the local residents with the freshest fruits and vegetables by driving to the warehouses themselves. They chose the items and hauled them to their store to avoid bruising and the usual rough handling of such delicate items. They had one of the most attractive fruit and vegetable displays while they were in New Richmond. The Hendrick's brothers last available advertisement was in the Montgomery County basketball schedule in 1947 and 1948.

Shep's Regal Market

Hayden B. Shepherd and his wife were in the grocery business in New Richmond from April 1948 to around 1954 or 1955. They were located in the Washburn building on the southeast corner of Wabash and Washington Streets.

Town Market

Chester "Chet" Bragstad conducted his grocery store in the Washburn block on the southeast corner of Washington and Wabash Streets in New Richmond from around 1955 to 1958. His store was listed as, "Bragstad's Town Market" in the local telephone directory.

Andrews' Market

E. Leonard and Lois Andrews began their grocery business in the center room of the Knights of Pythias Building located on the southwest corner of Washington and Wabash Streets in 1956. They moved their stock of groceries and equipment to the Washburn brick on the southeast corner of the two streets mentioned after Bragstad moved in 1958.

Andrews advertised in 1962, "Andrews Red and White Grocery, groceries, fresh meats, vegetables, health and beauty aids. Their last advertisement on June 21, 1963 offered "bacon, 49 cents per lb., Kraft Miracle Margarine, 29 cents per lb., Canteen Alaskan Salmon, 1 lb. can, 43 cents, hot house tomatoes- home grown, 25 cents per lb."

On the back of Andrew's last advertisement, they announced they had leased their store to Mr. and Mrs. Harley Stephens of Waynetown, and thanked their customers for their loyal support for the past seven years. The Andrews were back in the grocery business for a short time in 1972 and 1973.

Steve and Jerry's Red and White Grocery

Jerry Stephens, son of Mr. and Mrs. Harley Stephens, managed their New Richmond grocery, and the father continued the store in Waynetown. They advertised "groceries, fresh meats, dairy products, country style sausage, 49 cents per lb., Martha White mixes, 3 for 25 cents, Premium crackers, 25 cents per lb., and Jello, 3 boxes for 25 cents."

Stephens was in the grocery business in New Richmond from June 1963 until 1969. Jerry, his wife Patricia, and their three children resided in New Richmond for a number of years after he closed his grocery, but by 1983 they were residents of Chattanooga, Tennessee.

Barnes' Red and White Grocery

Mr. and Mrs. Frances Barnes leased the grocery building and equipment from Leonard and Lois Andrews in 1970 and 1971 and advertised a complete line of groceries, fresh meats, and dairy products.

Gould's Grocery

Don Gould leased the Andrew's grocery building and equipment for a short time in 1973, after Leonard and Lois Andrews recovered their stock and equipment, and were operating their grocery in 1972 and 1973. The town of New Richmond was without a grocery for a few months in 1973-74.

New Richmond Grocery

Don Fidler and his wife, Carolyn, of Indianapolis, purchased Andrews' grocery stock, equipment, and the building in March 1974. The family moved to New Richmond after the school term was completed that year.

Fidler's specialty was "the best of fresh cut meats." For a short time, they added a snack bar and game room to their store and also sold used clothing in one of the rooms.

On January 9, 1982, Don Fidler sold his meat counter equipment and part of the equipment in the grocery department. He discontinued the meat counter but remained in the grocery business. Mrs. Fidler managed the store and remained in the business until 1985. Don was the manager of the Southside Tavern in Linden at that time.

Meat Markets and Butchers

THE BUTCHER
She went to the butcher's for a spareribs and suet,
But found that some others had beaten her tuet.

She said she would settle for sausage and liver,
But the butcher insisted he had none to giver.
She pleaded for pork chops, for meat balls, for mutton,
The butcher said, "Lady, I just ain't got nuttin!"
   - Anonymous

Before the invention of refrigerators, meat was "harvested" on the coldest winter days. Butchering was done out of doors and the lard was rendered in large kettles in the backyard or barn lot. Almost every man and woman had the knowledge of how to cure and store meat without refrigeration, and smoke houses were an important structure on each lot in town at one time. Home cured hams and sides of beef were more handy than the community frozen food locker that came along many years later. The town people who attempted to raise livestock for their own meat could provide very little space for pasturing the cattle or hogs, so the need for a good successful meat market or butcher shop was in evidence from a very early day. Most of the New Richmond meat markets are listed in the following paragraphs.

In January 1887 Jack Smith operated a butcher shop, probably in connection with his general merchandise store located next to the railroad tracks on south Wabash Street. In March 1888 a Mr. Cadwallader had a new butcher shop almost completed. Cadwallader may have been the carpenter, because a month later, Henry Graves was mentioned as the "chief steak cutter" in the new butcher shop.

The New Richmond correspondent for the Crawfordsville weekly *Review* printed in May 19, 1888 the town people's complaint that, "twelve and one-half cents a pound for poor beef when the nearest town west was selling beef for only ten cents, was rather hard on the poor." A month later the price was reduced to ten cents. In 1888 another butcher, Mr. Templeton, informed a "certain woman in New Richmond that he couldn't get beef without bone, and she would have to try elsewhere." The writer for the *Review* was so successful in lowering the price of meat to ten cents, he decided to try and get prices even lower in December 1889, saying, "We do not see why beef should be ten cents a pound when you can buy the best in the market of butcher's stuff at two and a half cents a pound." He continued with, "Butchers pay two cents a pound for beef and sell it at ten cents are surely ahead. Someone must be making money, and it's not the one who eats it either!" At this rate, none of the butchers made enough profit from their shops to start their own bank in town.

Runyan & Fouts were operating a butcher shop in August 1889, and sold the shop to Mark Lucas and William Graves at this time. The 1890 county directory however, still listed the Runyan & Fout Meat Market.

D.M. Lucas' Meat Market was listed in the 1891-2 county directory, but in February 1892, Lucas took in another partner, a Mr. Morris, and they were to open a new meat market "in the near future." Lucas' Meat Market was one of the more successful meat markets and continued into 1904, possibly longer. Lucas sold elk meat from Dewey's elk farm, as well as beef, pork, and poultry. He advertised, "Farmers! Take notice, will pay the highest market prices for your beef hides, and tallow, or will sell you a quarter of beef, or butcher your beef at home at a reasonable figure. D.M. Lucas." He also offered "Dressed turkeys and chickens for Christmas-at Lucas' Meat Market." Lucas moved his meat market to the old Bunnell building in December 1903. Jones' butcher shop also was in operation at this time.

Samuel E. Magruder's meat market was listed in the 1891-2 county directory, and A.D. Snyder's shop was listed in the 1895 directory. In 1900-01, Foster & Schleppy Brothers were operating a meat market in New Richmond. The Schleppy Brothers continued on their own, advertising "Schleppy Bros., Dealers in fresh meat and fresh fish, smoked meat and bologna. See us when you have any stock or hides to sell, New Richmond, Indiana."

George W. Jones was offering the highest market price for some good choice butcher stock and feeders for his meat market in April 1902. Thomas Schleppy cut meat for Jones for a short time, but was replaced by Ed Wright from Hoopston, Illinois. Jones sold his meat market to Frank Hole in August 1903.

Hole and one of the Harriman brothers formed a partnership for a few months, then sold the butcher shop to Ben Rabourn, of Acton, Indiana in September 1903.

Ben Rabourn hired Fred Steck of Lafayette as his butcher, and Rabourn's advertisements promised to "butcher your hogs, render your lard and make sausage, and to get all out of your hogs but the squeal." He also offered "Sausage and Weinewurst-and other meats usually found in first class meat markets." Rabourn was more successful than the previous butchers and made several improvements in the shop, such as a new National Cash Register, a new automatic gasoline light plant, and a patent hog scalder, in his slaughter house. Rabourn's market stood on the grounds occupied in 1986 by the local telephone company on east Washington Street. The old frame building was removed many years ago.

Rabourn's (also spelled Rayburn's) Meat Market offered in 1922, "boiling meat and plate roasts for ten cents a pound, and farmer's 'threshing meat' delivered at your door." A year later oysters and fish, in season, were advertised. Butchers in Rabourn's meat market over the years were: Enoch Rabourn, Edward Byers, Jefferson Waye, and Jesse Rabourn, nephew of Benjamin. In later years (1920s) Rabourn's meat market was located on south

13 - John Utterback, L.P. Brown, Benjamin Rabourn, and Jefferson Waye inside Rabourn's Meat Market

Wabash Street in the frame building previously occupied by the Shotts' blacksmith shop. This meat market was still operating in April of 1923 when Rabourn sold to W.B. Shepherd.

Shepherd's Meat Market first advertised in April 1923. W.B. Shepherd had just purchased Benjamin C. Rayborn's Meat Market and was remodeling the building, (the former butcher's name has a change of spelling too). Shepherd offered "the best of meats at the best of prices," and his slogan was "Eat our meat-and get a treat!"

James A. "Art" Bell operated a meat market as early as 1907-8 in New Richmond. He sold his interest to Moses R. Binns with whom he was in partnership, in August 1908, and Binns and son Leverett ran the butcher shop a few years. Bell was listed as a traveling salesman in 1912, but kept his residence in New Richmond for his wife, Cora, and the family. He returned to his former line of work, and Bell's Meat Market offered, 'Fresh and cured meats, creamery butter, fresh fish, etc., in July 1920, and offered a delivery service on either Livingston's or Allman's grocery routes. He specified cash at the wagon. Two years later, he had his own blue and white meat wagon to make deliveries to the farmers near New Richmond.

Sherman and Charles Dwiggins were the proprietors of Dwiggins & Son meat market in New Richmond in 1912. Frank Ellis was the manager of this market, and the Dwiggins family continued their residence in Waynetown.

Charles M. Fruits operated a meat market at one time, possibly in the early 1930s. Dick Shotts worked in this market a short time before following the blacksmith trade.

Roy Carr had a meat market around 1935 in the neighborhood of the site now occupied by the local telephone office, the same building occupied by Rabourn's meat market. Carr had a blacksmith shop at the rear of this market. All the grocers had meat counters in their stores in later year.

New Richmond Frozen Food Locker Service

In the spring of 1941, a new business was established in the town of New Richmond—the Frozen Food Locker Service. The purpose of this new venture was to operate a food locker plant, rent frozen food lockers, supply general locker services, slaughtering livestock and poultry. They provided butchering and processing of all kinds of meat as well as storing vegetables and fruits. The locker plant also purchased containers wholesale and offered the same to their customers. Fruits, vegetables, and poultry were quick-frozen for their customers to store in their rented lockers for a small fee.

Associated with the frozen food locker in New Richmond—and their branch locker plant in Linden—were a Mr. Davidson, Robert and Geraldine Aaron, Arthur Sluyter, and Gordon Mefford. Mr. Davidson attended a meeting of the New Richmond town board November 17, 1941, hoping to purchase a strip of ground behind the locker in order to expand or to provide a space for their delivery trucks. This ground was owned by the town, which sold them a small parcel of the ground.

This new idea in food storage caught on very quickly, and many of the ladies in town discovered that freezing their fruits, vegetables, meats and poultry was the most convenient and the safest way to preserve food. The advantage of having the meat and poultry slaughtered, butchered, and processed in the locker plant year-round was certainly more convenient than having to wait for a very cold, frigid, winter day as they previously had to. I recall going to get the food our mother stored in our locker up town, and how the cold blast of air felt upon entering the refrigerated locker-room. It felt pretty good on a hot summer day, but didn't take long to freeze your hands while searching for a certain package of meat or other food.

The Frozen Food Locker advertised "Slaughtering, Processing and Curing of Fresh Home-killed Meats, and Frozen Foods, Wholesale Meats (the front quarter of beef was processed for 55 cents a pound)." They advertised "Snow Crop Frozen Foods at wholesale prices—in lots of twelve" and patrons could purchase frozen berries and cherries. A thirty-pound can of sweetened strawberries sold for $8.75 and pie cherries were $5.50, back in 1952. The locker also sold many other groceries as well as frozen foods and meats.

The New Richmond locker plant was destroyed by fire in the early 1950s, but a new structure was built, and business continued in the butchering and wholesale and retail lines. Home freezers were becoming very popular about this time, so the company did not install the lockers in their new building. Many New Richmond residents rented lockers in the Linden plant for several years, but Mr. Aaron closed the New Richmond store around 1955.

The Tri-County Telephone Company purchased the locker plant building and remodeled the structure several years later. It now serves as the telephone company's office building.

The Secretary of the State of Indiana published a legal notice in the Crawfordsville *Journal Review* November 25, 1969 revoking certain corporations unless a report was filed within thirty days—the New Richmond Frozen Food Locker Service was one of the corporations listed. Thus ended a once prosperous business in the town of New Richmond.

The Bakery Business in New Richmond

The most welcome business in the country must have been the bakery. What a chore it would have been for the pioneer woman with a large family, trying to keep bread on the table—and let's face it—not every housewife can master the art of baking light, tasty, homemade bread. There was no relief from this unwelcome daily task in the New Richmond area until the early 1890s.

My father, Forrest Waye, said when he first came to New Richmond, there were two or three large brick ovens behind the brick buildings occupied in 1986 by the New Richmond Bar & Grill and the Post Office, on east Washington Street. There were used by the local bakers for several years after his arrival in the town. They stood unused for many years and finally started to cave in, so they were removed and have never been replaced. In later years the grocery store owners purchased their bread and other bakery good from the Crawfordsville and Lafayette bakeries.

In 1891 there was mention of a bakery coming to New Richmond and later records indicate this was the one started by C.N. Boyland. William Dewey was operating a bakery in 1894, and the same year a Mr. Reeder was baking bread in the town. In 1896 two men were just starting in the bakery business—C.A. Taylor and "Daddy" Huff. Another twosome, Foster & Schleppy were operating a bakery according to the advertisement, but reading through the advertisement, only such items as fresh fish, celery, and oysters were listed, not a loaf of bread, cakes, or any other baked goods were listed; this was in 1899. The 1900-01 directory of Montgomery County listed Ebrite & Alexander's Bakery, and in the same years Dan Cleveland had his bakery in operation. Cleveland advertised, "Try Cleveland's Hot Soup, Fruit Cake. You Get the Best Bread in Town at Clevelands-Cleveland gives you 7-1/2 pounds of best bread for 25 cents." This was pretty expensive bread. Cleveland moved on to Cayuga where he started a restaurant.

The O.K. Bakery was listed in November 1900 and December 1901 in the New Richmond *Record*, the weekly newspaper. H.E. Strader listed a confectionery and bakery from 1902 to 1903, later adding a short-order restaurant to the bakery business. Strader employed C.N. Boyland as his baker for a while, and after he resigned, Sam Holliday of Linden came to work for Strader. Boyland had gone to Crawfordsville to a similar position.

It is interesting how this new type of business caught on, because in 1902 and 1903, besides the Strader Bakery, there were the following bakers listed in the advertisements: Albert A. Lucas, George Pebler, and Alec W. Hempleman's. Hempleman combined the bakery with a grocery, and was a little more successful, or it appears so at least, if advertising frequently is the measure for success. He advertised each week in the New Richmond *Record*. The *Record*, May 5, 1904 said, "We now have our new oven complete and are prepared to bake any kind of cakes, bread or pies, on short notice. Give us a trial order and be convinced, A.W. Hempleman & Co." A month later he was advertising, "Fresh Bread, 5 cents a loaf, 6 loaves for 25 cents, and Stale Bread, 2 for 5 cents. In December 1904, Hempleman had changed bakers, but he still guaranteed the "Quality of my bread and cakes to be held up to the high standard of quality that has marked our bakery products since last May," etc. Lucas started baking for Hempleman in 1905, and Hempleman was advertising "Per Alick's Graham Bread-Cakes-Buns-Pies-baked to order." By 1909, Hempleman had left New Richmond, and was a resident of Terre Haute, Indiana.

The New Richmond *Record*, Thursday, September 10, 1903, listed William F. Grigson's Bakery & Restaurant. He advertised, "Home-made bread, Pies, and Cakes. Special orders for fancy cakes given prompt attention! Short Order Counter in Connection! Fish & Oysters in Season..Fruits..Candies..and Nuts!" Grigson continued with his bakery into the year 1904 and may have been in the town later, but this is the latest record I have found of this business.

C.A. McLain started as early as September 1903, with his bakery and restaurant. McLain also had a grocery in connection with the two former lines of business. He continued in the grocery business up to 1912 in New Richmond. In 1907 and 1908, Joseph Hubler was listed as a baker in New Richmond. In 1913, G.L. and L.L. Bastion had made improvements, alterations, and repairs on their business house—a bakery structure—on part of lot No. 3 of the original plat of New Richmond in May and June of 1913; the repairs were completed by June 5, 1913. I have not located further records on this bakery.

DRUG STORES & DRUGGISTS

THE HOLLIN BROTHERS, JOHN W. AND WILLIAM H.

Early in the 1850s a young couple from Ireland came to America to seek their fortune, or at least the prospect of better living conditions in the new world. Michael and Mary Flynn Hollin were living in New

York City when their first child, William H., was born on April 16, 1853. The couple was not satisfied with life in New York, and two years later they had moved to Lafayette, Indiana, where their second son, John W., was born on August 16, 1855. When John W. was only six months of age, the two children were left orphans, having lost both parents during a cholera epidemic in Lafayette. The brothers spent their childhood and early manhood in Lafayette, attending schools in that city.

In January of 1879, the Hollin brothers first made their appearance in New Richmond, when John W. purchased the drug stock of Dr. Rainey, and entered the business world as a druggist. The brothers were residing in Dr. Manners Washburn's household in 1880. John W., age 25, was listed as a druggist, and William H., age 27, a drug clerk. The census taker mistakenly gave William's birthplace as Indiana, however.

The brothers' togetherness was carried over not only in their business ventures, but also in marriage when they married sisters. John W. Hollin and Lena King were married December 15, 1882, and William H. Hollin and Emma M. King were married December 31 the same year. The girls were daughters of Josiah and Sarah J. (Campbell) King. Both parents were from early pioneer families of New Richmond and Coal Creek Township. John and Lena (King) Hollin had three daughters; Orpha L., who died in infancy, Lelia N., and Gladys. William and Emma had no children to bless their union.

The Hollin brothers built identical homes, the first two houses north of their brick business block on north Wabash Street in New Richmond. The houses have been remodeled and their appearance has been altered on the outside, however. The two families lived next to each other until their death. John's death occurred January 19, 1927, and William died March 12, 1929. William's widow, Emma M. Hollin died at the family home October 4, 1935, and John's widow, Lena Hollin, on August 14, 1942. Their deaths erased all memories of the Hollin business establishment.

The Hollin building was divided into three business rooms on the ground floor; the room on the south served as the drug store, shoe and boots department, and the post office, all managed by John W. Hollin. The center section held the grocery department, managed by William Hollin, until later years when John took over the business. Miss Mexie Turvey designed and sold millinery in the north room of the building for several years, and for a short time, the brothers were listed as merchant tailors occupying the north room for this business venture.

The upstairs rooms were occupied by the Hollin Opera House, and various lodges such as the Odd Fellows and Modern Woodsmen met in the other rooms. The Henry Clay Lodge of the Knights of Pythias was organized in 1892, and a concrete marker was placed on the Hollin building at that time. This date was always confused by New Richmond citizens, thinking that was the date the building was constructed, but evidence shows the building was completed in December of 1890, and the drug store was in business at that time in the new building. The Knights of Pythias met in one of the rooms when they first organized.

John W. Hollin purchased Dr. Rainey's drugs in January 1879, as stated before, and a year later, John and Lowell Anderson had formed a partnership, and were operating drug stores in both Pleasant Hill (Wingate) and New Richmond. This same year, they added a stock of groceries. Both John and William operated the stores but it was usually listed as John W. Hollin's drug store.

The original Hollin drugstore was destroyed by fire in May of 1883, but they continued their business in another building in New Richmond until they built their new brick building. The new structure was almost destroyed by fire shortly after the Hollins moved in, by an explosion of a coal-oil lamp, but the fire was quickly extinguished.

John W. Hollin was appointed Postmaster in New Richmond, April 19, 1880, and served until December 29, 1884, when George F. Long replaced him. John was again appointed Postmaster July 16, 1901, and served until June 30, 1906. The post office was located in the north room of the new Hollin building for several years, then was moved to the rear of the south room with the drug and shoe store section.

John W. Hollin promised his customers "no matter what you buy-a penny's worth, to a double eagles worth-we aim to give you the best drug store service in the state, perfect goods-fair prices-a clean store-drug knowledge-careful attention-honest measure-accuracy, and strict attention to business." The store's most advertised products were Chamberlain's Remedies, Dr. Dade's Little Liver Pills, DeWitts Witch Hazel Salve, and Kodol for indigestion and dyspepsia. John's advertisements rotated between drug store items and shoes and boots, paints, varnishes, brushes, and gasoline. In 1912, John filed a bill with the New Richmond town board for $7 for 35 gallons of gasoline. In July 1920, Hollin's Drug store advertised, Edisons Diamond Amberola, priced at $100.

Mark Alexander, Will Lucas, and L.C. Carson were the only clerks employed by the Hollin brothers mentioned in the local newspaper, though they may have employed other New Richmond people.

Harry Wilson, Druggist

The earliest record of Harry Wilson as a New Richmond druggist was in April and October of 1891 when he visited his mother in Crawfordsville. There is no record in the newspapers as to his location in the town, but there were mere mentions of his drug store up to January of 1894. He was an agent for the Crawfordsville *Star* in New Richmond at that time.

Harry married in November, 1893, Katie Snyder, daughter of B.F. Snyder. Wilson had moved his drug stock to Waynetown, and in September 1904, sold his drug store to Stephen Davis, a former clerk for Wilson, and embarked in the life insurance business in that city.

F.M. Johnson's Drug Store

F.M. Johnson's drug store was located in John W. McCardle's frame building on the southwest corner of Washington and Wabash Streets across from the John W. Hollin and Company Drug firm.

The earliest record of Frank M. Johnson's drug store was an advertisement in the New Richmond *Enterprise*, Friday, May 28, 1897, and besides a receipt (recipe) for the cure and prevention of hog cholera, was the following, "Have you tried Johnson's Phosphates, the latest, and best temperance drink made?- JOHNSON'S DRUG STORE." For those who are not familiar with phosphates, it is a carbonated drink consisting of water, a fruit syrup, and a little phosphoric acid. New Richmond residents knew spring had arrived when F.M. Johnson opened his soda fountain. In the winter months, his hot chocolate was the rage. The F.M. Johnson drug store also carried school supplies, pure food chocolates, groceries, Queens Ware, tinware, and in 1905, the "new fountain pens, worth $1-but only 58 cents, garden seeds, household paints, and many over-the-counter remedies." One of his greatest medicines, Rocky Mountain Tea, had the following advertisement "When you wake in the morning feeling like the end of a misspent life, your mouth full of fir, and your soul full of regrets-take ROCKY MOUNTAIN TEA." This product also claimed to make children eat, sleep, and grow, and mothers strong and vigorous.

In January 1903, F.M. Johnson started a book exchange and rental service in his store which enabled his customers to read all the latest books on the market for a small fee.

F.M. Johnson's Drug store was noted for his "excellent" ice cream factory in New Richmond, and made express shipments of his most excellent ice cream on the Clover Leaf Railroad, both east and west, almost daily. On one Saturday in May 1903, he made 117 gallons. In August, the same year, his excellent ice cream was served to 120 people attending the Alexander reunion at the Montgomery County fairgrounds in Crawfordsville. Johnson hired the young boys in town to help manufacture his ice cream, and their pay was "all the ice cream they could eat." My father, Forrest Waye, was one of the ice cream manufacturers' helpers.

Johnson's drug store also carried valentines (comic and fancy), large blue mottled slop jars-for 50 cents, window glass, and liquid smoke-he advertised this product thus, "Don't burn your house down-smoke your meat with liquid smoke." A three-pound butter crock with bail and lid, "for delivering butter to your customers," was offered for 10 cents in April of 1906. In June that year he offered the "new and delicious ice cream cones-the latest craze."

All good things must come to an end, though, and F.M. Johnson's bankrupt stock of drugs was offered at a private sale, for cash, on October 10, 1908. The Crawfordsville Trust Company was the trustee in the bankruptcy. Johnson recovered from this set-back and was back in business the following spring.

He had installed a new "cashier," a National cash register, and was asking customers to save their printed check, with the date on it, and to return 50 cents worth of soda checks to receive a glass of soda water, FREE!

F.M. Johnson suffered a stroke in April of 1909, and went to Spiceland to take treatment. This is the last record of this once famous drug store in New Richmond who manufactured "the most excellent ice cream."

Frank M. Johnson and his wife, Maggie, lived on Wabash Street in New Richmond, and had a daughter, Mary, and sons Carl, Clarence, and Guy L. Carl attended high school at Ladoga, then entered Purdue University in the fall of 1904. He and his wife, Blanche, resided on Detchon Street, and Carl was listed as a druggist in the 1907-8 county directory.

Lynch Brothers Drug Store

The Lynch brothers operated drug stores in New Richmond and Linden in the early 1920s. Their drug store was known as "The High School Store," and was located in the Hollin brick building on the northwest corner of Wabash and Washington Streets. They advertised, "Dr. Hess's poultry supplies, and Wine of Cardui-a wonderful tonic for women, and Kirk's toilet soap-3 bars for 25 cents." There was no mention of a soda fountain in their advertisements, but I am sure they had one to entice the high school students.

The brothers were Ed and Earl Lynch, and Earl continued to run the drug store several years after Ed moved on. The latest known record of this drug store in New Richmond was dated August 30, 1923, but it is believed the Lynch drug store was in business until 1929 or 1930.

Shanklin Drug Store

Records show that Fred Shanklin had opened a drug store in New Richmond by May 1930. He was first located in the Hollin brick building formerly occupied by the Lynch brothers drug store. A short time later, Shanklin formed a partnership with Robert C. King. Shanklin was an undertaker in Linden at the same time, which he continued for over thirty years. He and King also formed a partnership in the undertaking business. After Shanklin's death in May of 1938, King purchased Shanklin's interest in the undertaking establishment and continued to run the business until 1955. After retiring, King worked in the Linden State Bank, and his death occurred in October of 1959.

Robert C. King Drug Store

Robert C. King moved to New Richmond in the early 1930s and had formed a partnership with Fred Shanklin in his drug store, as mentioned above, starting in the Hollin brick building. After the Corn Exchange Bank closed its doors, King moved his drug store across the street to the Knights of Pythias building into the former bank room.

Advertisements appeared from 1934 to 1943 under the name of "R.C. King Drug Store, The Coolest Spot in Town." He advertised patent medicines, toilet articles, sundries, and soda fountain.

King purchased Fred Shanklin's interest in the undertaking establishment in Linden, and moved his family to that city in the 1940s. He and his wife, Bernice Beard King, had three children; Norma, Shirley, and John.

After the King drug store, a line of drug stores occupied the former bank building, and the north room of the Knights of Pythias building is still referred to by many New Richmond residents as "the drug store" although a string of restaurants have occupied the room. The following drug stores were all located in the building.

The New Richmond Drug Store

Milford and Maude Andrews opened a drug store in the Knights of Pythias building in 1944. They operated under the name of the "New Richmond Drug Store." They advertised, "fountain service, candy, drugs, tobacco, gifts, films finished, and magazines." They were open seven days a week, and the last advertisement I have was dated October 21, 1949.

The New Richmond Drug Store was the favorite spot to spend intermissions during the summer street shows and the Saturday night band concerts. A group of girls and I made frequent visits to their soda fountain for cherry or chocolate cokes, or black and whites (vanilla ice cream topped with chocolate syrup and marshmallow topping). This was usually a much better treat than the moving pictures that were playing.

Kimbrell's Drugs Store

Bud Kimbrell operated a drug store in New Richmond in the early 1950s. His store was listed in the New Richmond Methodist Church History "Church Messenger" in 1951. Kimbrell's wife taught commercial studies in the local school in the late 1930s.

Coffman's Drug Store

Ruth Coffman (Mrs. Maurice Coffman) operated a drug store from around 1954 to 1957, the last year I have a record.

Stephenson's Sundries

Beulah Stephenson, widow of Milford Stephenson, operated a drug store a short time. Her store was listed in the local telephone directory in 1961, the only record I have. Beulah was the last person to operate a drug store in the town to this date.

Chapter 4 - Clothing & Beauty Services

New Richmond's Clothing Stores

Nicholas Washburn

The early settlers of New Richmond purchased their clothing, or material to sew their own clothing, from the stock of the dry-goods or general stores. It was in the late 1890s before the first store specializing in clothing appeared in the town. This store only carried men's and boys' clothing, therefore the ladies continued to do their trading at the local general store.

Nicholas Washburn was listed as the agency for a Chicago garment firm known as "Fred Kauffman—the American Tailor" in the New Richmond *Enterprise*, Friday, October 6, 1899. Washburn was in partnership with one of the Kirkpatricks for a short time, but was on his own a year later.

In September of 1902, Washburn moved into a new business room in his father's new brick building known as the "Bank Building," or the "Washburn Block" located on the southeast corner of Washington and Wabash Streets in New Richmond. He advertised, "Suitings and Overcoatings—Fall and Winter Wear—Fullam and Fullmore Overcoats—Wings and Polks—London Blue and London Smoke Shades—Union Suits—Shirts—Sox—Suspenders," etc.

In February of 1903, Nick's Men's Clothing Store advertised "Suits, from $15 to $45; Trousers, $4 to $12; and the much advertised Kingsbury Hat—in prevailing shapes and colors." Washburn was selling carpets by this time and advertised "Axminister, Wilton, Velvets, Amsterdam, Brussels, and Tapestries, the heaviest all-wool Longjohns." By July the same year, Washburn's Clothing Store was the place to purchase a new item, the "Automobile Caps." As the number of automobile owners in New Richmond was only five at the time, he was forced to reduce the price of the caps from $2.50 to $1.50 to move the new stock. At the same time, men's shirts were reduced to 95 cents, fancy vests to $1.25, straw hats, 75 cents; cigars, 1 cent to 25 cents each.

Washburn added boxing gloves to his stock in March 1905 and advertised, "A fresh supply of carnations-every Friday night" for the local gentlemen to present their special ladies on the big Saturday night engagements. In December the same year, he added Edison Phonographs to his stock of goods—and all the latest records. The phonograph from the Edison "Gem" to the "Concert size" were offered, and the records mentioned were: "'Old Grist Mill'; 'Golden Wedding'; 'Just Because I'm Lonely'; 'Calligan Called Again'; 'Razzazza Mazzazza' (the new march); 'My Name is Morgan, But it Ain't J.P.', by Bob Roberts; Collins and Harlan's 'Lazy'; and 'It's No Use to Knock When a Man's Down.'"

Nick Washburn sold his stock of Men's clothing to Robert E. Seaman in August of 1908. Washburn clerked for the Warner & Peck Clothing store in Crawfordsville until around 1922, and then moved to Lafayette, where he was employed as a salesman for the Rosenthal Clothing Company for a number of years. A few years before his death in 1952, he was employed in the advertising department of the Lafayette *Journal-Courier*.

Other Clothing Stores in New Richmond

Other merchants advertising clothing in New Richmond were: Robert E. Seaman's (Gent's Furnishings) from 1908 to around 1910. Seaman was selling real estate by 1912 in New Richmond. An advertisement in the New Richmond *Record*, Thursday September 24, 1908, and again on Saturday,

September 26, for his opening sale, advertised, "Kingsbury's Hats reduced from $3 to $2-and the Kingsbury's hats now out of style, now $1; The George C. Idle Gold Shirt, $1.50, now $1; the Silver Shirt, $1, now 80 cents; Work shirts while they last, 35 cents; underwear, 50 cents, now 35 cents, caps 50 cents, now 35 cents; ties 40 cents now 25 cents; ties 25 cents, now 15 cents; collars, any style, 10 cents; post cards 5 cents;" and he also advertised grocery items and carpets.

Also selling clothing in New Richmond were: Weymer's Department Store; Claypool and Fry's; C.A. McLain (agent for International Tailoring Co.—Men's Suits) in 1910; Busy Bee-1909-advertised Women's Suits, Skirts, Jackets-Tailored hats; Hanawalt and Son, selling men's furnishings, and men's, women's, and children's shoes and rubber footwear from 1910 to about 1930. Austin Hanawalt and his son Roy were the proprietors of this store. All the above stores stocked general merchandise as well as clothing, and are listed under general stores, except the women's clothing store, The Busy Bee.

Richard and Nancy Snyder purchased the A.D. Snyder brick building from Polly Buck in May of 1976, and a year later opened the Snyder's Tack and Apparel store, advertising "Tony Lama Boots—Gerry Down Baily Hats—Belts, Buckles—English Tack, etc. and Complete Western Outfitting—grooming aids for both cattle and horses—and Alfalfa Cubes." The alfalfa cubes were manufactured or processed about one-half mile west of New Richmond by the Don Miles family in their Emerald Acres factory. The Snyders sold their merchandise at a public auction held September 26, 1982, and went out of business.

TAILORS

ALLEN ALSTON

Allen Alston was listed as a tailor in New Richmond on the 1880 census.

ALOYS ANTON

Aloys "Al" Anton, was listed as a New Richmond Tailor in the 1882-3; 1884-5; 1887; and 1890 county directories. The Crawfordsville Weekly *Review* recorded some of the persons Al Anton made suits for. In January 1888 he was tailoring for the Amos Quick family, and the item said, "Al is a noted 'sewer' and goes far and near to work for customers." In March that year, he was making a suit of clothes for Dr. Washburn and doing other sewing. The "little Dutch Tailor from over the Rhine" was building new suits to the tune of about three per week, that year. The following year he was making a new set of clothing for a Wingate chap. Tailors remained in the patrons' homes until the clothing was completed to insure a perfectly fitted garment.

SWANK & CLARK

Swank & Clark were the leading tailors in New Richmond at one time. Practically all the tailoring in the town and surrounding country was done by this firm, according to the New Richmond *Record*, August 28, 1902. Clark came into full control later. The time period of this firm is unknown.

J.W. HOLLIN & CO. MERCHANT TAILORS

The 1895 directory listed J. W. Hollin & Co. "Merchant Tailors" in addition to their drug, shoes, and grocery store. Thomas D. Dillon was associated with the Hollin Brothers as the tailor, and was taking orders for Strauss Bros. Fine Clothing.

H.A. FRIESKE, TAILOR

H.A. Frieske opened for business in the north room of the Hollin Brothers block in June 1906. He offered to "take your measure and fit you out in a new hand-tailored suit just to your liking and has the newest and latest styles of goods on hand from which to make your selection, and he earnestly requests a call from you."

Philip Jones, The Tailor

Philip Jones was temporarily located with L.P. Brown until the new Knights of Pythias building was completed. He advertised, "Kahn Tailored Clothes, made to your measure. Prices from $20 to $45, five hundred pure wool patterns cleaning-pressing-repairing," in October 1910. He offered to "clean and block straw and Panama Hats," and "Suits made to order—Fashions Favored Fabrics for Fastidious Fellow," in 1911.

Other tailors included Robert C. and William F. Jones, Tailors, listed in the 1912 directory; Charles A. McLain, Merchant Tailor, Restaurant, and Grocery in 1912; Roscoe Plunkett, Merchant Tailor, offering "Cleaning, pressing & merchant Tailoring" in 1912; and Hanawalt & Son, tailoring, cleaning and blocking hats from 1921 to the 1930s.

Dressmakers and Seamstresses

Ella (Beal) Campbell, wife of William Campbell, the proprietor of the old **Pioneer Store**, was listed as a New Richmond dressmaker in the 1891-2 county directory. Ella moved to Chicago in October of 1893, and established a dress making business in that city. She was very successful and within a short time was working eight seamstresses, and received orders from Indianapolis and Lafayette besides her Chicago customers.

In 1903 the town had two dressmakers, Pauline Mitchell, and Mrs. L.E. Bigelow. The latter located her establishment in the rooms over Claypool and Fry's general store. Her dresses were very fashionable, and the local ladies were giving her their orders for clothing, and were trying to entice her to stay in the town. She was planning to make New Richmond her permanent home in February 1905, the last record known of Mrs. Bigelow.

Miss Mexie Turvey offered to do all kinds of sewing—plain, children's clothes, and shirtwaists. In April 1906, two other ladies, Mrs. Hinton and Miss Hobbs, placed an advertisement in the *Record* to do plain dressmaking and family sewing in May the same year.

Virginia Francis was listed as a dressmaker in 1912, Mrs. Wright Mason in 1921, and Fauniel Dryer advertised, "Fancy and Plain Sewing sewing needs, cards, and gifts in 1951. Her shop was located in the old Starr Dunn Bookstore, which has since been razed, next to the brick Dunn building.

There have been many ladies who sewed for people in New Richmond over the years, but did not advertise, and many ladies have made extra income by quilting—Jess Jones, Florence (Jones) Long, Fannie Ebrite, Inez Stephenson, and Gladys Swick, Daisy Fruits, and Ruth Todd, to name a few.

Milliners and Their Trimmers

The citizens of the little town of New Richmond took a back seat to no other town or city in Montgomery County when it came to the latest fashions. It is hard to believe the town was once so prosperous that specialty stores survived in the business section of town. While researching the history of the town, I was surprised to discover the number of women in the business of dealing in ladies' hats.

They started with the basic material, and decorated the bonnets, or hats, themselves, with the finest adornments. Those who stayed in this business for many years employed experienced trimmers who were from out of town, coming to New Richmond in the early spring and fall to work on the hats. The hats were decorated in time for the season's millinery openings—an exciting event for all the ladies about town. Some of the New Richmond milliners and their trimmers are listed in the following paragraphs.

Mrs. W.S. Bain was a milliner and Miss Mattie Youngblood was listed as a milliner and dressmaker in the 1891-2 county directory. In 1895 Miss Young and Miss Robinson were designing and selling hats. In

1897 Alice Mitchell and Flora Alexander had just received a complete line of spring and summer millinery goods, "far superior to anything ever shown in New Richmond." They engaged a competent trimmer who had studied this type of work for a number of years, and invited the ladies in town to call and inspect their trimmed hats. They were located the first door east of F.M. Perkin's general store.

Friday and Saturday, October 13th and 14th, 1899, were the dates set aside for the winter opening at the Dewey Millinery Parlors in New Richmond. They were to have music each evening during the opening. Miss Bessie Duncan was her trimmer.

In 1900-01, there were three millinery parlors in the town; Miss Washburn and Mrs. Dewey were partners, Miss Perkins and Mrs. Mitchell had a parlor, and Miss Mexie Turvey had a millinery parlor. Mrs. Alice Mitchell was the granddaughter of Squire Ebrite and mother of Glenn Mitchell, a well-known artist from New Richmond (see article on Mitchell).

Miss Mexie Turvey was a teacher in school district number one (Walnut Grove) in 1897, but was more interested in the millinery business. This became her vocation for many years, and her shop was known as Miss Turvey's Millinery Emporium. Miss Turvey's millinery opening, held in October 1899, was largely attended during the three days, and "her hats received many favorable comments," the New Richmond *Enterprise* reported.

Mexie Turvey rented the north room (ground floor) of the Hollin brick business block and moved her millinery parlor in September 1901. Each March, Mexie attended the wholesale millinery openings in Indianapolis to purchase her spring and summer stock. Each year in September, she attended the fall and winter openings for the same purpose. Her shop sold the handsomest, most stylish millinery ever shown in New Richmond. She advertised regularly in the local newspaper, such items as hand-made hats, trimmed or untrimmed, in the latest designs; beautiful ribbons, velvets, feathers, flowers and silks; tailor-made suits and skirts, hoods and fascinators and children's caps, and infant hoods. Ladies' turbans and little misses hats were offered in the fall of 1904.

The 1903 county directory listed "America Turvey's Millinery, located on Washington Street in New Richmond." The name was incorrect, and the Washington Street address was probably a mistake also, as the street in front of Hollin's building is Wabash Street.

The trimmers who added the finishing touches to Mexie's hats arrived in New Richmond as soon as the spring stock arrived in March, and stayed in town until the ribbons, feathers and other decorations were added to the hats, then returned to their homes at the close of each season. They arrived after the fall and winter stock was delivered to Mexie's shop in September, and finished about the second week in December.

Mexie did all her own trimming when she first started this line of work, but her shop was such a success she required a regular trimmer. A Miss Ellis trimmed for Mexie in November 1900. Miss Fannie Boone trimmed hats for Mexie from June 1902 to June 1904. Fannie was from Fairland, Indiana, and usually visited her sister, Mrs. Lewis Eiler, in Shelbyville, after completing each season as a trimmer in town. Fannie married William B. Mount, a well-known merchant and auctioneer from Darlington, in October 1904, and moved to that town.

Miss Mea Thompson of Judson arrived in town in September 1904 to trim hats for Mexie, staying until December that year. Miss Clara Trembly from Franklin arrived in April 1905, returning to her home in June. She returned to New Richmond in September, and finished her trimming in November that year.

Mexie Turvey moved her stock of millinery to her home on the corner of Franklin and Detchon Streets in 1906, and advertised all the usual trimmings for millinery.

Claypool and Fry had a millinery department within their general merchandise stock in New Richmond. Harry O. Fry attended the wholesale millinery openings in Indianapolis to purchase their stock each spring and fall. The trimmers in their millinery were (according to the New Richmond *Record*): Myrtle Herbert, March 1902; Miss Kerr of Hamilton, Ohio, March 1903; Grace Hopewell, April 1903; Effie Jessie of Lebanon, September 1903; Nellie Kerr, October, 1903—replaced Miss Jessie because of illness; Fleeta Cook of Ridge Farm, Illinois, March to June 1904; Nellie Smith of Muncie, March and October 1905; Alma Higert of Greencastle, March 1906.

Mexie Turvey's and Claypool & Fry's millinery openings were usually held during the same time. The New Richmond *Record*, Thursday, April 13, 1905, gave the following account of a spring opening. "The millinery openings held Thursday, Friday, and Saturday of last week at the millinery parlors of Claypool & Fry and Miss Turvey, were as usual, largely attended. The pretty pattern hats, ideals of the milliner's art, were greatly admired. Decided new colors and large hats predominate, and with a profusion of pretty varied colored flowers, ribbons, and all sorts of trimmings, the new hats for Easter, 1905, are prettier than ever. So fetching and so greatly admired were the new creations of Miss Smith at Claypool & Fry's, and of Miss Trembly, at Miss Turvey's, that on close of the opening, nearly all the pattern hats on exhibition were sold, but yet new creations by these ladies were shortly to be found on exhibition for belated buyers."

The fall openings of both the above millinery parlors took place in October, the same year, and Claypool & Fry's trimmer, Miss Mertz, designed a $50 hat, a ladies' hat, made up of forty-nine, one-dollar bills on a one-dollar frame as an advertising gimmick. Mr. David Scott, of Crawfordsville presided at the piano, playing good music all during the afternoon and evening.

George F. Long added a stock of millinery to his dry goods store in April 1904. Mrs. A. E. Lesley was in the millinery trade in 1909-10 in New Richmond. Ivy Smith, granddaughter of Jim Kincaid, was a milliner, but traveled to various cities to trim ladies' hats. In August 1909, she was in Lancaster, Kentucky; July 1916, in Leonard, Texas; she was listed in New Richmond as a milliner in 1912, but this was her place of residence. Ivy was a resident of Los Angeles, California, at the time of her death, December 12, 1980, at the age of 90 years.

SHOEMAKERS & SHOE STORES

Isaac H. Montgomery, an early Coal Creek Township pioneer, learned the shoemaker's trade, which he followed for twelve years. After his marriage, he became a farmer, but continued to make all the shoes for his wife and children doing the "cobbling" at night after working hard all day on the farm.

Checking into some of Coal Creek's pioneer's probate records, one discovers much information on their ancestors. The estate of James Kendall, for instance, listed one box of shoemaker's tools at 75 cents. David Oppy's estate, another early Coal Creek pioneer, also had shoemaker's tools among his inventory. There was hardly a household without a shoe maker's last standing by to be used when repairing badly worn shoes. My father, Forrest Waye, always repaired our worn out shoes, adding new soles and heels when necessary (not that we were pioneers).

It was the custom for shoemakers to stay in the pioneer's home during the necessary length of time required to make shoes for mom, dad, and all the children, in order to make properly fitted footwear. Shoemakers who made a living from this trade in New Richmond and Coal Creek Township are listed below.

The 1850 Federal census of Coal Creek Township listed Samuel Dinwiddie, age 52, born in Virginia, as a shoemaker; and his son, Adolphus Dinwiddie, 15, born in Ohio, was also listed as a shoemaker. Dinwiddie, a widower, had six children including Adolphus. They lived in the Patton Corner and Round Hill neighborhood.

Hiram Gobel, age 64, born in Pennsylvania, was listed as a shoemaker on the same census and lived in the Swank neighborhood between New Richmond and Wingate.

Joe Pender was listed as a shoemaker in New Richmond in the 1882-3 county directory.

Joe Kliter (also spelled Cliter or Kleiter), a German, opened his first-class shoemaking shop in William Campbell's building in September of 1886, but had moved into Wint Washburn's mammoth store, "and was pegging away from early morn to late night," by November that year. Joe placed a notice in the Crawfordsville weekly *Review* in 1888, saying he was looking for a Dutch woman for a wife (and cook) and mentioned his favorite food was apple pie. He must have had many ladies pursuing him because he placed another notice in the same paper about one year later saying he didn't like pie as well as he used to and all donations to that effect would be respectfully refused. There was no mention of any wedding.

After moving to New Richmond, Joe Kliter frequently corresponded with the friends and relatives he left behind in the old country. He received word of the death of his brother who left quite a substantial amount of money to Joe from his estate, but Joe continued his shoemaking trade in New Richmond. He had more business than he could handle and hired another shoemaker to assist him. His helper caused him more trouble than he was worth by being arrested for breaking into a store in Crawfordsville. Joe continued alone until December 1890 when he was having a large run of business and once again was compelled to hire extra help. The other cobblers names were not revealed. Joseph Kliter's boot and shoe shop was last mentioned in April 1891.

John W. Hollin & Company Shoe Store

John W. Hollin was the proprietor of a drug store and shoe store. At one time the shoe store was located in the center room of the Hollin building, but the two businesses were later conducted in the south room. The 1891-2 county directory listed Hollin's shoe store, and in 1895 Thomas D. Dillon was associated with the J.W. Hollin & Company, dealing in boots and shoes and Strauss Brothers Clothing. In November 1900 they advertised, "a Gigantic slaughter sale of Misses, Boys, Youths, and Ladies Calf shoes from 80 cents to $1." In January 1905 the following advertisement appeared in the New Richmond *Record*, "The Shoe Sale is On! 1,000 pairs of men's, women's and children's shoes at less than cost - at Hollins. You can't go out and steal a pair of shoes as cheap as you can get them at Hollin's Shoe Sale! You can buy yourself a $3.50 pair of shoes; your wife a $3 pair, and your girl a $1.75 pair and for the baby, a 75 cent pair, or $9 worth of shoes-all for $4.64 at Hollin's Shoe Sale!" Hollin's prices in shoes remained about the same, especially for the ladies and children, as late as 1910. Men's Florsheim and King quality shoes, most in patent leather, were $2 a pair; women's $1.50, and children's were half-price that year. He offered more expensive oxfords for men at $3, $4, and $5 a pair—for the more affluent customers.

Clem E. Heaton's Shoe Store

"Selz Royal Blue Store" was located on the west side of south Wabash Street. An insurance map gives the location on the corner of Madison and Wabash, but many older citizens of New Richmond remembered his store next door north of this location in the small building later occupied by Dr. Roth's dental office. Clem E. Heaton sold shoes in New Richmond in 1915 and 1916, offering "Colonial Shoes, $2.50, patent or dull, and cloth top shoes to keep the ankles warm, Comfort model Vicki Kid Flexible welt soles, $3.50; New Stage model cloth top, gun-metal vamp, $4; Cadet model, $3.

Hanawalt and Son Shoe Store

Hanawalt advertised, "Ball Band Artics" rubber foot wear in November 1921. They operated a general store, and men's clothing store until the 1930s. Fred Volz repaired shoes, and was associated with the Hanawalt firm in 1931.

Snyder's Tack and Apparel

Nancy Snyder sold "Tony Lama" Western Boots from 1977 to September 1982, the last dealer in footwear in New Richmond.

Beauty Salons

Although New Richmond ladies did not have a beauty salon available for many years after the town was settled, they were not without curls, or other vain additions to their daily "toilet." The men about town had been pampered in the local barber shops many, many years before the town had its first beauty salon. Experiments over the years to curl hair, and dressings to keep the hair in place appeared in every housewife's "receipt book." Combinations of such ingredients as aqua ammonia, colognep glycernet alcohol, pure soft water, or a combination of moist sugar gum Arabic and rose water was supposed to curl the hair. A combination of castor oil, cologne, alcohol, oil of lemon grass, and oil of bergamot was used as a dressing or hair oil. The addition of oil of lavender (English was the best, of course) and oil of citronella, or bay rum, gave the hair a striking essence–to please those who came near–and possibly to those who were not so near.

To keep hair in curl, the curling iron came into prominence in the early 1890s. The iron created tiny little ringlets after being heated over a coal-oil lamp. This proved to be a very dangerous way of curling the hair, as many accidents occurred from burns suffered from misjudging the location of the locks to be curled, and more than one lamp was upset, causing fires in the home.

A more safe way of curling the hair was to use strips of cloth, wound around locks of hair to create long curls, referred to as rag curls. This was a very painful way of creating beautiful spirals in little girls and their mother's hair. Some mothers went so far as to curl their little sons hair in this fashion, subjecting them to much teasing from playmates. This method required a lot of tugging and pulling to successfully intertwine the hair with strips of cloth.

We must not forget the metal curlers used in the 1930s and 1940s, and the pin curls made possible with a combination of bobby pins and gooey hair setting gel. Believe it or not, it was possible to sleep with the metal curlers, but it was not quite so painful sleeping with the hair 'done up' in pin curls.

The more affluent ladies from the little town of New Richmond traveled to Crawfordsville or Lafayette to have their hair styled, but those with less resources styled their own hair and their daughter's in the privacy of their own home. We must not forget the home permanents—my three daughters will never let me forget them!

The earliest record of a beauty salon in New Richmond was that of Mabel Lyon, in 1939 and 1940. Her shop was located in the back room of the Knights of Pythias building on the southwest corner of the square. How many of you readers can recall the electrically heated curlers that pulled down from a circular "gizmo" and were attached to the rolled hair? The solution applied to the hair had a very strong aroma that sizzled when the hot curler was attached. Mabel's shop went by the name of **The New Richmond Beauty Shop**.

Mary Murdock Wills opened her **Tiddy Toppe Beauty Shoppe** in 1949 on Osage Street in New Richmond, located in the family home.

Peggy Lyons Fyffe opened a beauty shop in the former office of Dr. Manners Washburn from 1953 to 1956. The doctor's office was moved to his location at the south end of Wabash Street previous to this time.

From 1962 to 1973, Gerrie Royer operated the **Swirl and Curl Beauty Shop** in her home northeast of New Richmond, on the north Linden road (a gravel road which leads to US 231 just north of Linden). She advertised "Hair Tinting and Wig Styling" in addition to permanent waves.

Betty Frey operated **Betty's Beauty Shop** in her home on Franklin Street from 1962 to 1964. She and her husband opened a restaurant in the town after she closed her beauty shop.

In the late 1950s, Lorene Davies, a graduate of Huffer's Beauty College in Lafayette, operated **Lorene's Beauty Shop** in New Richmond. Her husband, Chet, and their daughter, Linda, also entered the hair styling profession. Chet assisted Lorene in this shop located in their home northwest of New Richmond, and in 1961, Chet and Linda opened the **Davies Beauty Salon** in Lafayette. Lorene continued to operate the shop in New Richmond until 1973 when her health was failing.

Another rural beauty salon is that of Marcia Goings. **Marcia's Beauty Salon** is located north of the former location of the Davies family shop, just inside the Tippecanoe County line. She started around 1970.

The **Back Door Beauty Salon** was located in the frame building west of the Tri County Telephone office in New Richmond and was operated by Veronica Hartman. The earliest record of this shop was in 1974. It continued until the shop and equipment was offered for sale in May of 1978.

As of this date there is no beauty salon in the town of New Richmond. We ladies will have to go back to the long rag curls—electric curling irons are as hot as the earlier model, but not quite as dangerous.

Barbers—Tonsorial Artists Invade the Town

The 1870 Federal census of Coal Creek Township lists William Campbell, 22, Barber, in the town of New Richmond. Campbell later embarked in the general merchandise business, and continued barbering until 1890, when he sold his Pioneer Store, and his barber chair and equipment. He moved to the new little town of Kirkpatrick, Indiana. William Campbell was New Richmond's first barber.

Charles A. Taylor was listed as a barber in New Richmond from 1882 to 1888, when he sold his chair and equipment to Milton Wheeler and moved to Crawfordsville to ply his trade. There were several references in the papers of Taylor visiting his old friends in the New Richmond barbershops; he just was not happy in the city. He was listed as a New Richmond barber in 1890, and in 1903 he was listed as a barber and laundry agent. Taylor sold his outfit to J.M. (James) Alexander in March 1903, reducing the number of barbers in New Richmond to two shops. The price of haircuts was raised back to 25 cents each at this time. The New Richmond barbers had formed a little "trust" of their own, and placed notices in their windows stating that "henceforth and hereafter, your haircut will cost you 25 cents, two bits, or a quarter. The reason for the ad-vance is by the extortionate price of fuel, so says the barbers, but probably the real reason is because of the haircuts all over the face are in vogue. The fad of shaving off mustaches has just struck our little city, and the extra nickel is charged for their extra exertion in larger shaves, hereafter, thus hoping to get even." Taylor moved to Attica and followed his trade in that city. Other early barbers in New Richmond were: W.H. Howard, 1889; John Foster, 1891-2; Henry T. Vancleave, 1893; and A.D. Chauncy, around 1901.

Milton Wheeler, the "handsome young barber" of New Richmond, purchased Charley Taylor's shop in September, 1888, and a year later added a notion store to the business. Wheeler was soon doing a rushing business, and could shave as slick as the fastest of barbers. Wheeler died in 1903 after a lingering illness, at the age of 44 years. He left a wife and four children.

William Bell was a New Richmond barber from 1903 to 1916; and Benjamin Long from 1891 to 1895. Long's advertisement read, "Remember–when you want a shave or haircut–call Ben Long, The Leading Barber!" Ben moved to Champaign, Illinois around 1903, and continued barbering in that city. Ben's brother, John A. Long, was cutting hair in New Richmond the same year, and had the misfortune of having two fires in his shop–both fires were caused from a defective gasoline lighting apparatus. A.D. Snyder was sitting in the chair when the first fire broke out, and grabbed a nearby hand extinguisher, dousing the fire before the "Fire Laddies" arrived. The second fire damaged the shop more extensively, but the chairs, razors and other equipment were saved. John reopened his shop in March 1904 as one of the most up-to date shops in the vicinity, with a side line as a laundry service agent. The laundry was sent out on Tuesdays and was returned on Fridays.

John Long sold his barber shop to Clyde Alexander in March, 1905. He worked with Alex until July, then continued barbering with an unknown partner in New Richmond until 1908. They called themselves **Sonny & Burr**. They had the following advertisement, "Burr! Hair! Who Cut Your Hair? Burr!" Long was mentioned as one of the partners, but it is still a mystery as to whom the other man was. They sold their shop to a Mr. Nelson of Darlington, and Long went to Frankfort to barber. In 1907 and 1908, there were three barbers listed in New Richmond: J. M. Alexander, John A. Long, and Charles Michael.

J.A. McWhinney, of Danville, Illinois, rented the shop of Mr. Nelson, and was to start barbering in New Richmond in September 1908. J.W. Westfall and Ed Suitors were partners in the barbering business early in 1906. Westfall disposed of his interest, moving to Rossville, Illinois, to ply his trade, and Suitors continued to the end of the year. Another barber, Marcus Bowers, was mentioned as a New Richmond barber the same year. Bowers leased his shop to Suitors and went to Chicago to take a complete course in a barber school. He was to remain in the Windy City until the following spring.

Mrs. Fred E. Kincaid embarked in the haircutting business in 1906. Her advertisement read, "For the latest in hair cuts–call on Mrs. F.E. Kincaid." Pioneer women had been cutting their husband's and children's hair for years, so Mrs. Kincaid decided to branch out a little. Other short term barbers in the town of New Richmond were: Albert Redman, in 1912; D.L. Johnson, with Jack Arnold of Waveland, as a partner, in 1921. Their advertisement read, "JOHNSON'S BARBER SHOP Full line of Toilet Waters, Vanishing Creams Hair Tonics Hair Oils, and Shaving Soaps." They had as a sideline a tailoring shop and sold "SPENCER MEAD SUITS, prices ranging from $19 to $55.

Other barbers mentioned were: "Shorty" Jones, about 1920; and Elmore's Barber Shop, located in the northwest corner of the Washburn bank building, located on the southeast corner of the town square in New Richmond. His barber chair was placed right in the front window, and the time element was around 1930.

The Alexander family of New Richmond carried the barbering trade through many years. James Alexander was shearing heads as early as 1903 after purchasing Charley Taylor's second shop, and Clyde Alexander purchased John Long's shop in March 1905, as stated before. Long continued to work with "Alec" for a while, after selling out.

In 1904, a law was passed requiring all barbers to pass an examination before the State Board and more strict laws were passed requiring more sanitary shops, equipment, and supplies. In 1906 a bill was introduced making it unlawful for the barbers to cut hair on Sunday, but the New Richmond barbers had been closing on Sunday long before the bill was introduced.

Clyde Alexander added a shoe shining stand to his shop in 1906, and Roscoe Plunkett was preparing to "serve all the patrons with a shine that will outshine the sun" in Clyde's shop. Clyde had teamed up with his uncle James Alexander in 1912. The Alexanders usually had the laundry service with their shop. In 1905 W.C. Taylor was dry cleaning suits and clothing in Alec's Shop, and they also sharpened scissors for the citizens of the town for a few years.

J.M. (Jim) Alexander went to Indianapolis in March 1906, to ply his trade occupying the 7th of the 10 chairs in the Y.M.C.A. He then moved to West Lafayette and started a shop on State Street. He was not satisfied with city life, and returned to New Richmond "the best little town on earth." Clyde A. Alexander moved to West Lafayette and assumed possession of James' shop. J.M. decided to try West Lafayette again in August, the same year, but had returned to New Richmond in 1907-8. In 1910, J.M. Alexander's advertisement read, "J.M. Alexander, THE LEADING BARBER, agency for The Soft Water Laundry–Marion Steam Laundry."

James Alexander moved his shop into a room occupied by W.C. Taylor's cleaning establishment, and Taylor exchanged rooms with Alexander in January 1916. Jim excavated a basement under the building and installed a hot air furnace to heat his shop. He enlarged the building, adding a room to the rear of the shop, and brought his shop up to date. His nephew, James Alexander, brother to Clyde, was his partner at the time. They went by the name of **Jim & Jim—The Barbers**. The nephews, Jim and Clyde had moved to Gary, Indiana, by 1929.

Will Bell, a former employee of Jim Alexander's, opened his own shop in the Wray business room and was competing with him in 1916. Will's shop was open on Wednesday, Friday, and Saturday of each week.

Jim Alexander continued barbering, and another nephew, Byron Alexander, who was a half-brother to Clyde and James and also went by the name of "Alec," became his partner after graduating from New Richmond High School. They were selling Philco Radios as a side line in 1935, 1939, and perhaps later. Ralph Harwood and Byron were cutting hair in Alexander's (or Alec's) Barber Shop in 1940 and 1944. Jim Alexander was still listed as a barber in April 1948, the same year of his death.

Byron Alec continued until 1963, when he sold his chair and equipment to Bill Hon of Lafayette. Bill started a shop in the former office of Dr. Roth, a local dentist. Hon left New Richmond the following year and his shop caught fire, destroying the building and most of the contents–including Byron Alec's barbering chair. The town of New Richmond has been without a barber since that time.

Chapter 5 - Hospitality & Entertainment Businesses

Restaurants

William Campbell, in his New Richmond items August 27, 1887, said, "We have three or four 'chop houses' in town now." Bill neglected to list the proprietors of these eating places in New Richmond's early history, but we can easily see what the top choice of meat was during this period of time. The following restaurants and the dates they were mentioned in the newspapers are listed below:

Douglas Bunnell was the proprietor of a grocery, cigar, tobacco, and lunch counter in 1891-92.

H.E. Strader's restaurant was listed on June 5, 1902. In April 2, 1903, Strader's restaurant moved into Kincaid's saloon, but the building was owned by Boswell Clough.

John Reeder's restaurant opened in the old Bunnell building in August 1902.

G.A. Pence's restaurant opened July 30, 1903. Pence was a former resident of Mellott.

William F. Grigson purchased the bakery and restaurant from G.A. Pence September 3, 1903, and advertised, "Home made bread, pies, cakes, short order counter, fish, oysters in season, candies, fruit and nuts," and "this is the only place in town you can buy direct from the bakery. **Grigson's Bakery and Restaurant** closed its doors March 31, 1904. Leonard Baugh of Farmer's Institute owned the building in which Grigson's bakery and restaurant was located.

Hempleman's Grocery and Bakery was listed from December 25, 1902 to January 15, 1903, offering sandwiches and short orders.

Charles McLain purchased H.E. Strader's restaurant and bakery July 9, 1903. Charles' brother, Lawrence, was associated with him. McLain advertised, "Kokomo Ice Cream and cream soda." McLain remodeled his restaurant soon after he purchased the business, and the *Record* said, "The place is scrupulously clean, is prettily lighted at night, and is becoming a cool and inviting resort, and worthy of liberal public patronage." McLain's and Grigson's restaurants were both in operation at this time. McLain purchased a mammoth new soda fountain in April 1905, and informed the public, "the handsome piece of furniture and fixtures would soon be ready to give forth such delicious cool drinks as ever passed your lips." **McLain's Restaurant and Bakery** moved into new quarters in June 1906, and after the new Knights of Pythias building was completed, McLain moved into the center room. The first two locations are unknown.

George C. Livingston's Restaurant was listed in 1911 and 1912. Livingston combined the grocery and restaurant businesses in the latter year, and continued with his grocery until the late 1940s.

Jesse D. Hinman purchased a restaurant in March 1916, located in the southwest room of the Washburn building. He and his wife and daughter moved from North Vernon, Indiana, and immediately took possession of his new business, **The Sugar Bowl**, around the 16th of that month. Hinman's restaurant served seven dinners to parties serving on the election board on November 5, 1929, the last record available of this restaurant.

Shirley & Herbins Restaurant was mentioned in the New Richmond Record, April 5, 1923, and was listed in the 1923 New Richmond High School (N.R.H.S.) annual. They advertised, "sandwiches, short orders, candies, pies, soups, and ice cream."

Taylor's Restaurant was also advertised in the 1923 annual, "Don't divorce your wife because she can't cook–EAT AT TAYLOR'S RESTAURANT–and keep her for a pet. Regular meals, 35¢; school lunches 15 and 20¢."

Tortorella's Ice Cream Parlor and Lunch Counter–Joseph and Alice Ebrite Tortorella's ice cream parlor was located in the west room of the Washburn block. The Tortorellas lived in New Richmond in 1914-15 and in 1919. In between the two years mentioned, they lived in Chicago, and the date they operated their business in New Richmond is uncertain. They advertised "sand-wiches, ice cream, sodas, and lunch counter."

Levert Binns' restaurant was listed in 1934.

The New Richmond Restaurant, advertised in September and October, 1935, "Good hot lunches served at all times–sandwiches–all kinds."

The Black Hawk Cafe, "for good meals and home cooking" was advertised on November 21, 1936.

The Blue Hour Café, for "quality food, reasonably priced" was listed on August 13, 1937.

Magruder's Restaurant and Grocery, was located in the south room of Washburn's building in the 1930s.

Thomas' Cafe advertised in the N.R.H.S. class plays from March 25, 1938 to November 27, 1941, "Ice Cream, cold drinks, home cooked meals, short orders." Mae and Pearl Frances Thomas were the proprietors of this cafe.

Carr's Cafe was advertised in the N.R.H.S. class plays in 1939 and 1940.

Zeke's Cafe was listed in December 1940.

The City Grill was listed in December 1940 with Charles Shepherd, proprietor.

McMillin's Restaurant, Claude McMillin, proprietor, was located in the south room of the Knights of Pythias building. McMillin sold the cafe to the Baldwins in 1947. The date McMillin opened for business is uncertain.

Rose & Larry's Cafe was located in the east room of the Long building in 1950s.

The Dinner Bell Cafe was listed in 1947, advertising, "Fine Foods," the proprietor and location is unknown.

The **7 Day Cafe** advertised, "Meat and Eat at 7 Day Cafe–anything–anytime, good meals, tasty lunches, ice cream, T bone steaks, home baked pies." This cafe, owned and operated by Bill and Grace Baldwin, was located in the south room of the Knights of Pythias building from 1947 to 1951.

The **7 Day Cafe (No.2)** David and Margaret Easterly were the proprietors of the second cafe by the name of "7 Day Cafe" from 1951 to 1953 or '54. The June and July issues of the Shopper's Guide carried the following advertisement, "7 Day Cafe', a place to eat, that is clean and neat, with service fine and dandy; We also have ice cream, cigars and candy." The Easterly family moved to Lafayette in 1954.

Sylvester's Restaurant was located in the east room of the Long building in 1954, the proprietor was Lawrence Sylvester.

The New Richmond Cafe, proprietor, Bertha L. Carson, offered, "Meals and short orders" in the 1959 Chronicle.

Ruth (Priebe) Cunningham had a restaurant in New Richmond at one time, but the year and location is uncertain, possibly the Washburn block.

Ken & Betty's Cafe–Ken and Betty Frey opened a restaurant on July 1, 1964, in the south room of the Knights of Pythias building. They closed in August 1965.

Roy Kerr had a restaurant in the north room of the Knights of Pythias building, in the 1960s.

Kelp's Olde Town Restaurant–Durrell and Barbara Sue Kelp, proprietors, offered "Dining Room for small banquets available by appointment," from 1957 to 1971, and were located in the north room of the Knights of Pythias building.

The New Richmond Cafe, Mr. and Mrs. Roy Geiger, Jr. proprietors, was located in the north room of the Knights of Pythias building from November 11, 1971 to 1973.

Kelp's Restaurant–Durrell and Barbara Sue Kelp returned to the restaurant business by December 1973 and continued into 1974.

The New Richmond Restaurant–Don and Carolyn Fiddler purchased the restaurant building from Ralph Kunkel in October 1975 and opened for business in the north room of the Knights of Pythias building, for a short time.

Roxie's Place–Roxie Landis, proprietor, from 1975 to 1978. An advertisement in the *Messenger Crier* May 16, 1978 reads, "Roxie's Wednesday night special–Roxie's Cat Fish." This cafe was also located in the north room of the Knights of Pythias building.

West's Coffee Pot–Gerald and Dorothy West purchased Roxie's place in July 1978 and operated the restaurant until April 1983, when they sold the business to Stephen DePlanty.

Stephen DePlanty operated **Stephen's Fine Foods** from April 1983 until July 1, 1985, when he leased it to Linda Layton.

The New Richmond Restaurant, Linda Layton, proprietor, from July 1, 1985 to December 14, 1985. Linda's restaurant was renamed "Linda's Hickory Tree" for the movie *Hoosiers*, starring Gene Hackman, Barbara Hershey, Sheb Wooley, and Dennis Hopper. One of the scenes was filmed in the restaurant. Layton closed her restaurant shortly after the filming of *Hoosiers* was completed.

NEW RICHMOND'S SALOONS

SALOONS, BLIND TIGERS, BLIND PIGS, BEER JOINTS, BARS, COCKTAIL LOUNGES

Thomas Foster opened New Richmond's first saloon sometime between 1855 and 1860. The Daughters of Temperance Society organized in New Richmond in 1857 and only lasted about five years, but during this period of time they managed to buy Tom Foster's stock of liquors, pour the stuff on the ground, and set fire to it. Tom was in the grocery business, and being a native of North Carolina, he thought nothing of adding a keg of whiskey to his other kegs, or barrels of merchandise. His mind was changed very suddenly, however, and the "thirsty" quenched their thirst elsewhere.

Doctor Hostetter's Saloon—After Tom Foster's keg was destroyed, Doctor Hostetter "took the field" according to an early New Richmond historian, William Campbell. His saloon must have been short-lived, because it was not recorded on the 1860 census.

John W. Plunkett's Saloon—John Plunkett was another grocery store owner who added a keg of whiskey to his other merchandise. He was arrested for selling liquor without a license in June 1879. His grocery and saloon was listed on the 1860 census.

W.B. Wolls Saloon was listed in the 1882-3 county directory, although it should have been Walls.

William Campbell's Saloon and Grocery was listed in the 1884-1885, 1887, and 1890 county directories.

IRA STOUT

Ira Stout purchased a saloon in November 1886. He remodeled and refitted it with the latest style—bar fixtures, etc.—and was running the saloon in a decent and quiet way. Ira engaged various local men to tend his bar while he traveled all over the U.S.A. and abroad–in other words, he made a huge profit from the "thirsty citizens" of New Richmond. Ira was still selling liquor when another group of temperance workers began working toward closing New Richmond's saloons during the period covering 1903 through 1909. In March 1905, Ira purchased the storeroom formerly occupied by John E. Wilson's hardware, and fixed it up for a private "club room, so to speak, but not a Blind Tiger" [an illegal saloon, also known as a blind pig], Ira claimed. Ira sold his other saloon, The Zoo, to Tom Clark in 1890, but either purchased this saloon back from Clark, or purchased another saloon sometime before 1903.

Two months after Ira fixed up his club room, he offered for sale his business room, including all the "splendid bar fixtures, Balwood cash register, new pool table, box ball alley, etc., for less than half cost." In the same issue of the local newspaper, he applied for a liquor license and asked for the privilege of running pool, card, and billiard tables, serving lunch and cigars, tobaccos, and all kinds of non-intoxicating drinks in the same room wherein the intoxicating liquors were to be sold and drank. This license application gave the location as the ground floor, front room of a one story frame building situated on the north end of the east half of the north half of lot number three, block number one of the original plat of New Richmond (this would not have been the location of what was referred to as Smokey Row on south Wabash Street just north of the former railroad). Two remonstrances were filed against Stout, one for the business, and one for Stout himself. He failed to put in an appearance before the county commissioners, therefore, the saloon was closed for two years.

Ira Stout and Samuel Dean were running a blind tiger from June to October, 1906, before the temperance people brought suit against them for "maintaining a nuisance" in the town of New Richmond. This was a new approach in trying to rid the town of saloons. It was alleged that Stout owned the building, and Dean was running the place. Dean claimed to have a government license entitling him to sell intoxicants in quantities of five gallons at a time. The temperance people said they were running a disorderly and disreputable place, and in their opinion they were conducting a "tiger" in such a manner as to make it "odious" to the people in the township so they will refuse to sign a remonstrance, hereafter, all a part of a scheme of the defendants to get a license to run a saloon at a later date. They were accused of throwing beer bottles at the good citizens as they passed near the "blind tiger" which was located near the post office, churches of the town, and a thickly settled neighborhood. Ira Stout planned to go into the saloon business with Boswell Clough in Elston, after Clough was put out of the saloon business in town, but Clough changed his mind and backed out of the deal. In 1912, Ira Stout was listed as laborer in the town of New Richmond–his traveling days were over.

OTHER SALOONS

In July 1887, Charlie Peters was making two trips each week with his "wet goods wagon" to the "thirsty" of New Richmond. He was either a distributor of liquor, or a "rolling beer joint."

Kincaid's Saloon and Pool Room—James Kincaid's saloon and pool room was listed in the 1891-1892 county directory. Jim, Sr. applied for a liquor license in March 1902. His place of business was the same description as Ira Stout's saloon. Boswell Clough owned the building at this time. Jim was granted the license, and he assumed the saloon business of his son James Kincaid, Jr. In March 1903, Jim Kincaid had enough of the saloon business and closed his saloon "for good," he said.

Kincaid's Saloon—Samuel Kincaid, son of James Kincaid, Sr., applied for a liquor license in February 1903, and was to open another saloon in the old Bunnell frame building on east Washington Street.

Tom Cook's Saloon—Tom Cook, saloonist in New Richmond, was fined for selling liquor on Sunday in July 1891. The location of his saloon is unknown.

Sitting Bull Saloon—Boswell Clough's Sitting Bull Saloon was mentioned in August 1893; he also had a billiard hall in connection. Boswell sold the saloon equipment and stock to Oscar Stingley in March 1902. Oscar Stingley applied for a liquor license two years later in March 1904 for his place of business located at a place, "beginning 94-1/2 feet south of the center of the cross roads west of the old plat of New Richmond, etc., on the ground floor front room, one story frame building." A blanket remonstrance carried the names of 424, or a majority of 99 against Stingley, therefore his license was not granted. Oscar opened a "soft drink joint" in the old restaurant building two months later. The town had not one, but two blind tigers at this time, Stingley's and Clouser's.

Boswell Clough's Saloon (his second)—In December 1902, Boswell Clough was granted a liquor license–good for one year in New Richmond. His was the only saloon in operation the following April. He again applied for a license in November 1903, his place of business being located on south Wabash Street next door to the Snyder building–now the site of the town hall. Clough's license was not renewed, as he faced a "blanket remonstrance" from the Coal Creek Township temperance group. He withdrew from the conflict with all possible grace and this was the last saloon in Coal Creek Township to be closed by this group. Boswell Clough immediately opened up a "Temperance Saloon" and offered "Kentucky Cider" and "Hop Ale" to "mildly dampen the throats and stay the thirst of the thirsty," according to the New Richmond *Record* on December 17, 1903. There was a lot of interest generated throughout Montgomery County on the outcome of the saloon closings, and a comment was made about the thirsty having to quench their thirst at the town pump, but a citizen informed them New Richmond was dryer than most people thought because the old town pump had been "froze up" since the first frost came, and was twice broken. Clough sold his hop ale joint stock, and leased the saloon property for one year to

Nathan Fletcher of Frankfort. The place was immediately opened for business with John Clouser of Darlington, as his bartender. Boswell Clough sold his old saloon property in January 1906 to T.M. Layne, who stored buggies, farm wagons and implements in the building. The old ice house at the rear was also used as a storage room before he sold the saloon, however, John Clouser and others associated with the blind tigers kept the temperance people on the run while in this building of Clough's.

William Aulston's Saloon (Allston)—Willie Allston saved the temperance people a lot of trouble by destroying his own saloon. He attempted to clean out his chimney with gunpowder, which blasted the stove to pieces, threw fire all over the rooms, and burned the building to the ground. He had no insurance and his loss was estimated between $600 and $800—quite a large sum to blow away in 1895.

Elmer Plunkett's Saloon was listed in the 1900-1 county directory.

William Hayworth's Saloon—William Hayworth applied for a liquor license in May 1904 on Ira Stout's former saloon site (lot 3 block 1 original plat of New Richmond), but since there is no other record of his saloon available, he may not have been granted a license.

Hop Ale Joint (John Nelson Clouser's Saloon)—Boswell Clough leased his saloon, or "Hop Ale Joint" to Nathan Fletcher of Frankfort in March 1904, but due to the intervention of the temperance people, the "soft drink" joint was closed within a week. Fletcher (or Clouser) organized an "Independent Drinkers Association" and provided keys to the members for the purpose of evading the Nicholson law in April 1904, and continued to run his blind tiger despite the blanket remonstrance in effect in Coal Creek township at the time. The club was said to have a very large membership. There were many months of arrests, trials, and illegal moves made during this period in New Richmond's history, and Fletcher's bartender, John N. Clouser, bore the brunt of all the arrests and trials, Fletcher remaining a silent partner.

Clouser became known as New Richmond's Tiger and the trials were referred to as "another twist of the Tiger's tail." During one of the famous trials held in Justice Ebrite's court in New Richmond, a "hotly contested bottle" was passed around to see if it was an intoxicating or non-intoxicating brew. The jury tasted, smelled, and examined the stuff, called "Malt Mead" or "what not," and decided it *was* intoxicating. He was fined $25 and costs, and this case was "chalked up" as the first offense under the **Nicholson Law**.

The county prosecutor was John Murphy, a former Bristle Ridger, and a rising young lawyer in Crawfordsville at the time. He investigated several of the charges against Clouser. Murphy gave a man a dollar to purchase some liquor from the blind tiger, who bought four bottles of "mall mead" and a half pint of whiskey. He and a companion drank the four bottles of malt mead on the way home, but delivered the half pint of whiskey to Murphy, for the evidence he needed for the trial. The trial held in Esquire Ebrite's court was enjoyed by a large crowd which taxed the seating capacity of the high school room in the New Richmond School building.

The New Richmond *Record* of July 7, 1904, gave the account of the trial, saying, "The masterly orations of the attorneys in behalf of their clients took up most of the afternoon. There was much amusement for the spectators who enjoyed the laughable situations and funny jests. The evidence of one witness, John Hope, was particularly comical as he persisted in calling the beverage in question, 'Mead Malt,' he being from Kentucky, and the stuff was too weak and of too new origin for him to remember its rightful name. The oratorical efforts carried much amusement with them, too, a pleasant tilts between the attorneys in which 'bald heads,' 'marble tops' and other jesting comparisons were flung merrily at each other while their audience enjoyed their witty efforts. Clyde Jones, assisted by W.T. Whittington appeared as attorneys in behalf of the state, and Dallas Holeman of Frankfort, looked after the defense. The twelve serving on the jury were: A.D. Snyder, Ed Jones, Will Kite, J. C. Henderson, J.A. Lamson, Park White, J.A. Kirkpatrick, Chas. Zook, Homer Barcus, Jerre Harriman, R.A. Thomas and James Thomas." This particular trial cost Clouser $84.50 for running a blind tiger.

Other "twists of the tiger's tail" were continued into 1905, and the costs of running his blind tiger was too much for Clouser to bear. He decided to seek work on a nearby farm for a while. There were many attempts to open saloons in New Richmond around this period of time, but they very seldom got beyond the temperance people. A man named Baker, formerly of Stockwell, thought he could outsmart the local anti-saloonists, but a few small boys from New Richmond informed the local authorities they should take a look at his business enterprise. Some of the members of the Montgomery County grand jury "peeped under the canvas" of New Richmond's "Zoological Garden" and as a result, Baker was arrested on four counts of selling liquors without a license. His trial was held early in February 1905, and the results of running his blind tiger was entitled, "Baker Takes the Bakery" in the local newspaper. He was fined $100 for each case and served six months in jail. Judge Jere West presided, and informed Baker if the citizens of a township file a remonstrance against the sale of intoxicating liquors in their township, he believed their wishes should be respected.

Joseph Humbert's Saloon—Joe Humbert filed an application for a liquor license in August 1905, the place of business being the same description of Boswell Clough's saloon. He was turned down by the county commissioners, because the blanket remonstrance in Coal Creek Township was still in effect. Joe made an appeal to the circuit court, and Judge Jere West, in order to clear up a question concerning remonstrances, made a decision governing the signing of remonstrances by the power of attorney for the temperance groups, saying new cards signed since April 1905 (when the Moore law became operative) must be secured, and turned over to the temperance leaders. Humbert did not receive his liquor license, however.

George W. Harriman's Saloon—George W. Harriman applied for a liquor license in March 1906. His proposed saloon was in Ira Stout's old saloon, block one, lot three in the original plat of New Richmond. He may have been just testing the temperance leaders, as there is no record of his saloon available. Those desiring to keep saloons persisted throughout the years, and the temperance leaders were just as determined there would be no saloons in Coal Creek Township, but this is one sort of business that is still surviving in New Richmond.

Taverns Located at 4 East Washington Street

Ross Howe's Tavern was listed from 1939 to 1941 in the N.R.H.S. class plays. Ross paid for two rum table licenses in January 1939 to the local town clerk, and this may have been his first year as a New Richmond tavern and gambling room proprietor. The Howes moved to Frankfort in 1946-7 and their daughter operated the tavern.

Hackerd's Tavern—Paul and Pauline (Howe) Hackerd moved to New Richmond about 1946 and ran the tavern for her parents, the Howes. Their advertisement in the local class plays read, "Everything good to eat and drink." The Hackerds sold the tavern in 1962 to "Duke" Wright. Hackerd changed the name to "Hackerd's Bar and Grill" in 1962.

New Richmond Bar and Grill—Harold "Duke" Wright purchased the tavern from Hackerd in 1962 and called it the New Richmond Bar and Grill. The Wrights moved to Arizona in 1964 after selling the tavern back to the Hackerds. Paul Hackerd purchased the tavern from Wright in August 1964, but only kept it a year, selling to Roy Pendleton. The Hackerds moved to Florida where he operated a food store. Roy Pendleton, Sr. purchased the tavern in March 1965. He advertised, "Beer, wine, liquor, soup, and sandwiches."

The New Richmond Bar and Grill was offered for sale in May 1973, including the building fixtures and all the equipment and supplies. Jerry Matricia was tending bar in 1974 in the local tavern. In January that year he married Murlene Koehler, who was listed as a bar owner. In December of the same year, Donald and Mary Johnson applied for a liquor license, giving their place of business as the New Richmond Bar and Grill, Incorporated. Jerry Matricia's name was listed with the bar and grill in 1976, but not as the proprietor.

New Richmond Bar and Grill and Pizza King—On December 1, 1977, John Keith purchased the local tavern. In 1978 he advertised, "Cocktails, beer, wine, and "Try our Famous Pizza King—carryouts, we're here to serve." Keith sold the tavern to Denzil Flynn in 1981.

Denzil "Denny" Flynn purchased the tavern in 1981 and continued the Pizza King and short orders. He advertised, in 1984, "Catfish dinners, steaks, smelt, shrimp, clam strips, full grill menu, noon lunches," and added, "Come see our hats." Denny collected all kind of hats and displayed them all over the tavern, so the story goes. Denny and his wife, Helen, were still the proprietors, and both were running the tavern at the time of Denny's death, November 18, 1985. He was buried in Westminster, California. Mrs. Flynn sold the tavern to Mr. and Mrs. Long of Lafayette, February 1, 1986.

The Longs operated under the same name as the former owners. The New Richmond Bar and Grill was listed for sale in June 1987 in the Lafayette *Journal and Courier* (June 14, 1987). Bob Worland purchased the New Richmond Bar and Grill from the Longs.

TEMPERANCE CAUSES

It may be hard to realize there was a great need for a temperance society when Coal Creek Township was in its infancy, but the facts show the entire county was facing the problem of coping with early settlers addicted to the use of intoxicating liquors. When one stops to think about it, the pioneers used whiskey to cure everything from the common cold to snake bites, and after many illnesses it was very possible they became addicted without realizing it.

Richard Hargrave, an early Methodist Episcopalian circuit rider, delivered the first temperance lecture to the good people of Coal Creek Township around 1832 or 1833. The meeting was held in Absalom Kirkpatrick's log barn one mile west of New Richmond. The first temperance pledge was circulated and signed, although there was strong opposition to temperance movements at the time.

In 1893, temperance meetings were held in the township. Only two persons were mentioned as speaking out against the saloons at that time, Buck Stanley and Alice Ebrite. The opposition to saloons had some effect; in 1897, F.M. Johnson's Drug Store placed the following advertisement in the New Richmond *Enterprise*, May 28, 1897, "Have you tried Johnson's Phosphates—the latest and best temperance drink made?"

During the Quarterly Conference of the Methodist Church, held January 10, 1903, a committee was appointed to confer with like committees in Coal Creek Township with a view of circulating a remonstrance under the Nicholson Law for the suppression of the liquor traffic. On the east end of the township (New Richmond and vicinity) the committee was comprised of J.A. Bailey, Solomon Dewey, and George W. Pierce. Sol Dewey has been given most of the credit of ridding New Richmond of saloons, but it was the work of many dedicated people who attempted to make New Richmond a proud village in which to live.

There were many meetings held in all the local and nearby churches speaking against saloons. The Anti Saloon League sent speakers from the capital city on more than one occasion. Rev. A.L. Crim, a former minister of the New Richmond Christian Church, gave a prohibition speech at Center Church and in Hollin's Hall in June 1904. He was in town to make another speech in July that year, but Hollin's Hall was extremely warm (the thermometer reading was 122 degrees in the sun, 100 degrees in the shade, the day he was to speak), therefore the meeting was held under the tent of the Advent Christians who were holding meetings in town that week. Crim resigned as pastor of the Ladoga Christian Church in 1905 because some of the officers were in favor of open saloons. He decided that saloons existed in all the towns because the church members want them. Crim was an eloquent speaker, and ran for Secretary of State on the prohibition ticket in 1906. He spoke in New Richmond in October that year.

The people in favor of saloons used every available excuse to fight the temperance people. Some of the town "taxpayers" complained because their taxes were raised to make up for the loss of revenue collected from the saloon license. Temperance workers in both New Richmond and Wingate "hoisted a flag of victory" when the last two saloons were closed in September 1904, although the battle had just begun on both sides of the fence. The Coal Creek Temperance Society always worked within the legal laws—unlike the good citizens in Stockwell, who resolved to keep a saloon from opening by stoning the building, then warned the would-be saloonists that more disastrous steps would follow if they tried to stay open. The liquor laws always favored the saloon keepers, and the anti-saloonists had to keep on their guard to stay within the law.

In May 1906 there were 385 signers on a Coal Creek remonstrance to keep saloons out of the township. A bill was to be introduced in the Indiana legislature to increase the license fee to $1,000 for saloon keepers. This would have had the tendency to weed out the small ones, and the local temperance workers were in favor of such a bill, but there was too much opposition throughout the state for this bill.

14 - Temperance Parade March 1909

Prohibition Vote of March 1909

On Tuesday, March 23, 1909, a county local option election was held, and the anti-saloonists scored another victory. The results were printed in the New Richmond *Record* on the 25th. The entire county voted 4,958 against (dry); 2,155 for (wet); majority 2,803. Coal Creek precinct No. 1 voted, 230 against (dry); 80 for (wet), majority, 150. The temperance workers felt it was now time to celebrate in a big way. The New Richmond *Record* of March 25, 1909 printed the following item:

> The teachers and pupils of the New Richmond schools paraded the streets of the town Tuesday, making two parades, the first at 9 o'clock in the morning and the second at 1 o'clock, in behalf of the success of the "drys" in the local option election of the county. The line formed at the school building and headed by the New Richmond Band, every scholar bearing a flag, banner, or placard, and with a "Vote Yes for Me" tag pinned on every breast, marched downtown and through all the principal streets, singing patriotic songs as they marched. In the afternoon the schools were reinforced by a goodly number of the ladies of the town and vicinity, all carrying flags and bringing up the rear of the procession. Following the parades, the band went serenading, making the round of the "drys" of the merchants and clerks, and the "wets" too, if there were any.

A photograph was taken of this temperance parade, and a small boy is shown sitting next to a light pole near a storage container for gasoline on the corner of the Hollin brothers building. This disappointed little boy was the son of a saloon keeper or blind tiger, and his father refused to let him participate in the parade. My father, the late Forrest Waye, related the story, but could not recall the boy's name.

An article appeared in the New Richmond *Record*, August 12, 1909 stating, "THE COUNTY OPTION LAW WILL STAND!–will never be repealed–will liberate people from the evil that has been destroying the lives and characters of too many of its citizens." Unfortunately, this endless battle against intoxicants continues today.

Hostels & Boarding Houses

The Montgomery County commissioners fixed the following rates for tavern and inn keepers in the very beginning of the county's history: wine, per bottle, $1.25; brandy, per half pint, 50 cents; gin, per half pint, 25 cents; whiskey per half pint, 12-1/2 cents; victualing, per meal, 25 cents; oats, per gallon, 12-1/2 cents; corn, per gallon, 12 1/2 cents; horse, at hay, per night, 25 cents; lodging, per night, 12-1/2 cents.

The "Strawtown to Covington Road" was one of the more frequently traveled highways in the area of New Richmond in the early days. This road, running east and west, was nothing more than a trail used by the Indians, so it has been said, but was made a little wider from the use of the horse-drawn wagons, or carts. The road was very rough, and full of ruts made by the wagon wheels. Travelers were very badly in need of rest by the time they arrived in Coal Creek Township, and often were invited into the homes of the early settlers to partake of their food and to rest. Frequently, even strangers were invited to spend the night with these settlers. An extra, or spare bedroom, was unheard of back then, and the guest was asked to sleep on the hard, bare floor, with only a blanket to wrap around himself, and the children were asked to scoot over a little to share their already crowded sleeping quarters, if there were other children with the travelers. Crowding three or four children into one bed was often the rule.

One of the most noted resting places on the Strawtown to Covington Road was located a little over a mile west of New Richmond. It was situated on section eight, on the northeast corner of the above mentioned road, and the road north to Sugar Grove. The two-story log structure served as a boarding house, or hotel, and the stage coach made regular stops at this place in the early days of the township's history.

I have asked many former New Richmond residents to relate their versions of this famous hotel and corner, and their stories are always the same as the tales heard from those living in the town of New Richmond all their lives. The story goes like this, "Many years ago, there was a log, two-story building, or house, used as a hotel. The stage coach stopped there and the people riding the stage slept in the lofts or upstairs room of the log cabin. The place was fested with bed bugs, and soon the hotel acquired the name **Bed Bug Hotel**. The site to this day is known as Bed Bug Corner."

Hotels

The story of Bed Bug Corner has been handed down from generation to generation by the area residents, but it is very exciting to hear the tale related by people living on the east, or west coast, or the other faraway places, when they return to their old home town for a visit. No one ever admitted their ancestor owned the corner, or ran this hotel, however!

The Bed Bug Hotel anecdote was always followed by the fact that a huge log barn stood behind (or north of) the two story log house. My father, Forrest Waye, often played with some children who lived in the log house in later years when he was a child (around 1903-4), and said they usually played in the old barn. There were several stalls for the horses belonging to the travelers to rest under the shelter of this structure. I do hope the bedbugs were all gone by that time!

A sad incident occurred at the turn of the century when a young man residing with the family as a farm hand at this residence climbed to the very top beams of this huge barn, where he had laid some planks across as his final resting place, and attempted to commit suicide by swallowing carbolic acid. His screams were heard by the family members, and the local physicians gave him a large dose of salts, and a quantity of oil, and saved his life.

Forrest Waye also related an incident that happened to him in later years, saying, "Gypsies made yearly visits to the New Richmond area, and found the old Bed Bug Hotel, and barn, suited their needs as a resting place." Forrest and his brother Earl saw a beautiful black mare they had in their possession, and asked if they would trade this mare for their horse. After some haggling, a trade was agreed upon. Forrest and Earl came home feeling real smug for trading their tired, old, broken-down horse for such a beautiful animal. They hitched her to the wagon loaded with their painting tools and drove her to a house northeast of town where the two were painting. At the end of the day, they hitched her to their wagon and started for home. All went well for about a mile down the road, and then the horse began to show her true nature. She was tired, so she sat down right in the middle of the road. They tried pulling her, cracking the whip at her, kicking her; they even tried speaking nicely to her, but to no avail. Nothing would get her onto her feet. Along came a friend of theirs who told them to get into their wagon, where he joined them. He pulled out his six shooter, and fired into the sky above. The mare took off like "greased lightning." She ran about half a mile and again sat down in the road. The gentleman shot his gun again and the beautiful black mare ran as fast as any horse could travel, but every time she slowed down, the gun was fired, until the three men arrived in New Richmond. Forrest told his tale to a local horse trader, who traded the mare for a better horse. He must have had a customer he wanted to settle a score with, or perhaps he thought he could train the mare to stay on all fours.

These little anecdotes help to prove there was once a log building that served as a resting place for tired and weary travelers many years ago, but has been remembered best for its discomfort, instead of as a comfortable lodging place.

Other early New Richmond hotels mentioned in the county directories and newspapers are listed below.

The McComas Hotel was mentioned in July, 1880; T.N. Jones Hotel, 1882-3; J.H. Alexander had just started a boarding house in 1886, and George Livingston was "talking of starting a hotel" the same year, in connection with his livery stables. I searched the weekly news items following that announcement and found no record of his hotel, only the livery. A Mr. Blake was running a hotel or boarding house in January 1888, when he treated his boarders to an eighteen-pound roast turkey on New Year's Day. In March 1891, Mrs. Artimesa Wade was planning to erect a hotel in the town. No other record was found of her hotel, but Mrs. Wade was suffering from cancer, and she passed away in her home on Detchon Street on October 22, the same year. She had purchased some lots in town for her hotel, but did not live to fulfill her dream.

BLACK BEAR HOTEL

The boarding houses and hotels mentioned above were very poorly planned. They were quickly started to accommodate the increase in traffic in New Richmond caused by the coming of the new railroad in 1881. The railroad was changed from its original narrow gauge to a standard gauge in June of 1888, and the town was badly in need of a good hotel. The New Richmond correspondent made several pleas in the

15 - Black Bear Hotel

Crawfordsville newspapers for someone to start a hotel, as the travelers who stopped were having trouble finding a place to stay. The railroad men, too, needed a place to reside while working in the area.

If the correspondent of the Crawfordsville *Review* had done his research, he would have been aware of the plans in the making when his plea for a hotel was made, for on February 1, 1888, Ira Stout purchased the old grist mill (built in 1879 or 1880) from Charles Kirkpatrick. The old mill was a rectangular structure, and the only record of the building's reconstruction or conversion into a hotel was in June that year when Elisha C. Campbell was painting the old building.

In September 1888, the new hotel was "doing a good business and takes the place of a long felt want," so the *Review* quill pusher reported. There was no record of the carpentering, or the number of rooms, or any important facts concerning the new hotel in the papers at that time. A year later, Ira Stout had erected new gas lamps in front of his hotel, and he also erected a "tin pin alley" next to his hotel, for entertainment, or an added attraction for his customers. Stout also had a saloon he called The Zoo, and a small lunch room with a sign on the front of the building offering "Foreign and Domestic Fruits, Cigars, and Lunch." This little frame building was located between the Black Bear Hotel and the Zoo. North of the hotel was the bowling alley, and the South Wabash Livery Stables. These buildings situated on the west side of south Wabash Street, just north of the railroad tracks to Madison Street, was referred to as **Smokey Row** by the New Richmond residents in the late 1880s and 1890s. All of these building are long gone and forgotten; in fact, the residents in the town today have never heard of any of these business enterprises, or even Ira Stout.

Ira Stout was a character who made a living by building and starting the above business houses, then hired local residents to manage his saloon, hotel, and other enterprises. Ira managed to reap enough profits to enable him to travel to Europe in 1894. He formed a lifelong fascination for travel, and toured the United States and many other countries. Ira was listed as a professional lecturer and related his experiences on these trips to faraway places. He wrote of his travels and published the stories in the local newspaper, and Ira gathered the local lads around his places of business and filled their eager little ears with fascinating yarns about his travels as they sat spellbound upon the boardwalk.

Meanwhile, the manager of the Black Bear Hotel in New Richmond was Mrs. Anna, or "Hope" Kirkpatrick. Kirkpatrick did the cooking in the hotel, as well as serving as manager, and this hotel was soon known all across the Clover Leaf Line (railroad) for her excellent food and hospitality. The drummers claimed "New Richmond was the only town on the road where the 'Old Maid of Seventy Summers' would attract them and pin boquets [*sic*]on their coats." Now isn't that class for a small town hotel?

Ira Stout thought of selling the Black Bear Hotel in 1892, and considered moving to Darlington to start a new hotel in that city. He also planned to build a large addition onto the Black Bear the following spring if he could not sell the structure. An old photograph of Smokey Row shows only the grist mill section of the Black Bear Hotel, so the photograph had to be taken before the addition was made in 1893. Other photographs of the hotel show the large, square addition to the north side of the building. This picture was certainly worth a thousand words to me, as all the research I did for New Richmond's early history suddenly came to life when I first saw it!

Stout continued ownership of the Black Bear and gave the building a new coat of paint in April of 1904. In July, the same year, he installed two large windows on the front of the main room, and two smaller windows on the north—this spacious room served as the dining room. He added a large new kitchen to the rear of the dining room, then installed an electric alarm bell system to each room. His very famous "hostelry" was now up to date with all these improvements, but Prof. Stout was thinking of installing a spring bed contrivance, with a bath tub arrangement attached, which on the second call of guests to breakfast, could be operated by a push button from the office, thereby dumping the belated sleeper into the tub of cold water. "Auntie Hope" and Ira just could not tolerate tardiness, could they?

After all these latest improvements, Ira Stout decided to sell his famous Black Bear Hotel just a month later. An advertisement reads, "FOR SALE! BLACK BEAR HOTEL with all its contents (with some slight reservations), located on about one acre of ground–well set in fruit, situated in New Richmond, Indiana. Hotel of 25 rooms, all told, all furnished throughout, and equipped with electric bells. Very cheap for cash. Good reason for selling. Hotel doing a good business, will bear closest investigation. For terms, apply on the premises."

Thomas Martin Foster purchased the Black Bear Hotel from "Prof" Ira Stout in September of 1904. The New Richmond *Record*, September 15, 1904, says in part:

Mrs. Hope Kirkpatrick, under whom as a most generous, faithful, and patient hostess, the Black Bear has become a most noted hostelry, will retire from its management. Its most excellent table is known far and wide. Traveling men have worked hard, and stayed up late to make the BLACK BEAR HOTEL, much preferring its shelter and "Aunt Hope's" good table to any other. The hotel changes ownership for the first time in sixteen years. Mr. Foster will assume possession and management, shortly, and will strive to retain for the place its good name.

Mrs. Hope Kirkpatrick moved into one of Ira Stout's cottages in the south part of town a week later, and Thomas Foster and his wife, Cynthia, moved into the hotel. Their daughter, Musa, and her husband, Randall Baxter, moved from Lamb, in Switzerland County, Indiana, into the Black Bear Hotel to help operate the business. Following Randall Baxter and his wife from Switzerland County, was a long list of cousins, nephews, brothers, and other relatives to visit Randall at the Black Bear hotel. They nearly put the old folks out of business before they started. A year later, the Baxters moved to Tom's tenant house, and T.M. Foster, his wife Cynthia, and daughter, Myrtle, were to run the hotel. A granddaughter, Ruby, also worked in the Black Bear Hotel when she was young.

Thomas M. Foster and his wife leased the Black Bear Hotel to Harrison and Sarah Webb, and their son, William, of Wingate, in September of 1906. The Foster family moved back to their home just south of the railroad depot on south Wabash Street. Webb took possession of the famous hostelry on Monday, October 1st. Webb had many years' experience in the hotel business, and was welcomed to the New Richmond business circle by the local businessmen. Webb announced he would be serving Sunday dinners for 25 cents, and said dinner would be served at one o'clock. This was a welcome announcement for the ladies in the town, as they did not have to rush home from church to prepare a huge Sunday dinner.

The Webbs were listed in the 1907-8 county directory as the Black Bear Hotel managers, but the 1912 directory of New Richmond does not list the Black Bear, and the persons formerly concerned with the hotel (Foster, Baxter, & Kirkpatrick) were listed as farmers, or, as in Hope Kirkpatrick's case, no occupation listed. Thomas and Cynthia Foster sold the hotel for $5,000 on December 13, 1907 to Florence C. Helbig. Helbig sold the hotel July 15, 1908 to John A. Wilt for $5,000. Wilt sold the property to Joseph Hayes, July 28, 1908; again $5,000 was the going price. Hayes sold the hotel property to Zula Million on June 15, 1912, for $5,000. She, in turn, sold to George Akers for only $4,000 on February 13, 1914. Akers sold the property to Marshall L. Graves on April 7, 1914, consideration of $1.00 and exchange of other property. Graves was the last proprietor of the grounds on which the hotel was still standing. The hotel property had a $1,100 mortgage on it, at this time. The next transfer of property was Graves to John A. Frakes on February 26, 1915, for only $500. The following account gives the sad ending of the famous Black Bear Hotel.

HOTEL WAS BURNED

FIRE ENDANGERS NEW RICHMOND—TOWN WAS THOUGHT TO BE DOOMED WHEN FIRE SWEPT OVER IT FRIDAY NIGHT—HOTEL WAS ENTIRELY CONSUMED BY FLAMES—BUILDING WAS A GREAT FRAME STRUCTURE AND WAS DRY AS KINDLING, SPARKS SET THE ATTIC ON FIRE!

The New Richmond Hotel caught fire from a defective flue setting the attic on fire at 5 o'clock Friday evening of July 17 [1914], and burned to the ground. Most of the twenty rooms of furniture was saved except for one room. The hotel building was one of the oldest in the town, and was at one time one of the famed, country hotels of western Indiana. The property had ran down lately, and fell into the hands of outside parties, being frequently traded in later years, and was owned by Lafayette parties.

The hotel was said to have been traded the day before the fire occurred, but according to the abstract, Marshall L. Graves of Lafayette was still the proprietor of the hotel. A Mrs. Kincaid was managing the hotel a few days prior to the fire, but had sold the fixtures and furniture to the Clover Leaf railroad agent, Mr. Lane.

Calls to help fight the fire were made to Wingate, Linden, and Crawfordsville fire departments, and about 100 automobiles loaded with farmers came in to help fight the fire. The nearby elevators belonging to John Detchon and Charles Haywood caught on fire several times, but heroic efforts by men on the roof-tops with buckets of water put out the fires. The livery barn near the hotel also caught fire several times, but was quickly extinguished. The horses had been removed from the livery soon after the fire broke out to ensure their safety.

The fire burned furiously, the flames reaching high into the sky, for one hour, before completely destroying the famous, old, colorful Black Bear Hotel, New Richmond's last hotel.

SOME INTERESTING INCIDENTS OCCURRING IN THE BLACK BEAR HOTEL

In February 1891, a local businessman was trying to promote interest in prizefighting, but the event did not draw much of a crowd, so the prize fighters thought it best to leave town in a hurry. They threw their valises out the upstairs window of the hotel and slid down a pole, leaving the hotel with their unpaid bill to remember them by. The hotel lady was "on her muscle" and woe be to him that crossed her path. It was expected she would have had the first knockout! "Auntie Hope" knew how to deal with all types of characters, it has been said.

A more important event took place in the Bleak Bear when voters of the town met in the hotel on December 27, 1894 to determine whether the territory should be an incorporated town.

In March, 1904, a Clover Leaf train wrecked about one-half mile west of town and John Frye, a flagman, nearly had one of his hands cut off by the accident. He grabbed a signal light and ran for the New Richmond depot to warn other trains. He then went to the Black Bear Hotel and asked Hope Kirkpatrick to have someone summon a doctor for his wounds. Doctors Lynn and Washburn treated the cuts on his head and hand in the hotel.

When Zula Million owned the hotel, her children came down with a bad case of measles. The editor of the New Richmond *Record*, Edgar Walts, printed in bold, black headlines, "MILLIONS HAVE MEASLES IN NEW RICHMOND!" Fortunately, there was no panic due to this headline.

POOL ROOMS

In February 1886, Ed Shepherd and Frank Perkins purchased a lot from George Breed, then purchased the old church building at Prairie Chapel, moved the structure to New Richmond, and opened the first pool room in the town. What a terrible end to a house of God built by the pioneer worshippers in that neighborhood. A short time later, parents in the Round Hill neighborhood complained that too many young men were spending all their time at New Richmond's billiard table, and the married men in the area were spending their last nickel for a game of pool. This pool room was still in operation in 1889.

William Campbell thought he could make some easy money, and opened his "Y.M.C.A. POOL ROOM" in January 1890. He also carried a full line of confectioners, tobacco, and cigars for his customers' pleasure. James Kincaid's "Saloon and Pool Room" was listed in the 1891-2 county directory. It is possible the town always had a pool room, but records were not available between this date and the following— an early map of the town shows a pool room located east of the Washburn building in 1916. In September 1933, a Mr. Middleton applied to the New Richmond town board for a pool room license, but was refused because he had a liquor license.

Francis Myers was issued a license for two pool tables in January 1935, and was still in business a year later. Clell Terrill was issued a one-month license for one pool table, also in January 1935, and was still in business in October, that year. The town board instructed the Marshal "to notify the pool rooms not to let school children play pool and to control the profane language used in the rooms," when these two pool rooms were in operation. Others who were issued pool room licenses over the years are: Richard Thomas, July 1938; Clyde Wade, October 1938; Monroe Lyons, April 1939 and June 7, 1943—Lyon's Billiard Hall continued through 1947 (the last available record); John Patton, a license for a "Rum & Pool Table" January 1939; Anna Patton, John's wife, was issued a license for a rum and pool table in March 1939; Kenneth Frey opened a pool room in 1963, and Leonard Andrews' pool hall was in operation in 1964-65, the last in the town of New Richmond.

BOOKSTORES AND LENDING LIBRARIES

In 1890, mention was made of a public library in New Richmond, informing the people the library contained many good books that could be obtained by asking for them. This is the only reference made of this library. The schools in Coal Creek Township were constantly trying to raise funds to purchase books for their own libraries, and at one time the New Richmond Methodist Church conducted a lending library. Citizens donated their new and used books for this service.

George F. Long, a local dry goods merchant and jeweler, sold books in his store for many years. In March, 1904, Starr Dunn purchased Long's entire stock of books and was to open a complete book and stationery store. Work on the new addition to his existing business, a plumbing shop, was begun later in the month. The new building was a 12-by-30-foot, one story room on the east side of his brick building. Walter W. "Spud" Harriman was the contractor for the job. When completed the last of May, the same year, the editor of the New Richmond *Record* described it as a "regular little beauty, fitted with hard oak extension book cases with glass front, the inside furnished with birds eye maple. A partition divides the store the rear being used as Mr. Dunn's own personal library and office. The stock of books and stationery will be up to date and quite complete, etc." He continued to say, "the numerous volumes go out to a large membership of his friends who pay him a stipulated sum for their use. DUNN'S LIBRARY, BOOK, and STATIONERY STORE is a new accession to New Richmond which we should be proud of."

Single membership was one dollar per year, and only one book could be taken out at a time. Dunn stressed the importance of returning each book before taking out another. For those who could not afford the $1 per year, a fee of five or ten cents each book enabled the children to borrow books.

Dunn also sold school supplies, paper napkins for picnics and parties, bill boards, ledgers, box paper, envelopes, calling cards, Bibles and Testaments, assorted glass ink stands, paper weights, checkers, dominos, monthly magazines, valentines, book cases with a capacity of 300 volumes, fire cracker, torpedoes, masks, Jack O-Lanterns, candles and old fashioned candle sticks, souvenir post cards, Paul E. Wirt fountain pens, the popular card game Block, sheet music and song books.

Advertisements for Dunn's book store appeared regularly in the New Richmond *Record* and the New Richmond High School yearbooks for many years. Dunn purchased his stock in Chicago, choosing a very select list of authors and the latest books.

Starr Dunn's bookstore was a successful business for many years in the little town of New Richmond until his eyesight began to fail. In 1926 he and his wife, Martha, sold their home and business and moved to Florida, and spent their remaining years with their son, Stanley.

BOWLING ALLEYS

Ira Stout erected the first "ten pin alley" in New Richmond in March of 1889. The New Richmond scribe for the Crawfordsville weekly *Review* commented, "'All down but nine' will soon be heard in the vicinity of the Black Bear." Ira was the proprietor of the hotel.

In 1902 Frank Perkins purchased a bowling alley from Stout and Alston of Darlington, Indiana, in Franklin Township. Both of the latter gentlemen were former New Richmond residents. Stout had moved the equipment to Darlington after the fad wore out in New Richmond. Perkins installed the equipment in the old Washburn frame building that was moved south of the brick bank building on the southeast corner of Washington and Wabash Streets. All the "young male population" (and some of the older men) spent all their leisure time in this place of amusement. A month later, three men got into a heated argument which ended in a brawl-and a trip to Squire Ebrite's court. Frank advertised for sale "two bowling alleys-complete" in 1904.

Chapter 6 - Builders & The Housing Industry

Carpenters - Builders of Our Homes

Listed among the early carpenters in 1840s New Richmond was George Ebrite. Ebrite was also one of the earliest wagon makers who settled in the town. The earliest cabinet makers listed in Coal Creek Township were Joseph Shaffer and Noah Insley. They manufactured furniture directly from the forest, and it is probably a true statement when the early history of Montgomery County, Indiana, says that Insley was the first man who ever cut a stick of timber from Coal Creek Township for the purpose of making fine furniture. Insley resided northwest of New Richmond just inside the northern county line on road No. 700 West.

Jason Tribby was listed as a carpenter in New Richmond in the 1882 to 1885 county directories, and Samuel R. Tribby was listed in 1887. John McLain and his partner, a Mr. McCollum, were building houses and doing the woodwork on George F. Long's new brick building in 1886, and McLain continued as a carpenter up to 1895, at least.

In 1888 and 1890, Dan Ebrite and Levi Harriman were partners in the carpentry business, and were rapidly putting up houses. A Mr. Gooley was mentioned as a carpenter in November of 1888; he was erecting new wood houses, stables, coal bins, etc. at a rapid rate in New Richmond. Others listed as carpenters residing in or near New Richmond, and the dates mentioned were: A. Stafford, 1874; Joseph O'Connell; 1893; James P. Badgley, 1870; Buck Belt, 1889; Joe Phillips, 1904; Will Peek, 1906; Earl Peek, 1912; James Boyer, 1907 to 1912; Winton B. Shepherd, 1907 to 1912; George Dewey, 1912; Amos Ebrite, Esquire, was listed in the 1900-01 directory as a carpenter and followed the trade almost all his life. He was compelled to give up carpentry only a few months before his death in 1910. Amos and Dan Ebrite were sons of George Ebrite, the wagon maker, and carpenter. James W. Eller was listed as a carpenter in 1912, as were Garret V. and John Foster in 1903. Jim Kincaid's sons, James, Jr., Samuel, and William were all in the carpentry trade in 1903 and were working for a contractor who erected elevators all over the tristate area of Indiana, Ohio, and Illinois.

Not listed as a carpenter, but said to have built my house, was George Watkins, who was a minister of the New Richmond Christian Church from 1902 to 1904. The house is located on the southwest corner of Wabash and Stephenson Streets in New Richmond.

The Tribby family who settled in or near New Richmond produced a good share of carpenters. William Tribby emigrated from Nicholas County, Kentucky, around 1860 and settled near Romney, Indiana. He was a carpenter by trade and also farmed. William died two years later, leaving a wife and several children. The widow moved to Coal Creek Township and lived with her brother, John Myers, southeast of New Richmond. Leander, one of William Tribby's sons, was a farmer, but he knew the fundamentals of carpentry, and erected his residence and all the outbuildings on his farm. William's widow, Mahala, lived with Leander until her death in 1891.

In 1861 William's brother, George T. Tribby, died in Kentucky, and his widow, Nancy, and ten children all came to reside in Coal Creek Township, most of them settling in, or near New Richmond. There is a tombstone in the New Richmond Cemetery inscribed with George T. and Nancy Tribby's birth and death dates, although George was supposed to have died in Kentucky, according to their son, Benjamin's obituary in the New Richmond *Record*, Thursday, January 25, 1912.

Two of George Tribby's sons were well-known carpenters and resided in New Richmond. They were Jason and Samuel R. Tribby. Jason was listed as a carpenter as early as 1882 to 1885, and Samuel was first listed in 1884, and the years through 1895 directories of Montgomery County. He continued until he was no longer able to work at his trade. Samuel's two sons, Albert and Harvy B. worked with their father, and several homes in New Richmond were built by this family of carpenters. Among the homes were A.D. Snyder's, built in 1890, and Cy King's, built in 1891.

Samuel R. Tribby was better known as a builder of churches and erected the New Richmond Methodist Church in 1888, and possibly the Christian Church that same year, although there was no record of the carpenter of the Christian Church. Samuel built the new brick Sycamore schoolhouse north of New Richmond in 1891. In May 1902 Samuel had a contract to build a $6,000 church for the Methodists near Fairmouth in Marion County, Indiana. The people of this congregation had been so impressed by the building he erected at Wesley, Indiana, that Tribby had no trouble securing this contract. Starr Dunn and Alva Roberts did the tin work on the Fairmouth Church; both were New Richmond residents. In 1903, Samuel R. Tribby was granted the contract to build the new Methodist Church at Lizton in Hendricks County, Indiana, the cost to be about $4,127, and Starr Dunn and Alva Roberts also did the tin work on this church.

In March 1904 Samuel went to Whiteland, in Johnson County, south of Indianapolis, to build another Methodist church. His sons were still working with Samuel at this time. The church was completed and was to be dedicated Sunday, November 27, 1904. In May 1906 Samuel and his sons were contracted to remodel the Clark's Hill grade school, and in July, the same year, were awarded the contract to build a new brick school in Sugar Creek Township in Montgomery County. Samuel Tribby died in 1922 and is buried in the New Richmond Cemetery.

James and John Tribby, brothers of Samuel, were in the lumber business in New Richmond, and Harry Tribby delivered the lumber, so the Tribby family of carpenters played an important role in the early construction period of the town. John resided in Darlington before establishing the lumber company in New Richmond. He was in the process of building a new home in New Richmond in February and March, 1891, and moved into this new home upon its completion.

THE HARRIMAN FAMILY OF CARPENTERS

Levi Harriman and Daniel Ebrite had formed a partnership in the carpentry trade in 1888 and were still putting houses up very rapidly in 1890. Ebrite preferred farming and gave up carpentry, but Levi continued as a carpenter, and was listed in the 1891-95 county directories. In 1903, he and his two sons, Elmer W. "Pete" and Walter W. "Spud" Harriman were all listed as carpenters. In September 1905 the Harriman brothers established a carpenter shop in the east part of New Richmond, something the town was in need of for many years. They were to build fine cabinets and do wood repair work of all kinds. Their advertisement appeared in the New Richmond *Record* many times and reads:

> "Our shop is now open and we are equipped to do all kinds of cabinet work in hard or soft woods, and finish the same natural, or in imitation of the more expensive hard woods. New and satisfactory methods employed in finishing new and refinishing old furniture. We can upholster your old chairs and couches in PANTASOTE, VELOURS, or any covering that the worth of the article seems to warrant, and restoring the same generally to good serviceable articles of furniture. All kinds of Woodwork done at the CARPENTER SHOP. WORKMANSHIP THE BEST! Have your ideas in Cabinet Work realized at HARRIMAN BROS. CARPENTER SHOP!"

Walter or "Spud" Harriman continued his fine craft of cabinet maker and carpenter, into the 1940s and his work was excellent. He took great pride in his work. I recall a beautiful desk, or secretary, in the study of his home in the east part of town, and it made a lasting impression on my mind as a piece of fine craftsmanship. It was a great loss to the town of New Richmond when he passed away on December 26, 1949. He was a gentle and kind, easy-going type of man—a trait that most true craftsmen seem to possess, and he was a very good neighbor. His shop stood toward the rear of his home on east Washington Street in New Richmond. Levi Harriman, his father, built the home in 1891 that Walter later occupied. It was not situated square with the earth in order to make it "cyclone proof." He said he wanted his house to be unusual, and it certainly played havoc with one's sense of direction from the inside of the home—every window facing either southwest–northeast—or southeast and northwest—or was it?

Wint B. Shepherd was a carpenter in New Richmond, and was listed in the 1907-08 and 1912 directories of Montgomery County. Ivan Pollock came to Indiana in 1935 from Meade County, Kentucky, where he had worked in a sawmill. He held several other positions before moving to New Richmond, and in June of 1946 he acquired a position with the Parlon Lumber and Coal Company in the town as a salesman. In this new position, he was required to do a lot of carpentry for the company, and when the lumber company was sold in 1960, Ivan started carpentering on his own. He erected a large metal building in 1964, and sold all types of building supplies. Pollock sold all his building supplies at a public auction held on Saturday, September 17, 1980, but continued carpentry for a while. His building was purchased by the town trustees and now houses the New Richmond Fire Department's trucks and supplies. It is located on west Madison Street, just east of the New Richmond water tower. Pollock retired in 1984.

Monroe Lyon was building new homes and cabinets in the 1960s. He had done carpentry before this time, but did not advertise. Royce Whitehead was listed as a carpenter in the Robinson's Directory of Montgomery County from 1963 to 1981. Royce is now retired.

Painters and Decorators

As most of the residences in New Richmond were log structures up to the 1870-80s, there was not much of a demand for painters and decorators in the town before that time. Elisha C. "E.C." Campbell was the first painter listed in New Richmond, on the 1880 Census record. It was Campbell who painted the old dilapidated flouring mill and made an otherwise useless structure into a beautiful hotel.

In 1891 the town had the following painters: H.M. Mitchell and Jerry Pitts, who were partners, and Charlie Bennett. In 1895, Charles McClain was added to the list; Bennett and Pitts were still listed as painters that year. L.C. Carson was listed as a painter and paperhanger in 1904. Wallace White and Fred Harriman opened a paint shop in December of 1906. The 1907-8 County directory lists Frank Carson, Wallace White, and George Westfall as painters and decorators. In 1912, Thomas Conner, John W. Smith, and George Dewey were all listed as painters in New Richmond.

The year 1912 was also the beginning of a long tradition of painters and decorators in the Waye family. Forrest Waye learned the painting trade from George Westfall that year. Forrest and his brother, Earl Waye, formed their own company two years later. In 1916 they advertised, "See Waye Brothers for Paper Hanging and Painting–we give tickets (Phone 62, or 3 rings on 22)." Earl moved to Detroit a few years later, and was employed in the automobile factory, where he passed away in 1926.

Forrest painted alone for a while, then hired Alfred Allman to work with him in the late 1920s. Alfred said they loaded their painting equipment into Forrest's old Model T Ford, and painted several houses in Crawfordsville and the surrounding towns, and the two painted the interior of the New Richmond School one summer. Allman said Forrest Waye taught him so well, he never forgot the finer points in painting, and was complimented many times on the painting he did over the years–especially painting the trim around doors and window panes which is a difficult task for most people.

Forrest taught all his sons to paint and they all worked with him from the time they were old enough to hold a paint brush and climb upon a ladder. The oldest son, Gerald, started in 1932 when he was only fourteen. He continued with his father until he married and moved to Crawfordsville, joining a painting company in that city, and retiring in 1980. Charles started around 1934, and painted with his son Ron for many years. Charles served in the U.S. Army with the Engineer Corps from 1942 to 1945, part of which was spent in North Africa and Italy. Ron served four years with the U.S. Army, and his overseas duty was served in Germany and Vietnam. Ron resumed painting after returning from the army.

Twins Melvin and Malcolm Waye started painting during the summer months in the early 1940s. They both joined the U.S. Navy after graduation from New Richmond High School in 1945 and served in the States. They returned to join their father in the painting business. Melvin continued until 1961 when he accepted a position with the Crawfordsville Paint and Wallpaper Store. Malcolm continued until 1964 when he started working for Alcoa in Lafayette.

The youngest Waye son, Don, painted during the summer months in 1948 and 1949, then worked for the Mutual Electric Company in New Richmond. Don joined the U.S. Air Force and served in England. He returned in April, 1957, to join his father and brothers in the painting and paper hanging business. Don went to the Alcoa plant the same year as his brother Malcolm, and both worked there until retirement. All the Waye children graduated from New Richmond High School, incidentally.

Forrest Waye retired in 1968 after completing fifty-six years of beautifying many homes and business structures all over Montgomery, Tippecanoe, and Fountain Counties. He and his sons received many good compliments over the years from very prominent people they worked for. Those who appreciated their hard work and their ability to turn a drab old room or structure into a beautiful environment were rated highly by the Waye family painters. They all had a sense of pride in their work—they were truly artists in their own right.

I had the bright idea of joining the Waye painting company one summer. My father, Forrest, started my brother Don and I painting a board fence north of town in Tippecanoe County. We painted what seemed like miles and miles of fence, and the faster I slapped on the paint, the further the barn receded in the distance. We started at the barn and painted up to the road, across the front of the residence, and back toward the barn. I still chuckle when I see a beautiful white board fence, because my painting career ended when we finally reached that barn! I can vouch for the painters when they say it is very hard work—and I didn't even have to carry one of those heavy wooden ladders.

PLUMBERS AND TINNERS

Plumbers were unheard of in the New Richmond area before the late 1880s. Water for drinking purposes, cooking, and the laundry was drawn from the old hand pump in the back yard, or if you were lucky, the pump was installed in the back porch, summer kitchen, or kitchen. Once the well was driven and the pump installed, there was very little maintenance to the pump, except to replace a worn gasket now and then. This was usually handled by the man of the house. Bathroom facilities were unheard of back then, and the old outhouse served quite well. The laundry tub did double duty as a bath tub and never, never, gave grandma and grandpa any problems with stopped up drains. Therefore, there was no need for a plumber.

R.C. Snyder was listed as a New Richmond tinner in 1895. His work was possibly limited to applying tin roofs to buildings, and cutting and selling stove pipes. In 1898 Starr Dunn moved his family to New Richmond from Chicago, and opened a tin shop soon after. His shop and residence burned to the ground in July that year, but with the help from the local friends, Dunn started to rebuild his shop and residence a month later. Dunn's family lived on the second floor of the new building. Within a few years, Starr Dunn's tin shop was receiving contracts for plumbing and tin work on new churches and other buildings in Fairmount and Lizton in Indiana, in Mortimer and Ridge Farm, Illinois, and the Clark's Hill, Indiana, School, as well as contracts in New Richmond and vicinity. Alva Roberts worked for Starr Dunn as a plumber, and other men worked as part of his crew, but Roberts is the only person I have seen mentioned by name. It has been reported by several New Richmond residents that Starr Dunn manufactured metal shingles and roofed many buildings and residences in town with these locally manufactured shingles. S.R. Tribby, a local carpenter, who was referred to as "the builder of churches," provided Dunn with the cresting and tin work contracts on many structures. Ewing Mason clerked in Starr Dunn's tin shop when Starr was out of town on these jobs. Dunn's tin shop offered such items as, "Elliott's Anti rust Tin Ware" and the "Universal Bread Kneader or Mixer."

Starr Dunn and his crew installed the pipes for the gasoline lighting plants for John Detchon in many cities in Indiana. Dunn's shop was listed in the county PLUMBERS AND TINNERS directories from 1900 to 1907-8. In 1910 Dunn's son, Stanley advertised, "Auto Livery, Stanley Dunn, Proprietor–NEW RICHMOND AUTO LIVERY, and Automobile Repairs and Supplies." This was New Richmond's first garage. Starr Dunn moved his tin shop to the second floor of his building, and continued his plumbing business until 1926, moving to Florida, where his death occurred.

The Harriman Brothers, Pete and Spud (Elmer & Walter), were listed as plumbers and tinners in 1907-08. Augustus McMillin was listed as a plumber in New Richmond in 1912. William Warrick was the town's plumber in the 1930s and 1940s, advertising "Heating and Plumbing." Warrick moved from New Richmond in 1944.

Robert Reynolds was listed as a plumber in the 1960s and 1970s. Reynolds also did a lot of work in Linden, as his residence was between the two towns.

Kunkel Plumbing & Heating

Ralph Kunkel, a 1938 graduate of New Richmond High School, served in the U.S. Army in World War II. After returning to New Richmond he served as a plumber's helper, assisting William Warrick. He accepted a position with the Miller Plumbing Company in Crawfordsville, and worked for Miller a short time, then opened his own shop in New Richmond in August of 1945.

Ralph advertised as "Ralph Kunkel Plumbing & Heating" in 1947 and "Well Work" was added to his services a year later. His shop is located on south Wabash Street in the center room of the Knights of Pythias Building. Ralph has installed many bathroom fixtures, oil and gas furnaces, and air conditioners in New Richmond and the nearby cities and towns. Ralph Kunkel's son, Roger, joined his father in the plumbing business in 1962, and Ralph retired in 1980. Roger was listed as the owner of the Kunkel Plumbing and Heating in 1981. Roger had been the agent for the Philgas company from 1962 to 1976 in the New Richmond area. Russell "Bill" Lane worked with Ralph as a helper for several years, as did Carroll Puckett.

Ralph Kunkel erected a new building on south Wabash Street, and started a new business, KUNKEL'S MINI WASH, in 1970. This flourished for a few years, but was closed by 1976. The New Richmond Town Hall occupies the building at this time.

The Tile and Brick Industry

The pioneers of Coal Creek Township brought with them the knowledge they needed to adapt to any type of situation. Their first homes were made of crude logs, and as they prospered, more substantial brick homes began to appear.

Thomas A. Bell was listed as a brick-maker in the 1850 census of Coal Creek Township. The *History of Montgomery County, Indiana* by Beckwith (1881) tells of the early settlers building brick homes, all made from brick manufactured at the home sites. Thomas Ward, in 1845, erected a large brick house, and Samuel Dazey, in 1862, built a two-story, ten by twenty-six feet, with an ell of twelve by fourteen feet. Thomas Meharry erected his brick home in 1842 west of New Richmond.

The First Tile Made in Montgomery County

Walter Patrick Ward, a native of Leicestershire, England, son of Thomas and Mary (Patrick) Ward, came to America with his brother, Thomas. He entered eighty acres of land in section ten, township twenty, range five west, on July 27, 1829. He entered another eighty-acre plot in section twenty-one, township twenty, range five west on October 14, 1829. Both parcels were in Coal Creek Township, one within the town limits of New Richmond, the other south of New Richmond.

Walter, or "Wall" as he was known, is said to have made the very first drain tile made in Montgomery County, Indiana. This tile was made by hand in 1844 in Coal Creek Township. The cost of manufacturing this tiling was so great, Wall did not continue this early factory, therefore very little was ever sold in the county. His brother Thomas, however, purchased some of the tile in 1845 and ditched his fields with it. The tile was still in good condition and was being used as late as 1880 when Thomas visited the Crawfordsville *Journal* office and was relating the story about this early enterprise. He said James Heaton of Crawfordsville had the mold Wall used as proof of his statement. This mold would be lost or destroyed by the ravages of time by this time.

William W. Wilson made the next attempt to manufacture tile and brick in Coal Creek Township. Billie started sometime between the years 1864 and 1878. His brick kiln was located in section twenty-six, township twenty north, range five west, the same section as the Round Hill community. On the 1864 atlas of Montgomery County, the site was occupied by the old Asbury M. E. Church. The Methodists built a new edifice east of this location within the Round Hill community.

The Crawfordsville *Journal* of October 13, 1877 says, "Billie Wilson has been burning brick for a week." In the spring of 1878, he was going to supply tiling to everybody "that may be in need of it." The brick kiln shows up on the 1878 atlas, but it only lasted a few years and does not appear on later maps of the township. Billie moved his family to the Shawnee Mound neighborhood in Tippecanoe County in 1879 and there was no mention of anyone else running the brick kiln for him. He constructed another tile kiln near his residence four miles northwest of New Richmond and with this operation he ran a sawmill. Most of the tile manufacturers followed this practice, as they used the scraps of lumber to fire their kilns and sold the better lumber. William W. Wilson was killed on Saturday, March 14, 1891 by the bursting of some machinery he was working with at his tile kiln in Tippecanoe County.

In April 1881, Bristle Ridge was to be the next location of a tile mill in Coal Creek Township. Two enterprising Bristle Ridgers named Utterback and Applegate started this factory. They continued with their operation until the spring of 1885 when Sant Utterback decided to "let up" on tile making and returned to farming.

Another tile mill was mentioned in the Crawfordsville *Review* of November 17, 1883. The article says, "Ira Stout's Walnut Grove sawmill is now in motion again since last Monday week, it having ceased operations some time ago to furnish the motive power to Wards Tile Factory." Tom Ward owned several large tracts of land in Coal Creek Township, and none of the maps show a tile kiln situated upon them, therefore the location of this kiln is unknown to me.

The 1874 *Peoples Guide*, a directory of Montgomery County, Indiana, lists "W. Hunt, farmer and tile maker, four miles northwest of Darlington," etc. Evidently Hunt moved, because in April of 1882, Wilson R. Hunt resided in the Black Creek neighborhood and made a little trip on horseback to the little village of New Richmond. Bringing with him a pick and a spade or two, he dug a few feet into the ground and rode away with some samples of this soil. "Wills" showed his discovery to experienced tile men who pronounced it "A-number-one-dirt." The location of this proposed tile kiln was north of the railroad on South Wabash Street.

Coal Creek Township was blessed with many ponds and swampy low areas from its very creation. These ponds were a blessing for the wildlife, that is, but not so for the humans who lived near them. These beautiful ponds were the breeding place of many pests, and war was declared on them. Some of the early settlers in the township lost several members of their families by diseases caused by the stagnant water in the ponds. By draining these ponds, the farmers thought to benefit two ways; creating more acres of rich farmland; and improving the family's health.

Work of draining in the county had already commenced, but there was not enough tile being manufactured to supply the demand. There was only one kiln in operation in Coal Creek Township in 1882—that of Utterback and Applegate on Bristle Ridge. Newtown, Odells' Corner, and New Richmond were all in the process of having factories, or kilns, built by the first of July the same year.

Wills Hunt had his tile factory well established and began molding tile by the middle of August in 1882. In a short time he was turning out the finest tile ever made in Coal Creek Township. Wills, a former widower with children, had just remarried and moved his family to New Richmond to be near his kilns that demanded such close attention.

Mr. Smock, a local sawmill operator, brought his sawmill and attached it to the tile factory engine. This engine ground the clay, or pulverized it, into a smooth consistency. The proper amount of liquid was added to the clay and it was then forced into a mold to form the tile, or brick, depending on the demand of the consumer. A taut wire was used to cut the tile and brick in proper lengths. These were put into a drying shed for a few days, and then into a kiln to cure and fire. The kiln was cooled down gradually so the brick, or tile, would not crack or burst from the extreme change of temperature. The older style kilns had walls about two feet thick to contain the extreme heat needed to fire the brick and tile.

The summer of 1886 was a very busy year for Mr. Hunt. Dr. Detchon of New Richmond owned the ground north of town and this was a very low swampy piece of property. There was a small stream running through and the soil was of the consistency of peat. Detchon became the tile manufacturer's best customer. The Crawfordsville weekly *Review*, July 31, 1886 says, "Dr. Detchon has been a great help to our town by tiling the sloughs and ponds north of this place. We think there will not be so many cases of ague and fever as in days gone by." Wills Hunt was running the tile kiln on double time that summer. Dr. Black purchased half interest in the tile mill to help finance the operation. The physicians of New Richmond were doing their very best to rid the area of diseases caused by the swampy conditions. Repairs on the dry kiln were needed and the machinery up-keep was a constant problem and expense. Mr. Hunt ran the kilns from April through September, or until the temperature became too extremely cold to make tile. He closed down through the winter months.

The demand was so great Wills could not make the tile fast enough, and in the spring of 1887, the beginning of the new season, he sold the kiln to Maurice J. Lee and moved his family to Crawfordsville.

The Mr. Smock whose sawmill engine was used, was an interesting character and the following sketch of him was published in the Crawfordsville weekly *Review*, July 2, 1881: "James H. Smock, 54 years, native born, an ex-soldier, a miller by trade, and cursed by more misfortune that any other man in the township; having been bankrupted and turned out of house and home as surety for a worthless scoundrel; having come to this county four or five years ago; with a sawmill he had his right hand severed from his arm by the saw, and within less than a year the other hand was so mangled by the same saw, that he had only a poor excuse of fingers left. A few weeks ago he was knocked senseless by a crank in another mill; when giving up sawmilling as a bad job, Smock started home on a wagon loaded with tile—the horses became frightened and ran away throwing him from the wagon and running over him, fracturing the bones in the wrist of his 'excuse of a hand'—and yet, he lives! He is a widower, but it is not certain that he is a candidate for matrimony!"

"Dad Smock," as he was affectionately called, did return to sawmilling. He continued to be plagued by bad luck, for in December 1886, Smock was removing the irons of his sawmill that was burned at New Richmond and was preparing to rebuild it the following week. He was to have it in running order by Christmas. He had a 'first class' mill when things were going right for him, and he sawed all the lumber being used in the New Richmond vicinity. The Methodist church history mentioned that Mr. Smock, a local sawmill owner, sang for funerals, protracted meetings, quarterly conferences and other special meetings.

M.J. AND H.K. LEE TILE MILL

Maurice John Lee, son of Maurice and Cecelia (Runey) Lee, was born in Frankfort, Kentucky, on February 17, 1837. His parents were married in Pennsylvania, moving to Kentucky soon after, and remained there the rest of their lives.

Maurice Lee, their son, attended the schools in Frankfort and remained there until he was twenty-five years of age. He must have acquired the knowledge of brick manufacturing in Kentucky. Soon after he moved to Crawfordsville in September of 1862, he started the construction of his brick kilns on the same grounds as his home. He was very successful in this line of work and soon built up a very large business. He manufactured brick only until 1876 when he embarked upon the tile industry. There was a very large demand for drain tile at this time in Montgomery and the surrounding counties of Tippecanoe, Fountain, Parke, and Clinton. His new company was known as the M. J. Lee Drain Tile Company.

Maurice J. Lee married Margaret Keenan on April 4, 1864. A native of Scotland, Margaret came to this country at the age of four. She married Mr. Lee in Crawfordsville. They had one child, Henry Keenan Lee. Margaret died just before Henry's second birthday on November 16, 1866, and Henry was placed in the care of his grandmother Keenan, of Atchisan, Kansas. There he remained until he was eleven years old. His father remarried on January 29, 1870 to Katherine Alice Crow, daughter of Michael and Dorothy Beard Crow. While Maurice and Katherine had six children, only four were living in 1913, namely: Walter John, a resident of Chicago in later life; Catherine Helen, who married Dr. Chester J. Brittan; Maurice J. of Colfax; and Ruth Beard, of Crawfordsville.

Henry Keenan Lee, son of Maurice J. and his first wife Margaret (Keenan) Lee, was born in Crawfordsville, Indiana, on January 1, 1865. He married Nancy Price May 26, 1886 in Crawfordsville, and he and his new bride moved to Brockton, Illinois where they resided for three years. This was the birthplace of their two children: Agnes, who married Earl C. Overmyer (associated with the Lee tile factory and later the Francesville Tile company), and a son Maurice Franklin "Frank" Lee. This is the background of the New Richmond tile manufacturers, Maurice J. Lee and Sons.

In July 1881, Maurice J. Lee completed arrangements to establish a branch tile factory in Pleasant Hill (now Wingate). He formed a partnership with Daniel Curtis a year later, putting Curtis in charge of running this factory. The farmers of the Shawnee Prairie north of New Richmond and Pleasant Hill purchased most of this tile to drain their low, swampy fields.

Lee branched out again in March 1887 when he purchased the tile mill at New Richmond established by Wilson Hunt, located just north of the Clover Leaf Railroad in the west part of town. A month later he commenced renovating these kilns. T. J. "Barney" Wallace, a local bricklayer, rebuilt the kilns to Lee's specifications, enlarging and making them more productive. In a very short time Coal Creek Township was changing its appearance. Ditch diggers were "throwing" mud all over the place and nearly all the landowners were having tile laid in their fields. The tile business was becoming the business to be associated with. Lee was putting New Richmond on the map as far as this type of industry was concerned.

The men in Coal Creek Township who were in need of employment found it in the local tile mill—that is, if they could stand the hard work! Some of the old timers said Lee expected his workers to give him a good day's work and if he didn't he would never work for him the second day. Some of the hands dug the clay from the ground, others worked in the mill with the machinery and the cutting, others were needed to stack the tile on small rail cars to be placed in the drying shed, and later into the kilns to be burned. The mill gave steady employment to the local teamsters, who hauled the tile to the fields where the ditchers were working. The ditchers were also employed by the Lee Tile Company.

Lee purchased about twelve more acres of land of John Oppy to use in connection with the tile mill in April 1887. This was necessary for the timber—and for the clay. He purchased several acres of ground just for the timber for fuel to burn the tile. He was running the mill full blast, making tile and bricks as fast as possible.

The Crawfordsville *Weekly Review*, December 15, 1888 says, "Dr. Detchon raised corn this year where ten years ago people had to pull their horses and cows from the mire with ropes—sixty bushels to the acre, and all caused by a free use of ditching and tile." Good corn crops made the tile men very happy and it was almost impossible to keep tile supplied to the ditchers. One of the local farmers, Aaron VanHook, who farmed the Kincaid farm just north of New Richmond, displayed a stalk of corn measuring nine feet from root to ears; and the entire length was sixteen feet, and six inches of tape line was required to measure around it. It bore two ears that measured thirteen and one half and twelve and one half inches in length. He also carried with him in the buggy an enormous California Sweet pumpkin raised on the same farm. He explained that the pumpkin with him was a small one, as he had not enough men with him to load one of the large ones—and he wouldn't have room for himself in the buggy if he had. This farm of one hundred sixty-six acres was once a bog but was thoroughly tiled. He was sending them to be exhibited at the Traders National Bank in Chicago.

Mrs. Manners, George Washburn (New Richmond's Cattle King who resided at Patton's Corner), and Elias Perkins (William Kincaid's son-in-law who resided north of New Richmond just inside the county line) all had their fields ditched in the spring of 1888 and '89. Ditching contractors mentioned were James Harriman, George Cloud, Perry Wills, and in later years Joe Bennett, Charles Hyatt, D. M. Plunkett and Stephen Harriman.

The town of New Richmond was even rid of the continuous pesky mud. Tile was laid in the town; the Crawfordsville *Review*, June 29, 1889 made a note of this improvement to New Richmond's streets and walks.

In June 1889, Mr. Lee formed a partnership with Mr. Smock in order to operate a sawmill in connection with the tile mill. This provided the mill workers with year-round employment. They worked as "lumber men" in the winter months, cutting the timber and hauling it to the mill. The sawing was then started, the good lumber being sold for building material and the scraps were kept to burn in the furnaces to fire the brick and tile in the kilns. The tile operation closed down in October or November giving the men time to help with the corn husking, and when that task was completed it was time for the sawmill to start its cycle.

Mr. Smock tried to improve the delivery system of the tile mill and rigged up his traction engine and hauled four wagon loads of brick at once from Lee's Tile Mill. The writer for the Crawfordsville *Review* June 29, 1889 said, "Smock made the round trip in a day after loading the wagons—why is not steam power cheaper than horse power?" He did not mention the destination of the brick, however, on this eventful trip.

When the mill closed down in November 1895, Lee's tile kilns had made fifty-five kilns of tile since opening up in the spring. Each time the kiln was fully loaded for a "burn" it is referred to as a "kiln." There were two brick beehive style kilns in the New Richmond tile factory. according to early residents Forrest Waye and Chester Dunn.

Maurice Lee sold the New Richmond tile factory to his son, Henry K., in November 1900, but he continued to help run the mill. Other improvements were made before the seasonal opening in 1902. In April a large new boiler was installed, replacing the old worn out, overworked boiler, and operations began a week later. Besides the New Richmond factory improvements, Maurice J. and Henry Lee established another tile mill in Colfax in Clinton County. Maurice's son, Maurice III, managed this mill.

Henry K. Lee uncovered a "gold and gravel mine" on the tile mill site in New Richmond. In 1903 the township was in need of good gravel for the roads. The New Richmond *Record*, September 10, 1903 says in part, "Prospectors are hard at work in search of these genuine gold mines of gravel. There was much talk about the town the latter part of last week about the gravel found beneath the excavations made at Lee's tile factory. It is claimed that there, the gravel of good quality lies in a strata fifteen feet thick. There are several acres of it from which the top surface has been removed for the manufacture of tile." A week later machinery was brought in and scraping of the surface soil began. This large steam shovel scooped out a mountain of gravel and completed the task two years later. This little operation was unwittingly the beginning of the New Richmond Park. Wires and ropes were placed in position at the deep ponds at Lee's tile factory for the safety of those who began using the ponds for a swimming hole. The water was very pure and clear when they were first excavated.

The tile mill continued to prosper and Henry K. Lee formed a partnership in December of 1910 with Neal Casey, son of Timothy Casey, who resided north of Crawfordsville. Both were experienced tile makers and were expecting to reach out over a considerable territory and were going to increase their plant as the demand justified. Lee also took an active interest in the Corn Exchange Bank in New Richmond, serving as Vice President for a few years.

The first week of July 1911, Henry K. Lee and his new partner Neal Casey notified their employees they had sold their tile factory to the M. J. Lee Drain Tile Company and the equipment would be moved to Colfax. Henry was quitting the tile business entirely, he said at the time,

16 - New Richmond Park Shelter House

however, he remained in the tile business until his death. Casey purchased Henry's share of the big Colfax plant and was to serve as manager of that plant. The sale of the local factory came as a surprise, because Lee and Casey had just remodeled the New Richmond plant, adding new equipment, and they had been contemplating ten thousand dollars' worth of further improvements to their equipment. The railroad was building a new side track beside the local plant for the shipment of shale from Silverwood to improve the quality of the tile. The plant manufactured and sold more tile in 1911 than had ever been put out during any one whole year in the history of the plant.

Why the sudden decision to sell out? The neighbors were constantly complaining about the smoke nuisance, and the cost of installing a device to consume the smoke was too great. The lack of good quality clay and the necessity of having shale hauled in from a great distance would have been too costly, and the M. J. Lee Drain Tile Company (Henry's father) made some tempting proposals to combine the two factories into one large concern. All of these were the deciding factors to close the Henry K. Lee Tile factory in New Richmond.

At the time of closing, the tile factory employed twenty-two men who had to seek work elsewhere. Some of the men moved their families to Colfax to work in that plant, while others were left unemployed.

The editor of the New Richmond *Record*, Thursday, July 13, 1911 had this to say, in part, "Within six short weeks New Richmond's tile factory will be gone, her early morning waking whistle will be stilled, the buzz and grind of her wheels will not be heard; all the smoke will have vanished; and in a few short but dreary years only the black, ugly and falling in old tile shed will remain as the only monument of New Richmond's once greatest and thriving industry."

Henry K. Lee owned the land the factory occupied, and reserved the east wing of the tile shed to conduct business to sell off the ten thousand dollars' worth of tile on the yard for local trade, and as a distributing point for the M. J. Lee factory, but the tile kilns and remaining tile sheds were dismantled. A year later Lee sold the tile mill property to Charles Haywood, but leased the yard for another year to distribute tile.

The final story came when the old tile mill sheds were struck by lightning the last week of June in 1916. It was completely consumed by fire.

Some of the tile mill employees mentioned were: from 1887-89 Barney Wallace, Frank Dewey (night watchman), Gill Dearman, Perry Wills (engineer), Sam Dean, Frank Stover, and George Long. In 1903 John H. Cash, W. P. Coffman (engineer), James K. Shepherd, Winton B. Shepherd. In 1907-08 Mack Hobbs, Hugh Roark, William Tharp. Brick masons mentioned were: J. T. "Barney" Wallace, J. N. Beckley, Clarence Stephenson, and possibly others not listed in the directories.

The Lee family, Henry K., Maurices, III, Neal Casey and Mr. Lee's son-in-law, Earl C. Overmyer, continued to operate the huge plant in Colfax until 1923, when they heard of a great demand for tile in the Francesville, Indiana, area. They purchased the "Francesville Clay Products Company," in operation for several years, and built this company into a very large successful operation. Henry K. Lee dropped dead quite suddenly while working in the tile factory in January 1931 at Francesville.

THE LUMBER INDUSTRY—FROM SAWMILLS TO LUMBERYARDS

Early lumber dealers were simply the operators of the local sawmills. The early settlers who needed lumber purchased their building material, sometimes very roughly cut boards, on the grounds of the sawmill, thus eliminating the middleman.

In the vicinity of New Richmond, sawmills were operated by Ira Stout, who had his mill 'set up' in the Walnut Grove area just about two miles east of New Richmond. Ira was there at the right time and had the contract to saw 100,000 feet of bridge timber for the Frankfort and State Line Railroad, the first railroad running through the towns of New Richmond and Pleasant Hill, later Wingate.

The 1878 Atlas of Coal Creek Township shows a sawmill located on Thomas Ward's property on Section 13, township 20, range 5. Stout's steam engine later furnished the power to run the engines of Ward's tile factory.

George W. Washburn escaped serious injury when he was operating his sawmill in January of 1880. His clothing became entangled in the machinery and he was nearly pulled into the saw, but was able to free himself. He was luckier than most of the early sawmill owners; some of them lost a hand or arm before they went into other lines of work. George returned to farming and the raising of livestock after this accident. I am uncertain of the location of his sawmill. His residence was located about two miles south of New Richmond, but he also owned property just inside the Tippecanoe County line, in Jackson Township.

James H. Smock, a very unlucky man, tangled with his sawmill several times, as related earlier. He was always referred to as "Old Man Smock" or "Dad Smock" and he operated his sawmill in the town of New Richmond when the town was enjoying one of its big booms from about 1886 to 1890. The railroad had been converted to a standard gauge and was bringing the prosperity to the town of New Richmond that it had promised so long ago.

Smock would saw a huge pile of logs in New Richmond, and after completing this stack, he moved his steam engine, saws, and other machinery to Boston Store to work on a huge stack in that vicinity. He then would return to New Richmond, where another pile of logs was facing him.

In December 1886, Smock's mill suffered a loss by fire, but Smock, being used to bad luck, simply engaged a Mr. Armentrout to rebuild the structure the following week. Smock had removed the irons from the ashes, cleaned and repaired the saws and machinery, and he was back in business by the week of Christmas that same year. The writer for the Crawfordsville *Review* encouraged the residents of New Richmond, and vicinity, to purchase their lumber from Smock because "he has a first class mill and deserves the patronage of the people."

The operators of the sawmills fired up their big steam engines in the winter months, the trees being cut when the sap was down, then brought to the mill in New Richmond and placed in huge stacks. The logs were cut to the specifications, depending upon the carpenter's needs. Barns and sheds were constructed from the rough stock, and the better, smoother grade of lumber was used in the construction of homes and the business houses.

In 1889, Mr. Smock and Mr. Lee, the tile man, formed a partnership, and used Smock's steam engine to run the machinery for the tile mill through the summer months. In the late fall and winter, the sawmill operation began again, and continued until spring. The good lumber was sold for building material, and the scraps were used to fire the kilns in the tile and brick factory. Mr. Smock's identity as the New Richmond sawmill operator was lost when he joined forces with Mr. Lee. The concern was listed in the Directory of Montgomery County in 1891-92 as "M. J. Lee and son, Saw & Tile Mill" so it is not known for certain just how many years he worked in this partnership. The Lee tile mill continued several more years and the sawmill was in operation along with the tile mill, furnishing the fuel for the burning of tile. "Dad" Smock had the same arrangement with the former tile mill operator, Willis Hunt, in New Richmond in 1884.

Other early sawmills in the vicinity of New Richmond were the Dain & Cowan's Sawmill. An advertisement in the New Richmond Record, Thursday, May 13, 1915 reads, "Dain & Cowan's Sawmill at the Cowan Cross-roads south of New Richmond. Sawing done to order—frame material furnished on short notice. Bring us your logs!"

The 1878 atlas of Montgomery County, Indiana, shows a sawmill located on W. W. Tiffany's land on section 19, township 20, range 5 west; and one on J. Koon's land, section 27, township 20, range 6 west.

The first mention of a lumber contractor or dealer was a Mr. Graves, who was buying lumber near Linden in 1888 and trading with the New Richmond people. The newspaper did not indicate that he was associated with the railroad company, and perhaps securing lumber for them, but he did not establish a lasting business in the New Richmond area.

A year later the town was again in need of a good lumberyard, because the people had to go the Crawfordsville to secure building material and this was a terrible inconvenience for the carpenters. The builders had to wait until the following year, however, before a lumberyard was started in New Richmond.

W. B. Lynch and John Tribby, both of Darlington, formed a partnership and started the first good lumberyard in the town of New Richmond, in November, 1890. John Tribby was the manager for the firm, and Harry Tribby delivered the lumber by horse and wagon to the customers. This business was considered a blessing to the town, saving the local builders many hours that were formerly spent on traveling to the county seat to purchase lumber and other building materials.

Tribby & Lynch sold the lumber company to Orlando W. Mason, who operated the business under the name "New Richmond Lumber Company." This company was listed in the 1895 county directory.

Mason sold the New Richmond Lumber Company to a group of men from Tippecanoe County. The *Miscellaneous Records of Montgomery County*, Volume 6, page 439, recorded the articles of association on August 29, 1900. The stockholders were John W. Simler, Curtis E. Wells, and William H. Winnie. They formed an association to "buy and sell lumber", and the name of their company was The New Richmond Lumber Company, keeping the same name as the former owners. The capital stock of this company was $10,000 divided into shares of $100 each.

E. A. Bishop was the manager of this lumberyard for a short time, but soon accepted another position as yard foreman in a large lumberyard in Hammond, Indiana. Harry Cox of Lafayette came to New Richmond to fill the position as manager after Bishop left.

The New Richmond Lumber Company was the first really successful business along this line. In 1902, along with the lumber and coal, they advertised building brick and other supplies, and were also making available an assortment of house plans for the latest style houses with prices ranging from $500 to $4,000. The advertisement boasted 100 styles to choose from.

In 1903 the New Richmond Lumber Company supplied the lumber for the new Union Elevator, a rather large concern for the town, and a large contract for the lumber company. Threshing machines provided a year round need for a coal supply where otherwise there was only the need for fuel for homes or the local business houses.

The 1903 Directory of Montgomery County lists the New Richmond Lumber Company on Franklin Street and Clover Leaf Railroad, and the officers at the time were: W. F. Stillwell, President; A. H. Diver, Secretary and Treasurer; G. W. Clough, manager. George Clough continued as manager for several years. The company was a branch of the Henry Taylor Lumber Company of Lafayette, Indiana. In 1905, a large lumber shed was added to accommodate the expanding business. Harry Pullen of Lafayette supervised the building of the addition.

In 1910, the New Richmond Lumber Company was advertising "everything you need in the building line, including lumber, lath, shingles, sash and doors, posts, lime, brick, plaster, cement and roofing—also a full line of paints, oil, and varnishes." George W. Clough was still manager at the time.

The Big Four Lumber Company, owned and operated by J. T. Detchon, A. D. Snyder, and E. T. and William McCrea, opened for business in the summer of 1904. The first advertisements appeared in the June 23rd edition of the New Richmond *Record*. The company had just received a new shipment of twenty carloads of lumber and building supplies, and the company was "seeking a share of your trade," so the advertisement read. Their slogan was "Come and examine our coal, and if you don't say it's the best you ever saw in New Richmond, we will pay you for lying."

This lumberyard only lasted about two years, but brought lots more trade to New Richmond because of the sharp competition between the two companies. On the 15th of January, 1906, the Big Four Lumber Company stock was sold to the Henry Taylor Lumber Company of Lafayette, the sale amounting to about $7,000. The stock was moved, as soon as the invoice was completed, to the yards of the New Richmond Lumber Company—which, as stated before, was a branch of the Henry Taylor Lumber Company. The sale only included the stock, not the grounds or buildings of the Big Four, these being purchased by the Messrs. Haywood and Detchon of the Union Elevator. The Big Four was situated just west of the elevator on the former site of the New Richmond Canning Factory.

The New Richmond Lumber & Coal Company

James T. Parlon, owner and founder of the New Richmond Lumber & Coal Company, purchased the interests of the Henry Taylor Company, the New Richmond Branch, in 1908, and founded the New Richmond Lumber & Coal Company the same year. George W. Clough continued as manager for a while, but Jim soon took charge of the business. The year 1908 was another milestone in the life of James T. Parlon, being the year he married his life-long partner, Mary G. Creahan. She assisted her husband in the bookkeeping department of the Lumber & Coal Company for over 45 years. Both Mr. and Mrs. Parlon were natives of Tippecanoe County; Jim was born on a farm in Wea Township, June 2, 1880, son of Thomas and Anna (O'Shea) Parlon. He attended Purdue University. Mrs. Parlon was born March 26, 1878, daughter of Thomas and Catherine (Cleary) Creahan. She taught school at Wea and West Lafayette schools for eleven years. The couple had five children, namely: Mary Ann, Richard, John C., Alice, and Catherine. Richard went into the lumber business with his father-in-law, the J.O. Perkins Lumber Company of Lafayette, and John C. worked with his father in the New Richmond Lumber & Coal Company.

In 1924, Mr. Parlon expanded his business interests and constructed an elevator in New Richmond. This new enterprise went by the name of the New Richmond Grain Elevator, but eventually, most advertisements read The New Richmond Lumber and Coal Company. Estella M. Creahan was in partnership with Jim in both interests. The concern carried all types of "building supplies, fence, and other farm supplies, DUMORITE explosives—to rid the farms of large boulders and tree stumps—guaranteed not to freeze or cause headache!" They also carried, "DuPont, Dutch Boy, Bradley, and Vrooman Paints," over the years, and paint brushes and other painting supplies; "Coal-Anthracite, Bituminous and Pocahontas." In 1912, the company had acquired a new planing mill to handle all kinds of mill work more efficiently and promptly.

James Parlon continued with the lumber and grain business as long as his health permitted. After his death in November 1957, his son John C. continued to manage the business until 1960, when he sold the family business which had continued about 52 years in New Richmond.

Ivan Pollock worked for John Parlon in the lumber & paint department from June 1946 until the lumber company was sold. Ivan then went into the business of selling building supplies and carpentry until September of 1980, when he held a public auction, and sold out, retiring soon after.

Hardware Merchants

In the early settlement of New Richmond, hardware supplies were either manufactured by the local smithy, or could be purchased in the general stores. It was not until the middle 1880s that the store keepers began specializing in hardware. The following facts on New Richmond's hardware merchants have been recorded.

Jack Smith Hardware—Jack Smith sold his dry goods stock and he and his brother embarked in the hardware business in February 1886. They were still in this line in January 1890, when they added Tommy Patton's goods to their stock after he went out of business.

Thomas Patton's Hardware—Tommy Patton planned to erect a "handsome new hardware store" in August of 1887. The building was completed in January the following year, when Patton made a trip to Chicago to buy stock. He was from the Round Hill neighborhood, but moved to New Richmond to be closer to his business interests. Patton added farm implements to his stock and the expansion required more space. He erected a new building in October the same year. Wallace Brannon clerked for Patton while he conducted a writing school at the Patton Schoolhouse around this period of time. Tom was forced to give up his hardware store because of ill health in 1890; he sold his stock to the Smith brothers and his building to Blaine Archey.

Blaine Archey's Hardware—Blaine Archey purchased the grounds and building of Tom Patton's hardware in January 1890, and advertised, "Livery, feed and sale stable, and dealer in buggies and harness."

William Thomas' Hardware—William Thomas purchased Blaine Archey's hardware in 1891 and advertised, "hardware, stoves, tinware, furniture, and implements," in the 1891-92 Montgomery County directory.

H.O. Shelby's Hardware—Harry O. Shelby attended DePauw University several years, then embarked in the hardware business in New Richmond in 1895. Shelby married Annis Dewey and left a daughter, Edna, and his brothers, Evan and Clyde. Evan was in the hardware and telephone business in Linden for several years. Shelby sold his store to Snyder and Thompson in 1897, then moved to Chicago where he received religious training at the Moody Institute. He then moved to Oklahoma City, Oklahoma, and embarked in the real estate business. He died in Oklahoma City in 1904.

John McCallum Hardware—John McCallum of New Richmond purchased the hardware stock from Evan Shelby in April 1896. It is uncertain if McCallum conducted his hardware store in New Richmond or Linden at this time.

Albert D. Snyder

Snyder & Thompson Hardware–Albert D. Snyder and Walter Thompson purchased Harry O. Shelby's hardware stock in 1897. A year later they purchased a parcel of land from Charles F. Killen for the purpose of constructing a new building to house their expanding business.

Snyder and Thompson carried a large stock of furniture–parlor chair sets, dining room, oak stands, etc. The furniture was located on the second floor of the old frame McCardle block (later dismantled to make room for the Knights of Pythias building), and the general hardware was on the first floor.

Snyder and Thompson also carried farm implements that were displayed in the "Pritchard Bank Building," (also torn down). They advertised, DEERE wheel plows, OLIVER sulkey plows, DEERE riding cultivators, HAYES, TIGER & HOOSIER corn planters, tin ware, lawn mowers, and other garden tools, buggies, surreys, PHAETONS, and the finest lines of bicycles.

Albert D. Snyder's Hardware–Albert D. Snyder was born three miles west of Crawfordsville, and spent most of his life in Montgomery County, except for three years he spent in Missouri as a cowboy. He then followed farming, and in 1891 began buying and shipping stock, driving the stock to the markets, or to the stock pens in New Richmond and Linden, to be shipped by rail. Snyder became a New Richmond merchant as a butcher, which he continued until August 1896, when Walter Thompson and Snyder purchased H.O. Shelby's hardware store. In October 1898, Snyder bought out Thompson and continued alone in the hardware business. He erected a huge three story brick building in 1901 and 1902 to accommodate his mammoth stock of hardware, furniture, Queens Ware, farm implements, and buggies. In April of 1902, a new steel and sheet iron awning was added to the front of the building, which was removed many years ago. The Snyder Building is now owned by Bob Utterback of Utterback Marketing Services (112 South Wabash Street). The Utterbacks did extensive remodeling and refurbishing to both the interior and exterior of the building. They preserved the character of the original building by having a semi-open floorplan to the offices, and refinishing the original tin ceiling and oak woodwork.

Perry McLain clerked for Snyder and for the hardware merchants who followed Snyder in New Richmond. Charles M. Snyder kept the books for the concern. The China and Queens Ware department was located in the basement of his building when he first moved there. Alverta Hadley worked in this department around the holidays.

A.D. Snyder placed several full page advertisements in the New Richmond *Record* before Christmas in 1902, offering bookcases, sideboards, buffets, dining tables, chairs, couches, a complete line of rockers, and fine china. He advertised Morris chairs that year saying, "When your nerves are tired and deranged, your troubles begin, and remain, until you buy one of Snyder's MORRIS CHAIRS." A one-hundred-piece set of imported china sold for $6.50 in the spring of 1903, and a stronger line of buggies, with a one-year guarantee against breakage, was included in his stock.

On August 20, 1903, A.D. Snyder traded his mammoth hardware stock and building to John Fowler, of Cloverdale, for his 462-acre farm, livestock, implements, and crops. Fowler was a former "Coal Creek Boy." The hardware building was valued at $12,000.

Snyder was asking people to settle their accounts to the end of the year, 1903, in order to move to his newly acquired farm. He purchased another 80-acre farm in Putnam County and purchased a carload of goats in Kansas City to clear away the "briars and sage brush," he said. Farming, livestock trading, and cowboying was in his blood, rather than clerking inside a huge brick building. The loss of his wife in October 1902, after a lingering illness, was possibly another reason for selling his hardware. He returned to the New Richmond area and settled in Linden a few years later.

John H. Fowler Hardware (Snyder Building)

John H. Fowler, of Cloverdale, Indiana, purchased the A.D. Snyder hardware building and stock on August 20, 1903, and moved his wife and three sons to New Richmond about two weeks later. John was born and raised in the southwest part of Coal Creek Township. The family moved into Sam Jones' property in the east part of town.

Fowler's hardware advertised hardware, furniture, buggies, implements, harness, jump seat surreys, canopy top buckboards, and spring wagons. The famous MAJESTIC RANGE salesmen exhibited their stoves and gave away hot biscuits and coffee when Fowler first opened his store. They offered a free set of cooking utensils made of copper, steel, and enamel, worth $7.50, with each MAJESTIC RANGE sold from December 7-12, 1903. In 1904 he added two car loads of buggies to his stock. JOHN DEERE, or OLIVER sulkey plows sold for $32, all gang plows were $55 that year.

Employees of the Fowler hardware were Perry McLain, Nick Beckley; and James E. Twiddy. Fowler sold the hardware to Oliver Totten in June 1904, purchased a large hardware in Danville, Illinois, and moved to that city.

Oliver Totten's Hardware (Snyder building)—Oliver Totten purchased J.H. Fowler's hardware store and stock on June 9, 1904. Fowler traded Totten for a large tract of land near Mt. Erie, in southern Illinois. Oliver Totten was from Olney, Illinois. E.R. Yoke of Mt. Erie, a clerk for Totten's hardware, moved his family to New Richmond soon after the business changed hands. There was much confusion with this trade of the hardware, and the building changed ownership within a month.

John F. Wight Hardware (Snyder building)—John F. Wight, an attorney from Bloomington, Illinois, had taken possession of the hardware store in New Richmond on June 23, 1904. He reduced the stock and listed the prices of the merchandise on sale. In July the same year, Wight had disposed of his interests in the hardware to George Thomas. A.D. Snyder was collecting his accounts for him that month.

George Thomas' Hardware (Snyder building)—George Thomas, son of William M. Thomas, a former hardware merchant in New Richmond, purchased the hardware stock of John F. Wight of the Snyder building on July 24, 1904. A Mr. Martin clerked. Thomas sold hardware, furniture, and farming equipment, ROUND OAK and ESTATE heating stoves, scoopboards, shucking gloves, pegs, and mittens.

George Thomas sold his hardware stock to Theodore M. Layne, and he and his family moved back to Wingate. There was still conflicting records of ownership of the Snyder building at this time.

T.M. Layne Hardware (Snyder building)—Theodore M. Layne of Cloverdale, Indiana, acquired the large hardware building through a Sheriff's sale on January 4, 1905. The building was valued at $12,000. Layne traded the hardware for a well-paying hotel in Cloverdale, and a good farm near that city.

Layne purchased the hardware stock of John E. Wilson and moved it to the "Big Store" in the Snyder building. He employed James D. Martin of Cloverdale as manager, along with Wilford Byers of Hazelrigg and Lawrence McLain of New Richmond, to run his hardware in New Richmond. Layne also owned hardware stores in Greencastle, Cloverdale, and Darlington. J.W. Flannigan of Thorntown was employed as the farm implement sales clerk in February, 1905. Mr. and Mrs. Flannigan and their nine-year-old son moved to New Richmond, where they resided in the Henthorne cottage in the east part of town.

Layne advertised implements, buggies, wagons, horse blankets, furniture, stoves, folding beds, bedroom suits and sideboards. In July 1905, he offered reduced prices on all steel and rubber tire buggies and carriages, OSBURN vehicles, FISH BROTHERS, and SPRING VALLEY wagons, KLONDIKE wagon stoves, lap robes and horse blankets.

In September 1905, Layne made a trip to Chicago and purchased $2,500 worth of new stock of furniture for his hardware store. When fall came that year, T.M. Layne decided to enclose the elevator in the huge brick building in order to heat the structure more efficiently. He realized he could only heat the first floor and closed the other floors off.

In January of 1906, T.M. Layne purchased Boswell Clough's old saloon property to use as a carriage, buggy, wagons, and farm implements storeroom. Layne turned the old ice house that stood behind the structure into a storage room, and a large shed was constructed to connect with the frame building (saloon).

T.M. Layne sold his hardware stock and building to Henry K. Lee and Orlando W. Mason on September 16, 1907.

Mason & Lee Hardware (Snyder building)—Henry K. Lee and Nannie, his wife, and Orlando W. and Clara M. Mason, purchased the Snyder building from Theodore M. Layne September 16, 1907. The abstract shows another legal problem due to a mortgage that had not been settled.

Mason & Lee advertised in 1909, "Best AXMINISTER and WILTON 9 X 12 rugs" for $22. In 1910, Queens Ware, furniture, general hardware, farm implements, wagons, and buggies were among the items of this business establishment. Sam L. Rafferty clerked in this store. On January 1, 1911, Sam moved to Ridge Farm, Illinois, having purchased a hardware store in that city from Mason and Lee.

Teague and Sons Hardware (Snyder building)—James F. Teague traded his hardware store in Ridge Farm, Illinois, for the Mason and Lee hardware in New Richmond. The deal was settled on January 7, 1911. Teague had purchased a home in New Richmond from James M. Alexander in October of 1910, as the men had been negotiating the hardware trade at this time. Teague was to take possession of the residence the last of December that year.

J. F. Teague and Sons hardware and furniture store advertised in the NRHS 1911 annual as "The Big Hardware & Furniture Store." Items included heating stoves, ranges, tin ware, silverware, furniture, carpets, rugs, linoleums, farm wagons, and implements, buggies, gasoline engines, etc.

Operating and clerking in this store were J.F. Teague, Harry F. Teague, and Raymond B. Teague. On December 15, 1913, James F. and Nellie Teague sold the hardware stock and building to Theodore E. Christian, an unmarried adult, for $20,000.

Eichenburg and Christian Hardware (Snyder building)—The only record, other than the abstract of the building, available of this hardware in the Snyder building, appeared in the Crawfordsville *Journal* on April 8, 1914, relating an accident that occurred in the building. The crowded elevator dropped sixty feet, falling from the third floor to the basement of the store. Three persons were injured and fifteen were badly shaken up in the accident. They were attending a large auction of buggies and implements. Dr. Wray of New Richmond attended the injured.

T.E. Christian sold the hardware building to Marshall Smith on June 25, 1914. Other owners of the Snyder building who followed Smith were: James and Vina E. Courtney and Jonas E. and Julia E. Pershing; Oliver J. Frazee; Alva N. Harold; and Walter O. Bragg–all within the period of June 1914 to July 21, 1915. Charles A. Mauzy claimed to have purchased the building from Bragg and filed suit against the Corn Exchange Bank (et al.) to restrain the Sheriff from selling the property, due to a problem of ownership dating back to January of 1911.

L.P. Brown's Hardware (Snyder building)—Lonnie P. Brown was listed in the 1907-8 Montgomery County directory as a dealer in buggies, farm implements, and harnesses. He started this line of business in another location; however, on July 31, 1915, the sheriff of Montgomery County, Indiana, sold the Snyder building to Brown to recover $12,522.79 in principal and interest. Brown's bid was only for $4,000. The remaining amount involved the previously-mentioned short-time owners of the property.

L.P. Brown's hardware was advertising the BOWERS economy hatcher for chicks in March, 1916. Lonnie also sold LILY separators, farm implements, furniture, aluminum ware in five-, six-, seven-, and eight-quart kettles, with prices ranging from 79 cents to $1.49; and RADIENT HOME base burners, MAJESTIC RANGES. In 1920, HEIDER tractors, and COLUMBUS and ROCK ISLAND wagons were advertised.

Morrow Family Hardware (Snyder building)—Ebert (or Ebright) M. Morrow was the manager of this family hardware establishment in 1922. The abstract of the Snyder building includes a letter from Joseph C. Herron, dated July 10, 1924, to the Morrow Family Hardware, concerning the new proprietor of the building, John T. Detchon, to whom the Morrows were to pay rent from the first of July, the same year. An advertisement for the Morrow Family Hardware appeared in the New Richmond *Record*, July 6, 1922 which reads, "Some men buy washers–others marry them! Moral–consult the MORROW FAMILY HARDWARE."

The Morrow family also had a hardware store in the north room of the bank building in Linden, at one time.

A.R. Bowers Hardware (Boswell Clough's building)—The 1903 county directory listed A.R. Bowers, Hardware and Implements, in New Richmond. Bowers was from Kirkpatrick, and was later associated with John E. Wilson.

John E. Wilson Hardware (Boswell Clough's building)—While all the confusion was going on with the hardware merchants in Snyder's building, A.R. Bowers was trying to sell his hardware in New Richmond. Prospective buyers were Charles Haywood, and John E. Wilson, in July 1904. Wilson, of Clark's Hill, was looking for a new site in New Richmond and was interested in the old McCardle building occupied by F.M. Johnson's drug store. Instead, Wilson purchased Boswell Clough's old saloon property on Washington Street, which was occupied at the time by Oscar Stingley's soft drink establishment. Wilson and Bowers were partners in this hardware. Wilson moved his family from Clark's Hill early in September 1904 to Job Westfall's property in the east end of town. He announced the opening of his hardware store in the September 15th *Record*, and advertised, "JEWELL, GARLAND, MATTOON, and RADIENT HOME, base burners, ranges, heaters, and cook stoves. He also carried oilcloth, washing machines, churns, axes, barbed wire, blue enameled DELT WARE, cutlery, and horse blankets. John E. Wilson sold his stock of hardware to Theodore M. Layne in January 1905. Layne was located in the Snyder building.

Perry McLain and Sons Hardware (George F. Long's building, N.E. corner of Wabash and Washington)—Perry McLain was born at Connersville, Indiana, December 7, 1850. He moved to Greencastle at the age of eight, and to Jamestown at the age of fourteen, where he married and lived until 1872, when he moved to New Ross. In 1873 he moved to Thorntown, where he managed the Thorntown City Flouring Mills for four years. He later moved to Hillsboro where he lived for eleven years. In 1890, McLain and his family moved to New Richmond.

Perry McLain clerked in the following hardware stores in New Richmond: William Thomas for four years; H.O. Shelby's for two years; Snyder and Thompson for two years; A.D. Snyder for four years. He was head salesman and buyer in Snyder's store. Perry continued as clerk for the hardware merchants succeeding Snyder, except for a short time when he clerked in a hardware in 1904 in Veedersburg and in Clarks Hill in 1906. He was listed as a clerk in New Richmond in 1907-8.

Perry McLain and Sons were operating their own hardware store in January 1912, in New Richmond, advertising gas engines, washing machines, tubs, clothes wringers, sad irons, ironing boards, and DETROIT VAPOR STOVES. In 1920, he advertised ONE MINUTE washing machines—electric and hand power, and in 1923, he listed Chinaware, silverwares cutlery, stoves, and ranges for sale.

The latest record I have of McLain's hardware store was in 1923, but he may have been in the town for a longer period of time. His death occurred in 1932, and he is buried in the New Richmond Cemetery.

T.J. Oppy Hardware (George F. Long's building, N.E. corner of Wabash and Washington)—Thomas Jay Oppy was born near New Richmond on September 22, 1917, to Edward T. and Ruby (Foster) Oppy. Tom married Helen Lane in 1939, and they had the following children: Sandra, Sharon, Shelia, Sonya, and Thomas, Jr.

Tom operated a hardware store in New Richmond from 1945 until his death on February 19, 1959. He had suffered a heart attack a week or two before his death. Items offered for sale by T.J. Oppy's hardware in 1952 were REO and HUFFY lawn mowers, SHAWNEE Pottery, A.B.C. O'MATIC washers, PERFECTION and DUO THERM oil heaters, $69.95 and up. Tom always serviced what he sold and cleaned and reset the oil controls on the oil heaters. He sold KURFEE paints, SUNBEAM and G.E. appliances.

Lane's Hardware (George F. Long's building)—Richard "Beck" Lane managed T.J. Oppy's hardware for his sister, Helen (Lane) Oppy, after her husband Tom's death in 1959. After Helen's death on May 29, 1971, Beck purchased the hardware, and Lane's Hardware was first listed as such in 1973. Beck's brother Russell (aka "Bill") worked for him in the hardware on a part time basis. Beck tried to sell the store in 1976, but the deal fell through, so he continued to operate the store until the day of his death on June 1, 1983.

Bill Lane continued to operate the hardware on a part time basis after his brother's death, but his health was not very good. The store was closed in December 1984. On June 29, 1985, Elsie Lane, Beck's widow, held an auction to sell off hardware stock and building; however, the structure did not sell until later in the year, and the town of New Richmond was again without a hardware store. In February 1999, Gerald and Patty Ratcliff opened Coal Creek Center, a hardware and convenience store in the Hollin Building at 104 N. Wabash Street.

Furniture Stores

The early furniture dealers in New Richmond will be found within the history of the hardware stores in the town. William Thomas was the earliest on record to list furniture for sale in his hardware store, and was listed in the county directory in 1891-92. Before that time, homes were furnished with homemade furniture, or the local craftsmen, the cabinet makers, built the needed furniture.

The only store listed as a furniture store was **Alexander's Furniture Store**, listed in the New Richmond Telephone Company directory printed August 1934. He carried Philco radios, refrigerators, and records when he first started in this line of business. By the early 1950s, Alexander branched out and advertised Philco freezers in addition to the earlier appliances, and added Youngstown kitchens, Maytag washers, Futorian Custom furniture, Cosco products, Sunbeam appliances, Mainlainer bedroom suits, Kuehne and Arvin Kitchenette and Dinette sets, and other items.

In 1954 Alexander moved into the old Hollin brothers brick building on the northwest corner of Wabash and Washington Streets. He added gifts to his furniture and appliance store about this time. Alexander also continued to cut hair in his barber shop, located at the rear of his store, until he sold his chair in February 1964. Alexander's wife Bernice (better known as "Bill") added yarn and sewing supplies to their other stock around 1964. They carried Tell City; La-Z-Boy; and Madden Furniture in the 1960s.

Alexander's Furniture and Gifts Store was in business until 1985. Alexander died Sunday, January 14, 1996 at the age of 83 in St. Anthony Health Care, Lafayette, Indiana. He was buried at the New Richmond Cemetery. Alexander was one of New Richmond's most informative businessmen. He could recall many historic events and business locations of former years and enjoyed many visits from former New Richmond residents who swapped tales with him.

Bob Worland purchased Byron Alexander's building in 1988 and opened the **Hometown Furniture (Wholesale Furniture)** store in October that year. He went out of business in 1991. He moved another truckload of furniture into the same building in 1994 but loaded it up again in December 1996 and went out of business in New Richmond.

The Village Blacksmiths

The blacksmith was certainly the most important person in the early settlement of any section of the country. So important were they, early maps and directories showed the location of each smithy and were very exact in giving the mileage from the village to the blacksmith's place of business, usually next door to his residence. Shoeing the horses, pounding out the iron work required for the wagons the early settlers used for hauling and transportation, manufacturing the plows that turned under the wild prairie grass, and other farm implements, making nails and hinges for the homes, barns or other farm buildings were only a small part of the blacksmith's work. The ladies in the backwoods also depended upon the village smithy, for it was he who made the iron skillets, the Dutch ovens, the iron work for hanging the kettles over the fire in the fireplace, and many other cooking utensils—and the sad irons for ironing the clothing of the pioneer family. Many, many items too numerous to mention were manufactured by the local blacksmith.

Because of the important role of the blacksmith, it just so happens that New Richmond's first businessman was a smithy owned by Samuel Kincaid, who platted the town of New Richmond in 1836. Kincaid located his log cabin and blacksmith shop on the northeast corner of the crossroads of the Yountsville to LaFayette road and the Strawtown to Covington road—later the site of Beck Lane's Hardware in 1983. The Strawtown to Covington road was a former trail made by the Indians, a route they took to the Wabash River, and it is possible the other road mentioned was an Indian trail also. The white man decided the route was satisfactory for their needs, too, and used the road to transport their grain and other farm commodities to the mills, or by water way to the markets along the Wabash.

These two roads became well traveled within a few years because of a woolen mill purchased by Dan Yount in the early 1840s. Mr. Yount built the woolen business into a very large operation, and farmers came from every corner of Montgomery, Tippecanoe, and Fountain Counties to have their wool processed into cloth. The little crossroad village of New Richmond was enjoying its first little boom in a very short time.

Hogs, cattle, and turkeys were driven through New Richmond and on north to the markets in Lafayette. Public scale houses, blacksmith shops and the windmills were placed on the early maps of Montgomery and Tippecanoe Counties, showing where the livestock could be weighed and watered along the route. If the horses threw a shoe or if a wagon wheel broke down, they knew just how far it was to the nearest smithy so repairs could be made without too much loss of time. In the rainy season, the roads or paths all turned to a very soft mud because there were no graveled roads in the early years, and this created more work for the blacksmith as the horses had to be rough shod, that is, a pointed piece of metal was added and projected downward from the horseshoe to prevent slipping in the mud and maybe breaking a leg. This device was similar to the cleats on a football player's shoes.

Jacob C. Campbell, born in Northumberland County, Pennsylvania, on March 26, 1808, came with his parents to Coal Creek Township in 1832. He married in 1833, in Montgomery County, Mary Ann Pryor, daughter of Nicholas and Lucinda (Wilhite) Pryor. The Pryors lived west of New Richmond and settled here very early. Campbell farmed for a while, but in 1848 he opened a blacksmith shop in New Richmond. Jacob and Mary had nine children, but only five lived to maturity, namely: Mary E., Sarah J., Elisha, William, and Maria. The son William, opened a general store in the town of New Richmond in later years. Jacob continued as a blacksmith up to his last illness and his death on February 12, 1887.

The 1850 Census lists Jacob C. Campbell, James McComas, and Elisha Campbell as blacksmiths in the town of New Richmond. There were two Elisha Campbells in the town of New Richmond in the 1850 Census records. The Elisha who was a blacksmith was born in Ohio and was 35 years of age. His wife, Mary A., age 35, was born in North Carolina and his children were all born in Indiana, namely Sarah A., age 12; Ester, 9; John, 7; and Mary E., 2. The other Elisha Campbell was listed as a farmer, age 34, and was born in Pennsylvania. Jacob had a brother Elisha and it is difficult to know which was the brother—possibly the one born in Pennsylvania.

James McComas, age 29, a blacksmith born in Ohio, and his wife Nancy A., age 26, also an Ohio native, were listed in the 1850 Census records. All their children were born in Indiana, namely: William, age 5; John M. and Eliza A., twins, age 3; and Joseph, age 1.

The 1870 Census listed Jacob C. Campbell and James R. Thomas as blacksmiths in New Richmond. McComas was not listed. The *Peoples Guide*, a directory of Montgomery County, Indiana, 1874, lists the following blacksmiths in and near New Richmond: William Bennett, born in Indiana 1835, settled in Montgomery County, 1849–in New Richmond; T.J. Bennett, born in Ohio 1834, settled in Montgomery County, 1853, located 3-1/2 miles south of New Richmond (this was in the Round Hill neighborhood); J.C. (Jacob) Campbell born in Pennsylvania, 1808, settled in Montgomery County, 1832 in New

Richmond; T.S. Handley, born in Ohio, 1826, settled in Montgomery County, 1845, situated 1-3/4 miles northwest of New Richmond; S.S. Mitchell, born in Ohio, 1844, settled in Montgomery County, 1873 in New Richmond.

The 1882-83 directory of Montgomery County lists Jacob C. Campbell and Frank Cornell as blacksmiths in New Richmond. Cornell's name has been spelled these various ways: Carrell, Kernell, Cornell, Cernell, and Carnell. Cornell became so successful he had to hire a helper. James Harris came from Boston Store (later Elmdale) in February 1884 and started working with Cornell. He worked with him until March 1888, when he joined Charles Wolhever's blacksmith firm. Cornell was still listed as a blacksmith in the 1887 directory in the town of New Richmond. A man by the name of Brunis was listed as a partner with Harris in 1884-85. This was about the time Harris came to New Richmond, so they must have been partners before he (Harris) went to work with Cornell.

In January 1888 Thomas Cook, of Battleground, accepted a position in Frank Cornell's shop and they were listed as "Wagon Makers and Blacksmiths" in the 1890, 1891-92 County directories. A William Cornell also worked in the wagon and blacksmith shop with Frank.

Frank Cornell was appointed Postmaster of the town of New Richmond in 1889. This stirred up a lot of controversy and the citizens often complained because his shop was located in "a part of town least traveled, and was hard for the patrons to reach." Frank was the Postmaster, Curt Cornell the Postoffice Clerk, and Thomas Cook was the assistant Postmaster. Frank acquired the title "Chief Hot Iron" at this time. The townspeople soon accepted the location and things cooled down after a while, but there were a few hurt feelings from the change—not so much as the location, but the Postmaster before him was well thought of and some people disliked the change.

T.J. or "Jeff" Bennett was still listed in the 1891-2 directory. The Crawfordsville *Review* March 10, 1888 says, "Charles Wolhever has formed a partnership with James Harris, formerly connected with Frank Cernell." There seemed to be a problem in spelling the blacksmiths' names, because I have found Wolhever spelled Weliver, Wooliver, Weliever, etc. In August 1889 Dr. Detchon had just finished building a new blacksmith shop for Wolhever, and he and Harris were competing with Frank Cornell. Wolhever was connected with William Grannon in 1891-2. The Crawfordsville *Review*, April 11, 1891 said, "Charley Wolever has had enough of New Richmond and has moved to Darlington." William Grannon continued as a blacksmith until 1903.

C.K. Dueisbeck was listed in the 1900-01 directory as a New Richmond blacksmith and Levi Cheeseman was listed in 1903. H.G. Messer started blacksmithing in 1890, but in 1903 Messer (nicknamed "Daddy" Messer) was connected with Elisha B. Westfall. Their shop was located on west Washington Street in the area behind the Knights of Pythias building. They advertised "Messer & Westfall, General Blacksmith and Wagon Makers, Farm Implements, New Richmond." They continued their business together until September 1903, when Westfall accepted another partner, George Zachary. Zachary and Westfall opened a shop on the northeast corner of Washington and Franklin Streets, now the Christian Church property. They were going to specialize in horse shoeing only in that location. Westfall was still associated with Messer, but Messer was to run the west end shop, and was going to do only wood work and general repair blacksmithing. Messer is not listed after this as a blacksmith in New Richmond.

Elisha Westfall's Blacksmith Shop was listed in March 1905 and in June, the same year. There was to be a balloon ascension at Westfall's blacksmith shop in June and the location of his shop was given as Madison Street. He is still listed in the 1907-08 directory; in the New Richmond *Record*, April 15, 1909, the following advertisement appears, "See WESTFALL for your buggy painting, I have engaged an experienced buggy painter–bring in your old buggy and have it repaired and repainted to look as good as new." –E.B. WESTFALL, the BLACKSMITH.

The 1912 directory lists Hiland W. and Winters Beckley, HORSESHOEING and GENERAL BLACKSMITHING. In May 1915, A.E. Gaston purchased "Hi" Beckley's shop and hired William Burnes of Paris, Illinois, an "expert horse shoer", to do the work for him. The "Gaston Shop" changed hands again in September 1915, being leased to Ralph W. Wilson. His advertisement said, "I have had twenty years experience in horse shoeing and general blacksmithing, and I solicit the patronage of the general public."

J.A. Bryant had leased the "Gaston Shop" in May 1916 and was advertising, "General Blacksmithing and Woodwork...Horseshoeing a Specialty...All work Guaranteed, THE GASTON SHOP." I only found advertisements through May, June, and July 1916, but he may have been in New Richmond later than these dates.

Charles E. Smith was listed as a blacksmith in 1907-08, and 1912 directories, and Thomas McMillin was listed in 1912 as a New Richmond blacksmith.

Roy Carr advertised, "CARR'S BLACKSMITH SHOP...GENERAL REPAIR WORK" from 1935 to 1938 in New Richmond. His shop was located at the east end of Madison Street.

John and Sarah Shotts, parents of Theodore Morgan, or T.M. Shotts, settled in Madison Township in or near Linden, sometime after 1848. Shotts' brother Montgomery J. was born in Ohio and was 12 years of age in the 1860 Census. The next child was born in Indiana about 1851, so the family had moved in between the two dates. T.M.'s father was listed as a farmer on early census records. Besides the brother mentioned above, he had brothers William N. and John C.

The first recorded history of the Shotts family blacksmith—which was to become a family tradition for many, many years—was listed in the Montgomery County *Gazetteer* of 1903, "T.M. Shotts (wife Nora M.) Wagon and Repairs Shop, corner of Meridean [sic] and Water Streets in Linden, Ind." Their son, Grover C., worked in the wagon shop with his father in Linden and later in New Richmond.

Theodore M. Shotts and his wife, Nora Carman, had the following children: Benjamin Harrison, Grover C., Esther G., Lelia, Gay, Rose, Frances, Pauline, and the youngest son, Theodore Richard, known as T.R. or Dick.

The New Richmond *Record*, Thursday, September 10, 1903, printed the following advertisement: "NEW RICHMOND CARRIAGE AND WAGON WORKS–I have opened up my shop in the old Washburn Frame Building on South Wabash Street, and am prepared to do all kinds of Painting, Upholstering, Blacksmithing and Woodwork on BUGGIES, CARRIAGES AND WAGONS...Plow Work and Horse Shoeing. All work guaranteed. We solicit your patronage...AUTOMOBILE REPAIRING a Specialty. T.M. Shotts, manage New Richmond, Indiana."

17 - Shotts & Cox's Carriage Repair Shop, Painting, Horse Shoeing, and General Blacksmithing. Date Unknown.

In 1904 the son Grover was working with his father, and the shop was listed as "Shotts & Son's Blacksmith Shop"–the son Ben also was working in his father's shop. T.M. employed George Zachary to shoe the horses for him, so he could devote his time to building and repairing wagons and buggies. In 1905 Shotts was selling buggies and advertised a "Complete line of AUBURN BUGGIES of the best grade, all 1905 patterns. Price and Quality Guaranteed. We are also prepared to put on rubber tires of the best grade. NEW RICHMOND CARRIAGE WORKS, SHOTTS & SON."

The 1907-08 directory gives the residence of the T.M. Shotts family as Madison and Main Streets; this should have been Madison and South Wabash, since there was never a Main Street in New Richmond.

They lived on the northeast corner of this intersection. The sons Grover and Ben were also listed at the same address.

T.M. Shotts designed a new type of buggy called the "KLONDYKE BUGGY" and the advertisement said it was, "The lightest, strongest and most roomy of any element excluding carriage on the market, (Patent Pending). SHOTTS & SON MANUFACTURERS." There was a photograph of the framework of this buggy in the 1910 *Kole Kreke Kamera* yearbook. This buggy was advertised in the yearbook for several more years.

My father, Forrest Waye, was employed in the New Richmond Carriage Factory as a painter, painting the new buggies, and the detailed work of the thin stripe that gave the carriage that artistic, finishing touch. Shotts continued making buggies in this location until about 1920 when he constructed a new shop farther south on Wabash Street, on the west side of the street. Richard Shotts' sister-in-law, Ann McMillin, built a new National home on this site in 1962. In fact, the blacksmith shop was torn down to make room for this home. In 1923 T.M. Shotts was working alone, as the shop was listed as "T.M. Shotts, General Blacksmith, Wood working a specialty."

T.M. Shotts died in 1933 and his son, Theodore Richard "Dick" Shotts, was the next in line to carry on the family business. Dick was born February 17, 1911 in New Richmond. He attended the New Richmond school, graduating in 1929. He tried other lines of work—working in a meat market in town and the Hollin's grocery, where he made $1.00 per day. Having spent many hours in his father's blacksmith shop, Dick felt he was more qualified for this kind of work and returned to his father's shop. The New Richmond Telephone directory in 1934 lists "Shott's [sic] Blacksmith Shop...General Iron and Woodwork...Horse Shoeing." The 1937 advertisement lists, "Shotts Blacksmith...Wood Working...Trailers Truck and Body work a specialty."

18 - Dick Shotts in his blacksmith shop

In the 1940s came the Acetylene Welding–a completely new type of equipment used in general blacksmith work. This eliminated the time-consuming task of keeping the coals burning with the bellows formerly used for blacksmith work, thus freeing the hands for holding the material being forged or shaped. T.R. (or Dick) Shotts had the blacksmith shop to himself until 1941, when he took in a partner, Claude McMillin. Dick and Claude had grown up together and were always seen together. Claude was always known to everyone in New Richmond as "Pat" Shotts. Many people thought they were brothers, but they were actually cousins. Pat and Dick continued on with their business in the building Dick's father built in 1920, and advertised "Electric & Acetylene Welding." Later their partnership broke up and Claude went to South Bend to work for Armco Drainage and Metal Products, and Dick continued smithing alone most of the time. When Dick became too busy he hired part time help, Jim Murdock and Paul Goff and possibly others, but these two are all I remember working for him.

In the 1940s Dick moved his shop into a new concrete building located on the east side of south Wabash Street, across from the old shop. Carl Burnett had built a filling station and garage at the north end of this building and Dick occupied the south end. Verhey Erection was located in this building for several years. In 1962 Don Fouts became Dick's partner and they worked together until 1972. Their advertisement read, "Shotts and Fouts, Blacksmith & Welding Shop...Truck and Wagon Hoists...All types of Welding...Plow Sharpening...Portable Welding Equipment for on the job service...pipe thawing...construction and repair on all types of equipment...mill work…farrowing crates."

Don Fouts and his family moved to New Mexico after dissolving partnership with Dick, leaving the blacksmith shop in the possession of Dick again. Besides running the blacksmith shop, Dick also drove a school bus, starting with the New Richmond school system, later hauling students to the Coal Creek Central School. He continued driving after the new North Montgomery High School was built in 1971. He retired in 1976 after driving a school bus for 36 years. Dick also served as a volunteer fireman for the town of New Richmond and served on the town board.

Dick and his wife, the former Wanda Braman, had two daughters; Sarah Ellen, married to Dick Stephenson and residing in Georgia, and Mary Lou, married to a man by the name of Sprague, and living in Wallace, Indiana. Dick retired in 1979 and this ended the family tradition of Shotts' Blacksmith Shops in the town of New Richmond–and this ended the history of all blacksmith shops in the town. Farmers are now doing their own repairing of equipment, and thus eliminating the need of the local smithy. Dick and Wanda moved to Wallace to be near their daughter the following year. Dick Shotts died February 16, 1988 at their home in Kingman. His wife Wanda died October 20, 1995.

Horace Green Messer, blacksmith, was born May 27, 1834 at Rutland, Vermont, and died January 14, 1904 in New Richmond, Indiana. At eleven years of age, he came west with his father's family and settled in Ohio, and later came to Indiana in 1856. The family settled at Pittsburg, near Delphi, in Carroll County. From there he came to New Richmond in 1890.

Mr. Messer was probably the oldest veteran blacksmith in the state. From shoeing a horse at the age of eleven, he continued hammering away at the anvil until but a few days prior to his death. Before coming to New Richmond he opened up a wagon works at Delphi where he employed 15 hands, and of this 57 years of hard work, only five or six had in any way been given to other vocations of life. He held many positions of trust, and his life's living was an exemplary one.

While a resident at Pittsburg he was for eight years trustee of his home township, and on his coming to New Richmond he was one of the first fathers and earnest promoters of New Richmond's incorporation. The people of New Richmond nicknamed him "Daddy Messer" because of his position as one of the town's first trustees. (New Richmond *Record*, Thursday, January 21, 1904 p p. I c.4)

Chapter 7 - Farming, Husbandry, & Livestock Businesses

Livery Stables and Hostlers

The first recorded proprietor of a livery stable or barn in New Richmond was William R. Miller on the 1870 census, and John Wheeler was listed as an hostler on the 1880 census in the town of New Richmond.

George Oppy purchased a lot from George Phillips in February of 1888, and started a new livery. This was one of the more successful liveries in town and was "going full blast" by September the same year. There was no further record of Oppy's livery, but he may have sold his business to Uriah Copeland.

Uriah Coapland's (Copeland) livery was first mentioned in March 1889. Copeland hired Sam Mitty as his hostler and driver. The railroad's entry into the town of New Richmond created a need for a successful livery, for the traveling salesmen (or drummers—as they were called) required another mode of transportation when they arrived at the local train station.

Uriah Copeland had an unusual combination of business ventures going for him at the same time—his livery stable, a butcher shop, and an undertaking establishment. Mitty, his hostler, roomed in the undertaker's office, and slept in a cot while employed with Copeland. Mitty proposed to be ready when "Gabe" sounded his last trumpet, I suppose.

In January 1890 Copeland sold his livery stable to Billy Alston, and decided to try farming in December that year. Uriah Copeland again embarked in the livery business in October 1891, purchasing Blaine Archey's livery and feed barn.

William W. "Billy" Alston had only been in the livery business a short time when a wind storm blew the front off his barn around January 18, 1890. The storm did quite a bit of damage all over the vicinity of New Richmond, as well.

Billy was kept busy hauling drummers to and from the trains in New Richmond and Linden, and was having trouble keeping enough teams to transport his patrons. Billy kept first class teams, but he had one team that was not too fond of the noisy trains. One accident occurred after he met a couple who got off the train at Linden. The team became frightened and threw Billy and his passengers out on the ground and tore up the carriage. He upset another carriage load about the same time, shaking up the occupants pretty badly. Billy had other problems with the hostler he hired; the man returned to his stables unable to stand up, and the smell of whiskey was often very over powering in the stable.

The hay in Billy Alston's stables was also an attractive place for those requiring a place to sleep after a big night on the town. This concerned Billy because he was afraid they would set the place on fire. He hired Joseph Beel as hostler—and also fired him on three different occasions while he was in the livery business. Billy also placed a notice in a Crawfordsville newspaper stating his livery stable would no more be used as a hospital. These little incidents remind one of the old western movies. Billy Alston's livery was still in business in May 1891, the last date I found to be recorded.

A.D. Snyder erected a new house and a large barn in New Richmond in September 1892. His son, Willie, was learning the livery business from a local livery-man, and was to open his own stables in the new barn. There was no other record of Willie's livery.

On August 6, 1890, Blain (or Blaine) A. Archey purchased part of the old Methodist Church lot, located on south Wabash Street in New Richmond. A month later, he advertised, "B.A. Archey, Feed and Sale Stable an [sic] Dealer in Buggies and Harness." W.W. Alston was in the same line of business at this time, and Archey decided two livery stables were too many, and sold his livery and feed barn to Urias Copeland in October 1891.

In 1895, James Miller and Charles Killen both had livery stables in New Richmond. Frank Perkins was the proprietor of a livery on July 12, 1898 when the big fire occurred in town. His livery was saved, but he lost his general store and residence in the fire. Perkins' livery was in the vicinity of the grounds now occupied by the Tri County Telephone Company's office; it was across the street from his other properties.

Charles Killen and George C. Livingston operated a livery, as partners, in 1900 and 1901. In 1903 George was running the business alone, advertising, "Livery, Sale, and Feed Stable–on Washington Street." This location was either incorrect, or he moved his stables to south Wabash Street at a later date, because the 1907-8 county directory lists the Wabash Street location. The late Mildred "Punk" Tribby said his livery was across the street from the Black Bear Hotel on south Wabash Street, close to the site Dick Shotts' blacksmith shop occupied in Verhey's construction company (1985). Mildred said, "I can just see that plain as day. They had ropes hanging down, and an overhang. The big boys would always swing on the ropes which had knobs hanging from them."

Fern Patton was Livingston's hostler in 1903, and again in 1906. Aleck Hempleman kept his breeding horses in Livingston's livery barn and advertised this service in the local newspaper. Lew Roberts, a veterinarian from Veedersburg, set up an office each week at Livingston's livery to treat livestock. On Saturday, March 5, 1910, Livingston held a public auction at his livery barn in New Richmond, and offered the following property for sale:

HORSES–11 head
1 sorrel horse, 9 yrs. old
1 black horse, 10 yrs. old. These two horses are broke to all harness and safe for a lady to drive.
1 black mare 11 yrs. old, good single driver
1 bay mare 9 yrs. old, an awfully good driver and does not shy, nor scare at anything.
1 gray mare 9 yrs. old, double and single driver
1 bay horse 10 yrs. old, good driver
1 black mare 12 yrs. old, good double and single driver
1 bay horse 11 yrs. old, broke to all harness and gentle
1 bay pony 5 yrs. old, broke single and double, and gentle
1 team of ponies, 6 and 9 yrs. old, a pair of good drivers.

BUGGIES & CARRIAGES:
6 single top buggies, rubber tire, all practically new and of good makes
2 carriages one rubber tire, been used about 9 months, the other one a good steel tire
2 good trunk wagons
1 SHOTTS KLONDYKE (buggy)
HARNESS, ROBES, WHIPS, ETC.
4 sets of double buggy harness, 8 sets of single harness, 9 robes, 6 horse blankets, saddle and bridle, 1 STAR Storm front, 1 5-barrel galvanized water tank, and numerous other articles.
HAY–about 2 tons of Timothy Hay over $5, a credit of 9 months without
TERMS: $5 and under, cash. On all sums over $5, a credit of 9 months without interest with good freehold security, 8% interest from date if not paid at maturity. No property to be removed until terms of sale are compiled with, 4% off for cash.
GEO. C. LIVINGSTON
WRIGHT & SON, Auctioneers; Wm. Kirkpatrick, Clerk.

George Livingston went into the restaurant business after closing his livery, and in later years was a grocer.

Boswell Clough placed the following advertisement in the New Richmond *Record*, Thursday, August 21, 1902,

> "I will say to the public that John Sanders and Mark Lucas have retired from the livery business and the barn is now open again. Anyone can get their horse fed for 20 cents; tie-in for 5 cents; drive to Linden, 50 cents; drive to Wingate, 50 cents. If you don't believe it, call and see at the barn near the BLACK BEAR HOTEL! BOSWELL CLOUGH."

A photograph of the area known as "Smokey Row" shows the front of this livery north of the hotel on South Wabash Street. Boswell also had another livery on Bristle Ridge. The New Richmond *Record* mentioned that Mark Kenyon and Jake Zerface, both Bristle Ridgers, were re-roofing Boswell's structure.

Clough only continued the livery in New Richmond a few months, and Charles Neil of Attica opened a livery and feed stable in Clough's barn near the Black Bear Hotel. Neil only stayed with this business a few weeks.

Ora Stearman, also of Attica, purchased the livery stock from Charles Neil in December 1902. Stearman had been working for Neil. By December 25th, the same year, the south Wabash livery barn was again defunct; Stearman had moved his "bag and baggage back to Attica."

Henry Long was to take possession of Clough's Livery barn on April 7th, 1903. Henry moved his family to town, renting the Killen property in the north part of town. Henry advertised, "When in New Richmond, put your horse at Henry Long's Livery Barn, near the DEPT. Your buggy kept in the dry when it rains, and in the shade when the suns shines. If you want a first class livery rig to drive, you can get it here–all new rigs–and first class drivers."

Dr. Jasper Clough, a veterinary surgeon from Veedersburg, came to Henry Long's livery in New Richmond on Friday and Saturday of each week to treat livestock. Clough was a former Bristle Ridge and New Richmond resident, and treated livestock from 1903 to 1906 in Henry's stable. The last record I have of Henry Long's Livery was September 20, 1906.

Boswell Clough had moved his old livery barn, which stood on Wabash Street, to the west part of town, and connected it to another good sized barn, and was in the livery business again a few years later.

Fire destroyed Boswell Clough's huge livery barn, but the date of the fire is unknown. Mrs. Hugh Roark reported the fire to the telephone central, who sounded the fire alarm. Mrs. Roark was awakened by the light from the blaze shining through her window. The whole west end of the barn was in flames before the fire department arrived on the scene. There was no livestock in the building at the time, but Clough lost a buggy, hunting wagon, and harness. Allen Lewis's buggy and Sam L. Bayliss' big Automobile truck were destroyed. George Bunnel had recently rented the barn and stored two large wagon loads of hay in it. The fire was blamed on tramps who had gone there to sleep, but it may have been the hay that set the fire.

Flaugher & Son had a livery in New Richmond in 1916, advertising horse breeding. He kept registered Percherons, and a Jack in his livery for breeding purposes.

Samuel E. Magruder made the transition from the horse and buggy days with the following advertisement: "S.E. Magruder, proprietor of the Livery and Feed Stable, New Richmond, Ind. AUTOMOBILE FOR LIVERY, with good, careful and competent chauffeur. FIRST CLASS RIGS"

Sam advertised the above from 1910 to 1919. F. M. Monroe, a veterinary surgeon, had his office in Magruder's Livery barn in 1919. Will Peek was his hostler, at one time.

HORSES, HORSE BREEDERS, TRAINERS, RACES, SHOWS, ETC.

BILLY IS DEAD

"It's only a horse," some folks would say,

But when they took old Billy away,
It touched a spot right near the heart,
And for us, at least, it's sad to part
With dear old Billy.
For eighteen years, blow high, blow low,
In summer, winter, rain or snow,
He had never failed to do his best.
How many of us can stand that test.
Like dear old Billy?
He has done all this for little–say,
A stall, some corn and oats and hay.
And now he's gone, we don't know where,
But if there's an animal heaven,
Old Billy is there!

Billy the old gray pony belonged to Mrs. J.S. Vaughan, and made daily trips to town for the Wallace family, earning a spot in the New Richmond *Record* for his obituary. Billy had been a member of the Wallace stables since 1888, and died at the ripe old age of 26 years. He had been driven so long by the family that his faithfulness found for him a tender spot in their hearts. For years Uncle Barney Wallace, in his declining health, made daily, twice, or oftimes, thrice daily trips to town behind "Billy," and after Mrs. Wallace's death the family continued to use him as the family driving horse. Barney Wallace was a brick layer in New Richmond, who built many of the early brick structures, and laid the brick sidewalks in the town, some of which are still in evidence.

Living on the edge of the Shawnee Prairie (also known as the Nine Mile Prairie) in Coal Creek Township offered many advantages to the early settlers. Most important to the subject I now write was the native bluegrass, much of which was left undisturbed for many years after the white man entered the area. The prairie was a haven for horse breeders and other stock men, who grazed the stock on the tall, waving grasses, and watered the same at the many natural, spring-fed ponds near New Richmond. Because of these important factors, the horse rustlers, or thieves, selected this area, realizing the healthy livestock would bring them a large sum of money without having to work too hard. The local farmers lost so many horses they were unable to carry on their farming, hence, the birth of the Council Grove Horse Thief Detective Association, in the early 1840s, the first association of its kind in the country (see Chapter 19).

The early newspapers in Crawfordsville failed to record the early horse breeders and stock farms in the county, but a number of items in the later issues listed a few. The limited records include the following horse breeders, and traders.

The most noted horsemen of the New Richmond area were the Clough brothers, Jasper and Boswell, or "Bod." Jasper became a very well-known veterinarian, and was listed as such in the 1874 directory of the county. His residence was located two and one half miles southwest of town, but much of his time was spent in the local livery stables. I failed to locate a record of his veterinary schooling, but he was listed as a veterinary surgeon, practiced this profession many years, and was considered to be among the best in the state. Boswell Clough, brother to Jasper, also was born with the natural horse sense needed to raise and train horses properly.

Many stories were related concerning Boswell Clough's livery barn in New Richmond, and of his love of horses. Clough's first livery barn was near the Black Bear Hotel on South Wabash Street, but in later years, he was located on west Washington Street at the rear of the late Mae Fowler's residence. Clough raised some of the finest horses in the area, and treated them with tender, loving care. One New Richmond resident said Clough sold a fine stallion to a man in Lafayette, and while visiting the city one day, heard a horse nicker, and turning around, he saw a familiar horse—the horse he had sold a while back. It brought tears to Clough's eyes to think the horse remembered him. Another fine steed of Clough's was trained (he claimed) to locate coveys of quail. Clough rode his horse up and down the corn rows, and the horse threw up his head, or nickered, upon finding a covey. Clough would then signal the hunters to come to that spot to hunt. (I would like to note at this point, most horses would be a little startled upon the sudden flight of a covey of quail, but it does make a good horse story).

Clough entered his fine horses and mules in the nearby fairs and usually captured first or second premiums on his stock. Some of their names were: Abe Lincoln, Jr. (a jack), Billy Morgan, Robin, Billy Burns, Judge Mohawk, and others.

When Clough reached the age where his thoughts turned to making some final arrangements for his family and for himself, his last request was to have the New Richmond band play "The Old Grey Mare Ain't What She Used To Be" at his funeral. The request was honored, and Clough's casket was placed on a horse drawn cart followed by the New Richmond band, and the whole town of New Richmond walked to the New Richmond cemetery.

Other horse traders and breeders are listed below with some recorded dates and information: Will Clawson (located three miles southeast of New Richmond) 1909; Flaugher & Son, 1916, raised Percherons; Mart C. Graves, German Coach horses, Morgans, Percherons and mules. His advertisements appeared from 1902 to 1909, and included Hunold, an imported German Coach horse; Amero, a draft horse; Colonel Margrove; Axtell, and Jack Beauty, a large Spanish Jack; Orion, a coach stallion, the only government approved, stamped, licensed stallion in the county, Mart claimed. Aleck W. Hempleman raised and bred Hambletonian horses, 1904-5; Joseph Humbert raised coach horses, Belgians, and Morgans, 1905-7; Quin Kirkpatrick offered draft and coach horses, 1905. Thomas Foster was a horse trader in 1887.

Samuel S. (S.S.) Kirkpatrick of the Maple Shade Stock Farm, just north of New Richmond, raised Percherons and Standard bred draft horses, 1896-1909. Kirkpatrick was a member of the Horse Breeders Association of Montgomery and Tippecanoe Counties. In March of 1896, the following officers were elected to this association: Henry Leaming of Romney, President; W.C. Davidson of Sugar Grove, Vice President; S.S. Kirkpatrick, Secretary; Orlando W. Mason, Treasurer; and L.W. Cochran of Linden, Superintendent. There were about twenty stockholders in the association at the time, which included farmers and businessmen. The members were planning to import some fine English and Hackneys and introduce them to the area at that time.

Other horse breeders and traders were: Allie Lewis, 1906; Henry Long, 1906; George E. Marsteller, 1905; Sam E. Magruder, Morgans, 1905; D.C. Miller, 1905; Elias Ray—one of Ray's stallions, Bourbon J. brought $875, a trotting horse, brought $875, and two other stallions brought $350 each, during one of the largest auctions this section of the state ever held in 1910, with proceeds amounting to nearly $20,000. This was quite a large sum of money back then.

A.D. Snyder sold a horse to D.P. Simison for $390 in 1906, but unfortunately this fine animal wandered onto the Clover Leaf railroad track and was killed by a train. Snyder erected a large sale barn on his property in New Richmond and held regular auctions. His sale barn was located on the southeast corner of Detchon and Franklin Streets. Snyder was to have several of his fine stallions on exhibition in his barn on horse show day, Saturday, May 24, 1902. The horses were not to be entered in the show ring, but interested parties were allowed to see them in his barn. The latest horse breeder in the New Richmond area, was Monte Hicks, who offered his registered Paint horse for breeding purposes in 1983. Charles Swick and Son were to sell at auction a carload of Nebraska horses in August, 1908. These are the only available records of the horse traders, and breeders I have at this time.

There were a few amusing stories of unhappy deals concerning horse trading but two gentlemen from the Coal Creek Valleys, Cliff Dazey and Park Whites, traded horses one Saturday in January, 1904, and both gentlemen claimed to get the best of the deal—this was very unusual. One horse was traded by George Widner for eighty acres of land in Kansas—that must have been a good horse.

Horse Trainers

Almost every farmer who worked with horses was qualified as a horse trainer, but there were a few exceptions, therefore, horse trainers have always been active in Coal Creek Township. Among the trainers were: Evan (E.J.) Weyles, who offered to break colts for saddlers in 1916. Don Taylor was widely known at the horse racing tracks. He owned several trotters, training them on his farm south of New Richmond. He owned two famous horses, Taylor's Song–a two and three year old state champion in 1956-57, and a world champion pacer, Bye Bye Byrd, in 1958-59. His sons, Dick and Jim, are also harness racing enthusiasts. Don was a member of the U.S. Trotter's Association, and was a director of the Indiana Trotters and Pacers Association at one time.

Don Taylor's brother, Charles B. Taylor, also was active in the American Horse Show Association, serving as an announcer, and hunter-jumper in several horse shows in Georgia. Both men are now deceased.

Jack Lidester advertised, "Horse training, cutting and pleasure reining" in the late 1970s near New Richmond. Jack had the honor of riding his quarter horse for a reenactment of the pony express ride from Wingate to New Richmond, and back again for the 150th celebration of Wingate. He mounted his horse at the Wingate Post Office with his saddlebags filled with mail stamped with a special pony express stamp, riding cross-country to New Richmond. The round trip took one hour and eleven minutes. The events took place Saturday, June 5, 1982.

WILD WEST PARK

Early New Richmond gentlemen often boasted of their fine thoroughbred horses, and there were many occasions offered to prove just who owned the best, or the speediest steed. Spontaneous horse races often occurred on the streets of New Richmond. One such race occurred between Amos Humbert and James Ward, who raced their horse and buggies from the center of town to the east end. One of the buggies collided with a parked buggy, destroying the parked vehicle. The boys were charged with fast driving, and the incident cost the boys $9.50 each in "Squire Ebrite's Court." Another four-heat road race took place just west of town in 1916 between two well-matched road horses. Several admirers of a good horse watched this event with excited hearts.

One of the early horse shows in New Richmond was recorded in September of 1881, in the form of a "Colt Show." Bluford Clough (brother of Boswell and Jasper) offered premiums of $5, $3, and $2, for three of the best colts from his horse, Morgan. James A. McClure took first; Nat Hamilton, second, and Sam McGruder, third. Another gentleman, William Burris, also offered premiums of $10, $6, and $4, for three best colts from his Norman horse, and the winners were Newt Cowan, first; John Hiatt, second, and Harris Reynolds, third.

In June, 1890, the town of New Richmond was filled with about 3,000 horse show enthusiasts. Many of those attending were from the nearby towns, and Crawfordsville. Because of this large crowd interested in horse shows, Dr. Jasper Clough, the local veterinarian, saw the opportunity of a new business venture, and by September, 1891, he had a new race track almost completed. The track was located one-fourth mile south of New Richmond on Dr. Clough's farm, and was owned and controlled by him. This was a half-mile track and was considered in first class condition. Dr. Clough noted a purse was to be offered for the first and second best horses in a trotting, pacing, and running race at the new Wild West Park.

Saturday, September 26, 1891, was the date set for the first horse races in the Wild West Park. Charley Pittenger, of Elmdale, carried off $8 with his trotting colts at this race. Two weeks later, Samuel Kincaid's two-year-old trotter, Flory K., was the best of the day, making a mile in three minutes. She ran against two four-year-olds. Sam was offered $500 for her after the race, but turned it down.

A year later, on July 4, 1892, a big horse show was planned, and premiums were offered in all classes: trotting, pacing, and running. Prizes were offered for the best road team, best road horse, or mare single, and best pony, horse, or mare–and these were to be driven by a lady. In August, the same year, the Wild West Park was offering many great attractions, including horse and bicycle races

Dr. Jasper Clough's race track was considered a huge success, and in June 1893, the attendance was quite large for a small town race track during one of the horse shows. Many Crawfordsville horse racing enthusiasts attended the track, and a Kirkpatrick resident noted, "several of our people took in the horse show at New Richmond–or rather, the show took them in if reports are true. Boswell Clough, the saloon man, tapped an eight gallon jug every fifteen minutes, we are informed." Clough didn't want the folks to get thirsty during the show.

New Richmond's 7th Grand Annual Horse Show date was to be May 22, 1897. The classes, and premiums for the show were mentioned throughout the New Richmond *Enterprise*, Friday, May 28, 1897. Horsemen from New Market, Crawfordsville, Mellott, Waynetown, Hillsboro, Newtown, Wingate, Linden, Darlington, and Kirkpatrick were all on hand with good stock and carried away most of the premiums at this show.

In May 1902, all persons in New Richmond and the outlying area, were to set aside their worldly cares and enjoy a day of pleasure by attending the Annual Horse Show in New Richmond. The show had grown to include a merry-go-round, along with the horse races and show. The evening hours were to be filled by attending the Grand Ball in Hollin's Hall, the local opera house.

Prize winners were listed in the New Richmond *Record*, June 28, 1903 for the horse show, but the list is too long to include in this article. In 1905, the horse show was to be held in New Richmond on Saturday, June 24th. The event was organized by the Horse Show Association of New Richmond who promised a day better and bigger than ever before, with good cash premiums, a parachute leap from the heavens, and a balloon ascension to occur at 4:30 p.m. from Madison street near Westfall's blacksmith shop. Other attractions were sack races, foot race, greased pole, shows under tents, and music by the eighteen-piece Coal Creek Band. Automobile owners mutually agreed not to run their vehicles on the streets, to prevent scaring the horses.

The town trustees worked with the association to make this year's horse show a success. More than 300 loads of gravel were hauled onto the streets in town to put them in good condition. New Richmond always had a problem with muddy streets in her early days. Marshall Works was overseer of the local men who worked out their taxes by hauling and spreading gravel on the streets. The Horse Show Association elected George F. Long, President; and Edgar Walts, Secretary, that year. They announced a total of 174 entries in this show.

Horse shows continued into the 1920s and 1930s. The New Richmond Horse Show Association met with the local town trustees to work out the details of horse show day in August of 1935. Wabash street was to be closed in order to provide spaces for stands, as the Association was granted the right to sell stand rights and collect donations to meet the expense of the band.

Interest in the local horse shows had dwindled a few years after this, but in August, 1944, the local Lion's Club rekindled the fire in the horsemen in town. A race track was built on O.G. Hershberger's farm bordering the south end of New Richmond, on south Wabash Street. This club may have sponsored later shows, but in 1947 they announced their Third Annual Horse Show was to be held in August. Bleachers were erected on the Hershberger race track, and premiums were offered for the various classes of ponies, Western stock pleasure and parade horses, a mule race, Palominos, Hacknies, Tennessee Walking horses, and many others.

LIVESTOCK BUYERS AND SHIPPERS

Early farmers and cattlemen in the New Richmond area drove their livestock on foot to the markets in Lafayette, Chicago, Indianapolis, or Cincinnati, before the railroads crossed the state of Indiana. The railroad through Linden was a great improvement, but the little yard-wide into New Richmond was more convenient. After the railroad was changed to the standard gauge, buying and shipping of livestock began in earnest, and New Richmond was becoming noted as a shipping center of considerable importance. Livestock still had to be driven into the local stockyard, however, and the town residents soon became accustomed to the continuous noises from squealing hogs, and the mooing of cattle awaiting the cars to be shipped to the markets. Occasionally, outsiders brought their livestock to the markets in New Richmond. One weekend in August 1890, a Texas cowboy and his son appeared in town with seventy head of nice ponies for sale. They offered their stock to the local market at a much lower price compared to the usual price at the time, and undoubtedly had all the ponies sold before they left town. The ponies had been driven all the way from Texas to New Richmond. Cattle, sheep, and hogs were the principal stock bought and sold in the New Richmond area at that time.

Among the buyers and shippers of livestock in the town of New Richmond in 1888 were Jim Kincaid, Curtis D. Haywood, Dave Trout, and George Clough. They shipped the stock, mainly to Indianapolis, Chicago, and to Buffalo, New York, during this period of time.

Blaine A. Archey bought and sold livestock around 1891 to 1894, making trips to Omaha, Nebraska—as well as the before-mentioned shipping centers. Mart Lucas bought and shipped stock in 1891.

Albert D. Snyder and Dave Trout formed a partnership for buying and shipping livestock in March of 1890, although Snyder had been in this line of work before that time, driving his stock on foot to the railroad stock pens in Linden. After the railroad came into New Richmond he shipped on the new route. George W. Washburn gave Snyder quite a lot of trade with the cattle he fattened.

In 1905, Snyder leased a parcel of ground from the Union Elevator company and erected stock pens with a loading chute. These pens were built between the elevator and the Big Four Lumber Company, which stood south of the railroad, and west of the elevator on south Wabash Street. The railroad company made no effort to construct new pens after they were asked to dismantle the old pens they built when the railroad first came to town in 1881 and 1882. They had become a nuisance because they were placed too close to the residences, and they were not kept in clean and sanitary condition. The railroad company was a little miffed about the complaints. Snyder's pens were a great convenience to the farmers and stock men in the area. Snyder also built a large barn that was used as a sale barn for several years. It stood back of his residence on Detchon and Franklin Street. This was a very lively place on sale day, which usually occurred on Saturdays.

J. A. Lamson was a stock buyer and shipper in New Richmond from 1903 to 1908. Lamson first worked for A.D. Snyder, then joined Joe Bridge of Attica in the shipping trade–Lamson was in charge of the shipping from New Richmond. Lamson joined forces with G.A. Pence of New Richmond a year later, and they constructed stock pens under a roof in the west end of the old canning factory building. The town health officer was to inspect the pens regularly to see that they were kept in sanitary condition.

G.A. (Alpha) Pence of New Richmond was associated with J. A. Lamson in 1906, then joined forces with two Wingate stock dealers, Grennard and Crain (also spelled Crane). These three men bought A.D. Snyder's stock business and operated under the name of Grennard, Crain & Pence. Pence had been in the stock trade eight years at the time his company shipped a large shipment of cattle for George W. Washburn to Chicago. His cattle attracted much attention, bringing an average of $86.58 per head, which was quite a large sum back then.

Boswell Clough, brother of George, was listed as a stock dealer in 1912, and J.W. Timmons and Dayton Westfall were buyers and shippers of livestock in 1916.

W.W. "Wint" Washburn, son of George W. Washburn, purchased forty-two head of Scotch Shorthorn Cattle for his Villa Grove Stock Farm in 1914, and raised this breed of cattle several years. Harry Ackerman was the manager of Villa Grove, locate about two miles south of town, and was in charge of choice Shorthorns when they were shown at the International Stock Show in Chicago in 1916. "Wint" brought home several premiums from the state fair the year before for his Shorthorns. The Washburns were noted for their fine stock for many years.

One of the early stockmen in the New Richmond area was Ed T. McCrea. He was the first man in Montgomery County to raise Polangus Black cattle, and became widely known for his superior grade of cattle, finding a very ready market for this breed.

There were very few farms without cattle and hogs up to the 1940s, but the situation is now reversed—you very seldom see a farm that is fenced, having cattle or other livestock grazing in the pasture, or in the cornfields after the fields have been harvested. The stock pens were dismantled in New Richmond in the 1950s

DRAYMEN—TEAMSTERS—TRUCKERS

The following list of draymen, teamsters, and trucking companies was compiled from county directories, telephone directories, and advertisements in the New Richmond High School class plays:

1895   Thomas Bastian, Teamster; Henry Ross, Drayman.

1903   Winton S. Alexander, Drayman (also listed in 1912); William Livingston, Teamster; John Work was also a drayman from 1900 to the early 1920s.

1907-08   Garrett Bastion, Teamster; Adson Hayworth, Teamster

1920   Burnett & Son, Trucking Company, New Richmond, under contract with the Red Ball Transit Co. in Indianapolis

1921   Carl Burnett Trucking Co.

1923   New Richmond Transfer Co. Clifford Oswalt, Prop.

1932   Raymond Rice General Trucking Livestock, James Parker, driver

1934-36   Jake Austin Trucking Co.

1934-41   Dresden Todd Trucking Co. General Hauling Livestock

1934   J. M. Graham Trucking Co. General Hauling

1935-36   Forrest Patton Trucking

1935-44   J. M. (Milford) Stephenson Trucking Co. General Hauling (Buhner's Feed & Fertilizer)

1938   Stephenson & Haire (Sam Haire was associated with Stephenson in 1938)

1940-70s   Everett Pierce Trucking Co. General Trucking

1941-60s   Dick Thayer, General Trucking

1947   Cox & Snellenbarger Trucking Co. Gravel Hauling

1949   Sam Haire, General Trucking

1950-60s   John Swick, General Trucking

1960-79   Goff Livestock Trucking, Paul R. Goff.

1963   Glenn Pierce, Trucking

1970s   Linton & Sons Trucking Co.

1979-83   Kelp Bros. Trucking Co. (Bobby & Dennis) Hauling grain liquid fertilizer produce Interstate Transporting available.

1980-83   Charles Sturgeon Trucking Co.

POULTRY DEALERS

George Steele, was listed as a poultry dealer in New Richmond in the Crawfordsville Weekly *Review* from July 5, 1884 to April 11, 1891.

The *Record*, April 17, 1902, reported "a new poultry firm was the newest addition to New Richmond's business circle, the new firm starting up last week on the BUNNEL property, and as all great successes have small beginnings, the new enterprise has assured success before it, the beginning of their business being a borrowed old setting hen which they set upon fifteen eggs furnished by a party outside the syndicate. The name of the corporated firm is, JOHNSON, TAYLOR, KIMBAL COMPANY."

The 1903 county directory listed Winton C. Taylor, "Poultry Fancier."

The New Richmond *Record*, April 9, 1903 listed "Barred Plymouth Rock eggs for sale, 50 cents per setting of fifteen, Rev. George W. Watkins." Also in the same newspaper on April 16, same year, was J.W. Thomas of J.H. Fear & Co. of Frankfort opened up a branch of their poultry business at this place. Their office was located in George W. Washburn's frame building (they had moved to Wingate by June 4, 1903).

Mrs. Allen Lewis, 1.75 miles northwest of New Richmond, offered "Barred Plymouth Rocks" for sale in October 1905.

C. E. Kelsey, Poultry Dealer, offered "Buff Orpingtons" the new variety of chickens, beautiful birds, buff in color, good stocky body, splendid layers, good mothers, legs clean and free from feathers," in the October 11, 1906 *Record*.

The New Richmond *Record*, April 15, 1909 listed "Thorough bred 'White Plymouth Rocks' eggs, U. R. Fishel Straint, setting of eighteen for $1. Mrs. Henrietta J. Raub. The same issue listed "Rose Comb Rhode Island Reds the hens that lay are the hens that pay. The Reds are layers. Eggs for hatching, fifteen for $1. William Kirkpatrick." (Kirkpatricks's advertisement appeared in the 1910-1911 New Richmond High School Annuals and in the 1912 M.E. Church cook book). In the same issue of the *Record* listed, "Pure Bred S. C. Brown Leghorn eggs, fifty cents per setting, special price on incubator settings" Mrs. Fred Clough. (call over Pyke or Elmdale phones).

PHILLIP DEWEY'S DEER AND ELK PARK

Around 1896, Phillip Dewey, son of one of Coal Creek Township's early settlers, decided to try something new and different in the area, and commenced building extra high fences on his farm. The town folks–and his country neighbors–began to ponder, and they were very curious as to why Dewey needed such a high fence–what unique breed of livestock could possibly jump ten feet in the air and clear a fence such as he was building in his wooded area? Phil Dewey's farm was located northeast of New Richmond, on what is now known as road 1100 north on a very high ridge that runs east and west.

The questions were soon answered. Dewey spent considerable money and purchased many deer and elk to stock his new park. The herd multiplied, and very soon the neighborhood was enjoying a new taste of meat on their dinner table

Around the first of December of 1902, Dewey killed a very fine specimen of elk for a Christmas feast. He had enough left to offer some for sale at Jones' Meat Market in New Richmond, during the Christmas season, at 20 and 25 cents per pound. The four year old elk was getting quite ferocious, and Dewey had to dispose of him before someone was injured by the animal.

According to an announcement made by Dewey just before Christmas the same year, a crowd of around 300 people–men, women and children, from New Richmond, Linden, Crawfordsville, and the surrounding area, went out to Phil Dewey's deer and

19 - Phillip Dewey's Deer and Elk Park

elk park to witness the shooting of another buck elk. Wint Washburn, an experienced marksman, was given the honor of shooting the animal, bringing him down on the first shot. The two elks killed, each weighed around 800 pounds on foot. D.M. Lucas, the butcher, had the job of preparing this elk, and the steaks were placed on sale at Jones' Meat Market at 25 cents per pound. This elk was considered a splendid specimen by those who witnessed this event.

James J. Insley of Crawfordsville took the antlers, which measured four and one half feet, and was to send them to a taxidermist at Lebanon for mounting. Insley represented the Elks Lodge at Crawfordsville who paid $50 for the antlers. Each of the two tusks were disposed of by Mr. Dewey for $15. One was to be sent to Indianapolis, the other one to Seattle, Washington.

Dewey's only remaining elk was one buck and two does after this four-year-old was killed. This elk, as the other one mentioned, had become very ferocious and had killed four deer that were confined in the same park.

20 - Phillip Dewey's Deer and Elk Park

Phillip Dewey's elk farm was quite an attraction for the young lads who resided in New Richmond, and he never objected to the boys going out to visit his deer park, but, sometimes the crowd of town boys got a little carried away and prowled about his barns and other buildings, and even chased his stock. They were disturbing another neighbor of his by chasing his flock of geese all over the country, and the two men decided it was time to call the town marshal. They threatened to have them hauled into "Squire Ebrite's court" for trespassing.

In August 1904, Dewey's elk herd consisted of four old elk, one buck, and three does. One young elk was about three weeks old, and other one was only three days old. I have no record of the length of time Dewey continued his deer and elk park, but several of the older citizens had fond memories of this unusual farm near New Richmond. There is another story of this park in the article of George R. Holmes of his and Forrest Waye's adventure in the Phillip Dewey Deer and Elk Park.

Farm Implement Dealers

When the first settlers arrived in Coal Creek Township, the only farm implements brought to the wilderness were those which were easily transported, such as the old wooden mold board plow, made entirely of wood except for the share; it was a very heavy farming tool to be crowded onto the wagons. A cradle scythe for harvesting the grain and hoes for mom, dad, and all the children to help with the cultivating were all necessary tools for the family to survive. Thomas Meharry brought the first reaper into Coal Creek Township in 1845. Cyrus McCormick delivered the reaper to Meharry's farm for $100, and it was hauled in sections in a wagon from Chicago. Corn was still planted and harvested by hand at this time.

In February of 1887, Frank Dewey opened the town's first farm implement store, selling mowers and reapers for an Indianapolis firm.

Tommie Patton from the Round Hill neighborhood contracted Thomas or "Barney" Wallace to lay the brick for a new building in March 1888. Patton was planning to sell all kinds of agriculture implements and save farmers a trip to Crawfordsville or Lafayette to buy machinery.

Horace G. Messer was in the implement business in town around 1902-3. After his death, Joseph Humbert purchased his interests in the firm of **Messer & Westfall** in March 1904. **Humbert & Westfall** was the name of the new firm in February 1905. Their store room was located in the former John E. Wilson's hardware. Joseph Humbert and Elisha Westfall were the proprietors of this concern. Humbert & Westfall erected a new thirty-by-forty-foot implement storeroom in March 1905. W.W. Harriman was contracted to build the structure, located just south of Westfall's blacksmith shop. They advertised ROCK ISLAND OHIO CASSADAY, full line of plows, cultivators, and OSBORNE harvesting machinery; and the GREAT WESTERN manure spreader.

In January of 1906, Lon Brown purchased the interests of Elisha Westfall. The new firm operated under the title of **Humbert & Brown, Farm Implements**. They advertised "F.A. AMES High Grade Genuine Split Hickory Buggies; WEBER wagons; CASSADAY gangs and sulkys; ROCK ISLAND HAY LOADERS, sulkys, gangs, and corn planters; OSBORNE BINDERS, standard binder twine mowers, hay rakes, disc and springtooth harrows; SMITH GREAT WESTERN manure spreaders—all goods were guaranteed.

Humbert & Brown had dissolved partnership by November of 1906, and Elisha Westfall moved his blacksmith shop into the Humbert & Brown implement storeroom.

L.P. Brown's Farm Implement & Buggies firm was advertised in the 1907-8 County directory, and the New Richmond High School annual, *Kole Kreke Kamera*, in 1910. The New Richmond *Record* of Thursday, January 25, 1912, advertised, "L.P. Brown, Implements, KEMP'S TWENTIETH CENTURY NO. 3 manure spreaders, for $110 with terms to suit purchasers." Brown purchased the hardware building (Snyder's in 1915) and combined the farm implements with his hardware stock. (see Hardware Section).

T.M. Layne purchased Boswell Clough's old saloon adjacent to the big hardware store for a display room for buggies, wagons and implements in January, 1906. He advertised, "HOOSIER double spreader– friction, or cog gear, end gate seeders; JOHN DEERE'S full line of implements–disc, spike harrows, edge drop corn planters, hammock and rider cultivators; sulky and gang plows–all steel, three section rollers; EASTERN MOLINE'S FULL LINE OF IMPLEMENTS ECONOMY DISC AND CUTAWAY Harrows; GRETCHEN corn planters; DUTCH UNCLE riding cultivators; new GOOD ENOUGH sulky plows; GLADIATOR steel frame stalk cutter; SYRACUSE sulky with jointer and rolling Colter, the best plow on earth, etc."

J.F. Teague & Sons sold hardware, furniture, and farm implements in New Richmond in 1912. (see hardware section for more).

HARNESS MAKERS AND HARNESS SHOPS

One of the most important craftsmen needed in the pioneer villages was the harness makers, although many farmers and early settlers were capable of making their own. W.J. and Keziah McComb King moved from Ohio to New Richmond at an early date, and W.J. established himself in the harness business in the town. W.J. King was still living in 1893 at the age of 104.

William Campbell advertised his harness shop for sale in January 1891, and made the comment, "there are too many harness shops in town." John Clark was mentioned as New Richmond's new harness maker, the same month and year. John made all his own goods and was working on some "fine" harness for the spring trade. P.J. Clark was still listed as a harness dealer in the town in 1895. In April 1891, Henry Wray was mentioned as a harness maker in the town, but was moving to Darlington to work in a harness shop. Tom Bergin also was mentioned as a successful harness maker in the town in the same issue of the Crawfordsville *Review*. The writer of the New Richmond items said Tom, a bachelor, would make a good catch for an old maid in June that year, as he fell heir to 160 acres of ground near Garden City, Kansas.

The local hardware dealers sold harness, buggies, wagons, etc., along with their hardware stock. L.P. Brown and J.F. Teague & Sons usually listed harnesses.

"Harness Willie" was possibly the harness maker in the town of New Richmond with the longest record. William H. Long's harness shop was located in a small frame building that stood next door north of the A.D. Snyder hardware building. As a matter of fact, Henry K. Lee, and Nannie, his wife, added a clause to the deed of the hardware building granting William H. Long the right to use the brick wall for a south wall of his building. The town hall stands on this property today. William H. Long advertised, "harness, robes, blankets, and whips. General repair work a specialty." He was listed in the County directories from 1900 up to 1912, and the New Richmond High School Annuals, 1910, 1911, and 1923. He entered the new era with the following advertisement in 1923, "William H. Long, Harness, Robes, Blankets, Whips, General repair work a specialty, and FIRESTONE TIRES & TUBES, FORD SIZES." Long was still in business in the 1930s.

William H. Long's death occurred in 1946 and he and his wife, Nina A., are buried in the New Richmond cemetery.

THRESHING MACHINES AND RINGS

Bill Campbell said in his early history of the town, "Solomon Kite was the first man to run a threshing machine in the vicinity of New Richmond." Bill failed to give the time period for this first however, making it impossible to argue or prove his statement.

In 1886 Mr. Smock's steam engine served a dual purpose as the power to his sawmill operation and as a threshing machine. In September that year he just finished threshing over thirty thousand bushels of grain after forty days on the job

Dr. Allen of the New Richmond vicinity purchased a new thresher in July 1887. There were four different threshing machines operating in the New Richmond vicinity the last of that month, and the whistles of the steam engines could all be heard at once in the little town. That same month, John Massing and Mr. Elmore's thresher caught on fire while the workers were eating their noonday dinner; the entire engine, one hundred twenty-five bushels of wheat, pitchforks, coats, and other equipment were all destroyed.

Most of the threshing was completed in this area by the last of August each year, but often conflicted with the annual "Old Settler's Meetings" held in Meharry's Grove west of town, where unusually large crowds gathered to honor the pioneers of Coal Creek Township and the neighboring settlements.

By 1903 the "old time threshing dinner" was thought to be a thing of the past; with the improvements of machinery, the harvest was being completed more rapidly. The average crop was threshed in about half a day and the proprietors of the threshing machines furnished board for their crew. It was feared the excitement that used to characterize "the rush for the first table" was being replaced by a "hunt for a shady place behind the straw stack." In the early days when the grain was harvested by hand, all the neighbors and friends for miles around were expected to help each other with the harvest. The ladies, young and old, cooked the meal—and they were huge meals—for the men in the fields. These bountiful threshing (or thrashing) dinners continued into the middle 1930s, but with a slight change. The neighborhood farmwives, daughters, and mothers were sharing the cooking with the local church women's groups to help support their churches. The men came in from the fields in the hottest summer days and consumed large quantities of meat and vegetables and topped it all off with a large piece of pie, cake, or other rich dessert, and many glasses of iced tea and lemonade were available to wash it all down. After a short rest, they were back in the fields.

My sister remembered helping serve dinners to the threshing crews in the New Richmond Christian Church, and thinking back to the meals, said the men would fill their plates several times, then top it off with a rich caramel pudding. She said it was surprising they never became ill after eating so many rich desserts on the hot July and August days. The young lads in town earned a nickel or two carrying drinking water to the threshers while in the fields. My brothers were some of these enterprising young men. I watched the threshing crews from an upstairs window as they worked in the field behind our home. When oats were threshed near town we had oats-bugs all over the place, wriggling their way through the screen wire on the windows and doors.

Among the owners of threshing machines and outfits were Jake Zerface; John "Jack" Foster and Ed Jones; S.M. Mick; Thomas W. Banta; Frank and Arthur Allman; and the Long brothers—Henry, Homer, Dan, and Frank, who purchased a new COLEAN threshing machine in June 1906, operating two crews that year. While Homer was helping Dan and Frank move a threshing separator from the shed one day, his arm was caught between the machine and the side of the shed, cutting a large gash in his wrist and breaking a bone in his arm. His brother Frank, in his fright, lifted the heavy machine off Homer's arm and set him free. He was quickly rushed to Dr. Biedenkopf who stitched the wound and placed the broken arm in splints.

Settling up with the farmers was done at the end of the season. The following item paints a clear picture of the "Threshing Ring Feasts" held in August 1906.

> Threshing Ring No. 2, southeast of town, met Monday night at J. C. Henderson's for the purpose of settling up. All members and their families were present. The men furnished the [ice] cream and the women the cakes, and there was a jolly good time for all. Some of the best cakes one ever ate were there, many thanks for our good cooks.
>
> The ring settled up to a cent, everybody was well pleased with the work, and all think this is the only way to get the threshing done. Frank Allman did our threshing and we are all well pleased with his work. He did us good work and we have hired him for next year. The count of bushels of grain in the ring is as follows: Wheat, 3,477; Oats, 12,110; Total 15,587. We charge 8 cents a hundred for oats and 12 cents a hundred for wheat. This might sound cheap, but we average $1.70 per day. Our best yield in oats was 52-1/2 bushels per acre, and in wheat 35 bushels. The meeting adjourned at 10:30 to meet again sometime in 1907.
> J. C. Henderson, President; W. M. Clawson, Secretary and Treasure.

Two other rings recorded their settling up feasts the same year, one in the Round Hill area and one north of town. The northern Coal Creek ring reported, "Nine farmers just north of town who composed a threshing ring and their families held a 'settling up meeting and social' at the home of Mrs. Martha Miller on Saturday evening. Ice cream and cake were served and a general good time was enjoyed. The ring, too, were well satisfied with the season's work and voted Frank and Arthur Allman as 'number one threshing machine men.'"

Round Hill's ring reported, "The seventeen farmers, composing the Round Hill Threshing Rings and their families, held an ice cream supper at the Round Hill school house Saturday night and a big time was enjoyed by the sixty to seventy persons present. The ring met Tuesday night and made settlement for the year."

John Miller's account book revealed the following information during a threshing ring meeting held August 6, 1936. John Frey was elected president, John Miller, secretary. They voted to ask the threshermen to furnish their own breakfast and supper (except two men for breakfast). They stated the following threshing rates: Rye 5-1/2 cents; wheat 4-1/2 cents; oats 2-1/2 cents. Settling rate, Rye and wheat, 16 cents; oats 7 cents. This ring started threshing oats with Otto Jones on July 20 and finished on August 2 that year.

The Pierce family of Round Hill were the proprietors of two or three threshing outfits for many years. Henry and Virgil Pierce asked permission to use New Richmond's water supply to fill their threshing machines. They paid $5 for the entire threshing season in the summer of 1934, and $2 in 1937.

Other owners of threshing machines were Biff Dazey, who resided southwest of New Richmond, and John D. Merrill and his sons Avery C., Hugo, Ruben, and Ansel. The Merrill family operated one of the larger threshing rings in Coal Creek Township for many years.

Several of the men from the threshing crews went on to the Dakotas and other western and northwestern states after the harvest was completed in this area, to work in the fields. Those mentioned in the local newspaper during the period 1906 to 1916 were: Floyd Snyder, Frank Lee, Frank Long, Ed Ellis, Wallace White, Charles Reed, Lawrence McLain, Will Kincaid, Will Sandilands, Will Jones, David Holmes, Harry Magruder, Charles Wilson, Ernest Patton, Anson Thomas, Paul Mason, and Edd Magruder.

After World War II, the steam powered threshing machines were replaced by combines pulled by the new models of John Deere or Ford tractors. The new equipment made the harvest easier on the farmers, but put an end to a yearly tradition of fun, hard work, and social gatherings for the farmer's wife and children.

GRIST MILLS AND ELEVATORS

Early in the history of Montgomery County, when the first settlers had finally cleared enough land to raise enough grain for their own needs and had begun to expand their fields to grow a little extra, the problem of where to market this grain arose. Early residents had to load the grain into bags and onto their farm wagons, and haul it to Indianapolis or to Terre Haute. An early history of Coal Creek Township entitled "Bos-Ting" printed in the Crawfordsville Weekly *Review*, July 7, 1881 says, "Simeon Grenard, age 57 years, born in Kentucky, but came to this State when quite small, made his start in this world's goods with a dog and sled, and in the winter would harness his dog to the sled and with a grist of corn would go five or six miles to mill. A good trader, he soon became rich, etc."

Hauling the grain was a time-consuming task, and was very tiring for the people who had to make these long trips. Mills were soon erected in and around the Crawfordsville area. This made things better for those living close by, but it still was an inconvenience for the farmers living in the northern part of the county—New Richmond, Pleasant Hill (now Wingate), and Linden.

The first mill on record in the New Richmond area was found on an abstract of my property and a lot north of the railroad, formerly owned by the town of New Richmond. This was a transaction of a 360-

acre tract of Christopher J. Oppy's, deeding part of his land to his sons, Thomas F. and Edward T., on November 20, 1879. It gives the description as the N.E. 1/4 of Sec. 9, Twp. 20 N. Range 5 W., "except" two acres out of the northeast corner of said N.E. 1/4 of S.E. 1/4 for "Mill Purposes." The grantor, C. J. Oppy, "reserves the right of possession and the rents and profits of said real estate until grantees arrive at the age of 21." An early history says this mill was constructed in 1871, ran a few years and was torn down. A deed on the same property dated August 20, 1880 (consideration $650), Christopher J. Oppy to James H. Smock, the un-divided half of a two acre plot and one-half (1/2) the fixtures now in the flouring mill situated on said land. This indicates Oppy and Smock were partners in the mill. Mr. Smock was also New Richmond's first owner of a sawmill.

The Montgomery County directory, 1882-83 lists two flour mills: Logan and Swank's, and Samuel R. Tribby's. An item in the Crawfordsville *Review*, January 21, 1882, mentioned the town of New Richmond was to have another grain "warehouse" to be started by W.B. Montgomery. Montgomery had been in the grain business in Linden and was doing a good business there, but wanted to expand.

In New Richmond, G. S. Bruil was listed as a grain and coal merchant between the years 1884 and 1887. In this same period of time George Breed was listed as a grain merchant. Mr. Breed was plagued with machinery breakdowns, his corn sheller was in need of constant repairs, and the storage facility gave way and let large amounts of grain down to the second floor. He soon made the necessary repairs and continued to do business for a while, but finally gave it up and sold his warehouse and the grain therein, in June 1887.

Since New Richmond did not have an adequate water source for powering mills, the early mills might have been powered by horses. After 1860, steam engines were popular power sources for flour and saw mills.

Kirkpatrick Elevator

Charles Kirkpatrick, after graduating from DePauw University at Greencastle, Indiana, in 1886, struck out on his first business venture that was the purchase of an old warehouse or elevator at New Richmond. The first thing he did was to tear down the old building and began to erect a new and larger facility. The old building was too small for the large amount of grain now coming into the New Richmond markets. The railroad had been completed in 1881 through the town, and made the shipping of grain a very new and prosperous business to get into—that is if the right facilities could be made available. Kirkpatrick was going to do just that by erecting a first-class elevator.

By December 1888, Kirkpatrick's new elevator was being built with the capacity to handle a large amount of grain. The local merchants were afraid the town had already lost its chance for a large market to the neighboring towns of Linden and Whitlock (as Pleasant Hill was called at this time), but Mr. Kirkpatrick was doing a very good business in a short time and had the bills for freight, paid to the railroad company, to show for it. In two years he had paid $7,500. I suppose this is a small amount compared to the freight bills today, but it seemed quite large at the time. Kirkpatrick dug a large hole in the ground to burn the cobs and the flames "lit up the village like a natural gas town." He also purchased the latest machinery for manufacturing cornmeal to be placed in the elevator. This machinery was purchased in the east—he was going to furnish his patrons with the best meal in the market. Charley was so proud of his cornmeal, which was white as flour, he sent Henry Groves with samples to all the towns west of New Richmond, but restricting him to Indiana, and had him make "JOHNNY CAKES" to show just how good the meal would make up. I suppose he even furnished the butter and molasses to sop them in. This elevator flourished into January of 1890 and soon after he sold his elevator to John W. McCardle, so an early historian says. After a very careful search, the abstract does not show the purchase date, but does show a transaction of John W. McCardle to A.E. Malsbary later on. By October 1891 Kirkpatrick, "once our grain man", was now in the real estate business at Greensburg, Indiana.

McCardle Elevator

Under the New Richmond items in the Crawfordsville Weekly *Review*, March 8, 1890 has, "Our town suffered a great loss Saturday night, the elevator was consumed by fire. It was erected at a cost of $8,000 to accommodate the country for miles around. Mr. McCardle, the proprietor will certainly rebuild." Mr. McCardle's elevator at Wingate was also destroyed by fire in the same month and year. No record of the construction of a new elevator was found, but in April and May of 1892 the *Review* mentioned "J.W. McCardle, our popular and genial grain dealer had made a flying trip to Chicago," and he is listed in the advertisements and county directory as proprietor of the New Richmond elevator and as a grain dealer.

McCardle's elevator must have been a successful operation, because in 1902 he closed down the elevator for extensive repairs. The top of the structure was torn away and remodeled, and he equipped and enlarged the structure so it would be the best elevator in Western Indiana. He added a new tin roof over the scales and the office and gave the office a new coat of paint. John McCardle's son, Clyde A., worked with his father at the elevator and Bert Page, the engineer, kept the machinery running better than anyone had ever kept things going in the grain business, so reported the early residents.

In July 1905 the McCardle elevator in New Richmond was sold to Alfred E. Malsbary, who was to take possession on September the first. The structure sold for $19,000. Mr. Malsbary was operating a grain elevator at Francesville belonging to the Crabb-Reynolds-Taylor Company at the time of the purchase, and local people were at first led to believe Malsbary was representing that company, but it was discovered he had severed ties with that company upon purchasing the McCardle elevator.

A. E. Malsbary sold this elevator in August 1909 to Haywood and Detchon. This left the elevator business in New Richmond entirely in the control of these two men, as Haywood and Detchon were running the Union Elevator, as well. Malsbary assumed control of the big elevator at Remington and moved his family there.

W. R. Turvey was listed as the proprietor of a feed mill in the town of New Richmond in the 1895 Directory of Montgomery County, but there is no other information on this mill.

John McCardle purchased the old Turvey feed mill building in 1898 and tore it down. He used the lumber for a "suit of rooms" on the lot just south of the hotel.

Union Elevator

A group of farmers discussed, planned, and held many meetings, and finally, after many obstacles to overcome, the New Union Elevator for New Richmond was made a certainty. It was launched into existence at a meeting of the stockholders, held in Hollin's Hall, on the 2nd of April 1903. A Mr. McMillin had drafted plans and specifications of the proposed new structure and presented them to the group at this meeting. The meeting was called to start the payment of the subscribed shares of stock and to see if figures met the approval

21 - Union Elevator (also known as Haywood & Detchon, Furr & Cohee, and Farm Bureau Elevators)

of such stockholders. Mr. McMillin, the representative of the Reliance Manufacturing Company of Indianapolis, was the lowest bidder and was given the contract. The contract was to the effect that the building with the required machinery was to be in position, and with office and scales constructed, and all ready for business, by June 15, 1903. The contract price was an even $10,000.

The elevator business was now big business and the new elevator was a regular sky-scraper, being about 85 feet high with a guaranteed capacity of 45,000 bushels. Besides the main building there was a completely isolated brick engine room which reduced the danger of fire. The elevator was equipped with the latest improved machinery all the way through with a complete feed mill fitted to do all kinds of grinding, and the best "Marseilles Sheller" a machine so constructed that the worst break that might possibly occur could be repaired in eighteen minutes, as claimed by the manufacturers. The power was furnished by a new 50 horse-power "Atlas" engine and a 60 horse-power boiler.

This new elevator was built on the east end of the New Richmond Canning factory lot, south of and parallel to the Clover Leaf Railroad switch. The driveway was running east and west. The office was built near the street, facing south, and the scales were the best "Fairbanks" 22-foot scales, sufficient to weigh both wagon and team.

The Union Elevator Company was the style of the new firm doing business in New Richmond and was an incorporated company. The officers were Ed. T. McCrea, president; J. T. Detchon, secretary; and Charles Haywood, treasurer. The other two members of the board of directors were Stephen J. Beaver and Bayless Alexander.

The Articles of Incorporation, dated March 10, 1903, can be found in *Miscellaneous Record 7*, page 81 and reads:

> The Union Elevator Co., to The Record. We, the undersigned, incorporators desire to form a company for the purpose of constructing, maintaining and operating a grain elevator and of transacting the business incident to such company, which is to include buying and selling grain of all kinds and of grinding meal and feed of all kinds, and of buying and selling such feed.
>
> That the corporate name adopted by such company is THE UNION ELEVATOR COMPANY, the amount of the capital stock is $10,000.00 divided into shares of $100.00 each. That the term of existence of this company is 25 years. That the number of the directors shall be 5, who shall manage the affairs of the company for the first year, and their names are as follows: Albert D. Snyder, John T. Detchon, Charles Haywood, Stephen Beaver, and Ed. T. McCrea, and that the operation of this company is to be carried on at the town of New Richmond in Montgomery County, and State of Indiana.
>
> And we certify that the above is a true statement of the matters therein set forth. Given under our hands and seals this 10th day of March, 1903. Signed; A. D. Snyder, J. T. Detchon, Chas. Haywood, Stephen J. Beaver, Ed. T. McCrea. and acknowledged as by, A. D. Snyder, J. T. Detchon, Chas. Haywood, Stephen J. Beaver, Ed. T. McCrea, March 10, 1903 before Edgar Walts, Notary Public, Montgomery County, Indiana.

The list of stockholders in the new company were Chas. Haywood, Bayless Alexander, Grant Alexander, J. A. Kirkpatrick, W. T. Jones, D. W. Pierce, Wm. McCrea, Thomas F. Oppy, L. M. Tribby, Stephen J. Beaver, John R. Phillips, George B. Shelby, M. C. Graves, Mary Bible, John C. Oppy, Ed. T. McCrea, Jas. W. Tribby, Ed. H. McCrea, Charles W. Graves, Thomas Ward, John T. Detchon, Elias Ray, Edward Born, Michael Layden, Benjamin Martin, Addison Miller, and DeWitt Clinton Miller.

The New Richmond Lumber Company secured the contract for all the building material to be used in the new Elevator and Mr. L. G. McMillin lined off the plot of the structure, immediately started excavating the ground and hoped to have it completed by June 15th to be ready for "this year's crop of small grain."

The New Richmond *Record*, Thursday July 13, 1905 tells the story of the problems of the Union Elevator, "Suit for the receivership was brought by James Withrow, a director and stockholder of the company, and his complaint alleged that the affairs of the company were in bad condition—that the company had neither money nor credit with which to do business. He placed the indebtedness at $11,000, and also said the bank with which the company had been doing business with, the Corn Exchange Bank of New Richmond, refused to honor checks which had been issued by the company to the amount of $700, though that institution had been cashing them up until the time of the suit. The plaintiff alleged further, that the company's elevator was fully equipped and ready to handle the grain which would soon be ready for marketing and there were accounts collectable due the company outstanding amounting to $2,000. The plaintiff also said there should be plenty of grain raised near New Richmond to furnish ample business for two elevators and that if a receiver is appointed he believed the property could make money, etc. Thomas & Foley, attorneys for the elevator company appeared before the court Wednesday afternoon and admitted the truth of the plaintiff's complaint and also asked that a receiver be appointed, and on the same day Enoch F. Haywood of Lafayette was appointed receiver by Judge West, Mr. Haywood gave bond for $20,000, his bondsmen being John T. Detchon, James Withrow and L. M. Tribby, and he was given authority to borrow $1,000 in order to straighten out matters so the plant could continue running. The elevator was known as the "White Elephant" for a while and chances of another Farmer's elevator in New Richmond were believed to be gone forever.

The New Richmond *Record* July 6, 1905, says, "The late disruption of the Union Elevator of New Richmond only goes to prove further that a union of farmers is an abject impossibility and to put it plainly 'they will not stick together'." The editor goes on to say, "A union of the farmers and with their unity and cooperation backing it could make the greatest, the best and the mightiest trust with an unquestioned power and right, and all the financial interests of the world could be made to kneel at its altar for bread." He also said, "The Union Elevator had become to be conceded to be one of the best things that has ever come to the farmers of the vicinity of New Richmond."

E. F. Haywood, of Lafayette, came to New Richmond to reorganize the operation of the elevator, and in the 1907-08 Montgomery County directory, the elevator is still listed under the name Union Elevator, Wabash Street, New Richmond. The advertisement reads, "UNION ELEVATOR, Dealer's in grain and feed; J. T. Detchon, Charles Haywood, A. Walls, Manager."

The elevator narrowly escaped a serious fire in August 1908 and had it not been discovered by G. V. Foster, the Union elevator would have ended its history at that time. He discovered a small blaze in the cob bin where part of the firewall had fallen away on the side of the boiler and the heat had set fire to the dry husks and cobs. The employees quickly subdued the flames and saved the structure.

Another accident was the bursting out of a wall and spilling all over the ground the bulk of 15,000 bushels of new oats which were stored in the bin. The bursting and breaking and snapping of the timbers made such a great noise, it sounded a mile away like the falling of a large tree. The work of saving the mammoth pile of oats was immediately begun, and by the hard work of six teams and ten men, the oats were back in the main part of the elevator by 10 o'clock that night, with only a loss of about $500, mostly structural costs, as only a small percent of the oats were lost. Work began shortly after to reconstruct the bin to a stronger condition than the original structure. The advertisements in the 1911 New Richmond High School Annual read: "UNION ELEVATOR CO. Millers & Grain Merchants, Charles Haywood, J. T. Detchon, New Richmond, Indiana...Highest Market Price Paid for Grain...Dealers in WOOL, Call us for quotations." In 1907-08, there were two elevators in New Richmond still in operation, the Union and A. E. Malsbary (spelled incorrectly as Malsburg in the directory).

Now that the two elevators in New Richmond were in the possession of only two family groups, Haywood & Detchon having purchased the elevator of A. E. Malsbary in August 1909, the owners decided to form a new corporation. On June 10, 1912, a new corporation was formed and the corporate name remained the same as before, the "UNION ELEVATOR COMPANY."

The object and purpose was to carry on and transact the business of owning, constructing, maintaining, leasing and operating grain elevators or flour mills, or both, and to transact business incident thereto, including the manufacture of flour, meal, and all grain and cereal products, and the buying and selling of grain and cereals of all kinds, and the manufactured products thereof.

The amount of capital stock of this new company was $20,000.00, the same to be divided into 200 shares of the par value of $100.00 each. The corporation hoped to exist for a term of 50 years. The directors of this company were only three in number and Charles Haywood, John T. Detchon and Henrietta Haywood were to manage the affairs of the company for the first year.

The principal place of business to be located in the town of New Richmond, in the county of Montgomery and State of Indiana. This was signed on the 10th day of June 1912 by Charles Haywood, Henrietta E. Haywood, John T. Detchon, and Jemima T. Detchon. Henrietta was Charles Haywood's wife, and Jemima T. was the mother of John T. Detchon.

The 1917 map of New Richmond in the atlas of Montgomery County shows the Union Elevator just south of the railroad track on the west side of south Wabash Street. The elevator built by McCardle is shown, on this same map, on the east side of south Wabash Street, next to the railroad but north of the tracks. Metal grain storage bins that were built by Russell Linton in September 1965 are currently at this location.

Furr & Cohee Elevator

Furr & Cohee, partners in the elevator business, purchased the Union elevator at New Richmond in the 1930s. The Union Elevator was still being managed by Charles Haywood and John Detchon, his partner in the business. Bert Furr moved to New Richmond after purchasing the elevator and managed the business. Furr and Cohee owned several other elevators in other locations, according to Mrs. Furr's obituary. Mrs. Furr did the bookkeeping for the firm throughout their stay in New Richmond. After Bert's death in 1946, the elevator was sold to the Montgomery County Farm Bureau Co-op. Furr & Cohee had been in the elevator business for 40 years at the time of Furr's death, but not all those years were spent in New Richmond.

Farm Bureau Co-Op Elevator

The Farm Bureau Co-Op purchased the Furr & Cohee elevator after the death of Bert Furr and they continued to operate the elevator until it was consumed by fire during the Christmas Holidays, on Sunday, December 24, 1950. The loss amounted to about $65,000, burning to the ground the elevator that was built by the Union Elevator Corporation. The fire started in the feed mixing room on the first floor in the southwest corner of the elevator and was discovered by a passerby. The automatic siren did not sound, because the power was cut off before the fire reached it. The office also burned, but a coal shed containing coal was saved due to the direction of the wind. Two New Richmond fire trucks, one each from Crawfordsville and Romney, battled the blaze, burning a huge double elevator. In addition to the buildings, 4,000 bushels of soybeans, 1,400 bushels of corn, 1,400 bushels of oats, and about $4,000 worth of feed were destroyed. Harold Peacock was the manager at the time and said the loss was covered by insurance, but they did not rebuild in New Richmond. I remember quite vividly the debris falling in the lawns in the east part of town, and the sirens of the fire trucks from Crawfordsville and Romney screeching in the middle of the night. The Crawfordsville fire department sprayed water on the rooftops of all the homes and thus prevented any damage to the residential areas.

Parlon Elevator

In 1908, James T. Parlon purchased the interests of Henry Taylor & Company, a lumber dealer in New Richmond. Parlon, a native of Tippecanoe County, had just married Mary G. Creahan the same year they started the lumber business in New Richmond, and she assisted him with the bookkeeping department. The couple continued a lifelong business together which spanned a period of forty-five years, prior to the death of Jim in 1957. Parlon attended Purdue University and, after receiving his education, started the lumber business, building up a very large and successful business. In 1924 he expanded and entered into a new field—the couple built a new elevator in New Richmond that year. He continued to operate the lumberyard along with the grain and fertilizer industry. The elevator was located on the west side of south Franklin Street, just south of the railroad tracks.

John Parlon, son of James and Mary, carried on the family business from the time his father retired, in 1953, until 1960 when he sold the business to Lester B. Sommer of Crawfordsville. Sommer operated the business under the name of the "New Richmond Farm Supply."

New Richmond Farm Supply

22 - Parlon Elevator (also known as New Richmond Farm Supply and Montgomery County Co-Op Elevator)

Lester B. Sommer of Crawfordsville purchased the Parlon Elevator in 1960, operating under the name of the New Richmond Farm Supply. This name was continued through later owners of the elevator. John Crosby managed the elevator for Sommer at first, but in 1964, Russell Linton purchased half interest in the business and became the manager of the elevator, with Grover Wethington as his assistant. In 1980 Sommer sold his half of the business to Linton, thus giving Linton full control of the elevator. The New Richmond Farm Supply then became a family concern for the Lintons. Russell's son Randy became the business manager, while son Jeff was the fertilizer equipment operator, and Russell's wife Virginia and daughter Deana kept the books for the firm. Linton expanded the buildings and storage capacity during his ownership, adding three tall metal grain bins on south Wabash Street and two large pole buildings of metal. He also improved the office, bringing it up-to-date. He added a liquid fertilizer plant and three or four more metal grain bins on Franklin Street. In all, Linton had a grain storage capacity of a half-million bushels in his bins.

Linton continued the successful operation of the New Richmond Farm Supply until the last of December 1982, when he decided he was ready to retire and travel a little "before I get too old to enjoy it," he said. The Montgomery County Farm Bureau Co-operative Association agreed to purchase the elevator and once more went into the elevator business in New Richmond.

23 - Metal grain storage bins, New Richmond Farm Supply

Farm Bureau Co-Operative Elevator

On February 1, 1983 the Farm Bureau Co-operative Association began operating the elevator at New Richmond. The location on the Norfolk and Southern Railroad was of prime interest to the Co-op manager, because of future exporting facilities. The Co-op was operating four elevators in the county, as well as a petroleum plant in Crawfordsville at the time of the purchase of the New Richmond elevator. The surrounding area of New Richmond has always been excellent for grain farming and Linton had built up a very good business in the grain, feed, and fertilizer lines way up into the millions, in years prior to 1983. The co-op had been in business for more than 55 years when they returned to New Richmond. Linton's sons continued working in the elevator for the Co-op. Randy was made assistant manager, and Daryl Warren, a 1971 graduate of Linden High School and resident of Crawfordsville, was made the manager.

Bee Keepers

The mysteries of bee keeping were understood by the earliest white settlers who came to Coal Creek Township, and the very early estate records lists stands of bees as part of their inventory.

My father, Forrest Waye, kept bees at the back of our lot in the east part of New Richmond. Although I recall helping to assemble the frames for the combs, and helped place the comb, or foundation, in these frames, I did not fully understand the reason for doing so. Another vivid picture I have of my father, was the strange costume he donned when it was time to work with the bees, consisting of a veil, or netting, placed over a wide brimmed hat, a heavy jacket, two pairs of trousers, heavy gloves, rubber boots, and a strange little object called a "smoker" in which cotton rags were set fire inside a metal container. The container was closed in order for the rags to continue smoking. The new frames were placed into the hive at the same time for the bees to commence filling them with honey. I also recall getting stung on the lip by a bee as I walked too close to a puddle of water the bees were drinking from. I still lisp just thinking about this unpleasant encounter with honey bees.

Within most of our ancestors' kitchen cabinets was a book containing the answers to all survival needs. Some were referred to as the "Household Physician" or "Receipt Book" and included recipes, medical advice and remedies, house hold economy, etc., and everything the early settler needed to know about farming and bee keeping. The chapter on bee keeping covered everything: "how to commence bee keeping–what hive to use–how to procure the first colonies–how to give frames the starter, or foundation–how to take the honey from the hive—how to hive a swarm of bees–how to clip the queen's wings–how to winter the bees (either outdoors or cellar wintering)–how to make honey vinegar, which produced a better tasting vinegar than that made from cider.

On November 12, 1842, George Ebrite purchased two stands of bees from the personal property sale of James Kendall, and paid $2.50 for each stand. Compared to other items listed in this sale, this was quite a large sum. Incidentally, these two men were my early ancestors, but the readers of this article would probably discover the same items in their ancestor's inventories.

Another early bee keeper was Jacob C. Campbell, who kept bees for several years and traded honey for other necessities with the local residents. Upon his death in 1887, his son, William, carried on the family tradition as an apiarist. In March of 1891, William had moved to Kirkpatrick, Indiana, and advertised for sale, "twenty hives of bees–cheap–healthy bees–hives full of honey." He was not successful in unloading the bees. Evidently there were no bee keepers in the New Richmond vicinity at the time, or perhaps there were too many, at any rate, William proceeded to load the bee hives onto his old farm wagon and hauled them all the way to Kirkpatrick. I thought this would surely be the end of William Campbell, but there was no follow up on this trip, so he must have reached his destination without any incidents, such as his horses getting stung and running away. It is possible the grandfather of William may have brought bees to this new settlement in the early 1830s when the clan came to Coal Creek Township.

By 1903, Thomas M. Foster was gaining fame as the greatest bee keeper in the vicinity of New Richmond–if not in the state. From one stand of bees, a total of 108 pounds of the very choicest white clover honey was taken in one year. Four of the frames contained 16 pounds in each frame. His secret was to keep the colony at work with plenty of room. He said his swarm contained fully a half bushel of bees.

Jefferson Waye (my grandfather), father of Forrest Waye, secured his honey from hollow trees. Grandpa took Dad (Forrest) out to the woods and showed him how to locate a tree with honey, then to cut down the tree in order to extract the honey. This may have been easier if the tree wasn't too large. Grandpa was of tough pioneer stock, and tried to teach his sons how to survive in the woods by hunting, trapping, and hunting honey trees. His son, Forrest, kept bees from about 1920 into the 1940s. He gave his stands of bees to Robert Stephens in New Richmond. Stephens kept bees until about 1970.

John Baxter was a gardener and a bee keeper for many years, selling both the comb and the strained honey in many of the area supermarkets. Wayne Jones, a neighbor of Baxter, became interested in the bee keeping business and purchased Baxter's stands after his death. Wayne sold honey for many years. These last three men resided in the west part of New Richmond.

The Ice Harvest

As the mercury began to dip from around twenty degrees above, to around zero—or below, on the coldest, most miserably windy day—there was much excitement in New Richmond, as plans were being made for the annual ice harvest. Ice was harvested (or farmed) on the local ponds during the driest, coldest days of the year because any moisture in the air caused the cakes of ice to immediately freeze together again, making many problems for the workers. Another nuisance was removing any snow that had fallen into the ponds, especially after a very heavy snowfall. The ice had to be marked, cut, and stored as quickly as possible, and every available man, or boy was asked (or allowed) to help with this important annual event.

A circular saw, or groover, mounted on a horse-drawn sled, marked the ice into twenty-two by thirty-four inch blocks. The desired thickness of the ice was about twelve inches for easy handling. Every added inch on the bottom made too much weight for the workers to handle. The large blocks were then cut by a large-toothed saw, especially designed for this purpose, operated by the men and boys. The boys wouldn't miss the annual ice harvest for such unimportant things as school. The cakes of ice were then rafted, or floated, to the shore where another crew was standing by with the old Morgan horses and another sled ready to load the ice cakes onto the sled.

The ice was then transported over the packed, snowy roads, the runners of the sleds squeaking as they slid over the frozen snow, setting the teeth on edge of those driving the horses. The blocks or cakes of ice were then pushed onto heavy smooth planks into the ice house where they were neatly stacked, with a layer of sawdust sprinkled between the layers to keep the cakes from freezing back together. As the tiers of ice became higher, they were hoisted with the help of horses and pulleys—the same idea as used in storing the hay in the haymows.

At one time, there was a large pond located east of New Richmond near the site on which Charles Kirkpatrick later built his residence. The swimming pool occupies part of the hole left after the pond was drained (as told to me by the late Forrest Waye). Another very good source for the ice harvest was the man-made ponds in the local park. When Henry K. Lee excavated gravel from this site, the spring-fed ponds contained some of the purest, clear, water making the best quality of ice available in this area. This was before some thoughtless local residents began dumping their trash into the ponds and ruined the waters.

Ice Houses

A good, cheap ice-house was a bin-like structure made simply of rough boards about sixteen feet square, and roofed over, leaving a large opening in the front and sides. This type of structure would keep the ice over until the next winter supply was harvested. A layer of sawdust was placed about a foot thick onto the ground and stamped down as it was added. The blocks of ice were stacked in the center of the bin, about eighteen to twenty inches from the outer walls. Sawdust was then added, filling up the space between the stacks of ice and walls. The top of the ice blocks were finally covered with a foot to twenty inches more of sawdust. Some ice harvesters covered the ice with hay or straw when sawdust was not available. Ice would keep all through the summer, even with the sun shining into the openings in the ice house, and the cakes came out as square and perfect as when they were brought in from the ponds. The openings helped to carry off the moisture arising from the ice. My father Forrest Waye said Jim Kincaid's ice house (across the street from Dad's residence on east Washington Street) was constructed with a double wall, the space between filled with well-packed sawdust. Perry Coffman constructed his ice house with concrete blocks, although sawdust was packed around the ice blocks for insulation.

Before artificially made ice was available to the New Richmond residents, there were several ice houses in the town where ice could be purchased to make home-made ice cream, or for chilling meats and dairy products, etc. The owners and locations of the ice houses follow: George F. Long's ice house was probably next to his business place on south Wabash Street; the Black Bear Hotel's ice house was at the rear of the hotel on south Wabash Street; James Kincaid's ice house was at the rear of his residence on east Washington Street; at the rear of Boswell Clough's saloon on south Wabash Street (the town hall currently occupies the saloon site); and Frank M. Perkin's general store in the area of Perkin's brick building on east Washington Street (site currently is a storage building for Tri-County Telephone Company), Capt. Tribby was hauling ice for Perkins in March of 1891; an ice house was located at the rear of the residence on the northwest corner of Detchon and north Wabash Streets, this may have been William Long's ice house. Perry Coffman's ice house was located behind his residence on west Washington Street.

Ice Men

Each January and February (sometimes as late as March), the Crawfordsville newspapers mentioned the ice harvest in New Richmond, and sometimes mentioned the men who were putting up ice. George Long was harvesting ice in January of 1887; Frank M. Perkins, January, 1888; in February 1889, ice was being put up "at a rapid rate"—but there was no mention of the persons involved. Ice men had not been able to farm any ice in January 1890, and the supply from the previous year was depleted. This was a very bad year for those needing ice, and the meat markets, and other merchants who depended on ice, were buying it from Lafayette, Frankfort, and Crawfordsville. The next year was not much better, as only one man, Doug Bunnell, had harvested ice in March, but the ice he cut was of poor quality, due to the late season. The town people were hoping someone would start an artificial ice plant, but this plan was not followed through.

In December of 1903 the ice harvest produced one of the better yields. There were a few ice men who were putting up ice as late as 1905, but the new artificial ice plants in Crawfordsville, Lafayette, and Frankfort became an easier and a more dependable source of ice. Ten carloads came in on the Clover Leaf Railroad from Frankfort for Foster and Schleppy, Frank M. Johnson, James Kincaid, Sr., and Winton S. Alexander, in February of 1900. James Kincaid delivered ice in New Richmond from 1900 to 1912, and was listed in the county directory as an ice man, or ice dealer.

William Long hauled ice from Crawfordsville to New Richmond around 1914. A five-year-old son of John Harris suffered some broken bones in his hand from jumping onto the ice wagon to get chips of ice. As he reached down to the ground to pick up some fallen ice chips, the boy's hand was run over by the ice wagon. G.L. Bastion was delivering ice in New Richmond in 1916; and Perry Coffman hauled ice from Crawfordsville and stored an ample supply in his ice house in the 1920s and 1930s. Perry passed away in 1934 and is buried in the local cemetery.

An ice man was still making rounds in New Richmond in the early 1940s before electric refrigerators became available, or within reach of the less fortunate. In the early 1930s my brothers and I ran to the east end of town each time the ice man rounded the corner, hoping to get a handful of ice chips from the ice wagon. The wagon was an open flat-bed wagon covered by a heavy tarpaulin to keep the sun from melting the ice. My mother and grandmother didn't want me to climb onto the wagon as it wasn't "lady-like." This hurt my feelings, as my brothers were allowed to—but I lived through this big disappointment in life, somehow! Our parents had an ice box that held a seventy-five pound cake of ice. Our mother placed her ice card in the front window to order the amount that was needed. One side of the card read 25/50 lbs., the other 75/100. The card was turned to the amount needed, the top number being the required amount.

Ice Cream

Frank Perkins and George Long were more interested in the ice harvest for other reasons than preserving meat and other foods. The two men had purchased commercial-size ice cream freezers in May of 1887, and they were the first to introduce ice cream to the citizens of New Richmond. They were competing against each other, selling the new product for 5 cents a dish. Perkins was said to have given away three dishes for every two he sold during a horse show in the town. A year later, F. M. Perkins purchased a treadmill to run his ice cream freezer, and George Steele was to do the treading for him. Frank also purchased a milk shaker the same year, but two years later, Perkins, William Campbell, and other merchants, were purchasing ice cream from Frankfort to sell in their stores in New Richmond. F. M. Johnson's ice cream factory is mentioned in the drugstore section of this history.

Ice Cream Parlor

Joseph and Alice Ebrite Tortorella had an ice cream parlor in the west room of the brick Washburn building on the southeast corner of Washington and Wabash Streets in 1914 and 1915. This is the only store of this kind known to have been in New Richmond. The Tortorellas moved to Chicago the following year.

The Dairy Industry

There have been several attempts over the years to establish a successful dairy business in and near New Richmond. In 1887 John Dewey was delivering milk to "the thirsty" in the summer months. It is not known how long he was in this line of service. In 1890 Elias Perkins delivered milk in the town for 5 cents a quart, and in 1895, William Burris's dairy was listed in the Montgomery County directory. Joe W. Hainds (or Haines) had just discontinued his milk wagon service in New Richmond in May of 1897. A few years later, in January 1914, Merle Lovel had just sold his milk route to Walter Kemble because Lovell was moving to Clarks Hill.

W. T. Davidson's new dairy began delivering milk to its customers in New Richmond in January, 1922. His advertisement read, "Buy Davidson's Jersey Milk—Quality Counts." In 1936 there were two dairy companies in New Richmond. An advertisement for each appeared in the junior high school play program. One was the "Andrews Dairy—For Good Milk," and was located about two miles south of New Richmond on the old Washburn farm. The second dairy was The Western Indiana Dairy Association, New Richmond.

Charles W. Graves was in the dairy business in the 1930s and his grandchildren helped deliver milk door to door in New Richmond. His farm was west of New Richmond, about one and three-fourths mile.

There probably have been many other attempts of the dairy business that were not recorded, or that may have been recorded and I have not located their advertisements or other information.

Western Indiana Dairy Products, Inc.

In November 1936 the Civil Town of New Richmond, Indiana, and its Trustees, and their successors in office, purchased a lot on south Wabash Street just north of the Clover Leaf Railroad tracks for $1 and other considerations. This lot was sold to the town by the Union Elevator Corporation. Its president at the time was Charles Haywood, and its secretary, Henrietta Haywood. Charles Haywood presented one bill to the town trustees for the lot at the November 16th meeting the same year, for $400, and another bill on December 6, 1940, for $600 on the next meeting, for the payment in full, making a total of $1,000 which the town trustees paid for this lot. Incidentally, this lot was owned by the town of New Richmond until 1964.

The lack of information in the minutes of the New Richmond Town Board leaves a question as to why this lot was purchased at the time, but during the July 3, 1939 meeting, Earl Warren made a motion, seconded by Thomas, that a lease be drawn up between the Town of New Richmond and the Western Indiana Dairy Products, Incorporated, for the above lot, for $45 per year rent, the rent to begin at the completion of the building. A foundation had been laid, and a cornerstone laying ceremony was held; lumber was put on the grounds, and then the deal fell through, for some unknown reason. On February 5, 1940, the town trustees asked William Mason to move the supplies and papers, etc. belonging to the Western Indiana Dairy Products, Inc. from the town hall's office room. The office was vacated before the next town meeting.

An option was then offered to C. L. Snyder to use the lot owned by the town for a cheese factory. Snyder did not accept the offer and the offer was rescinded. The trustees were still offering to rent the lot to any interested parties for a factory site, or any other business establishment.

In October 1940 a gentleman from the Linden Lumber Company appeared at the meeting of the New Richmond town trustees in regard to a lien held by his company on the lot owned by the town. The town's attorney advised the trustees that the town could not be held liable for the material if there was no written lease between the town and the Western Indiana Dairy Products Company, and the materials were sold to Western which had planned to build on said lot. This problem was evidently resolved as there were no other comments on the lien, and this proposed dairy soon faded from the picture.

COAL CREEK DAIRY PRODUCTS, INC.

On February 26, 1940, a group of men decided to form a corporation and to establish another dairy or cheese factory in New Richmond. Paul A. Owen, James Hornbeck, and William W. Mason were the incorporators of this new enterprise. The name of the new dairy was the Coal Creek Dairy Products, Incorporated. The principal office was to be in New Richmond, Montgomery County, Indiana. William W. Mason was the resident agent. This company was organized with a capital of $2,000. The first board of directors was: Paul A. Owen, of Linden, James Hornbeck, Melvin J. Roth, and William W. Mason, all of New Richmond.

This cheese factory was located on west Detchon Street and the building was a concrete block structure; it now serves as a family garage. The cheese factory was a successful business from the start, and nearly everyone in the neighborhood of New Richmond who raised dairy cattle was selling their products to the dairy. However the factory was located in a residential district, and this became the downfall of the plant.

In October, the same year the factory was established, a group of citizens residing in the neighborhood of the cheese plant attended a meeting of the town board of New Richmond to complain of a very objectionable smoke nuisance that had prevailed for some time, and asked the board to try and correct the conditions. They agreed to meet with the directors to work out the problem. The directors promised to erect a new smoke pipe to control the nuisance. This addition did not eliminate the smoke, and the citizens again complained to the board. The board decided they could not take any action until the persons who were complaining signed a petition against the cheese plant officials. This was done, and the board talked to the town attorney who again advised them to require the factory to take the necessary steps to correct the smoke nuisance.

Several citizens who had signed the petition met with the board again in September of 1941, and Mr. Mason, Mr. Hornbeck, and Mr. Roth of the Coal Creek Dairy Products Company attended this meeting. After considerable discussion, the board declared the smoke condition of the cheese plant a nuisance, and informed the officials they would have to take all necessary steps to correct the situation. Written notice was also sent to the factory officials. The town attorney informed the board to meet with the prosecuting attorney, who would present the matter to the grand jury, making the problem a State case. The prosecutor agreed to take the matter up with the judge. The problem continued to disrupt each board meeting and was continued into the next year. Each meeting was spent discussing the smoke nuisance of the cheese plant. The officials finally agreed to put in a stoker, which was their way of showing some effort to remedy the smoke problem. The stoker evidently was not installed, because two weeks later, a town board member had another conference with the cheese plant authorities who promised early action. Both sides of the conflict were becoming very upset over the problem.

On March 2, 1942 the town trustees were relieved of the continuous problem that had taken so much of their time. Mr. Burnett reported the sale and the removal of the cheese plant, thus writing off the alleged smoke nuisance. But, this also closed a promising factory in New Richmond, and many jobs were lost at its closing.

The cheese making equipment was purchased by Gene Wehner, who made cheddar cheese in the Waynetown Dairy. Bill Kunkel had purchased a building, repaired the structure, and installed dairy equipment in another room of the building, and he and Wehner were in this dairy industry as partners.

Coal Creek Dairy

Frank Allhands and Leroy Young were the latest gentlemen to establish a dairy in the township. The Coal Creek Dairy was established in the 1960s. Their advertisements appeared in the Coal Creek Central Bearcats basketball programs through the 1960s and 1970s. This dairy continued into the 1980s and Young's son, David, was also associated with this dairy industry, which was located south of New Richmond on County Road 700 North.

The final chapter of the Coal Creek Dairy was closed in March 1986 when Leroy and Mildred Young retired from farming and the dairy business, and sold all their dairy herd. A public auction was held on their farm March 22, 1986 selling all their dairy and farming equipment.

Automobile Repair Shops

The first automobile mechanics in New Richmond were Starr Dunn and his son, Stanley. The day John Detchon drove the first automobile into town, Stanley Dunn's love affair for the horseless carriage began. Stanley was one gifted mechanic, and New Richmond automobile owners often went into the local school and asked Stanley to take a look at their disabled automobile. His father entered him in the school at Valparaiso in order to continue his education.

Starr Dunn's advertisements for his garage appeared in the county directory as early as 1912. Samuel Livingston was a mechanic in his garage at the time, and Roy Brown later worked for Starr. They sold Columbia batteries, and Fisk, non-skid tires (size 3 X 30 sold for $10.40 in 1916). Because of poor health, Starr Dunn sold his shop and moved to Florida in 1926.

Taylor's garage was listed in the town in 1919. He advertised Ford parts, repairing tractors and trucks as well as automobiles.

Maurice Coffman "Coffey" operated a garage until 1941. Coffey offered wrecking service, both day and night, from 1931, on. He also sold Cities Service gas and oil products. His garage was located on south Wabash Street in a frame building, the former site of Shotts' buggy factory. He repaired automobiles in New Richmond for thirty five years, according to his obituary.

Donald Todd was repairing automobiles in Coffey's garage in 1942 before he went into the army.

Tom Morris' garage was located on the southeast corner of Wabash and Madison Streets in 1936. For a short time in the 1930s, Tom Bailey repaired automobiles in a garage located in the old town hall and fire house, behind the New Richmond Christian Church. This was later a residence and burned to the ground in the 1960s or 1970s.

Wilbert "Web" Lyon's garage was in operation in 1930, during the same period of time Coffey's garage was in business. Web's son, Claude, worked with him repairing vehicles for many years. They were located in Starr Dunn's building on east Washington Street. They were still in business in the 1940s.

Toby's Garage was listed in the *Shopper's Guide* through the summer months of 1952.

Carl Burnett erected a concrete block building on south Wabash Street and his garage was listed in the advertisements from 1947 to 1949. He sold Cities Service gasoline, Koolmotor oil and grease, and Acme tires and batteries. Bob Dryer and Dave Cochran worked for Burnett as mechanics, while Carl delivered his gas and oil products by truck. This garage was on south Wabash Street and the building is now (1985) occupied by Verhey's Erection company.

Stull's Auto Shop was in operation from 1947 to 1949.

Fountain's Garage, operated by August "Augie" Fountain, was located in Maurice Coffman's building. He sold Mobil Gas, and Goodyear tires. He was in business from 1954 to around 1959.

The **New Richmond Garage**, operated by Wayne Jones, located on north Prairie Street, was listed in the local telephone directory and county directory from 1960 to 1980. Gerald Ottinger worked for Wayne in 1964. Wayne repaired automobiles in New Richmond up to the day of his death in 1980. He had a natural ability for locating problems in vehicles and was one of the best in this line of work. When called to our home to check out a problem with one of our vehicles, Wayne stood at the front of the car with his hands clasped under the bib of his overalls, told our daughter to start the engine, and without touching a part under the hood, discovered the problem and made a part to fix it. She had no more trouble with this part of the vehicle.

In 1972, the following garages were in operation in the town: P & R Garage, later named Perry's Mid Town Garage; New Richmond Garage, Wayne Jones, proprietor, Barnes' Garage, owned by Francis Barnes, and Swank's Garage, Doug Swank, proprietor. Swank's Garage was located one mile west of New Richmond. He was in this line of business from 1970 to 1972. Perry's Mid Town Garage was in operation from 1972 to 1976. He sold his equipment in May of 1977. He was located in the old Starr Dunn building on east Washington Street.

Dave's Repair Service, David Brown, proprietor, was located about one half mile south of New Richmond on the Linden road. He repaired vehicles from 1977 to 1983. William E. Swick "Bill," repaired automobiles in his garage next to his residence on east Washington Street in 1982 and '83. New Richmond has no automobile repair shop in operation at this time, but the need is still there.

Gas and Oil Products Agents in New Richmond

Standard Oil Agents

The Standard Oil bulk plant was located on the east side of south Franklin Street just north of the railroad. It has been dismantled.

Herbert White was an agent up to September, 1919, when he transferred to Shirley, Indiana.

George Neidigh, agent in 1923, advertised Polarine Motor oils, Red Crown gasoline, and Perfection Oil.

Fred Goodin, agent from 1934 to 1938.

Ora I. Newnum, agent from 1941 to 1972, advertised gas, oil, grease and fuel oil. Charles R. Fruits, Wayne Snouwart, and Dick Stephenson all drove the truck for Newnum.

Richard I. Stephenson, agent from 1972 to 1977, advertised Amaco heating oils in 1975.

Thomas "Tom" Kruse, agent for Standard Oil from 1978 to 1981. The Titus Oil Company carried Standard products, therefore, Tom was listed as an agent for both Companies.

Farm Bureau Petroleum Products, Alfred Patton, agent around 1935 to 1941.

Mobilgas Oil And Greases, Sam Haire, agent from around 1939 to 1948.

Tydol On Products, Richard "Dick" Thomas distributed Tydol products in 1949.

Cities Service Oil Company—the bulk plant was located at the very west end of Stephenson Street next to the railroad and was still in service in 1985.

Carl Burnett, agent 1925 to 1962. Carl distributed Cities Service Oil products for thirty seven years and retired because of bad health. An advertisement in 1937 offered New Bronze Koolmotor gasoline and oils, and in 1947 advertised Acme tires and batteries. In 1948 he sold Trojan and Koolmotor Oil. Al Boeldt drove Carl's truck from 1957 to 1960, and Bill Snellenbarger drove for Carl after his illness.

William Snellenbarger, agent for Cities Service Oil Company from 1961, is still in business. The Cities Service oil company changed its name to Citgo Oil Distributors in 1966 and was still listed under Snellenbarger's Citgo Oil Products in 1985.

Gasoline Dealers - The First

"The only place in town to get WHITE ROSE gasoline and NATIONAL light coal oil is at J.W. HOLLIN'S DRUG STORE," so Hollin's advertisement read in February of 1903. The price was not listed, but the late Forrest Waye said Hollin usually sold it for ten and fifteen cents per gallon. He stored gasoline in a square container that stood south of his store on the northwest corner of Washington and Wabash Streets. A photograph of a temperance parade in New Richmond shows this container.

Hollin's prices may have been the best, but he was not the only store owner who sold White Rose gasoline and National light oil in New Richmond during this period of time. F.M. Johnson's drug store and A.W. Hempleman's grocery and bakery were selling gasoline and coal oil in 1903. Hempleman's advertised the products, "at the right prices."

Gasoline Service Stations

Cities Service Stations - Maurice Coffman "Coffey" was probably the first Cities Service gasoline service station attendant in New Richmond. His garage and service station was located on south Wabash Street in the old Shotts' buggy factory building. This building is still standing–a frame structure with a concrete block front. C.W. Swick's garage now occupies the site.

Carl Burnett, agent for Cities Service products erected a concrete block building further south on Wabash Street in the late 1940s. Advertisements for this station and garage are available from 1947 to 1949, but he may have been in business in the early 1950s. He owned the building up to 1954. Bob Dryer and David Cochran were mechanics for Carl and pumped the gas. Carl distributed Cities Service products over the area by truck.

Francis Barnes erected a concrete block building on the northeast corner of Wabash and Stephenson Streets in 1974, and his sons sold Cities Service, or Citgo, gas and oil products for a short time in this location.

Standard Services Stations

Dick's Service Station Standard Products–Richard "Dick" Thomas and his grandfather, referred to by the town residents as "Uncle Dick," operated the Standard Service Station in New Richmond from 1939 to 1947, except for the month of November in 1941, when John C. Parlon and Oscar ran the station.

Gasoline Service Stations

Tim Hutchinson worked for Dick Thomas in 1940. The building is located on east Washington Street, and situated on lot three, block two of the original plat of the town of New Richmond.

Inskeep's Standard Service Station–John and Clara W. Inskeep purchased the Standard Service Station from Richard Thomas in 1948. His brother, George, operated the station less than a year, and sold out to Bob Thayer.

Thayer's Standard Service—On December 4, 1948, Robert M. and Frances W. Thayer made a down payment of $500 on the Standard Service Station in New Richmond, purchasing the property from John and Clara W. Inskeep. The deed was signed the 22nd of January 1949, and recorded the 29th, same month and year. The Thayers signed their first lease with the Standard Oil Company on February 4, 1949. Bob operated the filling station himself until 1957 when Morris Geiger became his partner. They advertised, "a complete line of Standard Products, tire repair, mufflers, and exhaust systems."

The Thayer and Geiger Standard Service sold Allis Chalmers mowers, lawn and garden equipment from 1975 to 1980. They were an authorized state inspection station when vehicle owners were required to have their trucks and automobiles checked each year in the late 1970s and early 1980s.

Morris Geiger retired in 1976, but continued to work part time when Bob was driving his school bus, or was attending his County Commissioner's meetings. Morris Geiger's death occurred August 1984.

24 - Thayer and Geiger Standard Service

Thayer celebrated his thirty-third anniversary in the same location from November 30 to December 5, 1981, by giving away free refreshments and offering extra specials to his customers that week. He enjoyed visiting and swapping stories with the New Richmond and area citizens too much to retire. His nephew, Roger Thayer, also worked at the station.

NEW RICHMOND CANNING COMPANY

Early in the spring of 1891, New Richmond businessmen realized the town had grown in population but was lacking in growth of business and industry. For many heads of households, there was no steady employment, and feeding and clothing their families was almost impossible at times. Suggestions were made in the local newspaper, the New Richmond *Times*, to correct this growing problem.

One idea was for the businessmen to get a chair factory to locate in the town. It was thought the buildings and machinery would not be too costly to get started. Another suggested a canning factory. The second idea proved to be the most acceptable of the two. George W. Washburn and Ira Stout made a trip to Brookston in October the same year to investigate the canning factory in that city, but no action was taken in New Richmond toward building one at that time. A lot of thought and planning was put into this type of enterprise later on; in fact, the wheels did not start in motion until 1898, when A.D. Snyder and O.W. Mason again toured the Brookston canning factory and decided to embark in the canning business.

On the 18th of March 1898, the New Richmond Canning Company was incorporated. The object of the company was to manufacture fruits and vegetables and to buy and sell the same. The amount of the capital stock of the new company was $4,000, to be divided into forty shares of $100 each. The incorporators expected the company to exist for fifty years. There were five directors to manage the operations of the company and the factory was to be built within the town of New Richmond, Indiana. Directors for the first year were Orlando W. Mason; Ed. T. McCrea; Wm. McCrea, John Detchon, and Thomas M. Foster. The directors, incidentally, were the only stockholders of the New Richmond Canning Company.

The company was now legally formed, and the next step was to interest the area farmers in planting tomatoes for the new factory. Tom Foster of New Richmond and F. M. Stoudt of Brookston contracted about 100 of the 200 acres needed within a month, but it took some time and effort to get the other one hundred acres—the canning company made up the remaining acres and planted fifty.

During this time the stone for the foundation was delivered to the factory site, the lumber was delivered, and a full description of the buildings was printed in the local newspaper.

The most important fact was the building was to be erected by local labor—donating their work for the enterprise. The local contractor, S. R. Tribby was to do the framework and supervise the work. Mr. Stoudt, associated with the Brookston canning factory, also served as overseer.

The buildings for the factory consisted of a ware room, work room and engine room. The ware room and main building was forty-five by ninety feet and two stories high. The upper story was for storage of empty cans and boxes, the lower for canned goods and shipping facilities. The workroom on the west was thirty-two by seventy feet and only one story, with a small dog-house passageway above, to be used in passing the cans from the storage room to the fillers. The size and position of the engine room was not decided upon at the time the article was published.

A great part of the lumber came from Arkansas (but was shipped by a Wisconsin firm from which it was purchased) and was to cost around one thousand dollars. The flooring was of Arkansas pine and about two thousand feet was needed, the greatest outlay of cash for the structures. Local painters, as well as the carpenters, donated their work.

The canning company was to employ about one-hundred twenty-five people, one hundred being peelers. Expected output of the factory was to be from twelve thousand to fifteen thousand cans per day. Only tomatoes were to be canned the first year but later other fruits and vegetables were added.

By the end of May the buildings were up, the siding on, the asphalt roofing was installed and a new well was drilled. The engine and boiler arrived the first of June and the Clover Leaf Railroad installed a new side track on the south side of the depot, alongside Mason's lumber and coal yard, and the New Richmond Canning Company's new buildings.

Local farm implement dealers Snyder and Thompson received the second handy labor-saving "Tiger" tomato planting machine for the area tomato farmers. The buildings were completed and the machinery was in place by the time the canning season was to start, about August fifteen.

The canning company's furnaces were lit for the first time on Thursday, July 7, 1898. The boilers, engine, and plumbing were tested. When the steam was up, deep low-toned sounds, as of a steamboat, came from her whistle for the first time. Whistles from the local elevator, the tile mill, and nearby threshing engines all gave a welcoming salute to the new enterprise. New Richmond resembled a huge factory town on this great day.

Charlie Taylor was the first to set out tomato plants for the new factory and was the first to deliver tomatoes for canning. George Pierce was another area farmer raising tomatoes for the factory. The canning factory was in operation by August twenty-third. The pay roll each week averaged about three hundred dollars for labor alone. There were ninety-six peelers, girls and women, and about forty men employed. The factory employees began labeling and boxing their first cans of tomatoes Monday, September 12, 1898.

By the end of September, five carloads of canned goods had been shipped from the factory. They had paid out five thousand, five hundred dollars for six carloads of cans, or about three hundred thousand cans. Employees came from Waynetown, Mellott, Crawfordsville, Linden, Bristle Ridge, and "other far-away points." The factory's output was about eighteen thousand cans of tomatoes daily. The first season the total output had reached about two hundred fifty thousand cans.

In October the first year, the tomato peelers at the canning factory struck for higher wages. The ringleaders were two "popular" married women of the town. The New Richmond *Record*, Thursday, October 13, 1898, said, "Some meddling fool told the girls other companies were paying four cents a bucket, and they should demand the same. They made known their demand to foreman, Foster Stoudt, who was in the wrong mood at the time and answered, "Go to h—— or to Congress—which he said meant the same thing. The girls realized it was too near the end of the season and went back to work.

The factory put in a new labeling machine, a great labor saver that would label about thirty-five thousand cans per day and was operated by hand.

The new factory opened up a new field for laborers and farmers, as well as provided work for the widowed mothers and young ladies in New Richmond. A few acres of tomatoes were more profitable at the time because of the low prices of small grains the farmers were receiving. Albert Dazey had probably the best yield of the first season delivering to the company—two thousand and eight bushels of tomatoes from a six and one-half acre field.

The New Richmond canning factory was very successful the first year, but the following year the crop of tomatoes was cut short by an early frost. The New Richmond *Record*, Thursday August 29, 1901, printed an article entitled "What is Failure," and the article reads in part, "What a good thing we didn't— It would seem ill grace to scoff at a failure of enterprise but just now what a good thing it seems that the New Richmond Canning Company died an honorable death with the bursting of the buds in the spring than to have died just at this critical time of year after the farmers had contracted and planted the required two hundred acres of tomatoes at twenty cents per bushel to find the drought had ruined the crop" etc. "Our company made money the first year or two but the enterprise seemed to have 'dropped through' just in the nick of time."

The following year, interest was revived in the New Richmond Canning Company and there was talk of running it again that summer. It was referred to as the "rotting-down canning factory air-castle," or "that big black hulk south of the railroad." The management asked people to raise tomatoes for twenty cents per bushel. Mr. Martz of Tipton looked the place over and considered leasing it for the season and contacted the area farmers for acreage for tomatoes. About the middle of August, Will McCrea, superintendent of the factory, placed an advertisement in the *Record* for tomato peelers. The first run of tomatoes was made a few days later. They also canned pumpkins that year and were paying farmers two dollars per ton for them. The factory, however, was run by the New Richmond Canning Company again, and not by Mr. Martz.

The factory enjoyed its most prosperous season in 1902, working steadily on tomatoes both day and night, and had from five hundred to fifteen hundred bushels on the platform. There were more than one hundred tons of pumpkins stored at the factory awaiting the slack in the tomato run. Employees were still hard at work labeling and packing tomatoes at the rate of fifteen thousand to eighteen thousand cans per day in December that year.

Orlando W. Mason sold his one-third interest to J. T. Detchon and Ed T. McCrea, the two other members of the company. They in turn sold Mason's third to Albert D. Snyder.

The 1903 Montgomery County directory lists the "New Richmond Canning Company; E. T. McCray (McCrea) Pres.; Will McCray, Manager; A. D. Snyder, Sec'y; John Detchon, Treas.; West on Clover Leaf R. R." By the time the directory was printed, the New Richmond Canning Company had died its second death. Rumor was the factory was to be moved to Charleston, Indiana, however, that deal fell through, and it was advertised for sale again.

In April that year, the New Richmond Canning factory merged with the "White Eagle Packing Company" of North Vernon, Indiana. The same New Richmond stockholders invested five thousand dollars and were the organizers of the company. The North Vernon *Sun*, Tuesday, May 5, 1903 says in part, "Last Thursday evening the stockholders of the tomato canning factory met in the city hall and organized The White Eagle Packing Company. Articles of incorporation were prepared, by-laws adopted and a board of directors elected. Capital stock for this company is $6,500. The board for the first year will be: A. A. Tripp, Pres.; Wm. McCrea, Supt. and Secretary; John T. Detchon, Joseph Powell and Ed Tech. The Treasurer and assistant secretary offices were not filled until later in the season. The directors met Saturday morning to make arrangements for the factory site, side tracks and buildings. The machinery is up to date and will be shipped from New Richmond at once." Plans were also being considered for rail facilities on the Pan Handle to the Big Four. Superintendent William McCrea drew up the plans for the "White Eagle Packing Company" buildings to be erected at once (these plans were printed in detail in the *Sun*).

The factory managers had the same problem at North Vernon as they did in New Richmond, that is the lack of interest among the farmers in this new proposition of raising tomatoes. One of their farmers said he could make more off tomatoes by peddling them door to door. The problem of townspeople not being able to support and feed their families was not the farmers' concern. The *Sun* also said, "Ed. T. McCrea and son William, and A. D. Snyder of New Richmond were down to help organize the 'White Eagle Packing Company.' These gentlemen are wealthy farmers and have faith in the tomato industry or else they would not invest $4,000 in our city. If these men made as high as ninety-seven per cent on their investment see money in the business why can't you?"

The machinery and fixtures of the old plant of the New Richmond canning factory were dismantled and loaded on the railroad cars to be shipped to North Vernon for the new White Eagle Preserving Company's plant the first week of July 1903, leaving the empty buildings as a monument of what was once one of the successful and thriving industries of New Richmond. The townspeople were once again without a means of supporting their families.

The canning factory buildings were moved out of the way for the new Union Elevator by John Ellis of Waynetown the last of July that year. They were later used for stock pens by Lamson and Pence, and in October 1907 were town down by the Union elevator company. The lumber was used in building a huge new corn crib near the elevator.

Some of the New Richmond people went to North Vernon to work in the factory, among them (besides the stockholders) were Morgan Foster and his wife and Mr. and Mrs. Charles Bastion. William McCrea moved his family down there and served as superintendent of the concern a number of years.

The local town board made another attempt to build a canning factory in the town of New Richmond in 1940, but this idea was soon forgotten.

Factories

New Richmond can boast a little about the factories that once occupied a tiny niche in her history. Some only thrived a short time, leaving no record of their existence, others, such as the tile factory and canning factory, prospered for several years.

Star Chemical Works

Among the lesser known factories was the Star Chemical Works. Edward H. McCrea was the manufacturer and dealer in extracts, perfumes, etc. The only record of this enterprise was one of his calling cards printed by the New Richmond *Record*. Naturally there is no date on the card, but it is possible he manufactured the products between 1896 to the early 1900s.

Wagon Factory

Early settlers in New Richmond and the Coal Creek area depended upon the local wagon-maker, George Ebrite, for their only transportation, the old farm wagon. George manufactured wagons from 1839 or 1840, until he purchased several acres of farmland and turned to farming in the 1860s. The local blacksmiths then manufactured the farm wagons and buggies.

Knockboard Factory

William E. Grannon invented a device called a knockboard for harvesting corn more efficiently. He secured a patent for the side-board designed to fasten to the farm wagon. He sold the patent to George W. Clough, who in turn, contracted Elmer Henthorne to manufacture the device in September of 1905. His factory was located in the sheds near Malsbary's Elevator on south Wabash Street. The knockboards were built of poplar end stays and white pine boards. Perry McLain, the local hardware man, took the model to Veedersburg, and other outlying areas, to sell the new device directly to the farmers for Clough and Grannon.

Slat & Wire Fence Factories (Picket Fence)

Samuel R. Tribby and J. W. McCollum (McCallum) rented a building from Mrs. Campbell in May of 1891, and opened a slat and wire fence factory in New Richmond. They soon had more orders than they could fill, as most of the residents in the town fenced their property to keep unwanted livestock from damaging the lawns and gardens. Joe Bennett of Round Hill invented a new type of fence and secured a patent in April the same year, and he, too, was manufacturing fence. H. B. Groves manufactured wire picket fence in New Richmond about the same time. The 1895 county directory lists W. S. Alexander and Henry Groves as partners in the slat fence factory, and J. W. McCallum was still in business with his slat fence factory the same year.

Mose R. Binns also manufactured slat (or lath) and wire fencing for a few years. He listed his "lath and wire fence machine" in his public sale held in 1904. Another fence manufacturer in New Richmond was Squire Ebrite. My father Forrest Waye said Ebrite's slat-wire fence factory was located back of what is now the Tri-County Telephone office building in New Richmond. Waye and other lads about town were fascinated by the machine, as it flipped the slats and twisted the wire around the slats quite rapidly. Ebrite may have purchased the Tribby and McCallum factory, as they were in the same location. Ebrite would have been in this line of business between 1900 and 1910.

Spark Plug Factory

The late Reuben Swank mentioned another factory in the town of New Richmond around 1914 or 1915. Three young men from the area manufactured spark plugs. This factory was located on Clyde Thomas' farm about one and one-half miles south of town (on the south Wabash Street road). This factory operated under the name Thomas, Conn & Conn. Those who remembered this factory said their spark plugs were well made and they could have been very successful had they continued their operation. Richard Martin later plowed into a pile of discarded pieces of the plugs while farming the former site of the factory.

The Surplus (or Mutual) Electric Company, Inc.

John T. Detchon purchased the A. D. Snyder brick building, located on south Wabash Street in New Richmond on June 15, 1924. The building was owned by Joseph C. Herron at the time, and the value of the property was listed as $8500. The building was occupied by the Morrow family hardware, but Detchon had other plans for the structure.

On the 15th of October 1924, John T. Detchon of New Richmond and William McCrea and Joseph Riley, both of Attica, Indiana (McCrea was a native of New Richmond), formed a corporation under the name of Surplus Electric Equipment Company. The purpose of this corporation was contracting in electrical work, wholesaling and retailing of electrical supplies, and manufacturing electrical equipment. The amount of capital stock this group started their business with was $10,000, with 100 shares of $100 each. The three gentlemen above were the only directors, and the office and place of business was to be located in New Richmond. The length of life of the corporation was listed as fifty years, and the first annual meeting was held on October 15, 1924 (the date of organization).

The Surplus Electric Company, Incorporated, was later reorganized under the Indiana General Corporation Act (approved March 16, 1929) on April 11, 1931, and recorded April 14, 1931.

The Surplus Electric Company continued to operate under that name until after World War II. Due to the confusion of the name Surplus Electric with war surplus—items offered for sale by the government after the war—the firm's officials decided that a name change was necessary. On May 12, 1949, the board of directors adopted the name of Mutual Electric Corporation, and operated under this title until the company shut down. The articles of amendment were filed in the Secretary of State's Office and recorded May 20, 1949.

Detchon sold the Snyder building to the Surplus Electric Equipment Company on June 3, 1930, and the former hardware store became the site of a busy little factory. Detchon was the President of the company, and Floyd Ellery Drysdale was manager, or foreman, over the employees. Employees assembled telephones and rebuilt the used or defective phones and other electrical equipment. Electric and telephone poles and other merchandise were sold by this company, and this provided employment to a few men who loaded and drove the truck which carried these products.

The Surplus Electric Company gave employment to many New Richmond residents through the years. Among the list remembered by local residents were Inez Stephenson (a school teacher who worked during the summer months), Clara Waye, Helen Oppy, Levert Binns, Dutch Fruits, Alfred Allman, Merril Clapp, Elsie Whipple, Louie Haywood, Ira Magruder, Richard Thomas, Eugene Stephenson, Elgie Whipple, Carol, Cecil, and Wayne Austin, Roy Hill, Don Waye (drove the truck), Mervin Jones, Leland

Oppy, Frank Lane, Teressa Lowe, Bert Goodin, Maurice Coffman, Mary Jones, Omer (or Homer) Miller, Charlie Todd, Grace Fruits, Byron Alexander and Ralph Kunkel.

After the death of John T. Detchon in 1951, the Mutual Electric Corporation sold the factory building and other buildings owned by the company to Polly Buck. The deed was recorded on November 22, 1952, and was signed by O. C. Buck, Vice President of the Corporation, and Floyd W. Young, Secretary-Treasurer, by the authority of its board of directors.

At the time of Detchon's death, telephone equipment and supplies were being stored in the upstairs rooms of the Knights of Pythias Building and the Hollins brothers' former building. There were many of the old crank-style wall telephones stored in these rooms, but these were eventually sold. The Mutual Electric Company was listed in the 1961 Tri-County Telephone Directory and the 1966 county directory. The Crawfordsville *Journal Review*, November 25, 1969, published a legal notice from the Secretary of State of Indiana, William N. Salin, revoking certain corporations unless an annual report was filed within 30 days. The Mutual Electric Company was one of those listed, indicating this company was no longer operating.

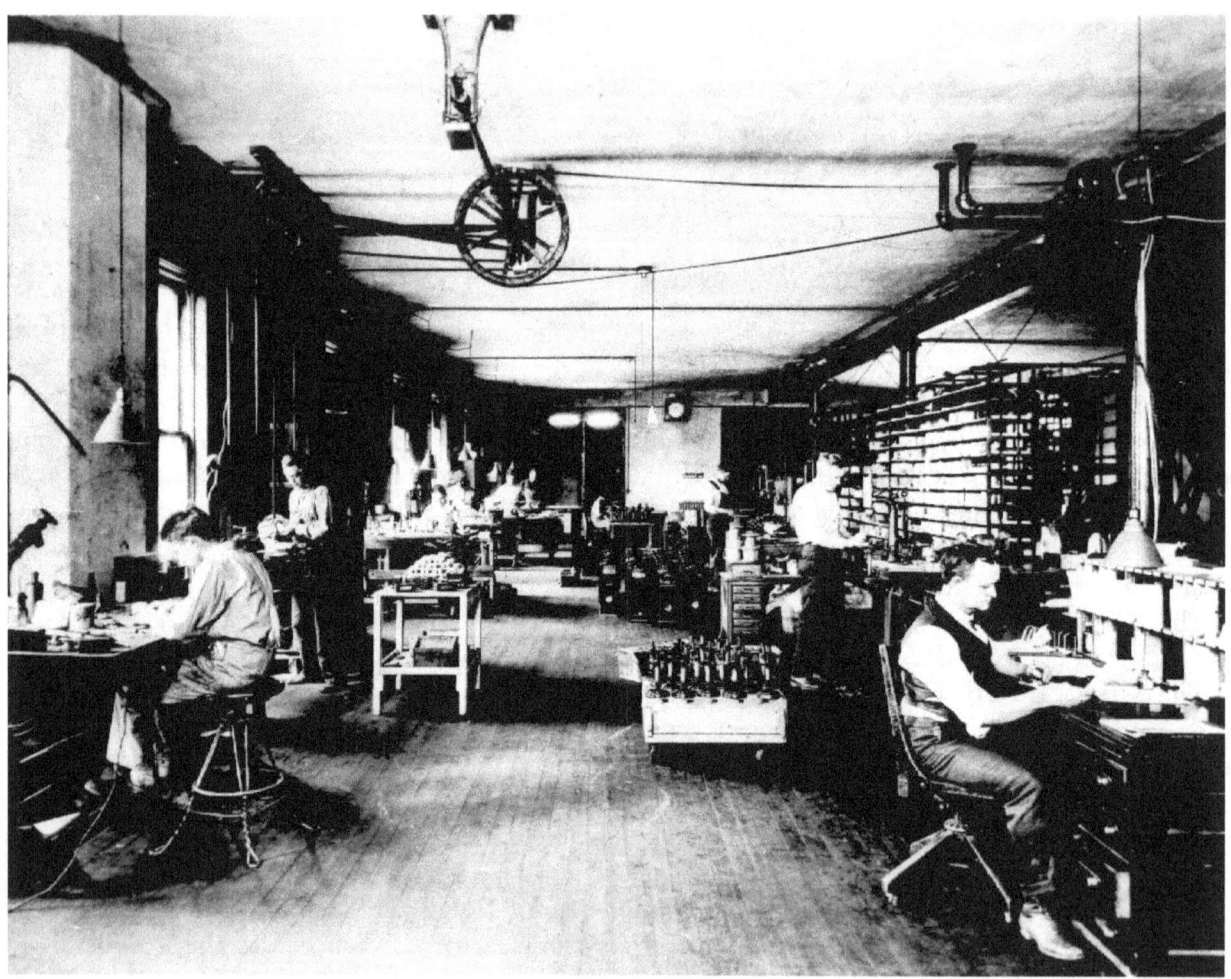

25 - Surplus Electric Company. Photo taken in 1930s or 1940s. F.E. Drysdale sitting at desk left front; Maurice Coffman standing second from right by window.

EMERALD ACRES (ALFALFA CUBES—THE BEST WAY TO FEED HAY)

While New Richmond residents were quietly going about their business, they were unaware of the birth of a new factory in the neighborhood. In the infancy of this factory, as in most new business ventures, there were many problems to be solved, and growing pains were to be suffered by the family members who were brave enough to embark in this new venture. There was no formal announcement of the opening of a new factory. Donald Miles and his family had a dream, in 1978, of manufacturing alfalfa cubes as a more convenient way of feeding alfalfa to livestock. After many discussions they decided to form a family corporation, and this was carried out. Their place of business was to be New Richmond, Indiana (Route 1). The officers at the beginning of the new concern were as follows: Don Miles, President; Scott Miles, Vice President (son of Don and Sandy); Mrs. Sandra Miles, Senior Vice President (Don's wife); Mrs. Carol Miles, treasurer (Scott's wife); and Miss Jill Miles, secretary (Don and Sandra's daughter.). They decided upon a pretty name for the new concern, EMERALD ACRES. A nearby farmer, Dennis Olin, worked part time for the new factory the first year.

Miles purchased his first cubing machine from the California Pellet Mill Company. This machine did not perform as well as expected so Miles made several changes and modifications. Don suffered another setback in October, the first year in business, losing three fingers while working on the machinery, but the family decided to continue the operation. Don and Scott operated the cubing machinery, while Sandy and Jill operated the bagging machine, until they became efficient in running all the machinery. The cubes when completed are one and one-quarter inch by three inches, and are shipped in forty-five pound bags to feed stores all over the area.

The large round bales of alfalfa, weighing from 1,500 to 1,800 pounds are used for their operation, as opposed to the square old-fashioned bales. The Miles family has a way of "making things do," and Scott rebuilt a school bus chassis into a vehicle for hauling the large bales of hay to their factory and secured a patent for his invention. This vehicle was an odd looking contraption but it served the purpose for which it was designed.

The large bales of hay are converted into small cubes by the following steps: The hay is chopped into small pieces in a device they refer to as a tub grinder, then goes into a machine called a Cyclone separator, and then into a surge bin. Moisture is added to the material at this stage in the mixing chamber. It is then ready to go into the final stage of the process, the cubing chamber, where the rectangular shaped cubes are compacted and extruded. They are now ready for the bagging process, or can be shipped in bulk form.

The factory produced 200 bags of alfalfa cubes daily the first year, and the business was to be a sideline occupation for the Miles family, but within a short time they were operating year round. Four years and three cubing machines later, the factory was producing six tons of cubes per hour, and the Miles family could not meet the demand of orders that were coming in. Their factory was the only alfalfa cubing factory in the Midwest, therefore, the market was wide open for their product.

In September of 1983, the Emerald Acres Alfalfa Cube factory was visited by representatives from twenty-six nations during the fourth International Agriculture Field Days. The visitors then spent two hours in New Richmond and were served lunch at the local park by the Montgomery-Putnam County Cattlemen's Association. The Miles family made an agreement to supply twenty tons of their cubes to a representative in Trinidad. Representatives from other foreign countries have visited the New Richmond cubing factory through the years to examine and place orders for the cubes.

Purdue University has fed the cubes from Emerald Acres with good success where a controlled diet is required for their animals. The cubes are also a convenient food for zoo animals.

The Miles family started their new factory in a small building on their farm about two miles south of New Richmond. They later purchased the former Merman Farms from M.L. Smith and were located about a mile west of New Richmond. A large metal building was erected on this site for the factory as expansion was necessary for the growth of the company. They hauled the large round bales of hay in large ventilated trailers and had a semi-truck for delivering their cubes to the various locations. Emerald Acres went out of business in the late 1990s.

Chapter 8 - Cemeteries in the New Richmond Vicinity

The New Richmond Cemetery

The land surrounding the old section of the New Richmond Cemetery was first entered by David Oppy on October 2, 1828, and Eli Elrod, on October 14, 1828, each entering an eighty acre tract in section nine, township twenty, range five. The land bordering the east of the old cemetery was entered by William Forbes, one eighty acre tract being entered on October 21, 1828, and another eighty acres on December 1, 1830.

The oldest recorded burial was that of Ezra Elrod (age 3 years, 9 months, and 21 days) on January 15, 1835. Less than a month later, Absalom K. Elrod (age 1 year, 6 months, and 17 days) died on February 3, 1835. These children were both sons of E. and R. Elrod (Eli). The Elrods lost a daughter, Harriett R. in 1843, age 6 years, and another unnamed infant - no dates on the tombstone. Another early burial was an infant son of Charles and Mary Forbes, on October 9, 1836.

Evidently there was no early deed made by either Eli Elrod or David Oppy to the New Richmond Cemetery trustees; at least, a careful search through the deeds in the Montgomery County courthouse failed to turn up any such record. After David Oppy's death in 1855, his son, Christopher John Oppy, inherited the land and the cemetery was part of his inheritance. David was buried in this old section. It was a custom in the early pioneer days to bury members of the family on a favorite spot of the family farm, but in this case, the Oppys and Elrods allowed their neighbors to bury their dead on the same section of ground, and this soon became known as the New Richmond Cemetery.

There were many burials in the 1840s through the 1870s in the New Richmond cemetery. Christopher John Oppy and his wife, Margaret, made their deed on January 22, 1879. They received $54.00 from the Trustees of the New Richmond Cemetery for a tract of land forty-seven rods north and south, by seven and one-half rods east and west, in section nine, township twenty, range five. This newly acquired land increased the size of the cemetery by one-half, and the deed was made to include the old section of the cemetery.

On December 18, 1878, a meeting was called for the citizens of New Richmond and vicinity, for the purpose of purchasing and enlarging the ground known as the New Richmond Cemetery. Dr. Stow S. Detchon was called upon to chair the meeting, and Mahlon J. Mason acted as secretary. Trustees elected at this meeting were: George W. Washburn, Cyrus Quinn Kirkpatrick, Stow S. Detchon, and Mahlon J. Mason. Mason was elected secretary of the newly formed association, but there were no other officers listed on this record. It is possible they made Detchon the chairman but neglected to record the office. This is the earliest record I discovered of a New Richmond Cemetery Association being formed.

As soon as the new ground was purchased from the Oppys, the association made plans to erect a fence around all the property. This was necessary to keep out the livestock which were always allowed to roam freely about the countryside. This new ground was staked off into lots, which were offered for sale for a small sum of about $5.00.

This cemetery served the community for many years, and it was decided the cemetery association should be incorporated. A group of New Richmond citizens met in the local schoolhouse on May 15, 1909 for the purpose of completing the Incorporation of the New Richmond Cemetery Association. John T. Detchon was elected chairman, and Orlando W. Mason, Secretary. Incidentally, John Detchon was the son of Dr. Stow S. Detchon who chaired the first organizational meeting of the New Richmond Cemetery

Association in 1878, and Orlando W. Mason was the son of the first Secretary, Mahlon J. Mason. The directors of the newly incorporated association were: Ed. T. McCrea–elected for one year; John T. Detchon, two years–was elected treasurer; O. W. (Orlando) Mason, three years–secretary; Samuel S. Kirkpatrick, four years–Vice President; Charles Kirkpatrick, five years–President for one year. The Incorporation of the New Richmond Cemetery Association was recorded June 1, 1910 by Henry D. Servies, Recorder of Montgomery County, Indiana, at 4.15 p.m.

Additional land was purchased through the years when expansion was necessary. On September 3, 1910, the land that is known as section three in the cemetery plat, was purchased from William D. and Susannah Graves. About the same time, on November 3, 1910, Henry K. and Nannie Lee, along with Lee's partner in the tile factory, Neil Casey, sold a strip of land running thirteen rods and seventeen feet north and south, by ten feet east and west, to the New Richmond Cemetery Association. The association paid $17.50 for this property. Lee and Casey had purchased this and the surrounding acreage for the timber and the clay underground. They had not removed the clay, as can be observed from the New Richmond Park. The field to the west of the park is some three to four feet higher than the park property where the clay was removed.

Thomas F. and Gertrude Oppy sold another ten foot wide strip on the east side of the cemetery at a later date. In 1959, Russell and Mildred Smith sold a one hundred foot wide strip of land that extended all the way from the black top road to the south end of the cemetery, for $100. This was located to the west of the old cemetery plat. Helen Oppy Binns donated another strip on the east side of the cemetery that extended all the way from the black top to the south end of the cemetery, and is known as section five on the plat of the cemetery. Contributions and income from a trust fund provide funds for the maintenance of the New Richmond Cemetery.

After many years of discussing the proposition of building a sidewalk from the town of New Richmond to the cemetery, it was decided to build a new concrete walk all the way to the west side of the graveyard, in September of 1915. The citizens of the town and the cemetery association were to raise subscriptions to finance the project. The walk was a great improvement to the town, and the cemetery.

In the very early years, the grass grew until it was tall enough to cut with a scythe, and before the fence was erected, livestock kept the grass down by grazing, but this also destroyed the gravesites, and many tombstones were pushed over and broken. I remember walking out to the New Richmond Cemetery with my grandmother, Fannie Ebrite, who pushed her lawn mower all the way from the east end of town to the cemetery to mow her lot where my grandpa was buried. The old part of the cemetery was so overgrown with weeds and brush, we never ventured to that part. After Garland Oppy took charge of the cemetery, he cleaned the old section, clearing away the brush and weeds, and reset the old stones. The association then planted Norway Maple trees around the graveyard and it is now a very well-kept cemetery.

Others who have served as trustees of the New Richmond Cemetery Association through the later years, and the offices they held are: David Nesbitt, President; Reuben Swank, Vice President; Roy B. Hanawalt, Secretary; Levert E. Binns, Treasurer (for 40 years); C. L. Martin; Melvin Waye; Roy E. Geiger; Garland W. Oppy, Secretary; Robert Mason (grandson of M.J. Mason); Ralph Kunkel; Ivan Pollock; Nyle Royer; Roger Kunkel, Treasurer; James Fenters; Richard Stephenson; and Donald Waye.

I tried to compile a list of gravediggers, and caretakers of the New Richmond cemetery, but realized a complete record does not exist. Among the names that could be recalled by longtime residents of New Richmond were: Sherman Lane, Oscar Lowry, Lawrence (Slim) Spears, Jim Harris, Isaac Fowler, Everett Pierce, and three generations of Kunkels—Fowler Kunkel, Ralph Kunkel, and Roger Kunkel.

The New Richmond *Record*, Thursday, June 1, 1905 printed the following list of OUR HONORED DEAD, buried in the New Richmond Cemetery: W.S. Foster, Civil War; Ab Kirkpatrick, Civil War, 10th Ind.; Zack Ellis, Civil; John Wheeler, Civil; George Phillips, Civil, Co., A., 63rd; John Crouch, Civil; Peter Clarkson, Civil; John Clark, Mexican; Howell Alexander, Mexican; R. Hobbs, Civil; Jack Mason, Mexican; Willis Mason, Mexican; Jacob Dazey, 1812; Curtis D. Haywood, Civil, 72nd Ind; James Foster; Confederate Soldier in Civil War; Milt Harper, Civil; Elisha Campbell, Civil; William Brown, Civil; William Lunger, Civil, died in Andersonville Prison; William Mershon, Civil, Co. G. 40th Ind.

Forbes Cemetery

The old Forbes Cemetery was located in Section 17, township 20 north, Range 5 west. The 1917 map of Coal Creek Township shows this cemetery located in the northeast quarter of section 17, southwest of New Richmond on the Oppy road between the railroad and Coal Creek. M.J. Westfall owned 95 acres surrounding the cemetery on this map. There are no records as to who was buried in this cemetery–was possibly the Forbes family plot. What became of the stones is a mystery, but one of the previous owners said her husband removed the stones and stood them against the fence, then plowed and farmed the land. She referred to the spot as "Forbes Hill," and wasn't the least concerned about her husband's actions. I have searched from the road in front of the location but there are no visible stones. Another question is why didn't this cemetery appear on earlier maps of Coal Creek township?

Park Cemetery

This cemetery has been referred to as the Alexander Cemetery, and in later years, the McCrea Cemetery, located in Coal Creek Township.

On November 13, 1877, Edward T. and Jessie L. McCrea deeded one acre of ground to the Trustees of the New Richmond Methodist Episcopal Church and their successors, to be used as a Burying Ground for the Dead of Montgomery County, Indiana, for seventy-five ($75) dollars. This plot of ground was described as: Part of the east half of the south half of the south-east quarter of section 10 township 20 north, range 5 west, containing one acre.

The cemetery is situated one and one-tenth mile southeast of the center of New Richmond on the Linden road. It is within the hilly wooded area behind the remains of Ed McCrea's residence–only an iron fence marks the site of the home today (1986). Family names of Alexander, Park, Ramey, Brannon, and Martin are buried in this family plot, and the latest recorded burial was that of Joseph Alexander, an early settler on this land. The New Richmond Methodist Episcopal Church members did not bury their deceased in this cemetery, although the McCreas deeded the plot to them. The following page is a list of tombstone inscriptions recorded by the W.P.A. many years ago; the stones are probably illegible today.

PARK CEMETERY
Sec. 10, TW. 20 N., R. 5 W. Coal Creek Township–inscriptions:

ALEXANDER, R.A.	died 5-30-1867	age 48
ALEXANDER, Joseph	died 4-3-1873	age 82
BRANNON, Experience	died 1-28-1853	age 23
PARK, Elijah	died 7-13-1844	age 51
PARK, Uwris, son, E. & E. PARK	died 2-2-1835	age—
PARK, Sarah E., dau. E. & E. PARK	died 7-10-1849	age 1
PARK, Elijah L., son, E. & E. PARK	died 9-5-1862	age 1 Mo.
PARK, Mary, dau. Micajah & Susan Brannon Park	died 9-11-1849	age 15 hrs.
PARK, Emily Ramey, w. of Omar Park	died 4-8-1858	age 29
RAMEY, Asa	died 10-3-1855	age 76
RAMEY, Mary, dau. L.J. & M.J.	died 9-18-1838	age 1
RAMEY, Infant, dau. L.J. & M.J. Ramey	died 7-14-1840	age—
RAMEY, William E., son of L.J. & M.J. Ramey	died 2-2-1849	age 2
MARTIN, John F., son J.P. & R. Martin	died 9-19-1862	age 1

A note made by the W.P.A. reads: This cemetery is located on a wooded hilltop, on the farm of Mrs. Mary McCrea, New Richmond, Indiana (owner in 1950). There is no fence around it and not one stone is standing–there are four posts with iron hooks embedded where a chain possibly was fastened. Hogs and other livestock range in this woods pasture and quite likely caused this damage.

Chapter 9 - Churches

Methodists in Coal Creek Township

Among the earliest religious groups in Indiana to form an organization were the Methodists, who divided the state into districts and conferences. The first district embraced all of western Indiana and extended from the Ohio River northward to the Great Lakes. The districts were then divided into smaller branches known as circuits, but even they covered quite a large territory. The circuit rider was required to publish the time and place of the quarterly meeting more than a month ahead of time. The people following this faith would come from miles away to attend these meetings.

In Coal Creek Township the most noted place of gathering to worship was in the famous Meharry's campground, located north of Wingate, just south of the Coal Creek bridge on what is now State Road 25.

The worshippers came on horseback, or in the old farm wagon—this being the most popular mode of travel due to the usually large families who attended these meetings. Some of the smaller families came in the more comfortable vehicle, the carriage, but many of the more hardy would arrive on foot.

Tents were erected soon after arriving, being scattered about the grove by many, but others preferred sleeping in their wagons, covered or uncovered, while some slept on the ground—whatever suited. The site of the campground was selected for the necessary shade, and was always near a creek or river for an ample supply of water for man and his faithful horse. Provisions were cooked ahead, enough to last a few days, and when the supply was exhausted, campfires were kept burning to replenish the supply.

To prepare for the religious services, a high, crude platform was erected so the minister could be seen by all attending these meetings. Surrounding this platform were seats; often they were only fallen logs on which the congregation seated themselves for the worship services. A rail fence was constructed to divide the area into two parts, one for the males, the other for the females. After the people experienced their religious 'awakenings,' both sexes were allowed to be together to sit, or exercise violently, shout, scream, clap their hands, jerk and swoon—or whatever effect the experience had on them, in a space down in front of the minister, or exhorter in charge of the meeting.

The group gathered for a morning service around 11:00 a.m., followed by the community noon meal, or love feast. The afternoon would find the group gathered together for a less formal service, shaking hands with the nearest neighbor, and repeating scripture, testimonies, etc.

The campground was lighted at night by fires built upon a raised platform that had been covered with earth to keep the fire from burning through. These platforms were placed on poles high above the ground to allow the light to radiate throughout the camp. Sentinels were placed about the grounds and the ladies were not allowed to go roaming about the grove alone after dark.

The evening services must have been a very inspiring experience for these worshippers out in the various groves. The sermon and prayers, and sometimes fervid exhortations under the stars would have created a lasting memory to many, especially the children, who attended. The bonds of society were surely strengthened after attending a week or two of these services.

As soon as the forests were cleared and the first crops were planted, the early settlers of Coal Creek Township began to turn their thoughts to public worship. One of the early families in the vicinity of New Richmond was the Kirkpatrick family. Absalom Kirkpatrick, a well read and learned man who came from Adams County, Ohio, was the first to open his home to a group who followed the Methodist faith. This group included the families of William Forbes, who incidentally was one of the first local 'exhortors,' and had twelve children; Jeremia Sherwood's; Alexander May and wife; James and Mary "Polly" Kendall and their family of eight children; Samuel and Sally Kendall and their eight children; and Elisha and Abigail Kendall and their three children. James, Elisha, and Samuel Kendall were brothers, all coming from Adams County, Ohio, before 1830—and all three were deceased before 1850. Samuel and Phebe VanPelt Kincaid came with seven children; it is believed that two of their children were deceased before coming to Montgomery County.

The pioneer log home often contained all the essentials of a home in one large room where meals were cooked, the Bible read, the family slept, and company was entertained. The home of Absalom and Elizabeth Van Pelt Kirkpatrick and their six children was 18 by 26 feet, with the usual fireplace at one end of the room. On the day of the meeting, the bedding was scooted off to one corner of the large room and the benches were put in place for the morning worship. After the services, the benches were placed around the table and the guests were invited to stay and partake of the Sunday dinner; hopefully Mrs. Kirkpatrick was assisted by the ladies of the group. This was the scene of the first meeting place of the Methodists in the New Richmond area.

In 1835 the group had grown to such a large number the Methodists decided it was time to build a meeting house. This was built on the Kirkpatrick farm and was located on County Road 500 West, about a quarter of a mile south off County Road 1100 North. This is the first road west of New Richmond, from the center of town, known as the Oppy road. This brick building was built on the west side of the road, and was 26 by 40 feet. It has not been recorded as to whether the bricks were made at the site or just where they were acquired. Many of the early settlers had the knowledge of brick manufacturing—the Meharry brothers all made their own brick at the site of their homes, and the group may have engaged them to make their brick. It is recorded that the building cost $900, quite a large sum in the early years for a newly formed congregation to gather. This church was always remembered as the "Old Brick Church."

This church was, like most churches, served by the circuit rider, or traveling preacher. Circuit riders had several churches to serve, so the congregation either had to hold services only when he could attend—which was sometimes every four weeks, occasionally every six to eight weeks—or they could have a local preacher serve on the days the circuit rider was elsewhere. One of the questions asked at the quarterly conference meetings was, "Are there any recommendations for license to preach?" and another question, "Are there any recommendations of local Preachers for orders?" Searching through Absalom Kirkpatrick's probate records, the sale bill listed several books on religion and the Methodist beliefs, indicating he had studied the literature enough to qualify as a local preacher, or class leader. Another local exhorter licensed to preach was William Forbes, who was also a class leader. These men carried on the services between the visits of the Circuit rider. This old Brick Church served the worshippers until they decided it would be more convenient for the town people if they would build in New Richmond.

Early historians gave the year 1853 as the date of the construction of the second Methodist house of worship, their first building in the town of New Richmond. This was built on the lot occupied by the Knights of Pythias block and the Snyder building, now the Utterback Marketing Services building. This building was a single-room, 30 by 40 feet structure and faced the north. Surrounding the building was a large churchyard to accommodate the hitching posts erected all about the structure to contain the horse and buggies or wagons. This churchyard was enclosed by a high board fence. The local school building stood south of the Methodist church building. The church services were often disrupted by the local boys playing ball and shouting so loud the preacher could not be heard. This building had two doors on the front of the building; the ladies entered on one side, the gentlemen, the other.

History is a little sketchy on the early life of the Methodist church, as well as other churches, before the Crawfordsville papers carried items from the small villages and towns in Montgomery County. However, it was recorded by some thoughtful person that Anna Bible was organist, Mrs. Barney Wallace and "Dad" Smock, a local saw mill owner, sang for funerals and other special meetings, such as the quarterly conferences when they were held in the local church. The Kirkpatrick family was active throughout the history of the Methodist church; Frank Kirkpatrick for many years was Sunday School Superintendent and S. S. (Samuel) Kirkpatrick served as Sunday School superintendent many years as well.

A copy of the deed of this property is printed below. You may note that the Methodist Trustees did not secure the land from Mr. and Mrs. McComas until 1856 and the deed was not recorded until August 30, 1875. This happened quite frequently with the church and school lots in the early years. This deed is copied as near as possible to the exact copy in the Montgomery County Recorder's office, Volume 40, pages 414-415.

> Montgomery County Indiana Deed book 40, pp. 414-415 Methodist Episcopal Church in New Richmond, Indiana (DEED)
>
> THIS INDENTURE WITNESSETH, That Samuel McComas and Maria McComas in consideration of Eighteen dollars and seventy five cents to them paid by Stephen Connel, Cyrus Q. Kirkpatrick, George Manners, Charles Forbes and John Alexander, Trustees in Trust for the Methodist Episcopal Church and their successors in office, the receipt whereof is hereby acknowledged, do hereby Grant, Bargain, Sell and Convey to the said Stephen Connel, Cyrus Q. Kirkpatrick, George Manners, Charles Forbes and John Alexander and their successors in Office, Forever, the following Real Estate in Montgomery County and State of Indiana, and described as follows to wit: Commencing at the middle of the Craws....States Rode West of the Town of New Richmond Known as the Thorntown and Covington Rode and Yountsville and Lafayette Rode; Thence West 8 rods thence South 15 rods; thence East 8 rods; thence North 15 rods, Containing Three quarters of an acre more or less: Being a part of the East half of The North East Quarter of Section 9, Township Twenty North of Range 5 West, Together with all the privileges and appurtenances to the same belonging, To Have and To Hold the same to the said Trustees and their successors in office, Heirs and Assigns Forever the grantor his Heirs and Assigns Hereby Covenanting with the grantee Trustees and their successors in office. So conveyed is Clear Free and Unincumbered that they are lawfully seized of the premises aforesaid, as of a sure and indefeasible estate of inheritance in fee simple; and that they will Warrant and Defend the same against all claims whatsoever.
>
> IN WITNESS WHEREOF The said Samuel McComas and Maria McComas his wife have hereunto set their hands and seals, this Fifth day of January A.D. 1856.
>
> Signed: Samuel McComas (Seal) and Maria McComas (Seal)
> The State of Indiana, Montgomery County Sct. Personally appeared before me the subscriber a Justice of the Peace in and for said County Samuel McComas and Maria McComas his wife, the Grantors in the above conveyance and acknowledged The same to be their voluntary act and deed.
>
> WITNESS my hand and seal this 5th day of January 1856. Edward P. Bennett, (Seal) Justice of the Peace
>
> Received for Record August 30th, 1875 at 5 P. M. and Recorded same day.
> T. N. Myers, R. M. Co.

In January 1879 there was talk of rebuilding the Methodist Church in New Richmond. The old structure was badly in need of repair by this time, but it continued to serve the congregation until 1888. The group decided they could wait no longer, and would have to part with the old building and build a new one.

In May 1888 the old building and lot was sold to Thomas S. Patton for $600. The deed said, "excepting such furniture as has been placed in the Church House thereon, since the erection of said house. Also, said Trustees reserve the right and full control of said described property on or about the first of November next." This deed was signed by the Trustees in Trust for the Methodist Episcopal Church at New Richmond, Indiana: Cyrus Q. Kirkpatrick, Ed. T. McCrea and Zebulon Zuck, and acknowledged before Amos Ebrite, a Justice of the Peace of Montgomery County, Indiana, on May 21, 1888.

William Campbell, the correspondent for the Crawfordsville *Weekly Review*, Saturday May 5, 1888, had this to say of the old building, "The old M. E. Church, one of the old land marks of our town, built thirty-five years ago, was sold Saturday to the highest bidder. It was knocked off to Mr. Patton, of this place at six hundred and eighty dollars. It looks like a sin to sell such an old landmark. People and heads of families all have sad feelings to see the old church go, but enterprise and push say it has seen its day and the place where our fathers and grandfathers worshipped will soon be a thing of the past. The old church has many memories that cling to those who witness with a sigh its downfall."

Mrs. Barbara Manners, widow of Dr. Manners, New Richmond's pioneer physician, gave three lots to the Methodist people on which to build and the remaining lots were to be used for a parsonage. Preparations were soon going on for the building of a new church. The ground was surveyed and staked off and soon the men with their teams hauled the stone and brick from Crawfordsville for the foundation of the church building. When Mr. Kirkpatrick started to lay the brick he found it out of square—he later discovered some small boys had moved the stakes—but this was corrected before any damage was done.

The carpentry contract was let to Joseph Tribby, he being the lowest bidder, and was to have the structure completed within 90 days, giving bond to that effect. The history of the church building presented at the time the building was remodeled said, "In November 1888 under the Pastorate of James Loder, a new church was dedicated upon the site of the present building. Samuel R. Tribby was the contractor, and the cost of the building was $3,400. It was dedicated by Rev. George W. Switzer."

The Christian congregation had already commenced building a new structure and the two were running 'neck to neck' as to which building would be completed first. By August both buildings were nearly completed and were soon ready for church services. Both structures were topped by brand new bells to call the New Richmond people to church. The writer for the Crawfordsville *Review* said, "they are both very nice and show up well."

M.E. Conference and Circuit History

Before we stray too far from the early history of the first two church buildings, a little history of the Conference and the Circuits follows, with short sketches of the sister churches within the same circuits.

The following is the Conference and Circuit history of the Methodist Episcopal Church at New Richmond:

> In 1859, '64, '66, the New Richmond church was in the Newtown Circuit, Lafayette District Northwest Indiana Conference. Heshbon Bethel (in the Meharry neighborhood), New Richmond, Prairie Chapel, Asbury Chapel (later Round Hill), Thompson's Chapel (at Boston Store or Elmdale), Pleasant Hill (or Wingate), Sugar Grove (in Jackson Township, Tippecanoe County) were all listed in this circuit. The LaFayette District conference records reported 358 members, 7 churches, with the value of the churches as being $7,000; there were 6 Sunday schools with 400 members.
>
> August 20, 1881, the Pleasant Hill Circuit, Crawfordsville District Pastor posted the following appointments: New Richmond, preaching at 11:00 a.m. August 21, 1881; Asbury, at 3 1/2 p.m.; and on August 28th: Pleasant Hill at 11:00 a.m., Thompson's Chapel at 4 p.m. The appointments appeared in the Crawfordsville Saturday Evening *Journal*, August 20, 1881.

November 24, 1889, New Richmond Circuit, Crawfordsville District Northwest Indiana Conference. Listed with this circuit were: New Richmond, Thompson's Chapel, and Asbury Chapel. The first quarterly conference was held at Wingate November 24, 1889 and David A. Rogers was the Pastor for the Circuit.

December 3, 1892, Wingate Circuit, Crawfordsville District, Northwest Indiana Conference. Listed in this circuit were: Wingate, New Richmond, Asbury Chapel, and Thompson's Chapel. This first Quarterly Conference was held at Wingate on December 3, 1892, H.M. Appleby was the Pastor of the Circuit.

November 4, 1895, New Richmond Circuit, Crawfordsville District, Northwest Indiana Conference. Listed in this circuit were: New Richmond, Sugar Grove and Asbury.

NOTE: Wingate and Thompson's Chapel were removed from this circuit at the First Quarterly Conference Crawfordsville District, held at New Richmond on November 4, 1895. J. P. Shagley was Pastor.

August 14, 1919, New Richmond Circuit, Crawfordsville District, Northwest Indiana Conference. Listed in this circuit were: New Richmond, services at 8:30 p.m.; Sugar Grove, 10:30 a.m.; and Round Hill, Sunday School at 10:30 a.m. The New Richmond Record, Thursday, August 14, 1919 listed the appointments.

Heshbon Bethel Church (M.E.) was built in 1837 on Thomas Meharry's property west of New Richmond. This church was connected with the Newtown and New Richmond circuits. The exact location is the grave of Polly (Meharry) McCorkle in the Meharry Cemetery. The building faced east.

Asbury Chapel, later Round Hill, was built in 1839 and was located one mile west and one fourth mile north of the Round Hill community. The building was moved to the Round Hill community and used as a house of worship for the Methodists in that area until it was replaced by a new brick building, dedicated in 1904. The Round Hill Church continued with the New Richmond circuit into the 1920s. Some of their members united with the Methodist Church in New Richmond, and some transferred their membership to the Linden Methodist church.

26 - Round Hill Methodist Episcopal Church

Pleasant Hill, later Wingate, organized in 1832 with 25 members. The congregation first worshipped in a log school until they built their first house of worship in 1852.

Thompson's Chapel, at Elmdale, organized in 1832 or 1833 with 30 members. They built their church in 1832, naming the building for Rev. Thompson, Pastor of the circuit, who was instrumental in the building of the church.

Sugar Grove, located in Jackson Township, Tippecanoe County, erected their first church in 1854, a frame building; they later constructed a handsome new brick structure in 1875. This building is still standing on the original site, but is being used to store farm machinery. The Sugar Grove organization united with the new Jackson Heights Church in Tippecanoe County in 1927.

Maintenance and Remodeling of the 1888 Methodist Episcopal Church Building

In November 1896 Mrs. Barbara Manners donated carpeting for the entire Methodist Church building. This served its purpose until it was replaced a few years later. In 1902 a committee was appointed to make plans to improve the building. On this committee were John P. Bible, James W. Tribby, and A.D. Snyder. It was estimated that $2,000 was needed to do the necessary improvements, and before the work was started, $1,500 had been raised to cover the cost. Improvements to the structure included new wallpaper, carpet, and varnish on the woodwork. The building on the outside was painted "white and drab" by L. C. Carson, the local painter.

In 1904 John T. Detchon installed a new automatic gasoline light plant in the building. There were nine lights with the lead pipes "buried" above the ceiling. The addition of new chandeliers was an added attraction to the beauty of the church. The house of worship was "most thoroughly and beautifully illuminated" for the first time in June of that year.

While researching the history of the church, I noticed that, when asked at the quarterly conference about insurance on the buildings of the circuit, only the New Richmond Methodist Church was insured. In 1905 it was insured for $2,500 and the value of the church was listed as $4,000.

Again in 1915, plans were made to remodel the structure, but this work was not started until July of 1917. The architect drew the plans with the idea of preserving as much as the original structure as possible. The size of the Sunday schools had grown and larger classrooms were needed. A large room was added to the rear of the building, to be used as a combination classroom and dining room for social events. This was a nineteen by thirty-two foot room. A spacious kitchen was added at the northeast corner, and four new classrooms completed the necessary room additions. The building was then covered with brick on the outside of the structure and stands almost the same as it did when this work was finished and dedicated Sunday, March 24, 1918. The steeple was removed in later years because of a safety measure; it was thought that the weight was causing the roof to leak in the entry room. Cost of remodeling the building was $10,000.

Trustees at the time of remodeling were: Samuel S. Kirkpatrick, chairman, John G. Utterback, Thomas J. Grantham, Charles Kirkpatrick, William Inskeep, John M. Malsbary, William Kirkpatrick, Charles Haywood, and Bayless Alexander.

The building committee members were the following: Chairman Charles Kirkpatrick, Pastor H. Earl Moore, Secretary Nettie Alexander, Treasurer Lenna Hollin, William Inskeep, Quinn McBeth, Susan Alexander, and John G. Utterback.

Services were held each evening of the week following the dedication. Former pastors preaching at these services were the Reverends M.H. Appleby of South Bend, Henry Clay Riley (Boswell), H.D. Dick (Argos), D.A. Rogers (Wolcott), and T.B. Wilber (Delphi).

Mrs. Barbara G. Manners gave to the Trustees of the New Richmond Methodist Episcopal Church Viz. James W. Tribby, Solomon Dewey, John P. Bible, Thomas Grantham and Ed. T. McCrea $1500, to be held as a perpetual fund for the church, the interest of which sum was to be applied to the preachers' salaries—who ever may officiate at the New Richmond M.E. Church or whatever name it may go by in the future. Besides this generous gift she gave $100 yearly to missions in memory of her late husband, Dr. George Manners.

The parsonage was built sometime before August 13, 1892, because the Trustees listed 1 parsonage in the circuit with probable value of $700. I failed to come up with the exact month and year it was built.

In April 1905 the congregation contemplated building a cottage to rent on the lot west of the parsonage, and by the middle of July, it was almost completed. This was to be a source of income to help support the church.

THE EPWORTH LEAGUE

In the minutes of the second quarterly conference held January 12, 1895, three Epworth Leagues (church groups) had been organized. The New Richmond, Sugar Grove, and Round Hill churches organized the groups. Charles Appleby was listed as the first president of the League at New Richmond. Others listed as Presidents of all the leagues were: James Hayes, Thomas Kerr, Brother Jakes, John Wilson, Samuel Rafferty (at Asbury), Raymond Alexander, and Minnie Cash. It is uncertain which church these people served, as all are recorded as Presidents within the circuit.

These young people were an active group who met each Sunday evening for prayer and social gatherings. They sponsored many programs, among them a series of lectures held in June 1904. Dr. Halstead of Indianapolis gave his famous lecture, "Fun on The Farm," Miss Helen Nell Lemmon of Zionsville, the elocutionist, presented "The Eve of Marriage," and the last of this series was a musical by local talent that included instrumental and vocals, assisted by musicians from sister towns: Miss Mustard (Lafayette), Miss Elizabeth Shoaf (Veedersburg), Miss Taylor (Bloomington, Ill.), and Mrs. J. Frank Simison (Romney).

The Epworth League and the Ladies Aid Society purchased a new organ from the D.H. Baldwin Music Company of Crawfordsville in March 1904. It was quite a mammoth piece of furniture and cost the two groups $700. It was an imitation pipe organ, "Estey" make and was formally dedicated at the children's day exercises in June 1904.

Officers of the Epworth League in 1918 were: Lela Hanawalt, President; Nelle Livingston, first Vice President; Elnora McNeil, second Vice President; Muriel Tribby, third Vice President; Ethel Turner, fourth Vice President; Gay Shotts, Secretary; Albin Raub, Treasurer; Muriel Tribby, Organist.

LADIES AID OF NEW RICHMOND METHODIST EPISCOPAL CHURCH

The Ladies Aid Society of the New Richmond Methodist Episcopal Church was organized between the year of the building of the church in 1888 and 1900. In 1939, this group was combined with the Missionary Society, and the Women's Society for Christian Service (W.S.C.S.) was formed.

The organization was active through the years, raising money to help support the church and the various missions. A "Peddler's Parade" was among the unique entertainment activities and fundraisers. "Lawn Festivals" were held on the lawns of the members of the group and on the church lawn. These festivals usually advertised good food, and musical entertainment. Sales such as the "Festival and Apron Sale" and "Apron and Bonnet Sale and Festival" were held in the Hollin Opera House or the Modern Woodman Lodge hall over Johnson's drug store. An "Afternoon Market" with all sorts of good eatables was held in the Perkin's business room. The ladies sold dressed chickens, homemade bread and cakes, fresh vegetables, ice cream, strawberries and cream, with cake. Annual festivals by the ladies of the Methodist Church continued into the early 21st century.

Another source of entertainment and a fundraising project was a lecture course, to be held in the "coming Winter days," according to the notices. Three of the programs were lectures and the fourth was a musical and was held during the holidays in 1905. A Halloween Festival was held previous to the lectures in the Washburn Building. New Richmond was not without social events in the early 1900s.

In January 1903 the ladies were to meet at the home of Mrs. Ed. T. McCrea, who lived just southeast of New Richmond. The ground was covered with snow, so Mrs. J.A. Kirkpatrick hitched up old "Dobbin" to a bob-sled and drove fifteen ladies from town out to the McCrea home and a jolly time was had by all.

The Ladies Aid Society of the Methodist Church, twenty-eight persons in all, went from New Richmond to Tecumseh's Trail, north of Lafayette, for an all day picnic. This was not quite as simple as it is nowadays to make a trip such as this. A few went in automobiles, some drove in horse and buggies, others rode horses, etc. to Linden, where they boarded the train. From the train they took the streetcar from the city to the trail.

"The group consumed about six dozen fried chickens along with all sorts of other good things to eat," the editor of the New Richmond *Record* said, and "the children and old folks alike enjoyed the dozens of lawn swings, rope swings, the May-pole, and they slid and skated on the dancing pavilion (they couldn't dance of course), and climbed the hill to visit the folks at the Soldiers Home." The editor also said that "no men should be allowed, but Lish Westfall got scared lest his folks might get run down by the 'Kyars' and he decided to go as far as the city on business, and John P. Bible went along to see that his daughter Miss Maud "chauffeured" their gasoline engine successfully. The group was captured by a "Kodak" (camera) while wading the Wabash River."

The New Richmond area has a very good record as far as Missionaries sent from the Methodist Church. The following pages tell of some of the work that has been done by these dedicated people.

Missionaries from the New Richomond Methodist Episcopal Church

Rev. William Clarence Davidson, born March 31, 1848 at New Richmond, was one of ten children of Gideon and Mary A. Davidson. William was educated in the local schools and furthered his education at the old Sugar Grove Academy in Jackson Township, Tippecanoe County, Indiana. He was converted during his first term in the academy and exhibited so much ability in the academy he was urged to prepare for the university. He was licensed by the quarterly conference of the Methodist Episcopal Church to "exhort" its teachings. He then entered DePauw University in 1871, and the Bishop gave him the opportunity to preach as assistant preacher in nine different churches. In 1876 he graduated from DePauw with the degree of A.M. and was immediately ordained to preach, his first charge being at Belleville, Indiana. On June 22, 1876 he married Miss Mary McDaniel, daughter of a Methodist preacher. He founded the M.E. Church at Greencastle, Indiana, during his course at the University.

In 1877 Rev. Davidson and his wife sailed for Japan as missionaries, teaching school at Hirosaki, then studied the languages for three months and began to preach at Hakadote and while there he was appointed United States Consul. After three years work in this field, he was transferred to Yokohama. The terrible strain that this work placed upon missionaries took its toll on the reverend and wife. They returned to the States after seven years in Japan, his wife passing away within three weeks after their return. They had no children.

After resting and regaining his health, Rev. Davidson accepted a pastorate at Plymouth, Indiana, where he met the principal of the high school, Miss Helen Oakes. On September 16, 1886, they were married at the home of her parents, Sanford and Mary Oakes, in Steuben. In the fall of 1887 Rev. Davidson and his new bride sailed for Japan and took up their residence at Yokohama. He entered his duties as presiding elder of the Sendai District. His new bride was unable to withstand the climate of Japan, so once again he returned to the States.

Rev. Davidson joined the Northern New York Conference and remained a member until his death. He preached at Verona one year, Clinton, two years, Herkimer, five years, Rome-on Liberty Street, one year, Oswego, Trinity, four years, and Lowville, two years. He retired in April 1902, purchased a home in Holand Patent and died at this home on October 29, 1903. He was buried in the Steuben Cemetery. He left his widow and four children, Fay, Marguerite, Hobart Oakes, and William Lucien, all at home, and brothers Prof. Albert, Lincoln, Nebraska; James, Lafayette, Indiana; John, Monitor, Indiana, and sisters Mrs. Amanda Edwards, Independence, Indiana; Mrs. Alice Black, and Mrs. Ella Phillips, New Richmond, Indiana.

Rev. Benjamin S. Haywood, born north of New Richmond, to Henry and Martha Sherwood Haywood, was a missionary to Mexico, New Mexico, Southern California, and San Juan, Puerto Rico. Benjamin returned home in the fall of 1904 and lectured to the home folks in the New Richmond and Sugar Grove Methodist Churches, dwelling reminiscently upon the happy days of his boyhood spent in the neighborhood of both churches. He then described the life and customs and the handiwork of the Mexicans and the other far-off people with whom he had labored. He was at that time preparing to leave for his new assignment as superintendent of the Puerto Rico Mission of the M. E. Church with headquarters at San Juan, Puerto Rico.

Rev. Benjamin Haywood paid another visit in October 1905, lecturing in the New Richmond, Sugar Grove, and Romney Methodist Churches. He was on a tour of lectures to the various missionary boards in Philadelphia and Brooklyn, and after these lectures was to fill an appointment to meet President Roosevelt and Secretary Taft in Washington concerning his splendid work as a missionary to Puerto Rico. He was to return to Puerto Rico on November 23rd of that year.

The Tribby Family—Not many parents are rewarded in the same manner as the parents in the brief sketch to follow. James and Mary Curnutt Tribby were blessed with, among their other children, three daughters and a son-in-law who became missionaries in Chile, South America. All their children were born near New Richmond.

Mary Curnutt Tribby was raised in the home of Dr. and Mrs. Manners; her parents both passed away when she was a child and the good doctor and his wife took her into their home, having no children of their own. The doctor and his wife were devout Methodists, giving generously to DePauw University, Ladoga Methodist, and the New Richmond Methodist Church. Dr. Manners was New Richmond's first physician and became quite wealthy, so Mary had a good life with her adoptive parents. After the doctor's death, Barbara Manners made her home with Mary and her husband James William Tribby and their children. The Methodist faith was carried on through this family, lasting throughout their lives. Between 1900 and 1916 three of their daughters had entered the missionary field, suffering many hardships along the way. Another daughter devoted many years as the organist in the Methodist Church in New Richmond. Their son Emory was considered a "prodigy to the song world;" once he heard a tune, it was never forgotten, and he declared at the age of six that he would be a preacher. If this is so, I have no record of his following this work.

Jessie Tribby, daughter of James and Mary Curnutt Tribby, married William Austin Shelley on June 1, 1904 at the home of her parents just southeast of New Richmond. The ceremony was performed by Dr. H.A. Gobin of DePauw University. Jessie and her husband entered the missionary field and left the following year in July, for Iquique, Chile, South America. Mr. Shelley was to teach in the English schools there. They traveled by train to New York, thence by steamship to Panama, thence a few hours train ride across the isthmus, and again boarded a steamer for Chile. The entire trip took about five weeks to their new home below the tropics. Their baby daughter, Mary Isabel, born April 19, 1905 at Greencastle, Indiana, made the trip with the parents. The following year she became ill and was near death twice, so the baby's physician advised the parents to move the baby from the seaside. They moved eighty-five miles inland, which probably saved the baby's life. Mary Isabel made two trips with her parents to visit Grandma and Grandpa Tribby, one in 1910 and again in 1916.

Jessie wrote letters to the editor of the New Richmond *Record* describing the customs of the people in South America. It made for interesting reading for the folks back home. In 1908 a son, James, was born to the Shelleys and the editor made the comment they were bringing their "little genuine South American boy who speaks nothing but Spanish" home to visit his grandparents. Mr. Shelley and the family returned to New Richmond for another visit in June 1916, making the trip to attend the Methodist International convention at Saratoga, N.Y. as one of the four delegates from South America. He gave a talk at the New Richmond Methodist Church while visiting home folks, describing his work beyond the tropics.

Etta Tribby Archey, daughter of James and Mary Curnutt Tribby, joined the Shelley family three years after the Shelleys went to South America. They were in Santiago, Chile, at the time. Etta graduated from New Richmond High School, then attended Madame Blaker's school in Indianapolis and later DePauw University. Etta's husband, William Archey, had died in 1902, leaving her widowed at a young age. She was a teacher in the mission school in Chile for many years. She was compelled to give up the work because of poor health and returned to the States with the Shelleys in October 1910. She was in charge of the Community House in Crawfordsville in 1916, and later remarried to Will Allen. Etta died in October 1964 at the home of her sister, Mary Pierce, in New Richmond.

Ruth Tribby, the youngest daughter of James and Mary Curnutt Tribby, left in November 1915 for her five-week journey to join her sister and family in Santiago, Chile. Ruth was to teach in the mission school with the Shelleys. She was a graduate of New Richmond High School and DePauw University, Class of 1915. She was married to Charles Morse Huffer, of Albion, Michigan, during her five years of service as missionary in South America. Charles was on duty as an astronomer in Santiago at the time.

Ruth and Charles returned to the United States in 1922, settling in Madison, Wisconsin, where he accepted a position as an assistant astronomer in the University of Wisconsin. They had one daughter, Helen Marie, who was only one year and eleven months old when Ruth died on August 22, 1923. Ruth died at the age of 30.

Mary Tribby Pierce, daughter of James and Mary Curnutt Tribby, served many years as organist in the New Richmond Methodist Church and was honored in November 1969 by the congregation on "Mary Pierce Recognition Day" for her many years of service. She was presented a plaque naming her "organist emeritus" of the church by the pastor, the Rev. Dale Seslar. Robert Fyffe gave a talk on Mrs. Pierce's early connection with the church through her mother. Mary was the widow of Lester Pierce.

THE NEW RICHMOND CHRISTIAN CHURCH

The First Church of Christ in New Richmond was organized in 1848 and a building erected. Bros. David J. Davidson and George Ebrite did the carpentry; Ebrite was a trustee of the church at the time. Oliver Wilson and William Young were the first ministers and Joseph Davis the last minister for this early group of worshippers. The building was a log structure and was located diagonally across the street from the Christian Church built in 1888 on East Washington Street. The 1864 Atlas shows the location at the northeast corner of Dr. Stowe Detchon's lot. This lot, used as a pasture in more recent years, was east of the Detchon residence.

The first school of the village also was held in this building. The school taught here was maintained by subscription and continued about two months a year. A description of this building was given in a 1938 letter to Mrs. Fern Davisson from Fanny (Cook) Copper.

> The First Christian Church in New Richmond was a rectangular building having double doors at the entrance and three or four little paned windows on each side. Inside, between each window, there was a tin holder for a candle and meetings were always announced to be held at early candle light.
>
> From the door to the opposite end of the building was a wide isle [*sic*]—in the center of the isle and midway of the room was to my childish eyes the biggest stove that could be made. The wood for the stove in winter, piled by the side of it, was two and a half or three feet long. The isle continued to the pulpit—no, to the place where the preacher stood, the floor was not even raised for a pulpit. There was just a plain table sitting on the floor and a long seat back of it. On the table were a large Bible, coal oil lamp and a pitcher and tumblers they called it, for water. The floor was perfectly bare, not even a rug by the table. This is the material picture of that Church building—poor-wasn't it? But it was rich spiritually. They were a Bible reading, New Testament Church.

27 - Log Church 1848 - 1873

> Among the Preachers that ministered to them were, John O. Kane, born in 1802; Blind Billy Wilson, born in 1808; Jacob Wright, born in 1809. John O. Kane lived in Crawfordsville for about 10 years and I think perhaps he organized the church at New Richmond, for he did a lot of starting new churches.

William "Blind Billy" Wilson, born September 23, 1808, died March 26, 1891, and is buried in the Hebron Cemetery in Putnam County, Indiana two miles southeast of Russellville. John O. Kane performed the marriage ceremony for James Cook and Margaret Mason, I do not remember seeing him but I remember B.B. Wilson and Jacob Wright, they were the oldest ones. I remember others were a man named Canfield that came, I think once a month for quite a while and two Evangelists—Abraham Plunkett and ___ Utter, don't remember his given name, and Kerr. But their main dependence always was Joseph Galbreath of Linden. Whenever they were without a preacher—as I remember-most of the time, Joseph Galbreath was always ready to help.

Just who the Charter members were I do not know. My earliest recollection is that from Linden there were four families that the parents came to New Richmond; the Johnsons, Ayedlotte's, Galbreath, Whetstone, there never was a Christian Church in Linden. The others nearest New Richmond were Davissons, Thomas, Fouts, Shewey, Kytes, Dewey, Hobble, Cook, Plunkett, Patten, Washburns—I suppose this is not all, but all I recall at present. John Plunkett was the first S.S. Superintendent that I remember. A Mr. Mosley (or Morly) also was S.S. Superintendent at one time.

Our literature was simply a New Testament-for each scholar. I still have one of them-and some small cards for the children as reward for committing to memory, verses of N.T. Scripture. It was a training I will never forget and am still thankful for having received it. ..About the last of the preaching in the old Church I do not know exactly, but it was, I think in 1879 or 1880. I remember we had meetings in the old Richmond schoolhouse. Kerr was the preacher. You know I think the Richmond Church is close to one hundred years old. Perhaps if you could go to the C. House and see the records you could find who it was gave the land for the Church and in what year, I would love to know...etc.

I would like to make a note about Mrs. Copper's letter at this point. The pioneer citizens called the town Richmond, eliminating the "New"—I know this for a fact, as my Aunt Jess Ebrite Jones always referred to the town as "Richmond." Also there was a Christian Church in Linden in later years.

On June 2, 1877 the following members of the New Richmond Christian Church held a meeting to elect three trustees: George W. Washburn, John Dewey, James Cook, John Patton, Gideon L. Davisson, William Burris, William Patton, Thomas M. Foster, Samuel McComas and Joseph Burris. George W. Washburn being called to the chair, the members proceeded to elect the following trustees: Gideon L. Davisson, Thomas M. Foster, and Levi Thomas. Washburn was elected Chairman and Samuel McComas Secretary.

It is interesting to note the caliber of people who attended this pioneer church in New Richmond. David J. Davisson practiced law in Lafayette, preferring the cases related to estate settlements and the small cases dealing with the local justice of the peace. He and his wife, Sarah (Shepherd) Davisson had six children and resided in Jackson Township, in Tippecanoe County. They both were natives of Adams County, Ohio. George Ebrite was a wagon maker, carpenter, and farmer; he served as township trustee and was a trustee in the Christian Church. He and his wife Mary (Wright) Ebrite had four children—three born in Adams County, Ohio, and the last child, Daniel, was born in New Richmond in 1840.

Joseph Galbreath, who was the minister of the Christian church, was a resident of Linden, was a Justice of the Peace for many years, and had a woodworking shop and a blacksmith shop in Linden, making wagons, plows, harrows and other farm implements. He and his wife Ruhama had seven children. Joseph was born in Missouri, his wife in Virginia.

Thomas M. Foster was a Justice of the Peace in New Richmond several years, kept a general store in the town, and was a farmer. Thomas was born in Mocksville, North Carolina. He and his wife Cynthia (Jolly) Foster had seven children.

James McComas, a blacksmith, was born in Ohio. He and wife Nancy A. had four children when they lived in New Richmond.

Samuel McComas was a Justice of the Peace in New Richmond twenty-two consecutive years. Sam and his first wife Maria Caw had ten children, two dying in infancy. After his first wife died, Sam married Susan Pitts and had eight more children. This family would have taxed the seating capacity of the small church. The McComas families were from Adams County, Ohio.

John Patton, born in Butler County, Ohio, was a wagon maker, farmer, and carpenter. John came with his parents to Montgomery County in 1830. He and his wife Nancy (Coons) Patton had eleven children; one died in infancy and two sons died in their youth. John and Nancy's remaining children continued as members of the church after the early deaths of both parents. John's brothers William and David Patton attended the New Richmond Christian Church in the early years.

William S. Turvey, born in Bracken County, Kentucky, and his wife Nancy Bowyer were the parents of six children. William ran a flouring mill for a while in New Richmond. William joined the Christian Church in New Richmond in 1851, then moved to Benton County, Indiana, in 1853. He returned to the town in 1894 and was killed by a Clover Leaf Train in New Richmond in 1905.

George Washington Washburn was born in Brown County, Ohio, and came to Montgomery County in 1833. George and his wife Louise J. Whetstone had three children; he founded the Corn Exchange Bank in New Richmond, was considered a wise counselor, and his services of good advice were sought by many. He became a large landowner and was known near and far as a man of keen business integrity and honesty.

James and Margaret (Mason) Cook were both born in Ohio, the husband settling in Coal Creek Township in 1850. James was a farmer and he and his wife had six children. They resided in the town of New Richmond, later moving one and one-half miles southeast of town. James was the last of the old settlers of the town to pass away.

NEW RICHMOND CHRISTIAN CHURCH, 1888 BUILDING

In January 1887, the congregation of the New Richmond Christian Church began making plans to build a new structure. The first Saturday in March, the group was to have a meeting in the New Richmond school house and a preacher from Richmond, Indiana, was to come and get the group properly organized. The Crawfordsville *Review*, March 5, 1887 published the following notices Saturday night, "meeting in the school house; minister from Richmond; purpose-to raise money to build a church for the Christian or Campbellite denomination." The New Richmond correspondent said, "There are several members and they could build a church and not feel the expense, as several members are men of means."

The group did not act immediately, because several months later, in October, they were still trying to raise the funds for the new building, and the writer for the *Review* said, "The Christian or Campbellites are quite strong and if they would only build a church, that would be an honor to this place, but their religion does not extend to their pocket books very strongly." The early newspaper correspondents were very outspoken. In December a decision was made to build a new church the following summer.

On February 15, 1888, the members of the Christian Church met at New Richmond and George W. Washburn called the meeting to order. Rev. J.P. Ewing was chosen as Chairman and W.G. Stites as Secretary. Stowe S. Detcheon (Detchon), Levi Herriman, and George W. Washburn were chosen as a building committee. Trustees for the above named church were also elected at this time; George W. Washburn, Stowe S. Detcheon and Thomas Foster being the persons chosen.

On motion of O.B. Groves, said building committee were authorized "to proceed to the erection of, at New Richmond, a Church house which they may seem fit and suitable for said church to worship in."

A carpenter and contractor visited the town of New Richmond to secure the church contract, the *Review* said, but failed to say who was to build the church. Samuel R. Tribby, a local carpenter, was known as the "builder of churches" and he may have built the Christian church. He did build the New Richmond Methodist church; it is recorded in the history of the M.E. church. In May 1888, big preparations were going on toward the building of the Christian church—and the Methodist congregation was also starting to make plans to build at the same time.

Dr. Stowe S. Detchon and his wife Jemima gave the land for this church building for "Love and Affection they hold for the Society of the Christian Church" the deed says. This deed was dated 3rd of May 1888.

The brick for the foundation and the chimney was purchased from the local tile mill. One of the "burns" of the brick kiln was a failure, causing a slight delay in the building, but the work soon continued, and in August the structure was nearly completed. The brand new bell arrived and was mounted in the belfry. This bell was cast in 1888 at the Buckeye Bell Foundry, "Vanduzen & Tift," in Cincinnati, Ohio, and was moved to the new brick church building built in 1921 by the Christian Church of New Richmond.

In September the two churches were finished as far as the carpenters were concerned, and the scaffoldings were removed. The two denominations were soon to be ready for services in their new structures. Both of these were frame structures having rather tall bell towers and steeples.

The ladies began circulating subscriptions for a new carpet, and the congregation was waiting for the new chairs to arrive so they could dedicate their new building. By the middle of December the seats had arrived and several members worked all week preparing for the big day. They had to try out their new bell before the opening day and it worked just fine—its grand tones were heard eight miles away across the wide open prairie that surrounds New Richmond.

On Sunday morning, December 30, 1888, the big day had arrived. The New Richmond Christian Church was dedicated. Rev. Ewing, the Christian State Evangelist, dedicated the building. The church would not hold all the people on the day of dedication, and the writer for the Crawfordsville *Review*, January 5, 1880, said, "A larger crowd is seldom seen in our village. Rev. Ewing preached a very fine sermon." The Bayless transfer brought a load of people from Crawfordsville to attend the dedication. Among the group was Samuel McComas, one of New Richmond's pioneers, the town's first Postmaster, and a Justice of the Peace. Another was Mike White, an attorney from Crawfordsville who the correspondent said "looked more like a preacher than a lawyer."

The church society raised enough money on the day of dedication to place them out of debt, and the members of the church became very hard and dedicated workers. Tom Cook made the statement that he "don't intend to quit talking Bible business until he gets all his associates to join church." A Sabbath school was organized Sunday, January 13, 1889, and the ladies organized their Ladies Aid Society in June the same year and started making plans to help support the church.

Rev. A.C. Smithers was the first minister of this new church building. He became quite popular with the congregation and was asked to preach another year. He did criticize the mode of living of some of the citizens for keeping stores open on Sunday, and this did not sit too well with some people. These stores were good loafing places for the men and boys.

This building was located on the north side of East Washington Street, just west of the old New Richmond School. It was a frame structure set back from the street. The baptistery was sunken so the top was level with the floor and was located under the pulpit. The pulpit had to be removed when new members were to be baptized. The water had to be carried by buckets from a pump which was located on the west side toward the back of the church lot, and emptied in the same manner. Some new members though still preferred to be baptized in the creek and they went to Coal Creek to a place made available west of town. It was equipped with a little shed for changing wet clothing after the baptismal service.

On the east side of the church was a hitch rack to hitch the old horse and buggy. There were two Sunday School rooms located behind the pulpit; the ladies would go to one room and the gentlemen to the other side. This was the custom of many churches in early days.

The members still living at the time of the reorganization of this church were: George W. and Lou J. Washburn, James and Mattie Cook, Hannah Burris, John Dewey and Catharine, Mrs. Nathan Quick, Levi and Margaret Herriman, O.B. and Jennie Groves, Thomas M. and Cynthia Foster, Clara Mason, W.G. and M.A. Stites, Mary E. Burris, Lou C. Banta, Sarah E. Stamper, Rhenhama (or Rheuhama) Galbreath.

George W. Watkins, minister of this church from January 1902 to January 1904, was the father of Maureen D. Watkins who wrote the play, *Chicago*, and other plays. George Watkins built the house where I lived when I wrote this book, and his wife taught in the local school. Maureen lived with her parents in New Richmond most of this time, except when she stayed with her grandmother in Kentucky while her mother took some courses at Valparaiso University.

Oscar W. Riley and Harry Martindale were the last ministers of this church. The first new members to be baptized in this church were Anna Long, Fannie Patton, Mattie Alexander, and George B. Banta. Twenty-one new additions joined the following evening, as services were held each night after the dedication of the church. Fannie Patton Ebrite, my grandmother, was the last charter member to pass away, on August 16, 1951.

After all the work and money spent by the two denominations to build new churches, it was amusing to read about a complaint the correspondent from New Richmond made in the Crawfordsville *Review* in June concerning the churches saying, "The nice groves around our village should be used more than they are, but instead, the people will crowd in the two churches to suffocation and put up with the torment, while if they would only put up seats in the grove they could enjoy the meetings and not be smothered and crowded to death..." He continued, "The leaders should make the change for the hot months."

The Christian Church organization used the subscription plan to support the ministers who served the congregation. Their agreement reads: "We, the undersigned, promise to pay the amounts severally subscribed by us for the support of the Pastor of the Christian Church of New Richmond for the year of 1889."

A list of the subscribers and their amounts were recorded and carefully marked paid upon receiving the payment. Services were held bimonthly because the early ministers usually served two churches, and because they lived quite a distance from New Richmond (except George Watkins). The ministers were "put up" by members of the congregation over the weekend while they were serving the local church.

Sunday School classes were held each Sunday morning. O.W. Mason was an early Superintendent of the Christian Church Sunday School. In 1899 Ella Phillips was the Organist for the church and E.W. Harriman was Musical Director. This same year the young people formed a group called the "Young Peoples Society of Christian Endeavor" (Y.P.S.C.E.). These young people met every Sunday evening for prayer and Bible reading. The society continued for many years, reorganizing several times as other young people came along. This group was still active in the 1940s and 1950s. O.W. Mason and Darwin Lane were very active leaders of the early group and Hay and Pearl Frances Thomas led the young people in the 1940s. M.L. Davisson also was a leader in the '40s.

The Missionary Society was organized at the time the church was built and continued throughout the lifetime of the church. Active members were Mrs. Fred Bible, Miss Fern Mason, Mrs. Thomas DeVault, and others over the years have supported the missionaries in various parts of the world.

My father, Forrest Waye, said he and his brother Earl painted the old church the last time it needed painting. The steeple was quite a challenge for the two. After the new church was constructed in 1921, the old building was torn down by William Inskeep and the lumber was used in the construction of a barn on his farm. Only the sidewalk remains—the only evidence of the church and a once active group of worshippers.

The Ladies Aid Society of the New Richmond Christian Church

On January 13, 1889 the ladies of the New Richmond Christian Church formed their Society for church enterprises to help fund the various programs such as missions, new piano, upkeep on the building, etc. The early days in New Richmond were filled with festivals from the two churches in town. The ladies planned lectures, lawn socials and other events. The lawn socials were held on the church lawn and the lawns of George Washburn and Henry K. Lee. George Washburn's woods, south of town, was the scene of a picnic and lawn festival. On this occasion the notice said there would be "all kinds of diversion of pleasure, including a baseball game and refreshments.

One of the more interesting gatherings was a "Colonial Festival" given by the ladies in Hollin's Hall. It was in the nature of Washington's Birthday Festival, the waitresses being costumed in Colonial fashion. Souvenirs given to the patrons were miniature U.S. flags. The New Richmond *Record*, Thursday February 25, 1904 said, "The several very pretty ladies who waited the tables, two to each table, looked even prettier in Martha Washington costume. Ewing Mason was dressed up as Little George Washington and assisted the ladies by distributing the souvenirs about the tables."

Henry K. Lee's lawn was the scene of another social. Entertainment included recitations, vocal and instrumental music, and refreshments of sandwiches, ice cream and cake. Oyster stew and chicken soup were really big in the early 1900s. The Modern Woodmen's lodge room and Johnson's Hall accommodated the Ladies Aid Society when the weather was unfavorable for outdoor activities.

The "festivals" became "bazaars"—Hollins' Hall was the scene of a Thanksgiving supper and Handkerchief Bazaar in October 1906. Fried chicken suppers came along in the 1940s and 1950s, then along came the hot dogs, hamburgers, and chili suppers in the 1960s.

In December 1906 a local general store, Weymer & Dudley's, turned their store over to the Methodist Church Ladies Aid one Monday and the next Monday to the Christian Church Ladies Aid. Each church was allowed three ladies to act as sales ladies for the whole day and they received ten percent of all the cash sales during their day in charge. This was a very nice gesture on the part of Weymer & Dudley.

Last, but certainly not least, were the famous dinners prepared for the "Thrashers" working around the town of New Richmond. There were at least three threshing crews in the vicinity who threshed the wheat and grain for the farmers. They employed a good number of men (and boys) who needed a good meal to sustain them throughout the day. The ladies gathered together early in the morning and started peeling the potatoes, baking hams, dressing chickens and preparing them either fried or in chicken and noodles, baking pies, cakes, hot bread, etc. At noon the church bell would be rung and the men would

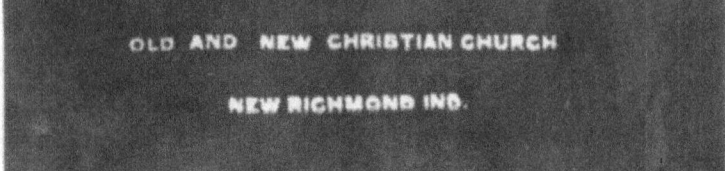

28 - On right, 1888 building. Top left, 1921 building.

come running in and stuffed themselves so full it is a wonder they were able to work the rest of the afternoon. The young ladies usually waited tables; this allowed the mothers to remain in the kitchen to keep the food supply plentiful.

The following is a transcription of the deed to the New Richmond Christian Church:

> THIS INDENTURE WITNESSETH that Stow S. Detchon and Jemima Detchon his wife of Montgomery County in the state of Indiana Convey and Warrant to Trustees in Trust of the Christian Church at New Richmond of Montgomery County in the state of Indiana for the love and affection they hold for the Society of the Christian Church the following Real Estate in Montgomery County, in the state of Indiana To wit
>
> A part of the West Half of the North West quarter of section Ten (10) North of Range five (5) West, beginning at the south East Corner of said lot, running thence North thirty two rods three and three quarters feet (32 R. 3 3/4 ft) to center of New Richmond and Crawfordsville free gravel road, thence West in the center of said road twelve rods to the point of Commencement, thence North thirteen and one third (13 1/3) rods thence West Six (6) rods, thence south thirteen and one third (13 1/3) rods to the center of said road, thence East six (6) rods to the place of beginning. Containing one half acre more or less. The said Trustees to have and to hold said described lot so long as they occupy it for church purposes, also to keep and maintain a good and substantial fence around said lot. IN WITNESS WHEREOF, the said Stow S. Detchon and Jemima Detchon his wife have hereunto set their hands and seal this 30th day of May A. D. 1888. Stow S. Detchon (seal) Jemima Detchon (seal) State of Indiana, Montgomery County. SS.
>
> Before me Amos Ebrite a Justice of the Peace in and for said County, this 30th day of May 1888 personally appeared the within Named grantors Stow S. Detchon and Jemima Detchon his wife and acknowledged the execution of the annexed Deed. WITNESS MY HAND AND SEAL,
>
> Amos Ebrite Justice of the Peace. Received for Record Aug. 17th 1893 at 10:20 O'clock A.M. and Recorded same day, Thos. T. Munhall R.M.Co. Montgomery County Deeds, Vol. 71 page 517-18

One of our distinguished citizens broke his usual rule last Sunday evening, and resolved to go hear Rev. O.S. Reed on "Opportunity" at the Christian church. He started to the church early and walked slowly up East Washington Street contemplating the improvements and viewing with much satisfaction the handsome homes in that part of town. He arrived at the church early and found that "business had not yet begun," as he remarked, but that the young people's meeting was in progress. His thoughts wandered back through time and he bethought to himself that the last time he was in that church was at a funeral when, because of the great crowd, he had crawled through a small window in front of the church, and he turned to look but the window was not there, and not until then had it dawned upon him that he was in the Methodist church instead of the Christian church. He told his friends, they say, of his mistake and they say, too, that he loses no opportunity to tell of the absentmindedness of his family before him and that he finds an excuse for his absentmindedness as a family heritage (New Richmond *Record*, Thurs. October 25, 1906).

New Richmond Christian Church, 1921 Building

On June 11, 1917 there was a call meeting of the members of the New Richmond Christian Church pursuant to a donation by Mrs. George F. Long of eight thousand dollars for the building of a new

Christian church, the congregation to raise an equal amount. The purpose of this meeting was to select committees and discuss plans for raising the additional money.

Brother W. Darwin Lane was chosen as chairman. The following members were chosen to serve on the building committees: Mrs. George F. Long, Thomas Devault, O.W. Mason, Fred L. Hunt, Frederick E. Bible, and Morton L. Davisson.

Since the above meeting of June 11th, one or two business meetings of the church board took place, the first of which was at Fred L. Hunt's home, and the other probably at the church, the minutes of either not having been recorded. The principal interest of these meetings was centered upon the following: the postponing of the building, or commencing to build, a new church until after the "Great War," or until the building committee and congregation should see fit. Postponing the building was also agreed to by the architect and building superintendent Honeywell. The money was to be invested in Liberty Bonds so that when they were ready to proceed with the construction the money would be guaranteed.

On August 2, 1917 the trustees of the church purchased the land for the new building from the trustees of the town of New Richmond. This lot was described as follows: 100 feet off of the south end of lot number 16 in Stow S. Detchon's Fourth Addition to the town of New Richmond, measuring from the outside of the walk. Trustees of the town were L.P. Brown, J.M. Conway, and J.M. Alexander. The trustees of the Christian church at this time were O.W. Mason, Thomas Devault, and Frederick E. Bible. The north end of lot number 16, to a width of 48 or 48.5 feet, housed the town hall and the firefighting apparatus in a small building.

In February 1918 the I-beams were delivered to the church lot, having arrived on the Clover Leaf Railroad, but the building of the church was at a stand-still and was not resumed until the summer of 1921.

The Corner Stone Laying Service was held Saturday, May 7, 1921 at 2:30 P.M. The Newtown Band furnished the music, and Rev. H.H. Martindale, after making some opening remarks, was presented the corner stone by the building contractor. The Grand Lodge F. & A. Masons had the privilege of laying the corner stone.

Orlando W. Mason gave a short history of the congregation's early churches, and Hon. Ed. Jackson, Secretary of State, gave the address. Former ministers gave short talks, and the Newtown Band accompanied the audience in the song, "America." Dr. John F. Clearwaters gave the benediction.

Sunday, November 13, 1921 will long be remembered as the greatest day in the history of the New Richmond Christian Church in the dedication of the newly completed church. Rev. George L. Snively of Lewiston, Illinois, was in charge of the dedication. The New Richmond Christian Church choir furnished music for the morning service. Rev. Snively gave a sermon on "The Fundamentals of Our Faith." The Ladies Aid Society furnished a free dinner to the crowd in the spacious new dining room in the basement of the church.

At 2:30 P.M. the Union Memorial and Communion services were held. The church choir sang several numbers, and the Wabash College Glee Club gave two numbers. Orlando W. Mason gave a memorial address, mentioning the early workers of the church who had passed on to the great beyond.

The evening's program began at 7:30 P.M. with Dr. Snively delivering the dedicatory sermon, then Rev. Martindale, the pastor, led the congregation in the dedication vows and petitions. Rev. Snively made the fund raising campaign during the three services, and had previously raised in pledges and cash the amount of $20,260. The Ladies Aid Society pledged $3,000, and personal pledges ranged from $2,500 down. The pledges were made payable in five yearly installments. Fred L. Hunt presented the keys to A.D. Long for the new church.

The new church, as it stood completed, was built and furnished at a cost of around $27,000, built of red brick, trimmed in stone, with memorial art windows, and is absolutely fire-proof. The main auditorium is a spacious one, its pews and pulpit furniture are of an attractive pattern, and like the woodwork finish, is of fumed oak. The ladies parlor is in the rear of the auditorium, and can be enlarged for large crowds by opening the folding doors to the auditorium. The choir loft is spacious enough for all its needs, and dressing rooms lead off from it.

The basement contains a large dining room and a well equipped kitchen, the furnace room, with a space for fuel storage (coal, wood, etc.), restrooms, and a Sunday school room, if needed. Construction on the new edifice was begun in March 1921.

Following the dedication services, a series of meeting were held, starting the next evening, in charge of Rev. J. Stanley West, of Brazil, Indiana, an Evangelist.

In order to raise money to pay off the pledges, the Ladies Aid Society served dinners to the "thrashers" in the area of New Richmond. They published a cook book that sold quite well, raising several hundred dollars, and served suppers for special events held in the town of New Richmond. The Men's Booster Club, made up of men in the community, held a rabbit hunt, killing hundreds of rabbits, dressed and hauled them to Indianapolis to sell. They also planned church suppers, pig roasts, and other events to raise funds. The most entertaining event the men provided was a womanless "Wedding" with a cast of men only. If the play was as amusing as the photograph of the group, it was quite an event. The play was performed on the New Richmond High School stage.

29 - Womanless Wedding – 1922 or 1923

Officiary on November 13, 1921 New Richmond Christian Church:

ELDERS Orlando W. Mason, Wm. Darwin Lane, Arthur D. Long, Morton L. Davisson.
DEACONS Frederick E. Bible, Frederick L. Hunt, Dennis Stuckey, Earl Waye, James Devault, J.M. Young, Orie Wagner, Forrest Waye, John D. Patton, and John Singleton.
TRUSTEES Orlando W. Mason, Thomas Devault, Frederick E. Bible.

TREASURERS A.D. Long. CLERKS Wm. Darwin Lane PIANISTS Mrs. Vera Waye; Assistant, Edna Lane. LADIES AID Pres. Mrs. Mabel Bible; Sec., Mrs. Bernice Shepherd; Treas., Mrs. Fannie Devault.

WOMAN'S MISSIONARY SOCIETY Pres., Mrs. Gertrude Oppy; Vice Pres. Mrs. Lewis Clarkson; Sec., Mrs. Myrtle Clark; Treas., Mrs. Fern Davisson.

TRIANGLE MISSIONARY CLUBS Pres., Edna Lane; Vice Pres., Margie Livingston; Sec., Ina Stuckey Treas. Rose Shepherd.

BIBLE SCHOOL: Superintendent, Dennis Stuckey; Sec. Mrs. Grace Allen, Treas., Morton L. Davisson.

BUILDING COMMITTEES Orlando W. Mason, Thomas Devault, F.E. Bible, M.L. Davisson, F.L. Hunt, and A.D. Long.

The following names appear on the windows of the New Richmond Christian Church as memorials: Levi and Elizabeth Thomas, George W. and Louise W. Washburn, Orlando W. and Clara M. Mason, Martha Ellen Hunt, Nancy Jane Smith, and son John Smith, Thomas Devault, Fannie Devault, John and Nancy Patton, William and Martha Thomas, David D., Sarah and daughter Nellie Davisson, George W. and Mary F. Jones, Ester Jane Mason, Rosetta Long, McMillions, and Florence Long.

30 - New Richmond Christian Church parsonage

In the fall of 1957, the house next to the church on the east was purchased for the purpose of providing a home for our ministers. This house was redecorated and remodeled by the various members of our congregation and was dedicated on April 18, 1958. The minister at the time was John Cachiaras. This was the first parsonage the church has owned.

DEED TO NEW RICHMOND CHRISTIAN CHURCH-1921

Deeds of Montgomery County Indiana Vol. 114, page 398

The Town of New Richmond, by L.P. Brown, J.M. Conway, and J.M. Alexander, Trustees of said Town, to Trustees of the Christian Church of New Richmond.

WARRANTY DEED, dated August 2, 1917; Recorded August 6, 1917; Deed Record 114, page 398; Consideration $600.00.

CONVEY AND WARRANT: 100 feet off the south end of Lot No. 16 in Stow S. Detchon's Fourth Addition to the town of New Richmond, measuring from the outside of the walk, to be used to erect the Christian Church thereon. Signed by Town of New Richmond, Ind., by L. P. Brown, J. M. Conway, and J. M. Alexander; Attests Ed King, Town Clerk.

Acknowledged August 2, 1917 by L.P. Brown, J.M. Conway and J.M. Alexander, Trustees of the Town of New Richmond, Montgomery County, Indiana, before Edgar Walts, a N. P. Montgomery County, Indiana. (L.S.)

Part of Lot numbered Sixteen (16), as the same is known and designated on the Recorded Plat of Stow S. Detchon's Fourth (4th) Addition to the Town of New Richmond, bounded as follows:

Beginning at the edge of the street on the south line of the sidewalk where the West line of said Lot would intersect, if extended South; running thence North along the West line of said Lot One Hundred (100) feet; thence East Seventy-four and One-fourth (744) feet to the East line of said lot; thence South One Hundred (100) feet to a point East of the beginning point; thence West Seventy-four and one-fourth (744) feet to the place of beginning. Situated) in Montgomery County, Indiana.

REGISTER OF MINISTERS, NEW RICHMOND CHRISTIAN CHURCH

Ministers of the old log church—dates unknowns:
Oliver Wilson
Abraham Plunkett

William Young_____ Utter
John O. Kane (O'Kane)_____ Kerr
William "Blind Billy" Wilson
Joseph Galbreath (listed in 1874)
Jacob Wright
Joseph Davis
____Canfield

NAME	DATE BEGAN	DATE ENDED
J.P. Ewing	Jan. 1889	Mar. 1889
A.C. Smither	Mar. 1889	May 1890
Geo. Hicks	Jun. 1890	Dec. 1890
M.B. McKinsey	Jan. 1891	Jan. 1892
T.J. Shuey	Jan. 1892	Jan. 1897
J.C. Ashley	Jan. 1897	Sep. 1897
O.W. McGaughey	Jan. 1898	Jan. 1899
A.L. Crim	Jan. 1899	Jan. 1902
Geo. W. Watkins	Jan. 1902	Jan. 1904
W. P. Shamhart	Jan. 1904	Jan. 1905
J.P. Ewing	Jan. 1905	Oct. 1905
O.S. Reed	Jan. 1905	Jan. 1907
J.C. Ashley	Jan. 1907	Jan. 1909
A.L. Carney	Jan. 1909	Jan. 1910
O.W. McGaughey	Jan. 1910	Jan. 1911
O.E. Kelley	Jan. 1911	Jan. 1912
F.E. Davison	Jan. 1912	Jan. 1915
Joseph Myers	Jan. 1915	Jan. 1916
W.P. Shamhart	Jan. 1916	Jun. 1916
C.C. Griggs	Aug. 1916	Dec. 1918
J.P. Wright	Jan. 1919	Sep. 1919
Oscar W. Riley	Nov. 1919	Oct. 1920
Harry Martindale	Nov. 1921	Dec. 1922
Chas. E. Cook	1 Jan. 1922	Aug. 1923
George F. Leonard	Oct. 1923	Nov. 1927
Henry Toogood	Nov. 1927	Autumn 1928
George F. Leonard	Autumn 1928	Dec. 1928
J.C. Burkhardt	Dec. 1928	Jan. 1931
Richard O. Lee	Feb. 1931	Jan. 1933
Lewis R. Hotaling	Mar. 1933	Jan. 1936
Keith L. McNeill	Apr. 1936	Aug. 1938
Don E. TerBush	30 Oct. 1938	18 Dec. 1938
Donald Dunn	Mar. 1939	1 Jan. 1942
Orville C. Miller	Apr. 1943	Oct. 1945
Harry A. Davis	1946	1 Apr. 1947
Harold Humphrey	20 Apr. 1947	1 Sep. 1947
Ray Britton	29 Feb. 1948	13 Nov. 1949
Thomas Alton Terry	1 Jan. 1950	31 Aug. 1952
Donald Monroe Tharp	14 Sep. 1952	Feb. 1954
John H. Cachiaras	4 Mar. 1954	7 Aug. 1960

NAME	DATE BEGAN	DATE ENDED
Phillip Bradford	28 Aug. 1960	30 Sep. 1962
Kenneth Buser	Nov. 1962	Aug. 1964
James Hannebohn	9 Aug. 1964	3 Jul. 1966
John M. Foxworthy	Aug. 1966	9 Aug. 1970
Richard D. Winson	27 Sep. 1970	12 Nov. 1972
Michael Pierce	10 Jun. 1973	Apr. 1974
Larry D. Call	16 Jun. 1974	1 Dec. 1977
Thomas Raymond Cash	18 Jun. 1978	Mar. 1980
Oren Rector	May 17, 1981	Oct. 9, 1983
Leonard Largent	5 Feb. 1984 (full time)	Dec. 1985
Stephen Carr	June 29, 1986	Oct. 16, 1988
David Finch	Apr. 9, 1989	Dec. 24, 1989
Joe Conarroe	May 6, 1990	Nov. 10, 1991
Thomas A Henes	Feb. 23, 1992	Aug. 28, 1994
Timothy Tretheway	Dec. 18, 1994	July 15, 1995
Darrell Cortez (part-time)	Feb. 23, 1997	June 14, 1997
Darrell Cortez (full-time)	June 15, 1997	Aug. 24, 1997
Darrell Cortez (part-time)	Sept. 1, 1997	May 31, 1998
Darrell Cortez (full-time)	June 1, 1998	Sept. 20, 1998
Darrell Cortez (part-time while attending Lincoln Christian College)		
Michael Black	Oct. 4, 1998	Mar. 5, 2000
Steve Wetterhan	Oct. 18, 1998	Mar. 14, 1999
Leon Langston	Dec. 13, 1998	
Ron Murphy	Nov. 1, 1998	Nov. 22, 1998
Tom Henes	Nov. 8, 1998	
Jim Wolf	Dec. 20, 1998	May 21, 2000
Ron Batts	Mar. 21, 1999	
Jim Lawler	Apr. 11, 1999	
John Kenneson	May 16, 1999	Jan. 30, 2000
Jerry Overman	June 20, 1999	
Jacob Jordan	July 4, 1999	
Jeffery Niles	July 18, 1999	July 25, 1999
Mike Fields	Aug. 22, 1999	
Mike Carmen	Sept. 12, 1999	Sept. 26, 1999
Charles Thomson	Oct. 10, 1999	Oct. 31, 1999
James Burgess	Nov. 21, 1999	Nov. 28, 1999
Brad Herbst	Dec. 12, 1999	Dec. 19, 1999
Johnny Cox	Dec. 26, 1999	Sept. 30, 2001
David Rush	Mar. 12, 2000	

Chapter 10 - Schools

Pioneer and Log Schools of Coal Creek Township

New Richmond Christian Church (and School) - Log Structure

Around 1848, the members of the Christian faith erected a log house in which to worship in the town of New Richmond. At the time, there was only a small number of houses in the little village, but the families living in the village, and nearby, realized they had neglected their children's education long enough, and they decided to remedy the problem.

Since there were not sufficient funds to build a new structure, it was decided to hold classes in the Christian Church edifice. This became the first school held in New Richmond, and was supported by subscriptions. Most of the early schools were financed in this manner. This structure stood on the east end of Stowe Detchon's lot on the south side of east Washington Street. The exact location can be seen on the 1864 Atlas of Montgomery County, Indiana.

The school terms lasted only two months each year. This building served the town as a school until the district school was built around 1856. David Davidson and George Ebrite, trustees of the church, did the carpenter work on this building. Early families with children attending this school would have been George Ebrite's children, Amos, Alfred, Catherine, and Daniel; the Campbell families—Jacob C. and Mary Ann (Pryor) Campbell's children, namely Mary E., Sarah J., Elisha C., William, Maria, Lucinda, John, Robert C., Emily; and Jacob's brother Elisha had one child, Nellie Leona, who would have attended the school. The children of James and Samuel McComas attended the New Richmond school—Samuel had ten children by his first wife, and eight by his second wife, but some of the children died in infancy, so it is uncertain how many attended the school.

Round Hill Log School

Sophia McGinnis, born in Hamilton County, Ohio, on November 4, 1827, came to Montgomery County, Indiana, in 1833 at the tender age of six. Her parents, Joseph and Sophia McGinnis, packed their belongings on wagons, and arrived in Crawfordsville when the village had less than a dozen log cabins. The older children took turns driving the stock they brought with them. The family stayed about two months in the county seat, then moved to their farm in Coal Creek Township, located near the Round Hill neighborhood. Here she grew to young womanhood, getting her education at the log schoolhouse on the same grounds the Round Hill district school later stood. She taught a subscription school in the same log house.

Sophia married William W. Wilson, and they built a large house, still standing in the heart of Round Hill—the only structure left to mark the little hamlet.

Pleasant Hill Log School (Wingate)

What was probably the first school house erected in Coal Creek Township stood two and a half miles south of Pleasant Hill (Wingate). Father Bingham taught in this pioneer school. This, too, would have been a log structure, and would have possibly been built in the early 1830s. In 1831, another log school house was constructed a short distance southwest of Pleasant Hill. James L. McKinney taught in this early place of learning. A History of Wingate written in 1912 by John Blacker mentions two log schools, "one in Boston Store neighborhood just west of Charles Goff's present house; the other stood in a field just west of S. M. Gilkey's present residence."

Meharry Neighborhood Log Structure - Heshbon Bethel Church (and School)

In 1837, the Methodists of the Shawnee Mound community decided to build a house of worship. (The Meharry neighborhood was called Shawnee Mound in early times). Not having the financial means to build, they resorted to the woods, and the whole neighborhood contributed their labor in raising the structure. The beams were fastened with heavy wooden pins, the lumber planed and dressed by hand, and there were benches without backs to sit upon. When the pioneers were settled and the timber was cleared away in order for crops to be planted, the homes were built, and their thoughts turned to educating their children. The log church mentioned above served the neighborhood as a school and stood in the center of what is now the Meharry Cemetery. It was called "Heshbon Bethel."

Edward P. Bennett Log School (Near Boston Store/Elmdale)

In the winter of 1830, a black bear was discovered and was given chase. He was chased up a large oak tree and was shot by George Allhands a mile and three-fourths northeast of Boston Store (Elmdale). The person writing about the bear chase said,

> "In those times there was not a frame school house in the township, and the day the bear was killed, the undersigned was at school in a log house on the farm of Edward P. Bennett, which was taught by Mrs. Harriett Siler, a sister of Edward P. Bennett. We got our education going to school not more than two days out of the five that were taught, and sat on hewed benches, and hewed split puncheon floors, with the writing desks fastened to the walls of the house and a fire place long enough to take in a back log six to seven feet long. The mud jams and backwall, and mud stick chimney would sometimes catch afire. The writer had the pleasure of eating a piece of that bear, the first and last he has ever eaten."

Absalom Kirkpatrick's Log School

The *History of Montgomery County, Indiana* by Beckwith (1881), in speaking of pioneer education in Coal Creek Township, says, "In the Kirkpatrick district, the education of the children was early looked to. The house of logs gave way to the present comfortable frame buildings, etc."

Reading through Absalom Kirkpatrick's estate records, the bill of sale lists many books on religion, law, Statutes, Indiana Justice, Medical Books, and school books such as: *Buck's Dictionary*, *History of U.S.A.*, Geography, Arithmetics, *Murray's Grammar*, *Webster's Dictionary*. Other books listed were, *The Life of Washington*, *Life of Marion*, *Life of Clay*, *Life of Scott and Taylor*, and *Paradise Lost*.

The home of Absalom Kirkpatrick, located about one mile west of New Richmond, was a log structure, and in the early settlement of the township, the Methodists held meetings in that home. This may have been the same structure used for school purposes; however, religious meetings were also held in Kirkpatrick's barn.

Pioneer Schools in Coal Creek Township

The first constitution of Indiana (Article IV, Section 1) provided a source of funds for school purposes by setting off a section of land to be sold at a later date, the money to be invested. The interest from the land sales was to be used to support the schools. Section 20, Township 20, Range 5, was reserved in Coal Creek Township.

In early days there were three trustees who were to call meetings of their inhabitants to make plans to support three-month schools. The trustees were to select suitable sites for the school buildings; the most important considerations were the drinking water and availability of fuel to heat the buildings. They decided what type of building material to be used, preferably native material. Frame buildings made their appearance in Coal Creek Township in the 1850s and 1860s.

The requirements of these structures were: they had to be at least one foot off the ground—they were supported by native stones to raise them from the ground; they were to be eight feet between floors and were to be lighted suitably by large windows. More comfortable seats and tables were added, according to the scholar's size, than the old log structures provided. The trustees made the decision as to how many buildings were needed, and were to place them in the most heavily populated areas. The trustees inspected the buildings upon completion, and if they met all the necessary requirements, the schools were numbered as they were completed, and then were given a name.

The buildings were named after the landowner who gave a parcel of land to the trustees on which to place the building, or in some cases, they were named for the setting, such as Walnut Grove or Round Hill. The trustees had the duty to employ the teachers, giving prospective teachers a test in English, Writing and Arithmetic, and if they passed, they were qualified to teach. Some of those who planned to teach attended a higher school of learning such as a near-by academy, or a short term at Wabash College or DePauw University (Asbury, as it was originally known).

The state of Indiana placed a tax levy on real and personal estate, of ten cents per hundred, on each house-holder to support the free schools in 1849. The beginning of mandatory state aid began when the Free School Law was passed in 1852, thus ending many subscription schools. By 1877, the schools of Montgomery County were supported by the following sources: a special school tax; a special tuition tax; common school fund income; Congressional school fund income; and liquor licenses.

In New Richmond, several years later, attempts were made to carry on with the subscription school concept by dedicated teachers. In 1886 Tommy Patton promoted his writing school for "those who desire good penmanship." In 1889 Mable Alexander circulated a subscription for summer school to be held in April and May. In April 1900, Nellie Franklin was teaching a two months subscription school. Twenty-eight pupils attended her school.

In 1904, Professor A. W. Krause offered a four week subscription school "for those who may wish to attend, but most particularly for the higher grades," the notice read. Only nine had enrolled in March, but there may have been more later after he reduced the term to only two weeks. Krause had mastered commercial work thoroughly, and the German language, which would have been very helpful for the higher grades. After leaving New Richmond, Krause became manager of the Cheyenne Business College in Wyoming, at a salary of $100 per month—quite a sizable salary for the teacher at the time.

DISTRICT SCHOOL BUILDINGS IN COAL CREEK TOWNSHIP

The Annual Reports of the State Superintendent of Public Instruction of Indiana recorded the following statistics: In 1860 Coal Creek Township had nine district schools; four new houses were built within the year valued at $2,700. The following year another building was erected, valued at $620. According to the 1863-64 report, these were all frame buildings. Another schoolhouse was constructed in the 1865-66 school year, bringing the total to eleven houses. This number was satisfactory until 1877, when a new structure was added. In March 1879 a new school was to be built two miles east of Pleasant Hill (Wingate). This brought the total to thirteen, and this school always went by the name of No. 13.

New Richmond's first brick school was constructed in 1887-88 and was valued at $2,140.28. The fourteenth building, a frame structure, and the last district school erected, was built in 1889-90 and valued at $600. This was the school named "Oklahoma," which was used only a short time.

In March 1881, the school superintendent of Montgomery County inspected all the district schools in Coal Creek Township—and their teachers. The school at No. 13 was the only building not constructed from the old pattern that had gone out of date twenty-five years before. It was the only building furnished with comfortable seats and desks. His report also said there were no maps, charts, globes, or dictionaries in any of the schools, and very little blackboard accommodations.

The superintendent raked the patrons over the coals, saying, "there is such a thing as being penny wise and pound foolish. Because many of us who are older had to go to school in an old log house, with undressed plank for a desk and the soft side of a split log for a seat, is no reason why we should not build comfortable and well-furnished school houses for our children."

The buildings did receive an occasional whitewashing, and the roofs were patched now and then. Some did not have fences around them and livestock roamed all around, and sometimes into the class rooms, causing quite a stir among the students.

The teachers—or the "Birch Wielders" or "Pedagogues," or "Hazel Manipulators," as they were always called—were expected to thoroughly clean the buildings, blacken the stoves, wash windows, scrub the floors, and sometimes cut the wood, and carry it in. Some of these jobs were doled out to the schools, however.

No attempt had been made to update the schools in Coal Creek Township as late as 1890, except the brick building in New Richmond. All the older buildings were in very bad condition and the patrons were asking the township trustee to give some attention to the architecture of the schoolhouses. The time of the square box at the country crossroads had passed!

In 1898 the old Center School was replaced by a new structure of the newer style, but was still a one-classroom building. It had a front foyer and cloakroom not found in the old buildings.

The old district schools could have told many, many stories, though, of the ciphering matches, spelling bees, box-suppers, cake and pie socials, the Christmas "Treats" and the Christmas "Trees." The treats were received from the teacher, or many pranks were played on him, usually barring him from the building until he treated the scholars. The trees were parties, and gifts were placed on the tree by the parents or the teachers. The following story about a Christmas Treat is a good example as told by J. J. Insley.

J.J. Insley as School Teacher

An Old Time Episode of a Christmas Treat—How a Hoosier School Master Conquered the 'Bristle Ridge' Boys.

"A way back yonder in the eighteen and fifties, before he had any beard but at the same time plenty of muscle and sand, J. J. Insley, of this city, was called on by some of his neighbors to teach school. He was wanted in one of those old timer districts in the center of Coal Creek Township where big, hard handed young roughs were used to have their own way with the school master. Jim was out in the barn one drizzly day playing checkers with the boys, when the committee called on him to try his hand at their school. The terms were satisfactorily arranged and the new teacher went on duty one morning in December and got along swimmingly until Christmas came near. On Christmas day the great tug of war would be made, Jim well knew, for in those days there were no legal holidays and the boys generally took the management of affairs in their own hands. The new teacher was posted on this, for he had been one of the boys himself, and therefore early Christmas morning, long before the rooster crew, James filled with a young arsenal the holes that his mother had made in his clothes for the receptacles of his mittens, husking peg and pop corn and repaired to the school house. The boys had taken time by the forelock, however, and had remained in the building all night that they might be on the premises early in the morning ready to bar out the "master" until he promised to treat. It wasn't the treating that hurt the teacher so much those days, but the humiliation of being made do it. The teacher in this case had provided himself with the necessary goods for a good treat, which he intended to use only if he came out conqueror. To make an entrance doubly sure, the master, before leaving the schoolhouse in the evening before, had removed two of the puncheons under his mammoth box used as a desk, so that he might crawl under the house and enter through the hole. This aperture was hidden by a large homespun curtain, which hung on the side next to the teacher's seat. As Jim approached the schoolhouse he discovered the presence of the boys by the dim light of the fire within, and without further noise he began the journey on his hands and knees under the house toward the opening he had prepared. Now it so happened that a skunk's nest was right under that hole and as the teacher approached on his under ground route, the said skunk being affrighted made its way through that hole and into the school house as the nearest means of escape. Then such a stampede as there was in that house for a few moments was never heard of. The boys had their doors so barred up to keep out the master that egress was not made until they had been sickened with the stench, while the teacher escaped by crawfishing to open air. It was a complete triumph for the master, while the boys were not only beaten at their game, but were compelled to go until the next Summer without their nice suits of school clothes. The skunk episode not only broke up the bulldozing Christmas-treat system of the boys, but was the further means of causing the old building to be burned and a new house put in place of it, and the new structure was for many years used as the voting precinct of the township. Some of those school boys, now well along in years (for some of them were older than the master at that time) have often wondered how Jim managed to catch that skunk and keep its perfumery down until he could throw it through the window."

The Crawfordsville Saturday Evening *Journal* October 22, 1881 printed this story about J. J. Insley's thrilling experience as a Bristle Ridge school teacher. J. J. was a cousin to Andrew Grady of Wayne Township, and a nephew of Noah Insley, who was one of the first settlers in Coal Creek Township.

COAL CREEK TOWNSHIP DISTRICT SCHOOL HISTORIES

DISTRICT NO. 1 WALNUT GROVE SCHOOL

Dewey-Walnut Grove
Deeded By: Richard Dewey and Katherine Dewey, his wife
Date of Deed: 5th October 1841
Recorded: 29 Dec. 1842
Amount Paid: $1.00
Amount of Lands: 1/3 acre
Deed Book: 10, Page: 302-303
Location: Sec. 11, Twp. 20 north, R. 5 west
Trustees (School Directors of Dist. #2): Elijah Parke, William Kincaid and Philip Lunger
Remarks: for the purpose of building a school house thereon and is to be applied to school purposes for said district, etc.
Note: Richard and Katherine Dewey sold their property to Charles and Malinda Swear and moved west in the early 1850s.

Dewey-Walnut Grove (second deed)
Deeded by: Charles Swear and Malinda Swear, his wife
Date of Deed: 29th September 1860
Recorded: 9th November 1860
Amount Paid: $1.00
Amount of Land: 1/2 acre, more or less
Deed Book: 25, Page: 165
Location: Sec. 11, Twp. 20, R. 5
Trustees: of Coal Creek township (not named)
Remarks: Samuel McComas, Justice of the Peace; George W. Alexander, R.M.Co.

Note: this school building had to be moved after the Frankfort and State Line Railroad was built, was moved to Sec. 14.

Dewey-Walnut Grove (third deed)
Deeded by: Thomas Cook (no wife listed on deed)
Date of Deed: 9 Aug. 1886
Recorded: 5 Aug. 1895
Paid: $20.00
Amount of Land: ½ acre
Deed Book: 75 Page: 534
Location: Sec. 14, Twp. 20 north, R. 5 west
Trustees: to trustees of Coal Creek Twp.
Remarks: Amos Ebrite, Justice of the Peace
Note: this building was located on Section 11 and was moved after the railroad was built in 1881. The railroad bed was located on, or near the road leading to the school which stood about one mile east of New Richmond.

Richard and Katherine Dewey made the first deed for the Walnut Grove School on October 5, 1841. The school trustees, three in number at the time, were Elijah Parke, Philip Lunger, and William Kincaid. Katherine Dewey and William Kincaid were children of Samuel and Phoebe Kincaid, who platted the town of New Richmond. This school stood about one mile east of New Richmond beside a road that no longer exists. This old road then turned north to join the north route to Linden, now County Road 1100 North. The Deweys moved west, and in 1855 Charles Swear, a native of Germany, and his wife Malinda, moved onto the Dewey property. The Swears then deeded the same piece of ground (Sec. 11, Twp. 20, Range 5) to the school trustee on September 29, 1860.

In 1881 the Frankfort and State Line Railroad was constructed parallel to the road on which the Walnut Grove School stood. For safety reasons, the school was moved to the south New Richmond-Linden road, now County Road 1000 North.

News items appeared in the Crawfordsville newspapers under the caption of "Walnut Grove," as there was a small settlement around the first location of the school. This can be seen in the 1864 atlas of Montgomery County in Coal Creek Township. Thomas Cook deeded one-half acre for the new location (Sec. 14) to the school trustee on August 9, 1886.

Some of the early teachers in the Walnut Grove School and the years they taught are: Sarah Widner - 1877; W. W. Hughes - 1879; Susan Miller - 1880; William G. Swank - 1881; Cynthia Warbitton - 1882; Emma King - 1883; Mollie Coon - 1888-89; Charles II. Turvey - 1901; Frank Wilson - 1903; Mabel Lynch - 1904-05; Carrie Dettbenner - 1905-06.

The Walnut Grove School was discontinued by the September term of 1908, but the building remained in the grove and stood next door west of Mr. and Mrs. Henry H. "Pete" Martin's home, one and one-half miles southeast of New Richmond. The Martins used this building for grain storage until the 1960s when it was dismantled.

31 - Walnut Grove School, District No. 1, Coal Creek Township.

District No. 2 New Richmond Schools

New Richmond School
Deeded By: Samuel McComas, and Maria McComas, his wife

Date of Deed: 1st June 1858
Recorded: 1st June 1858
Amount Paid: $12.00
Amount of Land: ½ acre
Deed Book: 23 Page: 186
Location: Sec. 9, Twp. 20 north, R. 5 west.
Trustees: not listed

Remarks: the land for the school was situated south of the New Richmond Methodist Church grounds—the church was located on the property now occupied by the New Richmond-Coal Creek Township Museum (1984).

New Richmond School (first brick building)
Deeded by: Stowe S. Detchon and Jemima Detchon, his wife
Date of Deed: 18 July 1887
Recorded 5 August 1895
Amount Paid: $250.00
Amount of Land: 1 acre more or less
Deed book: 75, page: 533
Location: Sec. 10, Twp. 20 north, R. 5 west
Trustees: Ed. McCrea, school trustee of Coal Creek Township.
Remarks: Amos Ebrite, Justice of the Peace; Thos. T. Marshall, R. M. Co.

Note: This was the site of the first brick building in 1887 and the second brick building built in 1894, which was remodeled in 1909 and served New Richmond until Coal Creek Central was built in 1953. The location was in the east part of New Richmond on the north side of Washington Street.

New Richmond's first school building supported by taxation was built around 1856. An early history of the town gives the year as 1856, another said in 1861. Samuel and Maria McComas deeded one-half acre of land to the township trustee on June 1, 1858 for school purposes, so it is uncertain when the actual construction took place. Many times the deeds were not made immediately, and the actual recording of the deeds was put off for many years, in some cases.

The first school stood on the northwest corner of Madison and Wabash Streets, but was back from the corner, or streets. This building served the town of New Richmond as a school until the first brick school was constructed. As early as 1879 the old school was showing signs of wear and tear, and by 1886, the building had 'played out entirely' and it was thought the children attending school in the building would freeze to death in the winter time.

The citizens of New Richmond were very disturbed because of the neglect of the building, and set about trying to remedy the situation. One complaint was "the building and premises looked as if they'd gone through the battle of Stone River." An appeal was made to the voters of Coal Creek Township to "find a man who will work to New Richmond's advantage occasionally."

District No. 2 New Richmond (or the "Mug Wump School")

The fight began in March 1886, when the Democrats listed the following candidates for township trustee: William Quillin, J. Utterback, Edward Goff, __ Vancleave, Daniel Ebrite, Elisha Campbell and J. H. Alexander; the latter three were from the New Richmond area. The Democrats then convened to nominate a candidate for trustee. There were five candidates at the start of the convention, but three more soon drew off, leaving Utterback (from the Elmdale neighborhood), and Ebrite to fight it out. Mr. Ebrite represented New Richmond, and the Democrats took a solemn oath that if their man was not nominated, they would vote for the Republican nominee. Such happened to be the case, and the aforesaid Democrats, true to their pledge, walked to the polls and did what was never done before in the township—elected a Republican trustee. Capt. Ed T. McCrea was the man they elected.

The Round Hill correspondent for the Crawfordsville weekly *Review* on April 10, 1886, showed his distaste for the whole "gang" of fellows for several weeks following, referring to them as "Mug Wumps," and made every effort to shame them publicly. William Campbell, the New Richmond correspondent for the same paper, a tried and true Democrat, straddled the fence for a while when the Bristle Ridgers entered the picture. The Constable, Pres. Swank of the Ridge, came to New Richmond one day looking for bacon that disappeared from a neighbor's smoke house, and the New Richmond correspondent said, "Mug Wumps" wont steal meet—will take the whole hog or none!"

This verbal war continued several months before the New Richmond writer asked the Round Hill scribe to define the meaning of "Mug Wump." He failed to come up with the definition except to say, "the New Richmondites have organized themselves into a band of deep, designing, and cunning politicians whose purpose will be to raise a candidate residing in that industrious city to the giddy heights of glory by making him trustee. Their object will be "A New Richmond Trustee or Bust, their Motto, Self Gain and Party Destruction!"

32 - The Mug Wump School, completed October 1887

The editor put an end to their fun by saying, "Our two Coal Creek correspondents—please understand, we have had enough personalities toward each other!" Whatever their methods, in January 1887, there was talk of a new school—a brick one—and hopefully it would be large enough to accommodate the public needs. Capt. McCrea began a search for proper ground on which to build, and the correspondent for the Crawfordsville *Review*, Bill Campbell, started after the landowners in the town to provide a parcel of ground for the building in May that year.

Dr. Stowe Detchon and his wife, Jemima, came forth, and sold an acre of land to the township trustee for $250. The building was to be started in June or July 1887, and was to be completed by the winter school term. Barney Wallace was awarded the contract for the brickwork, John Floyd, the plastering, and Samuel Tribby, the carpentry. Bill Campbell continued his political jesting by saying, "When the corner stone for the new school is laid, it should by all means be laid by a "Mug Wump."" When researching and writing this history of the New Richmond brick school, I couldn't help but dub it the Mug Wump School.

By October 1887, the steeple was being erected, and a month later, the bell was installed and tolling—calling forty-two scholars to their new school.

The old frame building and property was sold to George Washburn for $375. Ironically, this is the only building once used as a school, still standing in the town of New Richmond today. It has out-lived two brick structures—one of which was added onto in later years. The old building has served as a residence almost continuously, having been remodeled several times. The roof and ceiling was lowered in order to heat the house more comfortably. Dr. Manners Washburn, brother of George, lived in the beautiful little bungalow for several years after he sold his home on the corner of Washington and Franklin streets.

The new brick schoolhouse, "built at a tremendous expense to the taxpayers," was in a deplorable condition within two years. "The bricks are coming apart and the plastering is falling off—all due to Republican misrule!" said Bill Campbell. The brick building was valued at $2,140.28 when it was new.

New Richmond's Second Brick Building (1894)

Coal Creek Township's trustee, John W. Utterback, posted written notices in five public places in the township, according to law, stating he would file a petition on May 1st, 1894, asking the board of county Commissioners of Montgomery County, Indiana, to authorize him to incur indebtedness on behalf of his township, in order to erect a school building in the town of New Richmond. He stated in his petition that the existing school building was too small to accommodate all the children of school age in said town, and the

33 - Second brick school building, completed in 1894

building was considered dangerous and unsafe to use for school purposes. The taxpayers had filed a petition with the trustee asking that the old building be condemned and a new one erected. Utterback was given the authority to borrow the sum of $8,000, the amount he asked for, by the commissioners, namely: John W. Fullen, Allen Byers, and John Peters.

By July 1894, the trustee was making the necessary arrangements for contractors to do the work on the building. F.M. Alston, a tinner from New Richmond, was awarded the contract for the tin and slate work on the New Richmond School—the roof was slate. The new building was constructed on the same lot as the 1887 brick building, the old structure having been razed. It was only a four-room structure and, from early residents' description (my father Forrest Waye, Ruby Foster Oppy, and others), the building was a tall two-story brick, containing a large hallway both upstairs and downstairs. There was a third story room on the front of the building used as a practice room for the New Richmond orchestra. This building was considered a 'model school' at the time it was erected, and was equipped with the latest furnishings.

NEW RICHMOND'S NEW ADDITION TO THE SCHOOL (1909)

In January 1905, a new concept in school systems in Montgomery County was taking place: CONSOLIDATION! especially in the rural schools. It was believed the end result would be 'better schools at less cost.' Actually, consolidation was advised in 1856 by Caleb Mills when he was State Superintendent of Schools, so the idea was not totally new.

In March 1905, Coal Creek Township's trustee, Henry Vancleave, was to call the advisory boards together and make appropriations for enlarging the Wingate and New Richmond school buildings. Two new rooms were needed for each school. A number of the old district schools were to be closed over the township and the pupils residing near the two towns would be hauled to the town schools. This was tabled for a few years, however. During the fall term there were 140 pupils in the four-room school at New Richmond.

Sam D. Symmes of Union Township, in January 1906, read a paper at a meeting of the Trustees Association at Indianapolis, stating the benefits of the consolidation plan. He stated, "The old log school house with greased paper in the windows, a board with wooden pegs for legs, and serving for a seat without a desk, and the cross, crabbed, teacher with an armful of switches was good in its day, but have long since been placed in the background. Why? Because of improvements in education. The district schools were of a vastly more benefit than the old log house, but to be content in 'letting well enough alone' is to take a step backward." He continued by discussing the success of the city schools with its graded system, saying the same success could be accomplished in the consolidated rural schools. He made a special effort to remind the country people that their children could still breathe fresh air and commune with nature as in the past.

How to travel to these far-away schools was then discussed. The district schools were within walking distance of the scholars. He said, "Wagons could be purchased for this purpose and equipped with some kind of heating apparatus of a stove, or what is safer—foot warmers and robes. Hire men as drivers, as they must have charge of the children while in the wagon, and must keep order in every respect, etc ... pay drivers good wages-this will insure good work. Have wagons run on scheduled time so children will know when to expect the wagon to arrive, and can be ready. With good roads a wagon can go six miles in an hour, or perhaps a little more, and make stops for the children. Put on enough wagons to make the trips without being on the road too long or overcrowding the wagons."

One of New Richmond's school teachers attempted to enlighten the citizens about consolidation, saying, "we should not think of a few paltry dollars, but should provide the children with the best advantages in education where the grades could be taught separately by a teacher who was a specialist in his, or her, particular grade. Consolidation would be less expensive for the taxpayers with less buildings to maintain and heat, and in two years we could have a course of study in high school equivalent to that of the commissioned schools."

The inhabitants of Coal Creek Township balked at the idea of closing all the district schools, but the state authorities had other ways of making them 'see the light.' In October 1908, Dr. W.G. Swank, the Montgomery County health officer, was called to investigate conditions of the old district buildings. Wingate residents were already in the middle of a big fight over having their school, which had been built in 1891-92, torn down and replaced. Center School was closed for a while, until they corrected their "unhealthy" situations in the school.

Dr. Swank ordered two rooms closed in the New Richmond School because of over-crowded conditions. They had 72 pupils in a room which was only to accommodate 37 pupils in the primary room, and in the high school were 48 in a room that should have had only 37. Sixty pupils were thrown out of school, four grades being dismissed, until the township trustee could remedy the situation. All of the blame was put on him by the advisory board who said he had $300 with which to procure additional rooms. What the article failed to say was that the overcrowding was brought about by the closing of six district schools, and the pupils were transferred to New Richmond, Wingate and Elmdale Schools. The pupils were to return to school at the earliest possible moment—as soon as someone would furnish them room.

The Hollin brothers came to the rescue of the township trustee, and made their opera house available to the students. The class history of 1911 says, "We began our junior year in the opera house," etc. "Our place of residence so affected us we were inclined to think school but a mad and merry comedy in which we were the actors. Mr. Shanklin and Mr. Kesler soon changed our attitudes with assignments in History and Algebra." The class history continued with, "A short time before Christmas, as a reward for our good behavior, we were allowed to enter the new school building."

Getting back to the planning stages of the building, forty patrons met in the New Richmond School building on Saturday, April 10, 1909, to discuss the school building propositions. There were several views in the matter—one group was in favor of an entirely new building, another was in favor of adding only the necessary rooms to meet all the requirements made by the state, and still another idea was submitted—to re-open all the district schools in the country, and not improve the New Richmond school in any way. One member of the advisory board would not consent to tearing down the four-room building, but was in favor of improvements to correct the overcrowding.

J.D. Wilson, the township trustee, provided some rough estimates and specifications an architect had supplied, and discussed the possible cost of a whole new structure. The thought of building a new structure for the high school, and continuing the grades in the old building was also discussed.

It was decided the best plan was to add on to the old structure. The lower floor was to be given wholly to the grade school, and the upper to the high school. The estimated cost of about $11,000 was much easier to live with than the $30,000 building that had been erected in Wingate in 1907-08. The citizens of that town were still upset over the cost, for many years.

The laying of the corner stone of the New Richmond school addition was to take place on Friday, August 13, 1909. Patrons were told they could place any little trinkets, heirlooms, old coins or papers in the receptacle—a quart fruit jar, which was to be well sealed. Two issues of the New Richmond *Record*, dated April 15 and August 12, 1909 were to be included in the jar. Incidentally, I kept part of the contents of the jar, and the papers were so badly torn they were not of much value.

Shortly before Christmas 1909, the building with a new gymnasium was completed. The gymnasium was situated partially underground. Basketball enthusiasts met, and a team was organized. During the 1910-11 term, patrons decided to join the State High School Athletic Association. Officers of the local association were as follows: Roy Hanawalt, president; John Miller, secretary-treasurer, Professor Kesler, manager.

Most importantly, though, for the first time in the history of New Richmond, the school was listed as a commissioned high school during the 1910 term.

The New Richmond Parent-Teachers Association was organized in October 1914, a branch of the Indiana division of the National Congress of Mothers and Parent Teachers Associations. The first officers were: Nettie Alexander, President; Martha Dunn, Vice President; Altie Kirkpatrick, Secretary; Florence Tribby, Treasurer.

34 - New Richmond school building with students and faculty. Photo take December 12, 1913. Note the former Christian Church building in the background.

This school building served the town of New Richmond and the surrounding area until the new Coal Creek Central building was constructed in 1953, a consolidation of Wingate and New Richmond schools. Both the New Richmond and Wingate school buildings were sold on December 11, 1953.

A partial list of teachers in the early schools in New Richmond are: Mr. King - 1877; W.S. King - 1879; Wiley Tiffany - 1880; Paul Barcus - 1881; J. Martin McBroom - 1882; Emma King - 1883; Fred Burris and Miss Alice King - 1887; Thomas Patton and Eva McCallom, 1888 - 89 (E.E. Bailey, vice teacher for Thos. Patton, who was ill); Mr. Henry, Principal and Miss Eva McCallum, primary - 1890; E.M. Morrow - 1891; O.E. Kelley, Principal - 1893; S.S. Phillips (Stowe), Principal., John Murphy, Intermediate - 1895.

In 1901 - Lee J. Whelen, Prin., J.T. (John) Harriman, grammar, Samuel E. Jones, intermediate, Mary Courtney, primary. In 1903 - Fullor Combs, Prin., Walter S. Vaughan, Mrs. G.W. Watkins, Miss Nellie Franklin. In 1904 - Morton Dixon, Frances Wilson, Mrs. G.W. Watkins, Frances Bailey. In 1905 - M.J. Murphy, Prin., John W. Hutchinson, grammar, Robert Cowan, intermediate, Miss Cordella Fine, primary. In 1906 - M. J. Murphy, Prin., Lester Olin, grammar, Frances Bailey, intermediate, Cordella Fine, primary. In 1907 - Raymond Alexander, Prin. In 1908 - Oscar Swank, Prin. In 1910 - Howard Kesler, Prin., Edith Trout, Latin and German; Ida B. Shanklin, English and 8th grade; Lester Olin, 6 and 7; Caroline Dettbenner, 4 and 5; Ida Frances Epperson, 2 and 3; Lulu Greenburg, I A-B.

District No. 3 Brannon-Dazey-Bible School

Brannon-Dazey-Bible School
Deeded by: William Brannon and Artimesa Brannon, his wife
Date of Deeds: 13th October 1857
Recorded: 3 Jan. 1859
Amount Paid: $1.00
Amount of Land: ½ acre
Deed Book: 23 page: 470-471
Locations Sec. 8, Twp. 20 north, R. 5 west
Trustees: trustees of Coal Creek Township (not named)
Remarks: Samuel McComas, Justice of the Peace; Geo. H. Alexander, R. M.Co. this deed to hold good, so long as used only for school purposes, when used otherwise it shall fall back to said Brannon, his heirs or assigns.

Brannon-Dazey-Bible (second deed)
Deeded by: Albert Dazey and Carrie J. Dazey, his wife
Date of Deed: 20th January 1879 Recorded: March 21, 1879
Amount Paid: (sum of-crossed out) Amount of land: 180 feet x 110 feet
Deed Book: 44 page: 364
Location: Sea. 8, Twp. 20 north, R. 5 west
Trustees: (not listed)
Remarks: Amos Ebrite, Justice of the Peace; so long as it is used for school purposes

Brannon-Dazey-Bible (third deed)
Deeded by: John P. Bible and Anna L. Bible, his wife
Date of Deed: 16th March 1895
Recorded: March 19, 1895
Amount Paid: $1.00
Amount of Land: ½ acre, more or less
Deed Book: 75 page: 35
Location: Sec. 8, Twp. 20 north, R. 5 west
Trustees: trustees to John W. Utterback, trustee of Coal Creek Township
Remarks: Robert A. Osbum (Osborn) N. P.
Note: on the 4th of May 1910 the trustee of Coal Creek township conveys to John P. Bible for the sum of $21.50 the same parcel of ground, "the same has not been used for school purposes for more than 2 years."—Deed book 108 Page 256.

William and Artimesa Brannon made the first deed for this school, which stood two miles west of New Richmond, on the 13th of October, 1857. William signed the deed with his mark, an X, but his wife could write and signed her name.

The second deed was made by Albert and Carrie J. Dazey, on January, 20, 1879. In November 1883, the "Brannon-Dazey" school building was removed by the township trustee and placed near John Bible's residence.

John P. and Anna L. Bible made the third and last deed for this school on the 16th of March, 1895.

In 1910 the land was deeded back to John P. Bible, not having been used as a school for more than two years. Pearl (Kite) Bana said there were two school buildings on the Bible property; one stood next door to the Bible's home, and the children were so noisy, Mrs. Bible persuaded her husband to deed a piece of land on down the road so they would not disturb her. A new building was then erected on this lot. It stood on the south side of the New Richmond-Newtown road next to where Herman Keeney resided (1984). The old structure was then moved to the north side of the road across from Bible's residence and used as a tenant house. By 1970, the Bible home and both schoolhouses were all dismantled, and nothing remains to mark the sites.

Some of the school teachers and the years they taught are: Katie Frain - 1877 (Brannons); Harvey Bryant - 1878 (Brannons); E.M. Widner - 1879 (Brannon); William J. Cord - 1881 (No. 3-Brannon); Wesley Dazey - 1881 (Brannons); Mr. Tarpinning - 1882 (No. 3) Wesley Dazey - 1883 (Brannon-Dazey); Mr. Campbell (Brannon-Dazey) - 1883-84; John L. Shrum - 1888-89 (No.3); John Smith - 1899 (Bible); Robert Cowan - 1901 (Bible); Lester Olin - 1903 (Bible); Mary Alexander - 1904-05 (Bible); Will J. Irwin - 1905 (Bible) Sep. 7th, 1905; John Smith - 1905 (was listed in Sep. 14 list of teachers) (Bible); Note: Mary Alexander taught the 1904-05 term and one of the two men taught the 1905-06 term.

Trustee Vancleave almost closed the Bible School in 1906, but decided to continue at least another year. This was during the consolidation of the township schools, or district schools.

District No. 4 Oakland (Later Elmdale)

Oakland (this deed is back to owner)
Deeded by: trustee of Coal Creek Township, Orlando W. Mason
To: Guy O. and Minnie J. Widner
Date of Deed: 23 February 1901
Recorded: 6 Feb. 1901
Amount Paid: $30.00
Amount of Land: 1 acre
Deed Book: 86 Page: 167
Location: Sec. 30, Twp. 20 north, R. 5 west
Remarks: a careful search for an early deed for this school was unsuccessful.

Oakland school stood on a little knoll across the road to the west of the Oakland Cemetery. Just who gave the land for the school is uncertain, as a careful search for an early deed proved to be fruitless. The Montgomery County atlas shows the owners of the land surrounding the school property as follows: in 1864 - R. Riston; 1878 - A. P. Bible; 1898 - A. C. Widner.

A deed in the Montgomery County Recorder's office does show that Guy O. and Minnie J. Widner paid $30 for the one acre of ground on Sec. 30, T. 20 N., R. 5 W., on which the Oakland School stood, on the 23rd of February 1901. The land was no longer being used for school purposes at that time. The building was moved to the farm later occupied by Jacob Bunnell and family, but was dismantled many years ago.

A partial list of teachers in the Oakland School are: Ollie Allhands - 1877; Fred E. Weigand - 1879-1883; Henry Shotts - 1888-1889; and Wes Dazey - 1896. Fred Weigand was one of the more dedicated and successful teachers. The Crawfordsville Weekly *Review*, January 29, 1881 says, "Prof. Fred Weigand is a teacher of untiring energy and of superior skill. His order is perfect, and those who create disorder are promptly suspended, or expelled, and no favoritism is shown."

Oakland School was discontinued in 1898, and the students were transferred to the new school building in Elmdale.

District No. 4 Elmdale

Children of school age residing in, or near Boston Store (Elmdale) in the early days attended the schools of Oakland, Lud Thomas, No. 13, Oklahoma, and Hickory Corner. Hickory Corner was located south of Boston Store on the Wayne and Coal Creek Township line, but was included within the Wayne Township school districts.

Residents of Elmdale were looking forward to having the first school building erected within the village boundaries in February 1896. They had a two-year wait, however, because the new two-room structure was not completed until 1898.

Within a few years, the number of students in the Elmdale neighborhood had grown and more room was needed in the local school. On August 13, 1903, the Crawfordsville *Review* noted the opening of Coal Creek Township's schools was postponed until September 21st because another room was being added to the Elmdale School and the plastering was not completed. The new room was added to the rear of the original two rooms.

The New Richmond *Record*, Thursday, January 21, 1904, printed Coal Creek Township's annual report of the township trustee, listing the costs of the new addition: James Raisor was paid $1,525 for the Elmdale School building, Houlehan and Morrow received $137.50 for the heater at Elmdale, and Raisor also received $22.32 for the cement walks at the Elmdale School.

The school at Elmdale was discontinued in the 1932-33 term and the students were transferred to the schools at New Richmond and Wingate.

What happened to the Elmdale School building was a complete mystery to most of the residents residing in Coal Creek Township in 1979 when I asked questions concerning the school. When I read through some old New Richmond town board minutes, the answers suddenly appeared. On March 3, 1936, the trustees of the town of New Richmond made a motion to have two of the trustees, Charles M. Fruits and Clyde A. Thomas attend the sale of the Elmdale School building for the purpose of buying the building. The price to be paid was to be determined at a later date. During the April meeting they decided to pay for the building as soon as the money was available and on July 20, 1936, the town trustees of New Richmond paid the Coal Creek Township trustee, Grady Chadwick, the sum of $430 for the Elmdale School building. There was no mention as to what purpose the building was to serve the town in any of the meetings of the trustees.

On October 17, 1938, a resolution was passed by the trustees of the town of New Richmond, offering for sale the lumber from the Elmdale School building. An advertisement was placed in the Crawfordsville *Journal-Review*, and a special meeting was held to open the bids received for the lumber. None of the bids were acceptable so the town trustees let the lumber lie on the ground. At the March 4, 1940 meeting, the town trustees granted a ten-day option on the Elmdale School lumber lying on the town lot at a price of $350, the said lumber to be used in building a sale barn and stock yards in New Richmond.

The trustees of the town of New Richmond were still making plans to sell the lumber from the Elmdale School at the next meeting. Eventually, Lewis Withrow purchased most of the lumber for $351 in May 1940. The town marshal was instructed to sell the window sashes for 75 cents each, James Harris purchased $15 worth of the lumber, and frankly, I came to the conclusion that the purchase of the Elmdale School building was not the smartest move the trustees of the town of New Richmond ever made. There was no record of how much, if anything, was paid to the person, or persons, to dismantle the building and hauling the lumber to New Richmond's town lot. Reuben Swank thought Adam Bonebrake dismantled the building. Forrest Waye said he and Jim Kincaid went to the Elmdale School building in Jim's horse and wagon, to get a load of school desks to be used in the New Richmond Schools, after Elmdale School was closed.

The following is a partial list of Elmdale schoolteachers: 1900 - Matt Murphy; William Utterback; 1901 - M. J. Murphy, principal; Marion Westfall, Primary; 1903 - Lee J. Whelen, Prin.; Marion Westfall, Bertha Hormell; 1904 - Lee J. Whelen, Lester Olin; Bertha Hormell; 1905 - Lee J. Whelen, Prin.; Lester Olin, intermediate; Mary Hormell, primary; 1906 - Lee J. Whelen, prin.; Thomas Allen, intermediate; Mary Hormell, primary; 1910 - Ernest O. Kirkpatrick, Prin., and grades 6, 7, and 8; Mima Alexander, grades 3,4, and 5; Zelma Auter, grades 1 and 2; 1911-12 - Lawrence Pierce grades 6, 7, and 8 (was not listed as principal); Anna Stafford, grades 3, 4, and 5; Florence Goddard, grades 1 and 2.

DISTRICT NO. 5 PATTON SCHOOL

Patton School
Deeded by: John Patton and Nancy J. Patton, his wife
Date of Deed: 11th December 1858
Recorded: 7th April 1859

Amount Paid: $10.00
Amount of Land: 80 Rods, more or less
Deed Book: 24 page: 68
Location: Sec. 28, Twp. 20 north, R. 5 west
Trustees: of Cole [Coal] Creek Township
Remarks: Edward P. Bennett, Justice of the Peace; as long as same is used for school purposes, otherwise falls back to said John Patton, or his heirs.

John and Nancy Coons Patton deeded eighty rods of ground to the trustees of Coal Creek Township for school purposes on December 11, 1858. Both John and his wife could write and signed their names to the deed. The original deed places the lot in section twenty-eight, but all the maps in the Montgomery County Atlas places the school in section twenty-seven. The school stood about three and one-fourth mile south of New Richmond. The 1864 and 1878 maps placed the school on John Patton's land, but the 1898 map shows the land surrounding the school belonged to James N. Thomas. John and Nancy Patton both were deceased by that time.

Patton's schoolhouse was the scene of many political rallies and conventions, and was made a voting precinct in February of 1882. A Literary Society was "progressing finely" in January 1881 at the Patton Schoolhouse. Levi Thomas was president of this group. The students of Patton and Round Hill Schools competed in ciphering and spelling matches on many occasions.

Coal Creek Township was cursed by excessive mud, and in the early years, travel was almost impossible during the rainy spring season. In October 1887, the farmers along the road south of New Richmond were getting up a petition to raise money (and promises of work by the able-bodied residents) to gravel the road to Patton's Schoolhouse. Previous to the graveled roads, only muddy paths made by wagons or horses was the rule. They had very good success with the petition and contemplated building the road as early as possible.

Some of the teachers of the Patton School and the years they taught were: Amelia Widner - 1877; Eliza Quick - 1879 and 1880; Albert Wilson - 1881; David Shields - 1882; Susan Miller - 1883; Eva Morrow - 1888; E.M. Morrow - 1889; Fred E. Kincaid - 1901-03 (Kincaid resigned his position to take up the task of rural mail carrier and Miss Carrie L. Sibel, "a highly intellectual lady who holds a state license," finished his term); Fred Chelen - 1904; and Thomas Allen - 1905.

The New Richmond *Record*, Thursday, August 30, 1906, says, "Trustee Henry T. Vancleave gives a list of teachers for Coal Creek Township, and says the school at Patton's corner will possibly be discontinued and the few pupils there hauled to the New Richmond Schools." The late Mildred "Punk" Tribby said the Patton School, a frame building, was moved to the woods behind Clyde Thomas' farm, just west of Patton's corner on the north side of the road, and used for storage.

DISTRICT NO. 6 ROUND HILL SCHOOL

Round Hill School
Deeded by: Hiram Connell and Margaret, his wife, of Tippecanoe Co. Ind.
Date of Deed: 30th March 1846
Recorded: 1st March 1849
Amount Paid: (see remarks below)
Amount of land: 50/100ths acres
Deed Book: 13 Page: 378
Location: Sec. 26, Twp. 20 north, R. 5 west
Trustees: (not listed) only says, "residents of said district desire land for school purposes."
Remarks: Connell reserves for his own use all the timber on said lot, and the inhabitants are to pay, or exempt said Connell from paying tax for school or school house purposes on the balance of the 80 acres from which lot was taken for the term of 5 years from this date. (Signed by Hiram, and his wife Margaret's (X) signature).

Absalom Kirkpatrick, Justice of the Peace; James Heaton, R. M. Co.

Round Hill School (second deed)
Deeded by: James D. Wilson and Mary J. Wilson, his wife
Date of Deed: 26th January 1899
Recorded: 22 May 1903
Amount Paid: $43.50/100ths.
Amount of Land: 92 and 4/5th sq. rods
Deed Book: 91 page: 52
Location: Sec. 26, Twp. 20 north, R. 5 west
Trustees: to Ebbert M. Morrow, trustee of Coal Creek township
Remarks: Edgar Walts, N. P. Jno. Warbritton, R. M. Co.

Hiram and Margaret Connell, of Tippecanoe County, Indiana, made the first deed for the Round Hill School building on March 30, 1846. The building stood on section twenty-six and was located four miles southeast of New Richmond in the little hamlet of Round Hill, for which the school was named. The hamlet is now a ghost town.

James B. Pierce owned the land surrounding the Round Hill School for many years, but no deed was made by him to the school trustees. James D. and Mary J. Wilson made the second deed on January 26, 1899.

The school building was to be re-roofed and a new fence was needed in July 1877. Whitewashing of the old building was completed in October 1890, so these little country schools were maintained occasionally.

Early scholars attending this school would have been the children of Joseph and Sophia McGinnis, John A. King, William Campbell, Samuel Wilson, James Rankin, Moses Gillam, Sarah Bennington, John Killen, and others. Later students would have been the children of James B. Pierce, George Pierce's children, the Eshlemans, and the Tomlinsons.

Children of William W. and Sophia McGinnis Wilson, the second generation of two early families, attended the Round Hill School, and the old Wilson homestead was passed on to their son, James D. The children of James D. and Mary J. McClamroch Wilson, namely, Ethel, Stella, and Ralph L., all attended the Round Hill School.

Ralph L. Wilson, their only son, died from injuries sustained while playing a game of football between Wabash College and St. Louis University, on October 24, 1910. He was injured on Saturday and died the following day in Josephine Hospital, in St. Louis. A fractured skull was the cause of his death. Eight cousins acted as pallbearers at his funeral, and the honorary pallbearers were the ten members left of Wabash College's broken football team.

Crawfordsville, Wabash College, and New Richmond all disbanded their football teams after this terrible tragedy, along with other Coal Creek Township football teams. The sport was not played in the New Richmond Schools from that time on. Ralph L. Wilson was buried in the Oak Hill cemetery near Crawfordsville, and a banner on his tombstone is inscribed with, "Did Wabash Win?"—his last words spoken.

The New Richmond *Record*, Thursday, November 9, 1905, relates a story concerning the Round Hill School entitled "Three Plucky Girls." The three were Misses Mary Johnson, and Gretchen and Edna Kincaid, who walked from New Richmond to the Round Hill School to attend a festival being held there because they had been dared to by those who heard them mention going. After the festival was over they spurned the attentions of numerous gallant young fellows to see them home, and walked all the way back, arriving home about eleven o'clock. When asked why they did it, they replied, "we wouldn't be turkey, so we just went." The editor of the *Record* questioned, "how many young men about town will walk four miles in the country to a festival—or even to see his best girl? SPEAK UP!" Incidentally, the menu for the festival was oysters, ice cream, and cake.

An incomplete list of teachers at the Round Hill School and the years they taught were: Mina (Williamson) Johnson - 1877 (she was married just after the trustee hired her to teach); J.D. Wilson - 1879; King - 1880; Jas. D. Wilson - 1881; Nettie B. Stewart - 1882; Mrs. Mina Johnson - 1883; Joe Bennett - 1888; W. S. Vaughn - 1901; Robert Cowan - 1903; Blanch Loman - 1904; Mary Alexander - 1905; Chas. D. Fouts - 1910.

The Round Hill School was discontinued in 1911 and the students were sent to the New Richmond Schools. The Round Hill School building was then moved to the Pierce farm and was used as a storage shed—this seemed to be the fate of all the early district school buildings.

District No. 7 Center School (in Bristle Ridge)

Center
Deeded by: John Hiett and Mary F. Hiett, his wife, of Tippecanoe County, Ind.
Date of Deed: 7th June 1866
Recorded: 30 June 1866
Amount Paid: $50.00
Amount of Land: 8 rods x 13 rods; x 8 x 13 rods.
Deed Book: 31 page: 52
Location: Sec. 19, Twp. 20 north, R. 5 west
Trustees: to Trustees of Coal Creek Township (not named)
Remarks: for school purposes so long as it shall be used as such.
George C. Price, J.P. of Tippe. Co. – affidavit signed by William R. Ellis, Clerk of Tippe. Co.; H. I. Webster, R.M. Co.

The first deed found for the Center School district was made by John and Mary F. Hiett on June 7, 1866, however, there was mention of an earlier school being taught in the 1850s by J. J. Insley in Bristle Ridge. (see story of J. J. Insley's Christmas Treat and conquering the Bristle Ridge boys). Center School stood on section nineteen but adjacent to section twenty, which is said to be the heart of the Ridge, according to old timers.

The Center School house was at one time a voting precinct for the area, and many rousing Democratic Conventions and rallies were held in the old school house in the time period between 1870 to the early 1900s. In June 1904, what was said to have been the largest convention ever held in Coal Creek Township was held in the Center Schoolhouse to nominate delegates to the county convention. Again in 1906, there were 228 in attendance at the Democratic Convention at Center School. This certainly would have taxed the little building.

The same year, a Prohibition Convention of Coal Creek Township was held at Center Schoolhouse to nominate three members for township advisory board, two Justices of the Peace, and two Constables. An earlier 'rousing' meeting, held in February 1882 at Center, was a meeting of irate taxpayers of Coal Creek Township opposing the proposed tax donation of $21,150 for the Frankfort and State Line Narrow Gauge Railroad. They had been taxed previously for this railroad, and were thinking "enough is enough." They lost their fight, however, and had to pay again.

35 - Center School, District No. 7, Coal Creek Township. Copy of Reuben Swank's photo, used by permission.

Examinations for the eighth grade graduates of Coal Creek Township were held at Center School in 1904 and 1905 and perhaps in other years. Many socials were held in the schoolhouse, as well as entertainment of all descriptions.

The old Center School building eventually saw too many 'rousing' political rallies and had to be replaced by a new structure. This new building, completed in September 1898, was from a different pattern than the old 'square boxes' originally built in Coal Creek Township. The building had an entry room and a cloakroom, and a table for the water pail. The water pail was equipped with one drinking dipper to serve the whole school, according to Reuben Swank, who attended the School. The building was considered a 'credit to the Township' when it was new.

Thomas Allen, the teacher at the Center School in 1908, complained to the County health officer about the one-room school house—with eight large and two medium windows not having any shades or shutters to protect the scholars' or teachers' eyes from the glaring sun. Another complaint was that there was no trough to carry the water away from the pump, thus creating a health hazard from standing water. The school, upon visitation by the health officer, was temporarily closed until the problems were corrected.

The problem of appropriate money for such items was argued over between the township trustee Vancleave and the school board—a carry-over from the Wingate School squabble that continued a number of years. As it turned out, the school patrons furnished the shades for the windows, probably because they had heard enough of the conflicts between the board, the trustee, their attorneys, and the county health officer. The fuel for this fight started at the state level, forcing consolidation upon the district schools, and Coal Creek Township was not prepared financially to build, or support these schools. Center School was one of two district schools left in Coal Creek Township in 1908; Round Hill was the other. Center re-opened after the shades were installed.

An incomplete list of teachers at Center and the years they taught are: Luella Thomas - 1877; J.S. Henry - 1879; Mary Graham - 1880; Eliza Sprahan - 1881; J.D. Thomas - 1882; Lena King - 1883; A W. Dazey - 1889; Thomas Allen - 1901; John Hutchison (or Hutchinson) - 1903-1904; Fred Chelen - 1905; Thomas Allen - 1908; Oscar Swank - 1910; Charles C. Fouts - 1911-1912.

In the 1911-12 term, Center School was the only district school left in Coal Creek Township, and this was to be its final year. It was closed by the 1912-13 school term.

The Center School building was purchased by John Merritt and served as a tenant house. When John's son Eugene married, he and his wife moved into the school, after having it moved across the road to the east, and remodeled the structure in 1949. A kitchen was added and three rooms upstairs with a bath, making a nice home for the Merritts. Michael Merritt, son of Eugene, occupied the old Center School house in the 1980s.

DISTRICT NO. 8 TAYLOR-KENTWOOD-QUININE-COWAN'S CORNER

Taylor-Kentwood-Quinine-Cowan's
Deeded by: Thomas Taylor and Matilla Taylor, his wife
Date of Deed:19 June 1876
Recorded: Aug. 8 1876
Amount Paid: $15.00
Amount of Land: ½ acre, more or less
Deed Book: 41 Page: 83
Location: Sec. 35, Twp. 20 North R. 5 west
Trustees: Aaron H. Gilkey, trustee of Coal Creek Township
Remarks: John E. Hanna, Justice of the Peace; T. Y. Myers, Rec. M. Co.
Note: Kentwood school house, in the Cowan neighborhood, 5 miles south of New Richmond burned to the ground in January 1903.

Thomas and Matilda Taylor made the first deed for the Taylor School on June 19, 1876. Researching these early district schools can be very confusing sometimes, especially when they are referred to by so many names. I thought the above names were four individual schools at first, but after careful study, discovered only one building was involved.

Originally, the Taylor School was located five miles south of New Richmond, and about one-half mile east of Cowan's corner, but it was moved closer to the corner sometime before 1898. The Montgomery County atlas shows the School on A. B. and C. Harshbarger's property in 1898.

An interesting little story appeared in the Crawfordsville *Review*, November 25, 1893, under "Kentwood" items; it reads, "During the past summer, Jacob Swank has gained much notoriety as a jockey, but lately has proven himself superior in other lines. At an entertainment given at Kentwood Schoolhouse by Daniel Murphey and scholars, a cake that was baked by Mrs. John Lynch was placed as a prize to be captured by the best looking girl present, and sold for $17.90, being voted off at a cent a vote. The successful candidate being Miss Bell Patton. The entertainment was a success in every respect, but boys, you must remember that while you may 'out' Jacob on the outcome of a horse race, that it takes money to compete with him when the beauty of his sweetheart is at stake." By the way, Jacob married Bell a few years later.

Following is an incomplete list of teachers at Taylor-Cowan-Quinine-or Kentwood school and the years they taught (in parenthesis is the name (or No.) the school was listed as): A.W. Wilson - 1879 (Taylor); J.W. Johnson - 1880 (Quinine); S.A. Clevenger - 1881 (No. 8); Miss Carrie Warbritton - 1882 (No. 8); __ Hancock - 1883 (Quinine); Alice King - 1888 (No.8); Daniel Murphy - 1893 (Kentwood); Miss Hormell - 1903 (Kentwood and Quinine).

The township trustee discontinued school No. 8 in 1901, but must have re-opened it by 1903, because classes were being held in the school when it burned to the ground that year. The New Richmond *Record*, Thursday, January 29, 1903, gives the following account of the fire, "At an early hour last Friday morning, Kentwood, or Quinine schoolhouse, in the Cowan neighborhood, five miles south of town, burned to the ground. The origin of the fire is supposed to have been caused by a tramp that had taken refuge in the building from the cold, as one had been seen in the vicinity the day before. The wife of Ed Cowan who lived less than a quarter of a mile away, was probably the first to see the fire, but it had then gained too much headway to be extinguished.

Trustee O.W. Mason procured a room in the Ed Cowan residence, fitted it with seats and school fixtures, and the school was continued with only the loss of Friday. Miss Hormell is the teacher."

In August, 1903, the township trustee had decided not to rebuild the Kentwood School, and it was discontinued in the 1904 term.

DISTRICT NO. 9 (OR DIST. NO. 1 IN RANGE 6) HESHBON BETHEL-GREGORY'S-COUNCIL GROVE-MEHARRY'S

Gregory-Meharry-Council Grove
Deeded by: James Gregory (no wife listed)
Date of Deed: 7th February 1838
Recorded: April 6th 1838
Amount Paid: (not listed)
Amount of Lands: 6x6x6x6 Rods
Deed Book: 7 page: 227
Location: Sec. * Twp. 20 north, R. 6 west (*he owned 2 pieces of land in Sec. 12)
Trustees: (see remarks)
Remarks: the deed reads: WHEREAS, the inhabitants of School District Number one in Congressional Twp. 20 N. of R. 6 W. are in want of a piece of land on which to erect a house for School purposes, now therefore, know ye that I James Gregory, a citizen of said district, do for myself, and my heirs forever, have given, granted ...unto all persons while inhabitant of said district, the following parcel of land, beginning at a white oak tree standing in the section line between said J. Gregory and James Maharry etc. Attest: B. Sherwood, John Mann.

A. Kirkpatrick, Justice of the Peace; George Miller, R. M. Co.

Heshbon Bethel Church and School Council Grove-Meharry-Gregory
Deeded by: Thomas Meharry and Unity Meharry, his wife, of Mont. Co. Ind.
Date of Deed: 18th December 1847
Recorded: 22 Jan. 1848
Amount Paid: $1.00
Amount of Land: 1 acre and 84 purches
Deed Book: 13 page: 306-307
Location: Sec. 2 & 3 (on line of) T. 20 N., R. 6 W.

Trustees: Hugh, Thomas, and James Meharry, and Nathan Beach of Mont. Co., and David and Jesse Meharry of Tippecanoe Co.

Remarks: The deed reads in part, "Thomas Meharry has laid out a tract to be used as a burial ground and upon said land has been erected a building which is occupied as a school house and also a preaching station for the preachers of the Methodist Episcopal Church, etc ... the said Hugh, Thomas, James, David and Jesse Meharry and Nathan Beach (and their descendants forever) will act as trustees, to protect and keep in repair the said premises and also to use the same for the purpose of a burial ground for such of the members and relatives of their respective families as may depart this life and for such of the inhabitants of the neighborhood as may by their permission be interred therein and also to use the building now upon the premises or which may hereafter be erected by them or any of them as a school house for the education of youth, and as a place of divine worship in connection with the Methodist Episcopal Church, etc. Samuel R. Smith, Justice of the Peace; James Heaton, R. M. Co.

Witness: Samuel R. Smith and Jnas. Beach.

Heshbon Bethel Church & School-Council Grove-Meharry-Gregory
Deeded by: James Meharry and Nancy Meharry, his wife (2'd deed by Meharry's)
Date of Deed: 19th October 1856
Recorded: 13th July 1857
Amount Paid: $5.00
Amount of land: (not given)
Deed Book: 22 page: 438-439 Location: Sec. 2, Twp. 20 north, R. 6 west
Trustees: Levi Curtis, George Ebrite and Aaron Stephens, trustees in trust for Coal Creek Township.
Remarks: note the three trustees of Coal Creek Township on this deed. Samuel R. Smith, Justice of the Peace. As long as same shall be used for school purposes.

Heshbon Bethel Church & School Council Grove-Meharry-Gregory
Deeded by: Ira G. Meharry, Guardian of Allen N. Meharry (3'd deed by Meharry's)
Date of Deed: 27th September 1900
Recorded: May 22, 1903
Amount Paid: $32.50
Amount of land: ½ acre, more or less
Deed Book: 91 page: 53 Location: Sec. 2 Twp. 20 north, R. 6 west
Trustees: to the school trustees of Coal Creek Township (not named)
Remarks: It is agreed that in case said property should cease to be used for school purposes the same shall revert to grantors.

Gregory School: Land for the first school believed to have been in the Meharry neighborhood was deeded by James Gregory on February 7, 1838. The deed did not give a section number, only T. 20 N., R. 6W., so it is difficult to locate the site. The original Land Owners of Montgomery County, Indiana, shows that James Gregory purchased two parcels of land on section twelve, one on January 23, 1834, the other on April 5, 1836, so this school probably was located in Section 12.

The Federal census of Coal Creek Township in 1850 shows Samuel and James Gregory residing near Thomas Meharry. Coal Creek runs through section twelve and Meharry resided on the north side of the creek in section two. This deed was the only information found on this school.

Heshbon Bethel Church and School: The next deed for a school in this area was a building constructed by the Methodists for church purposes in section 2, Township 20 north, 6 west. The building also served the area as a schoolhouse. This deed was made December 8, 1847 by the Meharry family—the brothers and brother-in-law served as the church's trustees. (see history of the early log schools). The church was called Heshbon Bethel.

Meharry or Council Grove School: Another deed for a school site was made by James and Nancy Meharry on the 19th of October, 1856, to the Township school trustees, three in number, namely, Levi Curtis, George Ebrite, and Aaron Stephens.

The next deed was made by Ira G. Meharry, guardian of Allen N. Meharry on September 27, 1900. The Crawfordsville *Journal*, March 5, 1874, mentioned some "colored children" were attending the Meharry School. There was no explanation as to why they were in the neighborhood, or where they resided, only that they were well behaved and clean.

The famous Council Grove Horse Thief Detective Company (or the Council Grove Minute Men, as they were called) held their meetings in the Meharry schoolhouse for many years—almost throughout the existence of the group of law enforcers.

Clare Meharry said the Council Grove School building was moved east of the original site, and stood on the north side of the New Richmond-Newtown road in the corner of what is now Roy and Lee Meharry's field. The location can be seen on the 1864, 1878, and 1898 maps of Coal Creek Township in the Montgomery County atlas, in S. 2, T. 20 N., R. 6 W.

The incomplete list of teachers in the Meharry-Council Grove School is as follows: F.W. Gregory - 1877 (Council Grove); Berta Hartness - 1878 (Meharry); J.H. Bryant - 1879 (Meharry's, or No. 1 in R. 6); Lena King - 1880 (Council Grove); Lida O. Quick - 1881 (No. 9); Mrs. B.O. Hayes - 1882 (No. 9); Eliza Quick - 1883 (Council Grove); Charles Kellison - 1888 (No. 9); Miss Alice King - 1889; Miss Sadie Rust - 1901 (Council Grove); Frances Bailey - 1902 (Council Grove).

The Meharry-Council Grove School was discontinued in August 1903 by the trustee of Coal Creek Township, O.W. Mason. The students were hauled to the Wingate and New Richmond Schools in horse-drawn school hacks. Before this, they had walked to school or, in some instances, rode their horses.

DISTRICT NO. 10 PLEASANT HILL/WINGATE

Pleasant Hill-Wingate School
Location: Lot No. 16 Pleasant Hill Original Plat
No other information is known.

The first schools near Pleasant Hill (Wingate) were the log structures included in the first part of the history of Coal Creek Township schools. In 1860 a frame building was erected for school purposes in the village of Pleasant Hill, at a cost of about $1,800, the first school supported by taxation. The patrons promoting this school were the families of Mathias, Alexander, Beever, Hamilton McClure, John McJimsey, and John Ashenhurst. This school was to be a graded school and offered two departments.

The old building was showing considerable signs of 'wear and tear' and underwent the necessary repairs in April 1878. The Walker brothers repaired the building, and the opening of the spring term was delayed until they completed the work. This building was located on the corner of Vine and Main Streets in Pleasant Hill.

Pleasant Hill's 1891-92 Building

The above building served the village of Pleasant Hill until it was beyond repair. In October 1891, the township trustee, John W. Utterback, approached the county commissioners with a petition signed by sixty patrons to secure a loan of $3,000 to $4,000 to build a new brick schoolhouse for District No. 10 in Coal Creek Township (Wingate). By June 1892, Utterback reported to the Crawfordsville *Review* that Wingate's new school building was progressing nicely, and said, "when the building is completed it will be one of the prettiest structures in the county." This same year, all township trustees in the county contracted with an eastern firm to furnish the schools with slate blackboards. The price was to be twenty-one cents per square foot. This possibly may have been the first time the schools in Coal Creek Township had blackboards. The old frame building was sold to John Sprague in 1895, for $25 cash, a few years after the students had been attending classes in the new structure.

CONSOLIDATION—that horrid word that everyone despises had taken hold in Montgomery County by October 1905, and the Coal Creek Township trustee, Mr. Henry Vancleave, was being pushed by the state school authorities to close down the little district schools. The students were hauled in horse-drawn school hacks to the town schools at New Richmond, Wingate, and Elmdale. This created problems of overcrowding in these schools and the county health officer was asked to step in to inspect the conditions of the schools. In Wingate's school an over-crowded situation existed, and the only solution was to find a room in town to house the extra classes. The town hall was secured and another teacher, Miss Bonnie Grenard, was hired to teach these students.

In February 1906, plans for a new school building at Wingate were drawn by H.H. Richards and George W. Vancleave, associate architects of Chicago, and the cost was to be around $25,000. These plans were presented to the advisory board, and accepted by them, and they were approved by the State Board of Health. H.T. Vancleave, trustee of Coal Creek Township, was to advertise for sealed bids on the contract. The construction was to be commenced as soon as the school term closed in March, and to be completed by the first of September—in time for the fall term.

The Wingate school building was condemned by the State Board of Health around the first of April 1906, claiming the school had been in an unsanitary condition for some time, and pupils had become ill on account of the bad conditions. They delayed the closing of the school, however, because there was no other building to continue to the end of the school term. A deputy from Indianapolis represented the State Board of Health and viewed the building, pronouncing it unsafe.

The Coal Creek Township advisory board met in Trustee H. T. Vancleave's office in Wingate on February 28, 1906, to appropriate $32,000 for the construction of a new school building in Wingate. Attending this meeting were two-hundred remonstrators, or tax-payers, of Coal Creek Township opposing the construction of the new building, and with them was their attorney, Clyde Jones of Crawfordsville. Mr. Jones stated his clients "opposed the new building for two reasons: First, that it is not necessary to construct a new building, as the present one can be repaired and save the taxpayers thousands of dollars; Second, that the board cannot proceed according to law for the reason that the law requires ALL members to consent to such action, and as Mr. Cowan was objecting, no action of theirs would be legal." He further stated "that there were no objections to repairing the old building by adding on four new rooms to accommodate the growing classes."

In October 1906, a restraining order was issued by Judge West to stop the construction of the Wingate School building. Those opposing the building alleged fraud in the manner of the trustee's and his advisory board's procedure when the schoolhouse was ordered built. Special Judge Samuel R. Artman, of Lebanon, was appointed for the case. He was to render his decision the 25th of October.

The Coal Creek Township advisory board met in Trustee H.T. Vancleave's office in Wingate and awarded the contract for Wingate's new $30,000 school building to Peter Levandowsky, a contractor of Lafayette, early in November, 1906.

Jones and Murphy, attorneys for the taxpayers of Coal Creek Township, filed another complaint in November the same year, and Judge West again issued a temporary restraining order, this time against Trustee Vancleave and Peter Levandowsky, the Lafayette contractor who was to tear down the old building and erect the new one. A new advisory board had just taken office and had undone the work of the former board. The trustee of Coal Creek Township was not going to be supported in his plan to build a new $28,000 schoolhouse. The new board's desire was to appropriate $15,000 to build an addition to the old building and make it conform closely to the new Tuttle School building in Crawfordsville.

The Wingate School controversy continued to the end of 1906. Vancleave and Levandowsky were given time to prepare affidavits to show why a temporary injunction should not be issued against the building of the Wingate School. The attorneys, Jones and Murphy, had already presented affidavits trying to get another restraining order to stop the building of the school. Judge Claybaugh of Frankfort was appointed the special judge in the case. The temporary restraining order issued earlier was still in effect at this time.

After three days in court at the end of December 1906, the arguments for and against the Wingate School injunction were concluded, and Judge Claybaugh had a huge pile of affidavits and counter-affidavits to study. A decision was not likely to be made before the January term of court, beginning on Monday, January 14, 1907. The restraining order already in effect was to continue until the Judge made his decision.

The matter of the Wingate School building was partly settled by the middle of March 1907. A public auction was held in Wingate and several bidders were on hand to bid on the old Wingate schoolhouse. Peter Levandowsky, the contractor, made a bid of $500 and the amount was more than the rest wanted to offer, so he purchased the building for that amount. He was to tear the old building down to make way for the new structure, and he was to use some of the material from the old building in the new.

The Crawfordsville weekly *Journal*, August 9, 1907, gave the complete program for the ceremony of the laying of the cornerstone for Wingate's new schoolhouse. A large crowd attended in spite of all the difficulties in the previous months planning of the building. The structure was to be completed by December 1, 1907.

The Coal Creek Township advisory board was still fighting the building of the Wingate schoolhouse on September 1, 1907, by refusing to appropriate money for bonds. They met in their annual session with Trustee Vancleave, and by unanimous vote turned down every request or recommendation he made. They had their minutes already prepared—and written—before the meeting commenced. The tax levy was fixed so as to delay, in every possible way, the completion of the new schoolhouse, although the cornerstone had already been laid a few weeks before. They transferred $9,150 from the special school fund over to the Township funds so the trustee could not use it for building the school or to purchase school furniture. They cut the school fund levy from 50 cents to 25 cents on the $100, and refused to consider the bids submitted for the desks and other furniture for the school. They further refused to make any appropriation whatsoever to pay the interest on the bonds that had been issued for the schoolhouse. A big lawsuit was expected to come from their actions. This was not the end of the squabble, but the school building was eventually completed; after all, the trustee was only trying to comply with the state school laws.

The school term opened in Wingate's new $30,000 building, despite the Township advisory board's orders that school should not be held there, in the middle of September, 1908. The building stood on the corner of Bascom and Main Cross Streets. It was a magnificent structure and the residents of Wingate were very proud of the building for years to come. Students attended school, grades 1-12 in the same building, until decades later, when the dreaded word consolidation was brought up again.

In 1953 the two schools in Coal Creek Township, Wingate and New Richmond, were consolidated and the new Coal Creek Central School, housing grades 1-12, became the last school built in the township to this date. The old Wingate School was sold on December 11, 1953.

Following is an incomplete list of Pleasant Hill's or Wingate's early school teachers and the dates mentioned: C.H. Pease - 1860, Principal; Mr. Spillman - 1861 (an unknown assistant); John Ellis - 1861-64 (and an unknown assistant); W.C. and D.W. Gerard - 1865-68; Charles A. McClure - 1875 (and an assistant); Lettie Lee - 1877; Barbara Beever - 1878; C.A. McClure - 1879; Jennie Dunkle - 1880; C.A. McClure, Room 1 and D.A. (Dan) Murphy, Room 2 - 1881; Cornell - 1882; Jennie Dunkle - 1883; Charles A. McClure and Jas. Elmore - 1888; C. A. McClure, Prin. and James Elmore - 1889.

1901 - George B. Welty, Prin., and A.N. (Andrew) Foley, grammar, George Vancleave, intermediate, and Miss Frances Montgomery, Primary; 1903 - Matt Murphy, Prin., A.N. Foley, Geo. Vancleave, and Miss Frances Montgomery; 1904 - M. J. Murphy, A.N. Foley, Cordella Fine, and J. D. Finney; 1905 - H.M. Dixon, Prin., John W. Allhands, grammar, J.D. Finney, intermediate, Miss Blanch B. Loman, primary; 1906 - W. R. Allee, Prin., J.M. Allhands, grammar, Lena Thompson, intermediate, Velma Auter, primary; 1910 - Margaret Weesner, Prin., L.J.C. Freeman, Latin and Physics, Helena Johnston, English and 8th grade, Clara Vancleave, Music and Art, Susie E. Miller, 6th and 7th, Lucy McMullen, 4th and 5th, Nelle Templeton, 2nd and 3rd, and May Wood Talbot, 1 A-B.

DISTRICT NO. 11 (OR NO. 3 IN RANGE 6) GRENARD-TRACEY-RAKE POCKET

Grenard-Rake Pocket

Deeded by: Vezey Tracy and Nancy Tracy, his wife and by Simeon Grenard and Abigail Grenard, his wife, of Montgomery Co. Ind.

Date of Deed: 11th March 1856

Recorded: July 13, 1857

Amount Paid: $10.00

Amount of Land: 5x8x5x8 Rods (in each Sec.)

Deed Book: 22 page: 439 Location: Sec. 26/35 Twp. 20 north, R. 6 west

Trustees: Levi Curtis, Moses L. Burk and Aaron Stephens, School Trustees in Trust of Coal Creek Township.

Remarks: All four persons, Vezey and Nancy Tracy, Simeon and Abigail Grenard signed this deed with an (X) as they could not write their names. This is a double deed because the school stood on the grounds of the two families and on the section line between sections 26 and 35. Samuel R. Smith, acting Justice of the Peace witnessed the conveyance of land, to the school trustees.

The Grenard School was located two and one half miles south of Wingate. It stood on the section line between sections 26 and 35, in Range 6. Therefore, two deeds had to be made for the building. On March 11, 1856, Vezey and Nancy Tracy and Simeon and Abigail Grenard made the first deed for the school.

Mrs. Homer Goff enlightened me as to how the nickname "Rake Pocket" came about. She said there was a group of rough characters who hung out in the school building for the purpose of gambling, therefore, raking out their pockets. This name was used as often as the name Grenard, when the list of Coal Creek Township's teachers was printed in the Crawfordsville and New Richmond papers. I hope the gambling didn't take place during school hours!

The school had just received a coat of paint, applied by J. Wilking, in August 1879. Just a few months later, the building was broken into by unknown parties, who broke the lock on the door and carried off some books and notions belonging to the scholars. They also wrote 'vulgarisms' on the blackboard and seats. Someone must have decided to stop the gambling and locked the fellows out.

Following is an incomplete list of teachers in the Grenard School: Miss Rusk - 1877 (Rake Pocket); R.S. Osborn - 1879 (Rake Pocket); Joseph S. Henry - 1881 (No. 11); Wm. Dotson - 1882 (No. 11); Charles Sayers - 1883 (Rake Pocket); Wesley Dazey (or Daisy) - 1888 (No. 11); C.C. Kellison - 1889 (No. 11); W.J. Cord - 1892 (No. 11); John Hutchison - 1901 (Grenard); John Booe - 1903 (Grenard); Wm. Irvin - 1904 (Grenard), Clifford Coon - 1905 and 1908 (Grenard).

The Grenard School was discontinued in 1908. The building, a frame structure of the old square-box pattern, was auctioned off in 1910. Oliver Hopper purchased the building and moved it about one mile west of the original site. Hopper converted the building into a four-room house and used it as a residence. The building burned to the ground in November 1975.

DISTRICT NO. 12 (OR NO. 4 IN RANGE 6) THOMAS—OR LUD THOMAS

Thomas School

Location: Sec. 27, Twp. 20 north, R. 6 west
No other information is known.

The Thomas district school is shown on the 1864 map of Coal Creek Township on S. 25, Twp. 20 N., R. 6 W. Thomas Meharry owned 160 acres surrounding the school on this map, but in 1878 the land surrounding the school was owned by Polly Meharry.

The Thomas School stood on the north side of the road on what is now Old State Road 55, or the Attica road, as it was known earlier, about half-way between Elmdale and Wingate. No deed was found on this school when a search was made, but it may have been overlooked. Sometimes deeds were made, but the owner failed to have them recorded until several years later.

Just why it was called the Thomas School is not known. The Thomas family owned the land northeast of the school and Judith Thomas taught in the school at one time, but no record was found of Lud Thomas teaching in the school.

The teachers of Thomas School and the years they taught are: Judith Thomas - 1877 (Thomas); C.A. McClure - 1878 (Lud Thomas)—a spelling school was held in this school the same year and was taught by J.F. Drake; J.W. Ashby - 1879-80 (Thomas); C.B. Sayers - 1881 (No. 12); George Welby - 1882 (No.12); J.S. Henry - 1883 (Thomas); R.S. Osburn - 1888-89 (No. 12); J.T. Finney - 1901 (Thomas); Thomas Allen - 1903-04 (Thomas); John W. Smith - 1905 (Thomas).

The Thomas School was discontinued about 1908, but no information was found as to what happened to the building.

District No. 13 No. 13—Tailhoit—Hormell

No. 13 – Tailhoit-Thomas
Deeded by: Silas A. Thomas and Martha J. Thomas, his wife
Date of Deed: September 21, 1880
Recorded: May 1, 1882
Amount Paid: $30.00
Amount of land: ½ acre, more or less
Deed Book: 52 page: 295 Location: Sec. 13, Twp. 20 north, R. 6 west
Trustees: Trustee of Coal Creek Township
Remarks: reverts back to Silas A. and Martha Thomas whenever Coal Creek Township fails to use it for a school.

The Crawfordsville Saturday Evening *Journal*, July 17, 1880, says, "A new school house is to be built in this township about two miles northeast of town (Pleasant Hill items) in time to exhaust this years' crop of hazelbush." Incidentally, the hazelbush mentioned was to be used as switches, not building material.

Silas A. Thomas deeded one-half acre in Section 13, township 20, range 6, for this school on September 21, 1880. The Crawfordsville *Star*, January 20, 1881 gave an account of a fire that occurred shortly after the building was constructed saying, "The new school house near Mr. Fowler's (Lud Thomas' School) caught fire from the flue and burned a $50 hole in the roof and ceiling." This school was the thirteenth structure built in Coal Creek Township, stood on section thirteen, and was named Number Thirteen. If one were superstitious, it would make one think twice about the fire happening so soon after the building was constructed!

School No. 13 was the only building in 1881 made from a new pattern; the rest were made from the old box style that was terribly out of date by 1880. This was the only school furnished with comfortable seats and desks, and the township trustee was put under much pressure to leave them out, but he insisted upon the latest equipment for the new school.

The residents around the area of the No. 13 School soon became very proud of the building and the Crawfordsville *Journal*, November 19, 1882 said, "Number 13 is the name of the new school house J. E. Hanna erected two years ago in Coal Creek Township two miles east of Pleasant Hill, on the New

Richmond road, on the corner of Silas Thomas' farm, beautifully located one-half mile north of the narrow gauge railroad, surrounded by intelligent, industrious and school appreciative people."

The writer of the above statement failed to explain the nickname Tailhoit, but items had been appearing in the Crawfordsville newspapers under both captions, "Number 13" and "Tailhoit," since soon after the school was erected. It was assumed the name originated because it was to be the last district school built in the Township—at the tail end. This will do until someone can come up with a better explanation. The name "Lud Thomas School" was mentioned at the time of the fire at the new building, but this was the only time it was called by that name.

The following is a partial list of teachers and the years they taught at No. 13: James D. Thomas - 1881 (No. 13); Wesley Dazey - 1882 (No. 13); James D. Thomas - 1883 (Tailhoit); Israel Naugle - 1888-89 (No. 13); Fred Kincaid - 1890 (No. 13), Wesley Daisey - 1892 (No. 13); Miss Hormell - 1901 (No. 13 and Hormell's); J.D. Finney - 1903 (No. 13 and Hormell's); John W. Smith - 1904 (No. 13 and Hormell's).

No. 13 was last supplied with a teacher in September 1904. The following year, in September 1905, there were only schools numbered from 1-12 in Coal Creek Township's list of teachers, and No. 13 was not on the list. It is safe to assume the school was closed in 1905. The students were transferred to the Wingate Schools after the closing of No. 13.

District No. 14 Oklahoma

Oklahoma
Deeded by: The Traveler's Insurance Company
Date of Deed: 3 July 1890
Recorded: 12 September 1892
Amount Paid: not available
Amount of Land: 42/100ths acre
Deed Book: 69 Page: 411 Location: Sec. 36, Twp. 20 north, R. 6 west
Trustees: of Coal Creek Township
Remarks: Travelers Insurance witness: H.E. Fritts, Chas. S. Robbins, State of Connecticut, Hartford Co., Pres., J.G. Bortterson; Sec. Rodney Dennis. For school purposes, if abandoned for this purpose, to revert to the owner of adjoining land from which it was taken. Thos. T. Marshall, Recorder of Mont. Co. Ind.

In 1890 the list of Coal Creek Township schools included: 1 brick and 13 frame buildings. One building valued at $600 was erected during the year. The Oklahoma School, or Number 14, was constructed in 1890 and stood on Sec. 36, Twp. 20 north, Range 6 west. It was located due west of Elmdale on the north side of road 650 north, where road 750 west comes from the south to intersect, forming a "T." The school can be seen on the 1898 map of Coal Creek Township. Later maps of Montgomery County show the road numbers, making the location more easily found.

The fourteenth school, or Oklahoma School, was situated on a property line between the Traveler's Insurance Company and Louisa Brant's eighty acres. The Traveler's Insurance Company made a deed to the trustees of Coal Creek Township on July 3, 1890. The company owned 160 acres surrounding the east half of the school property. I failed to locate a deed from Louisa Brant, or why it was named Oklahoma.

I only found one entry of the schoolteachers of Coal Creek Township that included the Oklahoma School—this was in September 1901, and John W. Smith was the teacher.

The trustee of Coal Creek Township, O.W. Mason, discontinued the Oklahoma School in August 1903. It was the shortest lived district school in the Township.

Coal Creek Central School

On February 25, 1952, the taxpayers of Coal Creek Township met with the Township trustee, Levert Binns, and his advisory board, and were presented a plan of consolidation of the Wingate and New Richmond Schools.

The old structures in each town had served two generations, and in some instances, the third generation was attending classes in the old buildings. Forrest Waye and his wife Vera Ebrite both attended the New Richmond Schools; all seven of their children and some of their grandchildren attended the same school. There were others, perhaps, but their names cannot be recalled at this time.

I do not remember the condition of the Wingate School building, but the structure in New Richmond was very much in need of repairs in the 1940s. Plaster was constantly falling from the ceilings, the rooms in most of the building were very cold in the winter, and the restrooms were very outdated—not the little buildings behind the school as the district schools were provided with, but still very outdated.

The consolidation plan was voted upon and it was decided to make plans for a new structure. A site was to be selected halfway between the two towns, if possible, and this was accomplished.

In March 1952, township trustee Levert Binns and the advisory board met with architects Brunsma and Cashner of Lafayette in order to get an idea of the type and estimated cost of the structure. After much consideration and study, the plans and the proposed site was then presented to the state superintendent, who approved both after a few changes were made. The purchase of land was made by the school board and trustee on the 6th of March, 1953. The contract was awarded to Williams, Beck, and Hess of Crawfordsville to build the new structure, and the materials were delivered to the new site. Incidentally, some of the materials were damaged by a tornado that passed through the area on April 9, 1953.

The first concrete was poured for the foundation of the new school on April 22, 1953. It was decided to add more classrooms than the original plan called for, as well as a gymnasium. Bids were approved by the local school board and the state superintendent on the last day of September, the same year.

Students moved into their new school on October 5, 1953. Patrons toured the new facility the day before, more than one thousand people signing the register during the open house. The trustee, Levert E. Binns, appointed the following persons to select a name for the new building: Grace McBeth, Rosiland Clark, Mrs. Don Patton, Lester Olin, Fern Irwin, Lavonne Norman, and Mrs. Dan Gross. They selected the name "Coal Creek Central" because of its central location between New Richmond and Wingate.

The new facility cost the taxpayers $225,000. All twenty-four rooms were located on the ground floor, which was quite an improvement as both the old schools at Wingate and New Richmond had three flights of stairs to be climbed each day by the teachers and students. Grades one through twelve attended the Coal Creek Central School when it was first constructed. The greatest improvements were the spacious cafeteria and kitchen, and the well supplied library.

Within three years, the school was over-crowded and two classrooms were being added by the contractors who erected the original structure—Williams,

36 - Coal Creek Central School

Beck, and Hess of Crawfordsville. The rooms were to be completed by November 1, 1956. In 1966, the trustee and his board were in the process of leasing two portable rooms for Coal Creek Central to take care of the growing classes. The portable rooms were removed after the high school students moved to North Montgomery in 1971 and were no longer needed.

The Coal Creek Central School served the township students, grades one to twelve, until the new North Montgomery High School was constructed in 1971, about halfway between Linden and Crawfordsville. Coal Creek became a grade school with kindergarten through the eighth grade. In 1976 pupils in the sixth, seventh, and eighth grades at the Linden Middle School were transferred to Coal Creek Middle School. This move was to save the school board $40,000 in salaries by eliminating some of the teachers.

The latest consolidation in 1984 is the consolidation of all the grade schools in the North Montgomery school unit. Unfortunately, the little children now board the bus in the dark in the morning, and many do not arrive home in the evening until after dark in New Richmond, and they are only traveling to and from Coal Creek. Many hours are spent on the road to attend Pleasant Hill Elementary School, half-way to Crawfordsville.

Chapter 11 - Banks and Bankers

The New Richmond Bank

The early Indiana State Gazetteers, from a period of 1882 to 1890, list: New Richmond on Coal Creek, in Coal Creek Township, Montgomery County, Indiana–12 miles northwest of Crawfordsville Court House, the nearest banking place. The 1887 and 1890 directories gives the location as being 13 miles northwest of Crawfordsville, on the Toledo, St. Louis, and Kansas City Railroad (T. St. L. & K.C.R.R.).

In the 1880s, the people of New Richmond and the surrounding area were becoming a little more prosperous than they had been since the pioneer days, and realized a need for a bank a little closer to home. An appeal was made to the 'moneyed men' to start a bank in New Richmond.

Many times there were rumors that a banking institution was in the process of being organized, but they were just that–rumors. In the New Richmond items of the Crawfordsville Weekly *Review*, March 14, 1891, William Campbell, the New Richmond scribe, wrote, "Talk of a bank here went with the wind–if 15 cents would start a bank, this place might take one share of one cent each." A month later he was still pleading, "New Richmond wants a bank–and a lawyer."

The March 6, 1891, issue of the New Richmond *Times* informed the citizens, "New Richmond has a chance now to secure a first class bank, one that every person will have confidence in. Our best men are at the front, and mean business and we hope they will have the support of every businessman and every one that wishes our little city well…"

In September 1891 the New Richmond *Times* noted

NEW RICHMOND BANK–how does that sound? We are sure of it this time. Thomas Patton, the undertaker and rising young business hustler at New Richmond is to be the assistant cashier of the new bank at that place. On, or before November first 1891, the NEW RICHMOND BANK will open its door for business in the front half of the room occupied by T. S. (Thomas) Patton. Mr. Patton will build an addition and move his stock back, making room for the bank. Pritchard and son of Georgetown, Illinois, are the proprietors of the NEW RICHMOND BANK. L.F. Pritchard of Georgetown is cashier, and T.S. Patton, assistant.

Early in October it was announced,

The NEW RICHMOND BANK will be ready for business November 1st. The safe arrived Saturday and was placed in position Monday. Its weight is between ten and twelve thousand pounds and is absolutely fire and burglar proof. The second set of doors are proof against burglars, but to be more sure there is a money vault on the inside of the door which is controlled by a time lock that cost three hundred dollars alone, and it defies the workings of any burglar. The furniture for the bank is promised by the twenty-fifth of this month and as soon as it arrives it will be placed in position and the bank will be ready for business in a few days.

The New Richmond Bank opened Monday, November 2, 1891, in their "elegantly furnished room with a nice flourishing business–and a capital stock of $100,000". The furniture was placed in position and was "as nice, or even a little nicer than any of the city banks are furnished," and the "stationery was the best we have ever seen and everything needed to carry on the business" had arrived. The New Richmond Bank purchased their nice new carpet from George F. Long, a local dry goods merchant.

Within two months the New Richmond Bank, yet in its infancy, had done a wonderful amount of business and far exceeded the expectations of the officials. Pritchard & Sons were to erect a fine brick bank building 24 feet by 70 feet, built especially for bank purposes and furnished inside in the very latest style. The Pritchard family owned a bank in Georgetown, Illinois. Ed Pritchard was the cashier of that bank, and his brother Fred was the cashier of the New Richmond Bank. (There is no record of their new brick building).

The location of this early bank in New Richmond was in a frame building located next door north of the three-story Snyder brick building. The local town hall now occupies the site.

During the short existence of this bank, a panic was created in the town when the eastern exchange failed to reach the New Richmond Bank, forcing the men in charge to close the doors and suspend payment on all checks until the "vulgar" money arrived on the afternoon train. Before its arrival, however, two of New Richmond's prominent businessmen became engaged in a lively exchange of blows. Some of the bystanders condemned the bank management; the others sided with the bankers. For a time a general riot was threatened, and the fracture of many former personal friendships took years to heal.

The New Richmond *Enterprise* noted in November 1893, "The NEW RICHMOND BANK is paying off the depositors and will retire from business. There is talk of organizing a state bank in the spring with some cashier in charge." The New Richmond Bank continued to do business until June 1895, however, and a notice in the Crawfordsville Weekly *Review* said at that time, "The NEW RICHMOND BANK has decided to discontinue its deposit department and has paid its depositors."

Complete records are unavailable and it is unknown when the bank finally closed its doors, but this advertisement appeared in the New Richmond *Enterprise*, May 28, 1897, "The finest line of buggies, surreys, phaetons (touring cars), and bicycles ever in the town. Two car loads now on exhibition in the Pritchard Bank Building–Snyder & Thompson."

THE CORN EXCHANGE BANK

The mention of the Corn Exchange Bank in New Richmond immediately brings to mind its founder, a man who lived up to the image his parents must have had in mind when they named him George Washington Washburn. George W. Washburn, son of Nicholas and Jane (Potter) Washburn, was born January 10, 1829, in Brown County, Ohio. The family moved to Montgomery County, Indiana, settling near Waynetown in 1833, where the father operated a mill on the site later occupied by the Snyder Mill. In 1840, when Washburn was about eleven years of age, the family moved to Coal Creek Township, settling two miles south of New Richmond. At the age of twenty, Washburn received this eighty-acre tract of land, the old home place, from his father, and from this acreage he built his fortune. Washburn and William Winter then became partners in the farming and cattle business. The fear of becoming a poor old man was a driving force in Washburn, and the five years he and William Winter worked together were the busiest years in his life. William Winter sold his half to Washburn after the first five years. Washburn prospered, and was soon known as New Richmond's "Cattle King." The coming of the railroad through New Richmond was a great factor in his prosperity, as he was then able to ship his cattle from a nearby stockyard to the markets in St. Louis, and other points west and east. Much time was lost before the railroads came because of the necessity of driving the livestock to the markets.

George Washburn became one of the wealthiest men in New Richmond. At the time of his death, his wealth was estimated at $300,000. He owned 1,400 acres of land, some in Tippecanoe County, but most in Coal Creek Township. He owned several residence properties, 15 business blocks in New Richmond, and the Corn Exchange Bank. George Washburn married Louise J. Whetstone in 1857, and they had three children. The wife and one daughter, Ella, were deceased before Washburn's death, and his wealth was left to his two surviving children: William Winter "Wint" Washburn, and Jessica Louise

Washburn (Mrs. Charles Kirkpatrick). The son was named for the man Washburn had worked with and had admired throughout his life, William Winter.

In 1888, after a busy life of farming, trading, and raising choice cattle, Washburn moved to New Richmond to rest. He wanted to be near the churches, schools, and markets, and did not care to retire in a big city. George was not the type of person to rest, however, and soon after his move into town, he became more active in the New Richmond Christian Church, of which he was a member. He gave liberally toward the new building, which was built the same year he moved to town.

In 1895, he founded the Corn Exchange Bank of New Richmond with a capital stock of $10,000. He served as president, John McCardle vice-president, and Charles Kirkpatrick, cashier. George Washburn's son Wint later replaced McCardle as vice president, and also served as cashier of the bank at one time. In May, 1895, George Washburn erected a new brick building known as the "Bank Block." Myers and Swan, contractors from Crawfordsville, constructed the building, and Rappert and Son did the roofing and tinning. This block is still standing today on the southeast corner of the square in New Richmond. A biography of George Washburn appeared in the New Richmond *Record*, Thursday, December 11, 1902, that said in part, "A wise man from New Richmond once said of Washburn, 'His bank is as sound as the Rock of Gibraltar, and were I in London and should be told that every bank in the United States had collapsed but one, I'd known that the one was George Washburn's." Washburn served as president of the Corn Exchange Bank until his death on August 1, 1906. At the same time he was serving the Corn Exchange presidency, he held the position of president in the New Richmond Building Association, which was organized in November 1889. He was one of the incorporators and one of the original directors of the Association.

William W. "Wint" succeeded his father as president of the Corn Exchange Bank, moving up from vice president after his father's death. Wint Washburn had received a good common school education at New Richmond, attended Wabash College, conducted a general store in New Richmond for a few years, then traveled for a while. He, too, was very interested in raising and breeding fine livestock, especially Shorthorn cattle, which he often showed at the State Fair. His farm was known as the Villa Grove Stock Farm, on the old Washburn homestead.

Wint Washburn married a Crawfordsville girl, Mary Engle, and the same year of his father's death, he was elected as vice president of the Citizen's National Bank of that city, and was one of the six directors of the bank. He moved his family into their new home in Crawfordsville in December 1906 and resigned as president of the Corn Exchange Bank in New Richmond, severing all ties with that bank on March 1, 1907.

The Corn Exchange Bank was reorganized in December 1906, under the state laws. Jessie Louise "Lou" Kirkpatrick, one of the two heirs of George Washburn, became the controlling stockholder of the Corn Exchange Bank, and her husband Charles continued to manage and reorganize the bank. Persons who subscribed for stock in the newly organized bank were: Charles Kirkpatrick, Mrs. Charles Kirkpatrick, Bayless Alexander, A.J. Arnett, J.A. Bailey, Thos. O. Bailey, Homer C. Barcus, W.W. Boland, W.L. Bowles, J. Frank Chadwick, John Cutrell, Wm. T. Davidson, W.C. Davisson, Allen M. Deeter, Albert Dettbenner, Thomas DeVault, Daniel Ebrite, Thomas M. Foster, Jacob Fulwider, Thos. J. Grantham, John C. Henderson, W.H. Hollin, G.O. Julian, Jacob Kirkpatrick, S.S. Kirkpatrick, William Kite, John S. Lofland, Jr., Robert Long, C.A. Lydick, Frank M. Lynn, Albert C. Luse, S.E. Magruder, A.E. Malsbary, John V. Malsbary, Monroe Mason, Capt. E.T. McCrea, Boyd A. McMillin, Delbert W. Pierce, James Rust, Frank L. Rust, W.F. Shepherd, Justin Stanley, James H. Stewart, George A. Thomas, James N. Thomas, Capt. L.M. Tribby, Wm.P. Vess, Ira M. Wilson, and James D. Wilson.

Charles Kirkpatrick called his brother William home to take a position in the Home Exchange State Bank, as cashier. Will had been residing at Broken Arrow in Indian Territory for some time, and had to dispose of his business at that place before returning home. Jessie L. Kirkpatrick served as cashier of the bank and followed the same honest policies as her father, George Washburn. Henry K. Lee, J.A. Bailey, and John C. Henderson, all served as vice presidents of the Corn Exchange Bank over the years.

On the 27th of December, 1910, the Corn Exchange State Bank of New Richmond signed an agreement with the Henry Clay Castle Hall Building Association of New Richmond, to lease, for the sum of $3,000, the northeast room on the ground floor of the new Knights of Pythias (K. of P.) building in New Richmond. The lease was for a ten-year period commencing on March 1, 1911, and ending on the first day of March 1921. The bank officials were to pay $25 per month payable semi-annually on the first day of July and January of each year, and were promised the privilege of renewing the lease for another ten years after the original lease expired. The radiators, gas fixtures, vestibule, consulting room, director's room, telephone, and coupon rooms, were to be considered as a part of the fixtures of the party of the second part and were considered their personal property (the bank's property). The bank officials were to have the use of the furnace and light plant without charge, provided that they furnish their own fuel and gas. The lease of the K. of P. building was signed by George F. Long, secretary of the K. of P., and William C. Davisson, their president, and Corn Exchange State Bank President Charles Kirkpatrick.

The New Richmond *Record*, Thursday, December 22, 1910, tells of the bank's move into the new building:

> The work of the construction of the big fire-proof vault, 9 by 11 feet, in the new building was begun Monday of this week. This room was built especially for bank purposes, with high windows, plenty of north light, and when completed will be a beautiful new bank home.
>
> The new furniture will be of mahogany and marble. The woodwork of the room will be mahogany finished to match the furniture, and with marble baseboard around the lobby. The outer door at the southeast corner of the room will open into a vestibule with inside swing doors. Passing into the lobby you look straight back through beautiful grill work of the furniture into the fireproof vault. On your right you see the president's office on a raised floor of six inches, with counter railing and swing door. Back of this begins the office proper, of marble base and mahogany to a height of 50 inches, above this the metal railing.
>
> The fire-proof vault will be protected by the latest improved mechanism which will be a work of beauty as well as a great stronghold. The front of the outside door will be plate glass covering the outside workings of the time lock.
>
> Further complete equipment of the new home will be a private office and a directors' room, both of which will be enclosed by railing eight feet high and capped by a cornice moulding. The new bank home will be a thing of beauty and an enterprise in keeping with our handsome new K. of P. building, all of which New Richmond can be justly proud.

At a meeting of the stockholders of the Corn Exchange State Bank, held late April 1912, it was unanimously decided to increase its capital stock and to take into the bank all new stockholders who wished to get in. Thirty-three new shareholders were added within a few days, and within two weeks a total of sixty-five new stockholders were added. The bank reached the $50,000 mark for its working capital. Officers of the bank at this time were: Charles Kirkpatrick, President; Henry K. Lee, Vice President; William Kirkpatrick, Cashier; Jessie L. Kirkpatrick, Assistant Cashier.

In early morning of October 24, 1917, an attempt was made to rob the Corn Exchange Bank. The robbers cut two telephone cables before they started their attempt, but the report of three or four blasts of their explosives awakened nearby neighbors and when they turned on their lights the men were scared out of town. The night watchman at the livery barn, Professor Machen, and William H. Hollin, spread the alarm in a hurry, but the robbers were thought to have left in a machine [auto] just north of town.

The charter of the Corn Exchange State Bank of New Richmond expired the constitution's limitation in February 1927, and was converted into a private bank once again. The new officers elected were: W.W. Boland, President; John C. Henderson, Vice President; William Kirkpatrick, Cashier; and Anne Smith, Bookkeeper. The board of directors consisted of: Charles Kirkpatrick, William Inskeep, Ira Meharry, W.W. Boland, and John C. Henderson.

The Corn Exchange Bank of New Richmond did not survive the Great Depression. The Crawfordsville *Journal-Review*, Thursday, May 29, 1930, published the sad news, "CORN EXCHANGE BANK IS CLOSED FOR LIQUIDATION Majority of Stock of New Richmond Bank Owned By Estates–Depositors Probably Will Be Paid in Full–Will Be Re-organized Soon!" The title and sub-titles said it all. A notice was posted on the door Thursday morning, May 29, 1930, telling of the intention of the bank officers to seek voluntary liquidation. L.B. Holleman was the representative of the state banking department, and Foley & Foley, Crawfordsville attorneys, handled the legal affairs; the Corn Exchange Bank of New Richmond was on its way down. Officers at the closing of the bank were the following: John C. Henderson, President; William Inskeep, Vice President; and Charles Daniel, Cashier.

In December 1936 some of the depositors of the Corn Exchange Bank received seventeen percent payment on their deposits. They had received previous payments of ten and fifteen percent. The town board of New Richmond was put through a terrible ordeal trying to run the town without the funds that had been deposited in the Corn Exchange Bank when the doors were closed; the board had borrowed money from banks in Wingate, Linden, and Crawfordsville in order to make payments of town expenses.

THE NEW RICHMOND BUILDING LOAN FUND AND SAVINGS ASSOCIATION

Dr. Stowe S. Detchon and Mrs. Barbara Manners (Dr. Manners' widow), each made several additions to the town of New Richmond between 1885 and 1899. They sold the lots quite rapidly, but the cost of building new homes on these lots was too much of an expense for the people who purchased the lots.

The need of a banking institution, in the form of a building and loan, was suggested in 1887. Two years later, Thomas Smith, a New Richmond resident, accepted the agency for the National Building Association of Indianapolis, hoping to help the residents to finance new homes, but the citizens of the town were a bit skeptical and were not ready to borrow money or go into debt. This was a new idea, and the early residents of New Richmond always gave a lot of thought to any new ideas that came their way.

In November of 1889, several citizens of New Richmond came up with a better idea–they started a building and loan company of their own. A year later, the writers of the New Richmond items for the Crawfordsville weekly *Review*, on February 20, 1890, said, "There is a kick made at the Building and Loan Association, and a good many are pulling out," and he added, "where are the houses the association was going to build? Not a house yet, and no prospect of one." It seems they must have misunderstood the workings of the new association. The following is a transcription of the articles of incorporation of the New Richmond Building and Loan Association, taken from the Miscellaneous Record Book 5, pages 160-161. The book can be found in the Montgomery County Recorder's office.

> BUILDING, LOAN FUND AND SAVINGS ASSOCIATION:
> We the undersigned do associate ourselves together for the purpose of organizing a Building, Loan Fund and Savings Association.
>
> The name of the Association shall be, "THE NEW RICHMOND BUILDING LOAN FUND AND SAVINGS ASSOCIATION," and the place of business shall be in the town of New Richmond, in the county of Montgomery, and State of Indiana, in which county its operations shall be carried on.
>
> Its Capital Stock shall be One Hundred and Fifty Thousand Dollars.

The object of the association shall be to provide its members a safe and profitable investment of small weekly installments, and to loan them money on easy terms to enable them to purchase a home, or make other investments. The affairs of the association shall be managed by a Board of Directors, consisting of Seven Members, to be chosen annually from among the stockholders as provided by the by-laws. The following persons shall constitute the Board of Directors for the first year: George W. Washburn, Ed. T. McCrea, D.R. Black, H.M. Mitchell, Amos Ebrite, Samuel Tribby, Thomas M. Cook, Thomas Patton, Joshua Fisher, John McCallum, D.M. Washburn, Wm. Chrisman.

NOTE: All persons named above were the original Petitioners, and the first Board of Directors are the first seven in left column (1st seven listed).
STATE OF INDIANA SS.
MONTGOMERY COUNTY

Be it remembered that on the 22nd day of November 1889, before the undersigned, a Justice of the Peace, in and for the County and State aforesaid, duly commissioned and qualified, personally came Geo. W. Washburn, Ed. T. McCrea, D.R. Black, H.M. Mitchell, Amos Ebrite, Samuel Tribby, Thomas M. Cook, Thomas Patton, Joshua Fisher, John McCallum, D.M. Washburn, Wm. Chrisman, Who are personally known to me to be the same persons who executed the foregoing instrument of Writing as incorporators, and such persons duly and severally acknowledge the execution of the same.

In Witness Whereof, I hereunto set my hand, and affix my Scroll Seal, the day and year last written,

Walter D. Jones (Seal), Justice of the Peace
Received for Record November 26th, 1889 at 10 o'clock A.M. and recorded same day, Thos. T. Munhall, R.M. Co. (Recorder).

Originally, the New Richmond Building and Loan Association was to serve only the citizens of the town, and they did not advertise in the county newspapers, and only the 1895 Montgomery County directory listed the association with the other New Richmond business establishments.

In 1929, the association branched out into other communities. Levert E. Binns was elected Secretary-Treasurer that year. The association had assets of a little over $14,000 in 1929, and by the end of January 1963, had become New Richmond's first Million Dollar Corporation, with assets of $1,300,000.

In 1935, the New Richmond Building Loan Fund and Savings Association was reorganized. The Articles of Amendment listed the capital stock of $500,000 to be divided into 5,000 shares at per value of $100 each. Seven board members were to continue managing the association, as the original association stated, and the policy of electing directors annually, from among the stockholders, was continued throughout the existence of the association. Roy B. Hanawalt was president, and Levert E. Binns, secretary-treasurer, at the time of reorganization. The name was then shortened to the **New Richmond Savings and Loan Association**, which made a more convenient title.

"By 1964 the association was allowed, by law, to expand their operations to a radius of fifty miles from the home office, and was serving twelve counties at this time. Because of the early local association, the borrowers made stronger efforts to make loan payments; there had been only two foreclosures up to 1964. This banking institution was one of the lucky ones to survive the Great Depression of the late 1920s and 1930s, and did not miss paying a single dividend to its investors," the late Levert Binns said.

Other directors serving the New Richmond Building and Loan Association and some of their respective offices were: Frank E. Campbell (secretary-treasurer), William Kirkpatrick, John Hollin (secretary in 1895), M.J. Roth, Ed King, John McCrea, George C. Livingston, Perry McLain, Roy B.

Hanawalt (was serving as president as early as 1934), William McCrea, Dr. Ira Cole, James L. Hornbeck, Charles Oswalt, Harry Inskeep, Mary McCrea, Delmer K. Fruits, W. Maurice Coffman, John Parlon, Levert E. Binns (secretary-treasurer), Earl L. Warren (1st vice president), Wilbert Lyon (1st vice president), Ralph Kunkel (1st vice president), Paul Sayler (president), Robert M. Thayer (president), Garland W. Oppy (2nd vice president), Herbert M. Fruits, Richard Lane, Jack Fifer, and Donald Miles.

Levert E. Binns was elected to the Board of Directors of the association on April 3, 1923, and on November 29, 1929, was elected Secretary-Treasurer. He served in that capacity until he suffered a fatal heart attack in the office of the Savings and Loan Association on April 10, 1972. Levert was proud of his record of attending all but one of the 1,020 board and stockholder's meetings held during the forty-year period, up to 1963, that he served as director. He could not attend the one meeting he missed because his wife was hospitalized at the time. Levert praised the community for their loyalty, but no one was more loyal and devoted to the association than Mr. Binns. He managed the New Richmond Savings and Loan Association with pride and was always very kind to the investors and to those seeking and paying off their loans. His wife Helen assisted Levert as secretary, and succeeded him in the office after his death. Helen retired in October, 1974, after thirty-three years of service with the association.

The New Richmond Building Loan Fund and Savings Association office was originally located in the bank building, or Washburn Block, the brick building on the southeast corner of the square in New Richmond. Entry to the office was made on South Wabash Street; the door has since been enclosed. Helen Oppy Binns said when Levert became secretary-treasurer, the former secretary, Frank Campbell, was running the business out of his coat pocket–that is, they had no office space for the association. Levert used the same type of "office" (his coat pocket) until he acquired the back room of the bank building, on South Wabash, again.

A new concrete block office building was erected by Herbert and Charles Fruits. Maurice Coffman did the electrical work and the New Richmond Savings and Loan Company was ready for the dedication, which was held the last day of October in 1952. Levert Binns was very proud of this new building. The building is located on West Washington Street, behind the Hollin brick block, which later housed Alexander's Furniture and Gift Store and a convenience store (1999). The block building served as the association's office building to the end of the association's existence in 1975.

NEW RICHMOND BRANCH OF LINDEN STATE BANK

On July 17, 1974, the Linden State Bank filed an application with the Indiana Department of Financial Institutions, for approval of a branch office to be established at approximately 125 feet west of the intersection of Washington and Wabash Streets in New Richmond, Montgomery County, Indiana.

On Monday, October 21, 1974, the Crawfordsville *Journal-Review* published a notice of a special meeting of the Stockholders and Borrowing Members of the New Richmond Savings and Loan, to be held in the office of the said association on Wednesday, November 6, 1974. The main purpose of the meeting was to consider and act

37 - New Richmond Branch, Linden State Bank

upon a proposal for the voluntary dissolution of the New Richmond Savings and Loan Association. The necessary notices of dissolution were printed in the Crawfordsville *Journal-Review*, as required by law, and the board of directors appointed Ralph Kunkel as Liquidating Agent, after receiving approval from the State Department of Financial Institutions. The stockholders had approved of the voluntary dissolution, and Kunkel filed the necessary statements of all the assets and liabilities of the association with the Clerk of the Montgomery County Circuit Court. Harding & Henthorn, Crawfordsville attorneys, handled the legal duties of the dissolution. January 31st, 1975 was the date fixed that the creditors, shareholders, or any other persons, could assert any claims, or object to any allowances, or disallowances, recommended by the liquidating agent.

The Crawfordsville *Journal-Review*, Saturday, November 30, 1974, notified the public of the end of the New Richmond Savings and Loan Association, saying "LINDEN BANK ABSORBS NEW RICHMOND SAVINGS–It will serve as a branch bank of the Linden State Bank. Lloyd Faust, President of the bank, said a variety of new services will be offered through the New Richmond Branch, and the Tellers are, Lois Kunkel, and Ruthanna Oppy."

The office building, furniture, and other equipment, as well as the assets of the association, were purchased by the Linden State Bank, and were used by the new owners.

The last officers of the New Richmond Savings and Loan Association were the following: Robert M. Thayer, President; Ralph Kunkel, 1st Vice President; Garland W. Oppy, 2nd Vice President; and Helen Oppy Binns, Secretary-Treasurer. Directors were: Robert M. Thayer, Donald R. Miles, Ralph Kunkel, Herbert M. Fruits, Garland W. Oppy, Richard Lane, and Jack Fifer.

On January 1, 1974, the association was paying 5.5 percent dividends to the investors, and the authorized capital was $2,000,000. The New Richmond Savings and Loan Association went out in great style!

Chapter 12 - New Richmond's Newspapers

"New Richmond Needs a Newspaper"–the Patton's corner scribe (correspondent for the Crawfordsville *Review*) was trying to talk William Campbell of New Richmond into starting a daily newspaper in 1888. A year later Campbell was almost convinced he could take on such a venture, but he soon gave up on the idea. Another man by the name of Noggle considered starting a paper in October 1889. His plan was to combine New Richmond, Linden and Wingate, and issue a separate paper for each town. The New Richmond people thought this would be a very mixed up affair, and this idea was also dropped. In 1890 the New Richmond correspondent for the Crawfordsville *Review*, William Campbell, thought the town had grown sufficiently to support a local newspaper. The town was enjoying one of its building booms at the time. Several of the small towns in Montgomery County attempted to establish newspapers, and most of them had many ups and downs. New Richmond's early attempts at journalism followed the same pattern.

New Richmond *Times*

On March 6, 1891, George F. Long's first edition of the town's first newspaper, the New Richmond *Times*, made its appearance. Long, a local jeweler, published and edited the paper. It was an independent and very newsy paper put out for only fifty cents per year, and was the eighth county paper published in Montgomery County. The paper was printed in Frankfort when it first started.

In November 1891, Long relinquished the publication of the *Times*. Edwin D. Zook and O.A. Glover became its new editors. Glover was also the editor of the Hillsboro *Clipper* at the time. The new publishers installed their own printing equipment, thus eliminating the confusion of having an out of town printer doing the work. J.A. Booe was their typesetter and Nick Washburn was their printer's "devil" for a while.

The following February, the New Richmond *Times* had again changed hands. The new proprietors were W.E. Rogers and Joseph Smith. They purchased the equipment from the Long brothers–evidently the former owners had previously sold the equipment to George F. Long and his brother, possibly Arthur Long. W.E. Rogers was from Frankfort. The *Times* had suspended publication nearly two months before the new publishers took over.

By September 1892, the New Richmond *Times* was out of business, this time for good. The Crawfordsville *Review* had this to say:

> The Wingate GRAPHIC has followed in the footsteps of its arch enemy, the New Richmond TIMES, and climbed the golden stairs. By the demise of these two great literary efforts, both which succumbed while yet in the infancy of their glory, Coal Creek Township is left with two "long felt wants" on their hands which must remain unsatisfied until some "damphool" chances along and starts the Elmdale ELMPEELER on the ridge.

Ira Stout was the editor of the *Times* when the paper suspended publication.

NEW RICHMOND *NEWS*

There have been several references made to a weekly paper, the New Richmond *News*, established in 1892 by Joseph Smith and a partner. I have not substantiated the existence of a paper under this name. References of the early paper during the many changes of ownership always mentioned the New Richmond *Times*, and Joseph Smith and his partner, W.E. Rogers, purchased that in 1892.

Joseph Smith edited and published an agriculture paper, *The Montgomery County Farmer*, in Crawfordsville in 1902; the first copy was published in the middle of March that year.

NEW RICHMOND *ENTERPRISE*

One of William Campbell's most frequently used expressions in his New Richmond items of the Crawfordsville *Review*, noting a need for a new business or service of some type, was, "there is a long felt want for those needs." All the small town writers in Montgomery County poked a little fun at Campbell now and then, and frequently borrowed this term. In May 1893, the *Review* said "Robert Osborn is to launch the Yelper at New Richmond to fill that gaping 'long felt want' that was created by the sudden and untimely demise of the *Times*." Bob Osborn sold his newspaper, the Waynetown *Hornet*, to John W. Brant, and moved his printing equipment to New Richmond to follow his trade.

Bob Osborn's new paper, the New Richmond *Enterprise*, made its appearance on June 3, 1893. In 1895 R.S. Osborn was editor and publisher of the *Enterprise*. Mark Alexander and Charles Mitchell were printers for the paper.

The New Richmond *Enterprise* celebrated its fourth birthday in May 1897, and was rather successful for a small town newspaper, but another local paper, the New Richmond *Record*, had entered the picture in 1896.

The last publication of the New Richmond *Enterprise* was October 6, 1899. Robert S. Osborn and his son Othel L. owned the paper in October that year, and Frank E. Campbell was its editor and manager. The paper was printed every Friday morning, and the subscription rate was fifty cents per year.

In November 1898 Osborn purchased the Hillsboro *Times* and moved there to manage his new paper. He moved to Cayuga a little later where he established the Cayuga *Blue Pencil*. In 1903 he sold a half interest in that paper to Bert L. Graham of Humrick, Illinois. In 1904 Osborn moved his *Blue Pencil* to Perrysville; the first issue of the Perrysville *Blue Pencil* was published in August 1904. Osborn continued moving and establishing newspapers in Kansas, Iowa, Missouri and Oklahoma, in later years, but returned to his son's home in Waynetown in 1915 because of poor health. After his recovery he published the *Blue Pencil* at Hillsboro and the *News* in Wingate.

Bob Osborn had a way of stirring up the public everywhere he went, through his newspapers. A New Richmond man was ready to sue him only a month after the New Richmond *Enterprise* was established. He attacked the Crawfordsville *Star and Journal* because of some political issue–the excerpt from Osborn's *Enterprise* was printed in the Crawfordsville *Review*. Osborn tangled with the publisher of the Waynetown *Despatch* over another little issue, and the saloon keepers in Perrysville offered to buy him out in order to get him out of their hair. Osborn replied, "The privilege of telling the truth about them was worth about $2,000."

Robert S. Osborn died in March 1919 at the home of Dr. Roark in Waynetown, at the age of 79. He had been ill for two years previous to his death. He was married to Mary Grenard, who had preceded him in death many years earlier. They had two children, Othel L. and Bertha Osborn, both of whom survived him. He was buried in the Masonic Cemetery at Waynetown. Before his interest in newspaper work, Osborn had been a successful school teacher in Coal Creek Township.

THE NEW RICHMOND *RECORD*

The publisher and editor of the New Richmond *Record*, Edgar A. Walts, was born April 18, 1867, near Greenville, Floyd County, Indiana. He was a son of Samuel W. and Elizabeth Nance Walts. His mother died March 18, 1872, leaving five sons, listed in order of birth: Wallace S., Lawrence, Edgar, Wilbur A., and Samuel W. Walts. Edgar was almost five years old when his mother died; he was raised on his aunt's farm, where he remained until age fifteen. Edgar was educated in the schools near Lanesville, in Floyd County, taking the academy course at Salem, Indiana.

Edgar began his adult life farming for himself, but quit farming and went to Florida, taking a position as a bookkeeper at DeLand. He also spent a year working in the orange groves. He returned to Indiana, and in 1894 began his work in journalism with his brother in White County. On November 25, 1897, Edgar Walts married Rose L. Beaver Holmes, daughter of David and Matilda Grove Beaver. She was a widow with three sons, Harry, David, and George R. Holmes. Edgar and Rose had one son, Clyde E. Walts. All the boys were introduced to the newspaper business, working on the New Richmond *Record* at very young ages.

Edgar A. Walts, creator of the term, "New Richmond–the best little town on Earth," established the New Richmond *Record*, a newspaper printed each Thursday in the town of New Richmond, Indiana. The first issue made its appearance on July 16, 1896. This issue was printed on an old Washington Hand Press, which was used until October 1903. A new Monono Leverless Cylinder press was installed in the *Record*'s print shop at that time. A rapidly growing subscription list and an increase in the advertising section made the use of the old hand press a very arduous task, which was too time-consuming. Walts invited the citizens of the town to visit the *Record* office and watch the new press work. After the new press was in operation the *Record* became a six page paper, run on a gasoline propelled power press.

The *Record* was independent in politics and devoted much of the space to recording local happenings. The *Record*'s job department was considered one of the best in the county, printing note and letter heads, envelopes, wedding and other invitations, cards, hand bills, posters, programs, catalogues, and pamphlets.

Edgar Walts' column "Polite Politics" expressed his independence headed by this note, "Any items which may appear under this head are meant in no way to express the political views of the editor of the *Record*, and it is expressly asked of our readers to consider it so, but are merely in the middle-of-the-road observances from his elevated seat on the top rail of 'The Man On the Fence.'" The editors of the Indiana Associated Weeklies were invited by Edgar Walts to hold their spring meeting in New Richmond on June 9 and 10, 1911. The editors were cordially entertained by the *Record* force, assisted by numerous friends of the town and community. Walts arranged with the businessmen not to charge them for anything they wished to buy while in town, and they were to tell them their money was no good in New Richmond. A reception was held, and free entertainment was provided in the school assembly hall. Music was furnished by the New Richmond Orchestra, and readings by some of the best home talent were presented.

A photograph of the *Record*'s office force, consisting of Mr. and Mrs. Edgar Walts, Clyde E. Walts, and Miss Edna Kincaid, appeared with the announcement of the gathering. The visiting editors were very impressed with the welcome they received, and letters to Editor Walts appeared the following weeks in the *Record*, thanking him and the town of New Richmond for their gracious hospitality. The editors who attended were listed, along with their newspapers, in the June 15, 1911 *Record*.

The *Record* office and print shop was first located on the second floor above George F. Long's dry goods store. After having been in that location for seventeen years, the *Record* was moved into its own home over James L. Moulder's dry goods store. Walts had decided it was time to stop paying rent: he owned this room. The room was in the brick business room on the corner of Washington and Wabash Streets, and entrance was made on Wabash Street, or on the west side of the building, and at the rear of the Moulder store. An inside and easy stairway was an advantage of the new location, as well as more room, an abundance of light, and good ventilation. The editor of the Cayuga Herald said of the move, "The New Richmond *Record*, this week, hopped from the top of one dry goods store to a new home on top of another one." At this time a new electric motor was installed to power the presses. Editor Walts apologized for missing one issue due to the lack of power for the presses during the move.

On July 16, 1917, the New Richmond *Record* reached the age of twenty-one years, under Edgar Walts's continuous ownership and editorship. It was the only Montgomery County weekly paper that had not seen a change in ownership over such an extended period of time.

During World War I all publishers of newspapers had been asked by the government to conserve newsprint, and were advised to discontinue the subscriptions to readers who were not paid up, as a means of saving paper.

The *Record* was forced to suspend publication temporarily with the December 30, 1920, issue, because of the prohibitive cost of newsprint paper and the lack of office help. The editor's wife and son were his only helpers at that time. The job department continued printing sale bills, stationary, and commercial print jobs, however, and Walts informed the townspeople that contrary to the rumors, he and his family were not leaving New Richmond. No renewals were being taken for subscriptions as of January 1, 1921.

On June 2, 1921, the *Record* resumed publication. There was a great demand for the paper and "to fill a long, felt want" Editor Walts said part of the previous problems had been overcome. The annual subscription price was raised from $1.00 to $1.50, and was to be paid in advance. The increase was needed to cover the high cost of supplies and overhead expenses, as well as the ever-increasing postage.

"THE *RECORD* CHANGES MANAGEMENT!–with today's issue, November 2, 1922, Harry C. Bell is taking over the management and Edgar Walts is retiring." The new manager was to continue the *Record*'s policy in covering the home news in the best possible way, and in all ways standing for the best interests of "The Best Little Town on Earth" and her surrounding community. Harry C. Bell leased the paper from Walts after nearly two years of association with the *Record*.

Bell advertised for a young lady or man, out of school, to work in the *Record* office. The advertisements ran all through August (and possibly September and October). On November 29, 1923, the new publisher had to again suspend publication of the *Record* because he could not get office help. Bell had taken a trip to Norwalk, California, by the time the paper was on the stands, and was contemplating a relocation to Southern California.

Editor Walts took back the helm only to make the formal announcement to the *Record*'s subscribers that the end was upon them. "Reasons for suspending publication were: first–the lack of support of New Richmond's business houses as advertisers–only two display advertisements with only $2.70 income from them–the editor asked if anyone else in New Richmond would be willing to work for that amount; second, the lack of sufficient office help; third, other business demanding attention of the editor at this time."

In his departing letter Edgar Walts said in part, "The *Record* was established by the present owner and publisher on July 16, 1896, nearly twenty-eight years ago. The *Record*'s first business was to give its readers the very best service it could and stood always first and foremost for the best interests of New Richmond. The *Record* has never failed to be a booster for 'The Best Little Town on Earth'."

The editor and his wife were to leave in December that year for the South, to attend to business interests there. Edgar's father, Samuel W. Walts, had moved to Florida around 1880, and had devoted himself to raising oranges; Samuel spent winters in Florida and summers in New Albany, Indiana. Edgar continued the interests in Florida.

Edgar A. Walts died in New Richmond on Friday, September 29, 1933, in the home where he and his wife Rose had lived for thirty-six years. His survivors were Rose, a son Clyde E. Walts of Indianapolis, and three stepsons: Harry Holmes of Indianapolis; David Holmes of Battle Creek, Michigan; and George R. Holmes of Washington, D.C. Two brothers surviving were S.W. Walts of New Albany, and Wilbur Walts of DeLand, Florida; a nephew Samuel Walts of Michigan City also survived him.

The following is a list of employees of the New Richmond *Record* through its years of existence: Shelly B. Miller, Claud Work, Frank E. Campbell, Fred A. Taylor, Lemma DeArmond, Edna Kincaid, George R. Holmes, Clyde Walts, Harry S. Holmes, Mark Alexander, John Bunnel, Lorlie Harriman, Belle Wilson, Bessie Lehman, Frank Lane, Harry C. Bell, and Miss Switzer. Some of these employees went on to other newspapers throughout the country, and Walts kept close contact with them. His stepson George R.

Holmes became a very well-known journalist in a very short time. He managed and edited the *Record* when he was only fifteen years of age (Walts referred to him as "Squirt" Holmes back then), and by 1920 he had become manager, or chief, of the Washington Bureau of the International News Service. (See article on George R. Holmes in the "Noted Personalities" section of this book).

When Ed Walts had an attack of appendicitis, his son Clyde E. Walts edited the *Record*, at only eleven years of age. Clyde was the only person on the *Record* office staff who could run the Monono Leverless Press. Mrs. Walts was always in the *Record* office to help when needed. About two weeks after his illness, Walts caught his hand in the press and severely injured three fingers. Doctors Wray and Olin had to remove part of one finger and dress the hand. A fellow editor, A.J. Heuring of the Winslow *Dispatch*, came to Walts's rescue; he helped get out a large order of job work, all orders being shipped to Winslow. A second attack of appendicitis landed Walts in Home Hospital of Lafayette for the removal of his appendix. He required several months of rest in New Albany, Indiana, and then to St. Petersburg and DeLand, Florida, before he regained his strength. During this period he wrote home about the areas in which he rested, which added color to the home paper. The *Record* office force continued publication during his absence.

Another employee, Harry S. Holmes, was a linotype operator on the Indianapolis *Star* and other newspapers, and Fred A. Taylor also worked on several area papers. He established the *Farmers Review* in New Richmond after the *Record* ceased publication.

THE *FARMERS REVIEW*

Friday, November 6, 1931, marked the date of the first issue of the *Farmers Review*. Publisher Fred A. Taylor printed a greeting to his subscribers that reads in part, "Since the suspended publication of the *Record* (New Richmond), there has been no local newspaper. . . .Our aim is to make this a strictly local paper, giving news of New Richmond and vicinity. We start with the publication on Fridays with a very encouraging subscription list. Businessmen have responded readily–subscription price is $1.25 per year. We ask readers to contribute news items and invite the public to call on us and get acquainted. We are located in the room opposite the fire station."

Paul Mason was editor of the *Farmers Review* when it was first published, and his last editing was March 18, 1932. The Statement of Ownership dated April 1, 1932, says, "The *Farmers Review*, published weekly at New Richmond, Indiana, etc. the name and address of the publisher, editor, managing editor and business manager is Fred A. Taylor."

Fred Austin Taylor was a son of Charles A. and Artemesia Marie Campbell Taylor. He was born on August 18, 1884, in New Richmond. His mother "Rie" Campbell Taylor was also a New Richmond native and refused to leave the little town she loved so dearly for any reason. Her husband moved around quite frequently hunting for work, but she stayed put. Her parents, Jacob and Mary Pryor Campbell, were among the pioneers of the town. She had two other children—Mary, who died in infancy, and Winton.

Fred Taylor first married Ruth McNeil and they had two daughters, Bessie and Bernice. He had a son Frederick, Jr. by his second wife, Gertrude G. Ward.

Taylor served his apprenticeship on the New Richmond *Record*, and was listed as a printer in the 1903 directory of Montgomery County. He moved around to various newspapers, serving as editor or printer, and acquired the necessary knowledge in all departments of the news business. He served as editor-in-chief of the Romney *News* and published a monthly magazine, *The Eureka*, in New Richmond. He was also associated with the Linden *Reporter*, the Wingate *News*, New Richmond *Record*, the Frankfort *Crescent*, Star City *News*, Kewanna *Herald*, a paper in Urbana, Illinois, the Mt. Carmel *Register*, and papers in Villa Grove, Illinois, and Albion, Illinois. In Mt. Carmel, Illinois, he launched a new paper, the Wabash County *Record*; it was first published on April 24, 1919, but lasted a very short time, as he was on his way to Portland, Indiana, to take a printer's position on a paper. He was ad-man on a Muncie, Indiana, daily paper, but in January 1923, he quit that job to go to the Marion *Leader-Tribune*.

The *Farmers Review* office was moved a month after its establishment, into a room formerly occupied by Hinman's Restaurant. In February 1932, it was located south of Parlon's Lumberyard, south of the railroad. In April 1933, the newspaper plant was moved to Linden to cover both towns and to acquire more advertisers to support the paper. Linden was also without a paper at this time. A month later the *Farmers Review* had to move back to New Richmond. The publisher gave the reason of his failure as being deceived by unreliable parties in Linden, who had promised added business.

Taylor moved his *Farmers Review* to Stockwell in September 1933. He printed a "Greeting to this Community" in his first issue, September 22, saying, "in launching this paper in Stockwell, we feel that now, our first issue is the opportune time for a word of greeting and explanation. Stockwell has never had a newspaper printed in their city and we feel the territory is sufficiently large and the people were very anxious for a town and rural news paper.—We start with a very encouraging subscription list and expect to double the amount in a very short time. We will publish each Friday; the subscription price is fifty cents a year in advance. . . .we are located in the Oscar Youndt building."

The statement of ownership of the *Farmers Review* in October 1933, gives the name of the publisher, editor, business manager, and owner, as Fred A. Taylor, New Richmond, Indiana. The paper was entered in the New Richmond Post office as second class matter.

On January 1, 1934, Fred Taylor was asking for help from each citizen, as the newspaper could not survive without advertisements. The town of Stockwell was letting the publisher down; only a few loyal businessmen were supporting the *Farmers Review*, and there was concern about having to move to another town. In March 1934, the office had moved the plant back to New Richmond, but was to cover both Stockwell and New Richmond news items. Taylor moved the plant into the vacant room just north of the Christian Church, which had formerly housed the New Richmond Town Hall. Mrs. Roy Matson of the Sugar Creek Cream Station was to gather the Stockwell news items for the *Farmers Review*.

In August 1934, Taylor purchased the printing equipment owned by the late Edgar Walts, used in the publication of the New Richmond *Record*; he combined the two plants, making one of the most thoroughly complete newspaper and job plants in this section of the state. He enlarged the *Farmers Review* to a six-column paper and asked the readers to contribute news and job work of all kinds. The paper moved to the old *Record* room over the Shepherd's Grocery Store in the George F. Long building, on the northeast corner of Washington and Wabash Streets.

Taylor announced in his July 31, 1936, issue of the paper that "beginning with next weeks issue, the *Farmers Review* will be owned and operated by the new management, Mr. Charles O. Taylor, of Dunkirk, Ind., the transaction and transfer taking place this week. Mr. C.O. Taylor a newspaper man with ten years experience has operated and edited both weekly and semi-weekly papers. . . .Mr. Taylor received his education at Manchester College and Purdue University, Lafayette. The former editor and manager [Fred] A. Taylor, was forced to dispose of the business on account of poor health,–the new editor expects to install a linotype machine soon and to greatly enlarge the paper, and Fred and his wife bids all their friends good-bye."

Mr. Charles O. Taylor took over the management of the *Farmers Review* and he and his wife moved to New Richmond in August 1936. He added a four page comic supplement to the paper during this time. He continued the management of the paper until January 1938.

Charles O. Taylor sold the *Farmers Review* to Harry W. Campbell of Batavia, New York, in January 1938. He became the editor and publisher. C.O. Taylor was awarded a contract for a Star mail route and quit the newspaper business. He had been sending news items and advertisements to Waynetown to be printed. With the new owner, business was returned to the New Richmond office.

Harry W. Campbell, the new editor and publisher, extended "Greetings" to the readers of the *Farmers Review*, complimenting the former editor and publisher, C.O. Taylor, for his fine work; he promised to be helpful to subscribers and advertisers. He vowed to put the paper in the front ranks with the best weekly newspapers in the country. His motto was "one for all and all for one."

Campbell continued as publisher and editor of the *Farmers Review* into the 1940s. His son John worked in the composition department of the paper until he joined the Army Medical Corps in September 1940.

Subscription price on that date was $1.25 per year; $.65 for six months; $.35 for three months. The paper was published and mailed in New Richmond, Indiana. The latest issue recorded was September 2, 1940, which was a sample copy. The towns of New Richmond, Linden, Romney, Stockwell and Clark's Hill, were covered in this issue. The paper probably did not survive much longer.

Chapter 13 - Post Office and Rural Mail Carriers

The New Richmond Post Office was established on February 8, 1850. Samuel McComas was appointed Postmaster on that date. The following is a list of New Richmond's Postmasters taken from the National Archives Records on microfilm.

NAME	DATE OF APPOINTMENTS
Samuel McComas	8 February 1850
James S. McComas	18 February 1852
William B. McComas	15 July 1853
Aquilla S. Dilling	20 October 1854
Samuel McComas	23 March 1855
Elliott Detchon	23 June 1855
George H. Alexander	2 March 1863
Elliott Detchon	10 October 1863
Hardin Pottinger	15 February 1864
Daniel S. White	10 October 1865
Jeptha Bell	31 May 1866
Joshua Dilling	7 October 1869
John W. Plunkett	19 November 1869
James L. Anderson	25 October 1878
John W. Hollin	19 April 1880
George F. Long	29 December 1884
George F. Long	14 June 1887 (Mail Order office just begun)
Frank Cornell	22 April 1889
Thomas A. Cook	3 March 1891
Josiah A. King	1 February 1892
John W. McCardle	31 March 1893
Charles Kirkpatrick	7 April 1897
John W. Hollin	16 July 1901
Laura Kirkpatrick	30 June 1906
Frank E. Campbell	24 July 1914
Levert E. Binns	2 March 1922
Levert E. Binns	6 March 1926 (reappointed)
Levert E. Binns	18 March 1930 (reappointed)
John D. Patton	21 May 1934 (acting postmaster)
John D. Patton	1 June 1934 (assumed charge)
Mary M. Henderson	11 July 1935 (confirmed)
Mary M. Henderson	12 September 1935 (commission signed)
Mary M. Henderson	1 October 1935 (assumed charge)
Mary M. Henderson	1 July 1943 (President appointed)
Helen G. Oppy	1 March 1944 (assumed charge)
Robert Ervin Stephens, Sr.	23 September 1944 (appointed)
William F. Hockett	1 May 1971 (assumed charge)
Wilma Lewellyn	12 May 1984 (assumed charge)
Ann Lyons	PMR (postmaster replacement)

Virginia Waye	PMR
Vicki Martin	PMR
Gary Murphy	PMR
Terri Barnes	PMR
Ruth Goodin	PMR
Carol Myers	PMR
Kathleen Irvin	April 1996
Donna Yeagley	unsure of dates
Linda England	1 February 1997
Shari McCord	June 1997 – September 2001 (PMR)
Vicki Martin	November 2001 (clerk, PMR)

NOTE: Robert E. Stephens retired October 31, 1969, and Clarence (C.W.) Banta served as "Officer-in-charge" of the New Richmond Post Office until William F. Hockett was appointed, assuming charge May 1, 1971. Banta had served as clerk under Robert E. Stephens from June 1969 to the time he acted as officer-in-charge. Other assistants or postal clerks mentioned were: Curt Cornell, Post Office Clerk for Frank Cornell, Postmaster; Thomas Cook, Assistant Postmaster for Frank Cornell, Postmaster; Mayme Morris, Substitute Postmaster for Miss Laura Kirkpatrick; Gretchen Kincaid, Assistant Postmaster for Laura Kirkpatrick; Grace Haire, Assistant Postmaster for Mayme Henderson, Postmaster; Mrs. Fannie Stephens, Assistant for Robert Stephens, Postmaster (her husband); C.W. Banta, Clerk for William Hockett, Postmaster; Doris G. Palin, Part Time Clerk for Wilma Lewellyn, Postmaster; Carol L. (Katie) Myers, Part Time Clerk for Wilma Lewellyn, Postmaster.

38 - William F. Hockett

In February 1969, the President decided to take the selection of postmasters out of politics, and the offices are now filled on a merit basis. On July 1, 1971, the United States Post Office became the United States Postal Service.

In July 1877, the postal patrons in the New Richmond area circulated a petition to have their mail route changed so it would run from Crawfordsville instead of Linden. A year later, in Coal Creek Township, the New Richmond and Round Hill Post Offices were only having mail delivered twice per week, whereas Pleasant Hill and Boston Store were on another route and received mail three times per week.

Pleasant Hill, New Richmond, and Newtown were receiving mail three times per week in March 1880, on the Star Mail Route, but the Postmaster General changed the route to once per week at that time.

By 1890 mail was delivered to New Richmond on the railroad twice daily, at 12:15 and 2:30 p.m. At the time, the local postmaster notified the public they must mail their letters at the post office, and if they were not on time they could not go to the train to mail them.

In 1902 New Richmond was to have three mail deliveries per day. In addition to the two mentioned deliveries, there was to be a closed pouch made up at Veedersburg to be delivered to New Richmond on the 8:35 a.m. east-bound express. The New Richmond Post Office was to send a pouch back on the afternoon west-bound express. In July 1906 night mail was to be picked up at 12:55 a.m. on the west-bound express; there was also a Sunday morning delivery at that time. They made so many changes that year on the Clover Leaf Railroad that every postal official on the line was ready to throw in the towel, trying to keep the schedules straight. At one point it was decided the day mail service was as "rotten as it is possible." On the last day of June, 1916, New Richmond's Postmaster, Frank E. Campbell, received a

39 - New Richmond Post Office in 1986

notice from the Postal Department saying the Toledo, St. Louis, and Western Railroad Company would discontinue carrying the mail after July 31, 1916. Campbell was given authority to secure bids for carrying mails, two trips each way daily, except Sunday, between New Richmond and Linden, Indiana. Forms were sent to Campbell to complete, and he had less than a month to secure the bids. The Clover Leaf's main objection to delivering the mail was having to pay their night men to hang and receive the mail off the night trains.

It didn't take long for the neighborhood of New Richmond to rise up and let the railroad company hear their thoughts on this change of mail service. They said:

> Some ten or twelve years ago the rural route service was established to accommodate the farmers and this was a great advantage over the old Star Route. About the time everything was "in shape" the route was changed. This created many problems because all the mailing lists had to be changed. About a year ago, another change was made for a fifty mile motor change. The post office and patrons were just getting everything into shape again, and now the railroad that was built for the farmers' accommodation, has refused to haul our mail, but want to continue hauling our freight.

The farmers threatened to purchase motor trucks and haul their products to a railroad that would accommodate them. They were reminded of years gone by when livestock and grain were hauled to Chicago. They suggested the Clover Leaf Railroad officials should weigh the matter carefully and consider what the loss of freight trade could do to their railroad company. Their arguments went with the wind, however, and Postmaster Campbell arranged to have the mail picked up at Linden off the Chicago, Indianapolis, and Louisville Railroad. This proved to be a great inconvenience to the New Richmond Post Office and the patrons it served, but the railroad officials lost no sleep over the problem.

New Richmond residents continued to get their mail at the local post office but had to wait until the mail was picked up at Linden and brought to the local office to be sorted. This continued until the Postal Department began making the deliveries by truck, eliminating the use of railroad service. Now the mail from New Richmond is taken to Lafayette, sorted, and sent on to its destination.

Most of the New Richmond residents now over sixty years of age can remember the familiar name of Ira Chase, better known as "Bliskey," who hauled the mail twice daily from Linden to New Richmond and Wingate for many years.

Rural Mail Carriers

A man by the name of Charles White, the father of Mrs. Barbara Manners, was New Richmond's first rural mail carrier, as recorded by William Campbell, an early New Richmond historian. Campbell failed to give the dates White served in this capacity; however, Charles White died in 1855 at the age of fifty-six years. He was a native of Maryland, who immigrated to Ohio prior to the War of 1812, settled in Coal Creek Township (New Richmond) in 1828, and moved to Madison Township in 1833.

Mail came by stagecoach to the Oak Grove Post Office, established February 20, 1841. This post office was located south of the present town of Linden. The mail was delivered from this office to New Richmond and the rural areas until 1850. The Oak Grove Post Office was moved to the newly platted town of Linden on June 30, 1851, and the name of the post office was changed to that of the town. After the stage routes were discontinued, the mail was delivered to Linden by train. The mail was transferred to the post office, and government contracts were let to rural mail carriers.

There is no record of the early mail carriers that served the New Richmond area, other than Mr. White. Later carriers out of the New Richmond Post Office after the Rural Free Delivery system was established were: John McCrea, 1901-29 (his death) on Route No. 1 (or No. 33 on the Tippecanoe County system); Fred E. Kincaid, November 16, 1903-15 (his route, No. 2, was discontinued by 1915); Roy B. Hanawalt, 1930 to January 1960 (retired); Malcolm G. Waye, January 1960 to the summer of 1960 (temporary driver); Herbert M. Fruits, summer of 1960 to December 10, 1974 (his death date–died while sorting mail in Romney).

Substitute mail carriers for the rural area of New Richmond and the dates mentioned in the New Richmond Record were: William H. Burris, October 29 and November 19, 1903, for Fred E. Kincaid; Frank E. Campbell–took the examination for carrier on September 24, 1903, and July 6, 1905–for John McCrea; Mrs. John W. Hollin, July 7, 1904; Robert Seaman, November 1, 1906.

RURAL FREE DELIVERY

The Rural Free Delivery was established on an experimental scale in 1896. In 1901 Route No. 1 out of New Richmond was established and included all of the eastern part of Coal Creek Township and the southern part of Tippecanoe County. The route started northeast out of New Richmond, to Mason's Corner, to Goose-Nibble Crossroads, to Sugar Grove, and to the Shawnee Mound Road, then back to the post office via the New Richmond-Newtown Road.

NEW RICHMOND RURAL MAIL CARRIERS

The Tippecanoe section referred to as Route No. 33 was one of that county's thirty-nine routes in 1902. The mileage totaled twenty-two and a half miles of gravel roads and two miles of dirt roads. This route was reversed in 1902 to avoid retracing the miles, but served the same patrons. Added to the northern route out of New Richmond were approximately twenty-five miles in Coal Creek Township. The entire fifty-mile route was handled by John McCrea of New Richmond.

In January 1903 the U.S. Postmaster, Nye, threatened to discontinue certain routes in Montgomery County in the spring unless the dirt roads were put in first-class condition; however, the New Richmond rural area was being re-mapped for a new route. Ed T. McCrea, father of John McCrea, accompanied the rural route inspector, F.M. Dice, over the local route, mapping out the new route. It was simply a division of the route, to be handled by two carriers—one for the Tippecanoe section and one for Coal Creek Township. Fred E. Kincaid and Frank E. Campbell took the examination for carrier on the new route to be known as Route No. 2 out of New Richmond.

ROUTE NO. 1

The new Tippecanoe County route, Route No. 1, was a total of twenty-five and one-eighth miles, serving eighty-nine houses and a population of four hundred. John McCrea was the carrier. Captain McCrea's house was included in the route and John retraced approximately a quarter of a mile to the east end of New Richmond to McCrea's, then to the north. The "Corners" served in Tippecanoe County's route were: Malsbary, Mason, Withrow, Lydick, Greenburg, Cutrell residence, Peterson, Howey residence, Julian, Brown, Conn, Dettbenner, to Sugar Grove, Litka, DeVault residence–retrace to Washburn, then to the New Richmond Post Office.

ROUTE NO. 2

Route No. 2 in Coal Creek Township totaled twenty-five and seven-eighths miles. Fred Kincaid was appointed carrier for this new mail route. His route included the following "Corners": the Long corner northeast of New Richmond, to Wallace H. Montgomery, Wilkins, Jones, on to Round Hill, Burk, Quillen, Taylor, Coleman, McClamrock, J. Cowan, C. Cowan, Thomas, Patton Schoolhouse corner, to Beal's residence–retrace to Washburn's lane, to Washburn and Fulwider corner (Bristle Ridge), to the Newtown-New Richmond road, then east to the New Richmond Post Office.

Fred Kincaid resigned his teaching position at the Patton Schoolhouse in November of 1903 and started on his new mail route on November 16 that year. This route continued until 1914 or 1915, and

Fred resumed his teaching career after it was discontinued. The two routes were combined at the time, possibly because the motor vehicle would make better time than the old horse and carriage.

John McCrea continued the combined Routes No. 1 and 2 until his last illness and death in June 1929. John purchased a new mail wagon from the Terre Haute Carriage and Buggy Company in April 1902. It was painted black and red with white lettering. The New Richmond *Record* related an incident in 1903 concerning John, saying, "John McCrea went to see his sweetheart on Sunday in Indianapolis, was pointed to the wrong train by a depot guard, and went east instead of west, failing to arrive home until very late in the day. John carried no mail to his patrons on Monday."

The editor of the *Record* praised the two rural mail carriers out of New Richmond in March 1906 for getting the mail delivered to all their patrons during the "worst weather of the winter." The area experienced what was to be the heaviest, single snowfall for this section in several years. (I discovered another record of a thirteen inch snowfall hitting the New Richmond area in January of 1904. This was said to have been the deepest snow in eighteen years at the time; the mail carriers could not complete their rounds.) The Shawnee Mound (Meharry neighborhood) correspondent reported twenty-six inches of snow in eight days during March, 1906; the snow caused the passenger trains to be pulled by double-headers, and most traffic was completely stopped.

Fred E. Kincaid, carrier No. 2 out of New Richmond, completed his entire route, although his carriage upset twice in the huge snowdrifts and he had many other hardships due to the drifts. Kincaid's grandparents were among the earliest settlers of Coal Creek Township, settling in New Richmond; as a native of the township, he was familiar with the rugged winter storms.

John McCrea had to turn back on Route No. 2 because of the deep snow drifts, but approached the boxes from another route; he was able to deliver to every patron. McCrea's father, Captain Edward T. McCrea, settled about one-fourth mile southeast of New Richmond after the Civil War; John, too, was accustomed to the hardships of the area's severe winters. To this day, McCrea's corner southeast of New Richmond is the worst corner as far as snowdrifts are concerned, and still blocks traffic to Linden, despite the use of county highway department's huge snow plows that could prevent such an accumulation of snow.

The two early rural mail carriers always made their rounds during the spring rains. They were never prevented by mud from delivering the mail, as the roads on the routes were well-graveled. They were mindful of the fact that rural free delivery service belonged to the people and they were but paid servants.

After John McCrea's death, Roy Hanawalt became the rural mail carrier out of New Richmond. He continued on much of the same route as McCrea's combined route until his retirement in January 1960. Hanawalt died in June 1966, in the Veteran's Hospital at Marion, Indiana.

Malcolm Waye, a World War Two Navy Veteran, replaced Roy as a temporary driver. Waye and Herb Fruits passed the requirements on the Civil Service examination, seeking the rural route, but Herb was awarded the route because of a disability received during World War Two. Herb continued to deliver the mail until his death from an apparent heart attack on December 10, 1974. He was sorting the mail in the Romney Post Office at the time of his death.

Before his death, Fruits was transferred to Linden to serve on another rural route. The routes were consolidated, extending a forty-nine-mile Linden route to ninety-four miles. Fruits served a portion of the New Richmond route, and a portion of the Romney route in Tippecanoe County was added to Linden. The New Richmond rural route was discontinued during this reorganization, sometime around 1970 or 1971, and Harold Harshman delivered the mail to New Richmond until the consolidation plans were finalized.

Chapter 14 - Ghost Towns and Place Names of Coal Creek Township

Boston Store or Elmdale

The following history of Boston Store, later named Elmdale, was published in the Crawfordsville Weekly *Review*, April 16, 1887. It gave such a good account of the early settlers, I thought it should be reprinted as it was written:

ELMDALE

Thinking a short history of this place would be read with some interest, we will give you as near as can be given the origin of BOSTON STORE: In 1831 Edward P. Bennett bought a three cornered piece of land on the Crawfordsville and Williamsport state road in section thirty-one (31) township twenty (20) north, of range five west, all the land on the north side of the road that he owned out of the said farm of which now is owned by Jasper Hutchison. Daniel A. Bennett who was living at that time at Columbia, near Romney, wanted to leave that place and wanted to live near where he was raised, concluded that if E.P. Bennett would help him he would build a frame house on the east part of said three cornered tract of land, and in 1832 he built a dwelling with a store room in one corner. The carpenters were J.H. Miller, Beadle, known as Whitey, E.P. Bennett, J. S. Bennett and D.A. Bennett.

This was the first frame building there was in the place, and D.A. Bennett had a canvas with the words painted on it. "Boston Store - by D.A. Bennett." When he kept store in Columbia he had that canvas, and when he moved his goods into the new building he put up the same old canvas on the side of the store which could be read a good distance, and that is how the place came by the name of "Boston Store." At that time there lived in the vicinity of Boston Store, Joel Hixson, a farmer, the widow Prutsman, Abram Wilkinson, Michael Swank, Phillip Swank, and "Old Jacob," called Grandpa Swank, Wm. Mitchell, Isam Royalty, John Widener, all farmers. Time has told on them what it will tell on all, as there is not one of the old set we have named now living that lived in the vicinity of where stands good frame, buildings. Now some of the smart men of our country thought there ought to be a post office at Boston Store, and got one called Boston Store Post Office, but as there was some trouble with the name of "Boston Store" on account of some mail would come there that was not intended, they had the name changed to Elmdale. But we are a little ahead of our history. For several years after the first store was in running order, the land on the south and west of the road was layed out and was a nice place for the Invincible Guards to drill and they put in the time under Hardee's Manuel of Arms. Since then there has been added to the place on both sides of the road, and the place now holds G.W. Widener, where D.A. Bennett built the first frame house which has been pulled down and a neat residence in its place, and west of there on the same side of the road is as good a frame house as stands between your city and Pleasant Hill, and still west on the same spot of ground where Wm. H. Hixson did live, resides Doc. L. W. Olin. On south side Garret Larue where Joshua Dilling built, then Joe Boes where Andrew Battreal built, then the store building built by J. Dilling and the Grangers, then a small dwelling where Aunt Poly Smith now lives, then a good comfortable residence of J. Dilling, then south Bob and Gill Dearmands are both living, then on the corner Wm. Toat, our village blacksmith, then across on the corner east, Uncle Henry Oxley has a wagon shop, then a little east his residence that James Badgely built, then still east, one of the Vancleave's live, then Thompson's Chapel stands built by the Methodist in 1832, still a good house. Then east of that is John Harmon, a blacksmith and wagon maker, Dan Swank a farmer and teamster. Tiffany's fine residence now shows at a distance, on which farm there was at that time a large pond. In the winter of 1830 a black bear was discovered and chase was given him, and he was run up a large white oak tree a little over a mile and three quarters north east of this place, and was shot by Geo. Allhands, while Thomas Daisey's dogs were knocked head over heels by the bear. But the writer had the pleasure of eating a piece of that bear, the first and last he has ever eaten as he knows of up to this time. In those times there was not a frame school house in the township, and the day the bear was killed the undersigned was at school in a log house on the farm of Edward P. Bennett, which was taught by Mrs. Harriett Siler, a sister of Edward P. Bennett. We got our education going to school not more than two days out of the five that were taught, and sat on hewed benches, and hewed split puncheon floors with the writing desk fastened to the walls of the house, with a fire place long enough to take in a back log six to seven feet long. Mud jams and backwall, and mud stick chimney, which would sometimes catch a fire, surely the times of 1837 and the times of 1887 are very different. We have aimed to give you as true a history of Elmdale as could be made just from memory, having kept no memorandum of events.

Prairie Edge, in Wayne Township, located just south of Boston Store had a post office from June 7, 1855 to January 19, 1875, and John Shanklin was the postmaster for this office during its entirety. After this post office was discontinued, mail was sent to the Boston Store post office, which confused later historians into thinking the settlement had three names: Boston Store, Prairie Edge and Elmdale.

The name was changed from Boston Store to Elmdale on October 24, 1882, according to the official records of the post office. The main reason for changing the name to Elmdale was the post office constantly received mail addressed to other Boston Stores or Boston Stations and the postmaster decided to circulate a petition to have the name changed. Joshua Dilling was the postmaster at the time. There were enough signatures and it was decided to name the settlement for a large elm tree that stood in the village near the post office. The 1874 People's Guide gives another possible reason for choosing this name: "The Elm Dale Lodge, I.O.G.T.(Independent Order of Good Templar's), organized December 22, 1873 with a membership of 60, located at Boston Store." It is conceivable the post office adopted this name in honor of the lodge.

In 1883 the village of Elmdale had the following business establishments: J. Dilling, Postmaster—with three assistants, J.S. Bennett, Insurance agent, Leveritt W. Olin, Physician, G.W. Widener, salesman and farmer, J. Dilling and S. Dilling, groceries and dry goods; L. Dilling, store room (type of store not listed); J.H. Oxley, druggist, dry goods, groceries, glass and Queens Ware; Wm. Foot, blacksmith; Robert Dearmond, ditcher, Henry Oxley, and James Oxley wagon makers and carpenters; James Oxley, notary public; Jack Smith, clerk, teamster, and trader; and Thompson's Chapel Methodist Episcopal Church, built in 1851. (The church was organized in 1832 or 33).

The following is a list of Boston Store, and Elmdale postmasters and the dates of appointments. As you can see the Boston Store post office was established February 1, 1866. The information in parentheses was included with the records from the National Archives.

Postmaster	Date appointed	Other information
BOSTON STORE		
Jas. M.M. Collister	1 Feb. 1866	
James Green	6 Jun. 1867	
Wm. H. Simons	22 Jun. 1868	
Joshua Dilling	25 Dec. 1869	
William Patton	27 Apr. 1874	
Geo. W. Widner	26 Jun. 1874	
James Oxley	3 Aug. 1874	
Geo. W. Widner	24 Aug. 1874	
James Oxley	16 Dec. 1874	
J.W. Patton	11 Feb. 1875	
George H. Alexander	14 April. 1875	
Joshua Dilling	20 Feb. 1878	
Harry M. Mitchell	21 Apr. 1879	
Joshua Dilling	3 Dec. 1879	
ELMDALE	24 Oct. 1882	(changed from Boston Store)
Joshua Dilling	24 Oct. 1882	
Garrett Larew	3 Feb. 1887	(July 1895)
John R. Vancleave	24 Aug. 1895	(over Vancleave had off.rep/Sep. 20, 1895
Garrett Larew	3 Feb. 1887	(July 1895)
Clarence A. Widener	23 Apr. 1898	(This order rescinded Jul. 29, 1898)
Garrett Larew	3 Feb. 1887	
Garrett Larew	3 Feb. 1887	(N.B. Nov. 16, 1900)
James Swank	1 Jul. 1901	(rescinded 26 Jan. 1905, effective 31 Jan. '05)
James Swank	1 Feb. 1901	

Dis. (distribute?) mail to Crawfordsville 20 March 1905, effective 15 Apr.

The Boston Store post office received mail three times a week in 1878 and was carried by the same star route as Pleasant Hill (Wingate). Patrons of the Elmdale post office petitioned for daily mail service from Crawfordsville in January 1894, but this request was not granted until March 1898. Garrett Larue was serving as postmaster at the time, and had been trying for two years to resign. The post office records indicate Clarence A. Widener and John R. Vancleave were appointed during, or in between, Larue's term, but each only served a short time, for some reason or other.

The Elmdale post office was to be discontinued the end of January 1905, but many objections were made by the patrons, resulting in the postal authorities having to rescind the order. James Swank, the postmaster, tendered his resignation at this time, but remained in office until the Elmdale Post Office was permanently discontinued, effective the 15th of April 1905. Elmdale residents were informed they would be well supplied with free mail delivery out of Crawfordsville, as three rural routes would still run through the village, but it was a great disappointment to have the village post office closed forever, and another person lost his position as postmaster.

Elmdale residents had high hopes of growing into a thriving town. County Surveyor Ira McConnel surveyed the hamlet and numbered the lots, and the lots were sold in November 1881. There was a lot of interest in incorporating the town in 1896, but the plan was not followed through. The residents were in need of new sidewalks, hitching posts, and other conveniences that could be supported by town taxes. The village needed some laws made and someone to enforce them. Among the many problems were hogs running loose through the village, and a two-legged varmint was gathering up the turkeys and chickens from the residents' poultry lots.

The Methodists organized and erected a church in 1832 at Boston Store. This building, known as **Thompson's Chapel**, was standing in 1887. W. W. Tiffany, Vincent and John T. Utterback, and Jackson Quick were elected trustees of Thompson's Chapel during the Quarterly Conference a year later, 1888.

The Methodists erected a new edifice at a cost of $3,216, and the building was dedicated November 19, 1899. In 1971 the members withdrew from the United Methodist Conference and organized an independent church re-naming it the **Elmdale Community Church**. This church is still active today (1986) Alan F. Johnson the minister, has been with this church since 1981. The church building was remodeled in May 1983, adding new siding and roof.

The Old School Baptists Church was organized by the pioneers in the 1830s. This group has been referred to as Old School Baptists: Primitive and Missionary Baptists. After their old church burned around 1909 or 1910, a new structure was erected and dedicated in 1911, and named **Bethel Baptist Church**. The group met in the local school building between the date of the fire and the completion of the new edifice. This group disbanded in 1940, and the church is now a residence.

The Elmdale school history is included with the Coal Creek township schools.

The Waynetown and Elmdale Telephone System was established in Elmdale in February and March of 1896. Owners of this system were Alphonso C. Summer and William A. Wright, who sold the system to John T. Detchon of New Richmond on November 11, 1912. Detchon purchased the office equipment, switchboards, telephones, cables, poles, and wire—including all the country lines—and the supplies on hand for $20,000. He operated this system under the name of **Wabash Prairie Telephone Corporation** for several years. Indiana Bell purchased the Wabash Prairie Telephone company in the late 1950s.

Paris W. Kenyon conducted a general store in Elmdale, and had charge of the telephone exchange for a number of years. His wife Caroline "Carrie" Kenyon was in charge of the switchboard, and their son, Clayton M., was a lineman for the company. Kenyon was a native of New York, his wife from Virginia. Kenyon and his brother were carpenters in addition to the other occupations.

The community of Elmdale suffered extensive damage from high winds on May 1, 1983. The winds blew the roof off Mr. and Mrs. William Fultz's residence, leveled a barn owned by Earl Smith, uprooted several trees, drove some 2x4s three feet into the ground, and damaged bridges on two nearby county roads, closing the roads until repairs could be made.

As in many villages, progress has taken on a new definition, "regress," due to the automobile and other modern inventions; Elmdale is now but a few homes and the community church.

BRISTLE RIDGE

There are many various explanations as to how—or why—the name **Bristle Ridge** was given to a highland area in southwest Coal Creek Township. Most of the reasons are associated with hog bristles, but in one instance the name has to do with the vegetation. In order to keep the folklore in Coal Creek Township alive, I will record each. Beckwith's *History of Montgomery County, Indiana*, 1881, says,

> Near the center of the township (Coal Creek) is section 20, a high rise of ground known as "Bristle Ridge." This section of land was entered by a Frenchman, it is said, who upon beholding his purchase, hastily concluded he could not raise corn where there were so many trees, so leaving his farm unattended, he returned to his sunny vineland. Ere long, people whom we call squaters took up their abode on the hill in very small cabins they erected. These people were poor and squalid, and came but to exist a while upon food prepared for them. There were fifteen families on one section 20. There were immense quantities of moss in the region which after the early settlement of the surrounding territory became inviting to the swine for miles around, and here the hog grew fat. But his fatness proved his destruction, for those squaters, obeying the divine in-junction, did kill and eat abundantly. To escape suspicion they stowed away the bristles under the floor of their cabins. It is said that Isom Royalty, an early settler, purchased a farm having on it a

cabin, under the floor of which, when he destroyed it, he found twenty bushels of hog bristles. Whether this be true or not, it is true the squaters followed this plan of deception and hence the name "Bristle Ridge."

Ted Gronert, a Wabash College professor, gives his viewpoint of the area in his book *Sugar Creek Saga*, published in 1958 by Wabash:

> A highland area south of New Richmond was for years known as "Bristle Ridge." A band of hog stealers had infested the area for several years. They used a secluded cabin as an abattoir and flouted the law until forced to decamp by a vigilante committee. Some years later the cabin was dismantled and under the floorboards was found a great pile of pig bristles. From the time of the discovery, the place was known as "Bristle Ridge" and local news was sent to Crawfordsville papers under that heading.

Gronert also described Bristle Ridge in his column concerning the county's history in the Crawfordsville *Journal Review,* December 18, 1963 giving the same hog bristle theory.

Abraham (or Abram) Clough brought his family from Kentucky and purchased 240 acres in Coal Creek township in 1843. Abram built a log cabin from the remains of two cabins left by the squatters. Around fourteen years later, he erected a new story-and-a-half structure facing south, with a big, old-fashioned porch in the rear. The residence had four rooms downstairs and one large room on the second floor. Abram built his new home of the best native timber, using solid black walnut for the doors, the casings, cupboards, wardrobes, mantels, etc. This residence stood on a commanding knoll on Section 20 which is the center of the Bristle Ridge domain and the mile square of virgin soil to which is attributed the honor of giving the title to "Bristle Ridge." George W. Clough, son of Abraham, was born in the home shortly after it was finished, and after his father's death, George resided in the home. The house was destroyed by fire in August 1904.

The account of the Clough family residence being destroyed by fire is the first record of the theory of the name "Bristle Ridge" as being derived from the virgin soil, and should cause more than a little speculation as to why this soil was different from the surrounding territory.

Another early family settling on Bristle Ridge was the Utterbacks. In the spring of 1881, one of the Utterbacks, with a partner by the name of Applegate, erected a tile mill on the land "where the name Bristle Ridge originated," but they flourished only a short time.

All the "corners and settlements" carried on a friendly rivalry in the Crawfordsville newspapers by sending local news items under some very strange "place names." One account said,

> A citizen of Wingate informed us Saturday that "Bristle Ridge" had been annexed to the town and hereafter would be known as a suburb of Wingate, and the location of the Bristle Ridge paper to be known as the PORCUPINE was intended to civilize Wingate and Utah, a village lying between the two extremes of the combined towns. The Utah village had not as yet been broken into full fellowship, but negotiations were under headway, and the three towns would soon join hands. Eb Vanscoyoc, the boss carpenter, with a full supply of hands is erecting a fine dwelling for one of his Utah brethren which is to be known as "the half-way house" when the three towns have locked arms.

Unfortunately, the date and name of this newspaper was not saved with this item. The Crawfordsville *Journal,* January 3, 1891 reported "John W. Utterback is building a fine residence on "Holly Hock" street in Bristle Ridge." This may have been the dwelling mentioned above.

Another place-name near Bristle Ridge surfaced in April 1883 when items in the Crawfordsville *Review* appeared under the title of **Ashland**. At the top of the items was the following gem, "Bristle Ridge is now a three-cornered piece, one corner having been blown away by S.A.R. Beach, blasting stumps."

In 1891 Wingate was experiencing a building boom, and the Crawfordsville daily *Journal* dated November 6 printed the following item, "The boom that's on at Wingate is due to the enterprising citizens of Bristle Ridge. We have hauled them oak stove-wood, sorghum 'lasses, coon skins, and other valuable commodities as our fertile regions produce. It is the 'Ridge' that gives the town character."

The little one-room district school on Bristle Ridge, better known as **Center**, or School No.7, produced some very fine scholars who continued their education in the higher learning facilities, becoming school teachers and very well-known attorneys. The Murphys and Foleys were two families representing Bristle Ridge in the field of law, and they lived down the road from each other as children, on the road west of Patton's corner.

THE FOLEY FAMILY

John A. Foley and his wife, Bridget Coleman, came to America from their native Ireland and settled in Coal Creek Township in the vicinity of Bristle Ridge. They were the parents of ten children, but only five reached maturity. All the remaining children were sons, and of the five, three were farmers, and two were successful attorneys. A brief sketch of their sons follows:

Michael Emmett Foley, born September 14, 1872, attended the district school at Bristle Ridge. He taught school in the same township seven years, entered Wabash College, and graduated in 1899. He attended Columbia Law School in New York one year. In 1900 he joined Judge Thomas' law firm as a partner, and stayed with Thomas until 1909. He served as counsel for the Terre Haute-Indianapolis and Eastern Traction Co. in 1913 and was residing in Indianapolis at that time. Mike Foley rose early in the mornings and helped his father on the farm before riding to Crawfordsville in time for his classes in Wabash College. He always completed his lessons for the following day before returning to his home near Bristle Ridge. Mike was considered one of the most brilliant orators in the county.

Andrew N. Foley, born November 19, 1877, attended the school at Bristle Ridge. He taught school for a period of ten years with great success, during which time his services were in great demand, giving satisfaction to both pupil and patron, but his attention was turned to law. He entered the Indiana Law School at Indianapolis in September 1905, graduating with the class of 1907. He began practicing law at Covington, Indiana, as deputy prosecuting attorney, remaining there for two years. In 1909 he returned to his native county, Montgomery, and entered into partnership with Judge Thomas, where they established a large and lucrative clientele. Andrew and Michael Foley both worked very hard on their father's farm—and as school teachers to pay their way through law school. They were regarded as very honest Crawfordsville attorneys.

The *Attica Press* paid a tribute to "Two Poor Irish Boys" in December 1903:

> About fifteen years ago, in the schools of Coal Creek Township, Montgomery County, there were two farmer boys who were usually pitted against each other in the school debates held in that part of the county. Both were sons of comparatively poor and uneducated fathers, but both had ambitions to rise in the world and were hard students. The one was brilliant, ready spoken, and quick-witted, learning with ease and speaking with all the freedom of an old campaigner. The other, more slow in his manner of speaking and less brilliant in his speeches, but with a world of dogged determination about him, and a grasp of things that made his friends certain of his future. In the debates the first often got the decision over his slower opponent, but neither lessened his efforts to get an education, and to rise in the world. These two boys recently came into prominence, pitted against each other in the Myers murder case at Crawfordsville, and are known now as Mike Foley, the eloquent young lawyer of Crawfordsville, and John Murphy, the County Prosecutor.

The Murphy Family

Martin Murphy, a native of County Kerry, Ireland, came to America in 1865, residing in Montgomery County almost from the day of his arrival. He married a pretty Irish girl by the name of Margaret O'Brien, and they had three sons who made quite a name for themselves in Montgomery County—and Bristle Ridge.

John B. Murphy, born November 5, 1871, attended the district school at Bristle Ridge (Center). He went on to attend the old Normal Academy at Ladoga, and later graduated from Valparaiso University and Indiana Law School in Indianapolis. John taught school in New Richmond and other Coal Creek Township schools to pay his way through law school and worked on his father's farm. After graduating from law school, John practiced law with Clyde H. Jones in Crawfordsville for twelve years, first with Robert Williams, and after William's death, alone. John served as Montgomery County's prosecuting attorney from 1902 to 1904, and as Crawfordsville's City Attorney. He was known as an honest lawyer and ranked high in his profession by his colleagues.

Daniel W. Murphy, born May 10, 1875, attended the Center district school and Valparaiso University, and started teaching in 1881 in Coal Creek Township to earn his way through college. He taught in the following schools: Kentwood, Center, Wingate, New Richmond, and Elmdale. Dan quit teaching for a short time and operated a restaurant in Greencastle, but sold out in 1906, planning to move to Waynetown and practice law in that village. His early experiences as a teacher in the Coal Creek Township schools, however, made a lasting impression on Dan, and he decided to return to teaching. In addition to the Coal Creek schools, Dan Murphy was teacher and principal of the Smartsburg school for thirty-seven years before retiring in 1951. He taught, altogether, a total of fifty-eight years in Montgomery County schools.

Matthew J. Murphy, born August 9, 1878, attended the Coal Creek district school at Center; he taught at Elmdale, New Richmond and Wingate. He had served as principal and teacher for nine years by the year 1904, and was affectionately introduced as the "Past Grand Master of Bristle" when he presented diplomas to the Wingate High School graduates in 1904. Matt Murphy graduated from Indiana University Law School and began the practice of law in January 1911 with a partner, Silas Hayes, in Greencastle, Indiana, where he continued until his death in February 1953.

All three of the above Murphy brothers were teaching school in Coal Creek Township in 1896. John was teaching in New Richmond that year.

Center

The community of Center consisted of Coal Creek District School No.7, the Christian Church, and at one time, Arthur Young's small general store, and William Utterback's steam saw mill, and a little later, the Utterback and Applegate tile mill, mentioned in the Bristle-Ridge item. Center school history is included within the section on Coal Creek Township's district schools. The Center community is situated in the same general area of Bristle Ridge, and when one refers to either settlement, it is one of the same. The area farmers are the only residents of the community, as there was no plat made for a village. The view from the top of the "Ridge" is quite pretty overlooking many rolling hills, and I am drawn to the area by some unknown magnet when driving around Coal Creek Township. A brief history of the community church follows.

Center Christian Church

A group consisting of nine persons gathered together in 1866 (possibly in the Center School building) in the interest of forming a Christian Church Society in their neighborhood. This group was also said to be connected to the "Newlight Order of Christians" but the records show the church was served by the same ministers as New Richmond and Mount Pleasant Christian Churches who were not associated with the "Newlights," or "Campbellites." Attending this organizational meeting were: William Utterback and wife, Benjamin Roadhammel, James Morrow, Elisha Grenard, David Dazey, Garner Bobo, John Bennett, James Wainscot, and two Christian Church "rounders" or "Circuit Riders"—Lewis Bannon and A.L. Carney. The church society was duly organized in 1867, and Lewis Bannon served as the first Minister of the **Center Christian Church**. The group met in the Center school house - the gathering place for all the area's public meetings, during their first years as a society.

A meeting was held on December 13, 1871 in the Center School house to make plans for building a church for the Center Christian Society; the church was to be erected, "in William Utterback's southwest corner on the Lafayette Road." The following trustees were elected during this meeting: P. Wilhite, Thomas Johnson, Thompson Utterback, and Henry T. Wilhite, treasurer. William Utterback called the meeting to order and J.S. Bennett was elected clerk. William Utterback had been born in Virginia in 1817, and settled in Montgomery County in 1828.

For some unknown reason, the building was not erected at this time, although Mr. Utterback had offered a choice corner of his land on an easily accessible road. The most probable reason was a lack of sufficient funds to erect a new structure. In 1874, Rev. Thomas Quillen was pastor of the Center Christian Church and there were 100 members in the society at that time.

William Utterback raised the question of building a meeting house during a New Year's party given by A. L. Carney, their minister, in January 1880. Utterback and Benjamin Roadhammel created much enthusiasm by pledging money. Utterback offered to double any amount pledged to build the structure, and the amount needed was soon pledged. B. Merrill of Waynetown was awarded the contract to build a frame 35 x 45 church building at an estimated cost of $1,000. The church structure was completed and furnished at a cost of $1,200, and dedicated on Sunday, September 5, 1880. Brother A.L. Carney dedicated the new edifice, assisted by Thomas Quillen, Bros. Maxwell and Lindsey McCoy. McCoy was the minister of Center Church at the time. Center Christian Church is still standing today (1986) on section 19, township 20, range 5, or two miles east of Wingate, two miles north of Boston Store (Elmdale), and about three and a half miles southwest of New Richmond (as the crow flies).

In 1881 Center Christian Church had about 105 members, and the Deacons were William Utterback and James Morrow. David Dazey was clerk and Sunday School Superintendent that year. At the age of 80 years, Lewis Bannon, the organization's first minister, returned to Center to assist Pastor Kibby with a protracted meeting (revival) in February 1905. About a year later, the leaders of Center Christian Church became "incensed" with a general storekeeper, Arthur Young, because he kept his store open on Sunday, and disturbed their meetings by doing so. They also charged that Mr. Young sold cigars and tobacco to minors. Young pled guilty and paid a $12.55 fine and promised to be good thereafter. There were no other incidents recorded, so he must have kept his promise.

Formal Articles of Association of the Center Christian Church were filed January 28, 1889. The following is a transcript of the document:

> Miscellaneous Records of Montgomery County, Indiana, Volume 5, page 120.
> Articles of Association of the Center Christian Church of Coal Creek Township Montgomery County in the state of Indiana -
>
> We the undersigned persons who are residents of Montgomery County and state of Indiana do hereby voluntarily associate ourselves together for the object and purpose of organizing ourselves into a church society to be known by the corporate name of Center Christian Church of Coal Creek Township Montgomery County State Of Indiana pursuant to the statutes of the state of Indiana in such cases, made and provided said Church society shall elect yearly five Trustees who shall have and hold the title to said Church property and who shall have full control and management thereof and said Trustee shall hold their offices for the term of One year or until their successors are elected. The first election for trustees shall be held on the second Saturday in February 1889 and succeeding election of Trustees shall be held on the second Saturday in February in each year thereafter. Notice

of the election of Trustees shall be given at least ten days previous to any election by one publication in a newspaper of said county and also posting up one written or printed notice thereof on the door of the Church house of said society where all of the elections of the Officers of said Church shall be held and such notices shall state the time place and objects of such election. Said society shall have power to elect all other officers deemed necessary and proper and to pass all useful rules and regulations and fill all vacancies that may occur in the offices of Trustee by resignation death or removal at any meeting of said society called for that purpose provided that no trustee shall be elected to fill a vacancy or otherwise without the notice as provided above being first given at all meetings held by said society a majority of all the members present shall be necessary to elect any officer as (or) pass any measure or resolution." (all the names listed below gave their residence as Coal Creek except Sarah Dazey who gave hers as, "Shuger Creek. (Sic.)" William Utterback, Kezia Utterback, James Wainscott, Armilda Wainscott, W. H. Roser, Ellen Roser, Sarah Dazey, Sallie Bannon, Julia Swank, George W. Bunnel, Martha Calhoun, Susan C. Swank, Cathrine Brown, William E. Bunnel, Sviror (?) Dazey, Samuel M. Jackson, Voorhees W. Willhite, George W. Abbott, Eno Abbott, James C. Bannon, Pheobe Bannon, M. Z. Razor, F.In (?) Dazey, Hariet Morone, P. H. Swank, James Willson, Sarah Wilson, Louisa Crouch, John E. Dazey, Jane Harper, Eliza Jane Shafer, P.E. Bagby, John Mathew, Milton Mathew, James A. Bunnell, Maliah Williams, Elizabeth Utterback, C.A. Dazey, Amanda Dazey, Albert Harper, Abram W. Dazey, Boswell Bunnell, Elizabeth Razor (or Rozer?), Oswel Bunnell.

Received for record, January 28, 1889 at 8:45 A. M. and recorded same day, signed by John Johnson, R.M.C. (Recorder of Montgomery County).

Rev. David H. Williams is now the minister of the Center Christian Church, (1986) and the Society holds regular services in the little community church.

Mount Pleasant

The little community of Mount Pleasant was centered around the church and graveyard, situated on a small mound. The Christian Church was organized by the early pioneers; the exact date is uncertain, but the small cemetery known as the **Pioneer Cemetery** contains the grave of Rev. Benjamin Brooks, who died at the age of 76 on September 20, 1855. Also buried in this graveyard is William P., son of Rev. Benjamin and Mary Brooks who died at the age of 13 on December 6, 1834. There is no definite record, but it is believed the Rev. Brooks was an early minister of the Mount Pleasant Christian Church during this period of time. The Original Entry Record Book of Montgomery County, Indiana, shows Benjamin Brooks made several entries from a period of 1831 to 1835 in sections 23, and 36, in township 20, range 5.

Linden had no Christian church in the early years, and the followers of that faith attended the old Mount Pleasant Church in Coal Creek township until around 1852 when they decided to meet in the village's school house. Early pioneer ministers of the Mount Pleasant Christian Church were: Thomas Quillen, William Warbington, Thomas Allen, and A.L. McKinney.

On February 25, 1871, the members of the Mount Pleasant Christian Church met in a nearby school (across the line in Madison Township) known as the **Territory School House**, to re-organize and elect Trustees. Those elected were: Thomas Taylor, Joseph Jones, James Davenport, and James H. Vail. Vail was elected to serve as clerk of the organization. Beckwith's *History of Montgomery County, Indiana*, 1881, gives the location of the Mount Pleasant Christian Church as two miles south of Linden on the line separating Madison and Coal Creek townships, and the history also said the group was the "New Light Order of Christians." (This may-or may not be correct, as the Christian Church in New Richmond was incorrectly connected with the "New Light" and the "Campbelights" or Campbellites when they reorganized.) The Mt. Pleasant group erected their first church house (still standing in 1881) in 1875 at a cost of $1300. In 1881 they had fifty active members, and the organization was known as the **Mount Pleasant Christian Church Society**.

The building was located in Coal Creek Township on Section 36, township 20, range 5. The 1878 and 1898 atlases show the Mt. Pleasant Church on the Madison township side of the line, but the maps may be incorrect. Notices of meetings to be held in the Mount Pleasant Church were announced in the Crawfordsville *Review* under Round Hill and Cherry Grove items. In January 1894, it was announced there would be religious services at Mount Pleasant Sunday, indicating regular services were not held each Sunday. Children's Day was to be held on the fourth Sunday in June of 1890, so it is possible they only met on the fourth Sunday of each month. At the close of revival services held in the Mount Pleasant Church in January 1891, there were twenty-one new additions.

The Isaac W. (Billie) Patton family attended this church, and Ellis Burk was a prominent member of Mt. Pleasant, serving as deacon for twelve years, before his death in 1903. The Tomlinson's, Vails of Madison Township, S. D. Jones, and the Miller families all resided near the little settlement of Mt. Pleasant. The 1898 map of Madison Township shows three or four residences situated side by side in this neighborhood.

The members of the Mount Pleasant Christian Church met on May 26, 1922, to elect the following Trustees: P.A. Croy, Albert Vail, Fred Barr, Rose Young - Chairman, and Lydia Burk, Secretary. I could not find any information showing just how much longer this congregation held together.

Mount Pleasant Cemetery

The old **Pioneer Cemetery** was situated on Section 36, Township 20 north, Range 5 west. A record of the legible inscriptions on the tombstones date from 1834 to 1855; one infant was buried in 1875.

A new location was selected across the road located on Section 25. It is situated on a small mound and is a very well-kept cemetery. A record shows the Mount Pleasant Cemetery Association met in the Round Hill Church to elect officers in October 1911. Elected were: George Pierce, president, Ed Burke, treasurer, and Sam Miller, secretary. Mrs. Kate Goben and Mrs. Cynthia Tapp were to serve on the soliciting committee, and Mr. Prent Croy and Frank Nolan on the entertainment committee. No other records were available for this little community.

Round Hill

One of the more promising hamlets in Coal Creek Township was that of Round Hill. The farmers in the area realized the importance of educating their children at an early date, and a log structure was erected for school purposes in the 1830s. This school was supported by the subscription system, and one of the scholars attending this school was Sophia McGinnis, as well as other members of her family. Sophia's obituary said she taught school in this structure before her first marriage (at the age of seventeen).

After the township was a little more settled, land was deeded on March 30, 1846 by Hiram and Margaret Connell of Tippecanoe County, for a district school at Round Hill in section 26. This building stood on the same location as the old log structure. (More on this school in the district school section).

Asbury Chapel Methodist Episcopal Church

The old Asbury Chapel Methodist Episcopal Church stood three-fourths of a mile west, and one-fourth of a mile north of what is known as Round Hill. An early Methodist Episcopal Church minister, Rev. William Campbell and his wife Nancy, deeded one half acre - and one rod, of land the 23rd of November 1849 to the "Trustees in Trust of the members of the Methodist Episcopal Church in the United States of America." No church name was given on this deed, but the names of the trustees were:

Henry N. King, Samuel Wilson, Moses Gillam, Henry Campbell, and John A. King. The deed stated the trustees were "to erect and build thereon a house or place of worship for the use of the members of the Methodist Episcopal Church in the United States of America according to the rules adopted by the ministers of said church, etc." The deed also made some strict rules for the trustees and future ministers to follow concerning the use of the land.

According to the 1874 People's Guide of Montgomery County, Indiana: Asbury Chapel Methodist Episcopal Church, located four miles southeast of New Richmond, was built in the year 1839. The value of the property was $1500; the membership numbered fifty with the same number of scholars. Rev. Samuel Hays was the Pastor and John E. Shelburn was Sabbath School Superintendent at the time.

An article entitled "The Last Festival" concerning the old Round Hill Church, written in 1903 says, "the church has served as a temple for worship for about sixty-five (65) years." This too, places the date the old Asbury Chapel was built around 1839. The following is a transcript of the deed as it was recorded:

> Montgomery County Record Book (Deeds) 15, pages 192-193
> THIS INDENTURE made this 23'd day of November in the year of our Lord one thousand eight hundred and forty nine between William Campbell and Nancy his wife of the County of Montgomery in the State of Indiana of the one part and Henry N. King, Samuel Wilson, Moses Gillam, Henry Campbell and John A. King Trustees in trust for the uses and purposes hereinafter mentioned all of the County of Montgomery in the State of Indiana aforesaid of the other part
>
> WITNESSETH That the said William Campbell and Nancy his wife for and in consideration of the sum of Ten Dollars lawful money of the United States to them in hand paid at and upon the sealing and delivery of these presents the receipt whereof is hereby acknowledged, have given, granted, bargained, sold released confirms and conveyed and by these presents do give grant bargain, sell release confirm and convey unto them the said Henry N. King, Samuel Wilson. Moses Gillum, Henry Campbell and John A. King and their successors all the estate right, title, interest, property, claim and deman whatsoever either in law or equity, which he the said William Campbell and Nancy his wife, have in to, or upon all and singular a certain lot or piece of land situated lying and being in the County of Montgomery and State aforesaid abounded and butted as follows:
>
> TO WIT being a lot set off from the west half South East quarter Section twenty Seven Town (20) twenty north, range five west commencing fifty five rods from the South East corner of the above described tracts of land on the line running North, from thence running North Nine rods thence west nine rods, thence South nine rods, thence east nine rods to the place of beginning containing and laid out for one half acre and one rod of land, together with all and singular the Houses, privileges, appurtenances thereto belonging on in any wise pertaining
>
> TO HAVE AND TO HOLD all and singular the above mentioned and described lot a piece of land situated lying and being as aforesaid together with all and singular the houses and privileges thereunto belonging or in any wise appertaining unto them the said Henry N. King, Samuel Wilson, Moses Gillum, Henry Campbell and John A. King and the Successors in office forever in trust that they shall erect and build thereon a house or place of worship for the use of the Members of the Methodist Episcopal Church in the United States of America according to the rules and discipline which from time to time may be agreed upon and adopted by the Ministers and preachers of the said Church at their Annual Conferences in the United States of America and in farther [sic] trust and Confiden[t] that they shall at all times forever hereafter permit such Ministers and Preachers belonging to

the said Church as shall from time to time be duly authorized by the General Confere[nce] OF THE Ministers and Preachers of the said Methodist Episcopal Church or by the annual Conferences authorized by the said General Conference to preach and expound God's holy word therein and in further trust and confidence, that as often as anyone or more of the Trustees herein before mentioned shall die or cease to be a member or members of the said Church according to the rules and discipline as aforesaid, then and in such case it shall be the duty of the Stationed Minister or preacher who shall have the pastoral Charge of the members of said Church to call a meeting of the remaining trustees as soon as Convenient may be and when so met the said minister or preacher shall proceed to nominate one or more persons to fill the place or places of him or them whose office or offices have been vacated as aforesaid Provided the person or persons so Nominated shall have been one year a member of the said Church immediately preceding the nomination and be at least twenty one years of age: and the said trustees so assembled shall proceed to do and by a Majority of Votes appoint the person or persons so nominated to fill such Vacancy or vacancies in order to keep up the Number of five trustees forever, and in case of an equal number Votes for and against the said nomination the said Stationed Minister or Preacher shall have the casting vote.

Provided nevertheless, that if the said trustees or any of them or their successors have advanced or shall advance any Sum of money (_____) or shall be responsible for any sum or sums of Money on account of the said premises and they the said trustees or their successors be obliged to pay the sum or sums of money they or a majority of them shall be authorized to (raise?) the said sum or sums or money by a Mortgage on the said premises or by selling the said premises after notice given to the pastor or Preacher who has the oversight of the Congregation attending (_____) services on the said premises if the money due be not paid to the said Trustees or their Successors within one year after such notice is given and if such sale takes place the said Trustees or their Successors after paying the debt and other expenses which are dues from the money arising from such sale shall deposit the remainder of the Money produced by the said sale in the hands of the steward or Stewards of the Society belonging to all attending (_____) services on said premises which surplus of the produce of such sale so deposited in the hands of the said Steward or Stewards shall be at the disposal of the next annual Conference authorized as aforesaid which said Annual conference shall dispose of the said money according to the best of their judgment for the use of the said society, and the said Wm. Campbell and Nancy his wife doth by these presents Warrant and forever defend all and singularly the before mentioned and described lot or piece of land with the appurtenances thereto belonging unto them the said Henry N. King, Samuel Wilson, Moses Gillum, Henry Campbell and John A. King and their successors chosen and appointed as aforesaid from the claim or claims of him the said Wm. Campbell his heirs and assigns and from the claim or claims of all persons whatever.

IN TESTIMONY WHEREOF, the said William Campbell and Nancy his wife, have hereunto set their hands and seals the day and year aforesaid. Sealed and delivered in presence of us.
William Campbell (seal)
Nancy Campbell (seal)
James Heaton (sig.)
State of Indiana SS.
Montgomery County

I James Heaton Recorder of the aforesaid County do hereby certify that the above named William Campbell personally came before me and acknowledged the signing and sealing of the foregoing Deed of Conveyance to be his purpots and deed for the purposes therein mentioned.

And the said Nancy Campbell wife of the said William Campbell being by me examined separately and apart from and without the hearing of her said husband and being made acquainted with the contents and purports of said deed of conveyance, acknowledged that she executed the same of her own free will and accord and without any coercion or compulsion from her said husband.

WITNESS this 23'd day of November 1849. James Heaton R. M. Co.

THE LAST FESTIVAL

The New Richmond *Record*, Thursday, May 28, 1903 related the following sentimental final chapter of the old Asbury Methodist Episcopal Church building:

THE LAST FESTIVAL

The last social and festival in the old church at Round Hill was held on Monday evening, having been postponed from Saturday evening on account of the storm, and it was largely attended. Ice cream, cake, and all kinds of good things were served and the crowd was a merry one. The crowning feature of the evening was the sale at public auction of the old church building, Col. Albert W. Perkins crying the sale. James D. Wilson was the highest bidder and purchaser at $80.

A handsome new brick church is at once to be built on the site of the old church, the specifications and plans are now about ready to be submitted for bids on its construction, and the old church is to be moved off the ground by June 15th. The old building however, will probably (be) used for services until the completion of the new one.

In the passing of the old Round Hill church goes one of the old landmarks of the country. It has done service as a temple for worship for about sixty-five (65) years. The exact date of its building is probably not known but it was built by Rev. William Campbell, a pioneer minister, who gave the ground and was an active instrument in the erection of the structure on what is now the Homer C. Barcus farm, one and one-fourth miles west of Round Hill. Several years later it was moved to the present Round Hill site, the ground where it stands being then the property of the late Dr. Manners, who leased the lot for church purposes for an indefinite period, to revert to its owner when it ceased to be used for church worship. This land is now owned by Albert W. Wilson. The church has once been remodeled, and was the pride of that Christian community. The old building was built of heavy old fashioned barn timbers and save for a rotten sill under the door is said to be in good shape to be moved.

The 1864 map of Coal Creek Township shows the Asbury Methodist Episcopal Church on William Campbell's forty acres in section 26. J. Welliver owned this acreage in 1878, at which time the church was gone from the site and was located on section 25 on George Manner's 80 acre plot.

J. D. Wilson moved the old Asbury Chapel one hundred yards or so, to the southeast of the church site in July 1903 where it served the congregation until December. Services were held from that time until the following spring in the old Mount Pleasant church building.

The Asbury Methodist Episcopal Church was connected with the Pleasant Hill Circuit, Greencastle District, Northwest Indiana Conference, when a new board of Trustees was elected during the Quarterly Conference held in New Richmond on July 2, 1881. Lemuel McClamrock replaced James R. McClamrock, and George Pierce replaced William Wilson. In later years, Asbury (or Round Hill) was connected with the New Richmond Circuit.

The old Asbury Church building had served its members well, but was showing its age at the turn of the century. The members decided a new meeting place was badly needed and preliminary plans were begun to build a new structure. A $4,000 brick building was decided upon, and a meeting was held in April 1902 to discuss the project. Two thousand dollars were readily subscribed during this meeting, and it was decided the new edifice would be erected on the same site occupied by the old building. Plans were to start construction about the first of May that year, but construction was delayed until the following year.

The cornerstone-laying ceremony for the new Asbury Methodist church building at Round Hill was held October 11, 1903. The first part of the ceremony was held in the old church, with Reverends J.B. Coombs, L.O. Blake, and W.F. Clark conducting the services; the audience then moved to the scene of the cornerstone. Among the items placed in the receptacle were the names of the architect, contractors, brick masons, contributors to the purchase of a new bell, Sunday School books, song books and several Methodist Episcopal Church newspapers, and local newspapers, and other objects, and the receptacle was then sealed with Poston Brick. The face of the cornerstone, cut from Indiana's finest white limestone, bore the names of the committee on construction: J.D. Wilson, D.W. Pierce, and L.B. McClamrock. Construction was begun immediately, but bad weather in December delayed the contractors several weeks.

The New Richmond *Record*, Thursday, October 13, 1904, announced the dedication program of the new brick church "ASBURY" at Round Hill would take place the following Sunday. Rev. M.H. Appleby of South Bend was to have charge of the dedication, and the Reverends J.F. McDaniel of Crawfordsville, J.P. Shagley (Terre Haute), Charles Jakes (West Lafayette), and L.S. Buckles (of Thorntown) were to attend the ceremony. Because of the services there were to be no preaching services in any of the other churches of the New Richmond Methodist Episcopal Circuit.

On Sunday, October 15, 1904, the splendid new brick church at Round Hill was dedicated. The day was perfect, the people were happy, and the attendance was nearly double the seating capacity of the church. After Rev. M. H. Appleby delivered his sermon, Mr. James D. Wilson presented the church on behalf of the Board of Trustees, to be dedicated to the service and worship of Almighty God, and a new consecration was made by the people to the service of the Master.

The ladies of the church prepared lunch and served more than five hundred people in their new dining room at the noon hour. Services were held at 3 p.m. and 7 p.m. and the audience taxed the capacity of the new church during these services. A description of the new Asbury Methodist Episcopal Church edifice at Round Hill follows:

> The building of this pretty new church was begun a little more than a year ago, the laying of the corner stone occurring with fitting ceremonies on the afternoon of Sunday, October 11, 1903. The cost of the structure completed, amounts to more than $5,000 and the best part of it is that it is paid for in full and there is no debt hanging over that congregation. Much credit is due both the architect and the contractor, D.W. (Delbert) Pierce for its exterior and interior beauty. It is built of roughed Poston block and stone, cement steps, with cupola and bell, roofed with shingles, and has prettily painted steel ceiling. The windows are of beautiful colored glass and there are two memorial windows. The large and spacious basement is divided off into kitchen and festival hall, and the latter is of such proportions that 120 persons were at once comfortably seated at tables at the big dinner provided Sunday. It is provided with tables and seats and the kitchen with stove and

cooking utensils. The church is heated by a hot air furnace, and lighted by the automatic gasoline arc lights.

The auditorium was all beautifully carpeted, and seated with comfortable pews and handsome pulpit furniture, and hitchracks were built all about the church yard for the hitching of all horses, and everything was made ready in its entirety for the first service held in their new church.

Great credit is due to the enterprising people. They have not only built for themselves, but for their children and grandchildren, for this church ought to last for a hundred years. To say the very least it was a very signal and great victory.

The period between January 1921 and 1924 spelled disaster for the beautiful Asbury Methodist Episcopal Church at Round Hill. The members were transferring their membership to New Richmond Methodist Episcopal Church, to Linden, Elmdale, and many to Trinity and First Methodist Episcopal Church in Crawfordsville. The last date of removal was recorded April 17, 1935, but the church building was dismantled by that date. The bricks were salvaged and used as an addition to the brick building formerly erected by Starr Dunn in New Richmond.

The mystery of the conflict that destroyed the congregation of the Asbury church remains with the membership, but the dreams of those who played a part in the construction of the new brick edifice were badly shattered after a short twenty years of worship in a building expected to last a hundred or more years.

Among the family names who were members of the Asbury Methodist Episcopal Church at Round Hill in its final days were: Wilson, Myers, Peters, Patton, Patterson, Rafferty, Tribby, Vincent, Chadwick, Hall, Jones, McClamrock, Ames, Burk, Henderson, Pierce, and others.

ROUND HILL POST OFFICE

In July 1877, the citizens of the Round Hill neighborhood made an application to the department to have a post office established at Round Hill. The location given was eight miles north of Crawfordsville. The post office was established and John T. Tribby was appointed the first Postmaster of Round Hill Post Office the 25th of July 1877. Tribby served until the 18th of February 1878 when Thomas J. Bennett was appointed. The Round Hill Post Office was discontinued in December of 1879.

The 1878 Atlas of Montgomery County listed the Round Hill Post Office as having mail twice a week, but the patrons of the community were notified in January 1880 the Post Office at Round Hill was closed and their mail would be sent to Linden. This was one of the short-lived post offices in Coal Creek Township and was a disappointment to the neighborhood to have it closed.

The 1878 Atlas of Montgomery County, Indiana, shows that the little hamlet of Round Hill in Coal Creek Township consisted of the post office, School No. 6, Methodist Episcopal Church, a blacksmith shop (owned and operated by Thomas Bennett), and the residence of William W. Wilson. Dr. George Manners owned the land surrounding the Methodist Episcopal Church property, but the doctor and his wife, Barbara, were residents of New Richmond. Others in the neighborhood of Round Hill were: James B. Pierce, E. Burk, J. Alexander, Henry R. King, J. Welliver, J.W. Goben, W.R. Miller, Roda H. Jolley, Margaret and Charles Vancleave, and J. Eshelman.

The only trace of the Round Hill community today (1986) is the residence once occupied by William W. and Sophia (McGinnis) Wilson, whose descendants owned the home until a few years ago, selling to Mr. and Mrs. Stephen Waye and family.

The Wilson-Killin, or Asbury, Cemetery also remains as a ghostly reminder of the little hamlet of Round Hill, although it is north of the site of the hamlet. Land for the Asbury cemetery was deeded on the 17th of February 1851 by Samuel and Sarah Wilson and John and Sarah Ann Killen, to the trustees of Asbury Chapel of the Methodist Episcopal Church. The following is a transcript of the deed:

ASBURY CHAPEL GRAVEYARD
Deeds of Montgomery County Indiana, Volume 17, page 36.
Montgomery County Record,

THIS INDENTURE WITNESSETH, That W. Samuel Willson and Sarah his wife and John F. Killen and Sarah Ann his wife in Consideration of One Dollar to them paid by William Campbell, Sam'l Wilson, Moses Gillam Jno. A. King and Henry King Trustees of the Asbury Chapel of the Methodist Episcopal Church, the receipts whereof is hereby acknowledged do hereby grant, bargain, Sell and Convey to the said Trustees and to their Successors in office forever the following Real Estate in Montgomery County and State of Indiana and described as follows to WIT: a part of the South East quarter of the South West quarter of Section twenty three, in Township Twenty North of Range five west, and a part of the North East quarter of the South west quarter of the Same Section, Township and Range, and bounded as follows TO WIT: Beginning four rods South of the North East Corner of said South east quarter of South West quarter, from thence running due west Ten rods, thence due North eight rods, thence due East ten rods, thence due South Eight rods to the place of Beginning, Containing One half acre, the Same being hereby Conveyed for a grave yard together with all the privileges and appurtenances to the Same belonging.

TO HAVE AND TO HOLD, the same to the said Trustees and their successors in office forever. The grantors their heirs and assigns Hereby Covenanting with the grantees and their Successors in office that the title so conveyed is Clear, free and unencumbered, that they are lawfully Seized of the premises aforesaid as of a Sure, perfect and indefeasible estate of inheritance in fee Simple, and that they will WARRANT AND DEFEND the same against all claims whatsoever.

IN WITNESS WHEREOF, the Said Samuel Wilson and Sarah his wife and John F. Killen and Sarah Ann his wife who here by relinquishes all right to dower in Said premises have hereunto Set their hand, and Seals this 17th day of February 1851. sig. Samuel Wilson (seal); Sarah (X) Wilson (seal (her mark);
John Killen (seal); Sarah Ann Killen (seal)

WITNESS: Samuel W. Austin as to Sam'l Wilson and Sarah Wilson State of Indiana Montgomery County.

Personally appeared before me, the Subscriber a Notary Public duly Commissioned and Qualified in and for Said County Samuel Wilson and Sarah Wilson the grantor in the above conveyance, and acknowledged the Same to be their Voluntary act and deed.

And the Said Sarah Wilson wife of the said Samuel Wilson being examined by Me privately Separate and apart from, and without the hearing of her Said husband and the full Contents and purport of said Deed being by me made Known and explained to her acknowledged that she executed the Same of her own free will and accord, and without any coercion or compulsion from her said husband.

WITNESS my hand and Notarial Seal this 17th day of February 1851.
Sig. Saml W. Austin, Notary Public.

Place Names and Corners

While researching the history of New Richmond in the old Crawfordsville and New Richmond newspapers, news items appeared under very strange headings. Checking the family names under these headings, I discovered many were news items from the New Richmond area. At one time it appeared the writers were competing to see who could come up with the most unusual names for their columns, such as:

Vinegar Hill - located about one-half mile north of New Richmond. The Crawfordsville weekly *Review*, April 19, 1890, under the New Richmond items says, "There is a place not far from here called VINEGAR HILL. We suppose the name is derived from a sour lot of people living there." The late Dolly Miller, a resident of the hill, said she preferred to call her place of residence **Apple Hill**. It was possibly named for the fermented apple cider made from the apples grown on this hill.

Sleepy Hollow - located about three and one half miles southwest of New Richmond in the Clough family neighborhood, but the source of the name is unknown.

Bed Bug Corner - one and one-fourth miles west of New Richmond, named for a famous old log hotel that once occupied the corner during the stage-coach days.

Walnut Grove (First Location) - in Section 11, township 20, range 5, the 1878 map of Coal Creek township shows district school No.1 located about one mile east of New Richmond on an old road parallel to what later became the railroad. Nearby residences of Emma Alexander, two residences on J. Burris' land, Thomas Ward, Jr.; George W. Dewey - all were south and east of this school, and Charles Swier (Swear) owned the 160 acres surrounding the school.

Walnut Grove (Second Location) - Section 14, township 20, range 5, or one and one-half miles southeast of New Richmond. The Walnut Grove School (Dist. No.1) was moved to this location after the railroad was built through New Richmond. (1881)

Shawnee Mound - The Meharry neighborhood west of New Richmond was referred to as Shawnee Mound, and items concerning the Meharry family, and others nearby, were listed under this name, although the mound is several miles north-west of this area in Tippecanoe county.

Round Hill - located three miles southeast of New Richmond, situated on a little mound at the headwaters of Coal Creek.

Bristle Ridge - located about four miles southwest of New Richmond.

Roll's Run - located southwest of New Richmond, named for Aunt Polly Roll, a very spry old lady who is named in the Pleasant Hill Christian Church History.

No. 13 - southwest of New Richmond—near Wingate, near the Coal Creek bridge. The area was named for the 13th district school erected in Coal Creek Township. The school went by this name, and items appeared in the Crawfordsville newspapers under this title.

Utah - situated between Bristle Ridge and Pleasant Hill (Wingate).

Coal Creek Valley - located southwest of New Richmond near Center School.

Clarkson's Corner - located three miles west of New Richmond, named for the family residing on the corner.

Center - named for Center School, District No.7, and Center Christian Church, located at the nearest point in Coal Creek Township's center.

Patton's Corner - named for district school No.5, deeded by John and Nancy Patton, located three miles south of New Richmond.

Ashland - the remains of Bristle Ridge after S.A.R. Beach blasted stumps out with dynamite.

Cowan's Corner - located five miles south of New Richmond in the Cowan neighborhood. Kentwood, Taylor, or Quinine school stood on (and near) this corner.

Oakland - North of Elmdale, named for district school No.4, and the cemetery on the opposite corner.

Boston Store - later became Elmdale.

Pleasant Hill - later became Wingate.

Chapter 15 - Government

The Origin of Coal Creek Township

On May 4, 1829, the present township of Coal Creek was taken from Wayne Township. John Alexander and William Forbes were appointed fence viewers, and Charles Reed and Absalom Kirkpatrick were appointed overseers of the poor. The first election was ordered for the first Monday in August, 1829, to elect two trustees of the peace.

Absalom Kirkpatrick, a Whig, was a magistrate for fourteen years successively, until he resigned. He was employed to locate the public road from Covington to Strawtown, which he did, a distance of seventy miles, or more. He employed John Gilliland, of Crawfordsville to do the surveying. Absalom was the first incumbent of the office of land appraiser.

In 1836 there were fifty-six houses in Coal Creek Township. Josiah Hutchison, a life-long Democrat, made a trip to Crawfordsville and secured Mayor Bryce, a Democrat attorney, to make a speech for the Coal Creekers. Hutchison carried the news to every house in the township notifying them of the time and place. The speech was made and an election was held for Justice of the Peace. David Clarkson, of Clarkson's corner, was the Democratic nominee; Absalom Kirkpatrick was the choice of the Whigs. The Democrats won the nomination, but Clarkson, for some reason, dropped out shortly after, and the Whigs put Absalom Kirkpatrick in the office. Absalom Kirkpatrick witnessed the buying and selling of land in the New Richmond area and signed many deeds before his death on January 4, 1855.

Justice of the Peace in Coal Creek Township

Coal Creek Township was allowed, by law, two Justices of the Peace and two Constables, one each for the east part of the township and one each for the west. They were to keep law and order in the entire township and were elected by popular vote for terms of four years. The only compensation they received for their service was the fees they recovered from litigants in their courts. The same held true for those serving on juries. The Justices of the Peace who signed deeds in the township over the years and dates on the deeds follows (keep in mind this is not meant to be a complete record of the men or their terms):

Absalom Kirkpatrick, 1829-1846; Thomas Lamborn, 1838-1842; Samuel R. Smith, 1847-1856; Dan Mills, 1839; Samuel McComas, 1851 – 1876; Edward P. Bennett, 1856-1858; Joseph Galbreath, 1864; Moses L. Burk, 1860; David McDonald, 1882; Daniel Curtis, 1882; Thomas Foster (his obituary says he was a Justice of the Peace for a number of years – but no record of the dates); John G. Utterback, 1916 (John resigned because "business was too dull"); Amos Ebrite, Esq. 1870-1910 (served up to his death in 1910); 'Squire Earl, 1894; Walter D. Jones, 1889 (signed the Incorporation of the New Richmond Building, Loan Fund & Savings Association.)

On March 4, 1940, the trustees of the town of New Richmond discussed the need of a local magistrate and a petition was to be circulated for the appointment of a Justice of the Peace. The subject was brought up two months later, but the idea was dropped, and the town does not have a Justice of the Peace. The County Justices' offices were abolished several years ago.

Constables in the New Richmond Area

In an early history of the town of New Richmond, Nicholas L. Washburn was listed as the first constable in the New Richmond section of the township. Ben Swank was serving as Constable around 1879, and Elisha C. Campbell served around 1890 and 1891. During Campbell's term, a thief stole a "lot of jewelry and other stuff" from a New Richmond business establishment, and Constable Campbell shot at the man six times, and then hauled him off to the jail in Crawfordsville. He made several other arrests due to drunkenness and disturbances over the years. I am amazed at the number of times the constables tried to track down chicken thieves and smoke-house thieves in the 1880s. Many, many hams and sides of bacon disappeared about that time.

Squire Ebrite's Court

Squire Ebrite had the longest tenure (39 years) as a Justice of the Peace in the town of New Richmond. His grandson, Glenn Mitchell, said he certainly didn't hold the office expecting to make a profit, as most of the people brought before his court were "down and out". He often fined the individuals, and then paid the fine from his own pocket, so as not to take from the needy wife and children at home. Marshal Work settled many disputes between local residents by hauling them to Squire Ebrite's Court, most of them involving too much liquor.

One of the more entertaining cases was a case of property rights between a husband and wife. The case was venued from another court to Squire Ebrite's court. When the cases drew larger crowds of curious residents, Squire Ebrite held court in the local school house, such as the case below. The story was taken from the New Richmond *Record*, but to protect the innocent (myself) I will not reveal the dates, or the surname of the couple:

> Esq. Ebrite's court was occupied the greater part of the day Tuesday by the case of William _____ vs. Amanda, husband and wife, in a case of property rights, wherein a bay mare, supposed to be in the neighborhood of eight years of age, with a white spot in the forehead and sailing under the cognomen of "Maude," was the bone of contention. Three attorneys from Crawfordsville, two of which were Coal Creek township natives, M.E. (Mike) Foley and Matt Murphy, figured into the trial - on opposite sides of the fence, which made the local citizens take more interest in the trial. The jury to decide the legal ownership of Maude consisted of W.S. Turvey, W.H. Burris, Rev. G. W. Watkins, S.P. Harriman, G.L. Bastion, and James Smith.
>
> It seems there had been a split up in the family along the time the groundhog gently perambulated forth from Mother Earth in seek of his shadow, and from that time forth the dove of peace and domestic felicity has not hovered over the hearthstone of the _____ family, in fact since that time William and Amanda have ceased to be one, and while Wm. holds the fort at the old stamping grounds, Amanda has 'folded her tent' and now hangs forth in the classic village of Wingate. The bay mare Maude, according to William's version, was his—and his only, he having started in by securing a sow, which he paid for in work, that had raised pigs, which he traded for a calf, that grew to be a cow, that was traded for Maude when she was a two-year-old, and he had kept her until the severing of family ties, when upon one Sunday night she disappeared from the lot in which she was kept, and from that time forth, he has been led a jack-o-lantern chase trying to get her back. Now, Amanda's story is that she bought two pigs of Wm. for $2.50 and paid for them, that they were traded for the calf that grew into the cow, that was traded for Maude, and consequently said Maude is her property, and that she sent her son to get said mare out of the lot, that Maude was awarded to her by due process of law in Esq. Raisor's court at Wingate, and that on March 31, she sold said mare to one A. D. Snyder, New

Richmond's "John Judy," and she backed her claim up by the testimony of her son, daughter, and father. The case went to the jury about 3:30 p.m. and after due and grave consideration, the jury agreed to disagree, standing three in William's favor, and three in Amanda's favor. As for Maude, we knoweth not to whom she belongs.

A week later, Esq. Ebrite's Court was again occupied with the second round of William vs. Amanda's case of replevin. The two repeated their same stories and evidence, and a new jury was selected—who also decided to disagree, five in favor of Wm. and one for Amanda. They had wrestled with the case until 5 a.m. one morning. The Jury was A.W. Hempleman, Frank Smith, W.E. Grannon, T.B. Miller, James Clarkson, and H.G. Messer. The *Record* said, "the third trial of Wm. vs. Amanda will come up in Esq. Ebrite's court sometime the later part of this week, but as yet the date has not been named, and when it is, it will be but to declaim a legal holiday for New Richmond that all her citizens might once again hear the facts in the case in which the costs are already piling up most voluminously. It is anticipated to secure a jury of farmers to try the case this time—farmers, beware!"

The third, and which proved to be the final, trial of Wm. vs. Amanda to determine the ownership of the bay mare "Maude" was held in Esq. Ebrite's court on a Saturday, about a month after the second trail was held. The jury consisted of: Bayless Alexander, Al Bailey, John Henderson, William Kite, Thomas Cook, and Thomas Grantham, who reached a verdict and gave aforesaid "Maude" to Amanda! The plaintiff, William, had to pay the court costs of around $60 which was the worth of the mare, and he and Amanda "aired out all their domestic troubles" in public, but, was that the end of the story? NO! William had procured a pension improperly and had been drawing the pension, but it was stopped; and after the trials of "Maude" and lawing over everything in sight, Wm. and Amanda separated.

William moved to the Soldier's Home in Danville, Illinois, and Amanda left for Chicago. Things went quietly along the countryside until one day when they both appeared to dispose of the products of the farm (which was divided between the two). How they happened to arrive in town at the same time is mysterious, but they were both in New Richmond and had round four on the elevator grounds. Wm. threatened to use a large sized revolver on Amanda, and that clever lady hustled herself out of town before the threat was executed. The citizens of New Richmond were anxiously awaiting another chapter to the story, but I did not discover any. The editor of the *Record* was fond of the Maud Muller poems by Whittier, and printed several variations in his paper over the years; the following poem was published about the time of the famous trials above, it goes like this:

MAUDE'S BROTHER AND JAKE
Jake Muller on a summer's day, raked the meadows sweet with hay.
The mule, with which he raked the hay, was muckle dun with streaks of gray.
Jake's shirt was of hickory, and pants brown, with a patch on the place where he sits down.
Jake cussed in a way that was hard to see, for the mule went haw—when he said gee.
A bumble bee's nest in a stubble lay, where Jake and the mule raked the clover hay.
A tooth ran through the bumble home, and the bees came out and began to roam,
In search of the man that summer day, who raked the meadows of clover hay.
The bees swarmed inside of Muller's shirt and quickened the mule to a lively spurt.
It was tough on the mule, and worse on Jake, and worse still on the sulky rake.
for the mule turned loose in a promiscuous way and scattered the rake all over the hay.

NOTARY PUBLICS

The local Justices of the Peace were usually nearby to authenticate contracts, acknowledge deeds, take affidavits, depositions, etc., as well as carrying out his duties as the local judge. After the death of Squire Ebrite, there was a need for a local Notary Public in the town of New Richmond.

Edgar Walts, the publisher and editor of the New Richmond *Record*, advertised from November 1900 to July 6, 1922, "Edgar Walts, NOTARY PUBLIC, Pension papers, Mortgages, Deeds, and all kinds of legal papers acknowledged. Office, *Record* printing office." Other Notaries were: William L. Lee, 1899; Anne Smithe, 1920-1922; Starr Dunn, 1924; John L. McNeil, 1924; Estella M. Creahan, 1927; Maurice Coffman, 1931-1933; Robert C. King, 1936; Lon P. Brown, 1937; Boyd O. McNeil, 1934-1940; Helen G. Oppy, 1943; Levert E. Binns, 1951; Helen Oppy Binns, 1957-1974 (see Helen G. Oppy); Ruthanna Oppy, 1975-1977; Creo Pruett, 1980-1983.

ORIGINAL TOWN OF NEW RICHMOND AND ADDITIONS

The original plat of New Richmond was bordered on the north by Washington Street; on the west by Wabash Street; on the east by Vine Street. (Vine Street was vacated by the Dr. Detchon residence at a very early date, the house being erected on the very center of this street). No street was laid out on the southern border of the original plat, which reads as follows:

ORIGINAL PLAT OF NEW RICHMOND, INDIANA
Montgomery County Deeds, Volume 5, page 474

Town of New Richmond, laid out by Samuel Kincaid is situated in the W½ of the N. W. Qt. of Section ten T. 20 N. of R. 5 W. the lots are 74¼ Ft. front by 148½ back, with the exception of Lot 4 in block 4 which is but 66 Ft. front and lots in 1 & 2 in (___ ?) block 1-2-3 & 4 in block 3 are but 137 Ft. in Length, the streets cross each other at right angles and are all 60 Ft. wide as appears by the plan. The alleys are 10 Ft. wide. The bearing of the streets is N. & S., E. & W. Astronomically. The plan is drawn to a scale of 105 Ft. to the inch a true draught.

John Gilliland, C. S. (County Surveyor)

NOTE: (a map of the plat is drawn on this page in the deed book).
State of Indiana SS
Montgomery County
Personally appeared before me the undersigned

Recorder in and for said county, Samuel Kincaid and acknowledged the within Town Plat, to be his volluntary [*sic*] act and deed for the purposes There in contained. Given under my hand and Seal this twenty seventh day of July A. D. 1836.

G. Miller (Seal) Rec. M. C.
Rec'd for record 27th of July 1836
and Recorded 28th July 1836
G. Miller, R. M. C.

The name of the town and the name of the streets have never been changed and there is no record as to the reason for selecting the names. It is believed the town was named for Richmond, Virginia, birthplace of Samuel Kincaid. The road running north and south through New Richmond was known as the "Lafayette & Yountsville" road, the east and west road was the "Strawtown to Covington" road in early years.

The first owners of the lots of the Original Plat of New Richmond are listed below:

Lot No.	Grantor	Grantee	Date of purchase	Vol.	Page
BLOCK No. 1					
1.	Samuel Kincaid	David Oppy	Mar. 12, 1839	8	41
2.	Samuel Kincaid	Richard Gaines	Oct. 12, 1838	17	28
3.	Samuel Kincaid	David Oppy	Mar. 12, 1839	8	41
4.	Samuel Kincaid	Eli Elrod	Apr. 25, 1839	14	375
5.	Samuel Kincaid	Nathan Volra	Mar. 1, 1839	9	709
6.	Samuel Kincaid	Solomon Border	Apr. 25, 1839	9	441
7.	Samuel Kincaid	Solomon Border	Apr. 25, 1839	9	441
8.					
BLOCK No. 2					
1.	Samuel Kincaid	David Oppy	Mar. 12, 1839	8	41
2.[1]					
3.	Samuel Kincaid	William McBroom	Mar. 31, 1838	7	505
4.	Samuel Kincaid	William McBroom	Nov. 27, 1837	7	503
5.	Samuel Kincaid	David Oppy	Mar. 12, 1839	8	41
6.	Samuel Kincaid	David Oppy	Mar. 12, 1839	8	41
7.	Samuel Kincaid	David Oppy	Mar. 12, 1839	8	41
8.					
BLOCK No. 3					
1.	Samuel Kincaid	David Oppy	Mar. 12, 1839	8	41
2.	Samuel Kincaid	David Oppy	Mar. 12, 1839	8	41
3.	Samuel Kincaid	David Oppy	Mar. 12, 1839	8	41
4.	Samuel Kincaid	David Oppy	Mar. 12, 1839	8	41
BLOCK No. 4					
1.	Samuel Kincaid	David Oppy	Mar. 12, 1839	8	41
2.	Samuel Kincaid	David Oppy	Mar. 12, 1839	8	41
3.	Samuel Kincaid	David Oppy	Mar. 12, 1839	8	41
4.	Samuel Kincaid	David Oppy	Mar. 12, 1839	8	41

I did not locate deeds for lot 8 in block 1; or lot 8 in block 2, may have overlooked them.

Additions to the Town of New Richmond - In Chronological Order:

Name of Addition	No. of Add'n	Date	No. of Lots	Vol.	Page
Barbara G. Manners	1st.	30 Sep 1885	4	57	212-213
Stow S. Detchon	1st.	19 Nov 1887	5	61	40-41
Stow S. Detchon	2nd.	6 Mar 1888	1	61	411-412
Barbara G. Manners	2nd	12 Dec 1888	10	62	408-409
Stow S. Detchon	3rd	30 Mar 1889	8	63	287-288
James W. Tribby	1st	10 May 1890	9	65	109-110
Stow S. Detchon	4th	2 Oct 1890	4	65	523-524
James W. Tribby	2nd	17 Feb 1891	6	66	361-362
Stow S. Detchon	5th	21 Feb 1891	4	66	352-353
Barbara G. Manners	3rd	17 Apr 1891	8	66	573-574
Barbara G. Manners	4th	19 Sep 1892	10	69	444-445
Stow S. Detchon	6th	21 Mar 1893	4	71	54-55

---

[1] I was unable to locate a deed from Kincaid to William McBroom, but McBroom sold lots 2 & 3 in Block 2 in 1845 to George Ebrite.

Name of Addition	No. of Add'n	Date	No. of Lots	Vol.	Page
Stow S. Detchon	7th	17 Apr 1893	8	71	157-158
George T. Phillips	2nd	10 Feb 1896	2	76	543-544
(Official Plat of New Richmond)		4 Oct 1897		79	190-191
Stow S. Detchon	8th	8 May 1899	2	82	274-275
Orlando W. Mason	1st	21 Sep 1901	4	87	292-293
Thomas M. Foster	1st	10 Mar 1905	8	94	571-572
Geo. W. Washburn	1st	15 Mar 1905	7	95	289-290
Charles Kirkpatrick	1st	7 Jun 1911	23	105	604-605
Charles Kirkpatrick	2nd	2 Aug 1913	32	108	358-60

NEW RICHMOND BECOMES AN INCORPORATED TOWN

"If the non-taxpayers here who are so anxious to have the town incorporated would only attend to their own business, as well as they do other people's, how nice everything would be in our village."

"Some people here want the town incorporated, and especially those who pay no taxes, are loud in their talk of it."

"There is one person who could show a $10,000 bond as quick as he could a tax receipt, who is especially desirous that the town should 'take on city airs.' Now it will do for people who never pretend to pay taxes to swing their hats and want this place incorporated, but for the man who is taxed to death on gravel roads, it looks like robbery."

"The parties who talk of petitioning the Legislature to incorporate this place had just as well let up, as both sides can petition. Why do they want to force something on the people they don't want? It does look as if the majority of the tax-payers should have a hearing, and for non tax-payers to talk such stuff is entirely out of place."

"The 'slick-six' would like to show their hands if they could. They are going to incorporate our village, build factories, and play the devil, generally, to hear them tell it. They are not over-stocked with money-their strong hold is tongue-wagging, which is continually."

Can't you just imagine an old general store full of loafers, sitting around the old pot-bellied stove trying to decide how to put a stop to such an important event as incorporating the town in which they reside—each one trying to top the previous man's excuse for not incorporating, each one of them wanting progress "as long as it don't get in my way." In researching the history of New Richmond, I constantly played a little game of trying to decide just who the "slick-six" were, but I always came up with uneven numbers, such as three, five, or seven. Well, I guess we'll never know!

The talk against incorporating the town started soon after the railroad was constructed through the town of New Richmond. The first mention, which was of course against it, was in 1888. The town experienced a surge in building and in population about this time; although there were no recorded reasons for the incorporation, there were plenty of reasons not to, before 1890. The "slick six" decided to change their tactics, thinking maybe they should give some good concrete reasons for incorporating.

Bill Campbell, the New Richmond correspondent for the Crawfordsville weekly *Review*, decided to meet them half way and print their reasons, "Men who pay small taxes, and wanted the town incorporated gave the excuse that Charley Woliver's poor cow got a few mouthfuls of grass on the streets." He then asked the people of New Richmond to "look at the villages that are incorporated, and if our village does not compare, we will submit." Those pushing the incorporation were, at least, paying small taxes now, that should have helped their cause.

Campbell continues with, "One man said he wants to put a stop to drunkedness, and we will make the assertion that there are towns surrounding New Richmond that are incorporated, that has two drunken men to one in this place. When you want to pay high taxes and stand law-suits, INCORPORATE!"

"New-comers to our town who cry so loud for incorporation should remember that no one forced them to move here and they should not try to lead old citizens who have made the town what it is."

William Campbell's parents and grandparents had settled in New Richmond long before the town was even platted.

The question of incorporating the town was being discussed in other parts of the county, and one interested party wrote, "The question of incorporating the town of New Richmond is being strongly agitated. This is the proper spirit and we hope the efforts of those who have taken the matter in hand will be successful. New Richmond is one of the best towns in the county and the best is not too good for her." The *Review*, November 5, 1892, announced, "Thomas S. Patton, Charles A. Taylor, and J.W. Hollen (Hollin) are the petitioners to incorporate the town of New Richmond. If perseverance will win, these gentlemen will surely be in it." Well, we now know who one-half of the "slick six" were, but the petition was voted down in January of 1893. William Campbell had moved to Kirkpatrick previous to this date, and in his items (he now was the correspondent for Kirkpatrick) he said, "BULLY! Boys of New Richmond, you voted the corporation down and you never did a better thing. Success to you, stay with it. We say a town board for New Richmond and a blue coated Marshal—Bah!"

The town was becoming very unruly a year later and complaints of "Hoodlumism at New Richmond" were smearing the name of the little village. One article says, "Hoodlums collected upon the sidewalks along the street to the depot Saturday night and indulged in the pastime of insulting ladies who were compelled to walk in the middle of the street to get around the drunken wretches. A wide-mouthed desperado threw beer upon two of the group of four who were passing, and called them vile names, etc."

In another incident, a set of young thugs called out a participant in the Methodist church festivities and proceeded to "pommel" him. The writer of the article said, "stronger argument could not be offered for incorporation. The citizens will soon have upon their hands a mountain of disgrace if they tamely submit to the desecration of their churches by drunken, gambling thugs, that cannot be washed away by a spring shower. Until you have proper officers to command the peace and enforce the laws by severe punishment, you will be beset and tormented by just such hoodlums as visited the church Saturday night." New Richmond was the proud owner of a local newspaper, the *Enterprise*, by then, and the editor of the paper appears to be in favor of the incorporation of the town. The above editorial appeared in the *Enterprise* July 22, 1893.

The "slick-six" and other interested parties filed another petition to incorporate the village of New Richmond before the county commissioners on Wednesday, December 4, 1894, and to show the steps taken to incorporate the village, I have copied the following documents in their entirety.

COMMISSIONERS *Record* BOOK 21, page 221-222
The Board of County Commissioners of Montgomery County Indiana met Wednesday Morning December 5, 1894 in Regular Session
Present, John Peterson. Allen Byers. and Henry Harding.
State of Indiana
SS
County of Montgomery
Before the Commissioners of Montgomery County, December Session 1894
To the Honorable, the Board of Commissioners of Montgomery County.

Your petitioners would respectfully represent that they are citizens and legal voters of Montgomery County, Indiana. That they are all bona fide residents of the following territory situate in Coal Creek Township in said County of Montgomery, and State of Indiana, to wit:- Part of Sections nine (9) and ten (10) in Township twenty (20) North of Range five (5) West, bounded as follows: Beginning at a stone twenty (20) chains and forty (40) links South from the Northwest corner of the Southwest Quarter (¼) of said section ten (10) and running thence East eight (8) chains and ninety four (94) links, thence North nineteen (19) chains and thirty eight links, thence North 79° 15' East eight (8) chains and seventy nine (79) links, thence South 87° 45' East twenty four (24) chains thence North 8°

55' West seven (7) chains and fifty four links, thence North six (6) chains, thence West sixteen (16) chains and seventy five (75) links, thence North five (5) chains, thence West thirty seven (37) chains passing out of said section ten (10) into said section nine (9), thence South thirty seven (37) chains and eighty five (85) links thence East thirteen (13) chains and forty (40) links to the point of beginning containing one hundred thirty (130) acres.

That they caused an accurate survey and map of said territory to be made by William F. Hunt county surveyor of said county, and that the above description of the territory above described shows the courses and distances of the boundaries of said territory as furnished said Hunt in said survey and map.

That said territory according to the census taken by Robert S. Osborn contained Three Hundred and Sixty (p.222) inhabitants on the 5th day of November, 1894.

p.222 Your petitioners therefore pray an order, declaring that said territory with the assent of the qualified voters as provided by law be an incorporated town, by the name of New Richmond and they represent that there is no other town in the state of Indiana of that name. And your petitioners will ever pray.

p. 222 Commissioner's Record Book No. 21
Solomon Dewey, F. M. Smith, P. S. Turvey, O. W. Mason, R. S. Osborn, Ira Stout, Dora Ammerman and 59 others
State of Indiana
SS
County of Montgomery

In the matter of the petition of Solomon Dewey etal for the Incorporation of the town of New Richmond.

Comes now Solomon Dewey and sixty-five others, residents and legal voters of the territory sought to be incorporated, and file and present their verified petition, which reads in the words and figures following, (insert) and also a report of the census of said territory verified by the affidavit of the person taking such census. (here insert) and also a report of the survey of said territory and map thereof, verified by the affidavit of the surveyor making the same (here insert), and also file and present proof of publication of notice and posting of notices of this petition and application (here insert), and also proof of posting of census and survey (here insert). And said petitioners further file and present to the Board the affidavit of Robert S. Osborn, and introduce oral proof.

And this matter being submitted to the Board, the Board after hearing the evidence and being fully and sufficiently advised in the premises, finds that the whole number of legal voters in said territory is one hundred and twenty two (122), and that sixty six of them had signed said petition, being more than one-third thereof; that an accurate map and survey of the premises had been made showing the length courses and distances of the boundaries thereof and the quantity of land and number of acres within said territory; and that an accurate census of the resident population had been taken exhibiting the name of every head of a family, with the numbers composing each family, and the number and names of legal voters residing with in said territory on the 5th day of November 1894 not more than thirty days before the presenting of this petition, and that said survey, map and census had been each made and verified as the law directs and left within a convenient place within said territory for the examination and inspection of those having an interest in said application, for a period of not less than twenty days before the filing of said petition. And the Board finding that the law has in all things been complied with, that due publication and notices has been given and posted, It is therefore ordered by the Board that the said territory, to wit:-situate in the county of Montgomery and the State of Indiana be and the same is hereby declared with the assent of the qualified voters of said territory to be an incorporated town by the name of New Richmond.

And it is further ordered that the auditor cause to be printed in the New Richmond Enterprise and cause to be posted up in not less than ten public places with said territory a notice for the meeting of the qualified voters resident in said territory at a convenient place to wit: at a room, in the BLACK BEAR HOTEL in said town of New Richmond and with in said territory on the 27th day of December, 1894, to determine whether such territory shall be an incorporated town.

John Peterson
Allen Byers
Henry Harding Com's.

p. 292 COMMISSIONERS *Record* BOOK NO. 21
Regular Session, March 7, 1895
The Board of Commissioners of Montgomery County Indiana met in Regular Session, Thursday Morning, March 7, 1895
Present, John Peterson, Allen Byers and Henry W. Harding

In the matter of the Incorporation of the Town of New Richmond.

Come, now the petitioners in the above matter by Crane and Anderson, their Attorneys and file proof of the publication and posting of notices of the election heretofore at the December Session 1894, of this board, ordered to be held (here insert) and said petitioners now file the statement of the inspectors of such election verified by the affidavit of such inspectors (here insert statement verified by affidavit) and it appearing to the satisfaction of the Board by affidavits filed and by one proof that said election was duly and legally held in all respects according to law and in pursuance of the order heretofore entered and of the notices heretofore given in this matter and that at such election there were cast eighty-nine votes, of which sixty-two were cast in favor of such incorporation and twenty-seven against the incorporation.

It is therefore declared by the Board that said Town of New Richmond has been incorporated by and under the name and style of the Town of New Richmond.

Town Officials

1895 (The First Town Officials)

Horace G. Messer, (Trustees)Pres.
Orlando W. Mason
Stow S. Detchon
Marshal - Marion Smith
Clerk - George F. Long

Treasurer - J. P. Clark
Assessor - William Dewey
Town Attorney - Jere West (of Crawfordsville)

1899

Albert D. Snyder
Perry McLain
Bert E. Page
Clerk - George F. Long
Treasurer - W. S. Alexander
Marshal - John A. Work
Town Attorney - ?

1903 (Elected Monday, May 4, 1903)

A. D. Snyder - 1st Ward
B. E. Page - 2nd Ward
Perry McLain - 3rd Ward
Clerk - George F. Long
Treasurer - W.S. Alexander
Marshal - John A. Work

1906 (Elected November 7, 1905) Election held in Town Building on Franklin St.)

Albert D. Snyder - 1st Ward[1]
B. E. Page - 2nd Ward
Wm. H. Long - 3rd Ward
Clerk - Frank E. Campbell[2]
Treasurer - W. S. Alexander
Marshal - John Work
Town Attorney - Esquire (Amos) Ebrite
Health Officer - Dr. Frank M. Lynn

1911

L. P. Brown - 1st Ward (Pres.)
Frank E. Campbell[3] - 2nd Ward
William Kirkpatrick - 3rd Ward
Clerk - Ed King
Treasurer - Samuel Magruder
Marshal - John A. Work
Fire Chief - Joe Young

1914, January 1 (Elected Nov. 4, 1913)

L. P. Brown - 1st Ward

---

[1] Snyder resigned March 5, 1906-change of residence; Dr. Charles E. Kelsey appointed same date to complete his term. Dr. Chas. E. Kelsey resigned May 6, 1907; moved to Albuquerque, N. M. for his health; John P. Bible appointed to complete the term.

[2] Frank E. Campbell resigned as Clerk Oct. 5, 1908; Ed. King appointed Oct. 9th to complete Campbell's term.

[3] F. E. Campbell resigned; George F. Long appointed to complete term Sept. 11, 1914.

F. E. Campbell - 2nd Ward[1]
J. M. Conway - 3rd Ward
Clerk - Ed King
Treasurer - Orlando W. Mason[2]
Marshal - John A. Work

1916, January 1 (elected November 4, 1915)

L. P. Brown - 1st Ward (Pres.)
George F. Long - 2nd Ward[3]
Joseph M. Conway - 3rd Ward
Clerk - Ed King
Treasurer - Fred Hunt
Marshal - John A. Work
Fire Chief - Frank E. Campbell

1918, January 7

James T. Parlon - 1st Ward (Pres.)
William H. Hollin - 2nd Ward
Richard D. Thomas - 3rd Ward
Clerk - Ed King[4]
Treasurer - Edgar Walts
Marshal - John A. Work
Fire Chief - Clell Terrill

1919

James T. Parlon - 1st Ward (Pres)
William H. Hollin - 2nd Ward
Richard D. Thomas - 3rd Ward
Clerk
Treasurer
Marshal
Fire Chief

1923

George C. Livingston - 1st Ward (Pres.)
William H. Hollin - 2nd Ward
Richard D. Thomas - 3rd Ward
Clerk - Ann Smith (Sec)
Treasurer - [5]
Marshal - John A. Work

---

[1] F. E. Campbell resigned Sept. 11, 1914; Geo. F. Long appointed to complete term.

[2] O.W Mason resigned Sep. 7, 1916; Wm Kirkpatrick completed his term.

[3] George F. Long died Dec. 27, 1917; James Alexander completed term.

[4] Ed King resigned (date?); E. N. Sharp was to complete the term but resigned Jan. 5, 1920; Melvin J. Roth appointed same date to complete the term.

[5] John Henderson was Treasurer Dec. 7, 1922 meeting, but was not listed on the above list.

1924, January Meeting

George C. Livingston - 1st Ward
William H. Hollin - 2nd Ward
Richard D. Thomas - 3rd Ward
Clerk - Ann Smith
Treasurer - Arthur D. Long
Marshal - John A. Works (Work)
Fire Chief - Roy E. Brown[1]
Dog Police - E. E. Baldwin (first time this office is listed)

1926, January 1 Meeting

George C. Livingston - 1st Ward (Pres.)
Earl L. Warren - 2nd Ward
Melvin J. Roth (Dr) - 3rd Ward
Clerk - Ann Smith
Treasurer - A. D. Long
Marshal - John A. Work (appointed)
Fire Chief - Roy E. Brown
Town Attorney - A. N. Foley
Dog Police - E. E. Baldwin

1928, January 2 (Elected November 8, 1927) Great Depression Years-Many Changes

James T. Parlon - 1st Ward (Pres) elected four years
Earl L. Warren - 2nd Ward
Melvin J. Roth - 3rd Ward[2]
Clerk - Ann Smith[3]
Treasurer - Levi Thomas
Marshal - John A. Work[4]
Fire Chief - Roy E. Brown
Dog Police - E. E. Baldwin

1930, January 6 Meeting (Depression Years-Many Changes)

James Parlon - 1st Ward (Pres.)[5]
Edward King[6]
Levi Thomas - 3rd Ward (Levi was made Pres. after Parlon resigned)
Clerk - J. D. Hinman
Treasurer - C. W. Daniels[7]
Marshal - Sanford "Sant" Black
Fire Chief - Roy Brown
Health Officer - J. D. Hinman (appointed)

---

[1] Lynn Timmons resigned March 6, 1924 as Fire Chief; Roy Brown appointed same date

[2] Roth resigned Jan. 23, 1928; Charles Oswalt completed his term.

[3] Ann Smith resigned March 6, 1929; Ruth Coffman appointed March 15th to complete term to Dec. 31, 1929.

[4] Marshal John Work relieved of duties Feb. 6, 1929; Sanford Black appointed Feb. 8th 1929 to complete term.

[5] James Parlon resigned July 5, 1932; Boyd O. NcNeil to complete his term.

[6] Edward King died February 1931; James Alexander appointed to complete his term. Alexander resigned Sep. 2, 1931; H. D. Kindell to complete term, but he resigned July 7, 1932; Raymond Rice took oath of office to complete term-same date.

[7] Treasurer's job abolished June 16, 1931; combined with Clerk's office; Daniels resigned

Dog Police - E. E. Baldwin
Town Attorney - Foley & Foley
This year the dog police position and the fire chief position were abolished; Roy Brown resigned.

1934, JANUARY 1 MEETING (ELECTION HELD NOVEMBER 7, 1933)

Thomas Allen - 1st Ward[1]
Earl L. Warren - 2nd Ward
Charles Fruits - 3rd Ward (Pres.)
Clerk-Treasurer - Robert King[2]
Street Commissioner - J. D. Hinman
Health Officer - J. D. Hinman
Custodian of Fire Engines - J. D. Hinman
Custodian of Town Hall - J. D. Hinman
Marshal, when necessary - J. D. Hinman

1935, JANUARY 7 (TO NOTE CHANGES IN OFFICIALS)

Clyde A. Thomas - 1st Ward
Earl L. Warren - 2nd Ward
Charles M. Fruits - 3rd Ward (Pres.)
Clerk-Treasurer - Delmar K. Fruits
Marshal - J. D. Hinman
Street Commissioner - J. D. Hinman
Health Officer - J. D. Hinman
Town Attorney - Thomas E. O'Conner

1935, 1936, 1937 AND 1938

All officers are the same except in 1938 a Fire Chief, Maurice Coffman, was added to the list.

1939

Same as 1938

1940, JANUARY 1 (ELECTED NOVEMBER 7, 1939

Sheridan Geiger - 1st Ward
James M. Alexander - 2nd Ward (Pres.)[3]
Carl Burnett - 3rd Ward
Clerk-Treasurer - Lester W. Olin
Fire Chief - Morris (Maurice) Coffman
Marshal - J. D. Hinman
Street Commissioner - J. D. Hinman
Town Attorney - Thomas E. O'Connor

1946, OCTOBER 21

T. Richard Shotts - 3rd Ward (Pres)

---

[1] Thomas Allen resigned Nov. 5, 1934; Delmar Fruits completed term, appointed Dec. 3

[2] Robert King resigned Nov. 5, 1934; Clyde Thomas completed his term.

[3] J. M. Alexander resigned March 11, 1941; Charles Taylor appointed Mar. 15th to complete term. Carl Burnett was then made President-same date.

Forrest Waye - 1st Ward
Monroe C. Lyon - 2nd Ward
Clerk-Treasurer
Marshal - James Harris

1950 (?)

Ora Newnum - 1st Ward
Thomas Oppy - 2nd Ward
Ocie Hershberger - 3rd Ward
Clerk-Treasurer – Ora Perry

1952

Robert M. Thayer - 1st Ward (Pres.)[1]
George Inskeep - 2nd Ward
O. L. Hershberger - 3rd Ward
Clerk-Treasurer - Ora Perry[2]
Town Attorney - Walter Haney

1960, JANUARY (ELECTED NOVEMBER 3, 1959)

James Wright - 1st Ward
Thomas Lane - 2nd Ward[3]
Ivan Pollock - 3rd Ward
Clerk-Treasurer - Malcolm Waye
Marshal - Gerold Ottinger

1963

Same officers as 1960 except Bill Kindell who was added in 1962

1964, JANUARY (ELECTION ON NOVEMBER 5, 1963)

Royce Whitehead - 1st Ward
William Kindell - 2nd Ward[4]
Albert Boone - 3rd Ward
Clerk-Treasurer - Malcolm G. Waye
Marshal - Roy Kerr[5]
Water Works Commissioner - Malcolm G. Waye
Assistant water Works commissioner - Floyd Davis
Fire Chief - Robert Thayer

1968, JANUARY 10

James Wright - 1st Ward
E. Leonard Andrews - 2nd Ward

---

[1] Robert Thayer served two terms and was President three years.
[2] Perry served a short time, and was replaced by Ralph Wildman; Ralph moved away and Lester W. Olin completed his term.
[3] Tom Lane died February 20, 1962; William "Bill" Kindell completed his term.
[4] William Kindell resigned; Merle Rutledge appointed in June 1967
[5] Roy Kerr resigned, Howard Cox appointed in April 1964

Richard "Beck" Lane - 3rd Ward
Clerk-Treasurer - Malcolm G. Waye
Water Works Superintendent - Wayne Jones
Marshal - not selected in Jan.

1972, August 21

James Wright - 1st Ward[1]
Harold B. Widmer - 2nd Ward
Ivan Pollock - 3rd Ward
Clerk-Treasurer - E. Leonard Andrews

1976, January 15 (Elected November 4, 1975—First election in eight years.)

Morris Geiger - 1st Ward
James Fenters - 2nd Ward[2]
Terry Barnes - 3rd Ward
Clerk - Treasurer-Janet Brown

1980

Richard C. Vaughn - 1st Ward
James Cox - 2nd Ward[3]
Ted Kerr - 3rd Ward
Clerk-Treasurer - Janet Brown[4]

1981, October

Richard. (Rick) Vaughn - 1st Ward
Richard Verhey - 2nd Ward
Sheryl J. Puckett - 3rd Ward
Clerk-Treasurer - Linda Layton
Marshal - Oney Shoaf
Deputy Marshal - Mark Clapp
Water Superintendent - Carroll Puckett
Street Superintendent - Wm. "Bill" Lane
Fire Chief - Roger Kunkel

1984-1985

David Barker - 1st Ward
Richard Verhey - 2nd Ward
S. Joan Puckett - 3rd Ward
Clerk-Treasurer - Janet Brown
Fire Chief - Roger Kunkel
Water Superintendent - Carroll Puckett
Street Superintendent - vacant

---

[1] Wright moved away; Jerry Stephens completed his term
[2] James Fenters resigned; Keith Kelp completed his term-appointed 1978.
[3] Jim Cox resigned 1981-moved to the country; Richard Verhey appointed April 29, 1981.
[4] Janet Brown resigned December 1980; Linda Layton appointed January 1, 1981 to complete her term.

Town Hall

On December 27, 1894, the qualified voters residing in the village of New Richmond met in a room in the Black Bear Hotel to decide if they wished to incorporate the town. It was decided to go ahead, and proceedings to incorporate were followed. An election was held and eighty nine votes were cast. Sixty-two were in favor of the incorporation, and twenty-seven against.

A description of the three wards of the new Town of New Richmond, Indiana, was signed by Squire (Amos) Ebrite, William Winter Washburn, and Ira Stout. The first town officials met for the first five years in the same room in the Black Bear Hotel where the above historic meeting was held. The hotel stood on the west side of south Wabash Street, just north of the railroad. The town's first jail was erected across the street from the hotel.

The town's **first town hall** was located on north Franklin Street, and a description of the lot is included in the volunteer fire department chapter. The building was leased in 1899 from Stow Detchon; in December 1908 the trustees purchased the lot and building from Stow's widow Jemima and son John T. Detchon. The trustees met in this building a few years, but many of their meetings were held in the Corn Exchange Bank's meeting room, as the surroundings were more pleasant and comfortable.

40 - New Richmond's town hall, built 1970

The **second town hall** was located on east Washington Street, and was purchased by the town trustees on April 13, 1925. The trustees continued to meet in the Corn Exchange Bank until they built an office on the ground floor of their brick building in January of 1930. At this time the following bills were presented to the town board of New Richmond for remodeling and painting the town hall: Coffman's garage, electric material and labor - $122.02; Forrest Waye, painting town hall - $22.80; Walter W. Harriman, carpenter work on town hall - $52.50; Roscoe Cohran (Cochran), carpenter work on town hall - $85.50; Clell Terrill, for use of cement mixer for town hall - $12.00; New Richmond Lumber & Coal Co., for materials used on town hall - $188.52.

This building served as the meeting place of the town trustees until October 1981, when the building was sold to the Tri-County Telephone Co. The town's office was moved to a smaller brick building on south Wabash previous to this date. In September 1983, the trustees leased the building from Ralph Kunkel with an option to buy the structure. The fire trucks had been moved to another structure on west Madison Street in 1980.

Possibly the most trying times the trustees of New Richmond had were during the years of the Great Depression. The local Corn Exchange Bank had handled the funds for the town since the incorporation, but on May 28, 1930, the bank closed its doors and the town's funds were tied up in the liquidation proceedings. The Trustees were advised to borrow money from Citizen's National Bank of Crawfordsville to pay the debts of the town. The funds were later transferred to the Linden State Bank, as it was closer to New Richmond and more convenient. In March of 1933, the town's funds were again frozen when the Linden bank declared a "Bank Holiday." The trustees were again compelled to return to the Citizen's National Bank to borrow money to take care of the town's expenses. By July 1934, the Linden Bank had re-opened and was ready to handle New Richmond's town funds, but the Corn Exchange Bank in New Richmond had closed its doors permanently.

During the closings of the bank, the people of New Richmond felt they had suffered all the punishment they could endure; many had lost great sums of money. A lack of rainfall produced a hot, dry summer, and the dry, dusty streets became very unbearable that year. The trustees tried to purchase a sprinkling truck to lay the dust, but couldn't get the money to complete the deal. Eventually they purchased a vehicle and mounted a large tank for water and chemicals on the rear of this truck. This proved to be more of an expense than it was worth, requiring many costly repairs, so plans to black-top the streets were begun.

John Detchon loaned the trustees $500 until the Corn Exchange Bank could pay a dividend to the town, and an agreement was made with William M.E. Layne to "tarvie" all that part of Washington Street in town, comprising two blocks in the center of New Richmond between Franklin and Prairie Streets, from curb to curb, etc. and other streets that may be agreed upon. The cost was to be 25¢ per square yard. The contractor agreed to excavate all soil and gravel to required specifications, and to spread the streets with gravel—and to grade the streets. After the black-top was applied, he was to roll and compact the same to a smooth, level roadway. The agreement included precautions taken to prevent damages to persons and property by the contractor. I remember the day the black-top was applied to east Washington Street and the strong new aroma that filled the air, but I also remember the dust and dirt blowing through the streets. My father noticed several specks of tar on the front of our house, but decided this was not as bad as eating dust.

The $500 was to be paid to Detchon from receipts of the state gasoline taxes "from time to time," or from the dividends expected from the Corn Exchange Bank. This was the first black-topping of the streets in New Richmond.

During the Great Depression, many positions in the town's government were abolished because there simply were no funds to pay the men. The treasurer's job was abolished and combined with the Clerk's; the Dog Police and the Fire Chief's jobs were abolished and the Marshal was let go until they realized someone had to keep the town building warm enough for the fire truck to be kept in operating condition. E.E. Baldwin was hired for $10 per month to fire the stove and turn on the street lights. Trustees juggled positions, as everyone wanted out of their offices—especially the treasurer.

Somehow they all survived, and the town received its first dividend of $730 on April 15, 1935 from the Corn Exchange Bank's liquidated funds. A year later, a check for $1,273.95 was paid to the town trustees. By this time a few of the offices were being filled—by one man. J.D. Hinman was appointed as the Marshal, and was to fill all the vacancies, as Street Commissioner, Health Officer, Custodian of the fire house and fire engine.

Town Marshals

John A. Work - Town Marshal

"JOHN A. WORK-TOWN MARSHAL—The Old Lamplighter-Curfew Johnny—The Fearless, and most Efficient Marshal of the town of New Richmond—The Fear of the Wrong-Doer—The Champion of the Law."

The New Richmond *Record*, Thursday, January 11, 1906 pays the above compliments to a very faithful town marshal of New Richmond—one of the first marshals who stayed with the job that included duties of overseeing groups of men who hauled gravel and spread it upon the streets, keeping law and order, lighting street lamps, attending shows and horse shows to keep peace in the town, babysitting the young boys who lived upon the streets, and serving as Fire Chief. John A. Work was the marshal receiving the comments above, and in addition to all the town duties, he earned a living as a drayman in New Richmond.

John A. Work was born in Montgomery County in 1850, near the Wesley Church neighborhood. John also lived in the area of Liberty Chapel before moving to New Richmond. He married Miss Jennie Steele, and they had five children. One child and John's wife preceded him in death. The children who survived him were: Claude H. Work, Agnes Work Washburn, and Myrtle Work Lynn (Mrs. Dr. Frank Lynn).

Marshal John A. Work died at the age of 80 years, 4 months, and 4 days in the county home, on November 16, 1929. Work was buried in the Wesley Cemetery, near his birthplace.

The town marshals were elected when New Richmond was first incorporated, but from 1905 on they were appointed by the Board of Trustees. Work suited most of the local citizens, and he was considered the best marshal the town ever had. He was fearless, honest, and was determined to keep peace in the town. He often "stumbled" into gambling dens in the town, and on one occasion, broke up part of their furniture and carried away the rest. Another poker den was invaded after the sly official had learned the secret entrance of the den, and was within a few paces of the gamblers before he was detected. The Marshal gobbled up all the coins while the fellows begged for mercy. They were let go with a promise not to gamble again. Some fellow may have held four aces, but each gambler felt like he held a single jack when Work entered their den, no doubt. Work was directed by the town council to let them go with just a warning, and the money was returned later on—after he made them stew for a while. The Town Council always stood behind Work, and he followed their orders with respect, which worked for the best for both sides.

The town council purchased John a new Colt revolver in 1902. While John was showing off the new firearm to friends in Henry Long's Livery Barn, the gun went off and barely missed Henry's leg. The stray bullet went through the office door casing and made a big dent in the office stove. John decided to store the Colt away until it was needed. The town council purchased a new Colt Magazine revolver in 1905. John said all he had to do was just pump it, and eight shots in rapid succession would scare away all the hot-footers to taller timber!

In 1922, the president of the town board wanted to let Marshal Work go and to declare the office vacant at the end of the year; the President said, "Work was becoming inefficient in the last few years, and has overstepped his authority of different occasions, and has taken his cases before the HORSE THIEF DETECTIVE ASSOCIATION, instead of the town Board." The President said, "Since each and every member of the Horse Thief Detective Association has been issued legal papers giving them authority to make an arrest whenever necessary, the Board could save the taxpayers about $360 per year by declaring the Marshal's office vacant. The marshal's duties as street supervisor would be paid for by the hour." The two other members of the Board were not in favor of this proposal, so it was tabled.

Work served as the Marshal of New Richmond until he was relieved of his duties on February 2, 1929. He was nearly eighty years old at the time, and a month later, the citizens petitioned the Trustees to give him a bonus for his long and faithful service, but due to the depression, they could only give him $40. Work passed away in November that same year.

Marshal Johnny Work was often put to the test by the local youth who went out of their way to annoy him. They stole the marbles from a wire sign foot mat from in front of the bank, and while they were working hard at tearing the mat apart behind George Long's store, the big, strong Marshal appeared and gave the boys a fright to remember for years to come. The boys were destroying young maple trees by carving, tapping the trees, and peeling off the bark. Work threatened to disarm all the boys of their pocket knives for their "dark deeds."

A crowd of town boys, "pleasure bent," went roaming all over the country-side around New Richmond one Sunday afternoon, and visited Philip Dewey's Elk & Deer Park northeast of town. Now Phil didn't mind the boys visiting the park whenever they chose to, but they were beginning to prowl around the barn and sheds, and often chased his stock. This he *didn't* care for, as this breed of stock was easily excited and injured themselves when frightened. The boys made a stop at John Kirkpatrick's on this Sunday and came upon his flock of geese. They just couldn't resist temptation and "put them all to flight," killing one of the geese. They saw that Kirkpatrick had caught them and they picked up the dead goose and took off across the field, dropping the goose after they climbed across the fence. The Marshal was notified, and because the boys were identified, the Marshal published the story of their little caper in the local newspaper to shame them. They were warned publicly that they would be given the full force of the law if they tried it again.

Halloween and overturning of numerous outhouses went hand in hand, and the hoodlums dodged Marshal Work each year, usually succeeding in upsetting their quota. The town Council passed a Curfew Law in 1906, and hereafter, the marshal was referred to as CURFEW JOHNNIE by the boys who desired to stand on the street corners in all kinds of weather. To Johnnie, it was just another added duty to ring the curfew bell, and escort the little laddies home to their mommies and daddies—who were supposed to be responsible for them in the first place! Children under sixteen were to be off the streets between 8:30 p.m. and 7:30 a.m.

New Richmond was a lively town at the turn of the century and the town marshal was kept busy every now and then settling disturbances. One busy evening in 1902, he had more business than an "angling worm at fishing time," and forgot to light the street lamps. John carried a little four-foot stepladder over the town to light the gas lamps. For this chore he was paid $11.70 per month. In April 1906, the town "dads" decided to put up additional lamps, two in the south part, two in the east end, and one in the north end of town. This made a total of twelve lamps scattered about town for Curfew Johnnie to light. The late Forrest Waye said the lads about town followed John and snuffed the lights out as quickly as he lit them. (Hmm, I wonder how he knew this?) Bills were filed each month by George F. Long for dozens of mantels, chimneys, lamp galleries, and wire frames for the town's gas street lighting systems to keep them in operating condition.

When a new town council took office in January, 1906, and after Esquire Ebrite swore Marshal John Work into office, Mr. Claypool thanked Mr. Work, in behalf of the town council and the town citizens, for his tireless and unceasing efforts to maintain peace and harmony. From his coat pocket he pulled out a $19.50 Elgin 17-jewel movement gold watch as a token of appreciation of the citizens of the town. Johnnie was so surprised, and overcome by the honor that he nearly forgot the bushel of apples he had brought to treat the town officials. They reminded him and said, "Now, pass your apples, John!" He was indeed a well-respected law officer for the town of New Richmond.

Marshal James "Jim" Harris

Jim Harris was another long term marshal of New Richmond, serving from 1944 to 1961, a total of seventeen years. He began his duties of keeping law and order in the town, and was the street commissioner, water superintendent, and served as the town's volunteer fire chief a number of years. New Richmond's town Trustees gave a lot of responsibilities to one person, because there were never enough funds to cover the expenses for more than one person.

Jim Harris was born August 14, 1891, in Hardin County, Kentucky, son of James and Mary C. (Dowdale) Harris, and his death occurred March 16, 1970. Harris raised his three children as a single parent, and he was able to relate to the children in town because of this. They teased him and he returned the teasing, but he showed authority over them when it was necessary, and attended to his town duties with the same honest policies as Marshal Work. His heavy work as law enforcer was on Saturday nights, during the street shows, when the tavern experienced its surge in business. Jim had to keep the drunks from disturbing those who wished to enjoy an evening of entertainment in town.

I attempted to compile a list of New Richmond's town marshals, but due to missing record books, some may have been omitted. During the Great Depression the town's funds were tied up due to the closing of the Corn Exchange Bank, and from 1930 to 1934 the town was left without a law enforcer.

- 1895 - William Bunnell - served few months
- 1895 - F. Marion Smith
- 1897 - John A. Work appointed - served to Feb. 6, 1929 (32 years)
- 1929 - Feb. 8, Sanford "Sant" Black - resigned March 31, 1930
- 1930 - March 31, E. E. "Doc" Baldwin - job abolished soon after
- 1934 - Jan. 1, Jesse D. (J.D.) Hinman - job vacated Sep. 21, 1942
- 1942 - Sep. 21, Monroe Lyon - to Nov. 2, 1942
- 1943 - Feb. 1, Charles Oswalt - to 1944
- 1944 - James Harris - to 1961
- 1961 - Jack Dawson - served short time
- 1962 - Gerold Ottinger - to 1964
- Feb 1964 - Roy Kerr - to April 1, 1964 (resigned)
- April 16, 1964 - Howard Cox - to 1968
- Jan 1968 - Ernest Holt - to Dec 1968
- July 1, 1969 - Merton Allen - to Sep 1969

Sep. 30, 1969 - Nick Wood - to Nov 1969
Nov 1969 - Ernest Holt - to Feb 1, 1972
1972 - Nick Hood - served short time only
Feb. 7, 1972 - Roy Pendleton, Sr. - to Dec 1972
Dec 26, 1972 - Dale Dickson - to Mar 22, 1973
July 3, 1973 - Fred King - moved to Fla. few months later
Mar 27, 1974 - Charles Coy (from Crawfordsville) - to 1978
1978 - Onia Shoaf, Marshal; Mark Clapp, Deputy Marshal
1985 - Onia & Mark still serving[1]

NEW RICHMOND JAIL HOUSES

Three elderly residents informed me of an early jail in New Richmond, located on south Wabash Street across from the Black Bear Hotel. The cook at the hotel, Hope Kirkpatrick, was paid to take meals to the prisoners incarcerated in the prison. Squire Ebrite's residence was located in the same block, which made everything quite handy for everyone concerned with the jail. This old jail was always referred to as **The Oliver House**, but the reason for this name has not been revealed to me. Marshal Work was renovating the Oliver House in June of 1905 to make ready for horse show day in the town. Another incident involved a family of five who arrived on the Clover Leaf one day and were locked up in the Oliver House because it was thought they had smallpox, but they were sent on their way the following day after being examined by the doctor.

The town trustees leased a building on Franklin Street from Dr. Stow S. Detchon in November 1899; it stood on part of lot number sixteen (#16) of Detchon's fourth (4th) addition to the town of New Richmond. They later purchased the lot in 1908. This lot was the site of the local volunteer fire department, town hall, and a small building in which the jail stood. The jail was not moved from south Wabash Street to the new lot in 1899, but sometime after the trustees purchased the lot in 1908; the exact time period is unknown. When Levi Thomas sold the lot to William M. and Walter L. Todd on June 20, 1925, the jail and its building were still standing on the lot, and the old jail was reserved by Charley Haywood. The record does not state Charley's reason for purchasing the jail, and there is no record of its later history.

In April 1925, the trustees of the town traded the old town lot and building for a brick structure owned by Levi Thomas, located on east Washington Street. A new jail cell was purchased in October 1926 through a local hardware man, Perry McLain, for $206.46. The cell was manufactured by E. T. Barnum Iron Works of Detroit, Michigan, builders of Jail Cells, and was delivered unassembled. Charles Fruits, Sr., was paid $14.50 for assembling the jail and for night watch. This cell stood on the ground floor of the town hall, behind the fire trucks until the structure was sold. The jail was moved to the Snyder Tack & Apparel Shop in November 1981 to keep it within the town limits, for historical reasons, and stood for several years in this building, which had become the town's museum. Prisoners are now carted off to the county jail if such a problem arises.

VOLUNTEER FIRE DEPARTMENT

In July 1887, William Campbell, proprietor of the "Pioneer Store" and correspondent for the Crawfordsville Weekly *Review*, expressed his concern and fears of a big fire occurring in New Richmond. He had a very good reason for trying to get the townspeople to organize a "fire brigade," as he lost his residence—and his first business, a grocery—by fire in 1874. He was afraid the town would be brought to their senses only after the town was half burned down.

---

[1] In 2003, Mark Clapp suffered a fatal heart attack during a struggle with a suspect. He had served the town of New Richmond for 22 years.

Campbell mentioned the need of a fire brigade in his columns each week and was totally ignored for several years. Campbell was the victim of another fire the last of February, 1889; his Pioneer Store, a general merchandise establishment, burned to the ground, the fire smoldering for two weeks. This structure, as well as his first, was a log building and they usually smoldered for a longer period of time. In May 1879, Jane Washburn's residence burned, totally destroying the home and most of the contents. Jane, the mother of Dr. D. Manners Washburn, suffered a $1500 loss and had very little insurance to cover her losses.

The Hollin brothers lost their first drug store, building and contents destroyed by fire, in 1883. Campbell was still warning New Richmond residents to organize a fire brigade in August 1889, after Mrs. Allman's house was destroyed by fire. He said if the town had a hand engine (hand operated pump), the fire could have been controlled in twenty minutes, and he claimed a few dollars from each citizen of New Richmond could have bought the best hand engine on the market. The buildings in the town were constructed in such a manner the whole town would be consumed if a fire broke out.

In May of 1890, Campbell was trying to persuade the town to buy a fire engine that was for sale at Lafayette for half the original cost. "The engine could throw a stream of water over the court house at Lafayette, and would have extinguished any fire that might have occurred in the town. A few dollars spent for the engine would save thousands if another fire broke out," Campbell said. McCardle's elevator burned to the ground two months before he made this plea.

Campbell kept pushing for the Lafayette fire engine in July, August, September, and November, of 1890. He tried to convince the citizens their insurance would be lighter if the town had a good firefighting engine—the one at Lafayette was still for sale. In November the town was still without fire protection and he said, "Don't be surprised if you hear some day that New Richmond has vanished."

In January 1891, Campbell was proud to report that "nearly enough money has been subscribed to pay for the fire engine here-a thing we have been advocating for some time. The people are beginning to see the importance of our suggestion through this paper." A month later, however, Campbell was very upset with his fellow citizens and commented about their blowing about the growing town—but if they were asked to buy a fire engine, they look at you cross-eyed, and seem not to hear you." So Campbell gave up and moved to Kirkpatrick—and New Richmond still did not have a fire engine!

Well, his predictions came true—it finally happened! On Tuesday, July 12, 1898, about two o'clock in the morning, the "thrifty" little town of New Richmond was visited by a disastrous fire. The entire town turned out to fight the flames, but a whole row of frame buildings were in ashes before the fire was subdued. Andrew Townsley's dry goods store was the origin of the fire, his loss being estimated at $2,500—with $2,000 insurance; Douglas Bunnell's home—no insurance; James Carter lost two business rooms, occupied by Snyder & Thompson's farm implements—no insurance; Starr Dunn lost his tin shop and dwelling, and the family barely escaped with their lives. Dunn had very little insurance. Frank Perkins lost his general store and residence, with only a small portion of the contents saved. His loss was estimated from $3,500 to $5,000, although his livery barn was saved from the fire. George F. Long's dwelling was also saved from the fire. One account of the terrible disaster said, "the volunteer fire brigade worked nobly and credit should be given to those who assisted so materially in saving the town from total destruction." This statement mentions a fire brigade, at least, but there is no record of the hand pumped engine.

Finally, on July 3, 1900, the trustees of the town of New Richmond, namely: Albert D. Snyder, Perry McLain and Bert E. Page, passed an ordinance (Ordinance No. 16) establishing, and regulating the **Volunteer Fire Department of the Town of New Richmond, Indiana**. The Volunteer Fire Department was to consist of one chief, two assistants, and not more than twelve regular firemen. The chief was to be elected by the firemen, but was later appointed by the trustees of the town. All men in the fire department were to register with the town clerk, in order to be exempted from having to serve on the jury and from road labor (in the early days, all able-bodied men worked on the roads to help pay their property taxes).

The fire chief was given most of the responsibility and authority over the regulars. He was to see that all property and fire-fighting apparatus for the extinguishing of fires were kept in good order, report all fires during the year, and the expenses for the chemicals used at each fire. The two assistant chiefs were to see that the Chemical Engine No. 1 and 2 were kept in working order at all times.

It is interesting to note that the chief and the regular firemen were to serve without compensation, but the two assistant chiefs were to receive $5 each year for their services when the ordinance was passed; later, the chief was to be paid $10 per month, and all other members, 25¢ per regular meeting.

The late Forrest Waye said he remembered watching the old hand-pumped chemical wagon being pulled by the firemen to the fires. They did not bother hitching the horses to the wagon since the town was so small. He said it was a heavy load for the men and after arriving at the scene of a fire, they had to continually pump in order to keep the stream of water powerful enough to extinguish the flames, and the pumping also mixed the chemicals in the small tank. The fire company also had a hook and ladder wagon that required three or four men to pull to the fire.

After Starr Dunn lost his residence and business structures, he installed a water plant in front of his new building, and gave the town permission to hook their fire hoses onto his plant, in case of fire. The town had finally come to their senses, William!

New Richmond's First Fire House

On November 10, 1899, the Trustees of the Town of New Richmond, Indiana, signed an agreement to lease Dr. Stow S. Detchon's property from November 12, 1899 until November 12, 1909. The real estate was described as "Sixty-eight (68) feet, seven (7) inches off the north end of lot number sixteen (16) in Stow S. Detchon's third[1] addition to the town of New Richmond."

Trustees were to pay Stow S. Detchon an annual rent amount of five dollars ($5) at the end of each year, and pay all taxes imposed on improvement on said premises, the taxes on the ground—exclusive of buildings to be paid by Detchon. Trustees of the town at that time were: Stow S. Detchon, Horace G. Messer, and Orlando W. Mason. The lease was witnessed by Amos Ebrite, Justice of the Peace, and recorded February 2, 1900. The building was to serve as the town's first fire house and town hall, and the old jail was moved to this site on Franklin Street. The structure stood on the ground adjacent to the north of the New Richmond Christian Church, and was part of the lot on which the church was later built. The building was a small frame structure with a cupola situated upon the roof to house the bell. This bell was tolled as a fire warning, curfew, and to announce town meetings. Unfortunately, after serving many years as a residence, the building burned to the ground around 1980.

The **first fire alarm** sounded by the bell on the town building and engine house answered a call to the home of W. A. Turvey. There the ladies' aid of the New Richmond Christian Church were preparing a dinner to be served in the old 1888 church building that stood east of the present structure. The old cooking range was placed too close to the wall, and the wallpaper ignited. The blaze sprang up immediately, but the brave ladies extinguished the fire with a bucket of water before the **Volunteer Fire Company No. 1** arrived, although the firemen were very prompt. The New Richmond *Record*, Thursday, November 29, 1900 said, "Nick Washburn pulled the ropes on the first fire alarm. The bell's dreaded and doleful tones brought the populace out in a minute, and we hardly knew there were so many people in quiet New Richmond." Firemen answering the first fire alarm on November 28, 1900 were: Charles Boyland, Charles McClain, A. D. Snyder, and Frank E. Campbell. Their minutes say they arrived on time but the fire was "outened" by the time they arrived with Fire Engine No. 1.

Dr. Stow Detchon's son, John T., was appointed administrator of his father's estate after Stow's death, and John T. and his mother, Jemima, sold to the trustees of the town lot number sixteen (16) in Stow S. Detchon's fourth addition to the town of New Richmond, on December 12, 1908 for the sum of $600. The trustees at the time were: John P. Bible, Bert E. Page, and William Long. This was the same lot the trustees leased in 1899 on which the fire house and town building stood upon. The trustees sold one hundred feet off the south end of this lot (16) to the Trustees of the New Richmond Christian Church on August 2, 1917 for their new structure—which was not erected until 1921.

---

[1] This should be the fourth addition.

On April 13, 1925, George C. Livingston, W.H. Hollin, and Richard D. Thomas, Trustees of the town of New Richmond, met in the Corn Exchange Bank to buy and sell real estate. They traded the remaining forty-eight and one-half feet (48½) off the north end of lot sixteen in Detchon's fourth addition to the town of New Richmond, for a brick, two-story structure owned by Levi Thomas. Thomas was asking $2,000 for the building on east Washington Street erected by Frank Perkins around 1898-99, located just west of Starr Dunn's brick building. The new purchase was to be used as a fire station to store the new fire truck and firefighting equipment. A town office was built on the ground floor of this structure sometime later. This building was used as a town hall and fire house until 1980.

On August 14, 1980, the trustees of the town held a public meeting discussing the purchase of a large metal building owned by Ivan Pollock. The old brick fire house was having problems with a leaking roof, and it was believed the new structure would be less expensive to keep in good repair. The building was to be converted into a fire department building. Ivan was asking $10,000 for the structure, located on west Madison Street next to the town's water tower. The trustees purchased the building in September of 1980, and the firefighting equipment and trucks were moved into the structure soon after.

The old brick fire department and town hall on east Washington Street was sold to Ben Miller, representing the Tri-County Telephone Company, for $5500. As of this writing in 1985, it was serving as a storage building for the telephone company.

FIRE TRUCKS

New Richmond's first "fire truck" was an old Dodge truck Maurice Coffman converted by attaching the hand-mixed chemical apparatus to the truck, enabling the firefighters to make the fire runs a little faster. This would have been around 1915-20. The firefighters were in need of newer and more efficient equipment, and on June 5, 1922, a special meeting was called by the town trustees J.T. Parlon, R.D. Thomas, and William Hollin, to definitely decide to purchase a new fire truck. They decided to accept a contract submitted by J.M. Johnson, a representative of the **Obeuchain Boyer Company** of Logansport. The apparatus for fighting fires was a Boyer triple-tank chemical tank and equipment, to be mounted on a Ford Chassis. This truck was to cost the town $2,140, and terms were arranged to suit both parties. The Ford chassis was purchased through Jess DeVault, a Ford salesman (from the New Richmond area) who was to deliver the truck to Obeuchain Boyer Company, where the equipment would be mounted onto it.

The town trustees reduced Marshal John Work's salary from $40 per month to $30, because it was necessary to have a fire chief capable of operating and understanding the mechanisms of the engine and the chemical operations of the new equipment. Lynn Timmons was appointed to succeed Clell Terrill as fire chief, with a proposed salary of $10 per month. Terrill was a deputy fire chief at the time of Timmon's appointment, and the marshal was fire chief. A new law in 1906 specified the town marshals were to be fire chiefs. Both of the men lost their jobs on the fire department at this time.

One of the old fire chemical tanks was placed in the lumberyard, the other in Dunn's garage, and both were to be kept in operating condition at the town's expense. These were kept as an added security to the town. This Ford fire truck and equipment served the town for a number of years, but eventually became worn out and outdated. On March 17, 1941, the town trustees, Carl Burnett, Sheridan Geiger, and Charles Taylor, went to Crawfordsville with I.V. Borger, of Ligonier, to view their fire truck.

Two days later, the board met in a special session to consider the purchase of new firefighting equipment. Mr. Borger was present, and Mr. Bradshaw of the Delphi Body Works attended the meeting. Bradshaw proposed to equip any truck the board decided upon, using the ladders, reels, ladder-brackets, pike poles, and other equipment from the old fire trucks. He also proposed to install a two hundred gallon water tank, and would do the job for $200 on contract or on an hourly basis. No decision was made at this time.

The next meeting, held on the 24th of March, was spent opening, reading, and considering bids submitted by several automobile dealers in the area. A. T. Galloway submitted the lowest bid on a Chevrolet with the following specifications: "Chevrolet 1941 truck, one and one-half ton, with 134½ inch wheel base; dual rear wheels; tires, 650-20 all around, 6 ply Firestone; Body length, 108½ inches; width,

52 and 7/16 inches; 16 inches deep; overload springs, heavy duty 93 H. P. motor; the color is 'Swift Red.'" The price asked for this truck was $714 cash—and two Model T trucks (Fords). This was the accepted bid, and was signed by Clerk-Treasurer Lester W. Olin and Carl Burnett, President of the Town Board of New Richmond. At the April 7th meeting, Olin was ordered to write to Delphi Body Works to draw up a contract for building the fire truck body, which was presented to the board at a meeting held a week later, and accepted. The town paid $339.09 to Delphi Body Works, $710 to the American Fire Apparatus Company of Battle Creek, Michigan, for fire equipment, and $714 to A.T. Galloway for the 1941 Chevrolet truck.

The townspeople were very proud of their new fire truck, and a petition was signed by a number of New Richmond citizens in regard to the use of the new fire truck to fight rural fires. The town attorney advised them not to use the truck for rural fires, and a resolution was drawn and was to be published in the Crawfordsville paper saying, "The fire truck of the town of New Richmond shall not be taken out of the corporate limits to fight fires, or protect property of the rural areas. This action is necessary because of the ruling of the Inspection Bureau." This 1941 Chevrolet fire truck was sold on September 24, 1981 to Bill Kerns.

New Richmond Community Fire Department, Inc.

Realizing the farmers around New Richmond needed some fire protection, it was decided there was room for another fire truck to be stored in the town's building. In February 1949, a new organization was formed known as the **New Richmond Community Volunteer Fire Department Incorporated**. The first board of directors were: Carroll E. Irvin, New Richmond; Ewing F. Mason, Romney; Lewis J. Withrow, Romney; Kenneth F. Royer, New Richmond; and Richard Shotts, New Richmond. The Incorporators were: Alfred L. Henderson and Paul Sayler of New Richmond and Jerome Rund of Romney. The Romney people listed lived within a short distance of New Richmond, and the town was the nearest place to store their rural fire truck. Their rural fire truck was not to be used within the town of New Richmond unless the town truck had mechanical problems. Dick Shotts was the only person listed above with a New Richmond address who resided within the town limits, and he drove the truck to the rural fires.

Two other fire trucks were purchased for the fire department, over the years, one was a 1948 model and the other, a 1968 Ford.

Volunteer Fire Department

New Richmond's first volunteer fire fighters attended their organizational meeting on July 2, 1900. Albert D. Snyder was appointed as the town's first fire chief, and the regulars were: W.P. (Perry) Coffman, John B. Foster, Tom Kirkpatrick, Frank E. Campbell, Elston Philips, Park White (later replaced by Charles Shobe) Ellis Clark, Walter "Spud" Harriman, Charles McClain, Elmer "Pete" Harriman, Charles Boyland, Claude Work, Joe Wills, and John Patton. There were several changes of firemen over the years—too many to record all their names, unfortunately.

Most of the minutes of the early meetings listed the men as they answered roll call, but during one of the meetings, John Foster and Spud Harriman were to arrange for a bonfire (to test their skills at "outing" fires), on September 29, 1900. They reported the results of this trial run thus, "Engine No. 1 in the bonfire blew out a gaskett (sp), and engine No. 2 rushed gallantly forward and 'outened' the fire."

In 1902, they arranged with the local "central" (telephone operator) to give the fire alarms to those owning telephones. The meetings evidently were not exciting enough for the firefighters and they became a little lax in their attendance—their excuses were written into the minutes. One meeting recorded the following flimsy excuses. "Hank Lee was in Kansas inspecting timber; Charles McLain was seeing sights on the Pike; Westfall was 'all in' as a result of a Sunday fishing jaunt; Coffman was Loofing (loafing); F. E. Campbell was entertaining Hulligan; Burris wouldn't get away from his wife, and Snyder was called to Sugar Grove on short notice" (Snyder's girlfriend lived in the Sugar Grove area). Another meeting was held on the front lawn of the fire department, and "after three visious (sic) football rushes, those surviving answered roll call." If the firemen did not offer suitable excuses for not attending, they were dropped from the roll.

Because of incomplete records, there are a few names omitted, but among those serving as New Richmond's Fire Chiefs over the years are the following: The first fire chief was A. D. Snyder who served from 1900 - 1902; Mr. Harriman, 1903 - 4; Mr. Foster, 1904; Thomas Kirkpatrick, 1905; John Work, 1906; Nick Beckley, 1906 - 1909; Frank E. Campbell, 1909; Joe Young, 1909 - 1918; G.L. Bastion, 1918 - unknown; Lynn Timmons 1924 (resigned short time after appointment); Roy E. Brown, 1924 - 1931; Maurice Coffman, 1938 - 40; James "Jim" Harris in the 1940s; Robert Thayer served in the 1950s and 1960s as a fireman and completed twenty-eight years, serving as fire chief eighteen of those years; Ralph Kunkel served twenty-six years as a volunteer fireman, and he too served as fire chief in the 1970s. Roger Kunkel presented his father, Ralph, and Robert Thayer, plaques for their loyalty to the company on December 4, 1979. Richard Vaughan was the fire chief of the New Richmond Volunteer Fire Department 1985-1986.

TRUSTEES OF COAL CREEK TOWNSHIP

In 1831, a new school law was passed in Indiana, giving administration of the local school funds into the hands of three trustees, and took effect in the fall of the same year in Montgomery County. Records are incomplete on the early trustees of Coal Creek Township, but the following were listed on the school deeds:

October 1841	March 1856	October 1856
Elijah Park	Levi Curtis	Levi Curtis
William Kincaid	Moses L. Burk	George Ebrite
Phillip Sunger	Aaron Stephens	Aaron Stephens

Only one trustee was elected for each township by 1876, and was to serve a two year term. The following is an incomplete list of Coal Cree Township's trustees and the dates mentioned:

Aaron Gilkey	1876	Capt. Edward T. McCrea	1886-1888
J.E. Hanna	1880-1881	John W. Utterback	1888-1890
William Henry	1882-1886		

John W. Utterback was the first trustee to be elected after the four-year term was adopted. Again, there is not a complete record of the trustees available, but a partial list follows with the dates mentioned:

John W. Utterback	1890-1894	Glen L. Wilson	1933-1934
Ebright M. Morrow	1895-	H. Grady Chadwick	1835-1938
Orlando W. Mason	1901-1904	Homer C. Goff	1939-1942
Henry T. Vancleave	1905-1908	Isacc H. Montgomery	1943-1945
James D. Wilson	1908-1914	Glen L. Wilson	1946-1950
Orlando W. Mason	1915-1918	Frank Miller	1951-
John W. McCorkle	1919-1922	Levert E. Binns	1951-1958
Frank E. Campbell	1923-1926	Byron S. Alexander	1959-1966
Anson Thomas	1927-1932	Jacob Bunnell	1967-1974
James W. Fouts	1929-1932	Edith Fultz	1975-1986

Chapter 16 - Politics

Early Political Meetings

During the early 1880s and 1890s, politicians of both parties, Republican, and Democrat—yes, even the third party, the Prohibitionists—were very active in Coal Creek township. The Democrats held many "rousing conventions" in the little school house at Center, and after they finished nominating the various candidates, the Prohibition party gathered all their candidates together, in the same little school building to select their candidates. The Republican conventions were held either in Wingate or New Richmond—Hollin's Opera House was the setting for the meetings held in the latter town. Going back to the early years, a reporter from the Crawfordsville *Journal*, November 22, 1884, poked a little fun concerning a celebration of the New Richmond Democrats, rejoicing over the results of the election that year, saying,

> **NEW RICHMOND DEMOCRATS REJOICED OVER ELECTION—Gave a Big Blow-out here—Built a Huge Bon-fire in Public Square.**—Why, they built a bonfire in the public square that illuminated the city for at least ten feet in every direction and the principal Democratic store was gaily decorated with flags and brilliantly illuminated with one kerosene lamp and plenty of good Democratic Whiskey. A procession was formed and marched around the square headed by a wheel-barrow containing a man who had made a bet on the election and won it, and escorted by the military band, consisting of one fife and two drums, and lit up by a real Chinese lantern. The speakers for the occasion were G. W. Paul and Bayless W. Hanna, of Crawfordsville, who made brilliant speeches that fully convinced the Democrats present that the Republicans were all thieves. The band wagon from Crawfordsville, containing the drum corps and escort, arrived about 7 p.m., and repaired to the only boarding house here and ordered supper, which being eaten, the party informed the landlord that Wm. Campbell, who is famous for keeping Republicans from casting illegal votes, would pay the bill. The next morning the landlord waited upon said honest Democrat, and smilingly presented a bill for the supper of eleven men. The H. D.[1] after some demur, paid for six meals, but counted the other five out as illegal voters, or I should say eaters, so the poor landlord who belongs to the "Thieving Republican Party," had to whistle for his pay. etc..

Regardless of the above item, the town of New Richmond produced two state Representatives, which is not too bad a record for such a little town. A short sketch of the two follows.

Captain Edward T. McCrea - State Representative, 1894-1898

Edward T. McCrea was born April 20, 1836 in Shelby County, Indiana, and grew to manhood in that county. He received a common school education, and entered Franklin College at the age of sixteen in 1852. He also attended Hanover College for one and a half years. Ed was in the general merchandising business with his father when the Civil War broke out. He enlisted August 28, 1861 in Company D. 33rd.

---

[1] "honest Democrat"

Indiana Volunteer Infantry at Shelbyville and was immediately elected captain of that company. He fought in fifty-five battles and skirmishes and was discharged September 16, 1864. For this service, incidentally, McCrea received a pension of $24 per month.

Capt. McCrea was elected trustee of Coal Creek township and served one term, during which time he erected New Richmond's first brick school building. McCrea also served as trustee of the local Methodist Church many years. He was elected as representative to the state legislature in 1894, and again in 1896. The Crawfordsville *Review*, October 20, 1894, had this to say when Ed ran for the office of legislature the first term:

> The county Republicans nominated Capt. McCrea of New Richmond as their candidate for Representative. He seems to be little known. No one seems to know much about him. He remains away from any collection of people, and no one has heard him making any speeches or addressing the people....The people, however, want to know his views on public affairs.

41- Capt. Edward T. McCrea and his Civil War rifle

This item was followed by a list of questions with which the public was so concerned. Not on this list, however, was one of the most controversial issues that year—the Women's Suffrage Vote, and several ladies were turned away when they tried to vote in Crawfordsville, causing quite a stir.

After Captain Edward T. McCrea won the election by a majority of 525 votes, he became well known, and the Republicans nominated him for re-election for a second term—which he won.

CHARLES KIRKPATRICK - STATE REPRESENTATIVE, 1902

Charles Kirkpatrick (also known as "Kirk" or "Handsome Charlie") was born May 20, 1863 at Sugar Grove, in Tippecanoe County, son of Jacob and Mandy (Shuee) Kirkpatrick. His father, Jacob, made two trips to the gold fields of California and took up mining a few years, before returning to Sugar Grove to settle down on a farm. Charles Kirkpatrick attended the common school of Sugar Grove, later entering DePauw University, graduating in 1886. Charles married Jessie L. Washburn, daughter of George W. and Louise (Whetstone) Washburn, and moved to New Richmond. He served as the town's postmaster four years, purchased an elevator, and managed it for three years, and then sold out, moving to Anderson, Indiana, where he was associated with Lt. Governor William Combeak. A year later, Kirkpatrick went into the contracting business, building streets. He returned to New Richmond in September 1895 and joined his father-in-law's bank, the Corn Exchange Bank.

Charles Kirkpatrick became interested in politics, and served as state representative from 1902-1904, serving one term only. While serving in this capacity, Charles introduced in the house a phony "anti-chicken" bill, the framing of which originated with Tom Boraker of Crawfordsville, custodian of the Montgomery County courthouse. Boraker sent the bill to Kirkpatrick, who showed the same to several of his colleagues about the legislative halls and they insisted upon Kirkpatrick that he should read the measure, which the members class as among the batch of "freak legislation." The bill was to prevent the destruction of growing crops by chickens and ducks, and furnished no end of amusement for the legislators at the time. Boraker had planted a garden and was troubled with bothersome chickens and decided to have a little fun from his problem. The Indianapolis *Journal* published a cartoon of Kirkpatrick demonstrating his bill to prevent chickens from "scratching." In the picture, Mr. Kirkpatrick was posed eating a snack of drumstick sandwiches, one in each hand, and a wing protruding from a coat pocket.

On the serious side, though, Charles Kirkpatrick served as chairman of the House Committee on Banks during his term in office when a bill was introduced to regulate private banks. The bill, prepared by the Attorney General, would prohibit banks having less than $25,000 capital from doing business. Kirkpatrick, being a banker himself, opposed the bill, and the committee received many letters protesting against the bill because the bill would destroy the small banks.

Charles Kirkpatrick erected two new houses for him and his wife in New Richmond. The location of the first, built around 1902, was considered one of the prettiest and most convenient little homes in Montgomery County. It was possibly in Kirkpatrick's addition to the town of New Richmond, but the lot number is unknown. Kirk built his own water works plant for this residence since the town's water system was not built at the time. Kirkpatrick's beautiful country estate was erected in 1915-16 and is located at the extreme east end of New Richmond. A "Farm Home Tour" consisting of 125 Crawfordsville people in twenty-five vehicles, visited Kirkpatrick's new home in May 1916. The Crawfordsville *Journal*, June 2, 1916 described the visit like this:

> Just before starting for the home of Charles Kirkpatrick at New Richmond, C.B. Durham of the Hort. Service Company, demonstrated the Deleo System of electric lighting for the country home. The largest crowd of the two days gathered at the beautiful Kirkpatrick home at the eastern edge of New Richmond, and were given a sample of genuine hospitality by the hostess and host, both of whom spoke a few words. The speaker mentioned the evergreens, common hemlock, white pine, white spruce, well adapted for screening purposes. Mr. and Mrs. Kirkpatrick spent quite a time giving the guests a tour over all the house and grounds.

The Kirkpatrick's christened their new country home "Quiatenon." The article disappointed this writer, however, as it doesn't tell the style of home—English Tudor—nor did it describe the rooms within. I made a hurried search in the papers previous to this tour, but did not discover any items concerning this new home. My grandfather Jefferson Waye helped landscape the Kirkpatrick grounds, according to my father, Forrest. Polly and Olney Buck own the Kirkpatrick residence today (1986).

42 -At left, "Quiatenon" - former residence of Charles Kirkpatrick. At right, old carriage house of Kirkpatrick residence.

ROBERT M. THAYER - MONTGOMERY COUNTY COMMISSIONER

Although New Richmond, and Coal Creek township has lost the enthusiasm of the good old rousing conventions which were held in the early history of the area, there is still one politician in New Richmond who thrives on the day-to-day excitement his office creates. This politician is Robert M. Thayer who has served his hometown and Montgomery County for many years. A sketch of Thayer follows.

Robert Morris Thayer, son of Otis L. and Lona Bell Thayer, was born on a farm southeast of New Richmond on December 31, 1919. He was one of eleven children, and the family moved to a farm east of Romney where Bob and his brothers and one sister graduated from Romney High School.

Bob married the former Frances Waye and they were the parents of four children, namely: Sandra L. Graves of Crawfordsville; James R. Thayer, Florida; Linda K. Burkle, Linden, and Pamela J. Burns, New Richmond.

After graduation, Bob was employed with Lafayette's Alcoa plant until he was called to serve his country during World War II, serving with the U.S. Army. He was sent overseas, and was in the middle of the action of the European Theater. After returning from the service, he was employed with the Cecil Clark Painting Company in Crawfordsville. He purchased the Standard Service Station in New Richmond on December 4, 1948, and continued with the business until January 1986. During this time Bob also drove a school bus to Coal Creek Central School for thirty five years, retiring in 1986. He was director of the New Richmond Savings and Loan Association, serving as president many years. He was a member of the New Richmond Christian Church, serving as Superintendent, Trustee, Deacon, and Elder, as well as Sunday school teacher.

Bob Thayer had always been very interested in politics, and served eight years on the New Richmond Town Board; he was president four of those years. He served as a volunteer fireman from 1952 to 1980, and as fire chief for eighteen years. He was presented a plaque in December 1979 for his loyalty to the company, and was honored for his dedication and service to the community.

Bob entered the county political arena in May 1966, running for the office of county councilman, first district, and was elected to the office in November that year. He served two years as county councilman, and served four terms as county commissioner, representing the third district. During his terms as a county official he has been a part of many historical changes, such as: the erection of a new county jail; the establishment of the Solid Waste Authority—taking the landfill off the tax rolls; selling the old Culver Hospital to a for-profit health care corporation, American Medical International (AMI); and formulating plans to renovate the old Montgomery County courthouse.

Another historic moment in Montgomery County's history was the commissioner's signing of an agreement to allow crinoid exploration and research in the Crawfordsville area which is considered the world's richest crinoid beds. Dr. N. Gary Lane, professor of Paleontology at Indiana University, and Porter Kier, representing the Smithsonian Institute, combined their efforts for this research. Crinoids from the Crawfordsville area were sent all over the world in the 1880s. Bob served as Montgomery County's representative to the board of Wabash Valley Mental Health Care Center for several years.

All the above historical changes within Montgomery County required many hours of study, negotiations, and numerous meetings before suitable decisions were made. Wives of the county officials should receive special recognition for the hours they spend answering telephones, keeping schedules of meetings—and unscheduled meetings—straight on the calendar, and making certain their husbands attend the meetings. Bob Thayer was one of New Richmond's most devoted politicians, and support from his wife Frances was indispensable.

Chapter 17 - Professional Life

Physicians of New Richmond and Coal Creek Township, With Dates They Practiced

(Including students of medicine under local physicians)

Alphabetical List with Dates

Allhands, Frank Dallas (Wingate Physician)	1898-1940
Arnett, Arett Campbell (studied with Dr. Lynn)	1903-1907
Barcus, John Paul (studied with New Richmond Physicians)	1903-
Biedenkopf, Christian J.	March 19, 1904-Feb 24, 1910
Black, Dayton R.	1878-1897
Brown, L.L. (druggist and physician)	1903
Cole, Ira	1923-1929
Davisson, Vinton (studied with local physicians)	1904-1907
Detchon, Elliott	Around 1852
Detchon, Irwin Agnew	1881-1882
Detchon, Stowe Sylvester	1861-1888
Dewey, George W (New Richmond native – Liberty Chapel or Dewey's Corner physician)	- 1924 (year of death)
Ebrite, Alfred (studied with local physicians)	1870-
Gimmel, ? (associated with Dr. Stowe Detchon)	1873-
Hurt, William Johnston (studied with Dr. Stowe Detchon)	1870-
Johnson, John B. (listed as New Richmond Physician on Federal Census)	1850-
Jones, Samuel E.	May 1907-1909 Sep.
Kindell, Hurschell D.	1929-1978 April 15
Long, George Franklin (studied with Dr. D.M. Washburn, attended Indiana Medical College, but did not finish)	
Lynn, Frank M.	1894-1908 April
Manners, George (New Richmond's First Physician)	1843-1885 (died Jan. 5, 1885)
Mershon, William (studied with Dr. Stowe Detchon)	- 1886 (died Fall 1886)
Olin, Leverett W. (Elmdale Physician)	April 13, 1880 – 1924, May
Washburn, D. Manners	April 4, 1874-1941 (died Dec. 11, 1941)
Wray, Curtis M.	August 11, 1909-1923

A Chronological list of New Richmond Physicians

1850 Federal Census, Coal Creek Township—New Richmond
George Manners, Physician
John B. Johnson, Physician

1860 Federal Census
S.S. Detchon, Dentist (was a Physician at this time)
George Manners, Physician

1870 Federal Census
Stowe S. Detchon, Physician
Wm.G. Hurt, Student of Medicine-in Detchon's household
Alfred Ebrite, Student of Medicine
George Manners, Physician and farmer

1874 People's Guide - Directory of Montgomery County
Detchon, S.S., Physician (Dr. Gimmel was associated with Detchon in 1873)
Washburn, D.M., Physician
Manners, George, Physician (was not listed in People's Guide, but was a Physician)

1879 (articles in Crawfordsville Weekly *Journal*)
Dr. Manners Washburn
Dr. Dayton R. Black
Dr. Stowe Detchon

1882-83 Indiana State Gazeteer
Detchen, S.S., Physician
Washburn, D.M., Physician

1884-85 Indiana State Gazeteer
Black, D.R., Physician
Detcheon, S.S., Physician
Washburn, D.M., Physician

1887 Indiana State Gazeteer
Black, D.R. Physician
Detcheon, S.S., Physician
Washburn, D.M., Physician

1890 Indiana State Gazeteer
Black, D.R. Physician
Detcheon, S.S., Physician
Washburn, D.M., Physician

1891-2 Directory of Montgomery County, Indiana
Dayton R. Black, Physician & Surgeon
Stowe S. Detchon, Physician & Surgeon
D.M. Washburn, Physician & Surgeon

1895 Directory of Montgomery County, Indiana
Dr. D.R. Black, Physician & Surgeon
Dr. Stowe S. Detchon, retired Physician
Dr. F.M. Lynn, Physician & Surgeon
Dr. D.M. Washburn, Physician & Surgeon

1900 Census Coal Creek Township, Mont. Co. Ind. New Richmond P.O.
Stowe Detchon, Physician
Frank Lynn, Physician
D. M. Washburn, M. D.

1902 (Newspaper items)
Dr. D.M. Washburn
Dr. F.M. Lynn
Dr. S.S. Detchon, retired Physician

1903 Directory of Montgomery County, Ind. New Richmond
Brown, L.L., Physician and druggist, Post Office, Washington St.
Lynn, F.M. Physician & Surgeon (Mary E.) office E. Wash. St; house E.Wash. St.
Washburn, D. Manners (Sarah) Physician & Surgeon, Office E. Wash. St.; house, Franklin St.

1904 Co-Op Telephone subscribers' list
Dr. C.J. Biedenkopf
Dr. F. M. Lynn
Dr. D. M. Washburn

1907-08 Directory of Montgomery County, Indiana (New Richmond)
C. J. Bredenkaff, (sp) Physician, Wabash Street
Frank M. Lynn, Physician, Washington St.
D. M. Washburn, Physician, Washington St. (Sarah) Musa; house Franklin & Detchon

1909 Newspaper items
Dr. S. E. Jones (moved to Kirkpatrick in August 1909)
Dr. Ray (Wray) came to New Richmond in August from Monitor)
Dr. D. Manners Washburn
1912 Directory of Montgomery County, Indiana
Washburn, D. Manners, Physician (Sarah) Musa

1913 History of Montgomery County, Indiana (Bowen)
Dr. D. M. Washburn
Dr. C. M. Wray

A Little Humor from the Physicians

Master Harold Alexander's accident of a broken arm two weeks ago might best be explained by him like little four-year-old Harold in the *Youth's Companion* whose father asked how it happened. "Oh," said he, "I went upstairs, and there was a window open, I looked out, then I hollered out, and then I just followed the holler." – New Richmond *Record*, Thursday, November 10, 1904.

Physicians now say that those who sleep with their mouths closed have the best health, so if you awake in the night and find your mouth open – get up and close it. – New Richmond *Record*, Thursday, January 12, 1905.

A doctor is said to have permitted consumption to get the better of him so that he might study it. As the experience killed him, there is some curiosity as to what he intends to do with the knowledge acquired. (This just goes to show - some things you can take with you!) – New Richmond *Record*, Thursday, March 8, 1906.

How things have changed in the past quarter of a century. Fifty years ago, a boy would go out on a Sunday morning, climb a tree and get on the outside of a gallon of mulberries and top off on a pocket of green apples. The next morning his mother would diagnose his trouble as "worms" and he was made to swallow half a bottle of rhubarb and a quarter of a pound of Epsom salts, and turned loose in the cow pasture until supper time, when he would come in for a square meal all right, just as if nothing had happened. In those good old days, if a boy cut his finger off or run a nail through his foot, a piece of fat pork was applied to the afflicted member and in a day or two he would be entirely well. In these days of civilization and enlightenment, if a boy has a pain in the lower regions, he has appendicitis, and is hustled off to a hospital, starved within an inch of his life, half a dozen surgeons each take a whack at him with a pearl-handled knife and he is turned over to his friends and the undertaker. If he stubs his toe or is scratched by the cat he immediately has lockjaw or blood poison, or he is considered as behind the times. – New Richmond *Record*, October 15, 1903.

CONTAGIOUS DISEASES, EPIDEMICS, AND PIONEER REMEDIES OF NEW RICHMOND RESIDENTS

The swampy nature of the area in and around New Richmond and Coal Creek Township was a constant threat to the health of the early settlers.

Malaria, or Ague, as the disease was called in the early days of Indiana history, wiped out more than one family in Coal Creek Township between 1830 and 1850. Standing in the local cemetery and comparing death dates, one can see many losses of members of families. It is believed the Kendall family may have lost several members from this disease, and perhaps the Kincaids. Malaria had invaded the village of Pleasant Hill about 1845 and there were isolated cases near New Richmond in later years.

Scarlet fever raged through the area in 1886, killing five children from one family in April that year. Another epidemic broke out in 1903.

Measles and **chicken pox** were expected yearly. In early days children often died from these diseases, but new discoveries in medicine lessens the chances of complications which caused the deaths.

Smallpox - The dreaded disease in a community always causes panic and when New Richmond reported the first death from this, the townspeople and the whole county were in a state of fear. On March 4, 1902 the death occurred, and another member of the family who had the disease recovered. The rest of the family had been vaccinated and escaped the illness, but the townspeople were in a terrible uproar because the disease hit so close to them.

Consumption - White Plague, or Tuberculosis, as the disease is known today, was another illness that took the lives of complete families in New Richmond, until it was controlled by placing the persons afflicted in isolation. In 1903 the State Board of Health realized the illness may have been spread through the schools and made a rule that teachers or scholars suspected of having the illness should stop attending school. Sanitariums were built throughout the State to treat this disease about this time, controlling the illness. New Richmond had its problems with this disease in the early pioneer days. Many families who had the disease moved on west hoping to improve their health. Some improved a few years after, others died because the illness was too far advanced.

Diphtheria hit the New Richmond and Coal Creek Township area in 1893. One family lost three children in 1893, another child in 1894 and still another in 1895. Other families were stricken with this disease, and typhoid fever was taking its toll at the same time.

Mumps, measles, whooping cough and **diphtheria** were all rampaging in the area of New Richmond from January through April of 1889. Whooping cough struck again in 1903 and 1905 and was in epidemic proportions in 1934. There may have been other years as severe, but I do not have the records of others.

Grippe, an acute catarrhal disease resembling influenza, hit the town of New Richmond in epidemic proportions in January of 1890 and continued through December the same year. The Crawfordsville *Review*, December 20th that year says, "The grippe has lost none of its grip and still holds on with a death's grip. Quinine and whiskey are in demand. Doctors Washburn and Black are kept busy dishing out pills to the afflicted."

Typhoid fever hit Coal Creek Township in 1894 and continued into 1895. There were isolated cases through the years. In 1906 two or three families were suffering from the disease.

Pioneer Remedies

Whiskey was given to children as well as adults to cure every illness from a cold to snake bites. The local general store advertised good Kentucky Whiskey "for medicinal purposes" in New Richmond.

The local physicians followed the practice of "bleeding" patients by making a large orifice in the vein to allow the blood to flow until the patient either fainted or became very sick - and perspiring very heavily would soon be rid of his high fever and delirium. Within a few days the afflicted would be up and about, but a little weak. My Grandmother often talked about this method of treatment and I nearly fainted hearing the stories. Leeches were also used to bleed patients by some physicians.

Every pioneer mother had a section of home remedies in her cook book. Remedies were usually made from the herbs and roots found in the nearby wooded area. Salt pork was applied to festered wounds to bring out the poison. A slice of raw beet wrapped around a finger would draw a splinter right out. And this remedy—I have never seen printed in any pioneer medical remedies - was given to me by a great-aunt, "to cure a gathered ear - dig some earth worms, place them in a pie tin and bake them in the oven (alive) until the fat is extracted. The fat, when cooled to a comfortably warm temperature, was then dropped into the afflicted ear, and a short time later the pain would subside. This aunt suggested I treat my daughter's ear ache in this manner, and I quickly called the local physician for a more modern remedy. Besides, the ground was frozen and I couldn't possibly get the spade to break the ground—let alone get down to where the worms spend the winter. Maybe you weren't supposed to have earaches in the winter time back then.

There were many pioneer remedies that made sense and most illnesses were cured by the housewife—sometimes sewing up a severe wound with the common sewing needle and thread when a physician could not be reached in time to save a child from losing too much blood.

Small towns are without physicians today and may send people back to the home medical books. A person could lose too much blood from a severe wound before reaching the nearest big city hospital. That's progress? New Richmond is now without a physician, the first time since Dr. Manners first started to practice medicine in 1843.

Dr. Frank Dallas Allhands (Wingate Physician)

Dr. Frank Dallas Allhands, son of George and Sarah De La Hunt Allhands, was born November 23, 1869 in Clark County, Indiana. He was one of twelve children. His father was a farmer and in addition to helping with the farm chores, Allhands managed to attend the local schools and continued his education in the Borden Institute, Borden, Indiana.

Allhands taught school to earn money to pay his way through the Kentucky School of Medicine in Louisville, Kentucky, and graduated from that school as an M.D in 1897. He took post-graduate work in the New York Polyclinic.

Allhands began the practice of medicine in Wingate, Indiana, in 1898 and was a well-known physician throughout the counties of Tippecanoe and Fountain, as well as in Montgomery County.

On October 8, 1901, Allhands married Miss Georgia Goodwin, daughter of Columbus and Vashti Willy Goodwin; Georgia was born January 23, 1874 in Sellersburg, Indiana. They were the parents of five children: one dying in infancy, Dallas G. who died in April 1974 at Bellview, Washington; Tyler of Urbana, Ill.; Vashti Nanette and Franklin D., both residing at Route 1, New Richmond. Franklin D. was a school teacher and coach of the New Richmond and Coal Creek schools.

Allhands was a Mason, a member of several medical associations, Knights of Pythias and the Methodist Church. Besides a fine home in Wingate, he owned several farms.

Allhands had been a practicing physician in Wingate forty-two years before his death on January 8, 1953. He is buried at Oakland cemetery near Elmdale, Indiana.

Dr. Allhand's great-grandfather, John A. was a native of Pennsylvania, moving to Virginia, later Kentucky and thence to Indiana when it was just a territory. He settled first on the banks of the Ohio. Frank's father and grandfather were both named George.

Allhands made his rounds in the old horse and buggy until he was quite elderly, and then changed his method of travel to an old Ford automobile.

Note: This article was originally published in the April 1979 issue of the *Montgomery Magazine*.

Dr. Arett Campbell Arnett

Dr. Arett C. Arnett was born in New Richmond in 1882, son of Alfred Jefferson and Elizabeth McBroom Arnett. He attended the local schools and spent his youth in and around New Richmond.

Arnett studied medicine at the Indiana Medical College and Central College of Physicians and Surgeons in Indianapolis. He entered his studies there in 1903. Arnett returned to his home for a vacation after finishing the second year in the Central College, bringing with him the honors of his class—that carried with it a free scholarship for his remaining two years there. At the time he graduated in 1907, the Indiana Medical College was located at Purdue University. He served his internship in St. Elizabeth Hospital in Lafayette.

Arnett had many relatives in and near New Richmond and he made regular visits home to spend his vacations. He and two other New Richmond boys, M.L. Claypool and Fred Alexander, were vocalists in a musical in the Sugar Grove Methodist Episcopal church during one of his visits. He sang a solo at another event, a Mid-Summer Festival, also held at the Sugar Grove Methodist Episcopal Church. The New Richmond *Record* always noted Arnett's activities and his accomplishments.

On some of his visits home from Medical school, he assisted the local physician, Dr. Frank M. Lynn, with surgery on a few of his patients. This surgery was performed in the homes of the patients, although there were hospitals in Crawfordsville and Lafayette at the time. He accompanied the local doctors in New Richmond on their rounds observing and learning all he could about the medical profession and soon became one of the best in the area.

In 1908 Arnett married Ethel McKinstray and they had a son, Richard A., who was killed with his bride on their honeymoon in an airplane crash August 26, 1935 at Glendo, Wyoming. The son was a commercial flyer. He was their only child.

Arnett was very interested in aviation in the pioneer days of flying and encouraged Charles Shambaugh in the establishment of Lafayette's first airport. He was a student pilot in the beginning of this new venture.

In 1916, Arnett joined the National Guard and was called to duty on the Mexican Border. In August 1917, he entered the U. S. Army Medical Corps with the rank of Major, being assigned to the 42nd, the Rainbow Division, later was assigned to the American and French Armies operating his own surgical team.

Back in civilian life he became a prominent figure in the American Legion and was surgeon for the Lafayette Police Department, as well as Chief Surgeon for the Monon Railroad and other railroads serving the city. He also served on the staffs at the St. Elizabeth and Home Hospitals in Lafayette.

In 1922 Arnett and Dr. F.S. Crockett formed the Arnett-Crockett Clinic, starting in the Schultz building on Fourth and Main streets in Lafayette. They started with only four physicians. They erected their own building on Eighth and Ferry in 1929. Dr. Crockett retired soon after they moved into this building and since then the clinic has been known as the Arnett Clinic. The Clinic was a great success throughout the years and soon outgrew the old building and another building was erected on Greenbush Street and Elmwood Avenue. The size of this building has grown since its original construction, and there are around sixty physicians having offices in the building. The latest x-ray equipment and other modern facilities are found in this clinic. In 1983 the clinic built another structure located between 14th, 16th,

Tippecanoe, and Salem Streets in Lafayette. Twenty physicians had offices in this building, in addition to the other group in the Greenbush Street building.

Dr. Arett C. Arnett died April 2, 1955 and is buried in the Spring Vale Cemetery at Lafayette, but his name lives on through his clinic. Many of the New Richmond people have visited the Arnett Clinic due to illness and will continue to do so. Among the relatives the doctor had in New Richmond were Mary Grady Waye, mother of the late Forrest Waye. Forrest was my father and during his last years he spent many hours as a patient at the clinic and reminded his children of the relationship to Arnett. He was very proud of the New Richmond boy's accomplishments.

Dr. Paul John Barcus

Paul J. Barcus was born July 13, 1862. There are conflicting stories as to where he was born; his obituary says in Linden, another record says he was born near Lafayette, and the descendants of the Ebrite family (his mother's family) say he was born in his grandparents' home in New Richmond. His parents were Col. John M. and Catharine "Kate" Ebrite Barcus. Col. Barcus was a bridge contractor who built many bridges in Montgomery and the neighboring counties.

Paul's mother Kate died April 4, 1864, when Paul was less than two years of age. She was only twenty-six at the time of her death and is buried in the New Richmond cemetery beside her parents, George and Mary Wright Ebrite. His father John had enlisted in the 120th Regiment of Indiana Volunteers in January the same year, being the first man to volunteer from New Richmond during the Civil War. This left little Paul without either parent to care for him. Paul was taken into the William Davisson family home in New Richmond until his father returned from the war.

Col. John Barcus was fortunate enough to survive the Civil War, and soon after his return he remarried to Eliza Anna Davisson. They moved to Crawfordsville and resided there until John died. Paul was eleven at the time of his father's death and again he was moved into the home of the Davisson family, attending school at New Richmond. After completing the required eight years of studies and passing the examinations, he taught in the local school in 1881. He wasn't too successful as a school teacher in his hometown, judging from a report of the township schools, but the report did not blame him entirely. Part of the problem was the parents' refusal to purchase the necessary books for the scholars, preferring to spend money foolishly, etc., and the building was in bad repair—but the scholars were allowed to play "boisterously" in the house too much at recess. Paul, however, earned enough to enter DePauw University in 1882, for a five months' course, and continued working his way through.

Barcus then entered the Ohio Medical College at Cincinnati, graduating in 1887. He began practicing medicine in 1888 in the little town of Odell, Indiana. During the Spanish-American War, he enlisted in the 158th Indiana Medical Corps as a surgeon with the rank of Captain.

Barcus then located in Crawfordsville after his return from the war; the new Culver Hospital in Crawfordsville gave him the opportunity to perform the first surgery. Doctors Ristine, Swope, and Allhands assisted Barcus with this surgery. The patient was Mrs. Hattie Striley of Clinton, Iowa, sister of Dr. Allhands. Barcus has the distinction of performing the first Caesarean section performed in this part of the country on December 1, 1902. This type of surgery was frowned upon at first, but the public was informed that the surgery was done only to save the life of the mother or baby, and the procedure was soon accepted.

In August 1905, Barcus and his wife left for Boston to sail to Europe to further his education in medicine and surgery. He studied in London and in the University of Berlin, Germany. The studies were to last three months, but they didn't return until December the same year.

Barcus specialized in General and Abdominal Surgery and Disorders of women and was often called to attend patients in New Richmond by the local physicians. He was devoted to his profession and religiously lived up to the highest standards of medicine and surgery.

Dr. Paul J. Barcus married Susan K. Kirkpatrick, daughter of Jacob and Amanda A. (Shuee) Kirkpatrick. They had two children, Paul, Jr. and Gertrude. The doctor performed two operations the day before his death, suffering a stroke after he returned home from the hospital on Saturday. He died the next day, Sunday December 27, 1925, and is buried in the Oak Hill North cemetery in Crawfordsville, Indiana. To the end of his life he was a student and one of his most prized possessions was the fellowship he held in the American College of Surgeons, an honor extended only to a comparatively few of the leading surgeons of the country.

Dr. Christian J. Biedenkopf

Dr. C.J. Biedenkopf attended Wabash College and Rush Medical College of Chicago, graduating from Rush in 1903. He first practiced medicine at Union, Oklahoma, for a year, but his friends, the Vaughan family of New Richmond, encouraged him to come to New Richmond to practice.

The doctor arrived in New Richmond on March 19, 1904 and settled in the Black Bear Hotel while he made the necessary arrangements for a place for him and his wife to reside, and a place to rent for his office. He engaged a room over the bank—this would have been in the Washburn block, the brick building on the southeast corner of Wabash and Washington streets in the business district. The doctor's wife Bertha arrived from Union, Oklahoma, in April. She was an excellent trained nurse and worked beside her husband, nursing the patients back to health and assisting him during surgery.

Dr. Biedenkopf was the first physician in New Richmond to try grafting new flesh on an injury, and he also tried sewing the end of a finger that had been severed back to its original place. This operation was unsuccessful and had to be amputated.

A small boy was bitten on the lip by a horse, which took a piece about an inch long from his lower lip. The doctor had the rest of the family to try and locate the missing piece in order to graft it back to the lip, but they could not find it, and it was believed the horse had swallowed it. The parents decided the little boy would not suffer any material deformity by letting the lip heal with only the stitches the doctor had used to pull the wound together.

Biedenkopf and New Richmond's other two physicians, Dr. Lynn and Dr. Washburn, were all called to the scene of a terrible accident that occurred in New Richmond. Two men were painting on the new addition to the A.E. Malsbary elevator some forty feet off the ground when one of the scaffold pulleys gave way, leaving the scaffold swinging with the two men still on it. One of the men, Will E. Sims of Waynetown, caught onto a rope with his hand, thus breaking his fall, but the other, Emil Thurnblaser, a German, fell heavily to the ground, suffering internal injuries, a deep cut on the head, and a badly broken thigh and ribs. He was taken to Culver Hospital the afternoon of the accident and died the next morning. He was buried in the Masonic cemetery in Waynetown. A subscription was taken by his friends and citizens of Waynetown to bury him. He was an expert painter of thirty years' experience. He came from Hamburg, Germany, five weeks prior to the accident, but had been to America before and had painted about the tops of New York's twenty-six story buildings. He was a fine off-hand fresco artist. It was a tragic accident and the people of New Richmond and Waynetown were very saddened by his death.

Dr. C. J. Biedenkopf and his wife left New Richmond the latter part of February 1910. They had made many friends while living here and the editor of the New Richmond *Record* expressed his opinion of their departure saying, "The Doctor is a well-read 'materia medic' and his 'better half' is an excellent professional trained nurse. Their friends here will wish them success in their new field of labor."

The doctor was undecided as to where he would go to practice, but was considering Terre Haute, Vincennes, or Evansville, preferring the latter.

Dr. Dayton R. Black

Dr. Dayton R. Black was born in Bourbon County, Kentucky, in April 1852, son of Matthew and Zerilda (Berry) Black, both natives of Kentucky. Dayton was one of eleven children.

When Black was a little boy his parents removed from Kentucky, to Putnam County, Indiana, leaving behind many friends. His father was a farmer and Black and his brothers were expected to help with the farm work, but Black had developed a desire to read and study and was determined to pursue a professional life. Farm work was very hard work in the early settlement of our state and many young men had their fill of this type of work while in the parental home and often went out into the world seeking other means of livelihood. He attended the public schools in Putnam County and prepared himself for a college course.

Black entered the Asbury University in Greencastle, now DePauw University, at the tender age of seventeen, remaining there three years; he decided not to complete the course. When he reached the age of twenty-one, he had decided to pursue the medical profession and began studying under Dr. Wilcox, one of Indiana's leading physicians. Diligently reading medicine for two years, he then entered college in Indianapolis, and after completing his course of instruction at the College of Physicians and Surgeons, he graduated with honor during the 1874-75 term, and was ready to pursue his profession.

Doctor Black first located in Coatesville, Indiana, to practice his profession, remaining there two years. He was induced to remove to New Richmond in 1878 where he soon built up an extensive practice. He made many friends in the town and took an active interest in public affairs. At one time he owned half interest in the local tile mill in New Richmond. He was in partnership with Dr. D.M. Washburn until July 1880, when he joined Dr. Detchon. He and Detchon treated patients all over Coal Creek Township and received good comments from the Bristle Ridgers and Patton's Corner and Round Hill residents. He resided in the McComas Hotel in New Richmond before his marriage. Dr. Black had a fine sense of humor and was often telling funny stories in the local grocery and one at the expense of the weather—a cold January in 1887. Black said it was so cold that standing before the glass he had a life size picture of himself. He promised to hang it up in the office so he would always be there when his friends call.

On Sunday evening May 25, 1890, Dr. Dayton R. Black and Maggie E. Jones were married. The Crawfordsville *Star*, Friday, May 30th had this to say, "Dr. D. R. Black, the prominent young physician of New Richmond, and Miss Maggie Jones, daughter of George W. Jones, of Madison Township were married last Sunday evening at the home of Harry Mitchell in New Richmond. The ceremony was performed by the Rev. Rogers immediately after the adjournment of church services. A fine supper was prepared for the invited guests by Scott Steele, of this city. The bride and groom are well known in this county, and both occupy positions of high social standing. The Star is sincere in congratulating Dr. and Mrs. Black and wishes them mountains of success and happiness. They will begin housekeeping at once." The following year he and his wife took a belated honeymoon on a trip through the west.

Black continued to practice medicine in New Richmond until 1897, when he and his family moved to Terre Haute, Indiana. The doctor had many relatives in Terre Haute, and he soon built up an excellent practice in that city. He remained in Terre Haute until his death in May 1904, dying of pneumonia at the age of fifty-two. He left a wife and two daughters, Gretchen and Leona.

Dr. Ira Cole

Ira Cole was born in Fountain County, Indiana, around 1891 and was reared in Fountain and Warren Counties, where he received his early schooling. He attended Valparaiso University and taught school for two years. He entered the Medical School at Indiana University and received his Medical Degree from that school. He served his internship in Indianapolis and took post-graduate work at the University of Pennsylvania and also took special training at the New York Lying-In Hospital.

In 1921 Dr. Cole moved to Linden and commenced the practice of medicine, having his office in his home on Main Street. He located in New Richmond in 1923 practicing medicine and delivering many babies. My brothers, Melvin and Malcolm Waye were the first set of twins Cole delivered, and he also delivered me, Phyllis Waye. Our parents were Forrest and Vera (Ebrite) Waye. His office in New Richmond was located next door east of the Tri-County Telephone office; the little frame building still stands, but has been moved back from the street.

There are many people still living in the vicinity of New Richmond who were brought into this world by Dr. Ira Cole, and several expectant mothers continued to doctor with him after he left New Richmond.

Cole left New Richmond in 1929, locating in Lafayette, where he began to specialize in Obstetrics and Gynecology. He was associated with Dr. Lowell R. Johnson for eighteen years, and my path crossed

Cole's once again. Johnson was my physician and Cole covered for Dr. Johnson when he was otherwise detained, thus paying me a visit on more than one occasion.

Cole practiced medicine a total of fifty years and was to have been among twenty-four Hoosier physicians to be inducted into the Fifty Year Club in June 1971, at the 122nd Annual Convention of the Indiana State Medical Association in Indianapolis, but he was hospitalized at the time and was unable to attend. He served on the staffs of the Home and St. Elizabeth Hospitals in Lafayette, and was past president of both. He was past president of the Tippecanoe County Medical Association; member of the Indiana State Medical Association; American Medical Association; Fellowship in American Academy of Obstetrics and Gynecology, and Fellow in American Chapter of International College of Surgeons.

Cole married Mabel May Biser in 1911 at West Lebanon, and they had three children: Marjorie E., William I., and Victor Donald. The doctor's wife died in 1960, and Cole died on April 21, 1976 at the age of eighty-five years, and both are buried in the Springvale Cemetery near Lafayette, Indiana.

Dr. Elliott Detchon

Dr. Elliott Detchon was born in Portage County, Ohio, on March 15, 1828. Elliott married Martha Jane Agnew, daughter of Gibson Agnew, on July 4, 1848. They were married in Rockville, Indiana. Eleven children were born to this couple, five of whom were deceased before 1898. Those living were: Dr. Irwin Agnew Detchon, Mrs. William M. White, Mrs. E.B. Gonzales, Miss Harriet Detchon of Crawfordsville, Mrs. Dr. W.R. Garver of Indianapolis, and Seymour Detchon of Toronto, Ontario, Canada.

There is no record of Elliott Detchon's formal schooling, or where he studied medicine, but he was practicing, or studying medicine with Dr. Simison in Romney in 1851, and Dr. Stowe Detchon studied under the two doctors at Romney around 1860.

Elliott Detchon practiced medicine in Parke County, Romney, Pleasant Hill (Wingate), Newtown, New Richmond, and Crawfordsville. In 1871 he started a drug store in Crawfordsville located on the corner of Green and Main Streets, and was connected with his sons, Seymour and Irwin A. in the wholesale and retail drug trade. They later engaged in the manufacture of proprietary medicines, and established a branch office in Toronto, Ontario, Canada. Seymour was in charge of this branch and moved his family to Canada. Irwin Agnew, the other son, worked with his father, having an office at the same address as Elliott (Green & Main). Seymour was listed as an M.D., Physician and Surgeon.

Dr. Elliott Detchon and his wife Martha celebrated their Golden Wedding in July 1898. He was seventy years of age, and a man of magnificent physique; she was sixty-nine and still in very good health.

Dr. Elliott Detchon died January 29, 1905 in Crawfordsville and is buried in the Oak Hill cemetery. Martha J. died in 1908, and she too, is buried in the Oak Hill cemetery, as are most of their children.

Dr. Irwin Agnew Detchon

Dr. Irwin Agnew Detchon, son of Elliott and Martha Agnew Detchon, was born in Montgomery County Indiana in 1850.

It is uncertain where he studied medicine, but in November 1882, the rising young doctor married Ella Washburn, daughter of George W. and Louise Whetstone Washburn of New Richmond. Ella died a few months later, in March 1883 at the age of twenty-four years.

Dr. Irwin A. Detchon was practicing medicine in New Richmond in December 1881 and apparently there were rumors of his leaving the town, so he called on the Crawfordsville *Review* office and informed the public that he did not intend to leave New Richmond. Just a year later, however, he printed a notice in the Crawfordsville *Journal* that reads, "Irwin A. Detchon, M. D., Physician and Surgeon, office at Detchon's drug store, corner of Green and Main Streets; residence, third house south of Episcopal Church, South Green Street, Crawfordsville, Indiana. Prompt attention to all calls day and night."

The doctor was associated with his father Dr. Elliott, and brother, Dr. Seymour Detchon in the manufacture of proprietary medicines and was listed in the Montgomery County Directory of 1891-92 as a physician and pharmacist, and manufacturer of proprietary medicines at the same location of Dr. Elliott Detchon at the 1330 Main Street location in Crawfordsville.

Irwin Detchon married Annie Bell Lee on June 16, 1892, and they had two children, Irwin Lee Detchon and Esther. He and his wife moved to Chicago to manage the family business in that city in September 1893; their daughter Esther, was born in this city.

Dr. Stowe S. Detchon

Dr. Stowe S. Detchon was born in 1830 in what is now Mahoning County, Ohio, son of John and Maria (Hoadley) Detchon. Stowe attended the common schools in his native state and when he was twenty-one years of age removed to Montgomery County, in the town of New Richmond, Indiana. Determined to qualify himself for a profession, he first studied dentistry, practicing in Rockville, Parke County, and was listed as a dentist in the 1860 census in New Richmond. Not satisfied with his choice, he decided to become a physician. In order to pay his expenses in medical school, he taught school in Parke County, reading medicine in his spare time.

43 - Dr. Stowe S. Detchon residence

Dr. Detchon attended lectures at Rush Medical College in Chicago and then studied with Dr. Elliott Detchon and Dr. Simison at Romney, Indiana. Stowe's obituary said Elliott was his cousin, but another account states they were brothers, so I am not sure of the relationship of the two.

In 1861 Dr. Stowe Sylvester Detchon hung out his shingle in New Richmond; his office stood just east of his residence on East Washington Street. For nearly thirty years he gave his talents to the afflicted of that community, answering calls in sunshine or rain, by day or night, exposed to most inclement weather and various contagious diseases. In addition to treating the sick, he shared his knowledge of medicine with the next generation of prospective physicians. Studying under Dr. Detchon were: Billy Mershon; Alfred Ebrite in 1870; William J. Hurt, at the age of 19, was studying with him in 1870; and Dr. Gimmel in 1873. Dr. Dayton R. Black and Dr. Stowe Detchon became partners in July 1880 after Black and Dr. D.M. Washburn dissolved partnership.

Dr. Detchon unfalteringly went about his rounds until he resigned his practice in 1888. He kept his favorite pair of horses, George and Frank, said to be respectively 24 and 30 years old in 1891. The doctor drove them on his rounds while attending the sick and the pair retired on full rations to enjoy the fruits of old age. They were highly valued by the owner.

Dr. Detchon greatly aided in the development of New Richmond, laying out seven additions to the town and selling all the lots in each addition, so great was the demand for property. Not only did he make the lots available, but moved houses from other sites, placing them on his lots, remodeling, adding rooms, painting, and otherwise improving the homes to rent or sell. He had erected seven new homes by 1889. He built his own residence in December 1875, hoping to move in around the 11th of that month. He built another new residence in 1890 and had it piped for the use of natural gas, having faith in securing the gas to heat his home.

Dr. Detchon witnessed the burning of New Richmond and aided in the rebuilding of the burned portion of the town. He was one of the town's first trustees. He and his wife Jemima gave one-half acre of land to the trustees of the New Richmond Christian Church, "for love and affection they hold for the Society," the deed says, in 1888. The only requirement he asked was to keep and maintain a good substantial fence around said lot. This was to keep the livestock out—a common problem in the early days, when cattle were allowed to roam freely.

The doctor devoted most of his later years to agriculture, being the first farmer to lay drain tile on his land, thus ridding the town of the sloughs and the diseases carried by the ponds. This improvement made his farm one of the finest in the county, providing a rich productive soil. Other nearby farmers soon followed his example and in a few years most of the ponds were drained near the town of New Richmond. He became interested in livestock and raised some of the finest cattle and hogs ever to have been fattened on the prairie grass near the town. He purchased some large scales to aid the farmers in weighing their livestock and other farm products.

Dr. Detchon married Mary McComas in 1857; she died five years later, in 1862. He then married Jemima Thomas, daughter of James and Joanna (Bobo) Thomas. Two children were born to the doctor and his second wife—a daughter Tinna, who died at the age of five years on December 20, 1872; and a son John Thomas Detchon, born on February 5, 1874. Just before the doctor's retirement he and his wife decided to have a grand reunion of his family. He met the train at Linden with three teams to greet the relatives from Ohio.

Dr. Stowe S. Detchon was a member of the Montgomery County Medical Society, and the American Medical Association, and was sent as a delegate to the National Society in 1891, which convened that year in Washington, D. C.

Dr. Detchon's health began to fail and he suffered a paralytic stroke about a week before his death on November 12, 1902. His widow and son erected one of the largest monuments in the New Richmond cemetery for his grave. A Danville, Illinois, firm placed the stone, a handsomely carved stone which came in seven parts and stands about ten feet in the air. The base is five feet by eight feet and weighed about thirty tons.

Dr. George W. Dewey

George W. Dewey was born northeast of New Richmond on August 24, 1844. He was one of seven children of Washington and Elizabeth "Betsey" Gannon Dewey. George attended the nearby Dewey (later known as Walnut Grove) School.

On March 4, 1870, Dr. Dewey married Susan M. Alexander, daughter of Isaac H. and Asenith (Smith) Alexander. They had a daughter, Maude, who married William C. Breaks, and a son Claud, who died at the age of one year.

Dewey and his family resided seven miles northwest of Crawfordsville and practiced medicine in that neighborhood for over forty-five years. He was prominent in his profession during the trying period when physicians traveled on horseback or on foot. Many times he walked as far as ten miles to attend a patient, and did not think anything of it. Many early pioneers preferred to walk rather than take the time to harness the horse to a carriage.

Dewey died Sunday, May 11, 1924 at the home of his daughter in Crawfordsville at the age of eighty. His wife passed away October 9, 1921. Both are buried in the New Richmond cemetery.

Dr. Samuel E. Jones

Samuel E. Jones, son of George and Mary F. Champion Jones, was born in New Richmond, Indiana, August 5, 1875. He attended the local schools, graduating from New Richmond High School with the class of 1895. He had returned to the school after an absence of a few years to complete his studies. Sam attended the Indiana State Normal and taught school for two years in Montgomery County in order to pay his expenses to Indiana Medical School from which he graduated in 1906 with honors. At this time the Medical School was connected with Purdue University.

In May 1906, Dr. Samuel Jones and his wife were building a new home in Bowers, Indiana, where he was to follow the practice of medicine. Their home was completed and ready for their occupancy in June. Their first child was born in this home. The same year in October, Jones became a candidate for Montgomery County Coroner on the Democratic ticket; after winning the election, he served one term.

Jones and family moved back to New Richmond the following year, in 1907. He practiced medicine in the town, having his office in the little frame building later occupied by Doctors Cole and Kindell. This building still stands but was moved back from the street next to the Tri-County Telephone Office. He served as the town's Health Officer from April 6, 1908 to September 6, 1909, at which time he was preparing to move to Kirkpatrick to practice medicine.

Jones practiced medicine in Kirkpatrick only one year, moving to Lucerne, Indiana, where he stayed until 1920. From Lucerne, he went to Chicago, entering the Polyclinic Hospital to further his studies in order to specialize in the treatment of eye, ear, nose, and throat diseases.

After completing this course of studies he located in Crawfordsville in 1921. In 1924 he again moved his family, this time to Indianapolis, where he resided and practiced medicine until his death in 1937.

Samuel Jones was a half-brother to Edgar L. Jones, who resided southeast of New Richmond many years.

Dr. Hurschell D. Kindell

Hurschell D. Kindell, son of Hanson T. and Anna (Pittman) Kindell, was born January 15, 1901 near Wingate, Indiana. His father, Hanson, was a rural mail carrier in the Wingate area. Kindell spent his formative years in that vicinity and attended the Wingate public schools, graduating in 1919.

He entered the Medical School at Indiana University and received his Medical Degree in 1924. He served his internship in the U. S. Navy and commenced the practice of medicine in Newtown, in Fountain County, on August 13, 1926.

44 - Office of Dr. Hurschell D. Kindell

Kindell was persuaded to go to New Richmond upon receiving word that Dr. Cole, who was practicing there at the time, was to move to Lafayette, and the town was in need of a physician. This was in 1929 and the beginning of the Great Depression, not the best time in the history of our country for a young M.D. just starting in medicine—nor was it so great for his patients who did not have the money to eat—let alone get sick.

Many patients needing hospital care simply could not pay, so the doctor treated them in their homes as well as he could, setting broken bones—sometimes on the dining table—delivering babies, sewing up wounds, and treating the patients for various contagious diseases. The barter system was used on many occasions by the patients, or by the head of the family paying the bills. My father was a painter and paperhanger, and although we children were not ill too often, there were a few medical expenses to be met and Dr. Kindell and his wife would decide to have a room or two redecorated, enabling Dad to work off his bill. The area farmers kept his family in meat and poultry, and the town folks usually had gardens supplying the doctor and family with fresh produce.

Somehow we all survived. Gerald Waye, my brother, was Dr. Kindell's driver in the winter months of 1935 through 1937, and accompanied him on his rounds and to Culver Hospital in Crawfordsville. Gerald was always able to conquer the drifted snow on the roads without getting stuck, but on one occasion became so bogged down in the mud, they both thought they would never get out.

Dr. Kindell's first office was in the small frame building next to the Tri-County Telephone Company office. This building was moved back from the street and still stands today. His next office was located next to his residence.

This building stood between the Starr Dunn brick building and the Doctor's residence, both of which were built by Starr Dunn. The residence is on the northwest corner of Franklin and Washington Streets. In the 1950s Kindell purchased the brick house west of (and attached to) the Frank Perkin's brick building.

This served as his office until his retirement. The Frank Perkin's building served as the fire department and town hall many years.

Kindell was a member of the American Academy of Family Physicians. This organization required all the members to complete 150 hours of continuing education every three years, and held seminars on clinical, scientific, and technical exhibits. The headquarters of this medical association is in Kansas City, Missouri. He held membership in the Indiana Medical Association and was one of twenty-nine physicians inducted into the 50 Year Club on October 19, 1975. The special ceremonies were held during the 126th Annual Convention at French Lick, Indiana. He was also a member of the American Medical Association.

Kindell was selected as master of ceremonies for a homecoming picnic, sponsored by the C.I.N.R. Club of New Richmond in the town park in September 1960. He explained the purpose of the club—a community improvement group—and, after completing his talk, was presented a plaque in appreciation of his faithful service for over thirty years as a New Richmond physician. He also won the men's casting contest that afternoon. Fishing was the doctor's favorite pastime, and his vacations were usually spent in a boat with his fishing rods.

On Friday, August 13, 1976, several of Kindell's old patients and friends held a reception for him in his office. The businessmen of the town presented him with a large bouquet of flowers, and his first patient who came to him in his Newtown office, Robert Bacon, brought a decorated cake to share with the group.

The doctor was again honored by the New Richmond businessmen Sunday, April 16, 1978 at the Holiday Inn in Crawfordsville, upon his retirement after forty-nine years as a physician in New Richmond, and three years in Newtown.

He retired April 15, 1978, a dedicated physician to the very day of retirement. He had waited at the bedside of many patients, after administering medication, and doing all that was possible to cure them of their illness. His presence was a great comfort to the ill—and to other members of the family who were waiting with him.

Dr. and Mrs. Kindell moved to Crawfordsville, on the Country Club Road, in March 1970, but retained his office in New Richmond.

Dr. Hurschell D. Kindell had married Beulah Haas on August 2, 1924 at Danville, Illinois. They were the parents of two children: Shirley, Mrs. William Stoker, and William "Bill." His wife, Beulah, stood by the Doctor, answering the calls that came all hours of the day and night, and faithfully saw to his receiving and answering all the calls. More than one special dinner or family gathering was ruined or interrupted by a phone call from an anxious mother with a sick child—or an anxious expectant father unable to get the message straight, usually finished by the calm expectant mother. The wives and children of physicians are certainly to be commended.

After his retirement, the town of New Richmond was without a physician for the first time since Doctor Manners began the practice of medicine in 1843.

After a long illness, Dr. Hurschell D. Kindell passed away, on Friday, October 2, 1981, at the age of 80 years. The townspeople all felt as if they had lost a member of their family. He is surely missed.

Dr. Frank M. Lynn

Frank M. Lynn was born in Montgomery County, Indiana, on August 13, 1869. He spent his early life in Crawfordsville, attending the local schools. Frank was raised by his maternal grandparents, Andrew Jackson and Mary R. (Rearden) Clark. Mary was the only mother he ever knew. The Clarks were living in Mattoon, Illinois in 1904 when they removed to New Richmond and were still residents at the time of Mary's death in 1907 in New Richmond.

On October 15, 1890 Frank Lynn married Mary Elizabeth McLain, daughter of Perry and Nellie McLain. Mary had been born December 15, 1873 at Jamestown, Indiana. Her family had moved to New Richmond and was living there at the time of her marriage to Lynn. This marriage ended in divorce; they only lived together nine years. There were no children born to them.

Lynn then married Myrtle Work, February 28, 1910, daughter of John and Jennie (Steele) Work. John was the New Richmond Marshal. There were no children born to this couple either.

Lynn was working on the Monon railroad as a fireman in September 1891 when he was struck on the head by a low bridge and knocked "senseless." He was earning the necessary funds to enter medical school. He had graduated from Wabash College and was able to enter the Central College of Physicians and Surgeons in Indianapolis, in the 1891-92 term. He received his Medical Degree from Central in 1894.

Dr. Frank M. Lynn commenced the practice of medicine in New Richmond soon after receiving his degree and was listed as a physician in the 1895 Directory of Montgomery County. Dr. Arett Arnett studied under Dr. Frank M. Lynn and assisted him as he performed surgery on the local patients. Most of this surgery was still being performed in the homes at this time. Arnett was attending the Central College in Indianapolis at this time and worked with Lynn during his vacation and holidays. Lynn's office was in his residence on East Washington Street in New Richmond. He served as the city Health Officer in New Richmond until February 26, 1908, when he resigned the office; the resignation was to take effect at the April meeting.

Lynn moved to Peru, Indiana in April 1908, where he practiced medicine until his retirement in 1954. He served as City Health Officer in Peru eight years; was a member of the Miami County Medical Society, Indiana State Medical Society, and American Medical Society. He died March 15, 1958 and was buried at Peru.

Dr. George Manners

George Manners was born in Mercer County, Kentucky, January 29, 1816, son of James and Lettice (Hight) Manners. His father was a soldier in the War of 1812. When Manners was about two years old, the family moved to Monroe County, Indiana, where they stayed only two years. In 1820 the family moved to Putnam County, where the father helped plat the town of Russellville. The family made one last move—this time to Clark Township in Montgomery County in 1830.

In 1831 George Manners and his brothers, Joseph and Harvey, and his sisters, Percilla, (sp) Nancy, and Martha, attended a subscription school

45 - Dr. George Manners residence

held in an old log cabin vacated by Daniel Clark in 1829. It stood one-half mile east of the Ladoga cemetery. His first teacher was Miss Lettie Harrison, who only taught the summer of 1831, and married soon after. Her brother, Joshua, taught the next two winters. The first school house in Clark Township was built in 1835 and was one-half mile east of the log cabin, and was known as Shaver's school house. George Manners taught the first school in this house. He had taken a special course to qualify himself as a grammar teacher.

Manners' father was a farmer and he and his brothers and sisters were expected to help with the farm chores in addition to studying. Manners attended the common school until he was eighteen, and then entered Wabash College. In 1839 he entered Asbury University, taking a five month course. Asbury later became DePauw University and is located in Greencastle, Indiana. He taught school and worked at whatever jobs he could find to help defray the expenses of board and tuition.

At the age of twenty-two, Manners began to read medicine, and five years later began the practice of medicine in the town of New Richmond. He was twenty-seven years of age when he commenced his medical profession in 1843. Not satisfied with his limited knowledge of medicine, he decided to further his studies, and in the 1845-6 term he attended Louisville Medical College. On receiving his diploma from that school, he then entered Ohio Medical College during the 1846-7 term.

Manners was a sterling example of the pioneer spirit, starting with nothing but intelligence and energy, and a desire to learn a profession that would benefit many. He soon made a fortune. He owned 665 acres of fine farm land and became the wealthiest man in Coal Creek Township.

Some of the older residents of New Richmond have said Dr. Manners had his office in the town of New Richmond, but it has not been included on the early maps of the town. He did purchase Lot #4 in block 1 from Eli Elrod on February 23, 1844, and lot #3, block 1 from David Oppy May 28, 1847, so one of these locations may have been his office site.

Manners' residence was located just south of the railroad running through New Richmond, on the west side of the Linden-New Richmond road. It was a large two story residence that has been remodeled so extensively there is no resemblance of the original structure, but a home still stands at this location today (1983). He constructed a maple sugar camp across the road from his residence as another sideline; it produced a good supply of syrup and sugar for the townspeople as well as the Doctor and family.

Manners was not the type of character to sit and count his wealth at the end of each day; he put it to good use. When Asbury University was struggling to make ends meet and was facing bankruptcy, Manners, along with other Alumni, came to the school's rescue by donating $10,000 in 1879, and another $15,000 some time later. The Trustees of Asbury showed their appreciation by establishing the "George Manners Chair of Latin" in his honor. This honor is still in existence today and college students are benefited each year because of it. At the time of death, he had contributed between sixty to seventy thousand dollars, the exact amount was not known.

In addition to the endowments made to the University, he and his wife gave generously to the Methodist Episcopal Churches in Ladoga and in Coal Creek Township. A plaque beneath the windows in the bell tower of the Ladoga Methodist church reads, "Manner's Chapel Methodist Church, 1892." This tower was still standing in 1973; the church was closed three years previous.

The Round Hill, or Asbury, Methodist Church was built upon Dr. Manners' land in that neighborhood and Mrs. Manners gave the congregation in New Richmond land on which to build a church and parsonage on May 21, 1888, after her husband's death. In addition to the land, she purchased some of the equipment and furniture, and the carpeting. George Manners served on the Methodist church board many years in New Richmond.

Dr. George Manners married Barbara G. White on June 21, 1846. She was born in Ohio September 9, 1823, daughter of Charles and Mary (Leah) White. Charles White was New Richmond's first rural mail carrier. Dr. and Mrs. Manners had no children of their own, but raised several children. The Curnutt children were among the children they raised, after both parents died. Mary Curnutt married James Tribby and three of their daughters became missionaries from the New Richmond Methodist Church, carrying on the Manners tradition of giving.

Barbara Manners made four additions to the town of New Richmond containing thirty-two lots in all, to help with the growth of the town.

In September 1884, Manners met with a painful accident while walking to his home, falling on the slippery railroad ties caused by rains that had fallen. He fell with such force across the iron railing that his left femur bone above the center was fractured. Two men who happened to be nearby carried him to his home. The Doctor never completely recovered from this accident and died January 5, 1885. He was buried in the Oak Hill cemetery near Crawfordsville. The Crawfordsville *Journal*, January 10, 1885 had this to say of Dr. Manners,

"The community has lost one of the best friends, the church one of the main pillars, the profession, a good advisor, the wife a faithful husband. The widow has the sympathy of the entire community."

Barbara (White) Manners died August 8, 1900 and was buried beside her husband at Oak Hill, having lived to see the building of the Methodist church in New Richmond and the growth of the town fulfilling two of her dreams.

Dr. Leverett W. Olin

Leverett W. Olin, son of Ransom and Clara (Clark) Olin, was born near Kent, in Portage County, Ohio, February 12, 1851. The father died in that county in 1868, the mother in 1883. Leverett returned to his home to visit his mother in August, the year of her death. He was one of eleven children.

Olin was reared in Ohio, and attended the common schools in that state. He attended Buchtel College, at Akron, Ohio, and decided to pursue the medical profession. After four years reading medicine under Dr. E.W. Price, a physician in Kent, Ohio, he then attended two six-month terms at the College of Physicians and Surgeons, in New York City, this being the medical department of Columbia University, and graduated on March 12, 1880.

Dr. Leverett W. Olin moved to Elmdale, Indiana, and on April 13, 1880, commenced the practice of medicine in that neighborhood. He soon established a large and successful practice in Coal Creek Township and treated many patients in the New Richmond area. Dr. Stow S. Detchon and Dr. Olin met twice a week when Olin first started his practice - Detchon may have helped him get established. Detchon had been treating many patients near Elmdale and Bristle Ridge in addition to caring for his New Richmond patients, and that was quite a large territory to cover on horseback, or by horse and carriage. The two doctors may have been acquainted in Ohio, as they came from adjoining counties.

Dr. Olin met his lifelong companion, Effie Swank, and they were married September 2, 1883. She was the daughter of Benjamin and Ellen (Cowan) Swank, early settlers in the Elmdale and Bristle Ridge neighborhood. To this union were born eleven children, but only seven lived to maturity, the others dying from childhood diseases.

The children who survived to maturity were: Lester W., Blanche, Grace, Leverett R., Leland E., Ruth, and Reine.

Lester W. married Tessie Patton, and was a school teacher in the Elmdale and New Richmond schools for thirty-eight years, retiring in the 1950s. He taught three generations of several families in the New Richmond area, and was admired and respected by all three generations. This was before someone came up with the idea of a "generation gap." He began teaching after completing his eight years of common school, and by taking the required examination was qualified to teach.

Blanche Olin married Scott Cowan, a farmer in Montgomery County; Grace married Virgil Meritt, a farmer in Coal Creek Township; Leverett R. married Mary M. Crowder and was a foreman at the Studebaker plant in South Bend. He later farmed and was a race horse driver near Argos, Indiana. Leland E., a farmer, married May Harshbarger and resided south of New Richmond; Ruth married Mary's brother Ralph Crowder and resided at Waukegan, Michigan. Mary and Ralph Crowder were children of George and Melissa Crowder who resided in New Richmond around 1907-1912. The daughter Reine Olin, died in 1916, and was not married.

Dr. Olin's wife, Effie, died November 24, 1915 at the age of fifty-two and Dr. Leverett W. Olin died June 9, 1924 in his seventy-third year. He had practiced his profession near Elmdale for forty-three years, carrying on his work until within about a month of his death. He was one of the most prominent figures in the Elmdale community and a member of the Methodist Church of that place. Both Doctor and Mrs. Olin were buried in the Oakland cemetery, near Elmdale.

Dr. D. Manners Washburn

D. Manners Washburn, son of Nicholas L. and Jane Potter Washburn, was born August 3, 1850, two miles south of New Richmond. I have never found any record of his first name, but strongly believe it stands for Doctor, as he was named for Doctor Manners, New Richmond's first physician, who probably delivered him. Washburn spent most of his life in Coal Creek Township except a few years the family lived in Madison Township. His father purchased the farm south of New Richmond in 1840, and they were listed in Madison Township in the Federal Census in 1860.

Washburn started school in Linden at the age of six and completed the required examinations to teach school at the young age of fourteen. He taught in the New Richmond School one year and taught the following year in the Linden schools at age fifteen. He took a short course at the Ladoga Normal and, at the age of seventeen, began the study of medicine under Dr. McMurray, a Linden physician. McMurray later practiced in Frankfort, Indiana. Washburn read with Dr. McMurray for five years and in October 1873 entered the Medical Institute in Indianapolis, returning from the lectures in March the following year.

Washburn contemplated practicing medicine in Fowler in Benton County, but decided to remain in New Richmond, hanging out his shingle on April 4, 1874. He was first associated with Dr. Stowe S. Detchon, then with Dr. Dayton R. Black for about twelve years. After he and Dr. Black dissolved partnership, he was associated with Dr. Irwin Detchon for four years. Dr. Irwin Detchon moved to Crawfordsville to join his father, Dr. Elliott Detchon, in his medical office. After Dr. Irwin Detchon moved, Dr. Washburn continued to practice medicine in New Richmond alone.

The people in New Richmond were temporarily upset one morning over some rumors of Washburn getting his skull cracked—after which they were informed the skull belonged to his skeleton—the one he got from medical school. They decided he would recover from the accident without too much pain.

Washburn continued to study the latest medical discoveries, purchasing new books until he had acquired a fine, extensive medical library.

In addition to the knowledge found in medical books, he made several trips out into the woods with an Indian medicine man. The first trip he claimed to have been hunting prairie chickens, but admitted prairie chicks did not hide out in the woods. The next trip mentioned the two simply went hunting. The article said "two big medicine men together are enough to make one have a pain." Some of the older residents of New Richmond have said the doctor

46 - Office of Dr. D. Manners Washburn

was a firm believer in the use of herbs for medicinal purposes and he claimed to have a cure for cancer. Patients would come to his office for treatment and he would put them up in his home for a two or three weeks' treatment. The upstairs of his home contained one large room with small rooms off to one side that were used for treatment rooms, similar to a hospital room. This home was located on the southeast corner of Franklin and Washington Streets in New Richmond. The house still stands today. (1986)

A notice in the *Farmer's Review*, September 20th and October 11, 1935, reads, "Dr. D. M. Washburn, Specialist—Cancer and Gall Stones."

Studying medicine under Dr. Manners Washburn was George F. Long. George had studied and was almost finished in the Medical College of Indiana and would have received his sheep-skin in another six months, but lacked the funds to continue. He gave up his coveted vocation rather than to borrow money. George went into the jewelry business after this, later into the dry-goods merchandise business.

In December 1888 Samuel Mitty began the study of medicine with Dr. Manners Washburn. The writer for the Crawfordsville *Review* jokingly said, "The first degree is to build fires, curry

47 - Dr. D. Manners Washburn residence

horses - Sam will practice that the first year." A year later, in August, Sam Mitty, who was living with Dr. Washburn, had forsaken the livery stable. I was unable to find any record of his continuing the medical profession, so he must have not gone any further than the "first degree."

On July 6, 1870, Dr. Manners Washburn married Sarah Simpson, daughter of Samuel and Elizabeth (Wallace) Simpson of Montgomery County, formerly of Kentucky. They had two children, Nicholas L. and Musa C. Washburn. Nick had a men's clothing store and a cigar store in New Richmond many years. He later moved to Lafayette and clerked in a clothing store in that city.

Washburn was in the process of building a new home in the fall of 1879. It was nearly completed in September that year, and was destined to be the finest in town. His office was a little frame building that stood on Washington Street in the vicinity of the parking lot of the Tri-County Telephone Company.

He built another new residence that was almost ready for occupancy in September 1888. His brother George was to move into his old residence. It is uncertain which of these two homes was the two-story house that stands today on the corner of Franklin and Washington Streets.

Dr. Washburn enjoyed a large successful practice, keeping busy day and night, answering the calls during all kinds of inclement weather, on horseback, becoming exposed to all the contagious diseases, and performing surgery in the homes of the patients under adverse conditions.

Dr. Washburn and Warner Wilhite of Crawfordsville were "doubles" and were always being mistaken for the other, and when Warner went to New Richmond for a visit, everyone was constantly asking him about medicine. On the other hand, when the Doctor made a trip to Crawfordsville, he was asked, "when is my mortgage due," or some questions about an insurance policy.

Dr. Washburn died in his home in New Richmond, on Thursday, December 11, 1941. He was ninety-one years of age and one of the oldest persons buried in the New Richmond cemetery. He had practiced medicine throughout his last years, as long as he could get up and walk, never giving notice of a retirement.

Dr. Curtis M. Wray

Dr. Curtis M. Wray received his diploma from Indiana Medical College in 1906. He commenced the practice of medicine at Monitor, Indiana. On June 5th the same year he and Miss Gertrude Skinner, daughter of Mr. and Mrs. W.H. Skinner of Romney, were married, and were to make their home in Monitor.

On August 11, 1909, Wray's household goods arrived in New Richmond from Monitor. The wife, Gertrude, and their daughter, Bertha, were to move into the home in New Richmond the following week, and at the same time, Doctor Wray was to begin the practice of medicine in the town. His office was in the small frame building later occupied by Doctors Cole and Kindell, located just east of the Tri-County Telephone office building. The three physicians and their families also occupied the house next door to the office building on the east - as one moved out, the other moved in.

Wray was appointed to fill the unexpired term of Dr. Samuel E. Jones as health officer in New Richmond, in September the same year. He was elected to the office the following year, in 1910.

Wray was the first person to install a radio receiving station in New Richmond. This new radio was installed in 1922 and was as exciting as the first television set installed in the town several years later. All the neighbors had to come over to visit the doctor and listen to his radio.

Wray's office hours were from 1 - 2 and 7 - 8 p.m., having both afternoon and evening hours, as was the custom of the early physicians. He extended the evening hours to 9 p.m. later on, while he was still a physician in New Richmond.

He left New Richmond in 1923, when Dr. Cole arrived and occupied, as was mentioned before, the same house and office.

Physicians in New Richmond for a Short Term, or Studying with Local Physicians:

Dr. John B. Johnson - listed as a physician, living in the town of New Richmond in the 1850 Census. He was 33 years of age, born in Ohio; his wife Sarah A., 33, born in Virginia. They had two children; John P.H., age 3, and a female infant, age 1, both born in Indiana; no further record of this doctor.

Dr. Gimmel - was either studying under Dr. Detchon or was in partnership with him. They were mentioned as treating Dr. W.J. Hurt of Pleasant Hill for an illness in October 1873.

Dr. Alfred Ebrite - born in Ohio, son of George and Mary Wright Ebrite, was a student of medicine, listed in the 1870 census, age 29. Alfred served in the Civil War and his health was destroyed. He suffered a mental breakdown and was a resident in the county home, when he wandered away from the home and was found dead in a field near Smartsburg.

Dr. William "Billy" Mershon - studied medicine under Dr. Stowe S. Detchon but did not complete his studies. He ended his life by shooting himself in the head. He was New Richmond's first suicide victim.

Dr. L.L. Brown - was listed as a physician and druggist in the 1903 Directory of Montgomery County, however, the title of druggist was his correct title.

Dr. William J. Hurt - son of Absalom and Martha (Claypool) Hurt, born on a farm near New Richmond October 22, 1850. He studied medicine under Dr. Stow S. Detchon and was listed in the 1870 census in Dr. Detchon's household as a student of medicine at the age of 19. He then attended Rush Medical School in Chicago. He nearly lost his life from a bout with typhoid in October 1873 at his home in Pleasant Hill (Wingate) where he had started practicing medicine. He later went to Waynetown to practice medicine and remained there until his death in 1919.

Dr. Vinton Davisson - was born near New Richmond, son of William C. and Samantha Arnett Davisson. He attended the local schools and in 1904 entered the Central College of Physicians and Surgeons in Indianapolis. He and Dr. Arnett were attending college at the same time. Dr. Davisson practiced medicine in West Lafayette.

George F. Long - studied medicine under Dr. D. Manners Washburn. He had almost finished in the Medical College of Indiana and in another six months would have received his sheep-skin. He lacked the proffered funds, which he was loathe to accept as a short time loan, and gave up his coveted vocation.

THE DENTAL PROFESSION

Dr. Stowe S. Detchon, age 29, was listed as a dentist in New Richmond on the 1860 Federal census. He later studied medicine, and was a leading physician in the town for many years.

Dr. A.M. Miller was listed as a dentist in New Richmond in the 1895 Montgomery County directory, and the New Richmond *Enterprise*, Friday May 28, 1897, printed the following advertisement:

"The teeth nature gave are the best you will ever have.

They will never again be as good as they are to-day!

They can never be treated, or operated upon as easily and as cheaply as now. If your teeth need filling, don't hesitate to have them treated.

DR. A. M. MILLER."

DR. CHARLES EDWARD KELSEY

Kelsey, a New Richmond dentist, was born on a farm south of Crawfordsville, one of seven children. He began the study of dentistry in 1896 in the Ohio College of Dental Surgery of Cincinnati, graduating in 1899. He began practicing dentistry in Cincinnati the year of graduation, but in October the same year, opened an office in his residence on east Washington Street in New Richmond. He was a member of the Indiana State Dental Association. Dr. Kelsey soon built up an extensive practice and in October of 1903, he purchased the real estate office of O. W. Mason and remodeled the structure. When completed, the building contained a waiting room, an operating room, and laboratory supplied with hot and cold running water, marble top

48 - Office of Dr. Charles Edward Kelsey

washstands, and a fountain spittoon at the chair. Two nice features of his new office was the ground floor location, and the operating room received light from the north. The building was situated just east of the Starr Dunn building on Washington Street.

Dr. Kelsey attended the conventions of the Indiana Dental Association to keep abreast of the latest developments in dental surgery. He specialized in bridgework as early as 1900. In 1904 he made a careful study of anesthetics and used a preparation that was said to be both safe and efficient to be injected into the gums and contained no trace of cocaine to upset the nervous system, or to leave any unpleasant after-effects.

Dr. Kelsey's health began to fail in January of 1904, and surgery was performed on him by a New Richmond physician, Dr. Biedenkopf, in March of that year. He recovered from this surgery and practiced only a few months when he was admitted to Culver Hospital in Crawfordsville in November the same year. He was then taken to St. Vincent's Hospital in Indianapolis, where he underwent eighteen weeks of treatment, returning home in April of 1905. The doctor was able to attend the State Dental Association convention in Indianapolis in June that year. Dr. Kelsey was elected Councilman, first ward, of New Richmond, in March of 1906, succeeding Albert D. Snyder, but resigned the office on May 6, 1907, and soon after his resignation, moved to New Mexico for his health. Friends traveling west visited the former New Richmond dentist, and Dr. Kelsey returned for a visit with his old friends in 1916. He also visited his mother and sister in Indianapolis that year.

In 1920 he returned to the New Richmond area, and spent the summer in Wingate following his profession in that town, but the call of the west took him back to Albuquerque, New Mexico, where he practiced his profession. His hobby was photography, and he invented a folding tripod for cameras that was light weight, and could be folded, and converted into a cane. He designed the tripod in his laboratory in Albuquerque and his invention became a great boon to camera buffs.

The early residents of New Richmond had the highest regards for this early dentist, and regretted to have him leave the area.

Dr. Melvin J. Roth

Melvin J. Roth, born March 11, 1882 in Rossville, Indiana, was one of seven children of Joseph V. and Mary (Everetts) Roth. In 1904 he married Anna Beck, daughter of George W. and Eva N. Gregory Beck. They were married in Lafayette.

Dr. Roth attended the schools in Dayton, Indiana, where he had moved with his parents when he was a small child. He taught school several years in Pettit, Indiana, in order to pay his way through college. He attended Valparaiso University and graduated from Indiana Dental College in Indianapolis in 1908. After graduation Dr. Roth moved into Dr. Kelsey's former dental office in August of 1908. He later moved into a new office located on South Wabash Street in New Richmond, and practiced dentistry in the town thirty-eight years.

Dr. Roth's favorite pastime was hunting the foxes, and he usually returned home with some fine pelts to be made into beautiful furs for his wife. It has been said the doctor would leave his office so rapidly when the mere mention of a fox hunt was made that his patients were left with their mouths full of dental equipment. He preferred hunting them after a fresh new fallen snow and claimed he could catch their scent more easily in the snow.

In 1946 Dr. Roth and his wife moved to Colfax, Indiana, where he continued to practice dentistry until his death on May 20, 1958. He was buried in the Springvale Cemetery in Lafayette.

Dr. Robert R. LeGalley

Dr. Robert R. LeGalley, was born February 28, 1903 at Lafayette, son of Myron E. and Mildred (Rinker) LeGalley. In 1921 he married Helen H. Haywood.

Dr. LeGalley graduated from Jefferson High School in Lafayette, and in 1925 he graduated from Indiana University. After his graduation, he practiced dentistry with his father, Dr. Myron E. LeGalley, a well-established dentist in Lafayette. In 1940 he started his own practice in Linden, where he continued until 1976, when he retired. Dr. LeGalley and his wife were residents of New Richmond during the early years of his practice in Linden, and he treated many of the New Richmond people. Their children attended the New Richmond School. In 1960 the LeGalleys moved their residence to Linden. Dr. LeGalley died at the home of his daughter, Carol, at Crystal Falls, Michigan, on Sunday, November 23, 1980, and is buried in the New Richmond Cemetery.

Dr. Robert Newell Seaman

Dr. Robert Newell Seaman was born in New Richmond in a small house that stood east of the Thayer-Geiger Service station on east Washington Street. He was one of thirteen children of Robert E. and Elizabeth (Dewey) Seaman.

Dr. Seaman graduated from New Richmond High School and Indiana University. He practiced dentistry in Chicago for forty years, and then moved to his hometown of New Richmond in February of 1968. He purchased the Coffman property for his residence, and rented the north room of the Knights of Pythias building for a dental office, and continued his profession until 1971, when he moved to Henry, Illinois. He continued his dental profession in that city. Dr. Seaman first married Alta Graves, and had a son, William. His second marriage was to Marie (I couldn't find her last name), and they had a daughter, Jada.

Veterinarians

Jasper Clough, Veterinary Surgeon

Jasper began the practice of veterinary surgery around 1862 at the age of 24. Jasper was listed in the 1874 county directory as a veterinary surgeon and farmer, residing two and a half miles southwest of New Richmond. He was born in Ohio in 1838, coming to Coal Creek Township in 1842 with his parents. Records of his veterinary schooling are unknown, but it is highly possible he was a self-taught veterinarian. All the Clough men had an in-born knowledge of caring for their livestock, which was very common in the early pioneer days. Boswell, Jasper's brother, was well known for his wisdom in training and caring for horses, but was not listed as a veterinarian.

Dr. Jasper Clough was still treating horses and other livestock in New Richmond after he moved to Veedersburg around 1894. He notified the local liveryman, Henry Long, the day and time he would arrive in New Richmond to treat livestock and the nearby farmers drove their stock to the stable to be treated. Dr. Clough rode the Clover Leaf trains to and from New Richmond. Dr. Clough was regarded as one of the most skillful veterinarians in this area, and performed surgery on many valuable horses, prescribed medication, treated horses teeth, and all diseases of horses and cattle.

In March 1904, Dr. Clough advertised his new concoction, **Wild West Liniment**, for rheumatism, sore throat—a "general purpose remedy for MAN and BEAST" sold at all the drug stores in the New Richmond (and Veedersburg) area. He added **Wild West Healing Oil** a month or two later. The New Richmond *Record*, December 14, 1905, published a photograph of Dr. Clough, Veterinarian, who offered a $100 reward for any false statement found in the circular (or advertisement) concerning his famous Wild West Liniment and Healing Oil, and provided a complete list of ailments the medications would cure. Dr. Clough continued treating animals up to his last illness, and death, in 1911. He is buried in the New Richmond cemetery.

Other veterinarians practicing in New Richmond, and the dates they were mentioned in the New Richmond Record are listed below:

Dr. Howard Dewey, Veterinarian - New Richmond, June 12, 1902. Dr. Dewey was practicing veterinary surgery in Indianapolis in June 1904, and while taking his girlfriend for a carriage ride in that city, he was attacked by a rival (fighting over the girl) and three thugs. Dewey said the rival pulled him from the carriage, and Dewey knocked him to the pavement with some "straight arms and hooks" and covered his body with kicks. The three "seconds" of his rival rushed out to help him and Dewey put them all down—one—two—three—and out! He butted them all with his head, he said, the way he used to knock down horses when he was in college. Morton, his rival, threatened to even the score some day, and Dewey said, "All right, but be sure and bring more fellows with you the next time."

M.C. (Martin) Graves, Veterinarian - New Richmond. In 1894, Graves printed a folder including a pedigree chart of his breeding horses, listing one Standard bred, one Imported Shire Stallion, and one Imported German Coacher. Graves practiced veterinary medicine and surgery in New Richmond up to August 24, 1905, and perhaps later, as records are incomplete.

Fred W. Graves, Veterinarian - Fred Graves, son of Martin C. Graves, was born April 19, 1890 at Ladoga and attended school in Ladoga his first year. The family then moved to a farm near Wingate when he was seven. Fred attended the school known as No. 13, located between New Richmond and Wingate, then attended the Wingate School after the district school was closed. Fred was a graduate of Indiana Veterinary College, and began practicing his profession as a Veterinary Surgeon in New Richmond in 1909.

Fred Graves and his wife, the former Asena Alexander, resided in New Richmond at the time of their marriage in 1911, and he continued practicing his profession in the town until 1912, at least; then practiced in Wolcott, and Hillsboro from 1915 to 1924, when he moved to New York and accepted a position with the U. S. Department of Agriculture, inspecting dairy herds and products in Canada. He left the position in Canada and was associated with the New York Department of Health, where he continued inspecting milk. Dr. Fred Graves and his family were residents of Albany, New York, where his death occurred in 1952. He and his wife, Sena, are buried in the New Richmond Cemetery.

H.L. Boyland DVM - (Howard); Boyland, Veterinary Surgeon and Dentist, a graduate of the Terre Haute Veterinary College, opened his office in New Richmond in May 1915. His office was located one door west of Moulder's store, in the brick residence built by Frank Perkins, attached to the two-story brick building on east Washington Street. Dr. Boyland was still practicing veterinary surgery in New Richmond in 1916, but records are incomplete after that year.

Dr. Cooper, Veterinarian - Dr. Cooper moved to New Richmond in September 1918, and began practicing his profession. There is no further record of Cooper.

F.M. (Ferrell) Monroe, Veterinary Surgeon - Dr. Ferrell Monroe advertised in the New Richmond *Record*, August 14, 1919. His office was in Magruder's Livery Barn in New Richmond. There is no further record of this veterinarian.

E.E. Baldwin, Veterinary Surgeon - Dr. Baldwin advertised from November 17, 1921 to 1923. No records are available of his schooling, and those who remembered this veterinarian thought he was self-taught, but also claimed he was very knowledgeable on the subject of veterinary medicine. Dr. E.E. Baldwin was appointed "Dog Police" by the local town board in 1925. Baldwin also served as the town marshal and street supervisor during the period of 1925 to 1940.

UNDERTAKERS

Dority & Co, Undertakers - The following notice was placed in the Crawfordsville weekly *Review* in October 1888, "Mr. Doherty and Thomas Smith have formed a partnership and will start an undertaking establishment here. They will do well if they stand in with the doctors, one will help the other."

After reading the above notice, I certainly would have been skeptical, and hope my ancestors residing in New Richmond at the time kept one eye on the local physicians and the other on the undertaker, if they were "helping each other." This undertaking establishment operated under the name Dority & Company Undertakers as late as 1890.

Uriah Coapland, Undertaker - (also spelled Coopland-Copeland) Uriah was a very enterprising gentleman around 1889, running three business establishments: undertaker, livery stable, and butcher shop. In December, 1890, he decided to try farming and discontinued the above business enterprises.

T.S. (Thomas) and A.V. (Alvanza) Patton, Undertakers and Embalmers - Tom Patton erected a frame building on South Wabash Street, purchased a fine, new horse-drawn hearse from a company in Chicago, and the two cousins were ready to "supply the long-felt wants of this place" in July 1890. This partnership was dissolved when Tom's death occurred in 1894.

P.M. Brown, Undertaker - Records are incomplete for this undertaker, but in January 1894, Mr. Brown disposed of his undertaking establishment to Samuel Tribby.

S.R. (Samuel) Tribby, Undertaker - Sam Tribby was a local carpenter, and was in the undertaking business from January 1894 to 1901, in New Richmond.

H.B. (Harry) Tribby, Undertaker - Harry Tribby placed the following advertisement in the New Richmond *Record* from May to July 1903, "H. B. TRIBBY, FUNERAL DIRECTOR, All grades of work and furnishings-telephone calls, day or night—J. J. Birdsell, Embalmer and Assistant, New Richmond, Indiana." Another notice was placed in the same newspaper in May announcing the new business, and said J. J. Birdsell, his associate, had been in the business at Waynetown the past twenty-five years, was a member of the Indiana State Funeral Directors Association, and held a state license as an embalmer.

D.C. Barnhill, Undertaker - This Crawfordsville undertaker established a branch in New Richmond in the early spring of 1905, placing advertisements in the local newspaper up to April 1923, In March 1905 Barnhill moved into new quarters in Crawfordsville, a new brick two-story (22 by 150 foot) building with a basement the entire length, located at 134 West Main Street. Barnhill was doing most of the undertaking in New Richmond at the time. S. P. Templeton joined the firm as a partner of Barnhill in May 1915. Barnhill was listed as the general manager, and J. B. Swank and S. P. Templeton, licensed embalmers. They advertised, "BARNHILL-TEMPLETON, UNDERTAKERS AND LICENSED EMBALMERS, with lady assistant, modern motor ambulance service, motor or horse-drawn funeral cars furnished as desired. John G. Utterback, Assistant Embalmer, in charge of New Richmond branch—calls answered day or night."

In November 1921 and January 1922, Omer Nash had joined the firm of **Barnhill Undertaking Company**; Templeton was no longer a partner. John G. Utterback was listed as Director and Embalmer of Barnhill Undertaking Co., and Emit Grenard was listed as Barnhill's Assistant. M.J. Murphy was also listed as an assistant during these years. Barnhill was still in business in New Richmond in April 1923.

A map dated December 21, 1916, made by an insurance company, shows a building labeled UNDERTAKING, located between Dr. Washburn's office and a barbershop an East Washington Street. At this time there were two undertakers in town, **Barnhill and Templeton** and **M.A. West**. I am not certain which establishment was in this location.

M.A. West, Undertaker - Marcus and Nellie West purchased a residence on South Wabash Street in New Richmond on November 3, 1914, and sold the property February 10, 1920. West advertised, "M. A. WEST, FUNERAL DIRECTOR AND LICENSED EMBALMER, New private ambulance-lady assistant-calls answered day or night." This advertisement appeared in the local newspaper from early spring 1915 to August 1919. He offered "Auto Service, if desired" in 1919.

Fred Shanklin, Undertaker - Fred Shanklin's undertaking establishment was in operation in 1930 in New Richmond. A year later, he had taken Bob King as a partner and operated under the name **Shanklin & King Funeral Directors**, Linden and New Richmond. The business was moved from New Richmond to Linden a few years later, and Robert King continued to run the business after Shanklin's death.

Chapter 18 - Entertainment and Social Organizations

Meharry's Grove—"The Garden Spot of Indiana"

In April of 1827, four sons of Alexander Meharry left their home in Adams County, Ohio, in search of better farmland. Hugh, Thomas, James, and Jesse Meharry made this trip on horseback carrying with them only enough provisions to survive in their destination—the wilderness of Indiana. The prairie lands in northern Coal Creek Township in Montgomery County, eastern Fountain County, and the southern part of Tippecanoe County bordering Coal Creek Township, appealed to the brothers, and Hugh, Thomas, and James made several entries in the northwestern sections of Coal Creek Township between 1827 and 1832. Thomas entered several acres in Fountain County, and Jesse—and a brother David, who later joined his brothers on their return to Indiana—entered land at Shawnee Mound in Tippecanoe County. The brothers returned to Ohio to choose wives whom they knew would have to be very hardy to withstand the hardships of settling in the lonely new country. They brought their brides to Indiana, setting up housekeeping on their newly acquired acreage. Their sister, Mrs. Nathan Beach, came to Coal Creek Township in 1837, and another brother, Samuel, in 1846.

In the early days of Methodism, it was customary to hold "stirring" revivals and religious meetings. Since these meetings drew such huge crowds, the homes, which were the usual place of worship, could not possibly hold all these people, and as a result camp meetings became a necessity. These meetings were usually held in the summer months, and as the worshippers arrived, the first order of business was to set up camp. Soon the grounds would become a sea of tents, and by evening everything was in readiness for the first sermon under the stars and trees. These meetings usually continued for about five days.

49 - Coal Creek covered bridge

In Coal Creek Township, the Meharry brothers were among the first to help establish Methodism in pioneer Montgomery County. The date of these first meetings is uncertain, due to a lack of recorded facts. The first camp meetings were held in this area in James Meharry's grove, and then moved a few years later to Hugh Meharry's grove. The 1878 map of Coal Creek Township shows the campground just west of the Coal Creek covered bridge in section 3, township 20, range 6, on A. Meharry's land, or on the southwest corner of what is now the intersection of State Road 25 and the New Richmond to Newtown road. The campground contained forty acres and was in this location for forty years. The Meharry brothers formed an association and officers were elected each year to manage the campground and the Meharry Cemetery nearby. The campground was situated on a high and beautifully shaded place with plenty of pure, cold drinking water, and was equipped with a large number of seats. The grove was void of the thick underbrush usually found in the forest.

Many noted Methodist leaders spoke in the grove, and around 1875, a mammoth temperance rally was held at Meharry's Grove. Yes, there was a need for this type of rally for our early settlers. At one time cottages were erected on the historic Meharry's Grove campground. Samuel Meharry built a new cottage in 1892, and moved his old one to another location. Others were expected to build new cottages around that period of time, as well.

There were many Sunday School picnics held in Meharry's Grove by all the nearby church groups over the years. The young folks were transported to these outings on hayladders; the older parties traveled in buggies. The New Richmond Christian and Methodist Churches gathered one Sunday each year at the modern day Meharry's Grove further on down the road from the old historic campground, located at the rear of the Meharry Farm Service Center west of New Richmond, and held religious services, but the attendance never grew to the proportions boasted of by the pioneers.

OLD SETTLER'S MEETINGS

The first "Old Settler's Meeting" was held in Meharry's Grove on August 20, 1870. On Saturday, September 14, 1872, one of the best meetings ever held in the grove was enjoyed by invited guests from Tippecanoe, Montgomery, Fountain, and Warren Counties. One very special guest was invited to give a talk on the book he authored. Sanford Cox was the gentleman. His book gave an early history of the first settlers in Indiana, and was entitled "Old Settlers." Benjamin Ristine, one of Montgomery County's first settlers, also spoke at this gathering.

In August 1879, Old Settler's Day was observed in Meharry's Grove with ten thousand people attending. Capt. J.R. Carnahan gave the address, speaking for over an hour on "The Past, Present, and Future of the Country," and captivated his audience the entire time. The Waynetown choir performed and the pioneers told of their experiences as early settlers. The Crawfordsville *Journal*, August 30, 1879, gave an excellent coverage of the special day, saying in part:

> Thousands assembled from far and near to commemorate the first settlement of this part of Indiana. The old camp-ground was once used for religious meetings, but as the country became more settled, every neighborhood was supplied with a meeting house, and the necessity for camp meetings was gradually removed and the grove has not been used for that purpose for more than twenty years. Meharry's Grove is now a place to celebrate the Fourth of July, and the annual Old Settler's Day. Last Thursday was the annual recurrence of the meeting of the pioneers. The sun shone clear, the roads were good, and early in the morning the lanes and by-ways were lined with a dusty throng all tending in the direction of the grove. By ten o'clock the grounds were a densely packed mass of humanity, horses and carriages. The crowd was estimated at from seven to ten thousand. The old men and women brought with them many relics, they talked of the past—of the days they lived in log cabins with puncheon floors—of the days they swung the ax, clearing up the primeval forest—of the days of wooden mould-board plows and the flax brake—of the log rollings and house raisings—of the religion they enjoyed and the God they worshipped. Little did they dream when they came west fifty and sixty years ago that they were laying the foundation of so rich an empire, now enjoyed by their children and grand-children. Their posterity surely can rise and call them blessed, etc. Two hours were consumed in sampling the contents of the thousands of baskets after which an 'experience meeting' was held. Many amusing incidents were told by the gray-haired veterans illustrating the times in which they lived. Among the speakers were Sanford Gray, John Lee, William Birch, Lay Davidson, Elder McBroom, George Glasscock, William Talbot, and others. In August 1883, the old settlers gave their age, their former residence, and the year they settled in the area.

In 1885 the Newtown and Steam Corner bands discoursed sweet music to 4,000 to 5,000 people assembled at the 28th Old Settler's reunion at Meharry's Grove. Capt. DeWitt Wallace was the speaker. John Gaines, an early settler in Coal Creek Township, attended the Old Settler's Meeting in August 1890. He was said to be the first white child born in Indiana while yet a territory. John came to Coal Creek Township in the early 1830s and resided on the northern border of Montgomery County until his death.

Gaines and David Meharry gave an exhibition of wheat threshing with "flails" before a crowd of 6,000 in 1890.

An unfortunate incident occurred in 1898 during the Old Settler's Meeting when former governor Claude Matthews was stricken with paralysis while making a speech. He fell back into the chair he had occupied before speaking, and remarked to A.C. McCorkle at his side, "I can not understand this queer feeling." He attempted to move but paralysis made him unable to do so. He became unconscious and was carried to the home of Isaac Meharry, west of the campground. Physicians were called—Dr. Allhands of Wingate being the first to arrive. Dr. Olin of Elmdale, Drs. Stone and Kahlo of Indianapolis, and Dr. Baker, who was Matthews' physician from his place of residence in Clinton, Indiana, all arrived to care for the stricken man. Matthew's wife and their daughter Helen arrived on the midnight Clover Leaf train and were driven to his bedside. Another daughter and other members of his family were called when his condition grew worse. He was stricken on Thursday, and died early Sunday morning in Meharry's home.

By 1902, the crowds were growing smaller and the editor of the New Richmond *Record* suggested that several prizes should be offered to induce more people to attend—one for the oldest settlers, the largest family by the same name, the best collection of old relics, etc. The Old Settler's Meeting was the oldest of this type in the state, and he could not bear the thought of the historic celebrations being discontinued.

Between 1,500 to 2,000 people attended the Old Settler's Meeting on August 15, 1907, the last record I have of these historical meetings, although later ones may have occurred.

GLORIOUS FOURTH OF JULY CELEBRATIONS

Clementina and his Dora, on the FOURTH to Meharry's went,
Here they celebrated gaily—'til his money was all spent.
Homeward then their way they wended, full of love, ice-cream and cake, But alas! Their bliss soon ended—
both soon had a b_____,
No, it wasn't—you're mistaken—what I tell you is no fake,
Clem and Dora both were stricken—with a very bad headache.
- Author unknown

The exact date of the first celebration of Independence Day at Meharry's Grove is unknown, but was believed to have been in 1850, or possibly earlier. The Meharry's Grove Association met in the Wingate bank early each spring to elect officers and appoint committees for the annual festivities held in the grove.

In 1903 the following committees were chosen: Speakers—J.M. Hawthorne, E.J. Kirkpatrick, J.W. McCorkle, and C.R. McKinney; Music—A.J. Arnett, Melvin Hatton, and Ira G. Meharry; Hucksters—S.M. Mick, A.J. Arnett, and W.W. Boland; Advertising—J.D. Thomas, J.W. McCorkle, and M.M. Borum; Decoration—Mr. and Mrs. James Stewart, W.W. Black—with the authority to call on others as desired.

Plans were made at this time to schedule the year's celebrations, the main events being the Fourth of July, the Old Settler's Meetings, the local church picnics, and political meetings. The New Richmond *Record*, July 9, 1903, describes a typical Fourth of July celebration held in Meharry's Grove like this:

> Another grand and glorious old-time celebration at Meharry's Grove, known far and wide for its never failing and non-boisterous gatherings, is past and gone. At early dawn, the sound of the anvil told to the surrounding neighborhoods that it was time to be up and doing, preparing the dinner basket with fried chicken and all the dainties that composes the feast for such occasions and long before time to spread the white linen on Mother Earth, the conveyances began to come from all directions and by ten o'clock several hundred people were there to listen to the finest music heard upon the prairie in some years, rendered by the Newtown band, Invocation by Rev. C.W. Postil, Welcome address by Pres. George B. Hawthorne, reading the DECLARATION OF INDEPENDENCE by Lee B. Hawthorne, Addresses by Rev's W.R. Mikels and C.W. Postil, -this was the

morning programme. It was after all this, that you could see baskets headed in all directions to be unloaded of their burdens. At 1:15 p.m. the band gave twenty minutes concert—equal almost to one given by Sousa's. Master Hauk started the afternoon's entertainment with a select reading, followed by the principle address given by Rev. Mason of Attica, who was born a Scotchman and has lectured in all the countries on the globe, even in the courts of London. Miss Lelia Hollin gave a select reading and Rev. J.J. Claypool of Newtown finished the afternoon programme with an address. The crowd, which had 'ere this swelled' to more than a thousand, was most unceremoniously scattered by the appearance of a wind and rain storm which put a dampness on the fellowship meeting which always completes the celebrations of this historic old camping ground.—A Bystander.

Most readers have probably not heard of the old time **anvil shoot** or **firing of the anvil** mentioned in the previous description of the Fourth at Meharry's Grove. This was a forerunner of the modern day fireworks—and possibly just as dangerous. Black powder (blasting powder) is stuffed into a saucer-like depression in one of the anvils, where they are worn down from the constant pounding, and the second anvil is placed on top of the first one. A trail of powder is laid away from the anvil and a hot poker is touched to the powder trail. The loud blast could be heard for many miles—and the top anvil shot several feet into the air. I could not help but wonder how many pioneers were clobbered by a "flying anvil" during these celebrations.

The late Forrest Waye said Frank M. Johnson, a New Richmond drug store proprietor, manufactured ice cream in his store—with the assistance of several young lads about town, including Forrest—and delivered it to Meharry's Grove for the Fourth of July and other celebrations. Johnson's Drug Store was in New Richmond from 1897 to 1909.

In 1905, all the Sunday Schools in Coal Creek Township and the area were invited to participate in an old-fashioned Fourth of July celebration—New Richmond, Round Hill, Sugar Grove, and Shawnee Mound (Wingate was not mentioned, but I'm sure the town should have been among the crowd). The flag drill by the sixteen young ladies of the New Richmond Sunday School was the last—and best—feature of the program, and drills given by the boys and girls of Round Hill attracted much attention. Many patriotic recitations and musical numbers were presented, and reminded the older guests of the early celebrations. The Newtown band, the best band in the country, furnished music that year, playing "Marching Through Georgia" for the flag drill by the New Richmond schools.

The last record available of the Fourth of July celebrations at Meharry's Grove was the New Richmond *Record*, July 6, 1916, which said:

The New Richmond people celebrated the Fourth, generally, and though there was no observance of the day in town, our people and the community divided up among Meharry's Grove, Crawfordsville, Lafayette, and other places. At Meharry's Grove, a program of songs, recitations by the Sunday Schools, reading of the DECLARATION OF INDEPENDENCE, and speeches by John W. McCardle, of Indianapolis (a former New Richmond resident), and Hon. J. P. Goodrich, a republican nominee for governor. The Fourth was rather a quiet day in New Richmond for those who remained at home. Crawfordsville dedicated their new Milligan Park as part of their festivities.

How Grandma and Grandpa Spent Their Evenings

When our grandparents were in high school, it was really not all work and no play as they would have you to believe. They came up with some pretty good ideas on how to spend their leisure time. When Coal Creek Township was first settled, the whole community worked together building log cabins and log barns, then gathered together for a festival to dedicate the new barns. They referred to these parties as a "barn raising." The foxtrot, Virginia reel, and square dancing went on until the wee hours of the morning, accompanied by the local fiddlers. They also had their quilting bees, corn husking bees, and spelling bees to occupy their long winter evenings. Another work-related gathering in the form of "a wood-chopping and oyster supper" occurred at the home of Mrs. Garret near New Richmond in 1880.

Picnics were held quite frequently in McCrea's woods southeast of New Richmond around 1910 or 1915. "Moonlight picnicking" provided a lot of merriment with or without the moonlight. Or maybe they preferred a taffy pull, or a maple sugar eating contest. How about a marshmallow toast? All of these were popular pastimes when grandma and grandpa were kids.

Dancing parties were a big thing around the early 1900s and were all well attended. Local orchestras furnished the music for these dances. In 1903, Albert Dettbenner threw a big party to dedicate his new barn, located one-half mile north of Sugar Grove. The Sugar Grove Ladies Aid Society prepared the strawberries and ice cream for this party. Fifteen persons from New Richmond made up a wagon load, and took a "straw-ride" out to the Dettbenner's festival.

Hay rides, hayladder rides, or straw rides, always provided the young and old with an exciting evening. The freshman class of New Richmond High School planned a hayladder ride to Elmdale to attend a box supper one evening. Another outing was planned for a "progressive hay-ladder ride", but before reaching their destination, the wagon wheel "mysteriously" came off and the group was compelled to walk a mile or so.

A group of families in the Sugar Grove neighborhood—the Baileys, Nesbitts, Arnetts, and Davissons, some Illinois visitors, and Dr. Arthur Bible, of Cincinnati, Ohio, enjoyed a hay wagon ride to Wingate, returning by a circuitous route. The cider jug was passed around freely on the wagons on this outing.

Right up there in popularity were the sleigh-rides and the bobsled parties. Pierson King manufactured sleds for the communities of New Richmond and Round Hill in 1884, but there was always some carpenter around who was adept in building bobsleds, or any other items that required his skill. One of the New Richmond high school classes planned a bobsled ride for their outing in 1911, but was not successful until April 19th when the first snow fell. They said the ride was quite rough, but enjoyable. A few years later, Miss Gerhard, a teacher in the local school, tried to cram sixteen people onto one bobsled, but admitted later that twelve would have been more than enough.

Deep snows and zero-degree weather provided the correct conditions for good sleighing. In February, 1905, the thermometers ranged from 18 to 24 below zero, and everyone who owned sleighs and could brave the temperature was enjoying the rides. Young ladies of the junior class of New Richmond High School in 1910 and their invited partners enjoyed a "progressive bobsled Party." The first stop was Kittie Dunn's, where they were treated to oranges, then to Ruth Miller's for sandwiches, to Sene Alexander's for pie, to Mary Crowder's for fruit salad and cake, and the last stop was at Pauline Henderson's for toasted marshmallows and apples.

Fifteen ladies from the Ladies Aid Society of the Methodist church in New Richmond were driven out to Mrs. E.T. McCrea's to attend a meeting. Mrs. J.A. Kirkpatrick furnished the bobsled for the trip one snowy day in January of 1903.

The more settled ladies and gents preferred "Cinch parties," or "Cinque Parties" and a two- or three-course meal. The young people of the local Methodist Episcopal church were to hold their "barrel opening" at the home of Lena Hollins, and all who had barrels were to either bring or send them. A friend of mine often used her favorite expression, "stick around—I was just getting ready to open up a keg of nails" when she wanted me to visit her a little bit longer. I'm not quite sure what the term "barrel opening" covered; it would be interesting to know the answer.

A favorite pastime around 1904 was driving the old "hoss" and carriage all the way to Yountsville where the more rugged men or boys would "Shoot the Chutes." While the men were trying to break their necks, the "genteel" ladies were planning a weight social and were supposed to pay ten cents for every 100 pounds they weighed and five cents for every 25 pounds over. The group was to quietly put the money away and not reveal their weight. Ha! Music was furnished by Professor Ed H. McCrea for this party.

An "Old Maid's Tea" was held in September of 1906. It was to be a "Spinster's Experience Meeting" and each of the ladies was to give the reason why they were Old Maids. Incidentally, the same group of ladies formed a club later, called the D.D.D.S. Club. They were "to meet every two weeks, and was properly organized and governed by a constitution and by-laws that were rigidly fierce—and fiercely rigid." I imagined all sorts of names the letters stood for, but later discovered the name was **Dozen Dear Devine Sisters Club**. They allowed the editor of the New Richmond *Record*, the local preacher, and one "staid old widower" to attend one of their meetings, however.

Temperance Meetings were always cropping up, and the lecture courses. James Whitcomb Riley entertained in Frankfort one year, and the New Richmond people took the train over to enjoy his program. Many attended the concert of Sousa and his famous band at the Music Hall in Crawfordsville in 1905.

The tent shows—some good, some short of awful—were held on Washburn's cow pasture in New Richmond. A Wild West Show with a big troupe of Indians attracted a large crowd in town after only a few hours' notice, in 1906.

Now didn't our grandparents have fun? fun? fun?

Charivari

Webster's Collegiate Dictionary defines a CHARIVARI (shiv'-a-rē) as "a mock serenade of discordant noises, made with kettles, tin horns, etc."

Bells were added to the above noise-makers in New Richmond, as well as numerous other items. Charivaries were seldom recorded in the newspapers, but I uncovered a few that were. In 1902 Marion Westfall and his bride were awakened near the hour of midnight, and though the groom had a treat long laid up for the belated serenaders, the crowd failed either to get into the house or to get the sleepy groom out. The "belling" came late, but the extraordinary noise bespoke the pent-up energy reserved for the occasion.

Henry S. Jones and his bride Della Kirkpatrick drove quietly to Ladoga to get married by Rev. H.C. Weston, but news has a way of getting around, and at the peril of their lives from Henry's father's shotgun, their friends tendered them a noisy charivari.

Judd E. Meharry and his wife were awakened by about twenty people on their wedding night and they treated the group to cigars and doughnuts. Mrs. Meharry even sang a few selections for the group.

Jim Bible and his bride, Gretchen Kincaid, took a short honeymoon trip to Indianapolis, but did not escape a long, noisy charivari. The couple finally gave up and Jim promised to treat their noisy friends.

Wheelbarrows became the conveyance for the new groom to transport his new bride up and down the main streets in New Richmond, while rice was thrown all over the pair. Before the wheelbarrow was used, the groom had to carry his bride through the town and countryside, and quite frequently, the bride outweighed the groom.

Most of the groups were noisy but well behaved, and were only out to follow a tradition of welcoming the newlyweds into a new chapter of their life, but on occasion, the groups became a little wild and consumed enough alcoholic beverages to make them act repulsively–thus ruining another tradition. The tradition was carried on until the 1940s and maybe into the 1950s, but you never hear of them anymore.

Music, Music, Music

Since the beginning of time, man has expressed himself, and his many moods, through combinations of lyric poetry, set to melody and rhythm. A pleasing, harmonious, atmosphere surrounds the entertainer immediately as he begins to perform.

Among the inventory of one of New Richmond's earliest settlers, William Kincaid, was his fife. The widow, Deborah (Kendall) Kincaid, managed to keep his fife after the other personal property was sold at auction, perhaps passing it on to one of their children. The sale took place in 1847, and the value of the one fife was 25 cents. No doubt, William soothed their children with his sweet music many evenings in their home north of New Richmond.

Joe Kliter, a German shoemaker who made boots and shoes for the people in and near New Richmond, ordered a big Jews-harp from his native country and informed the people he would show the neighborhood where music first commenced. This was in 1887. There were several fiddlers and one or two violinists living near and around New Richmond in 1888, and the violin was heard above the "din of battle." Occasionally, entertainers came to New Richmond to liven things up and a group from Goosenibble came over with fife and drums to treat the citizens to some soul-stirring martial music in September the same year. Other entertainers were a "roving Italian and two of his girls" who entertained at the school house, he played the violin, and the girls danced clog.

As New Richmond and Coal Creek Township became more settled, attempts were made continuously to organize bands, orchestras, or small groups of musicians. Early bands mentioned in the township were the Wilhite Band, who was to furnish the music at the Old Settler's Meeting at Meharry's Grove, and the Coal Creek Sheepskin Band, who paraded with six miles of wagons and people celebrating "Democratic Day" in Crawfordsville in October, 1888.

The Knights of Pythias organized a band in New Richmond called the Knights of Pythias Cornet Band, in September 1891. They captured first prize at Shawnee Mound during a contest, giving them the confidence they needed. This band got off to a good start as they were asked to play in Crawfordsville for the Fourth of July celebration in 1892. They played at the Democratic Rally at Waynetown, along with the Waynetown and Crawfordsville drum corps. The band gave a concert and supper at Hollin's Opera House in New Richmond in March, 1893, and in July the same year, they supplied themselves with new instruments in time to play at Meharry's Grove on the Fourth of July celebration.

In September 1893 the New Richmond band, composed of fourteen members, entertained a large crowd on a Saturday night in Crawfordsville, giving a concert from the roof of the Fulton Market Building. They received a good review in the Crawfordsville *Review*, September 30, 1893: "The band executes most of the pieces of music in very good style, and steady practice will soon make it one of the first class bands in the state."

This New Richmond band was photographed by Al Champion, the Crawfordsville photographer, but I have not seen any copies of this group's photograph, or a record of the list of performers. It was interesting to read of the band taking the train from New Richmond to Linden to entertain the I.O.O.F. for their installation ceremonies.

New Richmond's fourteen-piece band was awarded the contract to furnish music for the Montgomery County Fair in August, 1894. They were among thirteen bands to make bids, and their bid of $100 was selected. They received the following comments after their week of performance in the Crawfordsville Weekly *Review*, September 8, 1894, "The New Richmond Band, which furnished music at the fair this year, gave the public better music than has been heard on the ground for years. Our home horn blowers, many of whom have been practicing for years, should either determine to give Crawfordsville a good band, or quit permanently, after allowing a little country band to 'skunk' them so easily."

The Commercial Club of New Richmond had organized a band by early April of 1900, and was furnishing music for the annual millinery openings in New Richmond. This was a big event for the ladies each year. The band also entertained the Old Settlers who met at Meharry's Grove on August 21, 1902. They reorganized a year later and practiced very regularly, striving for perfection.

The New Richmond horse show featured the New Richmond Commercial Brass Band in June 1903, and during their intermissions, John Ellis and Job and George Westfall furnished martial music throughout the day. This came as a complete surprise to the audience, and there was "much applause" after their performance. The boys always enjoyed playing, as it brought back fond memories of the days of 1861-65 when their flute and drum, in the self-same, soul-stirring strains, stirred the boys in blue to heroic deeds. Job marched and played his fife as long as he was able to walk. He participated in the state centennial celebration held in Crawfordsville in June 1916 where "he attracted worthy attention with his fife and martial music." Job would have been about 71 years of age when he marched in this parade. The late Forrest Waye said Job led the parade each year to the New Richmond cemetery to decorate the graves on Memorial Day.

Job also participated in the Knights of Pythias parade held in Wingate on Memorial Day in 1916. New Richmond's Henry Clay Lodge had ten members in the line, and Job Westfall was the only Civil War Veteran in the parade. Job Westfall served with the 63rd Indiana Volunteer Infantry in the War of the Rebellion from December 1863 to April 1866. He died in 1922 and is buried in the Pleasant Hill cemetery south of Wingate.

The Commercial Club reorganized their band in November of 1906. Elmer W. (Pete) Harriman was the new bandmaster, and had creditably filled engagements with all of the better bands in this section of the country. The following gentlemen are listed, and the instruments they played in this band: Glenn Mitchell, piccolo; E.W. Harriman, clarinet; Ernest Greenburg, clarinet; Lawrence McLain, Everett Leslie, Lorlie Harriman, and Lennie Beckley, cornet; Fred Harriman, Earle Way, Grant Dazey, alto; John Alexander, Wallace W. White, G.A. Pence, trombones; Walter W. (Spud) Harriman, bass; Will McLain, snare drum. There were openings for a bass drum and a clarinet player, not filled at the time of the writing. The New Richmond people were urged to encourage the new band members to make a success of it. This band made rapid progress, and within a month was ready to perform. They were preparing a minstrel show to raise funds for new uniforms.

The New Richmond Commercial Band and the townspeople received another pep talk in 1922. A large column appeared in the New Richmond *Record* on January 26. The editor was trying to get the community to boost the band and talk it up, in hopes the youth would have something to do besides "loafing and playing frivolous games." A year later in August, the New Richmond band played all week at the fair in Crawfordsville, and was to play for a Labor Day celebration in Rockville. They were having regular concerts each week in New Richmond besides the out-of-town performances.

The minutes of the town board of New Richmond recorded an appropriation of $75.00 for Band Concerts "this year" in July 1928. In 1929 the board gave $150 for ten concerts. The same year the board paid $75 to the 151st Infantry Band (National Guard) for five concerts. Several men from New Richmond played with this group. Maurice Coffman served as director of this band at one time. In 1933 Robert Campbell was paid $10 for services as band leader of the New Richmond band.

The New Richmond band practiced in the upstairs room of the town hall, which also housed the fire trucks and the firefighting apparatus. In 1930 the town board purchased lockers for the uniforms and other equipment. They paid $343.15 to Coffman's garage for the lockers in February that year. In 1934, the town trustees made a motion to furnish lumber that it had on hand to build a band stand; the motion carried. I remember the excitement of getting to go uptown to hear the New Richmond band play on Saturday nights, and Dad usually bought a small bag of candy for all of us to enjoy—a real treat in those trying years. Unfortunately, the band concerts were replaced by the Saturday night street shows.

A photograph of the New Richmond Band includes the following members as identified by residents of New Richmond: 1st row, left to right: Robert "Newt" Seaman, Raymond Oliver, John Westfall, Barney Bunnell, Harry McNeil, Estel Bell; 2nd row, left to right: Harold Bell, Floyd Swank (Reuben's brother), Charles Swadley, Orie Wagner, Joe Campbell, Ted McCrea (in white uniform—the band's mascot), "Dad" Harris, "Shorty" Harris, Paul Shepherd, Elmer "Pete" Harriman, Glenn "Punk" Neideigh; Back row, left to right: Clifford Ullman, Ed Neideigh, Lee Davis, Boyd McNeil, Raymond "Johnny" Bell, Bill Priebe, Edward H. "Prof" McCrea, John McCrea, Walter W. "Spud" Harriman.

Music boxes were a common item in the town of New Richmond in 1877. The scribe of the Crawfordsville *Journal*, October 13, 1877 made a note of a new craze, but failed to inform me who was so fortunate to own the little boxes. Ira Stout of New Richmond was showing off his talking machine in 1895 to the Wingate people—who boasted of two in that town "run by natural gas, but they were not quite so speedy as the phonograph," they said.

A "Phonograph War" was taking place in New Richmond in 1905. The editor of the New Richmond *Record*, Thursday, July 6, 1905 said, "A humorist of New Richmond makes a note of the fact that the town leads in automobiles, phonographs and dogs-numerically speaking. The town has survived the 'Gravel Road War,' 'The Saloon War,' 'The Elevator War' and the brethren are quarrelling among themselves and no longer dwell in unity. And NOW! Here comes the 'Phonograph War!'"

The reason for his concern was the fact that there were two merchants in town selling Edison Phonographs—Nick Washburn and J.M. Alexander—and the town resembled a resort, or a Midway, or the Pike. Washburn had a pretty window display of the Edison phonographs or "talking machines" and the records to play on them.

The New Richmond High School furnished some well-known entertainment over the years with various groups. In 1910 Professor Kesler, assisted by Everett Greenburg, Glenn Mitchell, and Mary Crowder, organized a six-piece orchestra. H.A. Kesler played the violin; Glenn Mitchell and Ernest Greenburg, clarinets; Everett Greenburg and Lorlie Harriman, cornets; and Mary Crowder, the piano. This group was known as the New Richmond High School Orchestra, although two of the members were out of school at the time. They practiced in the school building, and played for the school functions, church programs, and other entertainments in the town. Glenn Mitchell's father, Charles, was an accomplished musician, and played cornet for the Grand Opera House Orchestra in Lafayette and the opera house in Indianapolis, by the same name, and led the park orchestra in Fort Wayne. He also traveled all over the country with other bands. Glenn played clarinet at the age of fourteen with an Indiana band that toured the state during the summer months, and played the violin and piano. Glenn became a national and world famous artist in later years.

In 1923, New Richmond claimed to have had the only "Jazz Orchestra" in the Middle West. This group was known as "The Mystic Four." They were musicians of rare ability, and were in constant demand to perform at various functions. George Shepherd, Gene Hunt, Raymond "Johnny" Bell, and Miss Margaret C. Switzer at the piano made up this "Combo."

The New Richmond High School twenty-piece orchestra, organized in the fall of 1922, was directed by Miss Rachel M. Mathieu. This orchestra was composed of the following members and the instruments they played: Madge Chadwick, piano; Ruth Morrow, Paul Shepherd, Letha Fouts, George Shepherd, clarinets; Beulah Coffing, Harold Swank, Rose Shepherd, Ina Hornbeck, Gladys Burnett, Bertha Herrick, Eula Norman, Edith Bannon, violins; Margaret Rayborn, flute; James Malsbary, cornet; Eugene Hunt, Clifford Allman, saxophone (there were only eighteen students listed in this twenty-piece orchestra in the 1923 New Richmond High School annual, *The Jungle*).

New Richmond has produced many fine vocalists over the years—many received their early training in the local schools and churches. A quartet formed in the early 1900s consisted of Elmer "Pete" Harriman, Walter "Spud" Harriman, Melvin L. Claypool, and J. E. Burris. Other vocalists were John Turner, and Allie Deputy about the same time. Arett C. Arnett, M. L. Claypool, and Fred Alexander were vocalists around 1904. They entertained in the local churches and the Sugar Grove Methodist Episcopal Church. Prof. Ed H. McCrea played his violin for the Sugar Grove neighborhood the same evening. Arnett was cofounder of the Arnett-Crockett Clinic in Lafayette in later years.

Later harmonious groups formed within the New Richmond School were a sextet formed around 1938 with the following members: Edith Bunnell, Ruthanna Cox, Ruby Watts, Wilma Quigg, Martha Montgomery, and Theodora Murdock. In 1939 a quartet composed of Jean Harriman, Frances Sturm, Frances Waye, and Wilberta Quigg performed for many local functions.

In 1982 a group was formed called "The JoySings," with the following members: Wilma Lewellyn, Monica Swick, and Teresa, Shirley, Christine, Sandy, and Colleen Fruits, accompanied by Kathy Olin and Shirley Pence. This group, a New Richmond Christian Church group, performed for the New Richmond Christian Church Homecoming programs and other church functions in the county. They sang in 1983 and 1984 for the Fourth of July celebrations for the New Richmond, Coal Creek Township Historical Society Museum, and the Strawberry Festival at Crawfordsville in 1983. Monica Swick left the group in 1984 to enter college.

Another group organized in 1982 was the "Sounds of Joy" composed of the following members: Jane Remley, Karen Smith, Linda Kingry, Kathy Olin, Wilma Lewellyn, and Linda Miller. They appeared in many of the area church and school programs. Wilma Lewellyn resided near Wingate when the two groups organized, but later became a New Richmond resident. The others were from out of town.

The town of New Richmond was blessed with the musical talents of Edward H. McCrea who taught the fundamentals of excellent music to many, many, students in New Richmond and other neighboring towns and gave violin and piano lessons for many years. He played a big part in teaching music to the bands and orchestras formed in the town.

Edward H. McCrea was born June 6, 1869, one-half mile southeast of New Richmond, son of Captain Edward T. and Jessie Louise (Draper) McCrea. He died in the same house in which he was born, on Sunday, August 4, 1929. His obituary in the Crawfordsville *Journal*, Monday, August 5, 1929 says, "Mr. McCrea was a teacher of music, and a maker of fine musical instruments most of his life, receiving his education in Valparaiso, Indianapolis and Chicago." Ed McCrea possessed a rare, natural talent as a musician. He and his brother John played in the New Richmond Commercial Band, and John's son Ted served as the band's mascot. Ed, or Professor McCrea, as he was always called, composed classical music, as well as building fine instruments, and designed the artwork for his sheet music.

Incidentally, Vera (Ebrite) Waye was one of Ed McCrea's piano students. She played the piano for the New Richmond Christian Church for many years. When her children were very small, she sat them on the piano bench beside her as she played for church services, and as they grew, they occupied the pews close to the piano where she could keep one eye on them—the other on her music. Nine children got their start in this manner. How do I know? Because I was number seven. Many New Richmond people have said she was one of the best pianists they ever heard.

Howard A. Kesler taught Music, Violin, and Elementary Harmony and Theory in 1910, for fifty cents a lesson, in New Richmond. Miss Leila Hollin was a music teacher in 1911 and 1912 in New Richmond and in Mellott.

Grace Dettbenner, born east of New Richmond, July 29, 1887, was a daughter of Theodore F. and Augusta L. (Schumaker) Dettbenner. Grace attended the New Richmond schools, was a graduate of DePauw University School of Music, and did graduate work at the University of Michigan, Northwestern University, and New England Conservatory of Music.

Miss Dettbenner taught piano and voice until five years before her death on May 25, 1967. After she and her father moved to Crawfordsville, she drove to New Richmond and the surrounding area teaching piano and voice to students in their private homes. When her father became a semi-invalid, she brought him along, and he remained in the automobile while she taught the weekly lessons for many years. Such dedication is unheard of in this fast-moving world today.

My brother and sister, Don Waye and Frances Waye Thayer, were her pupils. Don took his first piano lessons at the age of six. Grace was very proud of his musical talent at such a young age. Don has played the piano and organ for the New Richmond Christian Church for many years, and played for many weddings and other events within the church.

Marianne Furr, once a New Richmond resident, was a very talented musician who played organ, piano, accordion, and vibraharp. She became a popular night club entertainer. During their residence in New Richmond, she and her mother participated in many amateur musical productions in the town.

William E. Sturm, son of Frank and Clara May Sturm, was lead guitarist for a group called the "Country Sunshine Band" and played with several other bands before he met an untimely death in an auto accident in December 1978.

Judith Perry, daughter of Albert and Marietta (Fruits) Perry, married Reynold "Rey" Cawley, one of the original members of the group Bill Hailey and the Comets. Both were killed in a head-on collision near Atlantic City, New Jersey, in July of 1980. Judy had served in the U. S. Army and Rey in the U. S. Navy and they were residents of Burlington, New Jersey, at the time of their deaths.

The list of talented musicians associated with New Richmond could go on forever, and the lack of complete records will have to be forgiven, as it is impossible to read 150 years of newspapers to be able to include everyone.

Social Life in New Richmond

The New Richmond businessmen made many attempts to keep up with the big cities, and when social events were increasing they provided space in their buildings for social affairs.

The Hollin brothers and William Campbell ran a pretty close race as to who was the first to provide a hall or opera house for these events. Campbell erected a two story frame building on the corner of east Washington and Franklin streets in December of 1889. The first floor housed his general merchandise, and the second floor was to serve as entertainment space. Campbell prepared his hall with seating capacity (he neglected to say the number his hall would seat in his column in the Crawfordsville *Review*) and made plans to book some type of entertainment. A troupe from Chicago was to "give a good show" in March 1890, and Lafayette parties tried to lease his hall for show purposes. Campbell was to give a "grand ball" shortly after his building was completed. Campbell's hall was not the smashing success he had hoped for.

He mentioned an early show, saying, "An Italian, and a bear were here performing tricks, and the boys hope another will come soon." He also mentioned "a good show gave two exhibitions in this place last week to good houses." Campbell booked a few prize-fights to entertain the male populace of New Richmond, but even they were a disappointment to those who attended. The Knights of Pythias were attempting to organize a lodge in New Richmond in November 1889; they tried to rent Campbell's Hall, but decided on the Hollin's Opera House building. Campbell's building was razed around 1904.

Magruder's Hall in New Richmond was mentioned in February, 1892, when the "Dancing Club" gave their first dance. This must have been their first - and last dance. There was no other mention of this club. The location of this hall is a mystery to me; its entrance and exit was as rapid as the dancing club.

Johnson's Hall - F.M. Johnson's drug store was located in a two-story frame building on the southwest corner of Washington and Wabash. The building was razed to make room for the Knights of Pythias building in 1910. The Ashland Temple of Rathbone Sisters gave a Hallowe'en Festival in Johnson's Hall in 1906. The hall was lighted with pumpkin heads, and the waiters were masqued. Prizes were given to the best masqued couple. There were church socials held in this hall occasionally, but most of these were held in Hollin's Hall.

Hollin's Opera House

John W. and William H. Hollin made their first appearance in New Richmond in January 1879, embarking in the drug business. They were successful in this profession, and erected a large brick building in 1890 on the northwest corner of Washington and Wabash Streets. The second floor of this building was the first meeting place of the Knights of Pythias, Modern Woodsmen, and other secret societies.

Various entertainments were held in Hollin's Opera House in 1892, but the town board did not set the amount for a license fee right away. On May 5, 1896, the trustees of the town of New Richmond, namely Stow S. Detchon, Orlando W. Mason, and Horace G. Messer, passed an ordinance fixing the amount of yearly license required for a certain place of amusement which reads:

> Be it ordained by the board of trustees of the incorporated town of New Richmond, Indiana, that any person, or persons desiring to exhibit within the following named place in said town for hire, or pay, or to let the same to other persons to so exhibit for hire or pay, any of the objects or things specified in ordinance number three (#3) may procure of the town clerk a yearly license and for such license, he, she, or they, shall pay the town Treasurer as follows for the place known as the HOLLIN OPERA HOOSE [*sic*], and situated on lot number nine (9) of Stow S. Detchon's third (3'd) addition to the town of New Richmond, Indiana, the sum of twelve dollars and fifty cents ($12.50) per year and a fee of twenty-five cents (25¢) to the clerk for issuing such license.

John Hollin managed the opera house in 1895, but his brother William also managed the hall as his partner over the years. Early entertainments held in Hollin's Hall were: The Ruth Kirby Company in

December 1892; the New Richmond Band gave a concert and supper; various persons in town sponsored dances; a "Panic Party" was held—where men were judged and fined for some breach of the rules, and if he was discreet enough to break no rules, was given a double portion for the offense of committing no offense; William Richmond's four-act comedy *Rip Van Winkle* entertained the local citizens one evening in 1896; a Chicago Comedy company, "held down the boards" the same year; New Richmond's Home Talent show presented a comedy entitled, *I'm Not Mesilf at All* in 1897. The New Richmond High School advanced pupils presented a play, *Tony the Convict* under the direction of Professor and Mrs. Welty. Tickets sold for 10 and 15 cents. A "Grand Easter Ball" was held April 11, 1898 with music by the Yountsville Orchestra. Thomas Kirkpatrick and Thomas D. Dillon were the managers of this ball. The tickets were fifty cents for numbers, and fifteen cents for spectators.

1902 was a big year in Hollin's Opera House. The Coal Creek Township commencement was held in Hollin's Opera house on May 28, 1902, the New Richmond Orchestra furnishing music. The Republican Convention met in the hall to select delegates to the state convention in Indianapolis on April 23 and 24. New Richmond's home talent presented a four-act comedy entitled, *A Woman's Honor*, assisted by the New Richmond Orchestra and Aeolian Quartette, to benefit the orchestra. This show was such a success they immediately started practice on a new play. Some of the members included M.L. Claypool and his wife, Raymond and Fred Alexander, and Arett Arnett. "The Deacon's Tribulations" was presented by Romney's home talent troupe in Hollin's Hall as a benefit for the Romney Methodist Episcopal church; The "Vitaschope" with all the latest moving pictures, *Cinderella and the Crystal Slipper*, McKinley Pictures, *Eruption of Mt. Pelee*, War and Naval pictures, comic, fight, serpentine dance, and others. (Admission 10 and 15¢).

In December 1902, Professors Matt Murphy, of New Richmond High School, and Marion Westfall, of Boston Store High School, booked Montgomery County poet James B. Elmore, "The Bard of Alamo," to appear in Hollin's Hall. His lecture and readings included many of his best and sweetest gems from his own pen under the caption, "Pure Literature." Hyde's Comedy Company of five people entertained in July and was to entertain the Wingate and Newtown people later in the month. The Wabash College Glee and Mandolin Club, composed of twenty-two members and accompanied by Byron Hughes, pianist, Walter Dorsey, soloist, and G.A. Eldredge, the impersonator, all of Crawfordsville, appeared in July.

The program for the Lecture Course of the 1902-3 Season, published in the New Richmond *Record*, April 10, 1902, included the following entertainers:

1. The Mendelssohn Quartette (for October) composed of Alpheno M. Applegate, first tenor, William C. Smith, second tenor, Howard Stewart Barnett, baritone, and Urban Leo Alkire, basso. Also included were Helen Faye, soprano, and Miss Marguerite Smith, "Queen of child impersonators."
2. Father Francis C. Kelley (Originally scheduled for November - didn't make the November date, but came in April) - His subject, "The Yankee Volunteer," portrayed a soldier's patriotism from enlistment to the terrors of warfare, honor and chivalry. He was introduced by Matt Murphy.
3. Hawthorne Musical Club, of Boston (December) - a concert comedy company composed of five gentlemen. The reviews said they proved themselves musicians and masters of every conceivable instrument - and encores counted as many numbers as the selections on the program.
4. Mr. De Witt Miller (January) Lecturer - his subject, "The Self Sufficiency of the Republic." A small crowd who braved one of the worst days of the winter and heard Mr. Miller were more than repaid for the effort.
5. Fred Emerson Brooks (February) - Poet and humorist, appeared in Hollin's Hall, but the inclement weather kept people in their homes. His Fourth of July poem brought him into prominence.

A representative of the Central Lyceum Bureau met with the managers of Hollin's Opera House, and made the contracts for the above entertainers. (Season tickets were on sale at the Corn Exchange Bank in New Richmond.)

1903 in Hollin's Opera House:

DeWitt Miller, Lecturer; and Fred Emerson Brooks, Poet and Humorist; New Richmond's Dramatic Club's presentation of the play, "The Spy of Gettysburg;" W. B. Townsend, Lecturer, given under the auspices of the local order of Modern Woodmen of the World; St. Valentine's Masquerade Ball; Father Kelly's Lecture; General Z.T. Sweeney's lecture, his new subject, "America's Civilization and Destiny," the Ladies Aid Society of the local Christian Church secured this lecturer (tickets were 50 and 35¢ - on sale at the bank).

A record-breaking crowd turned out to hear a performance of the Wabash Glee Club. The Glee Club had just finished a three-week tour of Indianapolis, Logansport, Frankfort, and Monticello. Elder J. August Smith of Rockford, IL, conducted Advent Christian Services in Hollin's Hall—a one week engagement that had very light attendance; the First Grand Ball of the season (October); Henry Clay Lodge No. 288 Knights of Pythias to sponsor the Famous Baldwin Quartette with Byron Hughes, the pianist. This was a charity program to benefit a widow and her four children; Ed Anderson and his Big Company of New York Artists presented the greatest of all great plays, "East Lynne." "Large audiences seem to be in full sympathy with the moral of the story, and laugh at Corny and Dill, Sympathize with Lady Isabel, weep at the death of Little Willie—truly a great play." (Admission -15, 25, and 35¢).

A long editorial printed in the New Richmond *Record*, November 26, 1903, accompanied the reviews of "East Lynne," concerning the disgraceful behavior at Hollin's Hall during the show, and read in part, "There was noise and confusion, etc. in the gallery, and such noisy boisterousness should be stopped and stopped well!" A meeting of the town trustees with the managers of Hollin's Hall followed soon after, and Marshal John Work was instructed, "to be present at all performances and keep order, so visitors to the local opera house will be assured they will not be molested, or disturbed any more."

Garrett L. Bastion was the great organizer of the "Grand Balls" presented on many special occasions in Hollin's Hall. "Monte Cristo" the greatest of all melodramas of the American Stage, was presented by the well-known company of Carl Ford. Jessie Colton, whose fame as an emotional actress was well established throughout the country, was the leading actress.

1904 in Hollin's Opera House:

Dr. Sam Bayliss, manager of the Hot Springs Remedy Company, was requested to give the New Richmond people a good show in January of 1904 (see Doc Bayliss). The Ladies Aid of the New Richmond Christian Church, gave a "Colonial Festival" where waiters were gentlemen and ladies dressed in Colonial dress. "The Woven Web" was presented by an amateur company from Waynetown. "Uncle Toby" "was played by T.H. Westfall, "Tim," by C.A. Summer, "Aunt Judy," by Miss Opal Hauk, and "Walter Hastings," by Paul Hurt. T.H. Westfall played the "sweetest music on eight ugly beer bottles." He and the whole Westfall family were blessed with a natural musical talent.

Prof. Guiseppe Marone, a talented Italian harpist, furnished music for the Coal Creek Township commencement held in Hollin's Hall in May, 1904. Every graduate of both eighth year and high school were to report at Nick Washburn's Furnishings establishment promptly at 7:45 to be ready for the program at 8 p.m. They were asked to be on time as, "the program cannot be delayed for any trivial matter" the trustee O.W. Mason stated. Matt Murphy, "Past Grand Master of Bristle" presented the diplomas to thirty-eight common school graduates.

"The Feast of Five Tables" was presented by the Epworth League of the New Richmond Methodist Church; Carlos Inskeep and his excellent company produced a show each night in September. Among their presentations were, "Joe Blossom," "Driven From Home," and "Damon and Pythisia." The Wells-Greenawalt Musical Company, a high-class musical and entertainment organization, presented a variety show. Such musical novelties as the wonderful organ chimes, xylophone, Swiss hand bells, saxophone, etc. interspersed with humorous and dramatic readings, impersonations and rapid crayon caricaturing were presented under the auspices of the New Richmond High School. Part of the proceeds was to go to the school library fund.

Mr. Goer, a blind man and a thrifty young lawyer of Lawton, Oklahoma, discussed political issues on the "Democratic Theories" "to a good crowd. Mr. Goer was a very fluent speaker and fuller of witticisms than a dog has fleas-his evening lecture was nearly one round of laughter," the reviews said.

The first number of the Lecture Course (1904-5 season) was Lee Francis Lybarger's splendid lecture on "How to be Happy—Whether Married or Single" presented in December; Hon. Charles B. Landis of Delphi spoke to a "good audience on Republican issues of the day" in October. He was introduced by the Hon. John C. Wingate of Wingate; the Republican Township convention was also held about this time in Hollin's Hall. The Ladies Aid Society of the Methodist Episcopal Church arranged a lecture course for the dull winter months of 1904-5: first Dr. W.R. Halstead gave his famous lecture "Fun on the Farm;" the second was a fine musical by the Rhineberger Ladies Quartette; and the third, Dr. Swadner's fine lecture "The Philosophy of Life." (Reserved seat tickets were 50¢ for the season, single, 25¢, Children's season tickets, 25¢, and could be procured at Claypool and Fry's store.)

1905 in Hollin's Opera House:

In January the New Richmond Lecture Course presented the Harry T. Butterworth Company, an excellent musical organization composed of Mr. Harry T. Butterworth, bass; Miss Fay Hill, soprano and accompanist; Miss Iona L. Senn, violinist and accompanist; Miss Mabel Marion Wallace, reader. Tickets were on sale at Nick Washburn's Cigar Store. Butterworth's solo, "The Song the Anvil Sings" was "one of the grandest ever heard in this section-his tones are profound, musical and of wonderful control," said the reviews in the Dublin, Georgia, *Courier-Dispatch*.

In February, Lou J. Beaucamp, a humorous philosopher, "a thinker who makes you laugh, and a humorist who makes you think," presented his lecture, "The Sunny Side of Life." *Eli and Jane Company* played to a good audience, and contained some thrilling scenes with many a hard laugh, but the play had a bit too much harsh language to be classed of the best. It was presented by a big comedy company with special scenery and calcium lights. Elder W.P. Shamhart of Champaign, IL, gave a free lecture in February.

The last lecture course number was "The Maryland Jubilee Company" on March 30th—all the reserved seats were sold out, but twenty-five more chairs were added to accommodate the patrons. The company presented, "A Black Frost Thursday Night," a company of five gentlemen of color gave an amateur performance to a large audience, "who were disappointed — to put it mildly, and it was without a doubt as hard a frost New Richmond has suffered in quite some time," the reviews said.

Mr. Earl Wilfley's most humorous and most popular lecture entitled, "Behind the Senes" [*sic*] at Hollin's Hall under the auspices of the Pythian Sisters (tickets on sale at Nick Washburn's Cigar Store); the American Biograph Company gave a performance of the latest moving pictures and illustrated songs at the opera house in October. "The Great Train Robbery," one of the best moving pictures, was repeated; the local Order of I.O.O.F. observed the anniversary of the organization by a free lecture given by Elder J.P. Ewing, an Odd Fellow of long standing, the lecture entitled, "Odd Fellowship." The Uncle Tom's Cabin Company, produced by the Harmount family under a mammoth water-proof tent, presented the "five-act play, divided into twenty-eight scenes in twelve tableaux, and a superb and awe-inspiring transformation scene." A band concert was held before the show. (Admissions -10 and 20¢).

The 1905-6 Citizen's Lecture Course included: George R. Wendling, lecturer; Cosmopolitan Concert Company, composed of Miss Edna Dorthea Rether, elecutionist, and Misses Rowena and Edythe Tyler (twins) violinists; Durno and Company—consisted of three persons with magic, music, illusions, imitations, and ventriloquism. Durno carried his own special scenery and was a sensation in 31 states. Also included in this show was Mr. Herman, a violinist, and five animals.

Voters of the town of New Richmond were called to meet in mass convention in Hollin's Hall in October, to nominate candidates for town office—trustees for first, second, and third wards.

1906 in Hollin's Opera House:

The Whitney Brothers Quartet made a big hit with the New Richmond people. Edwin N. Whitney, reader and impersonator, exhibited marked talent in this line. DeWitt Miller's lecture on "Reveries of A Bachelor" was filled with sound logic, quick wit, and eloquent appeals.

"An Evening with Opie Read" was presented by an author, entertainer, and a newspaper man—a leading writer on the Chicago Dailies for years—and appeared in Hollin's Hall in February. Opie Read's visit to Hollin's Hall was preceded by large reviews from other cities. "Being a southerner, his southern dialect comes freely and naturally, and his interpretation of the Negro dialect is especially true and rich. His personal appearance is such that he attracts attention every where—his long, black, bushy hair, and broad-brimmed hat of southern style, gives him the general appearance of a Kentucky Colonel he writes about." He spoke for an hour and a half in Hollin's Hall and the patrons of the opera house were so entertained they found it disappointing the show ended so soon.

The Keller and McCarty Stock Company gave a splendid repertoire in February; *The Noble Outcast*, a four-act comedy drama, was presented at Hollin's Opera House in March by the West Point dramatic club; Rev. Sam Jones, the noted "Southern Divine Lecturer," was well received by the local people; and the Fancher Company, composed of seven people, entertained for a full week in March. The last number of the 1905-6 Lecture Course was Miss Myla Card, entertainer, and reader. She gave readings from *Ben-Hur* and "Preciosa," and was assisted by Miss Mayme Galey of Wingate on the piano.

On March 22, the New Richmond *Record* printed Nick Washburn's financial statement for the season's lecture course in Hollin's Hall. Receipts from season tickets and door receipts amounted to $526.95, and the expenses were $565.00, a shortage of $38.05. Entertainment was a costly item in New Richmond in 1905-6. One of the entertainers cancelled his engagement, and another was secured to fill the void. The hall rent was only $35 per season—not a bad price for entertainment. Nick Washburn did not let the above financial figures frighten him, and he immediately made arrangements for the next season of lectures, and entertainment. The seven numbers follows:

1. In October, 1906, "Victor and his Royal Venetian Band" opened the 1906-7 season of lecture courses in Hollin's Hall. "The band consisted of twenty-five members, and was equal to Sousa's, Pryor's, Brookes' or any of the leading organizations now playing. The New Richmond School was dismissed for this concert, and the pupils were marched down the street to Hollin's Hall. One proud citizen, pleased by the spectacle, claims it took the procession thirty minutes to pass by, he was surprised to see so many pupils." This band was well received by the New Richmond citizens, but was poorly patronized by the Crawfordsville residents when they played in that city, although the reviews were quite good.
2. The Harmony Concert Company (November 14) - four ladies gave twelve numbers of voice, violin, flute, viola, and piano. Three Kirksmith sisters and Miss Daisy Higgins made up this company.
3. Floyds in Magic (December 26) - magic and mind reading. His great "Transformation Scene" changing from evening dress, to ancient magician, to a gorgeous suit of red, then disappearing, held the audience captive.
4. The Italian Boys (January 26, 1906) - with Elbert Foland as reader, humorist; Dominick Austrella, boy harpist; Tony Schillaci, flute soloist.
5. Col. H.W.J. Hamm (February 19, 1907) - the southern orator, whose subject will be, "The Snolly-Goster in Politics."
6. The Musical Five (February 17) - "they carry a reader, their own piano and have a quartette of merit."
7. Hon. George D. Alden (March 8) - "a new entertainer who has taken the country by storm."

In November, Life Motion Pictures and Illustrated Songs, presented *The Great Train Robbery* and *Meet Me At the Fountain*.

"Baltino's Show-a-weird" and comical performance of his marionettes was worth many items the price of admission. Mr. Slover, more familiarly known to New Richmond people as Mr. Baltino was from Grand Junction, Michigan. His wife was a sister to Mr. H.W. Beckley of New Richmond. Inclement weather lessened the crowd the November evening Baltino performed in Hollin's Hall, but he returned in December by special request by the local people who wanted to take their children to enjoy his show—as father and mother did when they were children. He presented his "Marionettes Resurgam, or the Haunted Church Yard," a fascinating show.

A masquerade party was given by the Rathbone Sisters in November. Messrs. A.E. Malsbary and Charles Kirkpatrick dressed as George and Martha Washington, Ralph Henderson and Miss Nesbitt as "Josiah Allen and wife," Beard Washburn and Mamie Patton as "Tom Thumb and his wife," Ralph Arnett as an Indian Chief, and Mrs. James Martin as a squaw, James D. Martin as a Chinaman, and dozens of others competed for the prize, but the first couple mentioned, "took the cake" as the best masked.

The Salisbury Family of ten people gave a musical entertainment in November; and the Christian Church bazaar and supper netted $159.90. Mrs. Leila Martin and Bert E. Page presided at the confectionery stand. Mr. Page was an expert taffy maker, and made it fresh in the booth—he could have sold much more than he did. There were many, many festivals and bazaars held in Hollin's Hall by the ladies groups of both churches, and other social groups, but a lack of space forces me to omit them.

1907 in Hollin's Opera House:

The 1906-7 Lecture Course program was listed with the 1906 pages because they started in the fall and continued through the winter into the following spring each year.

A debate between a team of colored gentlemen from Crawfordsville and a team representing New Richmond was given in January 1907, as a benefit for the school library, entitled "White and Black." I found no information on the outcome of the debate due to a lack of newspapers archives from that year.

In April 1909 the New Richmond High School staged a play entitled, *The Noble Outcast* and was given a good audience despite the inclement weather. Cast members listed Professor Jones as "Jerry, the outcast;" David Holmes, "the rich old Colonel;" Mayme Morris, "the Colonel's wife;" Ina Pence, "the good-natured France—the Colonel's foster daughter—and Worthington's sweetheart" was one of the best characters in the cast. Anson Thomas played "Jack Worthington- the dashing young lover;" Mae Coffman as "Sadie the faithful, but Free Maid;" Lewis Jones, as "James Blackburn, the Villain;" and little Everett Greenburg in Marshal Work's big police helmet looked formidable. The play was given in benefit of the school laboratory. This group presented the play at the Linden opera house later.

THE NEW RICHMOND COMEDY COMPANY

John R., Mark, and Bertha Alexander, all children of Winton and Flora (Thomas) Alexander, started a little theatre business called the **New Richmond Comedy Company** in an upstairs room over what is now Alexander's Furniture and Gifts (1986), but at the time was Hollin's Opera House. Flora Thomas was Amos Ebrite's step-daughter, and was often referred to as Flora Ebrite by the local residents. The comedy company played in Hollin's Opera House on many occasions, and they played in most of the neighboring towns' opera houses. One of their most famous plays was a comedy by C.A. Malby, entitled, *I'm Not Mesilf At All*, one of the most successful Irish plays that has ever been produced on stage in the line of comedy. The cast of characters were: "Phelim O'Rourke, Irish" by Mark Alexander; "Mr. Benjamin Pootles" by John A. Long; "Captain Debit," by Claude Work; "Laura Pootles" by Alice Mitchell (Amos Ebrite's daughter); "Mary, a servant" by Bertha Alexander.

Another amusing farce entitled *The Stage Struck Darky* was performed along with the former play, with the following cast of characters: "Johnny, the stage struck darky" by Mark Alexander; "Tommy, a tragedian" by John A. Long; and "Jenny, a servant girl" by Alice Mitchell.

The reviews on the two plays said, "The work of the company before a home audience was excellent all around, each member acting their part well. The company will present the same program with several new specialties at the Linden opera house tomorrow night and we believe those who attend will certainly get their worth of their money in fun and amusement." They were to play in the Mellott opera house at a later date.

John Alexander was co-owner of a circus for many years, was associated with the Ford Motor Company in Detroit, and left that company to form a motion picture partnership with his brother-in-law, Frank Carey. Frank's wife was Bertha Alexander who was mentioned above in the cast. They had theatres at Lebanon, Attica, Rockville, and Monticello. Their first venture was at Hammond.

Sam Bayliss' Big Sensation Show

Would you believe—New Richmond was a little circus town? The following account of the life of one early resident of the town should make a believer of you.

Samuel Lewis Bayliss, son of William F. and Ida (Epperson) Bayliss, was born July 15, 1871 in Evansville, Indiana. He attended the public schools in Evansville, and after leaving school went into the entertainment business, becoming part owner and player, in the early "Boat," and "Tent" shows. Bayliss became interested in the patent medicine shows, and for several years was affiliated with the **Hot Springs Remedy Company**.

Bayliss' father was a chef on the steamboats that plied the Mississippi and Ohio Rivers from his early youth, and continued throughout his active career. It is believed that Bayliss accompanied his father on many of his trips, and was exposed to the entertainment related to the romantic steamboat era. He became a very gifted banjo player, and a talented musician. He was a natural born entertainer with a charming personality who made many friends throughout his entire life.

In Bayliss' early show-business days he traveled by horse and wagons, later pulling his wagons with a Case tractor. After he became more successful, and to keep up with the modern times, he purchased a large parlor coach, containing twenty-one seats, to carry his show company on their tours.

Samuel Bayliss was residing in Marietta, Ohio, and was manager of the Hot Springs Remedy Company of Hot Springs, Arkansas, when he brought the show to the little town of New Richmond, Indiana, where he met his future bride, Agnes M. King, youngest daughter of Josiah and Sarah J. (Campbell) King. Sam and Agnes were married three weeks after they met on Sunday evening of November 25, 1900. They were married in the home of her parents in New Richmond. Agnes and her parents were all educated in the Round Hill and New Richmond schools. Her ancestors were early settlers of Coal Creek Township, and New Richmond.

In November of 1903, Sam "Doc" Bayliss and his wife and little daughter, Queen, visited his father, who was living at Tiptonville, Tennessee, at the time. Tiptonville was located on a considerably out of the way point on the Mississippi River, and the boats on the river only made the run once a week, each way. On the trip down, the Bayliss family missed the weekly boat, so Bayliss hired a skiff and had to row twenty-six miles down the river to his father's home.

Bayliss had a little daughter, Detty, from a previous marriage, who died in 1907 at the age of fourteen. He and Agnes had one child, Queen Ester. "Queenie," as she was referred to by New Richmond residents, received her education in the New

50 - Samuel "Doc" Bayliss' Big Sensation Show Wagons. Photo taken in front of Glen Pierce's residence south of New Richmond near Round Hill.

Richmond grammar and high school. Queen and her first husband, Joseph Million, eloped when he was a senior and she was only a sophomore. They were married at Crown Point, Indiana, January 11, 1919. Joe and Queen Million had a son, Rex King Million, born October 8, 1921, who was a very gifted musician. Queen married a second time to Oscar D. Crull, of Pendleton, Indiana, and they had a daughter, Iris

Eileen Crull, born December 10, 1929. Mr. Crull was connected with the Shore Line Bus Company. Queen married a third time to Jess Shekels.

After Sam and Agnes were married, New Richmond became the headquarters of the Hot Springs Remedy Company, and the young people about town suddenly became very interested in show business. The town already boasted of its own little theatre, the New Richmond Comedy Company, which included three of the Alexander children: Bertha, Mark and John, and Alice (Ebrite) Mitchell, Claude Work, and John A. Long. Mark soon became one of Sam Bayliss's favorite performers, and traveled with his show from that time on. He resigned his position in John Hollin's Drug and Shoe Store and became a showman.

The New Richmond *Record* reported the towns and cities in which Bayliss and his troupe were playing, and of their return to headquarters at the end of the winter and summer seasons. I do not have access to many issues of the *Record*, and some years will be a little skimpy—this does not mean his business was failing, however.

In 1903, the show was touring the northern part of the state of Indiana. Later, the town of Veedersburg was one of the stops in the New Richmond area. The summer season started in April, playing at Swazee, Sharpsville, and Sidney. Bayliss shipped his tent home in July that year and was to work with the company on the streets, because of the heat. The winter season started in September in Warsaw, Indiana—Mark Alexander was to have a "great big part" in the show there—then they traveled to Monon and Cayuga. An excerpt from the Cayuga *Blue Pencil* said of the show, "Dr. Sam L. Bayliss and Mark Alexander, the black-faced comedian of New Richmond, have been giving free exhibitions on the street and selling HOT SPRINGS CRYSTALINE. The Dr. leaves Sunday for the South to spend the winter healing the afflicted." Doc Bayliss was in Colfax, Indiana, with his show in November of 1903, and left for the south after this show.

The year 1904 was a very big year for Doc Bayliss. His show performed in many cities and had just played a week in Ridge Farm, Illinois, Markle, and Perrysville, Indiana, when they concluded the winter season and returned to headquarters in New Richmond. They were requested to perform for the hometown people, and the New Richmond Comedy Company joined in the performance held in Hollin's Opera House. The show was performed on a cold winter evening and the ground was covered with snow, but the show was greeted by an excellent audience despite the unfavorable weather.

Bayliss performed as a genuine Dutch comedian, and other lines of comedy, and he extracted music from almost anything he picked up, from a few inanimate pieces of wood, to tin funnels, and the best of string instruments. He was a very skillful banjoist and performed for all his shows. His wife, Agnes, was noted for her "Serpentine Dance" which she performed with very graceful movements.

Mrs. Dunning, known in show business as "Princess Neta," performed her skilled rifle shooting act, and as another part of her act, sang in a very strong baritone voice. Mark Alexander, the New Richmond boy, had his act as a black-face comedian make a lasting impression on the hometown citizens as a fine actor. Harry Germaine was well known for his female impersonations and succeeded in fooling his audience completely. He also performed his famous Clog Dance.

Samuel Bayliss expanded his show troupe to around twenty people in February, 1904, and because of a large profit made while showing at Ridge Farm, Illinois, he placed an order for a large canvas tent, 50 X 80 feet, and four or five smaller tents, and was to start on the road under a new style of show, **The Bayliss Big Sensation Minstrel Show**. The new arrangement was void of the medicine business and was to be a minstrel and vaudeville type of show, making one-night stands only. They were to make their drive from one town to another early each morning after performing the previous evening. This would have been a very exhausting experience for the players.

Doc Bayliss engaged New Richmond's blacksmith and wagon maker, T.M. Shotts, to build four new wagons to carry the paraphernalia. The band wagon was constructed to carry sixteen people. In all, six wagons and nine horses were required to carry the whole company. Doc Bayliss purchased nine good, strong horses from the local horse buyer. The name of the horse buyer was not recorded, but Sam S. Kirkpatrick raised registered Percherons and Mart Graves sold heavy draft and coach horses about this time. Boswell Clough was a local horse trader for many years in New Richmond, so one of these gentlemen may have been the lucky one to make this sale.

Sam Bayliss stored his wagons in a huge barn that stood on what is now a vacant lot just south of Byron Alexander's residence, on Cleveland Street in New Richmond. Each time the Bayliss show wagons entered or departed New Richmond during school hours, the teachers permitted the children to leave the class room to greet the show people. Three of these children, Forrest Waye, Elnora McNeil Nesbitt, and Opal Clapp, remembered very vividly how exciting it was to watch the circus go by, and no doubt, their little hearts went right along with them.

Everything was in readiness for the new Bayliss Big Sensation Minstrel Show, and Sam decided to give his first performance for the good citizens of New Richmond on Saturday, May 1st, 1904. An immense audience taxed the huge tent for standing room even. The New Richmond *Record*, Thursday, May 5, 1904, said:

> The show was one round of pleasure from beginning to end, from the first appearance of the laughable mute clowns in a very funny act, to the close of the last act in a side-splitting farce comedy. The show company of twenty-five people combines the marvelous acts by good athletes, funny and ridiculous situations of funny people, strange feats of the magician, good actors, comedians, orchestra, mirth and music! Special mention of the leading actors were: Kline & Neiser, the funny clowns in a most laughable act; Lemonzo, the human corkscrew - greatest contortionist in the world who comes from a family of contortionists, his father being one of the best circus contortionists; Lemonzo & Geiser do an interesting double act; Neiser is the slack-wire performer-and a good contortionist; on and off the wire; Prof. Kline performed his work in magic, too marvelous and too illusionary to admit a word of description; Geiser, a black-faced artist in song and dance- and is a great clog dancer; Mark Alexander, a New Richmond boy, does a new double impersonation of song and dance, entitled, "My Dear Old Mamma and I" which is captivating. Dr. Bayliss does all kinds of musical and comedy acts, and his wife, Agnes, the beautiful and picturesque Serpentine Dance. An entirely new program of music and specialties, and moving pictures made the show a performance worthy of all the appreciation accorded it as a New Richmond enterprise.

The Bayliss show only brought in a paid admission of about $150 that night, but you must remember Doc Bayliss only charged 10 and 15 cents admission to some of his shows, and often the shows were free.

Claude Work made plans to join the Bayliss Show Company, moving his wife, and their household goods from Lafayette, storing the goods at Shotts' place. Mrs. Work remained in New Richmond, and Work went on the road with the show.

The advertising paper, lithographs and other material, arrived in New Richmond, and Harry Germain was in charge of the advance wagon. The show played in Wingate, Waynetown, Ladoga, Greenwood (in Johnson County), the towns in the east part of the state, Linden, Kempton, Sheridan, Kirklin, Romney, Clark's Hill, Stockwell, and Reynolds. Bayliss added a new feature to the show, a comic acrobatic feat called the **Trick House** after the show went on the road. While showing in the town of Linden, the New Richmond citizens were treated to a band concert by the Bayliss Show Company's brass band.

Harry Germaine left Bayliss' Show and joined a theatre company in Nova Scotia in August, 1904. In October that year, Sam and his theatre-troupe were to start on the winter season, and were to play week stands in Opera Houses. They opened at Homer, Illinois, and played at Maroa, Illinois. Besides Dr. Bayliss and his wife, his company at this time included Mark Alexander, Henry Neiser, and E.E. Williams.

Dr. Sam Bayliss' winter show went back to the title of the Hot Springs Remedy Company, and spent all winter in Northern Illinois, played for a week in Galesburg, then played in Oxford, Indiana, for a week in March 1905.

The huge tent that Doc Bayliss and company performed in the previous summer became too much of a burden to carry, and he sold and shipped the tent, seats, and fixtures of his big wagon show outfit to an "Uncle Tom's Cabin Company" at New Martinsville, West Virginia. He then offered the rest of the wagons, harness, and other paraphernalia for sale. This ended the Bayliss Big Sensation Show chapter of Doc Bayliss' show business career.

The company continued playing under the name Hot Springs Remedy Show. The summer of 1905 found the company playing the streets in Greentown, Rossville, and Kewanna in Indiana; and Rossville and Tolono, Illinois; and Covington, Ohio, for week-long engagements.

In May 1906 the Hot Springs Remedy Company began the summer season in a tent show through Ohio. The troupe included Sam, Agnes, and Queen Bayliss; Mark and John Alexander; and Mrs. Alice (Ebrite) Mitchell. They concluded the summer season in Glandorf, Ohio, in August that year. The winter season opened in Spencerville, Ohio, in September 1906.

Mark Alexander was the only member of the show outside the Bayliss family, from New Richmond. They were playing the small towns in the vicinity of Toledo, Ohio, in December 1906.

The whereabouts of the Bayliss Hot Springs Remedy Company are a little uncertain from 1907 through 1909, as I have a limited number of New Richmond *Record* issues to search for the information. Sam Bayliss was listed as a showman residing in New Richmond in the 1907-08 directory of Montgomery County, Indiana, and the show was in Marion, Indiana, in August 1908. Some New Richmond people had "run into" the Bayliss troupe in their new automobile on their way to visit the home-town relatives. The New Richmond folks knew all about his new auto, because of the register number of the "machine" being sent to Doc in care of the New Richmond Post Office. One of his vehicles—a big open bus type of truck, was destroyed by fire in Boswell Clough's barn in the west part of New Richmond. There was an account of the fire, but the item was not dated. In 1908 Samuel Bayliss and Charles B. Snyder organized the Snyder-Bayliss Airplane Company at Osborn, Ohio, and he was associated with this for two years; however, Bayliss continued his show business tours while in this line of business.

Doc Bayliss and his company gave one of their "peerless shows" at the Hollin's Opera House in New Richmond on Saturday, April 24, 1909. Included in this show was "Sweet Music,-on many fine musical instruments, Comedy Acts, and Moving Pictures."

It is uncertain when Bayliss changed the format of his show, but in May 1915, the troupe went by the name of **The Bayliss Overland Electric Show**. They were showing in Sedalia, in Clinton County, at the time. Bayliss had rigged up a device to connect all his wagons together, inventing a type of tongue that would trail the tractor as the wagons turned the corners, but he failed to take out a patent on this device. A photograph shows six wagons being towed by the tractor. This show was lighted at night by an electric generator furnishing the power.

Bayliss installed a new maple floor in Hollin's Opera House, and purchased forty-eight pairs of roller skates, and started a new entertainment "emporium." Large crowds attended the skating rink, and this soon became a very popular place in New Richmond in 1916. The Crystal Theatre was also located in this emporium, where the early moving pictures were shown.

The Bayliss Overland Show was in Phillipsburg, Ohio, in August 1919. Sam was doing business "like in the old times" in the Ohio Tobacco Belt at the time, but this type of traveling show was on the way out in the early 1920s, and Samuel L. Bayliss decided he needed a more substantial business in order to earn a living and became interested in real estate.

In 1923, after a thirty year residence in New Richmond, Sam Bayliss entered another field of business—selling real estate in Hammond, Indiana. He was the senior partner in the real estate firm of Bayliss, Million & Million until 1927, when he went on his own as the Bayliss Real Estate firm. His new line of business soon made him a millionaire. He purchased large tracts of land and developed several subdivisions in Hammond. By 1931 he had erected a total of 555 homes. He sold all the homes except the residence he and his wife, Agnes, shared on Jackson Terrace, one of his better known subdivisions.

The last mention of him visiting the home town citizens of New Richmond was in 1935. He continued his interest in show business as a side-line after he started in the real estate venture. He helped develop the Lake Hills Country Club at Hammond, Indiana, and was a member of several lodges in the city.

Sam Bayliss was the author of two books: *The Master Key to Health* and a directory of farmers and businessmen he compiled for Montgomery County, Indiana.

Samuel and Agnes Bayliss retained their membership in the New Richmond Methodist Episcopal Church throughout their lives. This was always home to Sam, and he and Agnes are buried in the New Richmond Cemetery, along with her parents, their daughter, Queen Shekels, and Bayless' father, William.

Dr. Samuel L. Bayliss died June 4, 1942, age 72, at the home of his daughter, Queen Shekles, in Hammond, Indiana, and was brought home to his beloved little town of New Richmond for burial. His wife Agnes died in 1961 and was buried beside her husband.

Moving Picture Theaters

The Crystal Theater

The Crystal Theatre was the first motion picture theatre in New Richmond. Samuel "Doc" Bayliss, a medicine showman whose headquarters were in New Richmond in the early 1900's, was the promoter, or manager, of this early theatre. It is uncertain as to why the theatre was named "Crystal" but two possibilities are: 1, the first movie he presented to the local patrons was *Cinderella and the Crystal Slipper* in October 1902; or 2, he sold "Hot Springs Crystaline" for the Hot Springs Remedy Company.

The Crystal Theatre was located on the second floor of the Hollin Brothers' brick building, more commonly known as the Hollin's Opera House. The movies were shown between the lecture dates, or the many balls which took place in the hall.

Playing at the Crystal Theatre during the same month as *Cinderella* was a series of McKinley pictures, *Eruption of Mt. Pelee*; War and Naval pictures, comic, fight, serpentine dance, and others. Admission was 10 and 15 cents at this time. In November 1906, Life Motion Pictures and Illustrated Songs presented, *The Great Train Robbery* and *Meet Me at the Fountain*. The Crystal Theatre was going strong in May and June of 1915, and movies were shown each Wednesday and Saturday night. General admission was 10 cents, children under 9, only 5 cents. A Vitagraph in one act entitled *The Quality of Mercy* and *Essanay*—in two parts; *An Amateur Prodigal*, by Albert Payson Terhune, with Miss Ruth Stonehouse and Mr. Joseph Byron Totten, were just a few of the movies shown.

In June 1915, there was a call for sixty girls under 12, and sixty boys from 5 to 15 years of age to rehearse in the Crystal Theatre for *The Pied Piper of Hamelin*, a pageant to be presented in the "Grove" (Meharry's Grove) during the annual horse show in New Richmond.

In December 1916, Doc Bayliss added another attraction to his "Entertainment Emporium" in the Crystal Theatre by purchasing roller skates and turning the theatre into a roller skating rink. The rink was opened every evening, and the admission was FREE! There was no mention of his medicine show pitch to reimburse him for the cost of the skates, but the *Record* said Mr. Bayliss was doing everything he could to please his patronage, and his patrons were showing their appreciation of his efforts by attending and enjoying the skating and fun.

The Shadows Theatre

A map of New Richmond made in 1916 by the Hanover Insurance Company, shows the location of the "Movie Show" next door east of the Washburn block on East Washington Street (now the New Richmond Bar & Grill - 1986). The pool hall (now the local post office) was next door east of the theatre.

The earliest record available to me of the **Shadows Theatre** was in the New Richmond *Record*, Thursday, September 16, 1915, but the item indicated the theatre existed before this time saying, "The theatre, The Shadows, is to launch a new once-a-week feature policy beginning Saturday October 2. A contract for fifty-two special features, etc., produced by Thomas A. Edison and George Kleine was closed by managers Livingston (Samuel) and Plunkett with a representative of the Kleine and Edison Feature Film Co." Each of the fifty-two features contained from six to eight reels. They were to be shown Saturday afternoon and night, each week. The price of admission was 15 and 25 cents.

Around the first of January 1916, Miss Gertrude Herbert of Sullivan, Indiana, purchased the Shadows Theatre from Sam Livingston. Livingston left in March 1916 for Urbana, Illinois, to take a position in an auto agency. He had been an auto mechanic in New Richmond in 1912 working with Starr Dunn. Gertrude Herbert was a sister to Myrtle McLain, widow of Charles McLain, and moved into Myrtle's home while the two sisters managed the theatre. An older gentleman of New Richmond, now deceased, remembered the Herbert sisters as being very stern looking, and usually dressed in black clothing, and wearing tight-fitting hats when they sold tickets from the little box office at the entrance to the Shadows theatre. Another former resident said she and her brothers came to town with their parents each Saturday and the children spent the entire afternoon in the Shadows Theatre while the parents did their weekly trading. There was a player piano in the theatre for the silent movie films during this time.

The Herbert sisters (McLain & Herbert) sold the Shadows Theatre to Reuben Swank and Russell Weyles the last of June, 1920, and Swank & Weyles (seniors in New Richmond High School) took over the management on July 1st that year. The Herbert sisters purchased the **Joy Theatre** in Crawfordsville at the same time, and moved to that city.

Maurice Stribling was the projectionist for the Shadows Theatre during the McLain & Herbert management, and moved to Crawfordsville where he owned and operated the old **Ritz Theatre** and was the projectionist in the **Strand Theatre**. Stribling also owned and operated the Crawfordsville drive-in theatre for several years. Stribling enjoyed a forty-year span in the theatre business.

Maurice Coffman was a projectionist in the Shadows Theatre for a short time and purchased a theatre in Darlington in August 1919, operating in that city a number of years.

Swank & Weyles only managed the Shadows Theatre about two years, but the theatre was still in operation in August 1923. Later owners or managers are unknown at this time, but any information will be much appreciated. When my brothers and I were small children we attended a movie or two in a New Richmond theatre in the same location as the Shadows. This would have been in the late 1930s. I cannot recall the managers of the theatre, or the movies we attended, unfortunately.

Some of the movies shown in the Shadows Theatre throughout the years were: in 1915—*The Spoilers*, written by Rex Beach; *The Country Mouse*, with Adele Farrington, Myrtle Stedman, Rhea Haines, Marshall Stedman; and *Mrs. Black is Back*. In 1916—*Gretna Green* with Marguerite Clark, *Governor's Lady* with Edith W. Mathison; *The Unafraid* with Rita Govilet; *Fanchon, the Cricket*, featuring Mary Pickford; Paramount Pictures: Marguerite Clark in *Seven Sisters*, *The Woman*, *Puppet Crown*; Blanche Sweet in *Secret Orchard*; Elsie Janis in *Nearly a Lady*; Sam Bernard, the world's most famous comedian, in *Poor Schmaltz*; *The Impostors* (stars not listed); Hazel Dawn in *The Heart of Jennifer*; John Barrymore in *The Incorrigible Dukane*; *Esmeralda*; *Out of Darkness*; *Old Dutch*—a five-reel comedy, a special for the Fourth of July; *Madame la President*, with Anna Held; John Barrymore in *Nearly a King*; Charlotte Walker in *Trail of the Lonesome Pine*; Florence Rockwell in *He Fell in Love With His Wife*; Billie Rhodes in *Girl of My Dreams*; Enid Bennett in *The Marriage Ring*.

In 1919 the Shadows Theatre presented William Duncan in Vitagraph's big, high-powered serial pictures of the great open spaces, the lumber camps, football fields, mountains, streams and wind-swept prairies. The series contained fifteen two-reel episodes of "smashing melodrama of thrills-action-risks-and speed."

In 1920, performances included Louisa May Alcott's pretty story of Civil War days, *Little Women*, and *Girl of the Sea*. Admission to the movies was quite a bit higher by this time, being 20 and 25 cents. Ethel Clayton in *The 13th Commandment*; and *Black Beauty*, were playing in 1921. *Behold! My Wife*; *The Sky Pilot* was also shown, and in July 1922, *Fool's Paradise* was shown.

New Richmond joined in the National Demonstration for Better Motion Pictures in August 1923 and listed only Paramount Pictures to be shown at the Shadows:

September 4th – William C. deMille's *After the Show*

September 8th – Will Rogers and Lila Lee in *One Glorious Day*
September 11th – Elsie Ferguson in *Footlights*
September 15th – Jack Holt in *The Man Unconquerable*
September 18th – Jack Holt in *Her Husband's Trade Mark*
September 22nd – Thomas Meighan in *Our Leading Citizen*

THE OUTDOOR THEATER—FREE STREET SHOWS

On May 6, 1935, the Merchant's Association of New Richmond met with the local town trustees to discuss the possibility of presenting free street shows to the citizens. The town trustees agreed to pay $4 per week towards the expenses of the "talking movie-pictures" if the Merchants Association would pay the remainder. Movies were shown on the streets of New Richmond from the first of June through the first week in September, from 1935 to 1939. The cost to the town by then had risen to $6 per week and the trustees, thinking this was too steep, considered discontinuing the weekly free shows.

On May 6, 1940, a petition bearing the names of 42 citizens, mostly taxpayers, asked the town board to contribute toward free picture shows. After a motion was made by Geiger and seconded by Burnett, the board voted unanimously to pay $6 per week, and the clerk-treasurer was authorized to pay two weeks in advance. The town trustees continued to share the costs of the street shows through August 1942. The following year there were no records in the town minutes to indicate any payments toward the movies. The Merchants Association continued the street shows into the 1950s, but by this time the local citizens had recovered from the effects of the depression—and World War II, and the young lads drove their girlfriends to see the movies in the large and beautiful theatres in the nearby cities—an exciting era had just ended.

The movie screens were made of heavy white cloth, and were suspended by ropes between the Hollin and Long buildings on north Wabash, spanning the street. The projector was placed on its stand in the center of the street, and citizens gathered together, coming from the four corners of the town with their chairs or blankets from home, to sit in the center of the street, between the projector and movie screen. Many people removed the seats from their automobiles and placed them on the streets for a softer place to enjoy the movie, which was fine unless the crowd was quickly dispersed due to a sudden rain shower.

Popcorn was freshly popped during the movie in readiness for the crowd to purchase during intermissions. The local tavern owner, Ross Howe (and his grandchildren) popped and sold the corn. The local drug store usually enjoyed a sudden burst of business during intermission when many Cokes, sundaes, sodas, and ice cream cones were consumed. Quite a large amount of business was conducted in the local grocery—and the local tavern—before and after the movies. The merchants relied upon the big Saturday night trade to help pay for the rent of the movie reels and equipment. Ah! Those were the good ole' days!

SECRET SOCIETIES

"The first secret lodge in New Richmond was that of the DAUGHTERS OF TEMPERANCE, organized in 1857, and flourished about five years," said William Campbell in his early history of the town.

A Grange of the Patrons of Husbandry was organized in New Richmond in October 1873 to further interests of agriculture and general farming. This secret society only lasted about two years. Pleasant Hill and the Round Hill communities organized Grange societies during the same time period, and theirs lasted about the same amount of time.

William Campbell noted in January 1891 that "secret orders have struck our town, and breast pins from the size of a common field harrow, down to the size of a common dinner plate are in order. Joe Bennett wears one that covers his breast like the warrior's shield of the olden time." By February that year, New Richmond boasted of three secret societies, but I only found records of two—the **Knights of Pythias**, and the **P.O.S. of A (Patriotic Order of America)**.

The **Washington Camp No. 12, P.O.S. of A.** was progressing nicely and taking in new members almost every Thursday night by April 11, 1891. District president Samuel D. Symmes of Crawfordsville, accompanied by Sam J. Billman and Howard Griffith of Camp No. 6, installed the New Richmond Camp No. 12's new officers in January 1893 as follows: F.M. Smith, past president; W.P. Coffman, president; C.A. Taylor, vice president; Wm. Stites, master of forms; T.S. Patton, recording secretary; W.S. Alexander, financial secretary; S.R. Tribby, treasurer; Mart Lucas, conductor; George Steel, inspector; S.P. Harriman, guard; and the trustees were, Amos Ebrite, C.A. Taylor, and W.S. Alexander.

Knights of Pythias, Henry Clay Lodge No. 288

A group of men were in the process of organizing a local order of Knights in November of 1889 and were trying to rent Bill Campbell's hall for a meeting room. The Henry Clay Lodge No. 288 Knights of Pythias was chartered January 16, 1891, and in February the lodge members were busy carpeting the room on the second floor of the Hollin brother's brick building on the northwest corner of Wabash and Washington Streets, and otherwise improving the room for a meeting place. The officers of Henry Clay Lodge No. 288 Knights of Pythias on January 20, 1892, were: John W. McCardle, Chancellor Commander; Dayton R. Black; William W. Washburn; Harry Wilson; Samuel S. Kirkpatrick, recording and keeper of records; Dora Ammerman; Rob A. Bonnell; and the trustees were, Thomas W. Banta, William C. Davisson, and Richard. M. Bible.

On May 11, 1910, the Henry Clay Lodge No. 288 Knights of Pythias, formed a corporation by the name of **The Henry Clay Castle Hall Association**. The object and purpose of the incorporation was:

> to issue and sell stock or bonds, to purchase, acquire, use, enjoy, rent, lease and control, real and personal property, to erect and maintain a building or buildings for the use of Henry Clay Lodge Knights of Pythias, of New Richmond, Indiana, upon its real estate, and to rent and lease the said building or buildings or portions thereof, and to do all things necessary and proper for the erection, maintenance, repair and operation of the said building or buildings, and to receive, collect and disburse the income there from for the benefit of such lodge.

The new corporation began with a capital stock of twenty-five thousand dollars divided into shares of twenty-five dollars each. The principal place of business was New Richmond, Indiana, where all the regular meetings of the association were to be held. The incorporation was to be managed by a board of directors, composed of seven members to be elected annually by the stockholders of the association. The president and secretary of the board of directors were to perform their duties at all stockholders meetings, and each stockholder had one vote for each share of stock held.

The incorporators of the Henry Clay Castle Hall Association and the first board of directors were: Henry K. Lee, George F. Long, Charles Haywood, William C. Davisson, James H. Stewart, James D. Wilson, Charles A. Patton, and Orlando W. Mason. Edgar Walts, Notary Public in New Richmond, witnessed the articles of incorporation.

By October 20, 1910, the new Knights of Pythias brick building was almost completed on the southwest corner of Washington and Wabash Streets in New Richmond. The Henry Clay Castle Hall Association leased the north room to the Corn Exchange Bank of New Richmond on December 27, 1910, and the other rooms were soon occupied by other business establishments. The second floor meeting rooms were occupied by the Knights of Pythias Lodge, and the town board met in one of the rooms for several years.

In 1913 the Henry Clay Lodge Knights of Pythias No. 288 had a membership of 193, and the association was still active in the late 1920s. Some of the later officers were Charles Haywood, Wm. C. Davisson, W.W. Boland, Tom Banta, M.L. Davisson, and E.J. Mason.

Ashland Temple No. 160 Rathbone Sisters was instituted October 27, 1897 by Alice Lamphor, D.D.G.C. of Lebanon, assisted by Lily Temple of Crawfordsville. There was a disruption within this lodge in July 1902, and the fifty-nine members signed a petition against the two couples who were causing the problem. As a result, the lodge reorganized under the name **Ashland Assembly No. 1 Pythian Sisters** of New Richmond and the charter was dated September 18, 1902. There were forty-three charter members in the new organization. The first officers installed under the reorganized society were: Bessie Wallace, P.C.; Nettie Alexander, C.C.; Emma Hollin, V.C.; Libby Wilson, P.; Nina Long, K. of R. and R.; Anna Page, M. of F.; Clara Mason, M. of E.; Nannie Lee, M. at A.; Minta Ames, A.M. at A.; Clara Stewart, M.O.; Georgia Stewart, O.; Susan Alexander, I.G.; Elizabeth Stewart, O.G.; and the trustees: Maggie Tribby, Samantha Davisson, and Mrs. Nellie Vess.

The local lodge entertained the Pythian Sisters of the Fourth Indiana District in May 1912. It was the largest and best convention in point of attendance the Pythian Sisters of that district ever had, being their fifteenth annual convention. Twenty-one temples were included in this district, and all but two of the temples were represented. The New Richmond Ashland Temple had the finest lodge home in the district in which to entertain the convention, and was also the largest all-ladies temple in the fourth district at the time of this convention. They met in the new Knights of Pythias building, erected only two years before.

Modern Woodmen of America, New Richmond Camp No. 7594 was mentioned in August, 1902. Four members, Albert E. Luse, Will Bowles, Will Grannon, and George C. Livingston, attended the Modern Woodmen Log Rolling, held in Kokomo near that date. I could not find the date of the organization of this lodge or the first officers. The New Richmond *Record*, Thursday, December 1, 1904, listed the officers for that year, namely: William Bowles, V.C.; Sam Rafferty, W.A.; Albert E. Luse, Banker; George W. Clough, Clerk; Samuel Harriman, Watchman; George C. Livingston, Sentry. The Modern Woodmen of America, Camp No. 7594 held their meetings in F.M. Johnson's hall. This lodge was still active in October 1910, and met the second and fourth Thursday nights of each month. Officers at the time were: F.E. Campbell, William Bell, C.J. Biedenkopf, S.L. Rafferty, Lester Utterback, William Stites, Raymond Kemble, and managers: J.L. Jones, Arthur Bell, Thomas Davis; Physician, Dr. Sam E. Jones.

Blue Bell Lodge of Daughters of Rebekahs No. 621 New Richmond was mentioned in March 1904, but the date of organization of this lodge is unknown. In December that year, officers were listed in the *Record* as follows: Lennie Hollin, N.G.; Lillian Smith, V.G.; Bessie VanHook, Sec.; Millie McLain, Treas.; Flora Alexander, Warden; Ida Beckley, conductor; Lucy Groom, I.G.; John Cash, O.G.; Fannie Devault, R.S.N.G.; Bertha Kelsey, L.S.N.G.; Lizzie Coffman, R.S.V.G.; Mary Perry, L.S.V.G.; Ida Kincaid, Chaplain.

The Rebekahs met every Tuesday evening in the Odd Fellow's Hall in Frank Perkin's brick building on east Washington Street. They sponsored several old-fashioned box suppers and ice cream socials. During one of their festivals, a cake was to be given to the most popular young lady present, and the "boys" were urged to bring their pocket books and vote for the lady of their choice. They decided to give the girls a chance to vote on the most popular young man present, as well. Miss Hellie Long and Mr. J.M. Ward won the cakes that evening.

The Blue Bell Lodge of Rebekahs No. 621 were holding meetings in October 1910 and listed the following officers: Laura Malaskey, Sarah Ward, John W. Smith, Millie McLain, Ida Kincaid, Lizzie Coffman, Larkin Devault, George Malaskey, Lillian Smith, Millie Kemble, Mollie Lynn, Lenna Hollin, Allie Oppy, and Annie Devault.

Independent Order of Odd Fellows No. 748 New Richmond (I.O.O.F.) was instituted on the night of Saturday, October 31, 1903 in New Richmond. The camp of Crawfordsville headed by W.D. McClelland, D.D.G. of P., performed the initiatory work in the Odd Fellows Hall (second floor of Frank M. Perkin's building). The new lodge began with fifteen members (they expected thirty, but only fifteen joined) and was the sixth of the kind in Montgomery County—Crawfordsville, Shannondale, Ladoga, New Ross, and Waynetown all having organized before the New Richmond lodge. The Daughters of Rebekah served a full supper to the newly formed society and their visiting members in Hollin's hall, and a general festival was held during the evening. The New Richmond Lodge No. 748 Independent Order of Odd Fellows met every Wednesday night in their hall. The officers listed in the New Richmond *Record*, Thursday, December 1, 1904 were: Clell Terrell, N.G.; John W. Smith, V.G.; John Perry, Sec.; Ed C. Oppy,

F. Sec.; F. M. Lynn, Treas.; John Smith, Chaplain; Frank Bennett, L.G.; Charles Oppy, O.G.; and trustees Jasper Dick, John Oppy, and Perry McLain.

In October 1910, the Independent Order of Odd Fellows were meeting every Wednesday night in their hall on the second floor of the Washburn Block, and the following officers were listed: F.E. Campbell, Dennis Stucky, J.N. Beckley, Perry McLain, J.W. Hollin, Geo. Malaskey, Walter Kemble, Wm. Stites, Bazil Williams, G.L. Bastion, George Bunnell, Grover Shotts, Joseph Humbert, Eph Mears, Wm. Graves, A.C. McMillin; James Utterback, Joseph Humbert, and Grover Shotts were trustees. In 1912 the New Richmond Lodge No. 748 had a membership of sixty four. In 1916 Lodge No. 748 was meeting on the second floor of the Hollin brothers' brick building on the northwest corner of Washington and Wabash Streets.

Free and Accepted Masons, New Richmond No. 604 (F. & A.M.) was chartered May 26, 1896. The F. & A.M. Lodge met the Saturday night on or before each Full Moon.

Their meeting place was not listed through the years. The officers listed in the New Richmond *Record*, December 1, 1904 are as follows: Charles Kirkpatrick, W.M.; John C. Bible, S.W.; Nick Washburn, J.W.; E.T. McCrea, Sec.; T.M. Foster, Treas.; C.E. Kelsey, S.D.; Frank Shepherd, J.D.; George W. Clough, Tyler; James Battreal and William Kite, Stewards. The Masonic Lodge No. 604 New Richmond is one of two surviving secret societies in the town today (1985); the other is the O.E.S. The Masonic Lodge meets on the second floor of the Washburn block on the southeast corner of Washington and Wabash Streets.

Order of Eastern Star No. 377 (O.E.S.) New Richmond was organized in 1911. The society is still active in 1986. Mrs. Pearl G. (Kite) Banta, age 92, was pinned by her son, C.W. Banta, during a ceremony, for her 75th year as a member. She is a charter member of the New Richmond Chapter and has served forty-five of these years as an officer. The organization has eighteen offices, and Pearl held thirteen of the offices over the years. Officers in 1985 were: Nancy Matricia, Associate Matron; C.W. Banta, Associate Patron; Marilyn Coon, Secretary; Patricia Ferguson, Treasurer; Patsy Steele, Conductress; Doris Snellenbarger, Associate Conductress; David Snellenbarger, Chaplain; Candice Potts, Marshal; Robert Fyffe, Organist; Peggy Fyffe, Adah; Betty Leader, Ruth; Opal Miles, Esther; Bernice Snellenbarger, Martha; Mary Bean, Electra; Thelma Banta, Leader; and Roy Meharry, Sentinel.

Chapter 19 - The Horse Thief Detective Company

Minute Men Were Number One!

When the early settlers came to the northern part of Coal Creek Township, they were greeted by a wide-open prairie. This prairie was covered with an abundance of bluegrass and many spring-fed ponds. The setting was excellent for grazing and watering cattle, hogs, sheep, and—more important to this article—the horses. The settlers who farmed the area soon prospered, as they did not lose time by having to clear away the forests and brush. The livestock feeding on the tall prairie grass grew strong and healthy, and became a temptation for the ever-present thieves of the world. The most appealing to the thief were the fine horses the farmers used each day in their farm work, and for their transportation. They took a fancy to the Morgan horses in the area because of their strength and light qualities.

The pioneers were hardly settled into their new homes, when in 1844, about twelve horses were stolen between the New Richmond and Newtown neighborhoods, a distance of about ten miles. This left the farmer helpless, for without his horses, he had no way of making a living. Life was becoming unbearable for these victims, and something just had to be done about the problem.

A group of men who had suffered losses met one day in June of 1845 in Thomas Meharry's locust grove. They discussed their problem, and failing to come up with a solution, decided to meet again the following week. About twenty prominent citizens of the area who lived on the highway between New Richmond and Newtown met in the Heshman Bethel brick school house, four miles west of New Richmond. This building was erected for church purposes by the Methodists of the neighborhood and served as the first school as well. The exact location is now the grave of Polly (Meharry) McCorkle in the Meharry Cemetery–according to the Meharry family history. Before the meeting adjourned, they had organized their group. It is believed that James Gregory was named the first president, and the group called themselves the Council Grove Minute Men. The name was chosen because the group first met in a grove for council, and each member was to respond at a minute's warning when he was needed. The purpose of the group was to suppress horse stealing and all other criminal acts that were being committed, and were to capture and prosecute the thieves. The following Preamble was adopted:

> We, the citizens of Montgomery, Tippecanoe and Fountain counties in the state of Indiana, do pledge our sacred honor to assist each other to suppress horse stealing, house robbing, pickpockets and all other thieving, and to regain the stolen horse or horses and all other property, and to apprehend the thief or thieves, and for the better government of our social movements.

The organization limited membership to Montgomery, Fountain, and Tippecanoe counties and was not to exceed two hundred. They decided they would be more efficient if they kept the meetings secret. This was the origin of the Horse Thief Detective Association in the state of Indiana, and this was, and still is, believed to have been the first movement of the kind on record.

The group was very successful in capturing thieves, sending many to the state prison, and other areas who were having problems with horse thieves soon organized groups of their own. Before too long, the Council Grove company reached its limit of two hundred, and decided to limit itself to three townships: Coal Creek in Montgomery County; Jackson in Tippecanoe County; and Richland in Fountain County.

In February 1848, the Council Grove Minute Men incorporated. James Gregory, William Cosseboom, Absalom Kirkpatrick, James, Jesse, and Thomas Meharry, Christian Coon, Elias Moudy, John M. Thomas, and Edward McBroom were the incorporators. This group of men was formed by hardworking, religious people banding together for mutual protection. Coal Creek Township, from the beginning of its government, was allowed by law only two constables, one for the New Richmond area and one for the Pleasant Hill neighborhood. This was a large territory to police on horseback, and the policing was usually done after the fact, so the Minute Men were a great asset to the community. Their work attracted widespread attention because they had the horse thieves terrified of them. The most noted case was that of Joseph Cocran, a noted highwayman. He and his partner in crime, Martin Moore, were selling fraudulent land warrants to some members of the company, and when, after his arrest, he discovered he was in the hands of the Council Grove Minute Men, he feared for his life.

The second company to organize was that of Wesley, in Wayne Township, and was followed by Ripley, Beech Grove, Waynetown, and others. The companies were numbered as they formed organizations. In order to work more closely the companies met and revised the constitution and by-laws and formed The Wabash General Association of Horse Thief Detectives. James H. Johnson was the first secretary, followed by D.B. Hostetter, J.W. McCorkle, J.L. Crouse, and Ira G. Meharry. The detectives petitioned the state legislature for assistance and protection many times, and laws were enacted to aid them in their work. They continued to work in their local organizations, however.

The success of the Horse Thief Detective companies had influenced the neighboring states of Illinois and Ohio to organize companies. John S. Gray of Wesley helped organize the Illinois groups under the Indiana state laws. Because of the spreading of this type of work, a new constitution and by-laws were made, and a new association was formed and named The National Horse Thief Detective Association. This association, organized in 1860, was composed of delegates from each subordinate company. Each company was to have only one delegate to attend the annual meetings. The officers were bonded and were the Grand President, Grand Vice President, Grand Secretary, Grand Treasurer, and Grand Organizer. John S. Gray, or "Sant," was one of the more enthusiastic men in the association and gave many years to the work. He was referred to as "Father Gray" and served as the Grand Organizer. After his death, the association assisted the family in erecting a monument to his memory in the Wesley Cemetery.

In 1893, John S. Gray called all the Montgomery County companies to his grove near Wesley for a mass meeting. An ox was roasted or barbecued, and a huge social event took place. After the dinner, Gray expressed his reason for the meeting, informing the group that he believed the detectives needed a closer union to be more effective, and an organization called the Montgomery County Union Detective Association was formed. Their object was the same as the Council Grove Minute Men–to hunt down thieves and other criminals—and they were to meet the third Thursday in September each year. New by-laws were made to suit the new organization by William Monroe, James Swearengen, Jacob Snyder, and George Bratton, the committee members. Their first secret meeting was held in the Montgomery County courthouse on March 29, 1894, because of important business to be transacted. There was some controversy over this meeting being held in the courthouse because the union was a secret order, but they continued to hold meetings in the courthouse over the years.

G.N. Meharry, one of the oldest members of the Council Grove Minute Men, in 1895 had two gavels made from the root of the locust stump from one of the trees that stood in the grove where the first detective council was held. Ira G. Meharry, grandson of James Meharry, one of the original Council Grove Minute Men who helped organize the group, made the gavel. In June that year, Mr. Meharry presented one of the gavels to the Council Grove Company on their 50th anniversary as a souvenir; the other one, he presented to the National Horse Thief Detective Association to be used by their president.

James A. Mount was elected president of the national association at their meeting held in Frankfort in October 1893, and again in 1895 at Eaton, Ohio. Mount served as Governor of Indiana from 1897 to 1901, and was a resident of Montgomery County. The influence of the work of the Horse Thief Detective Association was to be felt in Indiana in October 1904 when W.N. Yencer of Richmond fathered a bill to be introduced in the following legislature making the crime of horse stealing in Indiana punishable with life imprisonment. This was to protect the farmers and liverymen. The law was a prototype of a criminal statute in effect in Ohio and was modeled after western laws. The law covered burglary and housebreaking where the offender enters a residence or other building inhabited at night for the purpose of stealing. The penalty of life imprisonment was affixed because, it was argued, a burglar enters with the intention of sacrificing, if necessary, a human life to secure his booty. There had been a number of convictions under the new law that were declared constitutional, but the new law made it possible for a jury to recommend clemency to an offender.

The annual meeting of the National Horse Thief Detective Association was held in Franklin, Indiana, in October 1905 and was attended by representatives of all the local companies. Ira G. Meharry, the Grand Secretary of the association for the previous two terms, was reelected to that office.

Thirteen new companies were added that year, making 218 companies. The total membership of these companies was more than 1000, and all within the states of Indiana, Illinois, and Ohio. House Bill Number 448, a bill for an act entitled "An Act Concerning the Workings and Institutions of Detective Associations," was approved March 9, 1907, repealing all laws, or parts of laws in conflict with them. Citizens of the State of Indiana were granted the right to form companies for detecting and apprehending horse thieves and other felons, etc., and could be incorporated under the laws of Indiana, could sue and be sued, plead and be impleaded, answer and be answered in any court of competent jurisdiction, and have a seal–and alter it at pleasure.

They also were allowed to receive donations in money or property and could assess dues and impose fines upon their members. The members were to have all the power of constables, and the names of the members were to be given to the board of county commissioners. After the board consented to the appointments, the commissioners were to empower the county auditor to issue certificates as constables. Constables were to have the power to pursue and arrest horse thieves and all other criminals against the laws of the state of Indiana, and to serve papers relating to the same, and to follow and pursue such criminals into and through any part of the state of Indiana. In the absence of a warrant, they were to have power to arrest and hold in custody without warrant for such time as may be necessary to procure a warrant. The companies organized under Sections 4491 to 4495 of Burns' Revised Statutes of 1901 were declared legal and valid provided the new act did not conflict with any pending litigation. When the Council Grove Minute Men first organized their company, the farmers in and near New Richmond were part of the First Horse Thief Detective Company, but as they grew in numbers, New Richmond formed their own company.

The earliest record of the New Richmond Company was in 1870. The Miscellaneous Records of Montgomery County, Indiana, (Book 2, page 56) reads:

> NEW RICHMOND MINUTE MEN–The undersigned citizens of Montgomery County and Tippecanoe County, State of Indiana, do hereby agree that we will form ourselves into an association for the purpose of apprehending and detecting horse thieves and other felons that we will assume the name of the NEW RICHMOND MINUTE MEN and will claim the right to sue and be sued by that name and style, that we will faithfully aid in assist each other in the recovery of any property that may be stolen from any member of Said association, that we will render due Obediance to the Constitution and by-laws which shall be adopted by said association and will do all other acts and things necessary for the protection of the members of this association against the depredations of Horse Thieves or other felons and this association shall continue in force for ten years.
> In Witness Whereof we have hereunto Subscribed our names with Statement of our Several Residences this 5th day of March 1870:–M.J. Mason, George W. Washburn, C.J. (or C.Q.) Kirkpatrick, David J. Davisson, Solomon B. Kite, Mosses Everson, Mosses F. Wilson, all of Tippecanoe County; Stow S. Detchon, Levi Thomas, Charles Swear, W.H. Cowan, George T. Phillips, Jonathan VanCleave, Jeremiah Stevenson, George Manners, James M. Plunket, John Dewey, Elles Burk, Wiley S. Foster, James Coleman, John W. Plunket, Amos Ebrite, Ed. T. McCrea, Isaac W. Patten (Patton), all of Montgomery County.

On the second day of October 1875, Amos Ebrite witnessed the signatures on an affidavit for a new group of men joining the New Richmond Minute Men.

Amos was the local Justice-of-the-Peace. From Tippecanoe County were: M.J. Mason, C.Q. Kirkpatrick, W.C. Davison, Joseph F. Steele, George W. Washburn, Jonathan Garret, Samuel Livingston. From Montgomery County were: Ed. T. McCrea, Amos Ebrite, Samuel McComas, John Patten (Patton), William H. Cowan, Richard Phillips (his mark), L.J. Steele, Joseph Phillips, James F. McCoy, John Swank, Ellis Burk, James Kincaid, James S. Bastin (his mark), James Coleman, Thomas Phillips, David R. Cowan, Isaac W. Patten (Patton), George Phillips, Charles Swear, John W. Plunket, James Wainscott, and Zebulon Zook. The signatures were also witnessed by M.W. Bruner, a Notary Public of Montgomery County, because Amos Ebrite was one of the members of the Minute Men.

Due to the changes made on the House Bill 448, in 1907 the New Richmond Minute Men reorganized and changed their name to the New Richmond Horse Thief Detective Company. The Articles of Association reads:

> Be it known that on this 2nd day of March, 1907, these subscribers hereto, Citizens of the Counties of Montgomery and Tippecanoe State of Indiana, under provision of an act of the General Assembly of said State in April 14th, 1866, and all acts amendatory thereto (See section 4431, 4432, 4433, 4434, 4435 of Burns' Revised Statutes of 1901) do hereby form ourselves into an association under the name of The New Richmond Horse Thief Detective Company for the purpose of Detecting and arresting horse thieves, counterfeiters, incendiaries and all other felons and bringing them to justice to aid each other in the recovery of stolen property, and for our mutual protection and indemnity against such thieves and felons as provided in said Acts and Amendment, and in the manner particularly set out in the Constitution and By Laws of this Association; and agree that this Association shall exist for the period of Ten (10) years, unless sooner dissolved by a vote of the majority of the members.

The list of New Richmond members and their residences are: J.D. Wilson, Bayless Alexander, O.W. Pierce, L.M. Tibby (Tribby), S.S. Kirkpatrick, W.W. Rawland, James Tribby, Jane Coleman, Nich Coleman, W.T. Jones, W.H. Wilson, Eber Hollingworth, Arthur Hollingworth, Joseph Hall, Chas. Lydich (Lydick), J.A. Bailey, Herman Lidikey, Sam Magruder, W.M. Clawson, W.M. Kite, John Royer, T.M. Cook, Jean Bailey, A.J. Arnett, Justus Oliver, H.K. Lee, John Tompson, Tom Devault, Joseph Steele, John Royer—Kirkpatrick, Lidikey, and Joseph Steele were listed as Tippecanoe County, the others in Montgomery County. From Linden (rural route) were: JE. Burh (Burk), James Blue, and Michael Woods. This affidavit was signed by the president of the company, J.A. Bailey, and the secretary, W.M. Clawson, and was recorded March 26, 1907. The men who were Tippecanoe County residents but listed as New Richmond residents lived just inside the Tippecanoe County line and their mail was delivered from the New Richmond Post Office.

The New Richmond Minute Men was the 35th company to organize. At the seventieth annual session of the National Horse Thief Detective Association, held October 7-8, 1930 at Indianapolis, Coal Creek township was represented by the Council Grove (#1) with 10 members; New Richmond (#35) with 43 members, and Elmdale (#42) with 9 members. Officers of the New Richmond group were: O.W. Mason, President; John G. Utterback, Secretary; M.L. Davisson, Captain. Meetings were held in the local school buildings and were well attended. Several gentlemen from Round Hill belonged to the New Richmond Company.

The local newspaper, the New Richmond *Record*, had the opportunity of printing 6,200 pamphlets containing 36 pages of the proceedings of the National Horse Thief Detective Association's meeting held at Richmond, Indiana, on October 6, 1903, and again in 1904 printed 7,500 pamphlets of 36 pages. It was quite a task for the small printing office, but was handled very successfully.

In 1922, one of the members of the New Richmond town board wanted to dispose of the local marshal and to declare the office as vacant, because Marshal John A. Works had taken his cases before the Horse Thief Detective Association and not to the board. He said since the H.T.D.A. members had legal papers giving them authority to make an arrest at any time, it would save the tax payers $360 per year by declaring the office vacant and would hereafter rely on the association for protection of the town and community. The motion was not carried and was deferred to the next meeting. Marshal Works was retained, however, during the next monthly meeting.

A monument erected in 1930, commemorating the organization of the Council Grove Minute Men, the first Horse Thief Detective Company, stands along State Road 25 about a mile north of the Meharry Cemetery.

On October 2 and 3, 1928, the sixty-eighth annual session of the National Horse Thief Detective Association was held at Crawfordsville, Indiana. The convention headquarters and registration clerks were stationed at the Masonic Temple. The welcoming committee presented each delegate and visitor with a convention badge on which his name appeared. The officers and delegates were headquartered in the Hotel Crawford.

Sherman A. Trout was in charge of a tour for the visitors, which included a visit to the Study of General Lew Wallace (author of *Ben-Hur* and other less known books), an artist, sculptor, music writer, and a diplomat. The group also toured the home for aged and invalids, the Ben-Hur Lodge, drove past the beautiful campus of Wabash College, past the Donnelley Printing Plant, which occupies acres of ground, drove through the famous Jack's Hollow, and on to Wesley Cemetery to view the monument of "Uncle" Santy Gray, one of the founders of the Horse Thief Detective companies. The monument bears the image of a horse's head on one side, and an inscription, "Erected in the Name of JOHN S. GRAY, by the Horse Thief Detective Association in recognition of his untiring zeal in the interests of said order."

A tribute was paid to Captain H.H. Talbot of Crawfordsville, a veteran of the Civil War and the oldest member of the organization. Talbot had stood on the 'firing line' for sixty-three years, making Indiana a better state in which to live. Mention was made of the original company formed some 68 years prior in Montgomery County, with the help of Tippecanoe and Fountain Counties, to protect the American home. The history compiled by E.W. Bratton was mentioned, but it was the history of the Council Grove Minute Men originally written in 1910 by James D. Thomas that appeared in the New Richmond *Record*, Thursday, October 27, 1910. The National Horse Thief Detective Association boasted of more than 10,000 members in 1928.

Capt. H.H. Talbot told the story of a company who was watching a horse thief. He was riding one, and leading another. The company caught him, and after questioning him, he admitted, finally, to taking the horses. When the foreman asked his name he said, "You can call me Jack, I won't give my other name." The hollow where he was caught was from that time on referred to as 'Jack's Hollow.'

Captain Talbot continued with the story of Jack:

> Some how or another that rope halter that Jack had been leading the lead horse with, got tangled around Jack's neck and the horse he had been riding was a little bit shy, and somehow or other, the other end of the rope got over a hickory limb and Jack was left hanging in the air. Right where you went over with your automobiles, Jack's bones, if they are not rotted, are still there. That was the way they had to do it at that early date. When they had to do business, they attended to it.

The Crawfordsville *Weekly Journal*, Thursday, September 2, 1858 relates the story of "Jack's Hollow" and why it was called by that name, saying it is "situated in the northwest part of Crawfordsville and is occupied by the graded road that leads down by Sperry's Mill, received the name from the fact that the sentence of Judge Lynch was there administered to one Allen Jack." The article tells the whole story about Jack and a drunken friend, who were raising a lot of hullabaloo in the town of Crawfordsville and were caught in the hollow where a fast trial was held; since there was no jail in the county at the time, he was hung by his neck from the nearest tree. This incident had taken place in the early days in Montgomery County before the country was well settled.

Chapter 20 - Noted Personalities

William Samuel Gaither - President, Drexel University

New Richmond High School has produced many outstanding scholars, and has made the residents back home very proud to have been a part of their early childhood days. One of the most outstanding alumni of the old N.R.H.S. is Dr. William S. Gaither, president of Drexel University, in Philadelphia, Pennsylvania. from 1981 to 1987.

William Samuel Gaither, born December 3, 1932 on a farm near New Richmond, Indiana, was the son of William M. and Frances Kirkpatrick Gaither. Frances was a descendent of Absalom Kirkpatrick, one of Coal Creek Township's earliest settlers. Bill Gaither's mother died in 1939 at the age of 38 years, leaving behind her husband, their son Bill, age seven, and their daughter Susan, age one year. Frances is buried in the New Richmond Cemetery. After her death, the children lived with their Uncle Frank and Aunt Dolly Miller. Bill and Susan spent their formative years in this home, one-half mile north of New Richmond. Their father remarried and moved to Ohio, but the children were well established in the Miller home and chose to remain with them, although their father provided for them and kept in close touch.

Bill Gaither began grade school in Jackson Heights, Jackson Township, Tippecanoe County, but transferred to the New Richmond grade school in his third year. He graduated from New Richmond High School in May 1950. Bill was active in high school athletics as one of the "Scrappin Cards," and the local chapter of Boy Scouts. He attended Purdue University as a science major in 1950-51, and was a member of the Purdue Varsity Glee Club. He enrolled in Rose Polytechnic Institute in Terre Haute in 1951 (now Rose-Hulman Institute of Technology), graduating in 1954 from the school of engineering.

After graduation from "Rose Poly," he enrolled in Princeton University and received two master degrees—in arts and engineering science—and received his doctorate degree from that school in 1964. Bill taught while at Princeton, and attended conferences, delivering lectures in Lisbon, Portugal. After graduation he accepted a position as Associate Professor of Engineering at Florida State University, in Gainesville, Florida, and served as chief engineer for port and coastal development with the Bechtel Corporation, and worked on projects as engineering supervisor for the Dravo and Meyer Corporations.

In 1967, Bill Gaither joined the University of Delaware faculty as an associate professor of civil engineering and was named to the American Society of Civil Engineering Technical Council on Ocean Engineering Education Committee. He was made a full professor in 1970. The year after joining the University, he organized and directed a Department of Defense program funded through the Office of Naval Research, concerned with the coastal and oceanographic environments, doing studies from Atlantic City, New Jersey, to Ocean City, Maryland.

In 1970, Dr. William S. Gaither was appointed Dean of the new College of Marine Studies, which he founded at the University of Delaware. He addressed a White House Conference on Youth, on the subject "Our Environment," before one thousand youth and five hundred adults from the fifty states. Bill was elected president of the Association of Sea Grant Program Institutions at Houston, Texas, in 1973. This association, which originated in 1966, consisted of 51 educational institutions and research centers participating in the study of marine resources, technology, environment, sociology, economy, and law. Dr. Gaither was also president of the Delaware Academy of Science that year.

Dr. William S. Gaither was one of six alumni of Rose Poly (now Rose-Hulman Institute) honored for outstanding achievement in 1975, and the following year was honored by the State of Delaware for contributing to improve the quality of life in the state. He appeared on the *Today Show* on April 23, 1976, describing his work on a special show honoring the state of Delaware.

Dr. William Samuel Gaither was named president of Drexel University in Philadelphia, Pennsylvania, on May 16, 1984 at the age of 51. He succeeded Dr. William W. Hagerty, who retired August 31 that year. He served in that post until 1987. J. Donald Rauth, Chairman of Drexel's Board of Trustees, cited Gaither's distinguished career as an educator, researcher, and administrator, and his record of public service in cooperation with government and industry. He said, "Dr. Gaither is an eminent civil engineer, an authority of marine transportation and ocean engineering, and is ably suited to steer Drexel through the coming years." Bill Gaither authored many articles on marine studies, and testified before Congress on oceanographic and environmental issues.

William S. Gaither married Robin McGraw of Appleton, Wisconsin, and they had a daughter, Sarah.

GEORGE R. HOLMES

NEW RICHMOND TO INTERNATIONAL NEWS SERVICE

In the year 1896, Edgar Walts established the New Richmond *Record*, a weekly newspaper of which he was publisher and editor. On November 25, 1897 he married Rose (Beaver) Holmes, a widow with three small sons: David, Harry and George. George R. Holmes was born on the Stephen Beaver farm in Jackson Township, Tippecanoe County, Indiana, on January 28, 1895. He was only two years old when his mother remarried; therefore Edgar Walts was the only father he ever knew. George grew up with the New Richmond *Record* and this became the background for his career in later life. It has been said by the older residents of New Richmond that he spent many hours in the *Record* office watching his step-father set up the newspaper and was extremely fascinated by the workings of the newspaper business.

My father, Forrest Waye, and George Holmes were very good friends when they were young lads and they had many good times together—especially the day George was visiting Forrest and they got into Grandmother Waye's apricot pie and nearly consumed the whole pie. They helped with the ice harvest which took place at the ponds located in the New Richmond Park and also delivered ice to Claypool's grocery to keep the perishables cold.

One day Forrest and George were walking northeast of New Richmond and decided to climb a fence at Dewey's Elk Farm to pick some beautiful paw-paws, or "Hoosier Bananas." They started picking up some good looking ones, but were interrupted by a large bull elk who decided they were trespassing on his property and took out after George, who climbed the nearest tree to make his escape.

Forrest must have been a fast runner because he made it back over the fence. This old elk kept George up the tree until sundown. Each time he started down from the tree, the elk charged right after him. Forrest finally got the elk's attention (he was still on the outside of the fence) and George was able to get down from the tree and over to the other side of the fence—and the two hungry, very tired boys walked the long trek back to New Richmond after dark.

Another time, a group of boys, including my father, decided to take George "Snipe" hunting. They went to what is now the town park in New Richmond, but back when they were boys, the area was the local tile mill. The top soil had been shoveled aside in order to dig up the clay needed for tile; about three to four feet of earth had been removed, leaving a swampy condition where water stood during the rainy seasons. They gave George a gunny sack and pointed to a rock in the center of this water and told George to stand on the rock and hold the sack open and they would drive the snipes into the sack. Beware George! They're up to no-good! Everyone knew about this age-old trick. Forrest and the rest of the boys left poor old George standing on that rock and went back to town, where a very tired, foolish looking George finally came straggling back to join them. Forrest felt very bad about playing this trick on him and apologized, but George was understanding and said, "That's okay, I fell for it myself. I should have known better." He probably forgot the incident long before Forrest did.

This is just a small account of his early boyhood experiences in New Richmond before George went out into the world and became a famous journalist.

George R. Holmes graduated from New Richmond High School in 1912. He attended the University of Wisconsin and at the age of 19 he began his career as a newspaperman, his first job with the Indianapolis *Sun*, where he worked for two years. He then went to New York where he worked first for the United Press, and then for the New York *Mail*.

In 1916 he joined the International News Service and the New Richmond *Record* reported George would soon go to Mexico as a war correspondent to cover events there.

His newspaper work was interrupted, however, when he enlisted in the Cavalry in 1917 during World War I. He served throughout the war, first gaining the rank of second lieutenant in the Cavalry, next assistant adjutant of the Seventy-eighth Division, then as observer in the Two Hundred and Fifty-eighth Aero Squadron, and served in France.

After the war, he returned to news work, covering important events in this country and all over the world. The New Richmond *Record* of Thursday, August 14, 1919 says, "George R. Holmes, who holds a position with the International News Service, is now doing newspaper work in covering the outing and summer vacation of Thomas A. Edison, Henry Ford, John Burroughs, H.S. Firestone, and others of their closest friends, in the Adirondack Mountains. The Indiana Daily Times of Saturday carried a story of his of these noted personages and their doings hidden away fifty miles from a railroad. The story was in the Times and appeared under the heading of 'FOUR U.S. WIZARDS HIDE IN A GHOSTLIKE VILLAGE.'"

In 1920 he became the manager, or chief, of the Washington Bureau of the International News Service, one of the great news agencies of the country. Between the years 1916 and 1936 he reported every major political convention and he knew intimately Presidents Wilson, Harding, Coolidge, Hoover, and Roosevelt. He was made president of the famous Gridiron Club, a Washington newspapermen's club.

He was there with the tools of his trade when his "big story" broke, and he received an honorable mention from the Pulitzer Prize committee for the story he wrote about the burial of the Unknown Soldier.

George R. Holmes died February 12, 1939 of heart disease at his home at 2338 Massachusetts Avenue, Washington, D.C., at the age of 44 years. In his obituary the Washington Post says, "President Roosevelt, himself ill, conveyed condolences to Holmes' family. Tribute and sorrow were also expressed by Vice President Garner, Senator LaFollette, of Wisconsin; Secretary of State Hull, Secretary of Commerce Hopkins, Jesse Jones, RFC chairman; Secretary of the Navy Swanson, Associate Justice Stanley F. Reed of the Supreme Court, Senator Barkley, of Kentucky, majority leader; Senator McNary, of Oregon, and Representative Martin, of Massachusetts, minority leaders."

Raymond Clapper, who succeeded Mr. Holmes as president of the Gridiron Club, said, "He was the best all-around newspaperman I have ever known." Earl Godwin, president of the White House Correspondents Association, named the entire membership as a committee to attend the services. Similar action was taken by the Standing Committee of the Congressional Press Galleries.

His obituary in the *New York Times* reads, "PRESIDENT MOURNS GEORGE R. HOLMES," "Many Others High in Official Circles Pay High Tribute to Press Bureau Chief." "…President Roosevelt, a close friend of Mr. Holmes, although ill abed himself today, sent a personal message to Mrs. Holmes expressing his sorrow. Mrs. Roosevelt, also a close friend of the Holmes family, dispatched another message of condolence." The *Times* also says, "Vice President Garner declared that 'the passing of Mr. Holmes is a loss to the nation.'"

Secretary Hull paid tribute, saying, "I am greatly grieved by the death of George R. Holmes. He was an able, courageous and brilliant correspondent, who always sought to be fair and objective in his reporting. An intimate friend and consultant of several Presidents, Mr. Holmes will be buried in Arlington National Cemetery."

George Holmes married Miss Catherine Early, sister of President Roosevelt's secretary, Stephen T. Early. They had two daughters, Mary Catherine, who was 16 at the time of her father's death, and Kathryn Early, age 7.

From the "Congressional Record" –

Senate, Mr. Harrison. "Mr. President, second only to the warmth of feeling which naturally grows among the Members of the Senate are the feelings and friendships that spring and grow between men in public life and members of the press. Within the last few days there has passed from the field of active journalism one of the most beloved and ablest members of the newspaper fraternity. He was a young man, and it seems cruel that fate should strike him down at the age of 44. Within that brief span of life he had accomplished great things. He had made a name for himself in the newspaper world. His writings were full of candor, frankness, and courage. He despised sham, pretense, and hypocrisy. He impressed the country by his daily writings. His career carried him not only throughout this country but to the capitals of the world. His name will live in the annals of journalism, and his fine work should be an inspiration to the youth of the land.…I pay this tribute to my friend and a man who, in my opinion, was able, sincere, and fine, and who possessed the true qualities of real manhood."

Mr. Barkley, "Mr. President, I wish to add just a brief word to what my friend from Mississippi, Mr. Harrison, has said about George Holmes. Life is not measured in years. It is not measured on the dial, but it is measured by what service may be crowded within a given space of time. If that is to be the standard, in my judgment George Holmes fully measured up to the requirements. In every sense of the word he was a gentleman. I believe he elevated the standards of journalism by his courage, by his frankness, by his ability, by his level-headedness, and by his fairness. Not only was he an outstanding journalist, studying, as all journalists who write for newspapers and who to a certain extent create public opinion, must do, but above his professional integrity and his professional ability, he was a charming associate, a man of sincerity, a man of honor, a man of learning.

In his public relations and in his private life, and especially in his family circle, no man has come within my acquaintance in a quarter of a century who was more sincerely beloved, who was more genuinely respected, and whose untimely end caused greater grief, not only in his profession, but among all who knew him."

The Indianapolis *Times* also carried his obituary and it says in part,

Mr. Holmes was an overseas veteran of the World War but thought little of that youthful interlude and rarely spoke of it. His life was bound up in the daily work of a Washington newspaperman. He never stepped out of that character. A couple of inches of type in Who's Who in America set out the foundation of dates and distinctions upon which Mr. Holmes established his national reputation. He was 19 when he broke in on the Indianapolis Sun in 1914 and he was 44 when he died.

He is survived in Indianapolis by his mother, Mrs. Rose Walts, two brothers, David B. and H.F. and a half-brother Clyde E. Walts.

George's obituary also appeared in the Lafayette *Journal-Courier* and this paper gives the residence of his mother; Rose Walts, as New Richmond. The Crawfordsville *Journal-Review* also gave his obituary, both appearing in Monday, February 13, 1939 issues.

This boy George, who spent his formative years in New Richmond, "The best little town on earth" as his step-father, Edgar Walts, the editor of the New Richmond *Record* called our little town, became a very distinguished, respectable, and successful journalist - who "rubbed elbows" with the greatest, including my dad.

The next time you "New Richmondites" visit the Tomb of the Unknown Soldier, take a look around for the tombstone of George R. Holmes—one of the greatest of the "New Richmondites."

GLEN MITCHELL, NOTED ARTIST

Glen Mitchell, son of Charles and Alice Ebrite Mitchell, was born in New Richmond, Indiana, on June 9, 1894. His maternal grandparents were Amos "Squire" and Mary Elizabeth Ebrite, whose parents were among the early settlers of New Richmond. Glen's father had his own band and traveled all over the country and at one time was traveling with the Owen Brothers show. They were in Montgomery, Alabama, in the Spring of 1905. Glen's mother was with a little theater group, which played in opera houses in the area of New Richmond, Newtown, Wingate, Linden, etc., called the New Richmond Comedy Company.

51 - Glen Mitchell as a budding artist

In November 1910, Mr. Kesler, the New Richmond High School principal, assisted by Everett Greenburg, Glen Mitchell, and Mary Crowder, organized a small orchestra known as the High School Orchestra. Glen, a freshman, played clarinet.

Glen's widow Frances wrote the following in a letter to me, "Glen was a great music lover, played clarinet at the age of 14 with an Indiana band that traveled the state during the summer. He also played piano and violin. Our home was always filled with art and music - and clicking cameras - as he was an amateur photographer and collected antique cameras and lenses."

As a child my family often visited Aunt Em and in her living room hanging beside her front door was a painting of a New Richmond elevator painted by Glen Mitchell. I often studied this painting and secretly wished I could paint as well as he. He may have painted the elevator scene from his own back door, as he lived right across the railroad from the elevator. Glen and my mother, Vera Ebrite Waye, were cousins.

Glen studied art at the Chicago Academy of Fine Arts and the Chicago Art Institute, receiving diplomas from each school. He also studied at the National Academy of Design in New York and the Academie de la Grande Chaumiere and Academie Colorossi, both in Paris. He did research, paintings, sketches, and drawings in galleries wherever he traveled and painted.

In the United States he painted in twenty four states. The foreign countries he painted in included Mexico, France, Germany, Egypt, Italy, Switzerland, Palestine, Spain and Canada.

Glen's art work brought him many awards. Among these are the Guggenheim Fellowship (foreign travel and study) in 1926-1927 and 1928; American Traveling Scholarship, Chicago Art Institute, 1918-19; first portrait award, three successive years; Chicago Art Institute, 1919, 1920, and 1921; first oil award, and first drawing award, Minneapolis Institute of Fine Arts; first oil award and first watercolor award, Minneapolis Spring Salon; first oil award, Minnesota State Fair, two successive years; first watercolor award, Hoosier Gallery, Chicago; and first watercolor award, Corcoran Gallery, Washington, D.C., 1939.

A Paris newspaper, the name and date of which were unfortunately not recorded, under the caption "Who's Who Abroad," has a sketch of Glen Mitchell and the following:

52 - Glen Mitchell in his New York studio

Mr. Glen Mitchell is one of the young American artists who are now over here. He has a studio in Montrouge, but is planning to establish himself more permanently in Florence. Before doing that, he will spend the winter in an extensive trip through the Near East, particularly Palestine and Egypt, to do some large canvases of historical subjects and some local color work....This is not his first trip abroad and on the present occasion he comes over covered with honors, for he is one of the artists to whom have been awarded, as men of promise, scholarships from the John Simon Guggenheim fund. These are given for foreign travel and study for periods of one or three years, and Mr. Mitchell's is for three years.

Indiana is Mr. Mitchell's native state. There he was born, at New Richmond in 1894. From 1915 till 1923 he studied at the Chicago Art Institute and has done most of his work in that city, he now has a studio in New York. In his years at the Art Institute he was noted as a student of great promise, and was the winner of many prizes. He was proclaimed by the internationally known painter, J. Wellington Reynolds, an instructor at the Institute, as one of his most brilliant pupils.

In the summer of 1938, the Minneapolis School of Art established an art colony in Mexico, the first one of its kind attempted by an American art school. Artists, art students, and photographers were enrolled in the school and the colony was under the direction of Glen Mitchell, instructor at the Minneapolis School of Art, and his wife, Frances Buholz Mitchell, also a Minneapolis artist. The Mitchells had spent the previous summer in Mexico. The artists met in Mexico City for ten days beginning on July 2nd; while there, they studied modern Mexican art, viewed the new murals, and visited museums. The colony then moved to Taxco, Mexico, and remained until August 14. The colony was arranged so the students and artists could go to Mexico at less expense. There were nineteen U.S. students in this first trip to Mexico and in 1951 he returned to Mexico with twenty students from the Parsons School of Design in New York.

Glen's teaching positions included: painting, advertising art and illustration at the Minneapolis School of Art from 1929 to 1941; summer classes at the Duluth Art Association; advertising art and drawing at Chicago Academy of Fine Arts; painting and advertising art at Parsons School of Design, New York, 1949 to 1954; and Assistant Professor of Painting and Display at the Fashion Institute of Technology, New York 1961 to 1971.

During World War I Glen enlisted in 1918 in the Air Corps and graduated from the U.S. School of Aeronautics, University of Illinois. He trained in Texas and Georgia. In World War II he painted for the War Department and Army Air Force.

He wrote an article for the Advertising Club News on "Development of Modern Art" which was published in two parts. The first one was published April 29, 1929. The last part, published on May 6, 1929, reads:

Finally, freeing himself entirely from nature, the artist endeavors to portray or interpret the moods and emotions of his inner self - there is truth and reality....This inner soul being at one with the Divine Creator must be of itself Creator. The spiritual vibrations moving the hands to set down forms and colors outwardly corresponding to those felt inwardly is the beginning of 'pure art.'

....The artist is now moved by spirit alone, thus advancing spiritually he turns away from the outer world and draws from the imperishable, inexhaustible fountain of spirit. On this new plane he need not fear his ground, even look or place a hand behind him for support....

Glen believed that the American scene has vast resources of inspiration for the American artist. In an article printed in the Minneapolis *Journal* Sunday, November, 1929, he says:

> A Minnesota boy, once he is taught something of 'organized' beauty, will surely be more successful in attempting a huge painting of flour mills or grain elevators than some far-fetched, second-hand conception of a castle on the Danube....America waits to be discovered. Our artists are gradually turning to the life and the landscape around them, but it is a slow process. We still have an uneasy feeling that a dash of the old world is essential in a work of art. Of course we must build on the great traditions of the past and most of those traditions come from the old world. But we must use our own material, and we must develop our own individuality.... Art is not something that is acquired overnight; it takes ambition, patience, and concentration.

In a newspaper clipping, source and date both missing, Glen says, "The problem of an environment in which the artist dwells offers the highest reality he can know; it is in interpreting this reality that beauty is created." He was showing about 40 paintings at the Nash Conley Galleries in Minneapolis, including "Railroad Crossing", "Midwest Silhouette", "The Blue Route", and "Fog in the Valley", which were painted on a trip through Iowa, Wisconsin, and southern Minnesota.

When Glen was teaching at the Minneapolis School of Art, he introduced for his advanced painting classes, for the first time and the first in the history of art schools, a regular period to the designing, carving, and finishing of appropriate frames. He said, "We stock the raw frames in our store, and then the students begin to design and carve, creating new designs. We finish, using all the modern materials we can lay our hands on, in such ways that I am sure we shall have an entirely new frame."

Glen wrote an article on Watercolors for the *American Artist* magazine which describes his feeling for this medium

> My initial plunge into watercolor was made during my first painting trip to Europe. I had planned to work in oil only, but soon I realized that carrying a growing catch of wet canvases around the country would slow down the mission. Wanting daily results, I thought I could make watercolor pinch-hit in the short stops, so I bought my first watercolor outfit. . . the lift I got from those first watercolors was terrific! I felt a great release and experienced the joy and ecstasy of this new medium. It was faster than thought, super-sensitive to touch, and responsive to any mood...the creative approach involves creative three-dimensional design as employed in all plastic arts, but its absence in so many watercolors is appalling...Height, breadth, and depth can be indicated with three strokes and it is the development of this point of view which is most important.

Art critics described Glen Mitchell as an "alert and sensitive painter. While his landscapes retain moderate fidelity to nature, they are always enriched by an artist's vision which is at once imaginative and analytical."

Another said, "Glen Mitchell belongs more to our own modern world. We find he is much more successful in the watercolors of the American scene and the quick, spontaneous sketches of nature than in the larger oils...a painting entitled Filling Station is gay, brilliant in color. He uses strong greens and reds and a checker-board roof with gusto...this is notably evident, too, in Ruby's Red Chateau. The painting Ruby's Red Chateau was described as being somewhat on the grim side despite the touch of life-at-leisure in the left-hand corner and the color is keyed high and rather bizarre."

The critic also said, "Mr. Mitchell finds himself at home in most kinds of scenery, and the bracing views of jagged mountains find their own technique as deftly as the more intimate town scenes find theirs. Much of his work has a breezy, sketchy quality as if the subject was caught on the wing, and this adds greatly to the spontaneity of the pictures." In London, his painting Reclining Figure was selected by editors of *Oil Painting of Today* as one of the best American pictures.

Glen exhibited his art work in the following galleries: Museum of Modern Art, New York; Whitney Gallery of American Art, New York; National Academy of Design, New York; Rockefeller Center, New York; Chicago Art Institute, plus two one-man shows; Pennsylvania Academy of the Fine Arts; Corcoran Gallery, Washington, D.C.; Civic Art Center, San Francisco; Colorado Springs Art Center; Kansas City Art Institute; Rockhill Nelson Art Gallery, Kansas City; John Herron Art Institute, Indianapolis; Milwaukee Art Institute; Minneapolis Institute of Arts; Dayton Art Institute; Columbus Gallery of Fine Arts; Minnesota State Fair, St. Paul; plus one-man shows at the last six places mentioned. Theaters in Minneapolis and Red Wing in Minnesota; Macy's, New York; Freeman's Toronto; Hect's, Washington, D. C.; and Filene's in Boston all have murals painted by Glen Mitchell.

Glen never forgot his roots and whenever he had the time he returned to New Richmond to visit relatives and friends. On his last visit I had the opportunity to visit with him—he thoroughly enjoyed sitting in our front porch swing and discussing art with our family, and he said the next time he came back home he would show me how to paint a scene out of doors, but this was not to be. In January 1972, Glen Mitchell passed away in New York and was brought to New Richmond for his final trip home.

Chapter 21 - Transportation

Pioneer Transportation

The pioneers who came to New Richmond and Coal Creek Township made the trip on horseback, or by covered wagons or carts pulled by horses or the sturdy oxen. It was not uncommon for the men of the family group to walk beside the wagon, or beside the animal pulling the wagon, allowing the women and small children to ride. When the women and children became tired of riding, they too, walked much of the distance. Many stories have been told of the pioneer men walking to their new homes in Coal Creek Township, building a shelter for the family, then returning to their former homes to settle business or to sell their land before making a permanent settlement in the new location. The old farm horses were the main source of transportation for many, but the smaller pony or riding horses were used for quick trips to the nearby village. It was much easier to saddle a horse than to harness the larger animals to the heavy farm wagon.

A new type of transportation was introduced to the people of New Richmond in July 1888, when the Indiana Bicycle Company sent three of their traveling agents to the town to sell Columbia Safety Bicycles. They made a few sales in the town, but it was not recorded as to how many or to whom the bicycles were sold. A couple of years later it was reported that the bicyclists had become expert riders. Ira Stout, of the famous Black Bear Hotel in New Richmond, and his friend Dora Ammoran both purchased bicycles in June 1891 and provided quite a bit of entertainment to the citizens of New Richmond as they were trying to learn to guide them. Ira was not a young man at the time. Evan Shelby was another early bicyclist and O.D. Thomas had purchased a Victor bike in 1893.

Crawfordsville bicyclists rode through New Richmond on many occasions. They had formed bicycle clubs and rode to the towns of New Richmond and Linden "in search of pure air and a good appetite." The cyclists rode through New Richmond to reach Lafayette, this being a better road during that period of time.

After the cyclists had mastered their wheels, they began to make longer trips. Theron Banta and Wright Mason, two New Richmond boys, decided to tour Kentucky, and at the time of their writing home had covered 185 miles. For recreation they were going boating and swimming–they still had energy left for more strenuous activity, young men being made of better stuff than they are today.

Roads in Coal Creek Township

On May 4, 1829, the present township of Coal Creek was formed and John Alexander and William Forbes appointed "fence viewers." Absalom Kirkpatrick was employed to locate a public road from Covington to Strawtown, a distance of seventy miles or more. John Gilliland of Crawfordsville surveyed the proposed road. This road runs east and west through the center of New Richmond's business district.

Coal Creek Township has always been troubled with slippery, black mud, and the problems associated with mud and road building have been handled in various ways over the years. The solution before the 1850s was to build corduroy roads, described in an early history of Indiana in this manner:

> A corduroy road is made of the unhewn boles of trees laid side by side on the earth. A slip is nailed across each end to keep them in their places, and the wheels, whether of carriages, or wagons, fall from bole to bole with the regularity of the thumps and stops, with which the wheels of a watch play into, and arrest each other. Sometimes, the hollow between

prostrate trunks of trees is partially filled up with earth, and then, of course, the jolts are less severe.

These sections of corduroy were usually constructed in the swampy or muddiest parts of the roads, the remainder being a simple wagon trail consisting of deep uncomfortable ruts in which to be jostled about inside the conveyance. A corduroy road was built between Linden and New Richmond in the 1830s or 1840s.

A more improved idea of road construction was the plank road system, introduced in Montgomery County in the early 1850s. Companies were formed and a board of directors was to oversee the construction and maintenance of these roads. Tolls were collected to defray the costs of building and maintaining the plank roads as well as the early private graveled sections of highways.

The New Richmond and Mark Street (Crawfordsville) plank road was 13.5 miles in length. It is doubtful that plank was laid the entire length, but would have been necessary over the low, muddy sections. This plank road was mentioned in the Crawfordsville *Journal*, August 30, 1879.

A plank road was described in "Readings in Indiana History" by an Englishman traveling on the Wabash Valley roads in 1850. The traveling party included Mr. Beste, his wife, and eleven young children. The Englishman wrote:

> ...very pleasant, a plank road is to travel upon. It may be slippery in wet weather, but now saved us from the dust that would have arisen from travel. The saw boards, or planks, about three inches thick, being nailed to sleepers at the two sides of the road, spanned it from side to side, and rose and sank under us with the elasticity of the floor of a ball-room. On each side of the plank tracks, between it and the worm fences that bounded the road, were holes and stumps and ditches of natural water courses that no wheels could venture amongst, etc. The plank roads were better suited for the rough and ready carriages, or agriculture teams that can get nearly five miles an hour with less fatigue to themselves than our heavy English teams creep over two miles an hour.

Some of the farmers in the vicinity of Wingate and New Richmond improved the old dirt roads by hauling and spreading gravel on them. Alex Meharry built a new gravel road east and west from New Richmond to Newtown in January 1874, making it one-eighth of a mile shorter than the original.

The Montgomery County commissioners hired a civil engineer and began building the "Free Gravel Roads," the first stretch of which was complete in 1878. The road running from Crawfordsville to New Richmond was started in 1879. Henry Clements had the contract to build this road, and in November of that year he was building at a rate of one mile per week. The New Richmond items in the Crawfordsville newspapers began with the following comments in January and February of 1880: "Mud! Need Gravel Roads!" "Mud, Maine and Measles" and "New Richmond has the muddiest sidewalks in the county" and last but not least, "New Richmond has sunk out of sight in the mud!"

The Crawfordsville and New Richmond Free Gravel Road was complete as far as Round Hill by May 22, 1880, and the New Richmond residents were rejoicing that fall because the road was graveled through town, to the Tippecanoe County line just north of town. The gravel was taken from the Black Creek Valley for this road. The road to Patton's schoolhouse was in "dire need of gravel," because it was impossible for scholars to attend school during the spring weather. Thomas M. Foster, J.H. Alexander, and Amos Ebrite were appointed fence viewers the following year, when Aaron Gilkey, Daniel Curtis, and others petitioned the county commissioners for a new highway in Coal Creek Township.

The probable costs estimate of the New Richmond and Crawfordsville Free Gravel Road was published in the Crawfordsville *Journal*, January 21, 1882. The road, 13.5 miles long, included the part of the Concord Road that was already built and was estimated to cost $15,986, or an average of $1,184 per mile. In February 1882, an election was held to vote on a proposition that the county buy the toll roads.

Farmers along these roads were to be assessed in order to extend these sections of roads and to construct new roads.

Better roads were still needed as late as 1887-1889 in the outlying areas in Coal Creek Township, such as Patton's Corner and Bristle Ridge, and the Meharry neighborhood referred to in early days as "Shawnee Mound." Farmers along the road south of New Richmond circulated a petition to gravel the road to Patton's schoolhouse in October 1887, and they were securing promises from men in the township to help build it. Another road from Round Hill to Bristle Ridge was being constructed by Johnny Patton that year. Jeff Bennett, the blacksmith of Round Hill, celebrated by firing his anvil twelve times when this road was completed past his shop in November 1887, and frightened his neighbors "half out of their wits by the loud noise." (Firing an anvil was the practice of shooting an anvil into the air using gunpowder.)

In January 1889 Thomas Shepherd was petitioning for a free gravel road to be called the New Richmond and Shawnee Mound Gravel Road, to be built in the summer of 1890. At the same time, Richard Bible was circulating a petition for a new road from his farm to Meharry's Grove, west of New Richmond.

Private roads were still being constructed as late as 1893. There were only three miles of free gravel roads built that year–the three miles of Meharry's Road in Coal Creek Township. The earlier gravel roads were in deplorable condition by that time. In May 1894 contracts were let to men in the county to repair these roads. Elias Burk won the contract for the Crawfordsville to New Richmond Road. In September of that year Leander Tribby, Phillip Dewey, and William McClamrock were appointed fence viewers for a public highway in Coal Creek Township.

By July 1903, Coal Creek Township had about twenty-five miles of gravel roads and seventy-five miles of mud roads. County Surveyor Harding prepared estimates and made maps of the proposed roads to be graveled in the township. These new roads ranged from one to eight miles in length, for a total of fifty-four miles of new road. The total cost was estimated at $63,528. All the roads and the right-of-way were to be from thirty-three to forty feet in width. A special election was held on Saturday, September 26, 1903, relative to the issuing of bonds for gravel road construction. Three hundred and ten voters signed a petition to have this election, which was the first step toward constructing the roads, although Coal Creek's roads were considered among the best in the state. The election resulted in failure, possibly due to a long editorial in the New Richmond *Record* stating the reasons taxpayers should vote against the so-called free gravel roads.

While the outlying highways were being debated, the New Richmond trustees were attempting to keep their streets passable, and in June 1904 Marshal John Work distributed ninety-two wagonloads of gravel on the streets. The gravel was purchased from Henry K. Lee's gravel pit near the local tile mill, and was considered to be of fairly good quality. Marshal Work was in charge of the men who worked out their taxes by improving the streets and shoveling snow in the winter.

The road supervisors in Coal Creek Township in 1905 were Robert Davidson, Carey Graves, W.J. Foxworthy, F.M. Bagby, Allen Brown, and L.M. Tribby. The duties of the supervisors were listed in the New Richmond *Record* on Thursday, April 27, 1905. One of these rules was that males from twenty-one to fifty were required to work on the roads two to four days each year, unless they were insane, idiotic, deaf and dumb, or served in the Civil War, Spanish War, or the Philippine Islands. Other rules stated that a superintendent who permitted a Canada Thistle to get six inches in length along a road over which he had control, could be fined one to ten dollars, and that a fifty dollar fine was to be imposed if a traction engine or automobile was not stopped when meeting a team.

Another election was to be held in the spring of 1905, to decide on the new gravel roads in Coal Creek Township. Detailed specifications were printed in the New Richmond *Record* in March, giving the names of the roads, the width, length, detailed grading descriptions of the streets in New Richmond and Wingate, and each span of roads included the estimated cost, totaling $68,000 for fifty-four miles of gravel roads. The roads mentioned were: Wingate to the township line; Wingate to Meharry's gravel road; Coleman; Elmdale and New Richmond; Fullwider; Oppy; Range Line Road; New Richmond and township line; Pattons; Washburn; McCrea; Phil Dewey; V.Y. Kennedy; Dinwiddie; Curtis; Wes Dazey; John Foley; Thomas and Elwood Swank.

As in all moves toward progress, there were many taxpayers opposed to the new gravel road system, and many problems had to be worked out between opponents and proponents of the new roads. The proposed gravel road system was defeated by a ninety-one majority in the second election. Taxes collected from the railroad helped pay for the improvements on the existing roads, and were maintained by the township trustee, who was in charge of the road supervisors.

The costs of the two elections were to be paid by those signing the petitions, and a meeting was held in the Center Schoolhouse to apportion the amount. Committees were created to close the entire business in the matter of payment of these costs. The first petition committee was made up of George W. Washburn, Bayless Alexander, O.G. Moser, Charles A. Patton, Oliver Crane, and Charles Kirkpatrick, who was named as treasurer to collect and pay all bills for the first petition. The second petition committee was formed by H.K. Lee, George A. Thomas, W.A. Murphy, Benjamin Brown, and Millard F. Buxton, who was treasurer.

Another petition was presented to the county commissioners asking for improvements on the Crawfordsville and New Richmond free gravel road in June 1913. George F. Long (clerk), L.P. Brown, and William Kirkpatrick, New Richmond trustees, signed and presented this petition. Hauling gravel onto the streets of New Richmond and the county roads was an endless task. The problem in town was solved by black-topping in the early 1930s, but continues to cause problems in the outlying gravel roads in Coal Creek Township.

THE LITTLE YARD WIDE

As early as March 1873, the people of Coal Creek Township were being stirred up about a railroad running through some part of the township. I.H. Montgomery was very instrumental in getting the railroad companies to investigate the possibilities of a great railroad future in this area.

One projected line was to run from Thorntown, by way of Linden, New Richmond, and Pleasant Hill, to some point of "little or no importance in the western part of the state," said a report in the Crawfordsville *Journal*. The people of the New Richmond area were not all that impressed to begin with.

A group of far-sighted businessmen from Frankfort, in Clinton County, had already formed a railroad company by the name of the Frankfort and Kokomo in 1872, and by the Fourth of July 1874 trains were running between those two cities. Their goal was to push westward to St. Louis, connecting to a line running from Toledo, Ohio.

In 1875 a railroad company by the name of the Frankfort and State Line was organized; this was to become the company to build the first railroad through Linden in Madison Township, and New Richmond and Pleasant Hill in Coal Creek Township. It was, however, a long wait before the citizens of the towns saw their first iron horse, though there was at that time a lot of railroad activity in and around Frankfort.

In May of 1879, while the Frankfort and State Line Company was still trying to raise subscriptions in the towns of Stockwell, Colfax, and Clarks Hill, the sub-contractors were continuing work on the line between Frankfort and Jefferson in Clinton County. Clarks Hill was to be the next destination and the line was to be completed within ninety days.

There was still some uncertainty as to where the line would run near New Richmond. One article, dated September 27, 1879, said, "the railroad will be built on the line running via 'Goosenibble' to Newtown and work will begin at once, and the grading completed across the township before cold weather." On November 8 of the same year, another notice appeared, saying, "We thought we had the Narrow Gauge located and the grading commenced, but now there is talk of having it follow the ditch along the road from New Richmond to Linden. This will be an improvement on having to lay down the fences for each passing train at 'Goosenibble.'"

The *Journal* reported, "The latest name for the narrow gauge is the TOLEDO, CORWIN, GOOSENIBBLE & SOUTHWESTERN." I know of two areas called Goosenibble. One was a school located in Jackson Township of Tippecanoe County, at Haywood's Corner–the southeast corner of the New Richmond Road and State Road 28. The other was a section on the east edge of Crawfordsville along the Monon tracks. Goosenibble was a name given to the Irish settlements–the Irish being the builders of the canals and railroads in the country, without whom railroads might still be a dream. I do not know of any section in Coal Creek Township or the area around New Richmond ever referred to as Goosenibble, so I am uncertain as to where the first proposed line was to run. Both above-mentioned Goosenibbles were contrary to the final direction the line was to take.

At the beginning of 1880, the town of New Richmond was still waiting for a railroad. The writer for the *Journal* had only this to say: "The narrow gauge is not dead, but sleepeth." On November 6, 1880, the *Journal* gives the results on an election held in Madison Township for a proposition to give "10,000 to the Frankfort and State Line Railroad. The vote went as follows: for the railroad appropriation, 80 votes; against, 44 votes." A week later the correspondent wrote, "Madison township anti-railroad people may as well take away their feet and let the spikes be driven." J.C. Wingate was at Indianapolis when the vote was counted and received a telegram from President Morrison announcing the "success of the railroad."

Another election was held to "pacify" some of the anti-railroad people in a special session of the common court on the same proposed donation of $10,000. The *Journal* said, "At the election held before, the greatest number of votes was against the appropriation, but enough of the tickets were found to be spurious and they were thrown out to carry the election in favor of the donation. Those opposing were not satisfied with this and declared the intention of going to law, when by the way of compromise another election was petitioned for and granted."

In the meantime the promoters of the narrow gauge had convinced the people of Linden and Madison Township that the railroad from Toledo to St. Louis had now become a matter of fact and would be completed within the year as far as Lodi, and the *Journal* of February 19, 1881, says, "The farmers and the laborers along the line should expect a general boom, and the merchant would have better facilities for shipping, and the grain and stock dealers would no longer have to wait for old 'Jerkwater' to furnish them cars." They were probably referring to the L.N.A. & C.R.R. as old Jerkwater. Enthusiasm was running full speed ahead, for the *Journal* continues, "The citizens of 'Old Quinine' township are wide awake to their best interests and propose to secure the road, if possible."

I would like to say at this point that, while researching the story on the railroad, I was very disappointed with the lack of coverage of this great moment in history on the part of New Richmond. The information had to come from Linden, Walnut Grove (and this was not even a town, but a school), Boston Store–alias Elmdale–and Pleasant Hill (a.k.a. Whitlock or Wingate).

Perhaps the New Richmond correspondent was the person mentioned in the next account. On March 5, 1881, the *Journal* reports, "While the engineers were surveying for the railroad between Linden and Pleasant Hill, George Niles, the transit man [*sic*] was arranging his glass to look through four miles of space when a 'dusky denizen of the forrest' [*sic*] stepped up to him and inquired how soon the 'engineers' would be coming through here. Niles told him he had better keep off the line, they were coming any minute!"

Another election was held in Madison Township to appropriate $20,000 for the Frankfort & State Line Railroad. The results were 146 votes for, 111 against. The *Journal* claimed that "Pleasant Hill now joins the 'Anvil Chorus' with Linden over the railroad prospects."

In June 1879 the Toledo, Delphos, and Burlington Railroad Company merged with the Frankfort and State Line. A collection of other small narrow gauge lines had already merged, incorporating on February 12, 1881; the subsequent company was going by the name of the Toledo, Cincinnati, & St. Louis, when it in turn merged with the Frankfort & Kokomo on May 20, 1881. The Boston Store correspondent referred to the road as the St. L & Toledo and said, "Many of the citizens of Coal Creek Township are rejoicing over the prospects of a railroad and the ties are being delivered!" Others referred to the railroad as the Frankfort & State Line.

By April 1, 1881, the workmen and tools for the grading of the narrow gauge were beginning to arrive and work was to begin soon after. The grading was to be completed to Charleston, Illinois, before July 1.

The work had commenced by April 9, but the railroad company was still having some trouble securing the right-of-way in some locations. Dr. D.K. Mitchell of Walnut Grove, for one, did not like the idea of having to move his house; but the work progressed, and a promise of a larger work force was to be fulfilled the following week. The grading would be pushed forward as rapidly as weather would permit. Eli Marvin and John C. Wingate finished their work securing the right-of-way as best they could and the pieces of land that were refused, were condemned. The railroad construction went on regardless of the landowner's sentiment.

To understand the location of the railroad running east of New Richmond to be located "following the ditch along the road to Linden" one would have to see the map of Coal Creek Township in the 1878 Atlas. It shows a road running east of town parallel to the path on which the railroad was located. The first school, Walnut Grove, was located on this road, as well as five homes. This road turns due north on the line between I. H. Montgomery's and Thomas Ward Jr.'s property, then joins the east-west road still in existence, County Road 1100 North. South of this road, which was to become the railroad bed, was another road to Linden, a forerunner of County Road 1000 North. This road started to run east on the north side of Captain McCrea's house, which burned to the ground in 1980, then it turned south a little piece, then followed a southeasterly direction for a time before continuing due east toward Linden. When my brothers and sister and I were young, we would walk on this old road north of McCrea's home to go back to their woods to hunt mushrooms. There was an old cemetery located on top of a hill, known as Park or Pioneer Cemetery; the stones may have been destroyed by now.

Persons in the vicinity of New Richmond selling land to the Frankfort & State Line Railroad were as follows: C.J. Oppy on February 18, 1881 (10.97 acres); George Manners on March 7, 1881 (3.61 acres); S.S. Detchon on March 26, 1881 (3.75 acres).

The Pleasant Hill item in the April 16, 1881, *Journal* says, "Surveyors, tie makers, and graders are all coming at once, and it is difficult to find accommodations. The hotel is full, not another soul could have been jammed in–we need a capacious boarding house! Mr. McJimsey has from fourteen to eighteen men constantly!"

John Cochran, the timber contractor, established headquarters in the area until all the timber they could purchase was cut and shaped for delivery; he was contemplating building a saw mill to prepare material for bridges, cattle guards, etc. Ira Stout of Walnut Grove was granted the contract for sawing 100,000 feet of bridge timber, and E.W. Cannon of Frankfort had the contract for grading 16 miles of the narrow gauge west from Clarks Hill. The parties who cleared the right-of-way on the narrow gauge used a very powerful blasting powder; as one reporter explained, "no matter how large or knotty the stump— one application of the explosive material would yank out everything except the hole." Men working for the railroad were paid $1.50 per day, and those with teams earned $3.50 per day, which was a good wage in those days. By April 23 the work was progressing well, but more teams must have been desperately needed, because the company was offering $8 per day, payable once a week. Colonel Craig, the president of the company, hoped to have the road completed from Linden east by June 1, 1881.

The *Review* said on May 7, 1881, "Pleasant Hill looks forward and contemplates her future greatness in the prospect and construction of the Toledo, Wabash and St. L. Narrow Gauge Railroad. The timber is all cut out of the right-of-way from this place to the Wabash and ties are strewn along the line by the thousands." (Notice the new name picked up here!) This article was almost certainly written by the railroad company itself as it tells of the great business capacity to be expected from the road, and that wealth and prosperity would surely come to everyone along the way, stretching across the most fertile belt of the country from Toledo to St. Louis–tapping coal mines of Indiana and Illinois—intersecting with the great transportation lines of the west and northwest to the vast lumber regions of the Unitah Mountains, traversing the Missouri region, the Bonanza Silver Mines of Nevada, the gold fields of California, the gold and silver belts of Colorado and the great wheat lands and pastures of Wyoming and Nebraska. "All in the future will pay tribute to the great Toledo, Wabash and St. Louis Railroad!"

On May 28, 1881, the *Journal* published a large column reporting the progress on the new railroad through Madison and Coal Creek Townships:

nothing creates more talk in a community than a young baby or a new railroad. You always find some jealous persons to speak of a sweet little baby, the idol of its parents, as an ugly brat, and when a new railroad begins to make its appearance the majority are always throwing dirt at it. The friends of the railroad always feel called upon to defend it, as fond parents defend their babies, and this sparring always brings out the full force on either side to swap views as seated upon the pine boxes in front of the corner grocery. This is the way it has been in Madison and Coal Creek Townships, over the Frankfort & State Line narrow gauge railroad, for nine months or more, everything has been narrow gauge out there, they plant corn in narrow gauge rows, eat narrow gauge custard pie and play narrow gauge seven up...The connecting link which is to complete the 440 miles of the railroad above referred to–from Toledo to St. Louis, is now under way of construction from Kokomo, [Indiana,] to Charleston, Illinois, a distance of 128 miles. It runs through two townships in this county, Madison and Coal Creek. After a severe struggle, Madison Township donated $10,000 to have it run through Linden, carrying the election by a majority of 34, but the greatest interest in it was manifested in Coal Creek Township where $21,000 was voted from the funds of the township and $9,000 was donated from private purses. The entire right-of-way was also given with the single exception of one farm, owned by a resident of Crawfordsville. The survey has been made and work goes rapidly on. The part under construction, starting at Kokomo, will strike the following points: Frankfort, Clark's Hill, Linden, New Richmond, Pleasant Hill, Veedersburg, Lodi and thence to Charleston, Illinois. A line is already built from Kokomo to Toledo and one is now in operation from Charleston, Illinois, to St. Louis, Missouri. The Frankfort and Kokomo road, a broad gauge, was bought and will be changed to a narrow gauge, and all this together will make 440 miles from Toledo to St. Louis. The Logansport *Journal* of last Tuesday, has this to say of the Frankfort and Kokomo branch of the road: "The name of the Frankfort & Kokomo Railroad has been changed to the Toledo, Cincinnati and St. Louis, and will be made a part of the narrow gauge system projected between these points. The work of changing the track to conform with that with which it is to be connected, will commence in two weeks." Though the iron is put down as narrow gauge, the grade is made 16 feet at the base and 10 feet at the top. Men are scattered along it at every mile and things are going with a whoop! The tie or timber men are cracking the bushes everywhere and the graders are ploughing and scraping like they expected the first train over next Monday. When that first engine squalls on the border of Pleasant Hill, that village will think the scream as sweet as a young mama does the crying of her new baby!

The Frankfort *Banner*, in the "Narrow Gauge Notes," printed the following facts concerning the railroad for the people of Madison and Coal Creek Township:

[A]bout $90,000 was paid out on May estimates from this place. The 15,000 tons of iron bought in Europe, and fifty miles from Cleveland, Ohio, cost not less than $800,000. There are employed on the line as tie makers and graders with shovels and teams, about 4,000 men. There are 15 miles of road completed this way from Charleston, Illinois, and at an early day, track-laying will begin both ways from Ridge Farm, Illinois. They expect to reach the Wabash River by August 1.

J.J. Daniels, contractor for the masonry on the Wabash River bridge, has notified President Craig that he could begin to put the superstructure on the masonry July 4, and he would keep out of the way with the masonry after that date. There is now at Frankfort 35 miles of iron, and enough more will arrive to lay to the Wabash River. The iron to be used west of the river comes from England, via New Orleans and Mississippi River to St. Louis, thence by rail, to be used on the road. The pay roll for the T.C. & St. Louis railroad for June was $100,000.

By September 17, 1881, the "Narrow Gauge Notes" reported that Gifford and Larson, who had the contract for grading the road between Veedersburg to New Richmond, had finished their work and had gone to another contract in Ohio.

"The YARD WIDE RAILROAD–Celebration of the Narrow Gauge Railroad at Pleasant Hill last Saturday–Neat Speeches and a Good Dinner–The Station Named WINGATE." On Saturday, October 22, 1881, a big celebration was held in John C. Wingate's grove near Pleasant Hill on the completion of the track laying of the Yard Wide Railroad, known as the Toledo, Cincinnati, and St. Louis Narrow Gauge Railroad. The celebration had been set for the Saturday before, but the track layers were delayed because the iron did not reach the village in time. The villages of Linden, New Richmond, and Pleasant Hill were joined by the bands of steel, to all the cities of the country, and the celebration consisted of "neat speeches, music and a tip-top dinner, one of those mammoth spreads which were common among the Coal Creek neighborhood. Speeches were made by the following people: General M.C. Manson, Hon. M.D. White and Hon. P.S. Kennedy, all of Crawfordsville; Eli Marvin, of Frankfort, spoke in behalf of the railroad; Col. J.B. Maynard, editor of the Indianapolis *Sentinel*; and E.H. Staley, of the Frankfort *Cresent*. A special train ran from Frankfort carrying a large number of people and many Crawfordsville people attended.

Following the dinner and speeches, a telegram was read from the superintendent of the railroad stating that as there was already a Pleasant Hill station on the road in Ohio, this Pleasant Hill station would be named Wingate, in acknowledgement of the most efficient work in behalf of the railroad that John C. Wingate had done. John Wingate then made a speech and Fred Sweitzer's Cornet Band furnished excellent music for about 1,000 persons who attended the celebration.

The renaming of the town caused quite a stir among some people in the town–well, that is putting it mildly–they were really raising a rumpus, and on November 5, 1881, the *Journal* said, "OUR PLEASANT HILL–through Eli Martin, of Frankfort, the Toledo, Cincinnati & St. Louis Narrow Gauge Railroad company, announced that its order in naming the station at Pleasant Hill will not be rescinded." This is given as final. The *Journal* on November 19 printed an article under the Pleasant Hill items entitled "Some Friendly Reasoning with Some Men of The Little Town on the Narrow Gauge" concerning the jealousy in regard to Wingate, which read in part:

> In addition to the tax voted to build the Toledo, Cincinnati & St. Louis Railroad through Coal Creek Township, a donation of $9,000 was asked for by the company. This was secured and the road is established, the track laid beyond Veedersburg, the telegraph posts put up to that point, the wire now going up, a telegraph office is located at Pleasant Hill, the water tank is completed and the village puts on the appearance of a railroad town....at a meeting held in the school house nearly a year ago, the following gentlemen could be mentioned as helpers in the work of securing the road: S.A.R. Beach gave $500; Alexander Meharry, $500; Isaac Meharry, $500; John Coon, $500; Aaron Gilkey spent untiring days and energetic work, securing the right-of-way for the most part through the township, gave $250; Jett & McClure, partners in the general store, gave $25; Levi Curtis, $500; and others gave according to their means, etc....We love to give "honor to whom honor is due," and in connection with the names before mentioned we gladly speak of the untiring efforts of John C. Wingate, who of his means gave all he could and has given tact, energy, labor, toil–both by night and day, to make this railroad enterprise a means of building up the town. It is not wrong, then, that he is honored by the railroad company.

The New Richmond people printed a card in the *Journal* saying, "The people of New Richmond would be glad to have an active man like Wingate to look after their interests of their village–if Pleasant

Hill is dissatisfied with the name of 'Wingate' transfer your railroad improvements with the name of New Richmond and you shall not hear of the 'growlers.'" Pleasant Hill answered with this note, "The name of the village has not been changed—only the station is to be called Wingate, in honor of a man we do not want to dispose of." The people of Pleasant Hill went on to say, "New Richmond had better work up a name of its own—how would 'Manner's Station' sound?" They continued with the idea of Dr. Manners and his good wife surrendering a triangular piece of land north of the railroad to use for railroad purposes. (The company had tried to secure this ground.) They concluded the note with, "New Richmond, to the front, or you will not gain much from this railroad built through your town."

On November 26, 1881, the *Journal* received word that "last Thursday, W.J. Craig, President of the Western Construction Company, turned over to the Toledo, Cincinnati & St. Louis narrow gauge railroad the completed line of forty-one miles from Frankfort to Veedersburg." In the same issue was printed less auspicious news of the railroad; recent deluges had caused several washouts along the newly-laid line, resulting in some train wrecks, one of which occurred near Pleasant Hill. Gen. J.M. Corse, president of the railroad, passed over the line from Frankfort to Veedersburg in a special train, accompanied by General Manager T.A. Phillips, and W.J. Craig, for a tour of inspection. President Corse decided that "this division could not be accepted until it was placed in better condition, and regular trains would not be placed on the road for about two weeks."

I would like to point out that in building these narrow gauge lines very little ballast was used. They had no way of hauling broken stone or gravel, and constructed the roadbeds with existing soil, native to the location of the roads. Quite naturally, washouts were frequent with each heavy rain.

On December 24, 1881, the *Journal* proudly reported, "THE FIRST TRAIN" over the Narrow Gauge Railroad from Toledo, through the county, to Veedersburg, and "the First Telegram is Sent Over the Wires from Station WINGATE.–On last Tuesday one of the finest passengers trains that ever passed through Indiana left Toledo and made the entire trip to Veedersburg, a distance of 250 miles, over the T.C. & St.L. R.R. (Narrow Gauge). The coaches were equipped with air brakes, miller platform and buffers, and the engine was of the most modern pattern and construction. The train was in charge of Superintendent Metheny and General Freight and Ticket Agent Lippincott." At Frankfort, Mayor Bayless and several others joined the crowd, and at Wingate Aaron Gilkey, J.W. McClure and John C. Wingate joined the party to go as far as Veedersburg, where they were greeted by a large crowd, and then returned to Station Wingate for another party in honor of Mr. Gilkey's 34th wedding anniversary.

The railroad company had promised to have a train of cars running from Toledo, Ohio, to Veedersburg, Indiana, before December 25, 1881, and they made good. Along with the transportation improvement came the communication—the first telegram left Wingate on the same day, over the wires opening an electric communication with its people and the world. Will McClure was in charge of Station Wingate at Pleasant Hill, as operator and station and express agent.

John C. Wingate, late of Pleasant Hill, now of Wingate-on-the-Narrow-Gauge, was appointed land commissioner of the Toledo, Cincinnati, and St. Louis Narrow Gauge from Frankfort to Veedersburg. His duties were to secure right-of-way for sidetracks, purchase lots for depots and to procure aid for building the same. He asked the county commissioners to levy a one percent tax in Coal Creek and Madison Townships, to aid in constructing the Frankfort & State Line Railroad. Both township taxes were granted in January 1882.

The citizens of Coal Creek Township were beginning to wonder why the railroad that supposedly would make them rich had begun adding a new tax every time they turned around. During the construction of the railroad, another tax levy had been ordered to pay for the "free gravel road" system, and this proved to be the proverbial straw that broke the camel's back. The voters called a meeting, held at Center Schoolhouse, to take initial steps toward defeating this last donation, which amounted to $21,150.

A committee had previously been appointed to talk to several attorneys, and the Terre Haute firm of Hanna & Spencer attended the meeting to discuss the problem. They informed the taxpayers of their fee, should they take the case; at this point, some attendees lost their nerve for this "dangerous scheme," but the majority wished to continue the fight.

Continue they did, and filed suit to prevent the collection of the tax. The case came up before Judge Britton in the circuit court, and was continued over several days. A motion was made that John C. Wingate be made a party to the suit on behalf of the defense, although the plaintiffs argued against this measure. It was sustained, however, and Wingate joined County Treasurer Dwiggins as a defendant. A motion was then made to dissolve the injunction and the plaintiffs; Hanna and others asked time to file counter affidavits. Time was granted and the case was set for the next Monday. To the surprise of all, when Monday came, the attorneys representing the taxpayers asked to have the case dismissed at the plaintiffs' cost, which was granted by the court, ending the lawsuit.

The attorneys claimed the suit was begun under a misapprehension of the facts. They had believed a consolidation between the Frankfort and State Line and the Toledo, Cincinnati, & St. Louis Companies had taken place, and consequently that the tax collection could not be legal. The aid was asked for the Frankfort & State Line Railroad Company, and the attorneys could not find sufficient evidence of the consolidation of the two lines. County Treasurer Dwiggins gave the taxpayers until the next Tuesday to pay the taxes without penalty; they did pay rapidly, but likely unhappily. The writer for the Crawfordsville *Star* opined they should not have complained in the first place, because after all, "wasn't a line from Toledo to St. Louis better than the short line from Frankfort to the Illinois border?" The narrow gauge at this point had a prominent attorney, M.F. Dickerson of Boston, looking after their interests, along with A.A. Thomas, president of the Frankfort & State Line Railroad and attorney for the T.C. & St. Louis Narrow Gauge.

The little "Yard Wide" was beginning to change the character of the villages in Coal Creek Township. Businessmen from all over the country began to descend upon New Richmond and Pleasant Hill (or Whitlock, as it was being called at that time), hoping to create new establishments such as tile mills, elevators, or grist mills. George Breed constructed a grist mill in New Richmond, and the firm of Casto & Chilcote located in Wingate. William Montgomery had a mill, or warehouse, in Linden, and later built one in New Richmond; all of them were handling large amounts of grain. George W. Washburn became New Richmond's "cattle king" along with other cattlemen Dr. Detchon, Capt. Ed. T. McCrea, Mr. Murphey, and Curtis D. Haywood–who lived north of town in Tippecanoe County but shipped cattle from New Richmond. George and Boswell Clough became regular shippers in the hog market, and sheep were also frequently sent from the area. In New Richmond the grain merchants were taking in 1,000 to 1,500 bushels of wheat daily and highest market prices were paid for the grain.

The colorful "drummers" carrying their carpetbags of samples began to invade the towns, until the citizens declared they were being "drummed to death." Jason Tribby, a carpenter from New Richmond, began building the Pleasant Hill Depot, and the side track was laid at New Richmond, though the town did not get a depot until later.

The poor struggling railroad was hit by another lawsuit, this time by Dr. E. Detchon to the tune of $5,000. He claimed the railroad damaged his property by entering one corner, pursuing a direct course through to the opposite corner, and that the railroad also used timber belonging to him for ties, without paying him for the timber.

John C. Wingate asked for another donation of $9,620.71 for the construction of the Frankfort and State Line Railroad in February 1883, which stirred up the taxpayers again, resulting in another court battle–again a total waste of time for the taxpayers. The little village of Pleasant Hill/Wingate was still having problems remembering its name, and the August 9, 1884, issue of the *Journal* mentions the change of Wingate to Whitlock; according to the article the name was received with general satisfaction, though it did not state why they had decided upon the name of Whitlock, or even why they felt it necessary to change the name of the village again.

Although there was a large amount of shipping done from this area, the little railroad was not making a financial go of it. From May 1 to July 9, 1885, the profits only amounted to $616.79, hardly enough to excite the big eastern syndicate, so the little train was put up for sale. On January 2, 1886, the *Journal* reported the sale of the T. C. & St. L Railroad, at auction in Indianapolis, for the price tag of $1,501,000. A representative of the Quigley Syndicate of bondholders, Sylvester H. Kneeland, made the successful bid. Both divisions of the road were included in the sale, the complete line of 450 miles from Toledo to East St. Louis.

The entire system was to be re-organized and the rumors that had been circulating around Coal Creek Township were confirmed as fact–the road would soon be changed to the standard gauge–four feet, eight and one-half inches between the rails. The writer for the Crawfordsville Weekly *Review* wrote under the New Richmond items, "Our little Yard Wide promises in the near future to be a star of the first magnitude." The various short lines were consolidated June 12, 1886, and were to be known collectively as the Toledo, St. Louis, & Kansas City Railway. The line was then nicknamed the "Clover Leaf" because of its supposed good luck–running through the fertile farmlands–and its trademark was a three-leaf clover.

The railway company gave the section hands orders to clear the right-of-way thirty feet on each side of the track to make room for the fence builders, who were progressing at the rate of five miles per day. By April 1887, the bridge builders had completed the widening of all the bridges from New Richmond to Toledo. New steel rails were already being laid this side of Frankfort by the middle of May 1887, and the switches at New Richmond were lengthened to nearly a quarter of a mile long. The railroad boss at New Richmond had orders to hire more hands at $1.10 per day, and boarding houses sprang up in the little villages; everyone who could "raise a bed" began taking in boarders for the railroad activity. The railroad workers invaded New Richmond in October and were working west of Pleasant Hill in the middle of December 1887 when they had to stop because of the cold weather.

The work of widening the railroad was resumed in May 1888. Ten more hands were added to the work force at New Richmond, and the June 23, 1888 issue of the *Review* said, "The narrow gauge railroad is to be made a standard today, and the citizens of Whitlock will rejoice."

On the same day the Frankfort *Cresent* reported, "Tomorrow, sixty-one miles of Clover Leaf road will be widened to standard from here to Eugene, Illinois, [*sic*] work began today and a large force of hands are at work. It will be completed by Monday morning." The railroad crew laid the standard ties on the widened roadbed, not interrupting regular train service a bit. The new steel rails were laid outside the narrow gauge. On June 23, 1888, the crews along the line threw the old narrow gauge rails off the track, and on June 24 the first standard engine rolled through Linden, New Richmond, and Pleasant Hill (aka Wingate-on-the-Standard-Gauge, aka Whitlock). The work was actually started at 5 a.m. on Saturday and finished on Sunday. New Richmond and the other towns had no trains Saturday and no mail reached the towns. The line from Toledo to Frankfort had previously been standardized on June 26-27, 1887.

The April 25, 1891, *Review* said, "The Little Yard Wide or streaks of rust is now a standard gauge and carries more freight than the Monon. It is the 'Clover Leaf' and is fast coming to the front, [*sic*] the men who made sport of the road are glad to get a job on it."

The Toledo, St. Louis, & Kansas City Railroad Company officials made a trip to England to borrow funds to complete the widening of the gauge to standard. There had been many complaints from the section hands concerning the low wages they were paid around the New Richmond area. The boss of the gang resigned his position and accepted a position with the local tile mill. The company didn't help matters when the pay car ran through New Richmond so fast the crew could not get their pay. The correspondent said, "The railroad people should receive no accommodations from the people here, for it is the most ungrateful corporation that exists." The employees on the road had to purchase supplies and groceries on time and this created hardships for all.

In August, 1888, the company had started a new practice of hiring Italian laborers because they worked for $1 per day. There were around sixty-five men working near Whitlock/Wingate in April 1889. The same year, in June, the company brought in two hundred Italians, who were to camp near New Richmond. The Linden correspondent said they camped in boxcars on the side track near that town. He made many derogatory comments about the Italians, calling them "lousy Dagoes" and claiming they took everything that was loose–thus giving them a bad name before they had a chance to prove themselves otherwise. He became very interested in their ways of life, saying, "one seems to be a baker and has a board he rolls his dough on for bread. He lays it down flat on the car floor, or ground, and gets down on his knees and rolls out the dough with a round stick." He continued, "All of them are merry as crickets and seem very polite."

The Italians were brought to the area to spread gravel on the railroad bed, and long trains of gravel were passing through New Richmond almost daily. The New Richmond correspondent gave a better picture of the Italians, saying they were doing fine work on the road and that they were very peaceable, causing no problems in New Richmond.

The nickname "Dago" was used by all the people writing about the Italians' introduction to Montgomery County, and all seemed fascinated by the meals they ate and the ways they prepared their food. A reporter from the Crawfordsville *Review* wrote, "The Dagoes Supper–The Clover Leaf is working several hundred Italians in spreading gravel over the road. The largest colony is quartered in tents near New Richmond and it was a *Review* man's pleasure to see them cooking and eating their supper Monday. Their principal dish and the one they seemed most fond of was noodles which was composed of a piece of soup bone boiled in water with slices of dough thrown in as a mixture. A large iron pot of this stuff consisted of all the supper a large party of them had." He continued, "they cook on a small furnace dug in the ground near their tent and only eat because it is a necessity to do so and live. They treat anyone pleasantly and are a race to be pitied." The real pity was the company officials were probably living high off the hog in the nearest city, leaving their hard workers to exist on practically nothing.

The gravel was spread on most of the road by August and the Italians were ready to move out of town. The New Richmond correspondent for the Crawfordsville *Review* said they were a nice lot of people and those who "throw stones at Italians do not know what they're doing, and the world could have used more people like [the Italians]." The gravel spreaders were in the area of Linden, New Richmond, and Whitlock from March to August 1889.

After the roadbed was graveled, the railroad company purchased several new engines for the line and the freight business increased. The management tried a little harder to accommodate the patrons and to improve relations along the line, hoping to increase passenger service.

This railroad, like so many others, went through many financial setbacks over the years, and by 1894 was on the decline. It was believed the railroad could be a success if the stockholders would remove half a hundred useless officers and "dudes–too many idle red-tape gents to support."

The Clover Leaf merged with the Nickel Plate in 1922, but retained its identity as the Clover Leaf District of that line. In 1964 the Nickel Plate merged with the Norfolk & Western, and in 1983 the Norfolk & Western merged with the Southern, becoming the Norfolk Southern Corporation.

During World War I four special trains of eighty cars passed through on the Clover Leaf one day, carrying soldiers and their equipment to the Mexican border. They were troops of the New York and New Jersey National Guards' Infantry, Cavalry, and Artillery. The soldiers traveled in forty-eight coaches, and the remainder of the train carried their horses, artillery, and other equipment. I remember seeing World War II troops on the Nickel Plate going through New Richmond many times. The boys always waved frantically at everyone they saw along the way.

Excursions

One of the most important items in the history of the railroad through New Richmond was the Excursions. The very first excursion was to be held on Saturday, October 15, 1881, but was postponed until the 22nd because of a delay due to the track not being completed. The time table read like this, "EXCURSION, OVER THE T.C. & ST. L. NARROW GAUGE RAILROAD, TO PLEASANT HILL, MONTGOMERY COUNTY, INDIANA–A Basket Dinner, Splendid Music and Good Speaking Among the Attractions–The Crawfordsville and Frankfort Bands will Positively Be Present. Take a Ride on the New Rail Road Across the "Garden Spot of Indiana." The time of arrival at the various stations, and fare for the round trip reads: Frankfort, 8 A.M., fare 60 cents; Jefferson, 8:15, 50 cents; Clark's Hill, 8:45, 40 cents; Beeville, 9:00, 40 cents; Kirkpatrick, 9:10, 35 cents.

In January 1903, the New Richmond *Record* received a pretty souvenir book from the Clover Leaf Route, containing time tables of the railroad's facilities and a picture of the Commercial Traveler, their famous fast train. The same year they advertised Excursions and Colonist fares to points Southwest and Southeast at greatly reduced rates to these points: St. Louis, MO; Chicago, IL; Indianapolis, IN; Richmond, IN; Anderson, IN; Boston, LA–all of these were for special conventions. They ran special excursions to Frankfort, Kokomo, and Marion, IN. At Marion the attraction was the National Soldiers Home Parade Grounds and Military Barracks.

In 1903 the Clover Leaf started making plans for new carriage equipment for the St. Louis Exposition traffic for the following year, and in June 1904, they advertised, "Low Round Trip fares to the St. Louis World's Fair Via the Clover Leaf Route, Toledo, St. Louis & Western, from New Richmond $10.90 Round Trip – any day" and offered "Pullman Palace Sleeping Cars, Café and Free Reclining Chair cars, Buffet, and Meals a-la-carte on all through trains."

In September 1904, the railroad was making special World's Fair Rates via Clover Leaf during the balance of the Fair at 1 cent a mile in each direction. In December they advertised special low excursion rates to see the DISMANTLING OF THE GREATEST OF ALL WORLD'S FAIRS. Admission was reduced to 25 cents. They advertised HOMESEEKERS to WEST & SOUTHWEST, CALIFORNIA, PACIFIC COAST–special rates. In 1905, LANDSEEKERS EXCURSION TO WESTERN & SOUTHWESTERN PARTS of the country were offered.

In July 1905 the Clover Leaf advertised its first annual Excursion of the year to Niagara Falls at $7.00 for the roundtrip. The same year in October, the Clover Leaf was offering half-fare rates to the "Hub City" during the big Annual Street Fair at Veedersburg. Principle attractions, the Ferri Brothers' Big Animal Show, and all kinds of amusements, etc., trains were to stop at New Richmond, Wingate and Mellott to accommodate the crowds who wished to attend.

In August 1906 the Clover Leaf advertised an excursion promoted by the Newtown Band to the Soldier's Home at Marion–the date for the trip was September 6 and the roundtrip fare from New Richmond was $1.00. The train was to leave New Richmond at 7:28 a.m.

Colonist tickets were available at very low fairs to points in Arizona, British Columbia, California, Idaho, Mexico, Montana, New Mexico, Nevada, Oregon, Saskatchewan, Utah, and Washington via the Clover Leaf Route, with fares from $30 to $40 as far as the Pacific Coast in August 1908. The same year there were low rates to the G.A.R. National Encampment–Toledo and return via Clover Leaf Route, and low rates for Homeseekers Excursions from New Richmond to Texas, Missouri, Colorado, Arkansas, Kansas, Oklahoma, and other southwestern and western states and territories.

Colonist fares via Clover Leaf were advertised at 25 to 30% savings to Alberta, Arizona, British Columbia, California, Colorado, Idaho, Mexico, Montana, New Mexico, Nevada, Oregon, Saskatchewan, Texas, Utah, Washington, and Wyoming, in October 1910.

In 1915 the Clover Leaf organized special parties for a tour to the Panama-Pacific Exposition in San Francisco. They also offered other tours to the coast, and Homeseekers rates to the southwest.

The latest excursion was a Labor Day excursion to St. Louis, in August 1952. The roundtrip fare from New Richmond was $9.15, leaving New Richmond at 1:30 a.m. on Sunday night; on return trip leaving St. Louis Monday morning at 6:30 a.m. The greatest attractions were sightseeing, zoo, parks, theatres, and a baseball doubleheader–the St. Louis Browns vs. Cleveland Indians.

New Richmond's Depot

The Toledo, St. Louis, & Kansas City Railway Company initially handled all their freight dealings through the local general storekeepers. Jack Smith was the first recorded express agent in New Richmond. W.W. "Wint" Washburn accepted the position a year later. The railroad company had a problem keeping someone in this job because they only paid $1 per month and the agents were to visit the train twice a day. The low salary was given as Washburn's reason to resign.

New Richmond stepped up into the big time in October 1887 when the railroad company erected a new depot in the shape of an old worn out freight car. The citizens of the town were very disgraced by their new depot, saying, "the old rat-trap of a thing is outrageous. The railroad company says they do more business at this place than any other on the line of the same size. It should be torn down and a ten bushel goods box erected." They continued with, "Mellot, a little station about eight miles from this place has a nice depot, one large enough for a place of fifteen thousand inhabitants and they do very little freight business."

The "Old, worse-than-a-hog-car" was still disgracing the townspeople the following year. Comments appeared in the Crawfordsville *Review* almost weekly showing the disgust of the people, such as, "the people of Coal Creek Township voted a heavy tax to the [rail]road besides many donations were given freely to build the road, and the business from New Richmond was greater than any point on the line and to the average Hoosier it does look like we should have a half-way respectable depot." Another comment was "poor railroad can borrow five million dollars and can't furnish the best station on the road with a respectable depot."

In August 1888, the people of New Richmond rejoiced when lightning struck the depot of the T.C. & ST. L. & K.C. Railroad and set it afire, burning it to the ground. William Campbell, the *Review* correspondent from New Richmond, said, "It was of little value and thank God, 'tis kind Providence came to the rescue, and the enterprising town may now get a good depot." He said a week later "the magnificent depot which was struck by lightning and consumed by fire caused the company a loss of $5. A judgement, we suppose, for putting up such a nuisance."

When the rumors started flying around town of the possibility of another freight, or hog car, being placed on the side track, Bill said, "May another streak of electricity come soon, if that is the case." It is not certain if the railroad company considered the next depot a step up, or a step down, as they put a poultry car on the road for the next place to do business. The people in town evidently decided they were fighting a losing battle and said, "it is quite an accommodation to merchants along the line."

By the middle of April 1889, New Richmond had a new depot. It was considered to be a "daisy" although it was not as large as it should have been. It beat the old box, or hog, or poultry car 'all hollow.' William Campbell then praised the Clover Leaf officials saying, the road was one of the best in the state, and the employees were very accommodating to those who did business with them.

Ira Stout deeded 11,175 square feet of land to the T. ST. L. & K.C. Railroad for the local depot for one dollar, and other consideration. The deed was not recorded until July 24, 1890.

The depot suffered a fire on March 20, 1913, and the building was thought to be doomed. The switch-light boy was getting his lamps lighted and a waste of oil on the floor of the freight room accidentally ignited. He closed the doors to await the arrival of the chemical engines, and by the time they arrived, flames were leaping up the sides of the interior of the freight room, but they were quickly extinguished by the chemicals. There was considerable fear that the depot would be consumed and that the nearby lumber company

53 - *New Richmond depot - Clover Leaf Railroad, circa 1924*

and the Haywood Detchon elevator across the track were in danger. The loss was only $100 to the building; the slate roof was torn away in places, windows were broken, the south door of the freight room was badly splintered, and the walls of the freight room were badly charred. The fire did not reach the waiting room or the agent's office and these rooms only received smoke and water damage.

The August 19, 1965 Wingate *News* published the following announcement: "In the matter of the petition of the Norfolk and Western Railway Company for Authority to discontinue maintenance of an agent at its station at New Richmond, Indiana; to make New Richmond a non-agency pre-pay station for car-load business only, under the jurisdiction of petitioner's agent at Wingate, Indiana; and to REMOVE its existing freight STATION facilities at New Richmond, Indiana." The Public Service Commission of Indiana was to conduct public hearings on this Thursday, August 28, 1965, and by December 1965 the station at New Richmond was dropped, and the building was torn down the following year.

The following is a list of Express Agents and Telegraph Operators of the New Richmond depot, and the approximate dates they served, taken from the New Richmond *Record* and the directories of Montgomery County, Indiana. In some instances there was a record of their next position.

Name	Position	Dates
George Howard	Exp.	Jan. 1886 to May 1886
Jack Smith	Exp.	May 1886 to Feb. 1887
W.W. "Wint" Washburn	Exp.	Feb. 5, 1887 to Feb. 4, 1888
Ellis Breed	Tel. Op.	1887
George F. Long	Exp.	Dec. 1888 to 1890
O.S. Bradford	Tel. Op.	Jun. 29, 1889
J.T. Vannatta	Exp.	Dec. 27, 1890 to 1892 (freight, ticket, Am. Exp. & Tel. Op)
J.H. Bowman	Sub.	Jul. 11, 1890
Fred Roberts	Tel. Op.	Mar. 1892
James Stewart	Exp. and Tel. Op.	1895 to Dec. 1899 to Alhanbra, Ill.
Amos M. Gross	Exp. & Tel. Op.	Jan. 1, 1900 to Apr. 1903 to Alhanbra, Ill.
Grover Garicher	Sub.	Apr. 1903-, to Brocton, Ill.
John A. Simpson	Agt.	Apr. 30, 1903 to Apr. 20, 1905
Homer C. Lydick	Agt.	Apr. 27, 1905 to Sep. 28, 1905, to Niles, Mich.
J.J. Hummer	Agt.	Sep. 28, 1905 to Dec. 21, 1905, to Delphos, Ohio.
J.M. Fredericks	Sub.	Oct. 5, 1905 to Dec. 1905, to Marion, Ohio
W.T. Bassett	Agt.	Dec. 21, 1905 to 1907
Homer A. Benjamin	Agt.	Sep. 24, 1908
Homer M. Bryant	Tel. Op. & Exp. Agt.	1912 to Mar. 1914, to Waterloo, Iowa
J.H. Lane	Exp. & Tel. Op.	Jun-3, 1915 to Jul. 6, 1922
Earl L. Warren	Tel. Op. & Agt.	Jan. 1921 to 1965; Depot at New Richmond Closed.

Earl Warren was born May 11, 1894 at Donnelson, Ill., and was only forty days short of having 55 years of service with the Nickel Plate Railroad. He was a member of the Railway Telegraphers Association, coming to New Richmond in January 1921, where he resided until his death in December 1968.

THE AUTOMOBILE COMES TO NEW RICHMOND

The Greek root of automobile is autos, "self," and mobilis, "movable." The theory of the automobile, or a road vehicle carrying its own motive power, was known to Solomon de Coste of Normandy as early as 1641. He wrote a book on the propulsion of carriages by steam power, and as a result was cast into a mad house.

Around 1680, Sir Isaac Newton developed a machine that had no gearing, and was propelled by the back action of a jet of steam. The first steam automobile was produced by the French inventor Nicholas Cugnot. This was a three-wheeled vehicle, the front wheel being the driver. This vehicle was designed to aid in transporting artillery and attained a speed of three miles per hour. Other experiments were designed by Murdock and Watt using Cugnot's design, but in the form of a wagon. William Symington built a steam carriage with the power plant in the rear, and Richard Trevithick produced a vehicle in 1802 with a crankshaft geared to the driving wheels.

There were numerous experiments with steam carriages in England after these early attempts, the most successful being a carriage built by W.H. James in which a tubular boiler was first used. Goldsworthy Gurny designed a vehicle in 1829 to carry fifteen passengers at the great speed of 12 miles per hour. England's experiments with the automobile were halted because of the enactment of the "Red Flag Act" in 1836. This law required that all self-propelled vehicles be preceded by a man carrying a red flag in daytime and a red lantern by night. The act also limited the speed to four miles per hour in the country and two in the cities. The reason behind this law was the farmers and coach drivers, and probably everyone else who depended upon a horse for conveyance, claimed that the steam vehicles frightened their horses. This law was not repealed until 1896.

Around 1867, Nicholas August Otto, a German engineer and inventor, and his partner, Eugen Langen, developed an early form of an internal combustion engine which operated on a four-stroke cycle. This was known as the "Otto Cycle" and was used principally in the later automobiles. Gustave Daimler, another German engineer, produced a high-speed gasoline engine operated on the principle of the Otto Cycle and this was the beginning of the modern period of motor car development. Daimler attached his engine to a bicycle. Carl Benz built a gasoline engine onto a three-wheeled carriage in 1884 but failed to take out a patent until 1886, so there was some controversy as to who invented the first automobile. Benz's inventions contributed to the amazing growth of the auto industry.

Americans were experimenting during this pioneer history of automobiles, and Charles Duryea developed a one-cylinder car in 1892 in this country. His automobile was followed soon after by such men as Haynes & Winton, Henry Ford, George Selden, Buick, Bristoe, Maxwell, Franklin, White, and several others. The models built by these men were generally powered by one-cylinder engines driving wooden wheels by chain and sprocket. Until 1903 there were more steam than gasoline driven cars. Henry Ford's first gasoline car was brought out in 1893, and could attain a speed of twenty miles per hour, a vast improvement over the European models. By 1894 there were a number of carriages in America and Europe that could attain speeds of ten to fifteen miles per hour.

About this time electric vehicles began to appear. These were propelled by electric motors with electrical current supplied by storage batteries. Electric vehicles were largely used by city folk, having a limited range of operation due to the necessity of recharging the batteries.

Many automobile manufacturers continued to make steam operated vehicles in America for several years, but these were bulky because the boiler had to be heated by oil or a compressed fuel.

The first automobile race in America was held under the auspices of the Chicago *Times-Herald* on Thanksgiving Day in 1895 and was won by Charles Duryea, the pioneer in American automobiling. His vehicle was of the buggy type with high wheels and single tube pneumatic tires, the first air tires in America. His vehicle is in the Smithsonian Institute in Washington, D.C.

The period between 1903-1915 produced every imaginable type of vehicle in America, ranging from one cylinder to sixteen. The country was well on its way to a new way of life. The standard of living was raised and manufacturers such as Henry Ford made it possible for almost every family to be able to afford an automobile because of his assembly-line production of the motor-car.

An early historian noted that John Detchon drove the first automobile into New Richmond in 1899, and that town residents had the distinction of owning the first five automobiles brought into Montgomery County. Setting out to prove these two statements, I drew a blank on both. John Detchon may have purchased the first auto, but the year was off. The Crawfordsville *Journal* (weekly) February 8, 1900 had the following, "John Detchon of New Richmond has purchased an automobile which is now on exhibition at the Dovetails Company office. It is a fine vehicle and touched John for $1,000. It weighs 400 pounds and has a speed capacity of forty miles per hour. John McCardle will also purchase one." I was very disappointed because the article did not give the make of the vehicle, and a search through later issues did not turn up any further information on his new automobile. (The Dovetails Company mentioned was a buggy factory in Crawfordsville.) Other residents of New Richmond took a wait-and-see attitude for a year or two and in August 1902 the editor of the New Richmond *Record* noted that "three of New Richmond's leading citizens are now critically ill with the automobile fever, with only slight chances of recovery."

In April 1903 the Indianapolis *Journal* challenged "any town the size of New Richmond in Montgomery County, Indiana, with a population of 360, according to the last official census, to equal, or surpass their record of five automobiles." This is as close as I could come to proving this report of town citizens owning the first five automobiles in the county. Four of New Richmond's leading citizens had ordered new Ramblers from the factory at Kenosha, Wisconsin. They were: Clyde A. McCardle, Charles Kirkpatrick, John P. Bible, and George F. Long. Two of the autos were delivered to the agent in Indianapolis on April 23, and when the gentlemen were notified of their arrival, there was quite a lot of excitement as to which two men were to claim these first two. McCardle was said to have "stowed a ham sandwich and a toothpick in his jeans and was off on the first hog train for the capital city to claim one," and a silver dollar was flipped to settle the friendly dispute as to the official owner of the second auto. George F. Long had to relinquish his auto to the Honorable State Representative Charles Kirkpatrick, and John P. Bible did not stand a chance for the other, as McCardle was "long gone."

All four autos were identical in color—a dark red or maroon—and were of the same style and size. They were all powered by gasoline engines. The two autos arrived in the town of New Richmond about 4 o'clock the same afternoon they had arrived in Indianapolis. Bert Page drove Charlie Kirkpatrick's auto home for him, and Clyde drove his own home. Page later drove for McCardle as his chauffeur, and often took spins in the new "Purple Streak" or "Auto Fiend" as they referred to the car.

The next Rambler arrived about the middle of May and John P. Bible hurriedly rushed to Indianapolis to claim the automobile (arriving before the auto made it to the dealer) and drove it "overland" to New Richmond," the *Record* said. Incidentally, John P. Bible of New Richmond was noted as being the first stockholder to make the trip to the Battleground Camp meeting grounds in an automobile, in August 1903.

George F. Long was the last to get his Rambler. It was shipped from the factory on Tuesday, May 12th. George went to the state agency to pick up his car and "drove the Red Terror home." I would like to insert at this point a story of Forrest Waye's in regard to the driving ability of these early automobile owners. He said when George Long first purchased his auto, he just let up on the gas pedal and coasted to a halt. When driving into his barn he let up on the gas and let the vehicle stop by hitting the end of the shed, yelling "Whoa!" as he entered. It is a wonder there were not more accidents than were reported; they had no driving experience whatsoever.

The first woes of automobilists were beginning; Clyde McCardle's new car was laid up for repairs only two months after he received it, needing a new chain "and other furnishings," and his wife went to visit some friends a few days, then his dog "Don" was run over by the car and died. He was feeling very low, saying, "My wife is gone, my dog is dead and my auto is out of repair, I just tell you, I'm in a deal of a fix."

Nick Washburn's Clothing Store received its first order of "Automobile Caps" with prices ranging from $1.60 to $2.50, and because of the limited number of automobilists, had to mark them down to prices of 50 cents to $1.50 to move them. Automobile caps were equipped with goggles to prevent a condition called "Automobile Conjunctivitis," a new disease of the eyes caused by fast riding in the autos—the rapid movement of the riders by the friction of the wind chilling the membranes of the eyes. The inflammation was confined to the Ocular Conjectiva, said the *Medical and Surgical Monitor* of Indianapolis. The treatment to correct this problem, besides washing the eyes three or four times a day with mild astringent washes using an eye-cup, was to wear close fitting goggles.

The town of New Richmond received a new name "Automobile-Burg" compliments of the Crawfordsville *Journal*. This paper also mentioned the possibility of an automobile factory in Montgomery County—but, the article said, "if there is a factory it will not be located in Crawfordsville, the county seat, but at New Richmond, the seat of Coal Creek Township." The article continues, "Representative Charles Kirkpatrick, John McCardle, Wint Washburn, Starr Dunn, and other monied men of that community, are talking over the feasibility of the scheme seriously and believe that such a scheme would be a money maker from the start. They see that the greatest development in the horseless vehicle is to come within the next five or ten years and being in the center of the good roads district of the county, they see no reason why New Richmond should not be a good distributing center for a product which is so dependent upon improved highways." Needless to say, this factory idea died a sudden death.

The editor of the New Richmond *Record* had to change the wording of local items a little, after automobile fever struck the town, as residents did not visit friends or relatives in other cities anymore—they automobiled here and there. The local Methodist church announced its first "Automobile Party" not the old fashioned picnic or outing party formerly held in the good ol' summertime.

Driving all over the countryside in their shiny new "Red Terrors" soon created more problems than the auto owners could handle, as every horse within a mile of the machines took fright. One day as Clyde McCardle rounded the corner at Johnson's Drug store in New Richmond and started north, a large valuable farm horse belonging to James Rust of Sugar Grove was tied to a hitch rack and took fright and lunged against a hitch-rack post with such a great force, it started bleeding profusely at the nose and continued bleeding until he died about one hour later. This happened in September 1903. There were many other incidents with horses, though not quite so dramatic, but some of the country people had already threatened to quit coming to New Richmond to trade because of the "too many automobiles and the fear of them scaring their horses." The editor of the *Record* cautioned the automobilists to be careful, and to assure their farmer friends they would not be annoyed by any reckless running of the "lightning speeders." The editor predicted there would come a time when the road horses would become as accustomed to the auto as they did to bicycles few years back.

Two years later the fight between farmers and automobilists was becoming a touchy subject, not only in the New Richmond vicinity, but all over the country. In February 1905 an automobile bill, the "Crumpacker Bill," was selected as the best of several automobile bills introduced and was adopted by the Senate. It stipulated that motor machines were to be run at

> reasonable and proper speeds, specifically, eight miles in the business or closely builtup parts of a city, or town, and 15 miles for other parts of a municipality, and 20 miles outside of municipalities. And upon signal from–a person riding or driving a horse that has become frightened, any motor vehicle must stop at the signal of a raised hand, and must remain standing until the horse is in control. If necessary to quiet the horse, the motor must be stopped. A white light in front and a red light behind a motor machine are required from one hour after sunset to an hour before sunrise. In addition, the machine must be equipped with brakes, a bell, horn, gong, or other signal to be used as occasion demands.

In April 1905 there were approximately 2,300 machines in Indiana and only 286 had taken out license as provided by the new law. The Secretary of State was to issue a certificate of registration for $1 and the owner received a small circular metal plate showing he had paid his taxes. For $2 more, he would receive a solid one-piece plate with the number of his machine on it.

The farmers tried another approach of stopping the automobilists by applying fresh gravel at frequent intervals. The automobilists claimed the gravel was put on in such a way as to make it difficult for them to get through, but the farmers declared it would soon pack and eventually become better roads for everyone concerned.

Accidents between autos and "skittish" horses were on the increase in 1905 and 1906. Charles McDaniel's team took fright at James Ward's auto, veering off the road and upsetting a wagonload of corn. Mr. McDaniel failed to give Ward the usual sign to stop and the latter, given his full share of the road, went around and sped away. The corn had to be loaded into another wagon to be taken on to the elevator. James Ward's auto also frightened James Withrow's team, throwing the driver, Lewis Withrow, from the wagon.

Another incident involved Evan Shelby and two young ladies, Frances and Mabel Haywood, who were out for a Sunday drive in their carriage when their pony was frightened by a passing auto and ran away, upsetting the buggy in the side ditch. This resulted in some painful injuries. Tilly Albright of Crawfordsville was driving along the road near Romney on a Sunday afternoon in her automobile and frightened the horse Mary Greenburg was driving, turning the buggy upside down in the ditch; the horse ran away. Miss Greenburg escaped injury by falling out through the back curtain of the buggy top. Miss Greenburg resided east of New Richmond.

A party of county officials out for a drive toward Ladoga one October day were held up at the point of a gun by an irate farmer near Clark Township's "capital." James Wilson, of Round Hill, Frank Maxwell, Charles McCullough, and Ab. Jones were "flitting by" in Jimmy Wilson's new Cadillac, when Wilson saw ahead a man, a horse, and a buggy. The man saw the auto, stopped, alighted, got his horse by the head, reached into his hip pocket and took out a gun. He gave the high sign. Mr. Wilson slowed down and approached the man, and as he approached, the revolver's size appeared to increase

> with great rapidity until when nearby the man, it assumed the size of Alf Lookabill's 13" gun, and was pointed dangerously in the direction of the occupants of the Cadillac. Mr. Maxwell asked the man with the gun, "You wouldn't shoot the sheriff, would you?" The Sheriff and his deputy were following the county commissioner's car. "You-bet-cher-life, I would or any other blankety-blankety man who tries to run by me without stopping," said the man with the gun. He then started abusing the party in the auto making each one feel like 30 cents-for how did they know if, or when, the gun might go off. Finally, the sheriff said to the deputy, "Let's arrest that man." The man with the gun, however, jumped into his buggy and with the reins dangling, started whipping his horse and at a run-away gait, and out-ran the deputy who was on foot trying to catch him.

This is one account of the more violent effects the automobile had in Montgomery County.

Another incident happened at Round Hill when Clyde McCardle and George F. Long were returning home from Crawfordsville one night. They ran into a huge pole that had been thrown across the road near the church. The obstruction lay in the shadow of a tree and a crowd of boys attending a church festival was standing "suspiciously" nearby. Luckily none were injured by the prank, nor did it wreck the auto.

When the New Richmond businessmen were planning a horse show in June 1906, it was decided as an added feature to have an automobile race with the local autoists as the competitors. The editor of the *Record*, said, "It will prove an interesting event and persons with scary horses need not stay away from the show on this account." Runaway horses presented the editor with some exciting stories to print.

John T. Detchon purchased another automobile, a handsome new Ford gasoline motor auto, a two seated carriage with the usual "red scare devil" color. The local autoists had run all the "goodie" out of their first autos and in February 1905 the men attended an auto show in Chicago. They just *had* to purchase new vehicles. Charles Kirkpatrick purchased an aluminum colored, 20 horsepower Winton and nicknamed it "Grey Wolf;" Clyde McCardle's big new 20 horsepower Stevens, a $2,500 auto with a gasoline motor engine, painted blue—with a top—arrived on the local freight. He nicknamed his "Blue Bell." Bert Page purchased a new 10 horsepower Cadillac and John P. Bible, a new four-passenger Cadillac. Bible decided to keep his old Rambler to "hack about in." He was one of the few early automobile owners in this section of the country to own and operate two autos. James M. Ward purchased a new Premier—a handsome auto that attracted all the girls in town—and James D. Wilson, as said before, had purchased his Cadillac the same year.

By May 1905, New Richmond boasted eight machines. The editor of the *Record* said, "New Richmond is making herself in one more way the far-famed town of New Richmond-"The Best Little Town on Earth."

Thomas Kirkpatrick became New Richmond's first automobile casualty from a blow with an auto crank. He received a badly bruised hand and threw his wrist out of place when cranking McCardle's car.

New Richmond played a small part in what is believed to be the first automobile theft in the state. Dr. Henry Jameson's auto was stolen from in front of his office in Indianapolis. The thief drove it to a suburb in the north part of the city and abandoned it. He returned to the city and spent the night, then returned to take possession of the auto again the next morning. Some boys, hearing of the theft, called the police and informed them where they had seen the auto, and about fifteen minutes after the thief left, the police arrived. The chase was on! The stolen car, with the thief as chauffeur, arrived in the town of New Richmond about 4:30 that afternoon, coming in from the south. He tore off the license number (#10 Indiana) and threw it away where it was found by William Bennett, who came up immediately after the thief passed.

The stolen auto went through New Richmond at a terrific speed, only hitting the high spots. The two autos in pursuit passed through New Richmond about 6 o'clock. The thief and the machine were found at George Shultz's, one mile north of Newtown, where the thief had stopped for the night. A pair of handcuffs were slipped on him. The owner of the car, Dr. Jameson, who was in one of the chase vehicles, drove his automobile back to Indianapolis. The thief gave a hard luck story saying he was a Chicago railroad "Butch" (news-boy) and was broke and wanted to get out of town, and that was the best way he could find. It is interesting that the road between New Richmond and Newtown was the same road the horse thieves took to reach their hiding place on the Wabash. One can wonder if there is a connection.

New Richmond's first drive-in church services were held on the Methodist Church lawn in August 1919. The New Richmond *Record*, August 14, 1919 said, "The event created a beautiful scene with the country folks in their automobiles forming the outer circle, and the town folks seated in chairs in the inner circle." They were to repeat this type of service on the 24th of August.

The New Richmond *Record* usually noted any new autos in the town and below is a list with the dates of the newspaper they appeared:

Name	Date	Car
W.W. Washburn	April 12, 1906	a dark green MARION
Charles Kirkpatrick	Oct. 4, 1906	WHITE Steamer
Samuel "Doc" Bayliss	Aug. 27, 1908	a big new automobile (make unknown)[1]
Samuel "Doc" Bayliss	April 15, 1909	Cadillac
George M. Martin	Aug. 12, 1909	a new REO[2]
Frederick E. Bible	Feb. 24, 1910	a new MITCHELL roadster
John P. Bible	Aug. 10, 1911	APPERSON JACK RABBIT touring car
Harry Ackermann	June 8, 1916	FORD roadster
John L. Cutrell	July 6, 1916	7-passenger BUICK
John L. McNeil	July 6, 1916	FORD touring car
John Grubb (of Shawnee Md)	June 15, 1916	PAIGE
Jasper Elmore	June 15, 1916	SAXON
Charles Kirkpatrick	July 1, 1920	MARMON
Frank E. Campbell	April 5, 1923	HUPMOBILE touring car.

Automobile Owners in New Richmond in 1920

Name	Model
Alexander, Bayless	Ford
Allen, J. Lee	Dodge
Andrews, E.W.	Ford
Andrews, F.L.	Ford
Austin, Jake	Ford
Bannon, Lewis	Ford
Blacketer, Charles	Ford
Brandenburg, John T.	Ford
Bratton, John S.	Oakland

---

[1] Bayliss had a large open bus to haul his company of entertainers of his Hot Springs Remedy Show.
[2] George was a former New Richmond resident, but had moved to Lafayette.

Bratton, Mills M.	Cadillac
Bunnell, Jacob W.	Ford
Bunnell, John W.	Ford
Bunnell, Thomas, E.	Elco
Chadwick, H. Grady	Ford
Chadwick, J.P. Frank	Hupmobile
Chadwick, J.P. Frank	Ford
Clapp, Alonza	Buick
Clapp, Lawrence	Ford
Clarkson, Louis E.	Lexington
Coffing, Theo. C.	Ford
Cook, T.M.	Dodge
Cowan, George A.	Ford
Davidson, William T.	Ford
Davidson, Robert	Overland
Dazey, Abram W.	Ford
Dazey, Barnum	Ford
Dazey, Ray C.	Ford
Dewey, Bert	Ford
Dewey, Philip W.	Oldsmobile
Ebright, Mrs. Jane	Buick
Felton, John H.	Ford
Fouts, James W.	Overland
Frame, William	Buick
French, Charles H.	Ford
Fulwider, Walter A.	Lexington
Geiger, S.L.	Ford
Glover, Orrin	Ford
Goff, Amos S.	Ford
Goff, Homer C.	Ford
Grantham, Thomas J.	Haynes
Graves, C.W.	Ford
Greenburg, Clyde	Overland
Grubbs, J.W.	Ford
Hamilton, Fay	Buick
Harris, Roscoe	Chevrolet
Henderson, Alfred L.	Oakland
Horn, Emmett	Ford
Hornbeck, James L.	Dodge
Inskeep, William	Overland
Jones, Charles R.	Hupmobile
Jones, Edgar L.	Buick
Jones, W.T.	Dodge
Kenyon, M.V.	Ford
Kirkpatrick, John M.	Ford
Kirkpatrick, Noah	Overland
Kite, William	Ford
Kochell, Charles	Dort
Kochell, F.E.	Overland
Lane, W.D.	Ford
Larew, Garret A.	Ford
Lewis, Allen M.	Buick / Ford
Litke, Herman	Buick
Livingston, Joseph	Ford
Long, Robert	Overland
Mason, Ewing T.	Ford
Mason, Monroe	Ford
Mason, William	Buick
McCrea, E.H.	Ford
Meharry, Judd	Lexington
Meharry, Mrs. Mary E.	Ford / Overland
Meritt, J.N.	Ford
Miller, John L.	Ford
Miller, Martha K.	Buick
Mitchell, Elliot O.	Dort
Mitchel, Ramond	Ford
Montgomery, Isaac H.	Ford
Morris, John N.	Haynes
Nesbitt, Herman B.	Ford
Oliver, Charles T.	Dodge
Oppy, E.T.	Overland
Oppy, Thomas T.	Buick
Patton, Arlie O.	Ford
Patton, Charles A.	Overland
Patton, Ernest C.	Buick
Patton, George T.	Chevrolet
Pierce, Delbert W.	Buick
Pierce, Henry S.	Cole / Ford
Quigle, Ira	Ford
Quillin, O.S.	Dodge
Rayborn, Benjamin C.	Overland
Rice, Raymond	Dodge
Sutton, Mrs. Ida D.	Overland
Swank, Harvey D.	Dort
Swank, W. Winton	Ford
Tatlock, Fred E.	Dodge
Taylor, Donald B.	Ford
Thomas, Anson S.	Ford
Thomas James N.	Overland
Timmons, J.W.	Hudson
Tribby, Gaylord	Buick
Utterback, James W.	Ford
Wainscott, Stephen	Ford
Waltz, Frank	Oakland
Westfall, John C.	Stephens
Whipple, David	Chevrolet
Wilkinson, William T.	Ford
Wilson, James D.	Ford / Studebaker

54 -Edgar and Jessie (Ebrite) Jones and their EMF Studebaker, manufactured from 1909-1913 at a cost of $1,250

Automobiles and New Richmond

The early automobile owners in New Richmond had very little knowledge of mechanics, and some of them hired chauffeurs to drive their automobiles and to keep them in good repair. Charles Kirkpatrick hired the following chauffeurs to drive for him over the years: Bert Page, Stanley Dunn, Arlie Binns, and Maurice Coffman. Dunn also occasionally drove for J.P. Simison of Romney, and Bert Page drove for John McCardle.

Then came the Automobile Taxi Service in New Richmond—among the first to carry on this service was Starr Dunn and his son, Stanley. They purchased two Hupmobiles and drove people around New Richmond, Linden, and Wingate, and occasionally longer trips were made over various parts of Indiana. The New Richmond High School yearbook *Kole Kreke Kamera* (1910) had the advertisement, "NEW RICHMOND AUTO LIVERY—also automobile repairs and supplies, Stanley Dunn, Proprietor." The same year and source listed another taxi, "S.E. MAGRUDER, Proprietor of the Livery and Feed Stable, New Richmond, Indiana. AUTOMOBILE FOR LIVERY, with good, careful and competent Chauffeur—First Class Rigs." This made a smooth transition into the automobile era. The 1915 New Richmond High School yearbook *N.R.H.S.-1915* had the following advertisement, "AUTO TAXI—call G.L. Bastian day or night for prompt, careful service." The 1923 *Jungle*, another N.R.H.S. annual, had the following advertisements, "HENDERSON'S TAXI—for prompt, careful service" and "FOR A TAXI, call George W. Shepherd."

Automobile sales dealers in New Richmond included John H. Turner, who in June 1916 advertised, "FORD! FORD! FORD! JOHN H. TURNER." And, in July 1920, BARKER AND HANAWALT for "FORD CARS AND FORDSON TRACTORS." Richard Thomas sold Hudson cars in 1951; his advertisement was in the Methodist Church history that year.

The earliest automobile mechanics were Starr Dunn and his son Stanley, who were believed to have been the first in New Richmond, although Wilbert Lyons claimed to be the first. Dunn had a garage as early as 1910, but the earliest record found on Lyon's garage was in 1930s.

"FOR SALE OR TRADE: Motor Car, four cylinder FULLER in running order. Will trade for Horse and Buggy! Thomas Morris, New Richmond, Indiana," from New Richmond *Record*, Thursday, March 16, 1916.

Automobiles and Little Boys

A certain very dignified citizen of New Richmond was walking along the street one day last week, and seeing several small boys playing together, he thought he would investigate and see what they were playing. As he approached he saw one of the boys walking on his hands, and another had hold of his feet, while still another was riding on the first lad's back. On asking what they were doing one of the youngsters replied that they were playing "automobile." Being satisfied, he walked on. About a block down the street he ran across a real small boy sitting on the curb, as though he was ready to cry, "Why my little man, why are you not playing automobile with those little boys down the street?" he asked. "I am," said the boy. "Why aren't you with them?" came the reply. "I have to stay behind 'cause I'm the smell!"

Automobiles and Big Boys

MAUD MULLER on a summer day, with her fellow ran away,
 in a benzine touring car, scooting to the preacher far.
Maud's father saw the fleeing pair—smelled the benzine scented air;
Caught a mule whose name was Jane, and galloped down the dusty lane;
The mobile very swiftly ran, but burned the oil all out of the can.
The motor stopped upon a hill, but Jane ran on just fit to kill.
Alas for maid, also for man, alas for empty benzine can.
Maud's daddy on the old gray mule, came and took her off to school.
The mule nigh wrecked the benzine cart, the feller died of a broken heart.
The moral of this tale so sad, "Don't steal the girl, go ask her dad."
— New Richmond *Record*, Aug. 23, 1906

Interurbans in New Richmond

"That Electric Road", "Electric Line Coming Our Way", "Electric Road Survey", "Another Electric Road", "That Proposed Interurban Road", "Interurbans Coming Our Way", "More Interurbans", "New Traction Line", "Interurban Trade", "Consolidated Traction Line is Assured", "Trolley Lines", "Farmer's Aids", "The Interurban Coming, Will Build Within Two Years", "Traction Talk", "Another Interurban Coming this Way", "Interurban to Attica", "Interurban Freight—Coal, Grain—Poultry and Milk, to be Northwestern's Revenue", "To Trolleyize the Clover Leaf", "Interurban Prospects", "Interurban Possibilities."

All the above were headlines in the New Richmond *Record* concerning the possibilities of an electric road coming through, or near New Richmond. One of the biggest disappointments of a person writing a history of a town is to spend hours of research on a subject and to write many pages on the same, knowing all the time the main topic of discussion never materialized. All the planning and preparation of the electric cars, or interurbans, through the town of New Richmond never got beyond the dreams of the big businessmen. There were many hours and dollars spent and wasted on these proposed interurban lines. None of the companies ever laid the first rail, or erected the first pole for the source of electrical power, and they kept the people of New Richmond and the surrounding towns up in the air from early 1900 to at least 1915, possibly later.

In 1902 there was some talk of a new interurban line between Indianapolis to Lafayette, via Crawfordsville and through New Richmond. This had been discussed some time before, and the citizens of New Richmond were being urged to take stock in the new enterprise. This same year, the Northwestern Traction Company was planning a line from Indianapolis to Lafayette and hoped to complete the line by the next June. The same company was then to build a line from Indianapolis to Crawfordsville.

A survey was being made on the line from Indianapolis to Crawfordsville for an electric interurban line the first of January 1903. The possibility of a line running west and northwest through Wingate, Newtown, Attica, Indiana Mineral Springs, and on into Illinois was being considered, but unfortunately this line was planned to bypass the town of New Richmond. The editor of the New Richmond *Record* was trying to promote interest in the line in order to have the line built east and west through the town of New

Richmond, as well as Wingate. It was pointed out the whole township would then be counted upon to vote for her subsidy to build the line if this was considered.

A month later, Surveyor James A. Harding had just completed maps for the Consolidated Traction Company, projecting a line to run from Crawfordsville, starting at the corner of Market and Washington Streets thence north to Lafayette Avenue, up the Lafayette Pike, over Sperry's covered bridge, and directly north to New Richmond. From New Richmond the line was to touch Wingate, Newtown, Rob Roy, Attica, and the Indiana Mineral Springs for a terminus. A branch line was proposed from Attica to Williamsport. The stretch between New Richmond and Wingate was to parallel the Clover Leaf Railroad, but elsewhere it was to run along the highway. The proposition for this line was to be submitted to eastern capital for consideration. "Electric line coming our way! Let 'er Come," was the reaction from the citizens of New Richmond.

The Tipton, Frankfort, and Attica Traction Company employed J.R. Brown and his force of five men to survey another route for an electric line. The nearest point of this survey to New Richmond was the half-section line just north of Charles Haywood's home, six miles north of town. There were to be three surveys for this proposed line, the second was to be farther north than this route just mentioned. The third was to be south of the first survey and was to touch Clark's Hill, Kirkpatrick, Linden, New Richmond, and Newtown. It was expected that the road would be built on the route on which the hardest "pull" was made. Mr. Brown, the surveyor, did the surveying for the Northwestern Traction Company on the Indianapolis to Lafayette line. Brown also surveyed a route for the railroad that runs through New Richmond, the Clover Leaf, but his survey projected the road some four miles north of the town.

In September 1903, the surveyors for the Tipton, Frankfort, and Attica Interurban Company, proposed a route for an electric road from Frankfort to Colfax, touching Linden in the extreme south, through New Richmond. The surveyors laid out two routes through New Richmond, one crossing the Clover Leaf Railroad on the curve and crossing the town just north of Henry Long's livery barn and south of the cemetery. The other route was to cross the Clover Leaf track just east of J.W. (James) Tribby's barn and follow Washington Street through the town, on west past the cemetery and then intersect the former route. This was the same surveyor and his gang of five men who laid out the former route several weeks previous.

The proposed interurban lines were studied and studied, and in March the following year, a decision still had not been made as to which route to consider. The straight, or the most northern route, was the shortest by only four miles, but the southern route had the greatest population per mile, which was an important factor in securing the financial aid necessary to build such a road.

Crawfordsville, in the meantime, was all agog over the arrival of their first green cars over the Northwestern's new interurban line around the first of July 1904. A big celebration was held and the first trolley party was held in the Crawford Hotel by the Commercial Club. The Northwestern Traction Company was the first company to consider building a line on to New Richmond.

Around the middle of July 1904, Honorable Charles Kirkpatrick met with the representatives of the Northwestern Traction Company in Crawfordsville. They made arrangements for a party, including a number of leading citizens from New Richmond, to go over the most advantageous, nearest, and best route from Crawfordsville to reach New Richmond, Wingate, Newtown, Attica, and with a terminus at the famous Indiana Mineral Springs. This is the same route proposed over a year earlier when the Indianapolis to Crawfordsville line was being planned.

The surveys were to be soon made after this group of men made their preliminary study, and the next step to be taken was to make the wealthy capitalists to see the advantages of this route. The advantages being, as the article said, "to run through the most densely settled country, with the best soil, some of the best crops the sun ever shown [*sic*] on, the thrifty farms, and thriving farmers, and above all, the best little town on earth" (meaning New Richmond, of course). This prospecting party was expected to be and "probably in the nature of an automobile party," headed by the Honorable H.L. Kramer, of Mineral Springs, Honorable Charles Kirkpatrick of New Richmond, and Messrs. Townsend, Reed, Wise and others of the Northwestern Company, were to be among the group.

A week later the Tipton, Frankfort, and Attica Electric Railway Company came forward with their proposition of the two routes mentioned earlier. The right-of-way had been procured for the northern route through Jackson Township in Tippecanoe County, and a force of men were at work securing the right-of-way through Linden, New Richmond, Newtown, and Attica. Col. Clark, the surveyor in charge and one of the promoters of the Clover Leaf Railroad in its early stages, was busy talking to citizens of New Richmond about the advantages of his new enterprise. Again, the problem of finding the necessary capital was holding back the construction of the road. The possibility of New Richmond being on the east and west line of interurban traffic was still uncertain.

By September 1904, the Tipton, Frankfort, and Attica Traction Company had secured the rights across northern Montgomery County with the exception of two or three farms. The promoters received part of this land as gifts, the donors expecting to see great returns from the interurban's convenience. The line was financed and work was to be started on this line the following spring. It was pretty certain that this line would be built.

New Richmond was still waiting for an interurban company to build a line in or near the town when, in April 1905, citizens of Crawfordsville were expecting their second electric railway line to be constructed. The Consolidated Traction Line was planning a line from Indianapolis to Crawfordsville.

This new line aroused the interests of the New Richmond people again. It was thought with the competition of two lines in Crawfordsville, New Richmond would have a better chance of a spur from one of the lines running through the town, but the idea soon was forgotten by the two companies.

The Tipton, Frankfort, and Attica Line tempted the citizens of New Richmond once again in August 1905. The headlines in the New Richmond *Record* read, "The Interurban Coming! ", "An Old Railroad Man Declares That the Tipton, Frankfort, & Attica Line is Coming Our Way", "Will Build within Two Years!" The railroad man who had "held the throttle on all kinds of trains on the Clover Leaf" during all its existence, declared the interurban would be built through the towns mentioned before, between Frankfort and Attica, and would not be built north of New Richmond on the shorter route surveyed. The editor thought it would be a good move and would make the Clover Leaf offer better accommodations for travel because of the competition. The citizens were still holding their breath for a line a week later.

In January 1906, still another electric line was being considered by Detroit and Attica capitalists. This line was to touch Newtown, Mellott, Wingate, and New Richmond, and they were trying to connect Crawfordsville to Attica. The men involved were J.W. Fewell and S.J. Hunt of Detroit and F.A. and A.P. Nave of Attica.

Articles of Incorporation of the Crawfordsville and Northwestern Railway Company, a traction line, were filed in January 1906 in Indianapolis. This line was to start at Crawfordsville and pass through the following towns: Wesley, Waynetown, New Richmond, Wingate, Attica, Hillsboro, Mellott, Williamsport, Kramer, Carbondale, Judyville, and Pence.

The capital stock of the corporation was $100,000, and the directors of the company were Spencer J. Hunt, A.L. Mason and John E. McFarland. The secretary of the corporation was to contact the commercial clubs of New Richmond, Wingate, and Newtown, seeking their cooperation in this new venture.

There were to be two routes: one was proposed as an "air-Line" to touch the towns of New Richmond, Wingate, and Newtown; while the other was to be a circuitous route, taking in the towns to the west and northwest of the city of Crawfordsville.

This traction line was planned as a heavy freight line–passenger business was to be of secondary interest. It was hoped to transfer freight from the steam roads to the smaller villages and to do a big business in milk trade with the farmers. The company negotiated with a large number of Hollanders to settle on farms along the line to cultivate the dairy business. Hollanders made a specialty of that type of farming, and made a success of it wherever they went. A direct route to Indianapolis each morning was the purpose of this route. Grain and poultry, too, were expected to be a large source of the company's freight income. They also planned to tap the coal fields of Fountain County and to set the "black diamonds" down in Crawfordsville, hoping to induce factories to be built in that city.

The problem with this line was getting the farmers and citizens of the towns or villages to vote for the subsidy. Attica, in Logan Township, had already gone the limit provided by law on subsidies; Richland Township was not expected to vote a subsidy, because the road was to pass through Mellott and they knew the Newtown residents would vote against it; and for some reason or another, the company decided to leave New Richmond off the line and pass through Wingate only, so they blew their subsidy vote from the New Richmond people. Their only hope for funds was in Union Township and the donations that had been promised. This line would have required a more solid roadbed for the heavy freight it intended to haul, and therefore would have been more costly to build.

The people of Union Township voted against the subsidy in June 1906. The results were: 759 for the line and 1,762 against it–more than two to one were against the subsidy. More than one-fourth of the voters stayed away from the polls, resulting in a very light vote. The Northwestern Traction Line was then said to be a "thing of the Past."

The belief in the electric cars did not stop altogether, for in December that year, plans were in the making to "Trolleyize" the Clover Leaf, and this would have become the "Greatest Electric Line in the World," had the plan succeeded. English, Belgian, and Canadian capitalists were planning to buy or lease the Clover Leaf. Canadian capital had helped build the traction systems in Central Illinois, and was known as the McKinley Lines, named for Congressman McKinley, the Champaign traction magnate. This line ran from Decatur, Illinois, to St. Louis, Missouri, with another line to Danville, Illinois. It was thought the rates of passenger service between Toledo, St. Louis, Cleveland, Pittsburg, and Washington could have been reduced to at least one and one-half cents per mile, and freight rates would have been reduced in proportion. This was expected to be a simple feat to change the cars to electric motor cars, and install their wires along the existing roads, and sell their huge steam engines. This change was never made, however.

"Bud" Johnston, a former Darlington citizen who was later associated with the law firm of Browman and Johnston in Indianapolis, was trying to stir up interest in another interurban line to run from Thorntown to Darlington, Linden, New Richmond, Newtown, terminating at Attica. Johnston met in the Campbell and Kersey drug store with several of Darlington's leading citizens to discuss his new idea on interurbans. This company was expected to bear the name of the "Thorntown, Darlington, and Attica Traction Line." This was in August 1908.

Traction companies stirred up the town of New Richmond at least one more time in August of 1911. A new company by the name of the Kokomo, Frankfort, and Western Traction Company proposed a line to run parallel to the Clover Leaf Railroad, and they hoped to connect to the McKinley line in Illinois. Again in May 1915, an "auto-line" was proposed between Attica and Crawfordsville, through Newtown and Wingate, but would probably have bypassed New Richmond. The coming of the automobile to New Richmond in 1900 solved the transportation problem for some of the more wealthy citizens, but it was many years before the average citizen could afford to drive and maintain an automobile. However, the citizens of the town of New Richmond never had the privilege of riding the trolley cars in their hometown.

AVIATION FEVER STRIKES THE TOWN OF NEW RICHMOND

The citizens of New Richmond were hardly over the excitement of the arrival of the first automobiles, when another fever invaded the town–the airplane. Although this new flying machine did not have the impact on the whole town as did the automobile, the young men in the town became very interested and excited. This was during the Great War, or World War I, and in order to learn to fly, the young men decided to let Uncle Sam foot the bill for their flying lessons. After all, they would have to fight the war and they thought they might as well choose their branch of service. Among the young men from New Richmond who entered the Aviation service were: William Fife Jones (better known as "Billie Fife"), Aetna Gail Elmore, Stanley Mangold Dunn, and Glenn Mitchell. No doubt these men discussed flying while they were gathered together in their favorite hangout in the town of New Richmond on more than one occasion. Lafayette citizens saw their first airplane on June 13, 1911 when Purdue University staged an air show, and perhaps many of the New Richmond boys attended this show.

William Fife Jones, son of William T. and Mary J. Smith Jones, was born April 20, 1892 in Mocksville, North Carolina. The same year of his birth, the parents brought him to New Richmond where he lived until he enlisted in the Aviation Service on August 31, 1916 at Indianapolis, Indiana. Jones attended the schools in New Richmond and had made many good friends; among those was my father, Forrest Waye. My father, incidentally, did not share the enthusiasm for flying, but did enjoy watching Billie's barnstorming act (with his feet firmly planted on terra firma, of course). Upon his enlistment, Jones was sent to Rantoul, Illinois, for training. He acted as a test pilot while stationed at the Wilbur Wright Field in Dayton, Ohio, and also served as an instructor, and remained in the States during the war.

During the war years, "Billie Fife" Jones flew all over the midwest to stage air shows in order to promote the sales of Liberty Bonds. He landed in Inskeep's field just north of New Richmond on one occasion and my father, Forrest Waye, who was in the Home Guard, was selected to guard his plane while he was in town. Forrest said he had already performed his stunts—he was a great barnstormer, and had settled down for the night. When he tried to take off the next day, the gasoline he had purchased in New Richmond for his plane did not have enough octane, or whatever it takes to get off the ground, and he told the spectators to go home and get a can, and he would give them the "Blankety-blank" stuff. He then had to ask someone to take him to Crawfordsville or Lafayette to get a better quality of fuel. He had no more trouble; the plane "took off like a big bird."

55 - Forrest Waye (at right) guarding the airplane of William Fife Jones

Jones was commissioned First Lieutenant October 3, 1917 and was promoted to Captain in 1919. He was sent to McCook Field, Dayton, Ohio, in January and was killed in an airplane accident the same year, on July 14, 1919. Jones and his mechanic George Buzane were testing a new type of airplane, a Curtiss, when engine trouble developed a few seconds after leaving the ground. The engine was cutting out to such a degree the plane was in a stalling position, then went into a tail-spin and crashed to the ground. They fell from about 300 feet and both men were badly crushed and mangled from the fall. Jones died instantly and Buzane died a few hours later at the McCord Field hospital. Buzane was an automobile racer of national fame and would have raced in the Speedway races at Indianapolis on May 31, but had a broken arm and could not enter. Jones was only 27 years of age when he was killed, and Buzane was 30.

The body of Captain William Fife Jones was accompanied home by Major Shroder and wife of McCook Field, Shroder being one of Jones' most devoted friends. An airplane from Dayton flew over the funeral procession from the Methodist Church to the New Richmond cemetery, where he was buried, and again flew over as the corpse was lowered into the grave, dropping flowers along the way. A good friend of his, Lt. Stanley Dunn, also flew a plane over the grave and scattered flowers. His comrades from McCook Field thought so highly of him they presented the family with a tombstone for his grave.

Aetna Gail Elmore, son of Jasper and Catherine Elmore, was born January 19, 1899, in New Richmond, Indiana. He enlisted December 5, 1917 in the Aviation Section of the Regular Army at Lafayette. He was sent to Ft. Thomas, Kentucky, and was later transferred to Kelley Field, Texas, where he contracted pneumonia and died January 20, 1918, his career as a flyer cut short. He was buried in the New Richmond cemetery.

Glenn Mitchell, another local boy, son of Charles and Alice Ebrite Mitchell, was born in New Richmond June 9, 1894. He attended the local school and played clarinet in the "High School Orchestra" in his freshman year. Glenn became a nationally and internationally known artist. Glenn enlisted in the United States Air Corps, and graduated from the U.S. School of Aeronautics, University of Illinois. He received his training in Texas and Georgia. During World War II, he painted for the War Department and the Army Air Force. He had a great love for the flying machines throughout his life.

Paul Seamon, another New Richmond boy, enlisted in the Aviation Department early in the war, but was not able to fly on account of a weak heart.

Stanley Mangold Dunn, the first child of Starr and Martha A. Mangold Dunn, was born in Chicago, Illinois, September, 28, 1891. When he was about six years old, the family moved to New Richmond. He attended the local schools and while in high school became very interested in the mechanics of automobiles. He and his father, Starr, started the first automobile garage in the town of New Richmond. Stanley was such a good mechanic he was often asked to leave the classroom by people with automobile trouble to work on their vehicles. He finished his high school in Valparaiso University because his parents were determined to have him complete his studies.

Being so interested in machinery, he naturally was one of the young men about town to have a desire to learn to pilot an airplane when they made their appearance. Stanley enlisted in the Regular Army Signal Corps Aviation Service on July 27, 1917 at Jefferson Barracks, Missouri, as a private. He was soon promoted to sergeant and completed his schooling of Engines and Rigging, and was appointed a cadet on January 26, 1918. He completed ground school on March 5, 1918, and was promoted to second lieutenant on August 13, the same year. He received advanced training at Ft. Sill, Oklahoma from September 6 to October 12, 1918, and completed Aerial Gunners School at Taliafero Field, Hicks, Texas, in December 1918. He was in no battles or skirmishes while in the service and was discharged from the Air Service on January 8, 1919.

Stanley Dunn returned to the New Richmond area after his discharge, and in July the same year, was engaged by Denton R. Craig, an automobile salesman in Lafayette, to fly his brand new Curtiss JN-4 Army bi-plane, and the two embarked in a new venture–Lafayette's first Aerial Taxi Service. In fact, the Craig airplane was the first private locally owned plane in the city of Lafayette. Lieutenant Dunn flew the plane from Grant Park, in Chicago, where Craig had purchased the machine through the Kokomo Aviation Company for $8,500. He stopped at Rensselaer for gas and oil, picking up his first passenger, N.C. Shafer of that city, and took him to Lafayette with him. Dunn left Chicago at 5:20 p.m. and landed in Lafayette at 6:50 p.m., at the grounds of the Orphan's home south of Lafayette, which was used as an early landing strip. This was the Catholic Orphan's home and has since been razed. The field is now occupied by the Central Catholic School and a residential area.

The Craig plane was of the Canadian type and was four hundred pounds lighter than the American Model. It had a 90 horsepower motor and was well adapted to commercial use. Dunn gave Walter Reser of Lafayette a short ride in the plane the evening he arrived in the city. The following day he flew over the funeral procession in New Richmond, of Captain William F. Jones who was killed in an airplane crash in Dayton, Ohio. They were lifelong friends and New Richmond schoolmates.

A few days later, Lt. Dunn was carrying a passenger, Earl Martens, to Fowler, where he intended to take more passengers for a ride in the plane. They landed in Fowler at 1:30 p.m. and were to take Lloyd White, assistant editor of the Benton *Review* for a ride, but White, who was to be the first, also became the last passenger of the day, as the motor began missing when the plane was but 25 feet from the ground. The plane took a nosedive and landed in a cornfield near the starting place. The impact broke a wheel and the propeller but the plane was repaired, probably by Dunn. There was no mention of any injuries of either of the two men.

A month later Lt. Dunn made his first descent on his hometown of New Richmond "in the first locally owned airplane" the article said, but later this plane was referred to as the Craig-Dunn airplane, so perhaps Dunn owned part interest. He had been carrying passengers in the surrounding towns, charging $15 for fifteen minute flights. He flew in from Veedersburg and landed on Inskeep's field just north of New Richmond on Friday, August 8, 1919. He did not carry any passengers from New Richmond that day, but flew on to Lafayette, then to Delphi, where he carried passengers on Saturday. On Sunday he flew to Brookston and gave several passengers a flight, and returned to New Richmond late that evening, landing on Inskeep's field after dark. That would have been quite an experience, to land on an unlighted air strip or field.

On Monday he took his mother, Martha Dunn, for her first aerial flight—she was "overjoyed with the thrill"—then his father, Starr Dunn, climbed in for a ride. Others taking their first aerial flight from New Richmond were: Clyde E. Walts, son of Editor Walts of the New Richmond *Record*, Fred Bible, one of the Devaults (*Record* was torn and the first name was missing), Mrs. Edgar Walts, (wife of the editor), and Margery Bible.

On Tuesday morning, Austin P. Barker and Mrs. John L. McNeil had their first flight. Mrs. McNeil was the oldest person to try the thrill of flying, and would have been about 62 years old at that time. The plane then went from New Richmond to Waynetown to carry passengers, then to Yeddo, to be a part of the annual "Old Settler's Meeting." Jim Alexander accompanied Dunn to Waynetown and returned to New Richmond by Ford (auto). The editor of the New Richmond *Record*, Edgar Walts said, "Well, how does the best little town on earth look to you from the sky?" I could not understand why he didn't take a ride and get the thrill first-hand–did he think, like my father, if man was meant to fly he would have been born with wings, or was it because his wife and son got there first and he could not afford a third fare?

On Tuesday August 12, 1919, the first "aerial mail flight" was made from New Richmond, Indiana. Frederic E. Bible of New Richmond wrote a letter to his cousin, Postmaster Bible of Waynetown, and the New Richmond Postmaster, Campbell, affixed and cancelled the requisite postage of sixteen cents for aerial delivery of an ordinary letter of first class mail, then James M. Alexander, a passenger on the Craig-Dunn airplane, carried the letter from New Richmond to Waynetown, flying over Wingate. Stanley Dunn was the pilot of the plane and the letter was delivered in fifteen minutes. Postmaster Bible said he would hold the letter from his cousin as a souvenir.

Lt. Stanley Dunn taught D.R. "Pappy" Craig how to fly and the two of them barnstormed all over the country. A cyclone destroyed their first plane, and a week later, Craig went to Dayton, Ohio, where he met the pioneer of Aviation, Wilbur Wright, and purchased two Jennies, or JN-4s. They made a fabulous sum of money from their Aviation Taxi Service, but most of it went back into the business for repairs and upkeep of the planes.

Another New Richmond native, Dr. Arett Arnett, was a pioneer promoter of aviation in Lafayette. One of the first local persons to own an airplane, he encouraged the late Charles E. Shambaugh in the establishment of Lafayette's first airport, in 1928. This airport was located at what is now 18th Street and Teal Road. Dr. Arnett was one of the first student pilots.

Another pilot associated with the town of New Richmond was Robert V. Dryer, a licensed pilot who owned his own airplane and resided on a farm south of New Richmond. He gave many of the residents in and around New Richmond their first airplane ride. His first wife was the daughter of Mr. and Mrs. O.L. Hershberger. Bob Dryer died July 1, 1964, from injuries he had sustained when his Cessna-150 crashed on the 29th of June about a mile northeast of New Richmond. His second wife had died instantly in the accident. He and his wife lived at Flint, Michigan and were visiting Mr. and Mrs. John Bianconi, when the plane started cutting out and lost altitude. The plane struck a utility pole and landed nose first into the field of J.H. Mahon. Dryer had circled the Bianconi farm to signal Mrs. Bianconi of their arrival in order that she could drive to the M.L. Smith landing strip about a mile west of New Richmond to pick them up after they landed at the strip.

Morris Lee Smith, son of Russell and Mildred (Morris) Smith, constructed a hangar and a landing strip one mile west of New Richmond in the 1950s for his own private plane. Other pilots used the facilities at the Smith landing strip. Ralph Kunkel learned to fly a plane as a hobby, or a form of relaxation, and became a licensed pilot. He stored his plane in the Smith hangar for some time, later using the hangar and landing strip of Clinton Wilkins, east of New Richmond just inside the Madison Township line.

Chapter 22 – Utilities

Gasoline Arc Light Plants

One of John T. Detchon's business ventures in New Richmond was installing gasoline lighting plants. The earliest record of his installations was in the new Snyder building completed by September 25, 1902. A description of the Snyder building, upon its completion, said, "The building is lighted by the new white gasoline arc lights, nine double arcs being necessary for the first floor, and when all of them are turned on, their effusive rays make the store ablaze with light that is brighter than day."

In 1904 John installed a plant in the New Richmond Methodist Church, John W. Hollin's drugstore and grocery, the new Round Hill Methodist Church, and the Masonic Lodge hall. This plant was sold in 1915. Edgar L. Jones' residence was equipped with gasoline lights and Detchon probably installed his plant.

Hollin did not limit his installations of the arc lights to the New Richmond area, but records show he installed the gas lights in Mellott (in Mellott and Livengood's store room, and Mellott Christian Church); Indianapolis; Darlington (in Kip Milner's store); and many other nearby cities.

George Milner of Darlington was one of four traveling salesmen Hollin hired to sell his gas machines for lighting purposes. Other employees of Hollin were Alva Roberts and Starr Dunn. In November 1904, Starr and Roberts installed one of Detchon's automatic gasoline arc light plants — one of the largest he ever contracted to install — in Mortimer, Illinois. The plant included sixty lights, all with electric ignition, which Detchon wired himself. The job required about two weeks to install. Dunn and Roberts installed a plant for Boswell Clough at Elston, Indiana, in 1905. There were possibly many others, but records were only available for the above mentioned places.

Electricity Comes to New Richmond

John W. McCallum Electric Co.

The days of kerosene lamps and gas lights were nearly over for the residents of New Richmond as early as 1896. There were many doubting Thomases however, and others were downright afraid of this new method of lighting up the family living quarters.

On January 13, 1896, the town trustees, Stowe S. Detchon, Orlando W. Mason, and Horace G. Messer, granted John W. McCallum the franchise or right-of-way for erecting and maintaining the necessary poles, masts, and towers for the purpose of supplying the town of New Richmond, Indiana, and its inhabitants with electric light and power. The trustees laid out the terms and conditions of said franchise and specified the type of wire (insulated), and size of poles (not less than 25 feet high), to be installed. The poles were not to be erected in such a place as to cause any inconvenience to public or private uses, or to interfere with drainage in the town.

The ordinance clearly stated that McCallum was not granted an exclusive franchise, but that, rather, other companies wanting to provide electricity to the town would have that opportunity. The length of the term of his franchise was for twenty-five years. I do not have the particular issue of the New Richmond *Enterprise* that it was to be published in.

There is no further information of the above electric company, but evidently there were a small number of subscribers for electricity in the town through this early franchise.

Fairbanks Morse Company

The next company planning to supply the town of New Richmond with electricity was the **Fairbanks Morse Company**. A representative of this company met with the town trustees of New Richmond on April 10, 1913, to submit plans and cost estimates of running the plant. The trustees decided to investigate some of the towns in which this company had installed their system before making any decisions. No further action was taken for the Fairbanks Morse Company.

Montgomery Light and Power Company

On September 4, 1913, the undersigned list of subscribers petitioned the honorable Board of Trustees of the town of New Richmond to borrow money and incur an indebtedness and liability to the town for the sum of $5,000. The money was to be payment of a subscription of that amount to the capital stock of the **Montgomery Light and Power Company** to install the electric lights and power system to residences, businesses, streets and alleys in New Richmond. The petitioners were as follows:

> William Kirkpatrick, Clelland Terrell, Sarah Washburn, Orlando W. Mason, George C. Livingston, D. Manners Washburn, Charles Kirkpatrick, Carl Flaugher, Curtis M. Wray, Edward King, William P. Coffman, Lula G. Brown, Frank E. Campbell, Lon P. Brown, Austin Hanawalt, Winton Alexander, Grant Alexander, Garrett L. Bastian, Charles A. McLain, James B. Shepherd, William H. Bell, Perry McLain, Francis M. Smith, William H. Long, James F. Teague, William R. Turvey, Arthur E. Plunkett, Monroe Mason, Artemesa M. Taylor, Maurice Coffman, James M. Alexander, Joseph Humbert, John G. Flaugher, Hiland Beckley, Joseph Young, William W. Harriman, Fred E. Kincaid, Melvin J. Roth, William H. Hollin, Samuel L. Bayliss, John W. Hollin, Charles Zook, John N. Beckley, John L. McNeil, Stephen P. Harriman, Jessie L. Kirkpatrick, Alice McNeil, Bayliss Alexander, Jerome B. Franklin, Samuel E. Magruder, and William C. Davisson.

The Montgomery Light and Power Company was organized on September 13, 1913. The purpose of this company was to supply electricity to the northern Montgomery County towns of Linden, New Richmond, and Wingate. The Crawfordsville Power and Light Company was to sell the power to the towns.

A notice was published in the New Richmond *Record* in regards to a proposed franchise and grant to the Montgomery Light and Power Company for electric light and power in New Richmond. A hearing was to be held on October 16, 1913. Trustees of the town of New Richmond at this time were: Lon P. Brown, Frank E. Campbell, and William Kirkpatrick. Ed King was clerk of the town at that time. After the third reading of the proposed franchise and contract, Kirkpatrick moved, and Campbell seconded the motion that the same be adopted and all three board members voted for the franchise.

An ordinance was passed November 6, 1913, granting the Montgomery Light and Power Company the right to establish and maintain an electric light plant and system in the town of New Richmond, Indiana. The company was to provide the facilities for supplying the town and inhabitants with electricity, and was to furnish ample current at all times to meet all requirements of the town.

The Montgomery Light and Power Company was to locate poles and equipment under the direction of the board of Trustees and not to obstruct the use of streets, alleys, and other public places. They were to install twenty incandescent series lamps, equivalent to a 200 watt street lamp, and were to furnish light for the streets from dusk until midnight on the "Moonlight Schedule." The town was to pay $50 per year for candlepower for each street light, and provisions were included if additional lighting was necessary. A minimum charge of $1 per month to private consumers covered the first eight kilowatt hours. In excess of the minimum, the rate was not to exceed 12½ cents per kilowatt hour. These rates included all meter rent, service charges, and repairs for the equipment—unless the consumer damaged the property. For heating and power, the following rates were to be charged: for the first 100 KWH, 10¢ per KWH; the next 200 KWH, 7¢ per KWH; the next 200 KWH, 5¢ per KWH; over 500 KWH, 4¢ per KWH.

The new company was to maintain an office in New Richmond for the transaction of business, and for consumers to pay their bills, etc. The term of this franchise was to be 25 years.

In March 1914, fifteen workmen began the task of constructing an electric branch line from the Crawfordsville Electric light plant to Linden and New Richmond. A car-load of poles was unloaded at Cherry Grove, and another at Linden. On Saturday, July 18, the same year, the current was turned on in Linden. New Richmond received their current a month later.

The Montgomery County Light and Power line is shown on the 1917 map of the county. From the Crawfordsville electric light plant it follows the Chicago, Indiana, and Louisville railroad tracks (Monon) to Linden, then follows the Linden-New Richmond road to New Richmond, then runs along the Clover Leaf railroad out west of town, then shoots off to a southwesterly direction to the Bristle Ridge road to State Road 25, and into the town of Wingate.

Before electricity came to New Richmond, the streets were lighted by gas lights, and the town marshall's job was to light each lantern in the early evening, and snuff them out around midnight. Marshall Johnny Work was New Richmond's "old lamp lighter," and Forrest Waye said the young lads in town followed Johnny around on his evening chore snuffing out the lights as quickly as he lit them. Yes! There were problem children in the early days—even in New Richmond, the best little town on earth!

Montgomery Light and Power installed the "park system" of lighting the streets, and buried underground cables furnished the power. In 1924 the company met with the town trustees to discuss replacing the ten year old cables, and they were trying to decide who owned the electric lighting system, Montgomery Light and Power or the town of New Richmond. It was decided the town still retained shares in the electric company and was entitled to service from the power company. At this same meeting, the town clerk reported receiving a check for $5,875 for dividends from their fifty shares in the Montgomery Light and Power Company. This power company furnished electricity to the town of New Richmond until it was sold to the R.E.M.C.

Montgomery Light and Power Company had erected several sub-stations within the city limits of New Richmond. One was located north of the railroad on South Wabash Street, another on the Linden-New Richmond road just north of the railroad, and another on lot #13 of Kirkpatrick's 1st addition to New Richmond, still another on lot 5 of the original plat of the town.

Long after the town of New Richmond received its electrical current, the area farms were still lighting their homes with kerosene lamps, and lanterns were carried to the barn to do the evening chores, such as milking the cows or feeding the livestock. The more wealthy farmers installed gas lighting systems. Edgar L. Jones and his wife Jessie were "the Joneses" in this case, and were always up-to-date on all the latest gadgets. They installed an acetylene gas plant in their residence around 1904-5. A large tank was buried in the ground near their home, and was partially filled with water, then a one-hundred pound can of carbide was lowered into the tank and when the carbide was released into the water, gas was formed. Uncle Ed's home had pipes installed in the living room, dining room, and kitchen, and if I remember correctly, he also installed a gas lighting fixture on the front porch. These gas lights flickered quite a lot, as I recall, when we visited their home after dark. Charles Waye, my brother, often helped Uncle Ed refill the tank, and it was quite a chore by the time the whole process was completed.

A group of farmers living west of New Richmond had formed their own electric company and installed an electric system for their own use before the Montgomery Light and Power Company came to New Richmond. This company was known as the **Oppy-Bible Company**. The members were as follows: Frederick E. Bible, John N. Morris, Edward Oppy, Thomas F. Oppy, John M. Kirkpatrick, and Charles and William Graves.

They generated their own current and installed poles, transformers, and electrical wires to their farm houses. Incidentally, while Jeff Waye and Maurice Stribling were walking west of New Richmond on the railroad track one day, Jeff pointed to a fire on top of an electric pole. Maurice ran ahead because he was much younger than Jeff, and discovered a man was on fire. Maurice ran all the way back to New Richmond from the Oppy road to inform the fire department. When he and the department arrived, they found that John Kirkpatrick had been killed instantly, when he came in contact with a live wire on a transformer at his farm. He had climbed a pole in front of his home to place a new fuse in a transformer. His clothing was burned completely by the fire. This occurred in January of 1925. The Montgomery Light and Power Company made an agreement with the Oppy-Bible Company to furnish them electric current in December of 1919, previous to this tragic accident.

TipMont Rural Electric Membership Corporation (REMC)

The Tipmont Rural Electric Membership Corporation (REMC) was incorporated on May 10, 1939. Preliminary meetings were held by each township during the planning stages, and easements for power lines were to be secured by leaders in their townships, making this task more simplified for the REMC.

Installing electrical lines in the rural areas was the main priority of the REMC as those areas were neglected by the earlier electric companies. Records show the Tipmont REMC purchased the Montgomery Power and Light Company in 1948, and it was after this date the work in New Richmond and the neighboring towns was commenced. Forrest Waye, Richard Shotts, and Monroe Lyon were the trustees of the town of New Richmond at the time the REMC came to the town.

New Richmond's Telephone Companies

An early New Richmondite said in 1888, "Our village needs a telephone connection to the outside world!" So, they waited a few years!

Evan Shelby's Telephone System

The 1895 County Directory lists, "SHELBY TELEPHONE COMPANY, New Richmond, Evan Shelby, manager." Shelby's was the town's first telephone system. In June the same year, D.M. Plunkett was digging the holes for the New Richmond and Wingate telephone line. Plans were to have the line completed to Meharry's Campground by the Fourth of July and a phone placed in position near the stand. Shelby was still devoting much of his time a year later to his telephone business, but it is uncertain as to what became of this telephone company. There was no telephone company listed in New Richmond in the 1900-1 directory.

The Tippecanoe Telephone Company or Pyke System

Dr. Albert D. Pyke, a Romney physician, decided he needed better communication with his patients. He and a group of stockholders formed a telephone company in 1893 under the name of **The Tippecanoe Telephone Company**. The main headquarters and switchboard were in the doctor's office; his wife Elizabeth (Leaming) Pyke, whose father was Dr. Leaming of Romney, operated the switchboard. This telephone company soon branched out and was serving several of the neighboring villages. Members of the board of directors for the Tippecanoe Telephone Company, elected in August 1902, were: J.M. Waugh of Colfax; H.C. Shobe, Linden; M.P. Gladden, Stockwell; C.E. Campbell, Lafayette; and Dr. A.D. Pyke, Romney. The officers elected at this time were: H.C. Shobe, president; M.P. Gladden, vice president; C.E. Campbell, secretary; A.D. Pyke, treasurer and manager; John W. Coffey, superintendent.

The Tippecanoe Telephone Company placed the following advertisement in the New Richmond *Record*, September 12, 1901, "The Tippecanoe Telephone Company will put you in a long distance telephone for five cents a day, and give you FREE connections with sixteen towns and stations. Why not give your order today. John W. Coffey, Supt." This advertisement was the earliest record I have of the Tippecanoe Telephone Company in New Richmond, but the poles may have been set and the lines strung before this date. My father Forrest Waye said the lines of the Pyke telephone system were strung along the fence rows, the large poles (tall enough to clear the tops of the tall hay wagons) used only to cross the country roads.

When this telephone company was mentioned in the early newspapers, it was sometimes referred to as the Tippecanoe Telephone Company, but more often was referred to as the **Pyke Telephone System**. This proved to be very confusing to me in compiling the history of the town, for it appeared the town had three telephone companies operating during the same period of time. George W. Jones and his wife, Mary, were put in charge of the New Richmond switchboard in August 1902 and the office or station was located on east Washington Street. The superintendent, John Coffey, accepted a position with the Home Telephone Company in Crawfordsville in April 1903, moving to that city. A few months later, the Tippecanoe Telephone System updated their local central office, installed new cables, new 35 foot poles, and made other improvements to offer better service in order to compete with the new Co-operative telephone system.

Mrs. Mary Jones and daughter Harriett (or Hattie) were the switchboard operators from 1903 to June 1905, when they resigned in order to travel to the West Coast. Mrs. Oliver Terrell accepted the job as "central" of the Pyke system, but decided to remain on the farm with her son, Clell, until fall. Her husband and two daughters, Misses Jennie and Mattie, moved to New Richmond and the girls took charge of the "board."

The Lafayette *Journal*, September 27, and the New Richmond *Record*, October 5, 1905 announced, "Dr. A.D. Pyke Sells the Tippecanoe Telephone Company's Plant to the Bell Company. Possession Changes October First." This was considered one of the most important telephone deals in this section of Montgomery and Tippecanoe Counties when Dr. A.D. Pyke sold the Tippecanoe Telephone System to the Central Union Telephone Company (Bell) for $22,000. The deal gave the Bell Company possession of seven stations and switchboards operated as the Pyke System, and an estimated seven hundred miles of wire and several hundred telephones. The article said, "The Tippecanoe Telephone Company was born twelve years ago and placed switchboards in several of the small towns in this section until it had grown to seven stations. The initial station was in Romney, and the towns of New Richmond, Linden, Colfax, Clark's Hill, Kirkpatrick, and Stockwell were all in direct connection." Many of the towns mentioned had new independent telephone companies with new, up-to-date equipment, and were giving good commercial service. New Richmond was one of these, with the new Co-operative Telephone System just organized two years earlier.

There were no changes made on the Pyke system's telephone line until February the following year, when the local central office was notified there would be some private individual coming to personally superintend the operation of the New Richmond plant. In March 1906, George Chapman, the new owner and manager of the New Richmond exchange of the former Pyke System, arrived from Royal Center, Indiana, with his wife, four children, and their household goods. George assumed control of his new telephone system shortly after his arrival.

Competition of this phone company and the Co-operative Telephone Company began in earnest, both adding a large number of new patrons. They published the lists of their new subscribers in the local newspaper. The local businessmen often referred to Chapman's telephone company as the Pyke System in their advertisements after it changed hands. Many New Richmond citizens paid bills for service on both lines. George Chapman decided he couldn't compete with the new Co-operative company and sold his telephone system to John L. McNeil who was from Chapman's former neighborhood, Royal Center, in Cass County. He traded his phone company for a 120-acre farm in Cass County. McNeil, his wife, and their five children arrived in New Richmond and Mrs. Chapman and daughters left the same afternoon for their new farm. Mr. Chapman and son, George, drove their horses through country and the household goods were sent by rail. The value of the **Chapman (Pyke-Tippecanoe) Telephone Company** was placed at $4,000, and the consideration for the farm in the deal was $75 per acre. The deal was closed in May the same year.

Local businessmen continued to list the phone numbers as the Pyke System after McNeil assumed management—old habits are hard to break sometimes. Harriet Jones was listed as a telephone operator in the 1907-8 County Directory, but the company she worked for was not listed. She may have returned to the former Pyke system on a part-time basis. John McNeil's daughter, Elnora (now Nesbitt) said the McNeil phone company was in their home, the second home east of the New Richmond Christian Church. McNeil's son, Boyd O., was a lineman for his father's telephone company. The McNeil telephone system was modernized with the installation of a new Sterling Hundred-drop Switchboard equipped with all the modern appliances and a power generator. McNeil followed the previous owner's policy by publishing his new subscribers and their phone numbers in the local paper. This also served as a phone book for those wishing to "jot down" the numbers.

The New Richmond Telephone System

"TWO TELEPHONE SYSTEMS MERGED—McNeil and Co-operative Plants to Become THE NEW RICHMOND TELEPHONE SYSTEM". On August 5, 1909, the contracts were signed by the managers of the Co-operative Telephone Company and the McNeil Telephone plant, merging the two companies. Alice R. McNeil was named as the "present owner" of the McNeil Telephone Company, and John L. McNeil was president and manager. The McNeils renamed the company **The New Richmond Telephone System** at this time. The lines were all transferred to the McNeil system and he then had the telephone field all to himself, with a combined list of two hundred phones.

The New Richmond *Record*, August 12, 1909, said in part, "Telephones are no longer a luxury, but a necessity, and the NEW RICHMOND TELEPHONE SYSTEM is here to serve our people with that commodity. Our businessmen will gladly welcome the condition of one telephone system instead of paying for both phones as they have for several years. Mr. McNeil contemplates many changes in the equipment for the betterment of the telephone business, and service to patrons."

The company connected with Bell and Independent lines. J.L. and Alice McNeil's new telephone company had a list of nearly four hundred subscribers in October 1910. Alma Roark was listed as a telephone operator in 1912, and Mrs. Ruth Taylor and Miss Lela Hanawalt attended a telephone operators' school held in the Fowler Hotel in Lafayette in 1915 to prepare for a position in the local telephone office.

In July 1918, John L. and Alice McNeil leased the New Richmond Telephone Company for one year to Elmer Brown of Waynetown. Brown was to take possession on August first.

In 1927 the New Richmond Telephone System was sold to John Dixon of Lafayette. Dixon sold the company to Wesley Thomas in 1930. For the rest of the story, see Russell Miller's New Richmond-and Tri-County Telephone Companies.

Co-Operative Telephone Company

There was much talk around the first of February 1903 of a proposed local co-operative telephone system, and a meeting was called for February 9th to be held in Hollin's Hall. About one hundred farmers and businessmen attended the meeting and all seemed to be very interested in the new enterprise. Several representatives of the Linden and South Raub Co-operative Companies attended and explained the workings, the plans of organization, and the cost of construction and maintenance of their systems. The Linden Co-operative Telephone Company started May 12, 1902 with twelve members, and had forty-eight members at the time of the meeting, with an additional twelve waiting for phones. The cost was $16 for installation, membership, and with the phone "ready to talk." Subscribers paid fifty cents per month for service. No decisions were made, but a committee was appointed to do more research as to the practicability of a local co-operative system in New Richmond. Arrangements for another public meeting were made at this time.

The second meeting, held the same week and place, only resulted in appointing other committees to do more studies on the cost of construction, to solicit probable members, or stock-holders, and to draft by-laws for the new organization. The South Raub and Linden companies were so satisfied with their companies, however, that they gave the local residents the push they needed. The third meeting held March 17, 1903 in Hollin's Hall proved to be a very enthusiastic meeting. The **New Richmond Co-Operative Telephone Company** was formed and a board of directors met the day before to file the articles of incorporation. Share-holders of the New Richmond Co-Operative Telephone Company were paying in their stock a month later, and those who were slow in paying were asked to do so, in order to have funds available to order the building material.

The newly elected trustees of the town of New Richmond, namely A.D. Snyder, B.E. Page, and Perry McLain, passed an ordinance (ordinance number eighteen) granting permission to erect and maintain a telephone system in the incorporated town of New Richmond on May 5, 1903 to the New Richmond Co-Operative Telephone Company, etc., its principle place of business being New Richmond, etc., granting the right-of-way through, in, upon, and over the streets and alleys of said town, for the use and purpose and thereon to erect, maintain, and use the necessary poles, posts, wire, and other apparatus which is necessary to successfully operate and use in a general system of telephone. The town trustees were to have the right to direct or restrict the location of poles and wires, so as to prevent interference with travel on streets or the flow of water in the gutters. The telephone company was to maintain the system in order to ensure the safety of the residents of the town, and reserved the right to grant other companies the same privileges—providing they didn't interfere with the Co-operative's system. The right was granted for a twenty-five year period.

The first construction material for the new lines of the Co-operative Telephone Company arrived in town May 4, 1903. Work was to be started as soon as the poles arrived. By the end of May, a six mile stretch of poles were erected north of town, the main poles in town were put up, the poles to Linden and South Raub were up, the lines to connect with Linden would soon be up, the stringing of wires was to begin shortly, and a new "one-hundred drop switchboard" was daily expected to be placed in position. Everyone was anxiously awaiting for the opportunity to talk over the free lines of the connecting Co-operative telephone companies.

The Co-operative company's new Sweedish-American switchboard arrived the last of June and was installed by an electrician furnished by the Sweedish-American Telephone Company. It was a new metallic system and the subscribers who were connected were highly pleased with the service.

By June 25th the new telephone company was ready for day service only, until the new telephone operator, Mr. Biddle moved in. Cecil Biddle, his wife and child, and Mrs. Biddle's sister, Miss Lulu Claypool, moved from Waynetown the last of June 1903, to the exchange rooms of the New Richmond Co-Operative Telephone Company over Claypool and Fry's Store, located on the southeast corner of Wabash and Washington-in the Washburn building. Entry was made on South Wabash Street. The ladies were to have charge of the "Central" and Mr. Biddle was employed as a lineman for the company. The connection was completed with Linden on July 8th.

The New Richmond members were well satisfied with their new telephone system, and several members met with interested parties in Waynetown to assist in a new organization of a co-operative system in that city. New Richmond Co-Operative Telephone Company had thirty-nine telephones, two trunk lines and a dozen more ready to be connected by July 9. A month later, forty-nine phones were installed with more to follow. A direct connection from Linden to Crawfordsville was completed by August, and by the last of April, 1904, seventy-eight members were connected to the new telephone system. In October 1905, negotiations were underway to connect New Richmond's Co-Operative and the South Raub Co-Operative with the Lafayette Telephone Company. They were to be connected to the Lutz Telephone Company at Odell, as well. Connections were to be made by the last of November or early December.

New officers elected during the annual stockholder's meeting held in the New Richmond school house in January 1906 were: William Graves, president; J.A. Bailey, vice president; E.W. Harriman, secretary; Job Westfall, treasurer; and L.M. Tribby, superintendent. Members of the Board of Arbitration were: J.A. Bailey, A.J. Arnett, T.J. Grantham, J.T. Detchon, and F.M. Johnson. The Co-Operative exchange board was moved to the Bailey Cottage near the Black Bear Hotel in March 1906. Workmen were busy stringing wires to complete the move. There was no reason given for the necessity of the new location. Arlie Johnson was the Co-Operative telephone operator up to the first of November, 1906. He then resigned and moved to Linden where he accepted a position with the American Milling Company. Mrs. Fred A. Taylor accepted the job as "central" to replace him.

In 1907-8 William McCrea was the manager of the Co-Operative Telephone Company in New Richmond, and W.T. Bassett and his wife Dora were the switchboard operators. McCrea had other telephone interests in Attica, Greenfield, and Mulberry.

A.L. Clark, a former Methodist Episcopal Church Minister, purchased the New Richmond Co-Operative Telephone System on April 1, 1909 and planned to make New Richmond his permanent home, but in four short months he was tired of New Richmond — and the telephone business — and was ready to leave. In August 1909, the New Richmond Co-Operative Telephone System merged. John L. McNeil purchased the Co-Operative system from Clark, and the two combined companies became **The New Richmond Telephone System**.

New Richmond Telephone Company

Lee and Mildred Miller, along with Lee's brother Russell, purchased the New Richmond Telephone Company from Wesley Thomas in November 1932. Russell was to manage their new telephone company and arrived in Indiana on July 5, 1933. Also included in their purchase were the Linden and Romney Telephone systems (formerly the old Pyke or Tippecanoe Telephone Company). They operated under the old company names until February 3, 1958, when the Tri-County Telephone Company was founded by Russell Miller. Miller purchased his brother's interests and was the sole owner by 1960.

Tri-County Telephone Company, Inc.

The Tri-County Telephone Company, incorporated in January 1959, was a consolidation of the telephone systems Miller had purchased throughout the years, namely The Kirkpatrick Telephone Company, purchased in October 1934; Akers, or Wingate-Odell, in November 1946; and the old Pyke and Co-Operative systems, including the South Raub Company. The Wingate telephone company included service into Fountain County, thus the name **Tri-County** (Montgomery, Fountain, and Tippecanoe). In April 1971 Miller purchased the Colfax Telephone Company, which served exchanges at Stockwell, Thorntown, Darlington, Clark's Hill, Frankfort, and Linden rural routes near Colfax.

56 - Tri-County Telephone Company business office

The old crank style telephones were replaced with the dial phones—New Richmond's being among the first in 1956, Romney in February 1961, and the Wingate-Odell in April 1961. New Richmond's dial phones were obsolete and were replaced with the newer style in May 1961; Linden also received the new dial phones at the same time. Push-button or touch-tone phones were offered to Tri-County patrons in 1973. The Tri-County Telephone Company provides all the modern equipment as the new improvements are made available.

The New Richmond Telephone exchange was located at one time on North Wabash Street in the residence at the rear of the Long brick building. The office was moved to the second floor of the Washburn building—the original site of the New Richmond Co-Operative Telephone Company's switchboard office. Miller continued in this location until the Tri-County Telephone Company was well established. The headquarters and business office is now on East Washington Street in New Richmond, in the building formerly occupied by the Frozen Food Locker Plant. The building was remodeled and is now a beautiful office with very modern equipment.

Among the switchboard operators for the New Richmond and Tri-County Telephone companies were: Bertha Oswalt (15 years); Stella Bunnell; Ethelynn L. Blair (22 years) June Bailey; Wanda Nicoson; Georgia Myers (8 years).

Russell Miller completed fifty years in the telephone business in New Richmond in 1983. He now serves as Chairman of the Board, and his son Bennet R. Miller was elected President of the company in 1983, and is still serving in that capacity (as of 1985).

Cable Television

Tri-County Communications Corporation Cable Television (CATV)

The **Tri-County Communications Corporation**, a subsidiary of the Tri-County Telephone Company, Incorporated, announced the arrival of a new cable television system on September 1, 1981, for New Richmond and the surrounding viewing areas. Previous to this time every household in New Richmond relied upon the television antenna placed upon the roof-tops, or on a tower beside the homes, for reception, and could only receive stations in Lafayette and Indianapolis. For those who were not glued to the T.V. set all day long, this was no major in-convenience, and for this reason—and the burden of another monthly bill to pay—some were slow to hook up to the new system.

Construction of the new one hundred seventy foot tower, with about a dozen antennas and a five-meter dish to receive satellite signals, was done by a southern Indiana firm, the Newkirk Communications Company. Plans were to have the cables strung and ready to hook up to by January 1982, and program schedules were sent to the Tri-County Telephone customers with information on the cost of connecting to the cable and the projected monthly rates. About four hundred customers were anxiously awaiting the arrival of the new cable by December 1981, but the cable was not completed until late spring or early summer of 1982.

Ben R. Miller is the president and business manager of the Tri-County Communications Corporation (as of 1986).

New Richmond Water Works

Completed June 9, 1941
(Photo by Cindy Boone)

New Richmond's Water Supply

The pioneers of New Richmond secured their water for drinking and other needs from the nearby springs or the brooklet which flows just north of town. This stream has been tiled, but there is still a very wet area indicating the spring or supply of water is active. There were many cases of ague in the early years, and the open running water used for drinking was thought to have been impure. This created a need for what was known as dug wells. Residents in the area did not have to dig very deeply before reaching a good supply of drinking water. These wells were usually left open and a bucket or other type of container was lowered into the well to be filled with the pure cold water.

In the 1870s wells were being driven to reach deeper into the ground for more pure water. Wind pumps were erected when larger amounts were needed to water livestock, but the residents drew their water supply with the old wooden style hand pump, and still later the iron pumps. New Richmond's first town drinking water supply may have been that of William Campbell's when he erected a wind pump in front of his Pioneer Store in August 1886. Livestock was driven through the little village, and to attract business, Bill notified the public he would have a good supply of cold drinking water available. This was very important to the cattlemen driving their stock to the markets; the early maps of Montgomery County showed the location of springs and ponds. One Tippecanoe County map listed the springs, ponds, wind pumps, and even included a cider mill location.

Early well diggers in New Richmond were John Foster in 1889, and W.D. Walker in 1891. A well was driven and a town pump was installed on the corner beside the Long Brothers' brick building sometime before July 1901, when A.D. Snyder placed a gasoline engine to pump water onto the streets in order to lay the dust. The Crawfordsville *Star* informed the public of New Richmond's "new Water works." A new electric pump was installed in September 1930 by William Warrick for this well, but a gasoline auxiliary engine was on hand in case of electrical failure. The reason for the pumps was to have an ample supply of water to fight fires in the business district.

New Richmond Water Works

The safety of many small villages' drinking water in Indiana was in question again in the 1930s because of the annual cases of typhoid, scarlet fever, and other illnesses. The State Board of Health made an effort to correct the problem by requesting the town officials to install deep well water systems.

The trustees of the town of New Richmond made plans to have an election in regards to a proposed water works system, and a resolution was drawn showing the need for the system, which was to be owned, operated, maintained, and managed by the town. The date for the election was set for May 20, 1939.

A complete pressure system for domestic and public use was to pump the water from deep wells to be piped to all parts of the town. Fire hydrants and connections with the pressure tank were to be erected and installed. The estimated cost of the new system was $22,402. Town board members were Charles M. Fruits (president), Clyde A. Thomas, and Earl L. Warren. Delmer K. Fruits was the Clerk-Treasurer at the time. On May 27 that year, the trustees met in the local depot to accept bids for the proposed water system. On June 10, the bids were opened, but no decisions were made until five days later, when bids were granted as follows—in accordance with plans and specifications:

Tower and tank - Pittsburg Des Moines Steel Co., Pittsburg, Pa.
Metne Box Covers, copper pipe, fittings, tapping machine - Mueller Co., Decatur, IL
Hydrants, valves, boxes - Rensselaer Valve Co., Chicago, IL
Pump - Central Rubber and Supply Co., Indianapolis, IN
Meters - Badger Meter Mfg. Co., Milwaukee, WI
Locks -Badger Meter Mfg. Co
Well - Roy A. Holt, Darlington, IN
Pipe - Central Foundry Co., Chicago, IL.

The trustees of the town accepted the proposal of Stifel & Nicolaus & Co., Inc. of Chicago to sell bonds to finance the construction of the New Richmond Water Works in July 1939. A month later the town purchased lot number eighteen of Charles Kirkpatrick's second addition to the town from M.J. Roth, for the water well and tower. In September the trustees advertised for bids for private construction, and the contract was awarded to H.N. Booe. Construction was to begin within ten days. The well was driven and a bill of $490 was presented to the board, who reminded the contractor he would be paid when the bonds were sold. There was a delay in the sale of the bonds and this stopped the project until the problem was settled.

A representative of the W.P.A. Office, Mr. Chelf of Lafayette, attended a meeting with the local town board in January 1940, and explained the possibility of building the water works system as a W.P.A. project. The board decided to go along with the W.P.A. plan and Mr. Chelf promised speedy action on their part.

H.Y. Dugan of Doyle O'Connor & Co. of Chicago and Kern G. Beasley, the attorney of the company, of Linton, Indiana, met with the town board to discuss the purchase of the remaining bonds for the water works. Dugan offered to buy the outstanding bonds if the transcript was properly drawn up. Beasley was to draw up the transcript for a fee of $150, when and if O'Connor & Co. purchased the bonds. There were many delays concerning the bond sales and the "properly worded transcript." Mr. Beasley, the attorney for the O'Connor Company, sent his transcript to the firm of Chapman and Cutler of Chicago for approval, who refused to acknowledge the document and said it would be necessary to start from the beginning of the proceedings—new petition, another election, and an entirely new transcript. Beasley offered to prepare the new proceedings and a new transcript for a flat guarantee of $500, and consider the original agreement ended (later records show he settled for $300).

A new petition for the building of the New Richmond Water Works was signed by thirty-five citizens and voters and presented to the town board in May 1940. Another special election was called for June 4, 1940 to determine whether the board should proceed with the building of the water works. A month later, a Mr. Wiest of Warsaw, and Mr. Caldwell of Claypool, Indiana, met with the local trustees and proposed to immediately purchase $9,000 of the bonds and to take the remaining issue within the next thirty days, which the board unanimously agreed. The W.P.A. director, Mr. J.M. Chelf, was contacted and steps were taken to begin construction of the New Richmond Water Works. The Pittsburg - Des Moines Steel Company was asked to send plans and specifications for the footings and foundation of the tower. The board decided to purchase a Peerless Pump from the Cook Pump Mfg. Co. of Lawrenceburg, Indiana, and asked the Central Rubber and Supply Co. to return the check and release them from their contract.

The main water lines were nearly completed, and the local citizens were informed the town would pay the rate of eight cents per lineal foot for digging and refilling the trench to the customer's residences. The trench was to be forty-eight inches deep at the water end, and slope to not less than forty inches at the foundations, was to be eighteen inches wide at the top and not less than twelve inches at the bottom. The board agreed to furnish three-fourths inch galvanized pipe to the customers at eight cents per lineal foot, if desired.

57 - New Richmond water tower

The Pittsburg Des Moines Steel company had not delivered the water tank and tower by January 1941, and the board asked the company to deliver it at once. The representative of the company agreed to paint the outfit aluminum instead of black, for $100 above the contract price. The tank was not delivered by March, and the Clerk-Treasurer was to wire the company concerning the delay. By May 19 the tower and tank had been erected, the pump house was ready to be painted, and grass seed was to be sown on the grounds surrounding the water system. Considerable time was spent making settlement for the service trenches. Mr. Chelf, the area engineer for the W.P.A., met to discuss the completion of the water system, and made a proposal to improve the streets. By June 1941, Mr. Chelf notified the board that the street and alley improvement project was approved by the state, and the W.P.A. was ready to begin.

The town board drafted a letter on June 9, 1941 to notify the patrons of the **New Richmond Water System** that the system was completed, was approved by the State Board of Health, and was ready for use. Customers were to make a meter deposit of $1 to be held in trust as a guarantee of payment of the water bill, which was due upon receipt of the letter, and was to be paid to the town's Clerk-Treasurer. The patrons who were supplied with pipe, fittings and other materials, were to pay for them at the same time. The trustees of the town of New Richmond at the time of completion were Carl Burnett, president; Charles Taylor; and Sheridan Geiger; the Clerk-Treasurer was Lester W. Olin.

Officials of the Nickel-Plate railroad made arrangements with the town to purchase water for their steam engines and a tower was erected; the remains of the foundation can be seen from the local park.

Jesse D. Hinman was appointed New Richmond's first Water Superintendent, along with his other duties as Marshal and Street Commissioner, for which he was paid $20 monthly.

The local water system was neglected throughout the years, the meters being in such disrepair they were not even read for many years. In 1962, the town trustees Ivan Pollock, James Wright, and William Kendall, and Malcolm Waye, the Clerk-Treasurer and Water Superintendent, made plans to repair the system. A new well was driven at a cost of $1,335, meters were rebuilt for $4,456, a new pump and fittings were installed at $2,942, the pump house was enlarged and a new furnace was installed at $978. After making the improvements, the income from the users of the water works increased, and by 1970 the system was debt free. The water rates were among the lowest in the state with a minimum of $1.50 for 2,000 gallons.

In 1978 the town board asked the Public Service Commission of Indiana for an increase in water rates due to the added expenses for repairs amounting to $7,900. The proposed rate of minimum monthly charge was raised to $3.38. There were 162 customers on the water system at the time. Due to inflation and a $3,000 repair to the water tank, another rate hike was required in September 1981. The proposed minimum monthly charge was to be raised to $6.26, but was lowered a few cents. Another rate hike was asked for in January and April 1982, but was not granted by the Public Service Commission. In September 1983, the trustees of the town met with the attorney for the Indiana Association of Cities and Towns concerning a proposal of taking the New Richmond Water System out of the jurisdiction of the Public Service Commission in order to set or regulate the rates in a less expensive and less complicated manner. A year later, the power of operating the water system was given back to the trustees of the town of New Richmond, as the original plan stated at the time of construction in the late 1930s.

Chapter 23 - Hollywood Comes to "Hickory, IN"

It would be impossible to write a history of New Richmond, Indiana, without mentioning the filming of the movie *Hoosiers*. In 1985 New Richmond was chosen as one of the locations for the film which starred Gene Hackman, Barbara Hershey, Sheb Wooley, Dennis Hopper, Fern Persons, and many local basketball players and extras who came from various Indiana towns, including New Richmond. Many of the town scenes were filmed in New Richmond including those in the barber shop, restaurant, hardware, feed store, and other various street scenes. Other local scenes were filmed at a house and barn south of town.

The September 9, 1985 Decatur *Daily Democrat* described the *Hoosiers* film as being "about a small town Indiana high school basketball team, which wins a state championship in the 1950s, using the "Miracle of Milan" as a base for a fictional story." The Milan team played Muncie Central in the state championship in 1954. The basketball scenes were shot in the Butler University Hinkle Fieldhouse in Indianapolis, IN, during the first week of December. Home game scenes were shot in the Knightstown school gym. The interior of a school was filmed in Ninevah.

Angelo Pizzo, a Bloomington native, wrote the movie script and his friend David Anspaugh, a native of Decatur, IN, was the director of the movie. Carter DeHaven, born in Los Angeles, was a co-producer.

The Indianapolis *Star*, September 5, 1985 stated that "Producers of...*Hoosiers* confirmed that their short list for a location includes Nineveh in Johnson County, Knightstown in southwestern Henry County, and Linden and New Richmond, both in northern Montgomery County." They go on to say that "About 80 communities have been in the competition to be the main filming location, according to the movie makers."

An article entitled "Linden, New Richmond are hoping to go to the movies", in the Crawfordsville *Journal Review*, September 5, 1985, states that "the crews are also looking to New Richmond for scenery shots. The rustic buildings of New Richmond, including the museum, are a bit more authentic looking than those located at Linden. Martha Swick of New Richmond said men from Hollywood were in town Saturday taking photos of the buildings and asking questions about the community."

In a Lafayette *Journal and Courier* article from September 8 of that year, Martha Swick said that "I've lived here all my life. I think it's the biggest thing to hit New Richmond." The *Journal Review* article of September 7 added, "New Richmond was selected because of its authenticity....the store fronts would be altered to represent a barber shop, drugstore, hardware, feed, seed and grain company, and so forth."

In a September 11 article in the *Journal Review*, Production Designer David Nichols of Hemdale Films of Los Angeles discussed his impressions of New Richmond. The article wrote, "Notice how the downtown area is relatively free of wires? He also mentioned there were not too many street lights if temporary ones need to be installed. He was impressed with the spaciousness of the downtown area where plenty of sky can still be seen. He also said traffic control should not be too difficult since no major highway runs through the town."

Rick Schmidlin, location manager for Hemdale Film Corp., Los Angeles, said "the downtown will remain about the same. The museum will take on the look of a hardware. The building just north of the town hall will have the face of a drugstore. The restaurant will get a new sign and could have its front extended, but Alexander's Furniture Store should see little change. Present plans are to turn the vacant hardware store into a feed, seed and grain company, perhaps with a loading dock on its east side. The old fire station will be used for that purpose in the movie. Across the street, Byron Alexander's old barbershop will once again echo the snip of scissors, but other buildings should see little change."

Town board meetings were called to discuss positive and negative aspects of having a film crew and hundreds of visitors in town. Safety and security of homes and businesses in town was discussed as well as community development and tourism and movie souvenirs. Residents had questions at the board meetings about child protection, potential traffic and parking problems, insurance liability, and restroom facilities. Later meetings discussed local extras needed for the movie and potential earnings for speaking and non-speaking parts.

The *Journal and Courier* of September 29 said that "While the doors to the New Richmond Town Hall were to open at 9 a.m., people began lining up between 7 a.m. and 7:30 a.m.," according to Linda Layton, owner of Layton's Restaurant. The article continued, "Extras with speaking lines can earn $361 a day. Those without speaking lines will be paid minimum wage."

Filming in New Richmond began on Friday October 18 and ran for about seven weeks. Many of the filming days were overcast and gloomy that fall which gave a soft light to the film. The town shop fronts were painted, the post office sign was changed from New Richmond to Hickory. Other signs were added for various businesses. A track for the film cameras had to be constructed. In one case, a freshly-painted building looked too new for the setting, so the movie crew sprayed mud on the exterior to age it.

"This is *the* town in the movie," says Ken Carlson, casting director, between sizing up the extras. "It is very pretty and isolated and it just has this wonderful feeling, the people here have been very cooperative." Source Indianapolis Star, Sept 29, 1985

In October, the town of New Richmond started to change, props like barber chairs, were unloaded and drapes made for a dress shop. "Sign painters altered several signs on business fronts at New Richmond Monday. There is now a Hickory Post Office and a Hickory Town Hall with a Hooks drugstore beside it," said the *Journal Review* of October 8, 1985.

On October 18, the *Journal Review* reported, "The very first field of footage for the movie "Hoosiers" was shot today in New Richmond. Popping over a knoll just north of New Richmond was the 1951 Chevy coupe which brought the new coach, Gene Hackman, into the town of Hickory for the first time."

"The Hemdale Film Co. moved its equipment to a farm site in the Liberty Chapel neighborhood near New Richmond Wednesday evening. They spent Thursday filming Thanksgiving scenes..." the *Journal Review* reported on October 25. "Thursday morning's filming included a scene in the barn, which smelled of freshly baled straw. The star was pictured lying on the bales of straw reading a book as rays of bright sunshine filtered through the open window. In one segment, the camera shoots over a field of drying corn stalks and focuses on the reverend's car as it passes Liberty Chapel Church and heads toward the farm."

The film crew went on to other sites after filming in New Richmond which included Knightstown, Nineveh, Brownsburg, Lebanon, Terhune, Danville, and Elizaville. They returned in the first week of December to shoot final scenes including the pep rally parade and barbershop scenes.

"Even though only five days of the seven week production schedule called for filming in New Richmond, the town received more publicity than most of the other "Hoosiers" sites in the state." Electric Consumer, Dec 1985, Rural Electric Pub Vol. 35, no. 6, State star-struck: On location with 'Hoosiers".

For a more in-depth look at the movie, I recommend reading a wonderful book by Gayle L. Johnson called *The Making of Hoosiers: How a Small Movie from the Heartland Became One of America's Favorite Films*, published in May 2010.

58: Clockwise from top left: Filming a New Richmond street scene; filming Gene Hackman driving; filming a victory scene with the Huskers team bus; Gene Hackman on the first day of filming in New Richmond.

Sources

Beckwith, H.W. *History of Montgomery County, Indiana, Together With Historic Notes on the Wabash Valley, Gleaned from Early Authors, Old Maps and Manuscripts, Private and Official Correspondence, and Other Authentic, Though, For the Most Part, Out-of-the-Way Sources.* Chicago: H.H. Hill and N. Iddings, Publishers, 1881.

Chapter 1 – Historical setting

Natural Wealth of New Richmond and Coal Creek Township

Original plat book of Coal Creek Township, Mar. 22, 1822, Recorder's Office, Montgomery County, Indiana
Crawfordsville Saturday Evening *Journal*, May 7, 1881 to May 4, 1887
Crawfordsville Weekly *Review*, Apr. 16, 1887 to Aug. 17, 1895
Crawfordsville Daily Argus News, May 29, 1888
New Richmond *Record*, Dec. 14, 1916
Crawfordsville *Journal-Review*, May 7, 1968
Star State Report, May 9, 1968
Author's notes and personal observation
Stories told by Forrest Waye, author's late father

Our Early Inhabitants

History of Montgomery County Indiana, 1881, by Beckwith, p. 526, Franklin Township; p. 435, Madison Township
Crawfordsville *Star*, Oct. 21, 1892, p. 1 c. 2 "Found an 'Injun' Cemetery"
Crawfordsville *Review* Weekly, Oct. 29, 1892, p. 1 c. 4 "The Gravel Pit Grave Yard"
Crawfordsville *Review* Weekly, Oct. 29, 1892, p. 6, c. 2 and Sept. 8, 1894, p. 1 c. 3; May 3, 1890, p. 4, New Richmond items
Crawfordsville *Journal-Review*, Aug. 21, 1964, "Ancient Skeletons Found in County May Be of Indians," Lois Irwin
Crawfordsville *Journal*, Oct. 9, 1903, p. 1, "The Mound Builders"
New Richmond *Record*, Oct. 22, 1903, p. 1
New Richmond *Record*, Apr. 14, 1904, p. 1, c. 5 and 6

Samuel Kincaid "Father" of New Richmond

Evans and Stivers, History of Adams County Ohio, 1900, pp. 332, 472
Adams County, Ohio marriage records, V.1, p. 67
Beckwith, History of Montgomery County Indiana, 1881, p. 117
Original Entries Montgomery County Indiana, Recorder's Office, Deeds
Probate Records of Hamilton County Indiana, Vol. B, pp. 384-385
Frances Kincaid Buss, Modesto, California, Thomas Kincaid's family
Sharon Lovell Gengen, Grand Island, Nebraska, Catherine Kincaid's family
Federal Census Records
Ohio Tax lists
Adams County Ohio Deed Records
Hamilton County, Indiana Deed Records

New Richmond's Pioneer Families

The Campbell Clan:
History of Montgomery County, Indiana, Together With Historic Notes on the Wabash Valley, Gleaned from Early Authors, Old Maps and Manuscripts, Private and Official Correspondence, and Other Authentic, Though, For the Most Part, Out-of-the-Way Sources, H.W. Beckwith, 1881, p. 505
Montgomery County Marriage Records, Crawfordsville Public Library
New Richmond Cemetery, tombstone inscriptions
Montgomery County Death Records, Crawfordsville Public Library
Federal Census Records, Microfilm, Crawfordsville Public Library

The Ebrite Family:
History of Montgomery County, Indiana, Beckwith, 1881, p. 510
Ebrite Family Bible, Birth, Marriage and Death Records
Adams County Ohio, Marriage Records
New Richmond Cemetery, tombstone inscriptions
Federal Census Records, Crawfordsville Public Library

The McComas Family:
Federal Census Records, Crawfordsville Public Library
Marriage Records of Montgomery County, Indiana, Crawfordsville Public Library
Death Records of Montgomery County, Indiana, Crawfordsville Public Library

Starr Dunn:
Taped interview with Ethel "Dunny" (Dun) Sparks of Lafayette, Indiana
Crawfordsville *Review* (weekly), July 16, 1898, p. 1, c. 5
New Richmond *Record*, Mar., 3, 1904, Mar. 15, 1906, Aug. 30, 1923 (items from *Record* 25 yrs. ago)

Chapter 2 – Buildings in New Richmond

Frame Buildings – Most of them Now Gone

Crawfordsville Weekly *Review*, Feb. 26, 1887, p. 1; Mar. 2, 1889; Mar. 13, 1886; July 16, 1898 (Big Fire in New Richmond, July 12, 1898); Aug. 27, 1887; Feb. __, 1888; Apr. 11, 1891
Crawfordsville *Journal*, Weekly, Feb. 1, 1879; May 17, 1883
New Richmond *Enterprise*, May 28, 1897
New Richmond *Record*, Oct. 9, 1902; Jan. 29, 1903, Sept. 10, 1903, Aug. 30, 1923 (items 25 years old)
Reminiscences of Forrest Way, an early resident of New Richmond
Reminiscences of Opal Clapp, a native of New Richmond

Brick Buildings in New Richmond

New Richmond *Record*, July 30, 1902; Oct. 9, 1902; Aug. 30, 1923 (items 25 years old); Mar. 17, 1904; Sept. 25, 1902; Oct. 20, 1910
Crawfordsville Weekly *Review*, July 5, 1890; Dec. 20, 1890; July 16, 1898, p. 1 c. 5
Crawfordsville *Star*, Weekly, May 2, 1895
Records of the Town Trustees, New Richmond, Indiana

Longs Dry Goods, Jewelry and Wall Paper Store

Emerson's City Directory, Crawfordsville, Indiana, A Gazetteer of Montgomery County, 1891-1892
Crawfordsville *Review* (weekly), Feb. 20, 1886; Mar. 13, 1886, and May 14, 1887
Crawfordsville *Journal* (daily), Mar. 6, 1891, p. 3 c. 2; Dec. 27, 1916, p. 1 c. 3
New Richmond *Enterprise*, Oct. 6, 1899

New Richmond *Record*, Nov. 29, 1900; Dec. 26, 1901; Mar. 19, June 3, July 9, Oct. 29, Nov. 12, 1903; Jan. 7, Mar. 17, Apr. 24, July 14, 1905; June 15, 1906, Aug. 27, 1908, Aug. 14, 1919, July 1, 1920; Apr. 5, 1923.
Tombstone inscriptions, New Richmond Cemetery

CHAPTER 3 – FOOD BUSINESSES IN NEW RICHMOND

GENERAL STORES, THE PIONEER STORE, WILLIAM CAMPBELL, PROPRIETOR

Crawfordsville Weekly *Review*, Saturday, Feb. 14, July 31, 1886, Feb. 26, July 2, and July 16, 1887; Mar. 31, Dec. 22, 1888; Mar. 2, Mar. 30, Aug. 24, Oct. 19, and Dec. 21, 1889; Jan. 10, Jan. 24, Apr. 11, Apr. 18, Apr. 24, 1891.
Crawfordsville *News-Review* (Weekly), July 2, 1901
History of Montgomery County, Indiana, Beckwith, 1881, p. 506
Directories of Montgomery County, Indiana, 1882-3; 1884-5; 1887

GENERAL STORES

Crawfordsville Weekly *Review*, June 7, 1879, p. 1 c. 3; Mar. 13, 1886; Feb. 26, 1887, p. 1 c. 8; Dec. 14, 1889; Apr. 18 and May 2, 1891; Jan. 4, 11, and 25, Apr. 4, 1896; July 16, 1898, Apr. 6, 1900
Crawfordsville Saturday Evening *Journal*, Dec. 6, 1879
Crawfordsville *Star*, Oct. 23, 1891
New Richmond *Record*, Dec. 26, 1901; Apr. 10, May 22, June 5, and Oct. 9, 1902; Apr. 9, Apr. 16, Aug. 18 and 28, Sept. 3, Oct. 15, 20 and 29, Nov. 5, Dec. 10 and 17, 1903; Mar. 3, May 19, June 2, and 30, Aug. 18, Sept. 15, Oct. 20, Dec. 1, 1904; Jan. 5, Mar. 9, May 25, Oct. 12 and 19, Nov. 2 and 23, 1905; Mar. 15, June 14, and 28, July 26, Sept. 13 and 27, Oct. 6, Nov. 1 and Dec. 6, 1906; Aug. 27, Sept. 24, 1908; Mar. 25, Aug. 12, 1909; Feb. 24, Oct. 20 and 27, 1910, Nov. 25, 1915; June 15, 1916; Aug. 14, 1919, Apr. 5, 1923.
Kole Kreke Kamera, 1910, New Richmond High School Annual
Federal Census Records, 1830-1880
Tombstone inscriptions, New Richmond Cemetery
Montgomery County Deeds, Vol. 52, p. 67
Directories of Montgomery County Indiana, 1882-3; 1887; 1891-2; 1900

DRY GOODS MERCHANTS

Montgomery County Indiana Atlas, 1878
Crawfordsville Weekly *Review*, Feb. 20, 1886
Crawfordsville *Star*, Mar. 20, 1898 (Sunday)
Crawfordsville Saturday Evening *Journal*, July 15, 1898, p. 3 c. 6
New Richmond *Record*, June 3, 1915, July 6, 1922
New Richmond Methodist Church Cook Book, 1912
N.R.H.S. - 1915 New Richmond High School Annual

NEW RICHMOND GROCERS

The Jungle - 1923; *Kole Kreke Kamera* - 1910; *The Cardinal* - 1943, New Richmond High School Annuals
New Richmond class plays (advertisements)
Federal Census Records, 1850, 1860, 1870, 1880
Crawfordsville Weekly *Review*, May 2, 1891; Jan. 26, 1896
Crawfordsville *Journal*, Jan. 31, 1880
Farmer's Review, weekly newspaper printed in New Richmond, Indiana, Sept. 20, Oct. 11, 1935; Aug. 13, 1937
Montgomery County Directories, 1900-1; 1903; 1907-8
New Richmond *Record*, Mar. 13, May 22, Sept. 25, Dec. 4, Dec. 11, Dec. 18, 1902; Jan. 8 and 22, Feb. 19, Apr. 16, Sept. 10, Oct. 15, Nov. 26, 1903; Mar. 17, 21, May 12, June 2 and 30, Oct. 6, Dec. 22, 1904; Apr.

13, May 4, June 1, Nov. 25, Dec. 28, 1905; Feb. 1, June 14, 1906; Jan. 3, 1907; June 22, 1916; Aug. 14, 1919; July 1, 1920, July 6, 1922.

MEAT MARKETS AND BUTCHERS

Crawfordsville *Review*, Jan. 22, 1887; Mar. 10, Apr. 7, May 19, June 2, Sept. 29, 1888; Aug. 24, Dec. 21, 1889; Feb. 20, 1892

New Richmond *Record*, Apr. 10, June 5, Dec. 25, 1902; Aug. 27, Sept. 24, Nov. 19, Dec. 10, Dec. 24, 1903; Jan. 7, Mar. 17, 1904; Aug. 27, 1908; July 1, 1920; July 6, 1922; Apr. 5, 1923

The Jungle – 1923, New Richmond High School Annual

Interviews with Louis Long, 1985; Richard Shots, 1984, Forrest Way, 1965, and Cecil Austin, 1985

Montgomery County Directories: 1890; 1891-2; 1895; 1900-1; 1907-8; 1912

THE BAKERY BUSINESS IN NEW RICHMOND

Miscellaneous Records of Montgomery County, Indiana, Vol. 9 p. 152

Montgomery County Directories: 1903, 1907-8

Crawfordsville *Review* (weekly newspaper published in Crawfordsville, Indiana

New Richmond *Enterprise* (weekly newspaper printed in New Richmond, Indiana)

New Richmond *Record* (weekly newspaper printed in New Richmond, Indiana)

DRUG STORES AND DRUGGISTS

Crawfordsville Saturday Evening *Journal*, Feb. 1, 1879; Jan. 10 and 31, 1880; May 17, 1883

Crawfordsville Weekly *Review*, Apr. 11, 1891

Crawfordsville *Star*, Oct. 30, 1891; Jan. 5, 1894

New Richmond *Enterprise*, May 28, 1897

New Richmond *Record*, Dec. 26, 1901; Apr. 24, 1902, July 31, 1902; May 28, 1903, July 23, 1903; Jan. 29, 1903; Apr. 7 and July 28, 1904; Nov. 9, 1905; Jan. 18, Apr. 5 and June 14 (through Aug. 9) 1906; Sept. 24, 1908; Mar. 25, Apr. 15, 1909; Nov. 17, 1921; Apr. 5, 1923; Aug. 30, 1923

Linden Observer (Historical Edition – not dated)

Interviews with the late Opal Clapp, Forrest Waye, Reuben Swank, and Byron Alexander

Farmer's *Review*, Sept. 20, 1935

New Richmond Town Board minutes, May 6, 1930 meeting

The Jungle – 1923, New Richmond High School Annual

New Richmond High School class plays (advertisements), Apr. 6 and Oct. 28, 1948; Oct. 21, 1949

3rd Annual Horse Show sponsored by the local Lion's Club – 1947

New Richmond Telephone Company directories

Tri-County Telephone Directories

The Chronicle – 1954, Coal Creek Central High School Annual

CHAPTER 4 – CLOTHING AND BEAUTY SERVICES

CLOTHING STORES

New Richmond *Enterprise*, Oct. 6, 1899

New Richmond *Record*, Sept. 25, 1902; Feb. 19, July 9, 1903; Mar. 9 and 16, Dec. 7 and 14, 1905; Mar. 8, 1906; Aug. 27, Sept. 24 and 26, 1908

Messenger Crier, May 16 and Nov. 14, 1978

Tri-County Telephone Directory, 1980, 1982 (advertisements)

MILLINERS AND THEIR TRIMMERS

Montgomery County Directories: 1891-2; 1895-, 1900-01, 1903, 1912

Crawfordsville *Review*, June 2, 1897

New Richmond *Enterprise*, Oct. 6, 1899

New Richmond *Record*, Nov. 29, 1900; Sept. 12, 1901; Mar. 13, June 5, and Oct. 30, 1902; Mar. 19, Apr. 9, Sept. 10, Oct. 1, Dec. 3, 1903; Mar. 17, Apr. 7, June 9, June 16, Oct. 13, Sept. 22, Dec. 8, 1904; March 9, April 13, Oct. 12, Nov. 23, 1905; Mar. 29, May 3, 1906; Apr. 15, and August 12, 1909; Feb. 24, 1910.

Shoe Makers and Shoe Stores

Federal Census, Coal Creek Township, Montgomery County, Indiana, 1850

Montgomery County Directories, 1882-3; 1891-2; 1895

Crawfordsville Weekly *Review*, Sept. 4, Nov. 27, 1886; July 2, 30, 1887; July 7, Dec. 1, 1888; Feb. 16, 1889; Dec. 20, 1890; Apr. 11, 1891

New Richmond *Record*, Nov. 29, 1900; Apr. 7, 1904; Jan. 19, 1905; Oct. 27, 1910; May 13, Nov. 25, 1915; Nov. 17, 1921

Kole Kreke Kamera - 1910, New Richmond High School Annual

N.R.H.S. – 1915, New Richmond High School Annual

N.R.H.S. – *Student*, March 1931, New Richmond High School Newspaper

Beauty Salons

Tri-County Telephone Directories

New Richmond Water Subscribers List

New Richmond High School Plays, 1939, 1940, 1949

Coal Creek Central Bearcats, Basketball programs, 1964, 1965, 1970, 1971

Tonsorial Artists Invade the Town

Crawfordsville Weekly *Review*, Crawfordsville, Indiana

Montgomery County *Gazetteers*, 1882 to 1887

Montgomery County Directories, 1890, 1891-92, 1903, 1907-8, 1912

New Richmond *Record*, a weekly newspaper published in New Richmond

New Richmond *Times*, a weekly newspaper published in New Richmond

Farmer's Review, published in New Richmond, Indiana

N.R.H.S. Annual, *Kole Kreke Kamera*, 1910

N.R.H.S. Annual, 1911

Letter from Herbert A. Lester, his memories of New Richmond

N.R.H.S. Junior and Senior Class Plays, advertisement sections

Robinson's Directory of Montgomery County, Indiana, 1963

Chapter 5 – Hospitality & Entertainment Businesses

New Richmond Saloons

Crawfordsville Weekly *Review*, Nov. 27, 1886; Feb. 26, July 2, 1887; July 25, 1891; Aug. 5, 1893; Feb. 23, 1895

Crawfordsville Saturday Evening *Journal*, June 7, 1879; Apr. 16, 1904

New Richmond High School Class plays, 1939 to 1949

New Richmond *Record*, Mar. 13, April 10 and Dec. 4, 1902; Feb. 19, Apr. 2, Dec. 10 and 17, 1903; Mar. 17, and 24, Apr. 7, May 12, June 9, July 7 and 14, 1904; Feb. 9 and 16, Mar. 2, May 10, June 8 and 15, Aug. 8 and 17, Sept. 21, 1905; Jan. 11, Mar. 1 and 8, May 3, Oct. 18, 1906

Bearcats Basketball schedules, Coal Creek Central School

Montgomery County Directories, 1882-3; 1884-5; 1887; 1890; 1900-01; 1912; 1963; 1975

Crawfordsville Journal *Review*, Jan. 12 and Dec. 10, 1974; Nov. 20, 1985

Messenger Crier, May 16, 1978; Oct. 3, 1984

Tri-County Telephone Directories

Lion's Club Horse Show, Program, Third Annual, 1947

Temperance Causes

History of Montgomery County, Indiana, Beckwith, 1881, pp. 25, 486
Crawfordsville Weekly *Review*, Mar. 4, Aug. 5, 1893
New Richmond *Enterprise*, May 28, 1897
New Richmond *Record*, Apr. 28, June 30, July 21, Aug. 28, Sept. 22, and Dec. 1, 1904; June 29; 1905; May 10, Oct. 25, Dec. 6, 1906; Mar. 29, Aug. 12, 1909

Hotels, Hostels, and Boarding Houses

History of Montgomery County, Indiana, Beckwith, 1881, page 122
Montgomery County Directories, 1882-3; 1907-8
New Richmond *Record*, Mar. 17, Apr. 14, June 9, July 14, Aug. 18, Sept. 1, 15 and 22, Nov. 17 and Dec. 1, 1904, Apr. 27, 1905; Sept. 13, 1906; Oct. 4 and 25, 1906
Crawfordsville Saturday Evening *Journal*, July 23, 1880; May 8 and July 17, 1886; Jan. 7, 1888, Mar. 21, 1891; July 18, 1914
Crawfordsville *Review*, Feb. 4, and May 5, 1888, June 30, Sept. 22, 1888; Jan. 26, 1889; Feb. 21 and June 6, 1891
Lafayette *Journal*, July 20, 1914
Crawfordsville *Star*, Oct. 30, 1891; Apr. 18, 1895, p. 1 c. 4
Interviews with Forrest Waye (author's father)

Bookstores and Lending Libraries

New Richmond High School Annuals: 1910 *Kole Kreke Kamera*
1911 *The Clarion*
1915 N.R.H.S.
New Richmond Methodist Church Cook Book 1912
New Richmond *Record*, Thursday, March 3, 1904
May 26, 1904
January 12, 1905, p.1, c.2
assorted dates of advertisements, Dunn's Book Store
Crawfordsville weekly *Review*, March 8, 1890, Saturday.
Memories of Forrest Waye of the Methodist Church lending library.

Chapter 6 – Builders & The Housing Industry

Builders of Our Homes – The Carpenters

Federal Census Records, 1850-1900
Directories of Montgomery County, Indiana, 1874-1912
Notes made by Phyllis Boone
Memories of Forrest Waye
Crawfordsville Weekly *Review*, May 1 and July 31, 1886; Apr. 7 and Nov. 3, 1888; Dec. 21, 1889; June 27 and Dec. 6, 1890; Apr. 11, 1891; Apr. 15, 1893
New Richmond and Tri-County Telephone Directories
History of Montgomery County, Indiana, Beckwith, 1881, p. 478
History of Montgomery County, Indiana, Bowen, 1913, pp. 1114-1116
New Richmond *Times*, Oct. 23, 1891 (extract in New Richmond *Record*, Oct. 20, 1910)
New Richmond *Record*, May 22, 1902; June 4, Sept. 17, Oct. 1, 1903; Mar. 3 and Nov. 10, 1904; Sept. 28, Dec. 7, 14, 21, and 28, 1905; January through March, 1906

Painters and Decorators

Federal Census, 1880
Crawfordsville *Review*, June 30, 1888; May 30, 1891
Montgomery County Directories, 1895; 1907-8; 1912
New Richmond Methodist Church Women's Cook Book, 1912
New Richmond *Record*, Feb. 25, 1904; Dec. 20, 1906; Mar. 16, 1916
Conversations with Forrest Waye and Alfred Allman

Plumbers and Tinners

Montgomery County Directories: 1895; 1900-1, 1903; 1907-8; 1912
Tri-County Telephone Directories
Crawfordsville *Review*, July 16, 1898
New Richmond *Record*, Aug. 30, 1923 (excerpt from Aug. 30, 1898); Aug. 28, 1902; Sept. 17, 1903; Apr. 7, 1904; Feb. 2 and Apr. 13, 1905; Aug. 30, 1906

The Tile and Brick Industry in the New Richmond Area

Original Land Owners of Montgomery County, Indiana, Montgomery County Recorder Office, Crawfordsville, Indiana
Crawfordsville Saturday Evening *Journal*, Oct. 1877 through Feb. 1910, published in Crawfordsville, Indiana
Crawfordsville Weekly *Review*, Crawfordsville, Indiana
Atlas of Montgomery County, Indiana, 1864-1917
Peoples Guide, Directory of Montgomery County, Indiana, 1874, Crawfordsville Public Library
Standard American Encyclopedia, Vol. VIII (author's home library)
Obituary of Maurice John Lee, May 20, 1922 (death date-name and date of newspaper not given on the obituary)
Abstract of title of the New Richmond Park
Convervation and recording of Chester Dunn, San Francisco, California, a former resident of New Richmond, recorded in 1963
New Richmond *Record*, published in New Richmond, Indiana

The Lumber Industry – From Saw Mills to Lumberyards

Crawfordsville *Review* (weekly), Jan. 30, 1880; Apr. 16, 1881, July 2, 1981; Nov. 17, 1883; Jul. 5, 1884; Apr. 17, 1886, Dec. 4, 1886; Jan. 22, 1887; Jun. 30, 1888; May 4, 1889, Jun. 8, 1889
Crawfordsville *Journal* (daily), Nov. 18, 1890
New Richmond *Record*, Nov. 29, 1900; Mar. 13, 1902, Jul. 31, 1902; Jun. 23, 1904, Jul. 14, 1904; Jan. 18, 1906; May 13, 1915
History of Tippecanoe County, Indiana, Vol. II, by DeHart, 1909, Purdue Univ. Library
1878 Atlas of Montgomery County, Indiana
1885 Directory of Montgomery County, Indiana
1900-1 Directory of Montgomery County, Indiana
Miscellaneous Records of Montgomery County, Indiana, Vol. 6, p. 439
N.R.H.S. Annual, *Kole Kreke Kamera*, 1910
Lafayette *Journal-Courier*, Jan. 4, 1960, obituary of Mrs. Mary G. Parlon
Lafayette *Journal-Courier*, Nov. 2, 1957, obituary of James T. Parlon

Hardware Merchants

Crawfordsville *Review*, Feb. 20, 1886; Aug. 27, 1887; Apr. 28 and Oct. 13, 1888; Apr. 11, 1896; Aug. 24, 1898; Jan. 4, 1890
Montgomery County Directories: 1891-2; 1903; 1907-8; 1912
New Richmond, *Enterprise*, May 28, 1897

New Richmond *Record*, Apr. 10, Sept. 25, Oct. 2 and 30, Dec. 11 and 25, 1902; Apr. 2, Aug. 27, Sept. 17 and 24, Nov. 12, Dec. 3 and 10, 1903; May 12, July 7 and 14, June 23, July 28, Aug. 4, Sept. 1, 8, 15, and 29 of 1904; Jan. 5 and 12, Feb. 2 and 23, Sept. 7, 1905; Jan. 11 and 25, Feb. 1, 1906; April 15, 1909; Jan. 25, 1912; June 8, 1916

N.R.H.S. Annual, *Kole Kreke Kamera*, 1910

N.R.H.S. Annual, 1911

N.R.H.S. Annual, *The Jungle*, 1923

Shopper's Guide, May through Sept. 1952

Prairie Farmer's Reliable Directory of Montgomery County, Indiana, 1920

Abstract of the Snyder Building in New Richmond

Tri-County Telephone Company Directory

FURNITURE STORES

Interviews with Byron Alexander

New Richmond Telephone Company Directory

Tri-County Telephone Company Directory

Shopper's Guide, Aug. 28, 1952

New Richmond High School Class Plays

The Chronicle, 1954-1971, Coal Creek Central High School Annual

NEW RICHMOND BLACKSMITHS

History of Montgomery County Indiana, 1881, Beckwith, pp. 481, 505, 506

Probate Records, Hamilton County, Indiana

Federal Census, Coal Creek Township, Montgomery County, Indiana, 1850-1870

Montgomery County Directories, 1874-1912

Crawfordsville Weekly *Review*, Jan. 1888-1895

New Richmond *Record*, Sept. 10, 1903-July 6, 1916

Farmer's *Review*, Aug. 13, 1937

New Richmond High School Plays, advertisements listed in various plays, 1935-1938

New Richmond Telephone Directories

Tri-County Telephone Directories

CHAPTER 7 – FARMING, HUSBANDRY, & LIVESTOCK BUSINESSES

LIVERY STABLES AND HOSTLERS

Federal Census, Montgomery County, Indiana, 1870, 1880

Crawfordsville *Review*, Feb. 4, Sept. 1, 1888; Mar. 2, Apr. 20, 1889; Jan. 4 and 18, Mar. 21, Apr. 5, June 21 and 28, Aug. 16, Sept., 13, Oct. 11, Dec. 6, 1890; Feb. 21, May 2, and Oct. 30, 1891; Sept. 24, 1892

New Richmond *Record*, Aug. 21, Dec. 11, 1902; Apr. 2, 23 and 30, and May 7 and 14, June 25, Oct. 15, 1903; May 12, 1904; July 12, Sept. 20, 1906; Feb. 24, 1910, Mar. 16, 1916; Aug. 14, 1919

N.R.H.S. Annual, *Kole Kreke Kamera*, 1910

Abstract to Snyder Building, New Richmond

Montgomery County Directories, 1895, 1900-1901, 1903, 1907-1908

HORSES, HORSE BREEDERS, TRAINERS, RACES, SHOWS, ETC.

New Richmond *Record*, Aug. 30, 1925 (excerpt from Sept. 1, 1898); Apr. 6, 1900; Apr. 10 and 24, May 22, Aug. 28, 1902; June 28, 1903; Jan. 28 and May 12, 1904; Feb. 2, Apr. 13, June 15 and 22, 1905; Feb. 1 and Dec. 6, 1906; Aug. 27, 1908; Apr. 15, 1909; Feb. 24, 1910; Mar. 16 and June 15, 1916

Crawfordsville *Review*, Apr. 30, 1887; June 27, 1890; Jan. 3, 1891; June 17, 1893; Mar. 7, 1896 (extract from New Richmond *Enterprise*)

Crawfordsville *Journal*, Sept. 3, 1881

Crawfordsville *Star*, Sept. 18, 1891, Oct. 2, 1892
New Richmond *Enterprise*, May 28, 1891
Farmer's *Review*, Sept. 20, 1935 (extract from New Richmond *Times*, Sept. 20, 1891)
Crawfordsville *Journal Review*, Feb. 1, 1965 and May 2, 1983
Messenger Crier, May 16, 1978
New Richmond Town Board, Special Meeting, Aug. 15, 1935 (minutes of meeting)
New Richmond's Third Annual Horse Show, sponsored by Lion's Club, 1947
Montgomery County Directory, 1874
Forrest Waye's memories of New Richmond (author's father)

LIVESTOCK BUYERS AND SHIPPERS

Crawfordsville *Review*, Feb. 4 and 18, July 7, 1888, Dec. 5, 1891
Crawfordsville *Star*, Mar. 21, 1890
New Richmond *Record*, June 1, 1905; Mar. 5 and July 26, 1906; Jan. 10, 1907; May 25 and Dec. 14, 1916
Lafayette *Journal-Courier*, Jan. 9, 1914
Montgomery County Directories, 1903; 1907-8, 1912
History of Montgomery County Indiana, Bowen, 1913, pp. 1122-23

PHILLIP DEWEY'S DEER AND ELK PARK

New Richmond *Record*, Thursday, December 4, 1902; December 25, 1902; March 24, 1904; August 4, 1904
Memories of Forrest Waye, Elnora McNeil Nesbitt, and Opal Clapp

FARM IMPLEMENT DEALERS

Crawfordsville *Review*, Feb. 5, 1887; Mar. 10, 1888
New Richmond *Record*, Mar. 17, 1904; Feb. 23, Mar. 9, Mar. 16, May 18, and June 1, 1905; Jan. 18, Mar. 15, Apr. 5, and Nov. 15, 1906; Jan. 25, 1912
Montgomery County Directories, 1907-8; 1912

HARNESS MAKERS AND HARNESS SHOPS

Portrait and Biographical Record of Montgomery, Parke, and Fountain Counties, 1893; Chapman Brothers, pp. 683-4
Crawfordsville Weekly *Review*, Jan. 10, 24; Feb. 21, Mar. 14, Apr. 11, June 6, 1891
Montgomery County Directories, 1907-8; 1912
Abstract of A.D. Snyder's Building, New Richmond
N.R.H.S. Annual, *Kole Kreke Kamera*, 1910
N.R.H.S. Annual, 1911
N.R.H.S. Annual, *The Jungle*, 1923
New Richmond Cemetery records

NEW RICHMOND ELEVATORS

Logan & Swank:
Indiana Sate Gazetteer, R.L. Polk and Co., Purdue University Library, 1882-3

Samuel R. Tribby:
Indiana Sate Gazetteer, R.L. Polk and Co., Purdue Univ. Library, 1882-3

Smock & Company:
Warranty Deed, Nov. 1879, Montgomery County Recorders Office, Crawfordsville, Indiana

G.S. Bruil:
Indiana State Gazetteer, R.L. Polk & Co., Purdue Univ. Library, 1884-5

Indiana State Gazetteer, R.L. Polk & Co., Purdue Univ. Library, 1887

Charles Kirkpatrick:
Indiana State Gazetteer, R.L. Polk & Co., Purdue Univ. Library, 1890
New Richmond *Record*, Nov. 3, 1888; Oct. 30, 1891

J.W. McCardle:
New Richmond *Record*, Mar. 8, 1890, Mar. 27, 1902, Oct. 2, 1902, July 6, 1905
Gazetteer of Montgomery County, Indiana, Crawfordsville Public Lib., 1891-2
Crawfordsville City Directory, Crawfordsville Public Library, 1895
Crawfordsville Business Directory, Crawfordsville Public Library, 1900-1
Resident, Business & Professional Directory of Montgomery County, Indiana, Crawfordsville Public Library, 1903

Union Elevator:
New Richmond *Record*, Apr. 9, 1903, July 13, 1905
Standard Directory of Crawfordsville and Montgomery County, Indiana, 1907-8, pp. 234-238, Crawfordsville Public Library
N.R.H.S. Annual, *Kole Kreke Kamera*, 1910
N.R.H.S. Annual, 1911
Montgomery County Gazetteer, Crawfordsville Public Library, 1912
Montgomery County-Crawfordsville, Indiana Directory, by Caron, 1914-15, Crawfordsville Public Library,
Miscellaneous Records, Recorder's Office, Montgomery County, Indiana ,Vol. 7, p. 81 and Vol. 9, p. 2
History of Montgomery County, Indiana, A.W. Bowen & Co., Indianapolis, Indiana, p. 1040, Biography of Charles Haywood, 1913
A.E. Malsbary: New Richmond *Record*, July 6, 1905
Standard Directory of Crawfordsville and Montgomery County, Indiana, Crawfordsville Public Library, 1907-1908

Haywood & Detchon:
New Richmond *Record*, July 13, 1905 and Aug. 12, 1909

Parlon Elevator:
New Richmond Telephone Directories
Lafayette *Journal-Courier*, Nov. 2, 1957, James T. Parlon's obituary
Lafayette *Journal-Courier*, Jan. 4, 1960, Mary G. Parlon's obituary

New Richmond Farm Supply:
Robinsons Directories, publishers of city and county directories, Hillsdale, Michigan, 1963, 1968-9, 1975, 1981

Farm Bureau Co-Op:
Crawfordsville *Journal-Review*, Dec. 26, 1950, p. 1 c 4 and p. 6, c 6 (fire)

Furr & Cohee:
Indianapolis *News*, 1960 (no date), obituary of Bess Florence (Plummer) Furr, wife of Bet Furr

BEE-KEEPERS

Reminiscences of Forrest Waye and Phyllis Waye Boone
Probate Records of Montgomery County, Indiana, James Kendall's Estate
Crawfordsville Weekly *Review*, Feb. 12, 1887, Mar. 14, 1891
New Richmond *Record*, July 23, 1903
Label from jar of honey, Wayne Jones, New Richmond, Indiana
Dr. Chase's "Receipt Book and Household Physician" by A.W. Chase, M.D. 1884, pp. 803-814, published by F.B. Dickerson Company, Detroit, Michigan and Windsor, Ontario, Canada

The Ice Harvest

Interviews or stories told to author by Forrest Waye
Crawfordsville Weekly *Review*, Jan. 22, 1887, May 14, 1887; Jan. 7, April 28, and Sept. 1, 1888; Feb. 16, 1889; Jan. 4, July 5, 1890; Jan. 10 and March 21, 1891
Crawfordsville *Journal* (Weekly), Feb. 9, 1900
Crawfordsville *Review* (Daily), Aug. 11, 1914
New Richmond *Record*, Dec. 3, 1903; Feb. 9, 1905; May 25, June 22 and July 6, 1916
Montgomery County Directories: 1907-8; 1912-, 1914-15

Automobile Repair Shops

New Richmond *Record*, Mar. 16 and June 16, 1916; Aug. 14, 1919
N.R.H.S. Annual, *The Jungle*, 1923
New Richmond *Student*, Mar. 1931, High School newspaper
Town Board Minutes of New Richmond, Indiana, meetings of June 4, 1930; Sept. 7 and Oct. 19, 1942
Conversations with Garland Oppy and Reuben Swank
New Richmond's Third Annual Horse Show, sponsored by Lion's Club, 1947
Shopper's Guide, May 15 to July 17, 1952
New Richmond High School Basketball Schedule, 1948-1949
Tax Duplicates of Montgomery County, Indiana
Coal Creek High School Annual, *The Chronicle*, 1956

Gas and Oil Products—Agents in New Richmond

New Richmond *Record*, Aug. 14, 1919
N.R.H.S. Annual, *The Jungle*, 1923
New Richmond High School Class Plays, advertisements
New Richmond Telephone Company Directories
New Richmond's Third Annual Horse Show, sponsored by Lion's Club, 1947
Tri-County Telephone Company Directory

Gasoline Dealers – Gasoline Service Stations

New Richmond *Record*, Feb. 19 and Nov. 19, 1903
New Richmond's Third Annual Horse Show, sponsored by Lion's Club, 1947
New Richmond High School Class Plays, 1939-1949
Receipt to Thayer's from Inskeep's
Tri-County Telephone Directories

Chapter 10 – Schools

The Crawfordsville Saturday Evening *Journal* October 22, 1881 printed this story about J. J. Insley's thrilling experience as a Bristle Ridge school teacher. J. J. was a cousin to Andrew Grady of Wayne Township, and a nephew of Noah Insley, who was one of the first settlers in Coal Creek Township.

Chapter 17 – Professional Life

Physicians of New Richmond and Coal Creek Township

Dr. Christian J. Biedenkopf: New Richmond *Record*, a weekly newspaper printed in New Richmond, Indiana, dated Thursday, March 24, 1904, July 28, 1904, September 27, 1906, February 24, 1910.
Dr. George W. Dewey: Crawfordsville *Journal*, Monday May 12, 1924, p. 1 c. 3, Obituary of Dr. Dewey; Montgomery County Marriage Records, Vol. 7, p. 433; 1850 Federal Census, Coal Creek Township.

Chapter 18 – Entertainment and Social Organizations

Sam Bayliss' Big Sensation Show

New Richmond Record, a weekly newspaper, published in New Richmond, Indiana Roll.
Charles, Indiana. *One Hundred and Fifty Years of American Development*. The Lewis Publishing Company. Chicago and New York, 1931.
Crawfordsville *Journal Review*, Saturday, June 6, 1942, page 8. column 4.
Tombstone inscriptions, New Richmond Cemetery

Chapter 21 – Transportation

Aviation Fever Strikes the Town of New Richmond

Gold Star Honor Roll, 1914-1918, Indiana-Montgomery County, p. 458, Captain William Fife Jones; p. 456, Aetna Gail Elmore
Indiana Daily *Times*, Indianapolis, July 14, 1919
Crawfordsville *Journal*, July 15, 1919
Lafayette *Journal*, Saturday, July 19, 1919
Lafayette *Journal*, Saturday, July 21, 1919
Ethel (Dunn) Sparks "Dunny," taped interview, and Stanley Dunn's handwritten notes of his military record. Compliments of Joan Oppy, Stanley's niece
Lafayette *Journal-Courier*, Apr. 2, 1955
New Richmond *Record*, Aug. 14, 1919
Crawfordsville *Journal-Review*, June 30, 1964
Crawfordsville *Journal-Review*, July 2, 1964
Miscellaneous Records of Montgomery County, Indiana, Vol. 1, p. 377

Note:
Crawfordsville *Review* (weekly newspaper published in Crawfordsville, Indiana
New Richmond *Enterprise* (weekly newspaper printed in New Richmond, Indiana)
New Richmond *Record* (weekly newspaper printed in New Richmond, Indiana)

Montgomery County *Gazetteers*, 1882 to 1887

INDEX

Regarding the index, every effort has been made to accurately record names and places. The index was perhaps the most challenging aspect of formatting and bringing the book to print. We apologize for any ommissions or errors. – ROC

7

7 Day Café, 64

A

A.R. Bowers Hardware, 95
A.W. Hempleman & Co, 40, 48
Aaron, Geraldine, 47
Abbott, Eno, 219
Abbott, George W., 219
Ackermann, Harry, 342
Agnew, Gibson, 268
Agnew, Martha Jane, 268
Ague, 262
Akers, George, 74
Albert D. Snyder's Hardware, 92
Albright, Tilly, 341
Alcoa, 82, 258
Alexander, 50, 60, 61, 96, 141, 143, 144, 165, 167, 169, 173, 174, 175, 176, 179, 183, 197, 239, 240, 270, 283, 298, 300, 306, 330, 342
Alexander Cemetery, 141
Alexander, Asena, 281
Alexander, Bayless, 119, 147, 193, 231, 312, 326, 342, 354
Alexander, Bernice, 96
Alexander, Bertha, 298, 299, 300
Alexander, Byron, 24, 34, 61, 96, 136, 253, 301
Alexander, Clyde, 60, 61
Alexander, Emma, 227
Alexander, Flora, 56, 307
Alexander, Flora (Thomas), 298
Alexander, Fred, 264, 291
Alexander, George H., 206, 213
Alexander, George W., 167
Alexander, Grant, 119, 354
Alexander, Harold, 261
Alexander, Howell, 19, 140
Alexander, Isaac H., 270
Alexander, J., 225
Alexander, J.H., 72, 169, 324
Alexander, J.M., 60, 61, 94, 158, 160, 241, 291, 351, 354
Alexander, Jim, 2, 61, 351
Alexander, John R., 144, 229, 290, 298, 299, 300, 302, 323
Alexander, Mable, 165
Alexander, Mark, 50, 200, 202, 298, 300, 301, 302
Alexander, Mary, 175, 179
Alexander, Mattie, 155

Alexander, Mima, 176
Alexander, Nettie, 147, 173, 307
Alexander, Raymond, 148, 173, 294
Alexander, Sene, 287
Alexander, Susan, 147, 270, 307
Alexander, W.S., 34, 134, 238, 306
Alexander, Winton, 11, 111, 125, 298, 354
Alexander's Furniture and Gift Store, 197
Alexander's Furniture Store, 96
Alkire, Urban Leo, 294
Allee, W.R., 186
Allen Jack, 313
Allen, Dr., 114
Allen, Grace, 160
Allen, J. Lee, 6, 342
Allen, Junis H., 6
Allen, Merton, 247
Allen, Thomas, 176, 177, 180, 187, 219, 241
Allen, Will, 150
Allhands, 164, 175, 186, 259, 263, 264, 265, 285
Allhands, Dallas G., 263
Allhands, Frank, 128
Allhands, Frank Dallas, 259, 263
Allhands, George, 2, 164, 212, 263
Allhands, John W., 186
Allhands, Ollie, 175
Allhands, Tyler, 263
Allhands, Vashti Nanette, 263
Allman, 42, 46, 81, 249
Allman, Alfred, 81, 135
Allman, Clifford, 291
Allman, Frank, 2, 115, 116
Allman's grocery, 42, 46
Allston, Willie, 67
Alston, Allen, 54
Alston, Billy, 103
Alston, F.M., 171
Alston, W.W., 103
Alston, William W., 103
American Legion, 264
Ames, 225
Ames, Minta, 307
Ammerman, Dora, 21, 236, 306
Ammoran, Dora, 323
Anderson, Ed, 295
Anderson, James L., 206
Anderson, Lowell, 39, 49
Anderson, Mr., 22
Andrews, E. Leonard, 242, 243
Andrews, E.W., 342

Andrews, F.L., 342
Andrews, Leonard, 76
Andrews, Lois, 44
Andrews, Milford, 52
Anti Saloon League, 69
Anton, Aloys, 30, 54
Apple Hill, 227
Appleby, Charles, 148
Appleby, Reverend M.H., 147
Applegate, 84, 215, 217
Applegate, Alpheno M., 294
Archey, Blaine A., 22, 91, 92, 103, 110
Archey, Etta Tribby, 150
Archey, William, 150
Army, 16, 41, 81, 83, 204, 258, 264, 292, 320, 349, 350
Arnett Clinic, 264, 265
Arnett, Alfred Jefferson, 193, 264, 285, 312
Arnett, Arett, 259, 264, 265, 273, 291, 294, 351
Arnett, Richard A., 264
Arnett-Crockett Clinic, 264, 291
Arnold, Jack, 60
Arvin, Stanley J., 43
Asbury M. E. Church, 84, 145, 146, 220, 221, 224, 225, 226
Asbury University, 267, 273, 274
Ashby, J.W., 187
Ashenhurst, John, 183
Ashland, 215, 227, 293, 306, 307
Ashland Temple, 293, 306, 307
Ashley, J.C., 161
Atkins, Samuel R., 10
Austin, Jake, 342
Austin, Saml W., 226
Austin, Wayne, 135
Auter, Velma, 186
Auter, Zelma, 176
Automobile Taxi Service, 344
Aviation Taxi Service, 351

B

Babourn, Enoch, 33
Back Door Beauty Salon, 59
Bacon, Robert, 272
Badgely, James, 212
Badgley, James, 79
Bagby, F.M., 325
Bagby, P.E., 219
Bailey, Al, 231
Bailey, E.E., 173
Bailey, Frances, 173, 183
Bailey, J.A., 69, 193, 312
Bailey, Jean, 312
Bailey, Thomas, 193
Bailey, Tom, 128
Bain, W.S., 55
Bakery, O.K., 48
Baldwin, Bill, 64
Baldwin, E.E., 240, 241, 245, 281
Baltimore and Ohio Railroad, 15
Bana, Pearl (Kite), 174
Bank Block, 24, 193
Bannon, Edith, 291
Bannon, James C., 219
Bannon, Lewis, 218, 342
Bannon, Pheobe, 219
Bannon, Sallie, 219
Banta, Clarence, 207, 308

Banta, George, 36, 155
Banta, Lou C., 155
Banta, Pearl G. (Kite), 308
Banta, Thelma, 308
Banta, Theron, 323
Banta, Thomas W., 115, 306
Banta, Tom, 306
Barber, 60, 61
Barcus Jr., Paul, 265
Barcus, Catharine, 265
Barcus, Col. John M., 265
Barcus, Gertrude, 265
Barcus, Homer, 67, 193, 223
Barcus, John, 13, 259, 265
Barcus, Katie, 13
Barcus, Paul, 13, 173, 265
BARKER AND HANAWALT, 344
Barker, Austin P., 351
Barker, David, 243
Barnes, Frances, 44
Barnes, Francis, 129, 130
Barnes, Martha J., 10
Barnes, Mary E., 10
Barnes, Phebe Ann, 10
Barnes, Terri, 207
Barnes, Terry, 243
Barnett, Howard Stewart, 294
Barnhill, D.C., 282
Barr, Fred, 220
Bassett, W.T., 337
Bastian, G.L., 344
Bastian, Garrett, 354
Bastian, Thomas, 111
Bastin, James S., 312
Bastion, Charles, 134
Bastion, Garrett, 111, 125, 230, 253, 295, 308
Bastion, Jeff, 20
Bastion, L.L., 48
Battreal, Andrew, 212
Battreal, James, 308
Batts, Ron, 162
Baugh, Leonard, 63
Baxter, John, 123
Baxter, Musa, 74
Baxter, Randall, 74
Baxter?, Ruby, 74
Bayless, Agnes, 302
Bayless, Sam, 302
Bayliss Big Sensation Minstrel Show, 300, 301
Bayliss Overland Electric Show, 302
Bayliss Real Estate, 302
Bayliss, Agnes, 300, 302
Bayliss, Detty, 299
Bayliss, Ida (Epperson), 299
Bayliss, Million & Million, 302
Bayliss, Mrs. Samuel, 11
Bayliss, Queen, 299, 302
Bayliss, Samuel, 105, 295, 299, 300, 301, 302, 303, 342, 354
Bayliss, William, 299, 303
Beach, Nathan, 182, 283
Beach, S.A.R., 215, 227, 330
Beach, Samuel, 2, 31
Beadle, 211
Beal, Ella, 12
Bean, Mary, 308
Beard, Ruth, 86
Beasley, Allen D., 9

Beaver, David, 201
Beaver, Stephen J., 119
Beck, Anna, 279
Beck, George, 279
Beckely, Hiland, 354
Beckley, Hiland, 98
Beckley, Ida, 307
Beckley, John, 308, 354
Beckley, Lennie, 290
Beckley, Nick, 93, 253
Beckwith, 5, 29, 83, 164, 214, 219
Bed Bug Corner, 71, 227
Bed Bug Hotel, 71, 72
Bedford, Elizabeth, 10
bee keeping, 123, 124
Beeckler, Charley, 2
Beel, Joseph, 103
Beever, 183
Beever, Barbara, 185
Bell, Arthur, 307
Bell, Cora, 46
Bell, Estel, 290
Bell, Harold, 290
Bell, Harry C., 202
Bell, J.A., 42
Bell, James A., 21, 46
Bell, Jeptha, 206
Bell, Raymond, 290, 291
Bell, Thomas A., 83
Bell, William, 60, 61, 307, 354
Bell's Meat Market, 46
Ben-Hur Lodge, 313
Benjamin, Homer A., 337
Bennett, Charlie, 81
Bennett, Daniel, 211
Bennett, Edward, 1, 144, 164, 177, 211, 212, 229
Bennett, Emma, 13
Bennett, Frank, 308
Bennett, George Frank, 13
Bennett, J.S., 211, 212, 218
Bennett, Jeff, 325
Bennett, Joe, 86, 134, 179, 305
Bennett, John, 218
Bennett, Opal Jane, 13
Bennett, Thomas J., 97, 98, 225
Bennett, William, 97, 342
Bennington, Sarah, 178
Bergin, Tom, 114
Bethel Baptist Church, 214
Betty's Beauty Shop, 59
Bianconi, 351
Bianconi, John, 351
Bible, A.P., 175
Bible, Anna, 143, 174
Bible, Frederic, 155, 158, 159, 160, 342, 351, 355
Bible, Jim, 288
Bible, John C., 308
Bible, John P., 147, 149, 174, 238, 250, 339, 341, 342
Bible, Mabel, 159
Bible, Margery, 351
Bible, Mary, 119
Bible, Richard, 306, 325
Biedenkopf, 115, 259, 266, 279
Biedenkopf, C.J., 259, 261, 266, 307
Big Four Lumber Company, 90, 110
Bigelow, L.E., 55
Bill Hailey and the Comets, 292

Billman, Sam J., 306
Binns, Arlie, 344
Binns, Helen, 140, 197, 198, 232
Binns, Levert, 46, 64, 135, 140, 188, 189, 196, 197, 206, 232, 253
Binns, Moses R., 46, 135
Birch, William, 284
Birdsell, J.J., 282
Biser, Mabel May, 268
Bishop, E.A., 90
Black Bear Hotel, 15, 16, 26, 72, 73, 74, 75, 104, 105, 106, 125, 244, 248, 266, 323
Black Creek Valley, 324
Black Hawk Café, 64
Black, Dayton E., 31
Black, Dayton R., 196, 259, 260, 266, 267, 269, 276, 306
Black, Gretchen, 267
Black, Leona, 267
Black, Matthew, 266
Black, Michael, 162
Black, Sanford, 240, 247
Black, W.W., 285
Black, Zerilda (Berry), 266
Blacker, John, 163
Blacketer, Charles, 342
Blaine Archey's Hardware, 91
Blake, L.O., 224
Blake, Mr., 72
Blatchley, 6
Blind Tiger, 65
Blue Bell Lodge, 307
Blue Hour Café, 64
Blue, James, 312
Boardman, Mr., 15
Bobo, Garner, 218
Boeldt, Al, 129
Boes, Joe, 212
Boland, W.W., 193, 195, 285, 306
Bonebrake, Adam, 176
Bonnell, Rob A., 306
Booe, J.A., 199
Booe, John, 186
Boone, Albert, 242
Boone, Fannie, 56
Boone, Phyllis Waye, 13
Boraker, Tom, 256
Border, Solomon, 233
Borger, I.V., 251
Born, Edward, 119
Bortterson, J.G., 188
Borum, M.M., 285
Boston Store, 89, 98, 145, 163, 164, 175, 207, 211, 212, 213, 214, 218, 227, 294, 327
Boswell Clough's Saloon, 66
Bowers, A.R., 95
Bowers, Marcus, 60
Bowles, W.L., 193
Bowles, William, 307
Bowman, J.H., 337
Bowyer, Nancy, 153
Boy Scouts, 25, 315
Boyer, James, 79
Boyland, C.N., 48
Boyland, Charles, 250
Boyland, H.L., 281
Bradford, O.S., 337
Bradford, Phillip, 162
Bragg, Walter O., 94

Bragstad, Chester, 43
Bragstad's Town Market, 43
Brandenburg, John T., 342
Brannon, Artimesa, 174
Brannon, Wallace, 91
Brannon, William, 174
Brannon-Dazey-Bible School, 173, 174
Brant, John W., 200
Brant, Louisa, 188
Bratton, E.W., 313
Bratton, George, 310
Bratton, John S., 342
Bratton, Mills M., 343
Breed, Ellis, 337
Breed, George, 75, 117, 332
Bristle Ridge, 7, 67, 84, 105, 132, 166, 167, 170, 179, 209, 214, 215, 216, 217, 227, 267, 275, 325, 355
Britton, George, 5
Britton, Judge, 332
Britton, Ray, 161
Broadlick, Thomas, 41
Brooks, Fred Emerson, 294, 295
Brooks, Mary, 219
Brooks, Rev. Benjamin, 219
Brooks, William P., 219
Brown, Allen, 325
Brown, Benjamin, 326
Brown, Cathrine, 219
Brown, David, 129
Brown, J.R., 346
Brown, Janet, 243
Brown, L.L., 259, 261, 278
Brown, L.P., 55, 94, 113, 114, 158, 160, 238, 239, 326
Brown, Lonnie, 94, 113, 232, 354
Brown, Lula G., 354
Brown, P.M., 282
Brown, Roy, 128, 240, 241, 253
Brown, William, 140
Bruil, G.S., 117
Bruner, M.W., 312
Brunis, 98
Bryant, Harvey, 175
Bryant, Homer M., 337
Bryant, J.A., 99
Bryant, J.H., 183
Buck Belt, 30, 79
Buck Stanley, 69
Buck, O.C., 136
Buck, Polly, 54, 136, 257
Bunnel, Douglas, 22, 30, 31, 39, 63, 249
Bunnel, George, 105, 219, 308
Bunnel, John, 202
Bunnel, William, 219
Bunnell, Barney, 290
Bunnell, Boswell, 219
Bunnell, Douglas, 22, 30, 31, 63, 125, 249
Bunnell, Edith, 291
Bunnell, George, 308
Bunnell, Jacob, 175, 253, 343
Bunnell, James A., 219
Bunnell, John W., 343
Bunnell, Oswel, 219
Bunnell, Thomas E., 343
Bunnell, William, 247
Burgess, James, 162
Burk, 209, 225, 312
Burk, E., 225

Burk, Elias, 325
Burk, Ellis, 220, 311, 312
Burk, Lydia, 220
Burk, Moses L., 186, 229, 253
Burke, Ed, 220
Burkhardt, J.C., 161
Burkle, Linda K., 257
Burnes, William, 98
Burnett & Son, 111
Burnett, Carl, 100, 111, 128, 129, 130, 241, 251, 252
Burnett, Gladys, 291
Burns, Pamela J., 257
Burress, Fred, 3
Burris, 40, 173, 252, 291
Burris, Fred, 173
Burris, Hannah, 154
Burris, J., 227
Burris, Jake, 31, 40
Burris, Joseph, 152
Burris, Mary E., 155
Burris, W.H., 230
Burris, William, 108, 126, 152, 209
Buser, Kenneth, 162
Buxton, Millard F., 326
Byers, Allen, 171, 235, 237
Byers, Edward, 46
Byers, Wilford, 93

C

Cachiaras, John, 160, 161
Cadwallader, 45
Caesarean section, 265
Calhoun, Martha, 219
California Pellet Mill Company, 137
Call, Larry D., 162
Campbell building, 30
Campbell, Artemesa Maria, 12
Campbell, Bill, 12, 19, 114, 170, 234, 306
Campbell, C.E., 356
Campbell, E.C., 30
Campbell, Elisha, 11, 12, 19, 73, 81, 97, 140, 163, 169, 230
Campbell, Ella, 30, 55
Campbell, Emily, 11, 163
Campbell, Ester, 97
Campbell, F.E., 238, 239, 252, 307, 308
Campbell, Forest, 12
Campbell, Frank, 12, 21, 196, 200, 202, 206, 207, 209, 238, 239, 250, 252, 253, 342, 354
Campbell, George, 12
Campbell, Harley E., 12
Campbell, Harry W., 204
Campbell, Henry, 221, 222
Campbell, Jacob, 11, 12, 19, 31, 97, 98, 123, 203
Campbell, Joe, 35, 43, 290
Campbell, John, 11, 97, 163, 204
Campbell, Lucinda, 11, 163
Campbell, Maria, 97, 163
Campbell, Mary, 11, 12, 97
Campbell, Mary E., 11, 12, 97, 163
Campbell, Mary H., 20
Campbell, Mr., 175
Campbell, Nancy, 220
Campbell, Nellie Leona, 12, 163
Campbell, Nola, 12
Campbell, Rev. William, 220, 223
Campbell, Robert C., 11, 163

Campbell, Sarah, 11, 97
Campbell, Sarah J., 11, 97, 163
Campbell, William, 11, 12, 19, 20, 22, 28, 29, 30, 31, 39, 57, 60, 63, 65, 75, 97, 114, 123, 126, 145, 163, 170, 178, 191, 199, 200, 208, 221, 222, 223, 226, 235, 248, 293, 305, 336
Campbell, William Kenton, 12
Campbellites, 153, 217, 220
Canfield, 152, 161
Carey, Frank, 299
Carl Burnett Trucking Co., 111
Carmen, Mike, 162
Carmichal, William, 2
Carnahan, J.R., 284
Carnell, 98
Carney, A.L., 161, 218
Carr, Roy, 46, 99
Carr, Stephen, 162
Carr's Café, 64
Carrell, 98
Carson, Bertha L., 64
Carson, D.M., 32
Carson, Frank, 81
Carson, L.C., 50, 81
Carter, James, 31, 249
Casey, Neal, 87, 88
Casey, Neil, 140
Casey, Timothy, 87
Cash, John, 307
Cash, John H., 88
Cash, Minnie, 148
Cash, Thomas Raymond, 162
Casto & Chilcote, 332
Catharine, Polly, 10
Caw, Maria, 14, 153
Cawley, Reynold, 292
Center, 69, 166, 172, 179, 180, 216, 217, 218, 219, 227, 255, 258, 284, 322, 326, 331
Center Christian Church, 217, 218, 219, 227
Center School, 166, 172, 179, 180, 217, 218, 227, 326, 331
Center Schoolhouse, 179, 326, 331
Central Lyceum Bureau, 295
Cernell, 98
Chadwick, 176, 225, 343
Chadwick, H. Grady, 176, 253, 343
Chadwick, J. Frank, 193, 343
Chadwick, Madge, 291
Champion, Al, 289
Charivari, 288
Charles Sturgeon Trucking Co., 111
Charles Swick and Son, 107
Chase, Ira, 208
Chauncy, A.D., 60
Cheeseman, Levi, 98
Chelen, Fred, 177, 180
Chicago, Indiana, and Louisville, 355
chicken pox, 262
Chrisman, Wm., 196
Christian, T.E., 94
Christmas, 2, 6, 37, 40, 41, 45, 85, 89, 92, 112, 121, 166, 172, 173, 179
Cinque Parties, 287
Cities Service Oil Company, 129, 130
Civil War, 11, 13, 140, 210, 255, 265, 278, 290, 304, 313, 325
Clapp, Alonza, 343
Clapp, Lawrence, 343
Clapp, Mark, 243, 248
Clapp, Merrill, 13, 135

Clapp, Opal, 22, 30, 301
Clark, Daniel, 273
Clark, Ellis, 252
Clark, J.P., 238
Clark, John, 114, 140
Clark, Mary R. (Rearden), 272
Clark, Myrtle, 160
Clark, P.J., 114
Clark, Rosiland, 189
Clark, Tom, 65
Clark, W.F., 224
Clarkson, David, 229
Clarkson, Della, 34
Clarkson, James, 231
Clarkson, Louis E., 343
Clarkson, Mrs. Lewis, 160
Clarkson, Peter, 140
Clawson, W.M., 312
Clawson, Will, 107
Claypool & Fry's, 24, 31, 32, 34, 42, 57
Claypool & Lacy, 34
Claypool and Fry's, 54, 55, 296
Claypool, Arthur, 32, 34
Claypool, Charles, 34
Claypool, J.J., 286
Claypool, Melvin L., 32, 33, 34, 264, 291, 294
Clements, Henry, 324
Cleveland, Dan, 48
Clevenger, S.A., 181
Cloud, George, 2, 3, 86
Clough, Abraham (or Abram), 215
Clough, Bluford, 108
Clough, Boswell, 63, 66, 67, 68, 94, 95, 105, 106, 108, 110, 113, 125, 280, 301, 302, 353
Clough, George, 90, 91, 110, 134, 215, 307, 308, 332
Clough, Jasper, 105, 108, 280
Clough, Mrs. Fred, 112
Clouser, John, 67
Clover Leaf Line, 73
Clover Leaf Railroad, 50, 86, 90, 119, 125, 126, 132, 158, 207, 208, 346, 347, 348
Coal Creek, 1, 3, 4, 5, 6, 7, 8, 9, 10, 11, 12, 13, 14, 19, 20, 21, 25, 28, 39, 41, 49, 57, 60, 66, 67, 68, 69, 70, 71, 76, 79, 83, 84, 86, 88, 92, 93, 96, 97, 101, 106, 107, 109, 112, 113, 115, 116, 123, 127, 128, 134, 141, 142, 153, 154, 163, 164, 165, 166, 167, 168, 169, 170, 171, 172, 173, 174, 175, 176, 177, 178, 179, 180, 182, 183, 184, 185, 186, 187, 188, 189, 190, 191, 192, 199, 200, 207, 208, 209, 210, 211, 214, 215, 216, 217, 218, 219, 220, 223, 225, 227, 229, 230, 235, 253, 255, 256, 257, 258, 259, 261, 262, 263, 267, 274, 275, 280, 283, 284, 286, 289, 291, 294, 295, 299, 309, 310, 312, 315, 323, 324, 325, 326, 327, 328, 329, 330, 331, 332, 333, 336, 339
Coal Creek Band, 109
Coal Creek Center, 96
Coal Creek Central School, 101, 128, 169, 173, 185, 188, 189, 258
Coal Creek Dairy, 127, 128
Coal Creek Dairy Products, 127
Coal Creek Sheepskin Band, 289
Coal Creek Temperance Society, 69
Coal Creek Township, 1, 3, 4, 5, 6, 7, 8, 9, 11, 12, 13, 14, 19, 20, 21, 25, 28, 39, 41, 49, 57, 60, 66, 68, 69, 71, 76, 79, 83, 84, 86, 88, 93, 97, 106, 107, 112, 113, 115, 116, 123, 141, 142, 153, 163, 164, 165, 166, 167, 168, 169, 171, 172, 174, 175, 176, 177, 178, 179, 180, 182, 183, 184, 185, 186, 187, 188, 191, 192, 199, 200, 207, 208, 209, 210, 211, 214, 216, 217, 218, 220, 223, 225, 227, 229, 235, 253, 259, 261, 262, 263, 267,

274, 275, 280, 283, 284, 286, 289, 291, 294, 295, 299, 309, 310, 315, 323, 324, 325, 326, 327, 328, 329, 330, 331, 332, 333, 336, 339
Coal Creek Township Historical Society Museum, 291
Coal Creek Valley, 107, 227
Coapland, Uriah, 103, 281
Cochran, Dave, 128
Cochran, David, 130
Cochran, L.W., 107
Cocran, Joseph, 310
Coffey, John, 356
Coffing, Beulah, 291
Coffing, Theo. C., 343
Coffman, 52, 129, 241, 244, 252, 280, 290, 298
Coffman, Lizzie, 307
Coffman, Maurice, 52, 128, 130, 136, 197, 232, 241, 251, 253, 290, 304, 344, 354
Coffman, Perry, 21, 88, 124, 125, 252, 306
Coffman, Ruth, 52, 240
Coffman, W. Maurice, 197
Coffman, William P., 354
Cohran (Cochran), Roscoe, 244
Cole, Ira, 197, 259, 267
Cole, Marjorie E., 268
Cole, Victor Donald, 268
Cole, William I., 268
Coleman, 209, 325
Coleman, Bridget, 216
Coleman, Ed, 2
Coleman, James, 311, 312
Coleman, Jane, 312
Coleman, Nich, 312
Collister, Jas. M.M., 213
Colton, Jessie, 295
Combs, Fullor, 173
Commercial Club, 289, 290, 346
Conarroe, Joe, 162
Connel, Stephen, 144
Connell, Hiram, 20, 177, 178, 220
Connell, Margaret, 178
Conner, Thomas, 81
Consumption, 262
Conway, Joseph M., 158, 160, 239
Cook, Charles E., 161
Cook, Fleeta, 56
Cook, James, 20, 152, 154
Cook, T.M., 312, 343
Cook, Thomas, 66, 98, 154, 168, 196, 206, 207, 231
Coombs, J.B., 224
Coon, Christian, 309
Coon, Clifford, 186
Coon, John, 330
Coon, Marilyn, 308
Coon, Mollie, 168
Cooper, 281
Co-Operative, 122
Coopland, 281
Copeland, 103, 104, 281
Copeland, Uriah, 103
Copper, Fanny (Cook), 151
Cord, William J., 175, 186
Corn Exchange Bank, 23, 24, 25, 51, 87, 94, 120, 153, 192, 193, 194, 195, 244, 245, 247, 251, 256, 295, 306
Corn Show, 33
Cornbeak, William, 256
Cornell, 98, 185, 207
Cornell, Curt, 98, 207
Cornell, Frank, 98, 206, 207
Cornell, William, 98
Cortez, Darrell, 162
Corwin, Mr., 31
Cosseboom, William, 309
Council Grove, 106, 181, 182, 183, 309, 310, 311, 312, 313
Council Grove Horse Thief Detective Company, 183
Council Grove Minute Men, 183, 309, 310, 311, 313
Council Grove School, 183
Country Sunshine Band, 292
Courtney, James, 94
Courtney, Mary, 173
covered bridge, 283, 346
Covington, 97, 144, 216, 229, 232, 302, 323
Cowan, David R., 312
Cowan, George A., 343
Cowan, Newt, 108
Cowan, Robert, 173, 175, 179
Cowan, Scott, 275
Cowan, William H., 311, 312
Cox & Snellenbarger Trucking Co, 111
Cox, Harry, 90
Cox, Howard, 242, 247
Cox, James, 243
Cox, Johnny, 162
Cox, Ruthanna, 291
Cox, Sanford, 284
Coy, Charles, 248
Craig, D.R., 351
Craig, Denton R., 350
Crane, Oliver, 326
Crawfordsville, 1, 2, 3, 4, 5, 6, 8, 13, 14, 19, 23, 28, 29, 33, 34, 35, 36, 45, 47, 48, 50, 53, 54, 57, 58, 59, 60, 67, 72, 75, 76, 81, 82, 83, 84, 85, 86, 87, 89, 92, 94, 98, 103, 106, 108, 109, 111, 112, 113, 114, 116, 117, 118, 121, 122, 125, 132, 136, 143, 145, 146, 148, 150, 151, 153, 154, 155, 157, 163, 167, 168, 170, 175, 176, 178, 181, 183, 184, 185, 186, 187, 188, 189, 190, 191, 192, 193, 195, 197, 198, 199, 200, 207, 211, 213, 215, 216, 217, 220, 224, 225, 227, 229, 230, 234, 238, 244, 248, 251, 252, 255, 256, 257, 258, 260, 262, 264, 265, 266, 267, 268, 269, 270, 271, 272, 274, 276, 277, 278, 279, 281, 282, 284, 286, 288, 289, 290, 291, 292, 293, 294, 297, 298, 304, 306, 307, 313, 318, 323, 324, 325, 326, 327, 329, 330, 332, 333, 334, 336, 338, 339, 341, 345, 346, 347, 348, 349, 354, 355
Crawfordsville Review, 2, 3, 72, 84, 87, 89, 98, 114, 117, 145, 153, 154, 155, 170, 176, 181, 184, 199, 200, 215, 220, 256, 262, 268, 276, 289, 293, 334, 336
Crawfordsville Weekly Review, 29, 54, 86, 111, 116, 118, 145, 175, 191, 192, 211, 248, 289, 333
Creahan, Estella M., 91, 232
Creahan, Mary G., 91, 121
Crim, A.L., 69, 161
Crockett, F.S., 264
Crosby, John, 122
Crouch, John, 140
Crouch, Louisa, 219
Crouse, J.L., 310
Crouse, Mr., 30
Crow, Katherine Alice, 86
Crow, Michael, 86
Crowder, George, 275
Crowder, Mary, 275, 287, 291, 319
Crowder, Ralph, 275
Croy, P.A., 220
Croy, Prent, 220
Crull, Iris Eileen, 300

385

Crull, Oscar D., 299
Crystal Theatre, 302, 303
Culver Hospital, 258, 265, 266, 271, 279
Cunningham, Ruth (Priebe), 64
Curnutt, Mary, 150, 274
Curtis, 86, 90, 110, 140, 182, 277, 326, 332, 354
Curtis, Daniel, 86, 229, 324
Curtis, Levi, 182, 183, 186, 253, 330
Cutrell, John, 193, 342

D

D.D.D.S. Club, 288
Dain & Cowan's Sawmill, 89
Daisey, Thomas, 1, 212
Daniel, Charles, 195
Daniels, C.W., 240
Daniels, J.J., 329
Danner, Catherine, 10
Danner, Margaret, 10
Daughters of Rebekahs, 307
DAUGHTERS OF TEMPERANCE, 305
Daughters of Temperance Society, 65
Davenport, James, 219
Davidson, David J., 151
Davidson, Gideon, 149
Davidson, James, 149
Davidson, John, 149
Davidson, Lay, 284
Davidson, Prof. Albert, 149
Davidson, Rev. William Clarence, 149
Davidson, Robert, 325, 343
Davidson, W.C., 107
Davidson, William T., 126, 193, 343
Davies Beauty Salon, 59
Davies, Chet, 59
Davies, Linda, 59
Davies, Lorene, 59
Davis, Floyd, 242
Davis, Harry A., 161
Davis, Joseph, 151, 161
Davis, Lee, 290
Davis, Stephen, 50
Davis, Thomas, 307
Davison, F.E., 161
Davison, Mr., 47
Davison, W.C., 312
Davisson, David D., 160
Davisson, David J., 152
Davisson, Fern, 151, 160
Davisson, Gideon L., 152
Davisson, M.L., 155, 160, 306, 312
Davisson, Morton L., 158, 159, 160
Davisson, Nellie, 160
Davisson, Samantha, 307
Davisson, Vinton, 259, 278
Davisson, William, 193, 194, 265, 278, 306, 354
Dawson, Jack, 247
Dazey, 116, 173, 174, 175, 180, 219, 343
Dazey, A.W., 180
Dazey, Abram W., 219, 343
Dazey, Albert, 132, 174
Dazey, Amanda, 219
Dazey, Barnum, 343
Dazey, C.A., 219
Dazey, Carrie J., 174
Dazey, Cliff, 107

Dazey, David, 218
Dazey, Grant, 290
Dazey, Jacob, 140
Dazey, John E., 219
Dazey, Ray C., 343
Dazey, Samuel, 83
Dazey, Sarah, 219
Dazey, Wesley, 175, 186, 188, 326
Dean, Samuel, 66, 88
Dearman, Gill, 88
Dearmands, Bob, 212
DeArmond, Lemma, 202
Dearmond, Robert, 212
Deeter, Allen M., 193
Democrat, 170, 229, 255
Democratic Conventions, 179
Demoret, County Sheriff, 7
Dennis, Pearl, 36
Dennis, Rodney, 188
DePauw University, 92, 117, 149, 150, 165, 256, 265, 267, 273, 292
DePlanty, Stephen, 65
Deputy, Allie, 291
Detchon, Dr., 4, 22, 31, 85, 86, 98, 232, 267, 269, 270, 277, 278, 332
Detchon, Dr. Stowe, 28, 37, 151, 170, 259, 260, 268, 269
Detchon, E., 332
Detchon, Elliott, 206, 259, 268, 269, 276
Detchon, Esther, 269
Detchon, Haywood, 336
Detchon, Heaman (or Herman), 19
Detchon, Irwin A., 259, 268
Detchon, Irwin Lee, 269
Detchon, J.T., 90, 119, 120, 133
Detchon, Jemima, 121, 244, 250, 269
Detchon, John, 75, 82, 95, 119, 120, 121, 128, 131, 133, 135, 136, 139, 147, 214, 245, 250, 269, 270, 338, 341, 353
Detchon, Maria (Hoadley), 269
Detchon, S.S., 260, 261, 328
Detchon, Seymour, 268
Detchon, Stowe, 22, 139, 154, 157, 158, 160, 163, 169, 170, 195, 233, 234, 237, 248, 250, 259, 260, 261, 269, 270, 275, 276, 278, 293, 311, 353
Detchon, Tinna, 270
Dettbenner, Albert, 193, 287
Dettbenner, Augusta L. (Schumaker), 292
Dettbenner, Caroline, 173
Dettbenner, Carrie, 168
Dettbenner, Grace, 292
Dettbenner, Theodore F., 292
Detty, 299
Devault, Annie, 307
Devault, Fannie, 159, 160, 307
Devault, James, 159
DeVault, Jess, 251
Devault, Larkin, 307
Devault, Thomas, 158, 159, 160
Devault, Tom, 312
Dewey Millinery Parlors, 56
Dewey, Albert, 10
Dewey, Bert, 343
Dewey, Catharine, 154
Dewey, Claud, 270
Dewey, Elizabeth, 10, 270
Dewey, Ephraim, 19
Dewey, Frank, 88, 113
Dewey, George, 79, 81, 227, 259, 270

Dewey, Harriett, 10
Dewey, Howard, 3, 280
Dewey, John, 10, 126, 152, 154, 311
Dewey, Katherine, 167, 168
Dewey, Maude, 270
Dewey, Mrs., 56
Dewey, Phebe, 10
Dewey, Philip, 19, 112, 246, 326, 343
Dewey, Phillip, 112, 113, 325
Dewey, Richard, 9, 10, 167
Dewey, Samuel, 10
Dewey, Solomon, 69, 147, 236
Dewey, Thomas H., 10
Dewey, William, 10, 48, 238
Dewey-Walnut Grove, 167, 168
DeWitt Clinton Miller, 119
DeWitt Miller, 295, 297
DeWitt Wallace, 284
Dice, F.M., 209
Dick, H.D., 147
Dick, Jasper, 308
Dick's Service Station Standard Products, 130
Dickson, Dale, 248
Dilling, Aquilla, 206
Dilling, Joshua, 206, 212, 213
Dilling, L., 212
Dilling, S., 212
Dillon, Aquilla, 19, 39
Dillon, Thomas D., 54, 58, 294
Dinner Bell Café, 64
Dinwiddie, 57, 326
Dinwiddie, Adolphus, 57
Dinwiddie, Samuel, 57
Diphtheria, 262
Dixon, H.M., 186
Dixon, Morton, 173
Doctor Hostetter's Saloon, 65
Donnelley Printing Plant, 313
Dority & Co, 281
Dorsey, Walter, 294
Dotson, Wm., 186
Dowen, Nancy E., 10
Dozen Dear Devine Sisters Club, 288
Drake, J.F., 187
Dresden Todd Trucking Co., 111
Dryer, Bob, 128, 130, 351
Dryer, Fauniel, 55
Dryer, Robert V., 351
Drysdale, Floyd Ellery, 135
Dueisbeck, C.K., 98
Duncan, Bessie, 56
Dunkle, Jennie, 185
Dunn, Chester, 15, 87
Dunn, Donald, 161
Dunn, Ethel, 15, 16
Dunn, John, 15
Dunn, Kittie, 287
Dunn, Martha, 16, 17, 76, 173, 351
Dunn, Mildred Elizabeth, 16
Dunn, Ruth, 15, 16
Dunn, Stanley, 15, 16, 24, 76, 82, 128, 344, 348, 349, 350, 351
Dunn, Starr, 15, 16, 17, 23, 24, 55, 76, 80, 82, 128, 129, 225, 232, 249, 250, 251, 271, 279, 304, 339, 344, 351, 353
Dunn, William, 15
DUNN'S LIBRARY, BOOK, and STATIONERY STORE, 76
Dwiggins & Son, 46
Dwiggins, Charles, 46

E

Early, Catherine, 317
Easterly, David, 64
Ebright, Mrs. Jane, 343
Ebrite & Alexander's Bakery, 48
Ebrite, Alfred, 13, 163, 259, 260, 269, 278
Ebrite, Alice, 11, 12, 63, 69
Ebrite, Amos, 12, 19, 79, 145, 157, 163, 168, 169, 174, 196, 229, 250, 298, 306, 311, 312, 319, 324
Ebrite, Catherine, 13, 163
Ebrite, Daniel, 10, 12, 13, 19, 79, 80, 152, 163, 169, 193
Ebrite, Elizabeth, 13
Ebrite, Emma, 12, 30
Ebrite, Fannie, 1, 140, 155
Ebrite, Flora, 298
Ebrite, George, 12, 13, 19, 79, 123, 134, 151, 152, 163, 182, 183, 233, 253, 265, 278
Ebrite, Jessie Lola, 13
Ebrite, Margaret Emma, 13
Ebrite, Mary, 12, 13
Ebrite, Mary Alice, 11, 12
Ebrite, Mary Elizabeth, 12, 319
Ebrite, Mary Wright, 12
Ebrite, Squire, 56, 77, 108, 113, 135, 230, 231, 238, 248
Ebrite, Vera, 10, 13, 189, 319
Eichenburg and Christian Hardware, 94
Eiler, Lewis, 56
Eldredge, G.A., 294
Elisha Westfall's Blacksmith Shop, 98
elk, 45, 112, 113, 316
Elks Lodge, 112
Eller, James W., 79
Ellis, Ed, 116
Ellis, John, 134, 185, 289
Ellis, Miss, 56
Ellis, William R., 179
Ellis, Zack, 140
Elmdale, 1, 98, 108, 112, 145, 146, 164, 169, 172, 175, 176, 184, 187, 188, 199, 211, 212, 213, 214, 217, 218, 225, 227, 259, 264, 275, 285, 287, 312, 325, 327
Elmer Plunkett's Saloon, 67
Elmore, Aetna Gail, 348, 349
Elmore, James, 185, 294
Elmore, Jasper, 342, 349
Elmore, Mr., 114
Elmore's Barber Shop, 61
Elrod, Absalom K., 139
Elrod, Eli, 139, 233, 274
Elrod, Ezra, 139
Elrod, Harriett R., 139
Elrod, R., 139
Emerald Acres, 54, 136, 137
England, Linda, 207
Engle, Mary, 193
Enterprise, 200, 235
Epperson, Ida Frances, 173
Epworth League, 148, 295
Eshelman, J., 225
Everett Pierce Trucking Co., 111
Everson, Mosses, 311
Ewing, J.P., 153, 161, 296

F

Fairbanks Morse Company, 354
Farley, Henry, 19

Farm Bureau Co-operative Association, 122
Farm Bureau Petroleum Products, 129
Farmers Review, 203, 204
Father Bingham, 163
Faust, Lloyd, 198
Faye, Helen, 294
Felton, John H., 343
Fenters, James, 140, 243
Ferguson, Patricia, 308
Fewell, J.W., 347
Fidler, Carolyn, 64
Fidler, Don, 44
Fields, Mike, 162
Fifer, Jack, 13, 197, 198
Fifer, Ralph, 13
Finch, David, 162
Fine, Cordella, 173, 186
Finney, J.D., 186, 188
Finney, J.T., 187
Firemen, 250
First Church of Christ, 151
Fisher, Joshua, 196
Flannigan, J.W., 93
Flaugher & Son, 105, 107
Flaugher, Carl, 354
Flaugher, John G., 354
Fletcher, Nathan, 67
Floyd, John, 170
Flynn, Denny, 69
Flynn, Denzil, 68
Flynn, Helen, 69
Foley, Andrew N., 186, 216, 240
Foley, John, 216, 326
Foley, Michael Emmett, 216, 230
Foot, Wm., 212
Forbes Cemetery, 141
Forbes Hill, 141
Forbes, Charles, 139, 144
Forbes, Sarah Ann, 39
Forbes, William, 8, 139, 143, 229, 323
Ford, Carl, 295
Forrest Patton Trucking, 111
Foster & Schleppy, 45, 48
Foster, Cynthia, 74
Foster, Garret V., 79, 120
Foster, James, 140
Foster, John, 60, 115, 252
Foster, Morgan, 134
Foster, Myrtle, 74
Foster, Thomas, 39, 65, 73, 74, 107, 123, 131, 152, 153, 155, 193, 229, 234, 308, 324
Foster, Wiley S., 140, 311
Fountain, 7, 10, 82, 85, 97, 129, 263, 267, 271, 283, 284, 297, 303, 309, 313, 347
Fountain, August, 129
Fountain's Garage, 129
Fouts, Charles C., 180
Fouts, Chas. D., 179
Fouts, Don, 100, 101
Fouts, James W., 253, 343
Fouts, Letha, 291
Fowler, Isaac, 140
Fowler, John, 92, 93
Fowler's Hardware, 93
Foxworthy, John M., 162
Foxworthy, W.J., 325
Frain, Katie, 175

Frakes, John A., 74
Frame, William, 343
Francis, Jim, 7
Francis, Virginia, 55
Frankfort and State Line Railroad, 88, 168, 327, 332
Franklin Township, 5, 77
Franklin, Jerome B., 354
Franklin, Nellie, 165, 173
Frazee, Oliver J., 94
Fredericks, J.M., 337
Free and Accepted Masons, 308
Freeman, L.J.C., 186
French, Charles H., 343
Frey, Betty, 59
Frey, John, 116
Frey, Kenneth, 64, 76
Friedman, Mr., 35
Frieske, H.A., 54
Fritts, H.E., 188
Frozen Food Locker Service, 47
Fruits, Charles, 26, 241, 248
Fruits, Charles M., 46, 176, 241
Fruits, Charles R., 129
Fruits, Christine, 291
Fruits, Colleen, 291
Fruits, Daisy, 55
Fruits, Delmar K., 241
Fruits, Delmer K., 197
Fruits, Dutch, 135
Fruits, Grace, 136
Fruits, Herbert, 197, 198, 209, 210
Fruits, Sandy, 291
Fruits, Shirley, 291
Fruits, Teresa, 291
Fry, Harry O., 32, 56
Frye, John, 75
Fullen, John W., 171
Fullwider, 325
Fultz, Edith, 253
Fultz, William, 214
Fulwider, Jacob, 193
Fulwider, Walter A., 343
Furr & Cohee, 121
Furr, Bert, 121
Furr, Marianne, 292
Fyffe, Peggy, 59, 308
Fyffe, Robert, 151, 308

G

Gaines, John, 284
Gaines, Richard, 233
Gaither, Susan, 315
Gaither, William M., 315
Gaither, William S., 315, 316
Galbreath, Joseph, 152, 161, 229
Galbreath, Ruhama, 152
Galloway, A.T., 251
Garicher, Grover, 337
Garret, Jack, 3
Garret, Jonathan, 312
Gaston, A.E., 98
Geiger Jr., Roy, 64
Geiger, Morris, 130, 131, 243
Geiger, Roy E., 140
Geiger, S.L., 343
Geiger, Sheridan, 241, 251

George C. Livingston's Restaurant, 63
George Thomas' Hardware, 93
George W. Harriman's Saloon, 68
Gerard, W.C., 185
Gerard, Winnie, 36
Germaine, Harry, 300, 301
Gilbert, John A., 34
Gilkey, Aaron, 253, 324, 330, 331
Gilkey, Aaron H., 180
Gilkey, S.M., 163
Gillam, Moses, 178, 221, 226
Gilliland, John, 229, 232, 323
Gimmel, 259, 260, 269, 277
Girl Scouts, 25
Gladden, M.P., 356
Glasscock, George, 284
Glover, O.A., 199
Glover, Orrin, 343
Gobel, Hiram, 57
Goben, J.W., 225
Goben, Kate, 220
Goben, Will, 31
Goddard, Florence, 176
Goff Livestock Trucking, 111
Goff, Amos S., 343
Goff, Charles, 163
Goff, Edward, 169
Goff, Homer, 186, 253, 343
Goff, Paul, 100, 111
Goings, Marcia, 59
Goodin, Bert, 136
Goodin, Fred, 129
Goodin, Ruth, 207
Goodrich, J.P., 286
Goodwin, Columbus, 263
Goodwin, Dallas G., 263
Goodwin, Franklin D., 263
Goodwin, Georgia, 263
Goodwin, Tyler, 263
Goodwin, Vashti Nanette, 263
Gooley, Mr., 79
Goosenibble, 289, 326
Gould, Don, 44
Graham, Mary, 180
Grand Annual Horse Show, 109
Grand Lodge F. & A. Masons, 158
Grange of the Patrons of Husbandry, 305
Granger Store, 12, 30
Grangers, 212
Grannon, W.E., 231
Grannon, William, 98, 134, 307
Grantham, Thomas, 147, 193, 231, 343
Graves, C.W., 343
Graves, Carey, 325
Graves, Charles, 119, 126, 355
Graves, Fred W., 281
Graves, Henry, 45
Graves, M.C., 119, 281
Graves, Marshall L., 74, 75
Graves, Martin, 107, 281, 300
Graves, Sandra L., 257
Graves, William, 45, 140, 308
Gray, Jack, 5
Gray, John S., 310
Gray, Sanford, 284
Great Depression, 195, 196, 244, 245, 247, 271
Green, James, 213

Greenburg, Clyde, 343
Greenburg, Ernest, 290, 291
Greenburg, Everett, 291, 298, 319
Greenburg, Lulu, 173
Greenburg, Mary, 341
Gregory, 181, 182
Gregory, F.W., 183
Gregory, James, 181, 182, 309
Gregory, Samuel, 183
Grenard School, 186
Grenard, Abigail, 186
Grenard, Bonnie, 184
Grenard, Elisha, 218
Grenard, Mary, 200
Grenard-Rake Pocket, 186
Grendard, Simeon, 116, 186
Grennard, Crain, 110
Griffith, Howard, 306
Griggs, C.C., 161
Grigson, William F., 48, 63
Grigson's Bakery and Restaurant, 63
Grippe, 262
Gronert, Ted, 215
Groom, Lucy, 307
Gross, Amos M., 337
Gross, Mrs. Dan, 189
Groves, H.B., 134
Groves, Henry, 117, 134
Groves, O.B., 153, 155
Grubb, John, 342
Grubbs, J.W., 343

H

H.O. Shelby's Hardware, 92
Haas, Beulah, 272
Hackerd, Paul, 68
Hackerd, Pauline (Howe), 68
Hackerd's Tavern, 68
Hackman, Gene, 65
Hadley, Alverta, 92
Hagen, Anna, 35
Hainds (or Haines), Joe W., 126
Haire, Grace, 207
Haire, Sam, 111, 129
Hall, 69, 83, 109, 118, 148, 156, 204, 225, 241, 244, 246, 288, 293, 294, 295, 296, 297, 298, 307
Hall, Joseph, 312
Hamilton County, 8, 9, 10, 11, 163
Hamilton, Fay, 343
Hamilton, J.B., 21
Hamilton, Nat, 108
Hanawalt & Son, 43, 55
Hanawalt and Son Shoe Store, 58
Hanawalt, Austin, 35, 54, 354
Hanawalt, Lela, 148
Hanawalt, Roy, 35, 54, 140, 173, 196, 197, 208, 210
Hancock, 181
Handley, T.S., 98
Haney, Walter, 242
Hanna, B.W., 29
Hanna, Bayless W., 255
Hanna, J.E., 187, 253
Hanna, John E., 180
Hannebohn, James, 162
Harding & Henthorn, 197
Harding, Henry, 235, 237

Harding, James A., 346
Hargrave, Richard, 69
Harmon, John, 212
Harness Willie, 114
Harold, Alva N., 94
Harper, Albert, 219
Harper, Jane, 219
Harper, Milt, 140
Harriman Brothers, 83
Harriman, Elmer W., 80, 155, 252, 290, 291
Harriman, Fred, 81, 290
Harriman, George W., 68
Harriman, J.T. (John), 173
Harriman, James, 86
Harriman, Jean, 291
Harriman, Jerre, 67
Harriman, John E., 31
Harriman, Levi, 79, 80
Harriman, Lorlie, 202, 290, 291
Harriman, S.P., 230, 306
Harriman, Samuel, 307
Harriman, Spud, 252
Harriman, Stephen, 86, 354
Harriman, Walter W., 24, 76, 80, 244, 252, 290, 291
Harriman, William W., 354
Harris,, 290
Harris, James, 98, 176, 242, 247, 253
Harris, Jim, 140, 247
Harris, John, 125
Harris, Roscoe, 343
Harrison, Joshua, 273
Harshbarger, 181
Harshbarger, A., 181
Harshbarger, B., 181
Harshbarger, C., 181
Harshbarger, May, 275
Harshman, Harold, 210
Hartman, Veronica, 59
Hartness, Berta, 183
Hatton, Melvin, 285
Hauk, Mary C., 14
Hawthorne Musical Club, 294
Hawthorne, George B., 285
Hawthorne, J.M., 285
Hawthorne, Lee B., 285
Hayes, B.O., 183
Hayes, James, 148
Hayes, Joseph, 74
Hayes, Silas, 217
Haywood, Charles, 75, 88, 95, 119, 120, 121, 126, 147, 248, 306, 346
Haywood, Curtis D., 110, 140, 332
Haywood, E.F., 120
Haywood, Frances, 341
Haywood, Helen H., 279
Haywood, Henrietta E., 121
Haywood, Henry, 149
Haywood, Louie, 135
Haywood, Rev. Benjamin S., 149
Hayworth, Adson, 111
Hayworth, William, 67
hazelbush, 187
Heaton, Clem E., 58
Heaton, James, 83, 177, 182, 222, 223
Helbig, Florence C., 74
Hempleman, Alec W., 40, 41, 48, 104, 107, 231
Hempleman's, 22, 41, 48, 63, 130

Henderson, 195, 225, 298, 343
Henderson, Alfred L., 252, 343
Henderson, J.C., 67, 115
Henderson, John, 193, 195, 231, 239
Henderson, Mary M., 206
Henderson, Mayme, 207
Henderson, Pauline, 287
Hendricks Brothers, 43
Henes, Thomas, 162
Henry Clay Castle Hall Association, 306
Henry Clay Castle Hall Building Association of New Richmond, 194
Henry Clay Lodge, 49, 290, 295, 306
Henry Long's Livery Barn, 105, 246
Henry Taylor Lumber Company, 90
Henry, Joseph S., 180, 186, 187
Henry, Mr., 173, 184
Henry, William, 253
Henthorne, Elmer, 134
Herbert, Gertrude, 41, 304
Herbert, Myrtle, 56
Herbst, Brad, 162
Herrick, Bertha, 291
Herriman, Levi, 153, 155
Herriman, Margaret, 155
Herron, Joseph C., 95, 135
Hershberger, O.G., 109
Hershberger, O.L., 242, 351
Hershberger, Ocie, 242
Hershey, Barbara, 65
Heshbon Bethel, 145, 146, 164, 181, 182, 183
Heshbon Bethel Church, 146, 164, 182, 183
Heshman Bethel, 309
Hiatt, John, 108
Hickory Corner, 175
Hicks, George, 161
Hicks, Monte, 107
Hiett, John, 179
Hiett, Mary F., 179
Higert, Alma, 56
High School Store, 51
Hill, Roy, 135
Hinman, Jesse D., 63, 240, 241, 247
Hixson, Joel, 211
Hixson, Wm. H., 212
Hobbs, Mack, 88
Hobbs, R., 140
Hockett, William, 206, 207
Hole, Frank, 45
Holeman, Dallas, 67
Holliday, Sam, 48
Hollin, 11, 12, 22, 24, 39, 48, 49, 50, 51, 54, 56, 58, 69, 70, 96, 100, 109, 118, 130, 148, 156, 172, 197, 235, 249, 255, 289, 292, 293, 294, 295, 296, 297, 298, 300, 302, 303, 305, 306, 307, 308, 353
Hollin Opera House, 11, 24, 49, 148, 255, 289, 291, 293, 294, 295, 296, 297, 298, 300, 301, 302, 303
Hollin, Emma, 307
Hollin, Gladys, 49
Hollin, J.W., 54, 58, 235, 308
Hollin, John, 11, 31, 36, 39, 49, 50, 58, 196, 206, 209, 293, 300, 353, 354
Hollin, Lelia, 49, 286
Hollin, Lenna, 147, 307
Hollin, Lennie, 307
Hollin, Michael, 48
Hollin, Orpha L., 49

Hollin, W.H., 39, 193, 251
Hollin, William, 11, 49, 194, 239, 240, 251, 293, 354
Hollin's Opera House, 255, 289, 291, 293, 294, 295, 296, 297, 298, 300, 301, 302, 303
Hollingworth, Arthur, 312
Hollingworth, Eber, 312
Hollins, Lena, 287
Holmes, David, 116, 201, 202, 298, 316, 318
Holmes, George R., 113, 201, 202, 316, 317, 319
Holmes, H.F., 318
Holmes, Harry, 201, 202, 203, 316
Holmes, Kathryn Early, 317
Holmes, Mary Catherine, 317
Holmes, Rose L. Beaver, 201
Holt, Ernest, 247, 248
Hometown Furniture, 96
Hon, Bill, 61
Hood, Nick, 248
Hoosiers, 38, 65
Hop Ale Joint, 67
Hope, John, 67
Hopewell, Grace, 34, 56
Hopper, Dennis, 65
Hopper, Oliver, 186
Hormell, 176, 181, 187, 188
Hormell, Bertha, 176
Hormell, Mary, 176
Horn, Emmett, 343
Hornbeck, Ina, 291
Hornbeck, James, 127, 197, 343
Horse Show Association, 108, 109
Hostetter, D.B., 310
Hot Springs Remedy Company, 295, 299, 300, 301, 302, 303
Hotaling, Lewis R., 161
Hotel Crawford, 313
Houlehan and Morrow, 176
House, Oliver, 248
Howard, George, 337
Howard, W.H., 60
Howe, Ross, 68, 305
Huff,, 48
Huffer, Charles Morse, 150
Huffer, Helen Marie, 151
Hughes, Byron, 294, 295
Hughes, W.W., 168
Humbert & Brown, 113
Humbert & Westfall, 113
Humbert, Amos, 108
Humbert, Joe, 68
Humbert, Joseph, 68, 107, 113, 308, 354
Hummer, J.J., 337
Humphrey, Harold, 161
Hunt, Eugene, 291
Hunt, Frederick, 158, 159, 160, 239
Hunt, Gene, 291
Hunt, Martha Ellen, 160
Hunt, S.J., 347
Hunt, Spencer J., 347
Hunt, Wilson, 84, 86
Hupmobiles, 16, 344
Hurt, Absalom, 278
Hurt, Martha (Claypool), 278
Hurt, W.J., 277
Hurt, William J., 259, 269, 278
Hutchinson, John W., 173
Hutchinson, Tim, 130
Hutchison, Jasper, 211
Hutchison, John, 180, 186
Hutchison, Josiah, 229
Hyatt, Charles, 86

I

ice harvest, 124, 125, 126, 316
Ideal Ladies Tailoring, 36
Independent Drinkers Association, 67
Independent Order of Good Templar's, 212
Independent Order of Odd Fellows, 307, 308
Indiana Bell, 214
Inskeep, George, 130, 242
Inskeep, Harry, 197
Inskeep, John, 130
Inskeep, William, 147, 155, 195, 343
Insley, J.J., 166, 167, 179
Insley, James J., 112
Insley, Noah, 3, 79, 167
International Agriculture Field Days, 137
Invincible Guards, 211
Irvin, Carroll E., 252
Irvin, Kathleen, 207
Irvin, William, 186
Irwin, Fern, 189
Irwin, Will J., 175

J

J. M. (Milford) Stephenson Trucking Co., 111
J. M. Graham Trucking Co., 111
J. W. Hollin & Co, 54
J.O. Perkins Lumber Company, 91
Jack Smith Hardware, 91
Jackson Heights Church, 147
Jackson Quick, 214
Jackson Smith, 31, 36
Jackson, Andrew, 272
Jackson, Ed., 158
Jackson, Samuel M., 219
Jake Austin Trucking Co., 111
Jakes, Brother, 148
Jameson, Henry, 342
Jessie, Effie, 34, 56
Jett & McClure, 330
Jim & Jim, 61
John E. Wilson Hardware, 95
John F. Wight Hardware, 93
John McCallum Hardware, 92
John Nelson Clouser's Saloon, 67
John O. Kane (O'Kane)_____ Kerr, 151, 152, 161
John W. Hollin's Drug Store, 49
John W. Plunkett's Saloon, 65
Johnson, Alan F., 214
Johnson, Blanche, 51
Johnson, Carl, 51
Johnson, Clarence, 51
Johnson, D.L., 60
Johnson, Donald, 68
Johnson, F.M., 40, 50, 51, 69, 95, 130, 293, 307
Johnson, Frank M., 50, 51, 125, 286
Johnson, Guy L., 51
Johnson, H.C., 22, 40
Johnson, J.W., 181
Johnson, James H., 310
Johnson, John, 19, 219, 259, 277
Johnson, Lowell R., 267

Johnson, Maggie, 51
Johnson, Mary, 51, 178
Johnson, Mina, 179
Johnson, Thomas, 218
Johnston,, 348
Johnston, Helena, 186
Jolley, Roda H., 225
Jones, 38, 45, 55, 61, 93, 112, 116, 152, 184, 185, 209, 217, 225, 259, 267, 270, 271, 297, 298, 317, 343, 349
Jones,, 61, 349
Jones, Ab., 341
Jones, Charles R., 343
Jones, Clyde, 67, 184
Jones, Ed, 13, 20, 67
Jones, Edgar L., 13, 271, 343, 353, 355
Jones, George, 2, 270
Jones, George W., 45, 160, 267
Jones, Harriet, 34
Jones, Harriett, 34
Jones, Henry S., 288
Jones, J.L., 307
Jones, Jess, 55
Jones, Jessie, 355
Jones, Joseph, 219
Jones, Maggie E., 267
Jones, Mary, 38, 136
Jones, Mervin, 135
Jones, Philip, 55
Jones, Robert C., 55
Jones, S.D., 220
Jones, S.E., 261
Jones, Samuel, 173, 259, 270, 271, 277, 307
Jones, Sarah Florence, 38
Jones, W.T., 119, 312, 343
Jones, Walter D., 196, 229
Jones, Wayne, 123, 129, 243
Jones, Will, 116
Jones, William F., 348, 349, 350
Jones, William T., 349
Jordan, Jacob, 162
Joseph Humbert's Saloon, 68
Journal-Review, 176, 195, 197, 198, 318
Joy Theatre, 304
JoySings, 291
Julian, G.O., 193

K

K. of P., 22, 24, 25, 194
Keenan, Margaret, 85
Keeney, Herman, 174
Keesee, Nellie, 38
Keir, Nellie, 34
Keith, John, 68
Kelley, Francis C., 294
Kelley, O.E., 161, 173
Kellison, C.C., 186
Kellison, Charles, 183
Kelly, Mary Jane, 12
Kelp Bros. Trucking Company, 111
Kelp, Durrell, 64
Kelsey, Bertha, 307
Kelsey, C.E., 308
Kelsey, Charles Edward, 278
Kemble, Millie, 307
Kemble, Raymond, 307
Kemble, Walter, 126, 308

Ken & Betty's Café, 64
Kendall, Adason, 20
Kendall, Debby, 9, 10, 20
Kendall, Elisha, 143
Kendall, Isabell, 20
Kendall, James, 14, 20, 21, 57, 123, 143
Kendall, Leah, 20
Kendall, Mary, 20
Kendall, Milton, 20
Kendall, Polly, 20
Kendall, Samuel, 143
Kennedy, P.S., 330
Kennedy, V.Y., 326
Kenneson, John, 162
Kentwood, 180, 181, 217, 227
Kentwood Schoolhouse, 181
Kenyon, Caroline, 214
Kenyon, Clayton M., 214
Kenyon, M.V., 343
Kenyon, Mark, 105
Kenyon, Paris W., 214
Keplar, Joe, 23
Kernell, 98
Kerns, Bill, 252
Kerr, Miss, 56
Kerr, Nellie, 56
Kerr, Roy, 64, 242, 247
Kerr, Ted, 243
Kerr, Thomas, 148
Kesler, H.A., 291
Kesler, Howard, 173, 292
Kesler, Professor, 173, 291
Kibby, Pastor, 218
Killen, Charles, 92, 104
Killen, John, 178, 225, 226
Killen, Sarah Ann, 226
Kimbrell, Bud, 52
Kincaid Jr., James, 66, 79
Kincaid Jr., Samuel, 8
Kincaid Jr., Thomas, 10
Kincaid Sr., James, 66, 125
Kincaid, Albert, 10
Kincaid, Catherine, 8, 9, 10, 11
Kincaid, Deborah, 13, 21, 288
Kincaid, Edna, 178, 201, 202
Kincaid, Elizabeth, 8, 9, 10
Kincaid, Elizabeth Jane, 10, 11, 13
Kincaid, Ella, 10
Kincaid, Emily Josephine, 10
Kincaid, Franklin, 10
Kincaid, Fred, 60, 177, 188, 208, 209, 210, 354
Kincaid, Frederick H., 10
Kincaid, Gretchen, 178, 207, 288
Kincaid, Horace Greely, 10
Kincaid, Ida, 10, 307
Kincaid, Isabel Frances, 10
Kincaid, James, 8, 10, 66, 75, 125, 312
Kincaid, Jim, 57, 66, 79, 110, 124, 176
Kincaid, John, 8, 9, 10
Kincaid, Lydia, 10
Kincaid, Margaret, 10
Kincaid, Martha Ellen, 11
Kincaid, Martha J., 10
Kincaid, Mary, 9, 10
Kincaid, Mary A., 10
Kincaid, Mary Ellen, 10
Kincaid, Phebe, 8, 9, 10, 11

Kincaid, Polly Catharine, 10
Kincaid, Russell, 8, 9, 10, 11
Kincaid, Samuel, 7, 8, 9, 10, 11, 19, 32, 66, 79, 97, 108, 143, 232, 233
Kincaid, Thomas, 8, 9, 10
Kincaid, Will, 116
Kincaid, William, 8, 9, 10, 13, 20, 21, 79, 86, 167, 168, 253, 288
Kindell, Anna (Pittman), 271
Kindell, Bill, 242
Kindell, Hanson T., 271
Kindell, Hurschell D., 259, 271, 272
Kindell, Shirley, 272
Kindell, William, 242, 272
King, 42, 49, 51, 58, 68, 86, 114, 168, 173, 178, 179, 180, 181, 192, 221, 226, 238, 282, 299, 304
King, Agnes, 11, 299
King, Alice, 173, 181, 183
King, Bernice Beard, 51
King, Cy, 80
King, Ed, 42, 160, 196, 238, 239, 354
King, Edward, 11, 240, 354
King, Elizabeth L., 11
King, Emma, 49, 168, 173
King, Fred, 248
King, Henry N., 221, 222
King, Henry R., 225
King, John, 51, 178, 221, 222
King, Josiah, 11, 49, 206, 299
King, Lena, 49, 180, 183
King, Lenna L., 11
King, Norma, 51
King, Pierson, 287
King, Robert, 51, 232, 241, 282
King, Rose, 11
King, Sarah J. (Campbell), 49, 299
King, Shirley, 51
King, W.J., 114
King, W.S., 173
Kingry, Linda, 291
Kinnett, George, 9
Kirkpatrick, 8, 16, 30, 31, 32, 60, 73, 74, 75, 95, 104, 107, 108, 109, 117, 123, 142, 143, 144, 164, 173, 176, 177, 182, 193, 207, 229, 235, 239, 246, 248, 249, 252, 256, 257, 261, 265, 271, 311, 312, 334, 339, 343, 346, 354, 355
Kirkpatrick, A., 182
Kirkpatrick, Absalom, 69, 140, 142, 143, 164, 177, 229, 309, 315, 323
Kirkpatrick, Altie, 173
Kirkpatrick, Amanda A. (Shuee), 265
Kirkpatrick, Charles, 16, 72, 117, 124, 140, 147, 193, 194, 195, 206, 234, 256, 257, 298, 308, 326, 339, 341, 342, 344, 346, 354
Kirkpatrick, Cyrus Q., 107, 139, 144, 145, 311, 312
Kirkpatrick, Della, 288
Kirkpatrick, E.J., 285
Kirkpatrick, Ernest O., 176
Kirkpatrick, Frank, 144
Kirkpatrick, J.A., 67, 119, 148, 287
Kirkpatrick, Jacob, 193, 265
Kirkpatrick, Jessie, 34, 193, 194, 354
Kirkpatrick, John, 246, 343, 355, 356
Kirkpatrick, Laura, 34, 206, 207
Kirkpatrick, Mandy (Shuee), 256
Kirkpatrick, Mr., 31, 117, 145, 256
Kirkpatrick, Noah, 343
Kirkpatrick, Samuel S., 107, 140, 144, 147, 193, 300, 306, 312
Kirkpatrick, Susan K., 265
Kirkpatrick, Thomas, 253, 294, 342
Kirkpatrick, William, 112, 147, 193, 194, 195, 196, 238, 326, 354
Kite, Solomon, 114, 311
Kite, W.M., 312
Kite, William, 67, 193, 231, 308, 343
Kliter, Joe, 57, 58, 289
Klopfer, Charles, 34
Knights of Pythias, 15, 24, 25, 44, 49, 51, 52, 55, 59, 63, 64, 83, 92, 98, 136, 143, 194, 263, 280, 289, 290, 293, 295, 305, 306, 307
knockboard, 134
Kochell, Charles, 343
Kochell, F.E., 343
Koehler, Murlene, 68
Kole Kreke Kamera, 100, 113, 344
Krause, Professor A.W., 165
Kross, Jim, 2
Kruse, Thomas, 129
Kunkel, Bill, 128
Kunkel, Fowler, 140
Kunkel, Lois, 198
Kunkel, Ralph, 64, 83, 136, 140, 197, 198, 244, 253, 351
Kunkel, Roger, 83, 140, 243, 253
Kunkel's Plumbing and Heating, 26

L

L.P. Brown's Farm Implement & Buggies, 113
L.P. Brown's Hardware, 94
Ladies Aid Society, 148, 154, 155, 156, 158, 159, 287, 295, 296
Lafayette String Band, 30
Lamborn, Thomas, 229
Lamphor, Alice, 306
Lamson and Pence, 134
Lamson, J.A., 67, 110
Landis, Roxie, 64
Lane Hardware, 23
Lane, Bill, 7, 96
Lane, Darwin, 155
Lane, Edna, 159, 160
Lane, Frank, 136, 202
Lane, J.H., 337
Lane, N. Gary, 258
Lane, Richard, 96, 197, 198
Lane, Russell, 83
Lane, Sherman, 140
Lane, Thomas, 242
Lane, W. Darwin, 158, 159, 343
Lane, Wm., 243
Lane's Hardware, 96
Langston, Leon, 162
Larew, Garrett, 213, 343
Largent, Leonard, 162
Larue, Garrett, 212, 213
Lawler, Jim, 162
Layden, Michael, 119
Layne, Darwin, 32
Layne, T.M., 25, 67, 93, 94, 113
Layne, Theodore M., 93, 94, 95
Layne, William M.E., 245
Layton, Linda, 65, 243
Leader, Betty, 308
Learning, Henry, 107
Lee, Agnes, 86
Lee, Annie Bell, 269
Lee, Catherine Helen, 86
Lee, Cecelia (Runey), 85

Lee, Frank, 116
Lee, H.K., 85, 312, 326
Lee, Hank, 252
Lee, Henry K., 85, 86, 87, 88, 94, 114, 124, 140, 155, 156, 193, 194, 306, 325
Lee, III, Maurice, 87
Lee, John, 284
Lee, Lettie, 185
Lee, Maude, 42
Lee, Maurice, 85, 86, 87
Lee, Maurice J., 85, 86
Lee, Nannie, 114, 307
Lee, Richard O., 161
Lee, Walter John, 86
Lee, William L., 232
LeGalley, Carol, 280
LeGalley, Mildred (Rinker), 279
LeGalley, Myron E., 279
LeGalley, Robert R., 279
Lehman, Bessie, 202
Leonard, George F., 161
Lesley, A E., 57
Leslie, Everett, 290
Lewellyn, Wilma, 206, 207, 291
Lewis, Allen, 105, 343
Lewis, Allie, 107
Lewis, Mrs. Allen, 111
Liberty Chapel, 245, 259
Lidester, Jack, 108
Lidikey, 312
Lidikey, Herman, 312
Lily Temple, 306
Linda's Hickory Tree, 65
Linden, 2, 15, 16, 24, 26, 32, 33, 43, 44, 47, 48, 51, 59, 75, 83, 89, 92, 93, 95, 99, 103, 105, 107, 109, 110, 112, 116, 117, 122, 127, 129, 132, 141, 146, 148, 152, 168, 189, 195, 197, 198, 199, 203, 204, 205, 207, 208, 210, 219, 225, 244, 257, 265, 267, 270, 274, 275, 280, 282, 289, 298, 299, 301, 312, 319, 323, 324, 326, 327, 328, 329, 330, 332, 333, 334, 344, 346, 347, 348, 354, 355, 356
Linden Lumber Company, 127
Linden State Bank, 26, 51, 197, 198, 244
Linton & Sons Trucking Co., 111
Linton, Deana, 122
Linton, Jeff, 122
Linton, Randy, 122
Linton, Russell, 121, 122
Linton, Virginia, 122
Literary Society, 177
Litke, Herman, 343
Little Dixie, 33
Livingston, George, 37, 42, 63, 72, 104, 105, 196, 239, 240, 251, 307, 354
Livingston, Joseph, 343
Livingston, Louie, 42
Livingston, Margie, 160
Livingston, Nelle, 148
Livingston, Samuel, 128, 304, 312
Livingston, William, 111
Loder, James, 145
Lofland Jr., John S., 193
Logan and Swank, 117
Loman, Blanch, 179, 186
Long brothers, 37, 199
Long, A.D., 38, 39, 158, 159, 160
Long, Anna, 155
Long, Arthur, 38, 159, 199, 240

Long, Benjamin, 60
Long, Carrol, 39
Long, Dan, 115
Long, Doris, 39
Long, Florence, 39, 55, 160
Long, Frances, 39
Long, Frank, 115, 116
Long, George, 22, 23, 37, 38, 49, 57, 76, 79, 88, 95, 96, 109, 125, 126, 192, 194, 199, 201, 204, 206, 237, 238, 239, 246, 247, 249, 276, 278, 306, 326, 337, 339, 341
Long, Hellie, 307
Long, Henry, 105, 107, 115, 246, 280, 346
Long, Homer, 115
Long, J. Chester, 39
Long, John A., 60, 298, 300
Long, Louis, 38, 39
Long, Mrs. George F., 157, 158
Long, Nina, 114, 307
Long, Robert, 193, 343
Long, Rosetta, 37, 160
Long, Ruby, 38
Long, William, 114, 125, 238, 250, 354
Lovel, Merle, 126
Lowe, Teressa, 136
Lowry, Oscar, 140
Lucas, Albert A., 48
Lucas, Arlie, 41
Lucas, D.M., 45, 112
Lucas, Mark, 45, 105
Lucas, Mart, 110, 306
Lucas, Will, 50
Lunger, Philip, 167, 168
Lunger, William, 140
Luse, Albert C., 193
Luse, Albert E., 307
Lydich, Chas., 312
Lydick, C.A., 193
Lydick, Homer C., 337
Lynch brothers, 51
Lynch, Ed, 51
Lynch, Mabel, 168
Lynch, W.B., 90
Lynn, F.M., 260, 261
Lynn, Frank, 193, 238, 245, 259, 261, 264, 272, 273
Lynn, Mollie, 307
Lynn, Myrtle, 245
Lyon, Claude, 128
Lyon, Mabel, 59
Lyon, Monroe, 76, 81, 242, 247, 356
Lyon, Wilbert, 128, 197, 344
Lyon's Billiard Hall, 76
Lyons, Ann, 206
Lyons, Dema, 42
Lyons, Monroe, 76
Lyons, Wilbert, 344

M

M. J. Lee Drain Tile Company, 85, 87, 88
Machen, Professor, 194
Mackey, Mary, 8
Madison Township, 5, 99, 208, 219, 220, 267, 275, 326, 327, 329, 331, 351
Magruder, Edd, 116
Magruder, Harry, 116
Magruder, Ira, 135
Magruder, Samuel E., 45, 105, 107, 193, 238, 312, 354

Magruder's Hall, 293
Magruder's Livery Barn, 105, 281
Magruder's Restaurant and Grocery, 64
Mahan, Jim, 5
Maharry, James, 181
Mahon, 7
Mahon, J.H., 351
Malaria, 262
Malaskey, George, 307, 308
Malaskey, Laura, 307
Malsbary, Alfred E., 117, 118, 193, 266, 298
Malsbary, James, 291
Malsbary, John M., 147
Malsbary, John V., 193
Mangold, Martha, 15
Mann, John, 181
Manners, Barbara, 145, 147, 150, 195, 208, 225, 233, 274
Manners, Dr. George, 1, 20, 147, 225, 273, 274
Manners, George, 19, 144, 259, 260, 273, 274, 311, 328
Manners, Harvey, 273
Manners, James, 273
Manners, Joseph, 273
Manners, Lettice (Hight), 273
Manners, Martha, 273
Manners, Mrs., 86, 150, 274
Manners, Nancy, 273
Manners, Percilla, 273
Manners, Robert, 12
Manson, M.C., 330
Marcia's Beauty Salon, 59
Marcus and Nellie West, 282
Marshall, Thos. T., 169, 188
Marsteller, George E., 107
Martens, Earl, 350
Martin, Benjamin, 119
Martin, C.L., 140
Martin, George M., 342
Martin, Henry H., 168
Martin, James D., 93, 298
Martin, Jennie, 34
Martin, Richard, 135
Martin, Vicki, 207
Martindale, Harry, 155, 161
Martindale, Rev. H.H., 158
Mason & Lee, 94
Mason, A.L., 347
Mason, Clara, 94, 155, 160, 307
Mason, E.J., 306
Mason, Ed, 32, 34
Mason, Emma, 13
Mason, Ester Jane, 160
Mason, Ewing, 5, 82, 156, 252, 343
Mason, Fern, 155
Mason, Jack, 140
Mason, M.J., 140, 311, 312
Mason, Mahlon J., 139, 140
Mason, Monroe, 193, 343, 354
Mason, Orlando W., 90, 94, 107, 131, 133, 139, 155, 158, 159, 160, 175, 181, 183, 188, 234, 236, 237, 239, 250, 253, 278, 293, 295, 306, 312, 353, 354
Mason, Paul, 13, 116, 203
Mason, Robert, 140
Mason, William, 127, 343
Mason, Willis, 140
Mason, Wright, 55, 323
Masonic cemetery, 266
Masonic Lodge, 308, 353

Massing, John, 114
Mathew, John, 219
Mathew, Milton, 219
Mathias, 183
Mathieu, Rachel M., 291
Matricia, Jerry, 68
Matricia, Nancy, 308
Matthews, Helen, 285
Maurice III, 87
Maurice J. Lee and Sons, 86
Mauzy, Charles A., 94
Maxwell, Frank, 341
May, Alexander, 143
McBeth, Grace, 189
McBeth, Quinn, 147
McBroom, Edward, 309
McBroom, Elder, 284
McBroom, J. Martin, 173
McBroom, William, 233
McCallom, Eva, 173
McCallum, Eva, 173
McCallum, John, 92, 196, 353
McCardle Elevator, 22, 118
McCardle, Clyde, 118, 339, 340, 341
McCardle, John, 22, 40, 50, 117, 118, 193, 206, 286, 306, 338, 339, 344
McClain, Charles, 81, 250
McClamrock, 209, 225
McClamrock, James R., 224
McClamrock, L.B., 224
McClamrock, Lemuel, 224
McClamrock, William, 325
McClelland, W.D., 307
McClure, C.A., 185, 187
McClure, Charles A., 185
McClure, Hamilton, 183
McClure, J.W., 331
McClure, James A., 108
McCollum, Mr., 79
McComas Hotel, 14, 72, 267
McComas, Arvilla, 14
McComas, Barbara M., 14
McComas, Charles Franklin, 14
McComas, David C., 14
McComas, DeLoss, 14
McComas, Ed, 14
McComas, Eliza A., 14, 97
McComas, Hattie, 14
McComas, James, 14, 19, 97, 153, 206
McComas, Jeanette, 14
McComas, Jemima, 14
McComas, John, 14, 97
McComas, Joseph, 14, 97
McComas, Louella, 14
McComas, Maria, 14, 144, 168, 169
McComas, Mary, 14, 270
McComas, Nancy, 14, 97, 153
McComas, Robert, 14
McComas, Samuel, 14, 19, 144, 152, 153, 154, 163, 167, 168, 174, 206, 229, 312
McComas, Stowe (or Stover), 14
McComas, Susan Pitts, 14
McComas, William, 14, 97, 206
McConnel, Ira, 213
McCord, Shari, 207
McCorkle, A.C., 285
McCorkle, J.W., 285, 310

McCorkle, John W., 253
McCorkle, Polly (Meharry), 146, 309
McCoy, James F., 312
McCoy, Maxwell, 218
McCrea, 110, 119, 133, 135, 141, 148, 169, 170, 209, 210, 256, 287, 290, 292, 326, 328, 343
McCrea Cemetery, 141
McCrea, Ed, 141, 292
McCrea, Edward H., 119, 134, 287, 290, 291, 292, 343
McCrea, Edward T., 3, 119, 131, 133, 140, 145, 147, 148, 193, 196, 210, 253, 255, 256, 287, 292, 308, 311, 312, 332
McCrea, Jessie Louise (Draper), 292
McCrea, John, 196, 208, 209, 210, 292
McCrea, Mary, 141, 197
McCrea, Ted, 290
McCrea, William, 90, 119, 131, 133, 134, 135, 197
McCullough, Charles, 341
McDaniel, Charles, 340
McDaniel, Mary, 149
McDonald, David, 229
McFarland, John E., 347
McGaughey, O.W., 161
McGinnis, Joseph, 163, 178
McGinnis, Sophia, 163, 178, 220
McGraw, Robin, 316
McGruder, Sam, 108
McJimsey, John, 183
McKinney, A.L., 219
McKinney, C.R., 285
McKinney, James L., 163
McKinsey, M.B., 161
McLain, C.A., 41, 48, 54
McLain, Charles, 41, 55, 63, 252, 304, 354
McLain, John, 79
McLain, Lawrence, 63, 93, 116, 290
McLain, Mary Elizabeth, 272
McLain, Millie, 307
McLain, Myrtle, 41, 304
McLain, Perry, 92, 93, 95, 134, 196, 238, 248, 249, 272, 308, 354
McLain, Reid, 41
McLain, Will, 290
McLain's Restaurant and Bakery, 63
McMillin, A.C., 308
McMillin, Ann, 100
McMillin, Augustus, 83
McMillin, Boyd A., 193
McMillin, Claude, 100
McMillin, Thomas, 99
McMillin's Restaurant, 64
McMillions, 160
McMullen, Lucy, 186
McMurray, 276
McNeil, Alice, 354
McNeil, Boyd, 43, 232, 290
McNeil, Elnora, 148, 301
McNeil, Harry, 290
McNeil, John, 232, 342, 351, 354
McNeil, Ruth, 203
McNeill, Keith, 161
McWhinney, J.A., 60
Mears, Eph, 308
Measles, 262, 324
Mefford, Gordon, 47
Meharry, 113, 142, 143, 145, 146, 164, 181, 182, 183, 210, 227, 283, 285, 288, 309, 310, 313, 325, 343, 356
Meharry Cemetery, 146, 164, 283, 309, 313
Meharry, A., 283

Meharry, Alexander, 283, 324, 330
Meharry, Allen N., 182, 183
Meharry, Clare, 183
Meharry, David, 182, 283
Meharry, G.N., 310
Meharry, Hugh, 182, 283
Meharry, Ira, 182, 183, 195, 285, 310, 311
Meharry, Isaac, 2, 285, 330
Meharry, James, 182, 283, 309, 310
Meharry, Jesse, 182, 283, 309
Meharry, Judd, 288, 343
Meharry, Mary E., 343
Meharry, Nancy, 182, 183
Meharry, Polly, 187
Meharry, Roy, 183, 308
Meharry, Samuel, 283
Meharry, Thomas, 83, 113, 146, 182, 183, 187, 283, 309
Meharry, Unity, 182
Meharry's campground, 142, 356
Meharry's Grove, 115, 283, 284, 285, 286, 289, 303, 325
Meharry-Council Grove School, 183
Men's Booster Club, 159
Mendelssohn Quartette, 294
Meritt, J.N., 343
Merman Farms, 137
Merrill, Ansel, 116
Merrill, Avery C., 116
Merrill, B., 218
Merrill, Hugo, 116
Merrill, John D., 116
Merrill, Ruben, 116
Merritt, Eugene, 180
Merritt, John, 180
Merritt, Michael, 180
Mershon, Billy, 269
Mershon, William, 140, 259
Mershon, William, 278
Mertz, Miss, 33, 34, 57
Messer & Westfall, 98, 113
Messer, H.G., 98, 231
Messer, Horace G., 113, 237, 250, 293, 353
Messer, Horace Green, 101
Methodist Episcopal Church, 144, 145, 147, 149, 182, 212, 220, 221, 223, 224, 225, 226, 274, 296
Miami, 7, 273
Michael, Charles, 60
Mick, John, 30
Mick, S.M., 115, 285
Middleton, Mr., 75
Mikels, W.R., 285
Miles, Carol, 137
Miles, Don, 54, 137
Miles, Donald, 137, 197
Miles, Donald R., 198
Miles, Florence, 34, 35
Miles, Jill, 137
Miles, Opal, 308
Miles, Sandra, 137
Miles, Scott, 137
Miller, A.M., 278
Miller, Addison, 119
Miller, Ben, 251
Miller, D.C., 107
Miller, De Witt, 294
Miller, Dolly, 227, 315
Miller, Frank, 253, 315
Miller, J.H., 211

Miller, James, 104
Miller, John, 116, 173
Miller, John L., 343
Miller, Linda, 291
Miller, Loucinda, 10
Miller, Martha, 116
Miller, Martha K., 343
Miller, Maude, 33
Miller, Omer (or Homer), 136
Miller, Orville C., 161
Miller, Ruth, 287
Miller, Sam, 220
Miller, Shelly B., 202
Miller, Susan, 168, 177
Miller, Susie E., 186
Miller, T.B., 231
Miller, W.R., 225
Miller, William R., 103
Million, Joe, 299
Million, Joseph, 299
Million, Rex King, 299
Million, Zula, 74, 75
Mills, Caleb, 171
Mills, Charles, 19
Mills, Dan, 229
Milner, George, 353
Miss Turvey's Millinery Emporium, 56
Missionaries, 149
Missionary Society, 148, 155
Mitchell, Alice, 56, 298
Mitchell, Charles, 11, 12, 200, 291, 319, 349
Mitchell, D.K., 328
Mitchell, Elliot O., 343
Mitchell, Frances, 319, 320
Mitchell, Glenn, 12, 56, 230, 290, 291, 319, 320, 321, 322, 348, 349
Mitchell, Harry, 81, 196, 213, 267
Mitchell, Mrs., 56
Mitchell, Pauline, 55
Mitchell, Raymond, 343
Mitchell, S.S., 98
Mitchell, Wm., 211
Mitty, Samuel, 103, 276
Mobilgas Oil And Greases, 129
Modern Woodmen of America, 49, 156, 293, 295, 307
Monon, 264, 273, 300, 327, 333, 355
Monroe, Ferrell, 281
Monroe, William, 310
Montgomery & Zook, 40
Montgomery County Union Detective Association, 310
Montgomery Power and Light Company, 356
Montgomery, Frances, 186
Montgomery, Isaac H., 57, 328, 343
Montgomery, Isacc H., 253
Montgomery, Martha, 291
Montgomery, T.F., 35
Montgomery, W.B., 117
Montgomery, W.H., 2
Montgomery, William, 332
Montgomery's Woods, 1
Montgomery-Putnam County Cattlemen's Association, 137
Moore, Martin, 310
Moore, Pastor H. Earl, 147
Morone, Hariet, 219
Morris, John N., 343, 355
Morris, Mayme, 207, 298
Morris, Mr., 45

Morris, Thomas, 31, 39, 128, 344
Morrow Family Hardware, 95
Morrow, Ebright M., 95, 173, 177, 178, 253
Morrow, Eva, 177
Morrow, James, 218
Morrow, Ruth, 291
Moser, O.G., 326
Moudy, Elias, 309
Moulder, James, 32, 36, 201
Mound Builders, 4, 5, 6
Mount Pleasant, 217, 219, 220, 224
Mount, James A., 310
Mount, William B., 56
Mumps, 262
Munhall, Thomas T., 157, 196
murals, 320, 322
Murdock, Jim, 100
Murdock, Theodora, 291
Murphey, Mr., 332
Murphy, Daniel, 181, 185, 217
Murphy, Gary, 207
Murphy, John, 67, 173, 216, 217
Murphy, M.J., 173, 176, 186, 282
Murphy, Martin, 217
Murphy, Matt, 176, 186, 217, 294, 295
Murphy, Matthew J., 217
Murphy, Ron, 162
Murphy, W.A., 326
Musa, 74, 261, 277
Mutual Electric Company, 82, 136
Mutual Electric Corporation, 135, 136
Myers, 24, 144, 180, 193, 207, 216, 225
Myers, Carol, 207
Myers, D.A., 5
Myers, Francis, 75
Myers, John, 79
Myers, Joseph, 161

N

Nash, Omer, 282
National Guard, 264, 290, 334
National Horse Thief Detective Association, 310, 311, 312, 313
Naugle, Israel, 188
Nave, F.A., 347
Navy, 81, 210, 271, 292, 317
Neideigh, Ed, 290
Neideigh, Glenn, 290
Neidigh, George, 129
Neil, Charles, 105
Neiser, Henry, 301
Nelson, Mr., 60
Nesbitt, David, 140
Nesbitt, Elnora McNeil, 301
Nesbitt, Herman B., 343
New Richmond Band, 70, 289, 290, 294
New Richmond Bank, 23, 191, 192, 195
New Richmond Bar and Grill, 47, 68, 69, 303
New Richmond Bar and Grill and Pizza King, 68
New Richmond Beauty Shop, 59
New Richmond Building Association, 193
New Richmond Café, 64
New Richmond Canning, 90, 119, 131, 132, 133
New Richmond Cemetery, 10, 12, 13, 14, 42, 79, 80, 95, 96, 139, 140, 280, 281, 303, 315
New Richmond Cemetery Association, 139, 140

New Richmond Christian Church, 12, 14, 34, 69, 79, 115, 128, 151, 152, 153, 154, 155, 157, 158, 159, 160, 163, 193, 250, 258, 269, 291, 292, 295
New Richmond Citizens Band, 25
New Richmond Comedy Company, 298, 300, 319
New Richmond Commercial Brass Band, 289
New Richmond Drug Store, 51, 52
New Richmond Enterprise, 50, 53, 56, 69, 109, 192, 200, 237, 278, 353
New Richmond Farm Supply, 122
New Richmond Garage, 129
New Richmond High School, 42, 61, 63, 76, 81, 82, 83, 111, 112, 113, 114, 120, 150, 159, 270, 280, 287, 291, 294, 296, 298, 304, 315, 317, 319, 344
New Richmond Lumber & Coal Co, 91, 244
New Richmond Lumber Company, 90, 119
New Richmond Methodist Church, 41, 52, 76, 80, 147, 150, 151, 169, 274, 295, 353
New Richmond Methodist Episcopal Church, 141, 147, 148, 225, 303
New Richmond News, 200
New Richmond Orchestra, 201, 294
New Richmond Park, 3, 87, 140, 316
New Richmond Record, 6, 19, 23, 33, 34, 35, 40, 41, 42, 48, 53, 54, 56, 57, 58, 63, 66, 67, 70, 71, 73, 75, 76, 79, 80, 87, 88, 89, 90, 92, 95, 98, 99, 101, 105, 106, 109, 111, 112, 113, 120, 132, 134, 140, 146, 148, 150, 156, 157, 173, 176, 177, 178, 181, 193, 194, 200, 201, 202, 203, 204, 209, 210, 223, 224, 230, 232, 245, 250, 261, 262, 264, 266, 280, 281, 282, 285, 286, 288, 290, 294, 295, 297, 300, 301, 302, 303, 307, 308, 312, 313, 316, 317, 318, 325, 335, 337, 339, 340, 342, 344, 345, 347, 351, 354, 356
New Richmond Restaurant, 64, 65
New Richmond Savings and Loan Association, 26, 196, 197, 198, 258
New Richmond School, 39, 67, 81, 154, 168, 169, 171, 172, 176, 177, 178, 179, 183, 188, 189, 275, 280, 291, 297
New Richmond Telephone, 43, 96, 100
New Richmond Times, 37, 131, 191, 199, 200
New Richmond Transfer Co., 111
New Richmond's Tiger, 67
New Richmond-Coal Creek Township Historical Museum, 23
Newlights, 217
Newnum, Ora, 129, 242
Newtown, 84, 109, 145, 146, 158, 174, 183, 207, 209, 268, 271, 272, 283, 284, 285, 286, 294, 309, 319, 324, 326, 335, 342, 345, 346, 347, 348
Nick Washburn's Men's Clothing and Cigar Store, 24
Nickel-Plate, 334, 337
Niles, Jeffery, 162
Nine Mile Prairie, 7, 106
No. 13, 165, 175, 187, 188, 227, 281
Noggle, 199
Nolan, Frank, 220
Norfolk and Western Railway Company, 337
Norman, Eula, 291
Norman, Lavonne, 189
North Montgomery High School, 101, 189
Northwestern Traction Line, 348
Number 13 School, 5

O

O'Brien, Margaret, 217
O'Connell, Joseph, 79
O'Conner, Thomas E., 241
Oak Hill North cemetery, 266

Oakes, Helen, 149
Oakes, Sanford, 149
Oakland, 175, 227, 264, 275, 342, 343
Oakland Cemetery, 175
Odd Fellows, 49, 296, 307
Oklahoma, 92, 165, 175, 188, 200, 266, 296, 335, 350
Old Brick Church, 143
Old Jacob, 211
Old School Baptists Church, 214
Old Settler's Meeting, 115, 284, 285, 289, 351
Olin, Blanche, 275
Olin, Clara (Clark), 275
Olin, Dennis, 137
Olin, Doc. L.W., 212
Olin, Doctor, 203
Olin, Grace, 275
Olin, Kathy, 291
Olin, Leland E., 275
Olin, Lester, 173, 175, 176, 189, 241, 242, 252, 275
Olin, Leverett R., 275
Olin, Leverett W., 259, 275
Olin, Leveritt, W., 212
Olin, Ransom, 275
Olin, Reine, 275
Olin, Ruth, 275
Oliver Totten's Hardware, 93
Oliver, Charles T., 343
Oliver, Justus, 312
Oppy, 95, 96, 103, 117, 136, 139, 141, 143, 171, 198, 232, 325, 343, 355, 356
Oppy Jr., Thomas, 95
Oppy, Allie, 307
Oppy, C.J., 328
Oppy, Charles, 308
Oppy, Christopher J., 14, 117, 139
Oppy, David, 57, 139, 233, 274
Oppy, E.T., 343
Oppy, Ed C., 307
Oppy, Edward, 355
Oppy, Edward T., 95, 117
Oppy, Garland, 140, 197, 198
Oppy, George, 103
Oppy, Gertrude, 160
Oppy, Helen, 135, 140, 197, 198, 206, 232
Oppy, Joan, 16
Oppy, John, 86, 119, 308
Oppy, Leland, 136
Oppy, Margaret, 139
Oppy, Ruby Foster, 95, 171
Oppy, Ruthanna, 198, 232
Oppy, Sandra, 95
Oppy, Sharon, 95
Oppy, Shelia, 95
Oppy, Sonya, 95
Oppy, Thomas, 95, 117, 119, 140, 242, 343, 355
Oppy-Bible Company, 355, 356
Orr, John, 34
Osborn, Bob, 200
Osborn, Othel L., 200
Osborn, R.S., 186, 200, 236
Osborn, Robert, 200, 236
Osburn, R.S., 187
Osburn, Robert, 174
Oscar, 66, 95, 130, 140, 155, 161, 173, 180, 204, 299
Oswalt, Charles, 197, 240, 247
Oswalt, Clifford, 111
Othel L., 200

Ottinger, Gerald, 129, 242, 247
Overman, Jerry, 162
Overmyer, Earl C., 88
Owen, Paul A., 127
Oxley, Henry, 212
Oxley, J.H., 212
Oxley, James, 212, 213

P

P & R Garage, 129
Page, Anna, 307
Page, B.E., 238
Page, Bert, 11, 118, 238, 249, 250, 298, 339, 341, 344
Palin, Doris G., 207
Parent-Teachers Association, 173
Park Cemetery, 17, 141
Park, Elijah, 167, 168, 253
Parke County, 2, 268, 269
Parker, James, 111
Parlon Lumber and Coal Company, 81
Parlon, Alice, 91
Parlon, Catherine, 91
Parlon, J.T., 251
Parlon, James T., 91, 121, 239, 240
Parlon, John, 91, 122, 130, 197
Parlon, Mary Ann, 91
Parlon, Richard, 91
Patriotic Order of America, 305
Patten (Patton), Isaac W., 311, 312
Patten (Patton), John, 312
Patterson, 8, 225
Patterson, Mary, 8
Patton, 23, 91, 113, 145, 153, 165, 173, 176, 177, 181, 191, 209, 220, 225, 282, 298, 311, 312, 343
Patton School, 91, 176, 177, 209
Patton Schoolhouse, 91, 177, 209
Patton, A.V. (Alvanza), 282
Patton, Alfred, 129
Patton, Anna, 76
Patton, Arlie O., 343
Patton, Bell, 181
Patton, Charles A., 306, 326, 343
Patton, Ernest, 116, 343
Patton, Fannie, 1, 13, 155
Patton, Fern, 104
Patton, George T., 343
Patton, Isaac W. (Billie), 220
Patton, J.W., 213
Patton, John, 76, 152, 153, 159, 176, 177, 206, 227, 252, 325
Patton, Mime, 34
Patton, Mrs. Don, 189
Patton, Nancy, 160, 176, 177
Patton, T.S., 191, 306
Patton, Tessie, 275
Patton, Thomas, 23, 91, 113, 145, 165, 173, 191, 196, 235, 282
Patton, William, 152, 213
Patton's Corner, 2, 6, 86, 227, 267, 325
Patton's Schoolhouse, 177, 324
Pattons, 326
Paul, G.W., 255
Pease, C.H., 185
Pebler, George, 48
Peed, Isaac, 20
Peek, Earl, 79
Peek, Will, 79, 105
Pence, G.A., 63, 110, 290

Pence, Shirley, 291
Pender, Joe, 57
Pendleton Sr., Roy, 68, 248
Pendleton, Roy, 68, 248
People's Guide of Montgomery County, 84, 97
Perkins, Col. Albert W., 223
Perkins, Elias, 86, 126
Perkins, Frank, 22, 24, 31, 32, 75, 77, 104, 125, 126, 249, 251, 281
Perkins, Lucy, 31
Perkins, Miss, 56
Perry McLain and Sons Hardware, 95
Perry, Albert, 292
Perry, John, 307
Perry, Judith, 292
Perry, Marietta (Fruits), 292
Perry, Mary, 307
Perry, Ora, 242
Perry's Mid Town Garage, 129
Pershing, Jonas E., 94
Peters, 171, 225
Peters, Charlie, 4, 66
Peters, John, 171, 235, 237
Peterson, John, 235, 237
Philip Dewey's Elk & Deer Park, 246
Philips, Elston, 252
Phillips (Stowe), S.S., 173
Phillips, Charles, 21
Phillips, Ella, 149, 155
Phillips, George, 103, 140, 234, 311, 312
Phillips, Joe, 79
Phillips, John R., 119
Phillips, Joseph, 312
Phillips, Richard, 312
Phillips, Thomas, 312
Pierce, 116, 150, 151, 176, 178, 179, 224, 225, 343
Pierce, Delbert W., 16, 119, 193, 224, 343
Pierce, Everett, 111, 140
Pierce, George, 69, 132, 178, 220, 224
Pierce, Glenn, 111
Pierce, Henry, 116, 343
Pierce, James B., 178, 225
Pierce, Jesse, 33, 34
Pierce, Lawrence, 176
Pierce, Lester, 151
Pierce, Mary Tribby, 151
Pierce, Michael, 162
Pierce, O.W., 312
Pioneer Cemetery, 219, 220, 328
Pioneer Store, 12, 20, 22, 28, 29, 30, 31, 39, 55, 60, 248, 249
Pittenger, Charley, 108
Pitts, Bertha, 34
Pitts, Jerry, 81
Pitts, Susan, 14, 153
Pleasant Hill, 2, 49, 86, 88, 116, 117, 145, 146, 163, 165, 183, 184, 185, 187, 190, 207, 211, 213, 224, 227, 262, 268, 277, 278, 290, 305, 310, 326, 327, 328, 329, 330, 331, 332, 333
Pleasant Hill Depot, 332
Pleasant Hill Elementary School, 190
Pleasant Hill-Wingate School, 183
Plunket, James M., 311
Plunket, John W., 31, 36, 65, 206, 311, 312
Plunkett, Abraham, 152, 160
Plunkett, Arthur E., 354
Plunkett, D.M., 86, 356
Plunkett, John, 31, 36, 65, 152, 206
Plunkett, President, 31

Plunkett, Roscoe, 55, 61
Pollock, Ivan, 81, 91, 140, 242, 243, 251
pony express, 108
Pool Rooms, 75
Postil, C.W., 285
Postmaster, 14, 19, 49, 98, 154, 206, 207, 208, 209, 212, 213, 225, 351
Pottinger, Hardin, 206
Potts, Candice, 308
Powell, Joseph, 133
Prairie Chapel, 75, 145
Prairie Edge, 212
Price, George C., 179
Price, Nancy, 86
Pritchard & Sons, 192
Pritchard, Ed, 192
Pritchard, Fred, 192
Pritchard, L.F., 23, 191
Prohibition Convention, 179
Prohibitionists, 255
Pruett, Creo, 232
Prutsman, Widow, 211
Pryor, Lucinda, 11, 97
Pryor, Mary Ann, 11, 97
Pryor, Nicholas, 11, 97
Public Service Commission, 337
Puckett, Carroll, 83, 243
Puckett, S. Joan, 243
Puckett, Sheryl J., 243
Pullen, Harry, 90
Purdue University, 51, 91, 121, 137, 204, 264, 270, 315, 349
Pyke Telephone System, 356
Pyke, Albert D., 356
Pyke, Elizabeth (Learning), 356

Q

Quartette, Aeolian, 294
Queen, 294, 299, 303
Quiatenon, 257
Quick, Eliza, 177, 183
Quick, Lida O., 183
Quick, Mrs. Nathan, 154
Quigg, Wilberta, 291
Quigg, Wilma, 291
Quigle, Ira, 343
Quillen, Rev. Thomas, 218
Quillen, Thomas, 218, 219
Quillin, O.S., 343
Quillin, William, 169
Quinine, 180, 181, 227, 263, 327

R

Rabourn, Ben, 45, 46
Rabourn, Enoch, 46
Rabourn, Jesse, 46
Rafferty, 94, 225
Rafferty, Rena, 34
Rafferty, S.L., 307
Rafferty, Samuel, 148, 307
Rainey, Dr., 22, 49
Raisor, James, 176
Rake Pocket, 186
Ramey, 141
Range Line Road, 325
Rankin, James, 178

Rappert and Son, 24, 193
Rash, Floyd, 43
Ratcliff, Gerald, 96
Rathbone Sisters, 293, 298, 306
Raub, Albin, 148
Raub, Mrs. Henriette J., 112
Rawland, W.W., 312
Ray, Elias, 107, 119
Rayborn, Benjamin C., 343
Rayborn, Margaret, 291
Raymond Rice General Trucking Livestock, 111
Razor, Elizabeth, 219
Razor, M.Z., 219
Rector, Oren, 162
Redman, Albert, 60
Reed, Charles, 116, 229
Reed, Minton, 32
Reed, O.S., 157, 161
Reeder, John, 63
Reeder, Mr., 48
REMC, 356
Remley, Jane, 291
Republican, 169, 170, 255, 294, 296
Reser, Walter, 350
Reynolds, Harris, 108
Reynolds, Robert, 83
Rice, Raymond, 343
Richards, H.H., 184
Riley, Henry Clay, 147
Riley, Joseph, 135
Riley, Oscar W., 155, 161
Ristine, 265
Ristine, Benjamin, 284
Riston, R., 175
Ritz Theatre, 304
Roadhammel, Benjamin, 218
Roark, Hugh, 88, 105
Robbins, Chas. S., 188
Roberts, Alva, 80, 82, 353
Roberts, Fred, 337
Roberts, Lew, 104
Robinson, Miss, 55
Rogers Blake and Company, 36
Rogers, D.A., 147
Rogers, W.E., 199, 200
Roll, Aunt Polly, 227
Rose & Larry's Café, 64
Roser, Ellen, 219
Roser, W.H., 219
Ross Howe's Tavern, 68
Ross, Henry, 111
Roth, Joseph V., 279
Roth, Mary (Everetts), 279
Roth, Melvin J., 1, 127, 196, 239, 240, 279, 354
Round Hill, 2, 16, 29, 57, 75, 84, 91, 97, 113, 116, 134, 145, 146, 148, 163, 165, 170, 177, 178, 179, 180, 207, 209, 220, 221, 223, 224, 225, 227, 267, 274, 286, 287, 299, 305, 312, 324, 325, 341, 353
Round Hill Methodist Church, 353
Round Hill School, 177, 178, 179
Roxie's Place, 64, 65
Royalty, Isam, 211
Royer, Gerrie, 59
Royer, John, 312
Royer, Kenneth F., 252
Royer, Nyle, 140
Rue, John, 19

Rum & Pool Table, 76
Rund, Jerome, 252
Runyan & Fouts, 45
Rush, David, 162
Rusk, 186
Rust, Frank L., 193
Rust, James, 193, 340
Rust, Sadie, 183
Ruth Kirby Company, 293

S

Saloon and Pool Room, 66, 75
Sanders, John, 105
Sandilands, Richard, 41
Sandilands, Will, 116
Sayers, C.B., 187
Sayers, Charles, 186
Sayler, Paul, 197, 252
Scarlet fever, 262
Schleppy Brothers, 45
Schleppy, Thomas, 45
School No. 13, 187
Scott. David, 33, 57
Seaman, Dr., 26, 280
Seaman, Elizabeth (Dewey), 280
Seaman, Jada, 280
Seaman, Marie, 280
Seaman, Robert, 32, 34, 35, 53, 209, 280, 290
Seaman, William, 280
Seamon, Paul, 350
Servies, Henry D., 140
Seslar, Rev. Dale, 151
Shadows Theatre, 41, 303, 304
Shafer, Eliza Jane, 219
Shafer, N.C., 350
Shaffer, Joseph, 79
Shagley, J.P., 146
Shambaugh, Charles, 264, 351
Shamhart, W.P., 161, 296
Shanklin, Fred, 51, 282
Shanklin, Ida B., 173
Shanklin, John, 212
Shawnee, 2, 4, 7, 84, 86, 106, 164, 209, 210, 227, 283, 286, 289, 325, 342
Shawnee Mound, 7, 84, 164, 209, 210, 227, 283, 286, 289, 325
Shawnee prairie, 2, 4
Shekels, Jess, 300
Shekels, Queen, 303
Shelby, Clyde, 92
Shelby, Edna, 92
Shelby, Evan, 92, 323, 341, 356
Shelby, George B., 119
Shelby, Harry O., 22, 92, 95
Shelley, James, 150
Shelley, Mary Isabel, 150
Shelley, William Austin, 150
Shepherd, Bernice, 159
Shepherd, Charles, 43, 64
Shepherd, Ed, 75
Shepherd, Frank, 308
Shepherd, George, 291, 344
Shepherd, Hayden B., 43
Shepherd, James, 88, 354
Shepherd, John, 20
Shepherd, Paul, 290, 291
Shepherd, Rose, 160, 291

Shepherd, Thomas, 5, 325
Shepherd, W.B., 46
Shepherd, W.F., 193
Shepherd, Winton B., 41, 79, 81, 88
Shepherd's Meat Market, 46
Sherwood, B., 181
Sherwood, Jeremia, 143
Shields, David, 177
Shirley & Herbins Restaurant, 63
Shoaf, Oney, 243
Shoaf, Onia, 248
Shobe, Charles, 252
Shobe, H.C., 356
Shotts, Benjamin Harrison, 99, 100
Shotts, Dick, 46, 101, 104, 252
Shotts, Esther G., 99
Shotts, Frances, 99
Shotts, Gay, 99, 148
Shotts, Grover, 99, 100, 308
Shotts, Henry, 175
Shotts, John, 99
Shotts, Lelia, 99
Shotts, Mary Lou, 101
Shotts, Montgomery J., 99
Shotts, Pauline, 99
Shotts, Richard, 100, 252, 356
Shotts, Rose, 99
Shotts, Sarah, 101
Shotts, T. Richard, 241
Shotts, T.M., 23, 99, 100, 300
Shotts, Theodore Richard, 99, 100
Shotts, William N., 99
Shrum, John L., 175
Shuey, T.J., 161
Shultz, George, 342
Sibel, Carrie L., 177
Sibel, Jennie E., 12
Siler, Harriett, 164, 212
Simison, 30, 148, 268, 269
Simison elevator, 30
Simison, D.P., 107
Simison, J.P., 344
Simler, John W., 90
Simons, Wm. H., 213
Simpson, Elizabeth (Wallace), 277
Simpson, John A., 337
Simpson, Samuel, 277
Simpson, Sarah, 277
Sims, Will E., 266
Singleton, John, 159
Sitting Bull Saloon, 66
Skinner, Gertrude, 277
Sleepy Hollow, 227
Sluyter, Arthur, 47
Smallpox, 262
Smith, Ann, 239, 240
Smith, Anne, 195, 232
Smith, Charles E., 99
Smith, Earl, 214
Smith, F.M., 236, 247, 306, 354
Smith, Frank, 231
Smith, Ivy, 57
Smith, J. August, 295
Smith, Jack, 45, 91, 212, 335, 337
Smith, James, 230
Smith, John, 81, 160, 175, 187, 188, 307
Smith, Joseph, 37, 199, 200

Smith, Karen, 291
Smith, Lillian, 307
Smith, M.L., 137, 351
Smith, Marguerite, 294
Smith, Marion, 237
Smith, Marshall, 94
Smith, Mildred, 351
Smith, Morris Lee, 351
Smith, Nancy Jane, 160
Smith, Nellie, 34, 56
Smith, Poly, 212
Smith, Russell, 140, 351
Smith, Samuel R., 182, 186, 229
Smith, Thomas, 195, 281
Smith, William C., 294
Smithe, Anne, 232
Smither, A.C., 161
Smithers, A.C., 154
Smock,, 89, 143
Smock, James H., 85, 89, 117
Smock, Mr., 84, 85, 87, 89, 114, 117
Smokey Row, 65, 73, 105
Snellenbarger, Bernice, 308
Snellenbarger, Bill, 26, 129
Snellenbarger, David, 308
Snellenbarger, Doris, 308
Snellenbarger, William, 130
Snouwart, Wayne, 129
Snowbird Custard Shop, 41
Snyder, 22, 23, 25, 40, 54, 58, 66, 92, 93, 94, 95, 107, 110, 113, 119, 127, 132, 135, 143, 192, 238, 248, 249, 252, 302, 353
Snyder & Thompson, 22, 23, 92, 95, 132, 192, 249
Snyder Mill, 192
Snyder, A.D., 22, 25, 26, 40, 45, 54, 60, 67, 80, 90, 92, 93, 95, 103, 107, 110, 114, 119, 131, 133, 135, 147, 230, 238, 250, 253
Snyder, Albert, 25, 92, 110, 119, 133, 238, 249, 252, 279
Snyder, B.F., 50
Snyder, C.L., 127
Snyder, Charles, 92, 302
Snyder, Floyd, 116
Snyder, Jacob, 310
Snyder, Katie, 50
Snyder, Nancy, 58
Snyder, Nolen, 32
Snyder, R.C., 82
Snyder, Richard, 54
Snyder-Bayliss Airplane Company, 302
Sommer, Lester B., 122
Sonny & Burr, 60
Sounds of Joy, 291
South Wabash Livery Stables, 73
Spanish-American War, 265
Spears, Lawrence (Slim), 140
Sperry's Mill, 313
Spillman, 185
Sprague, John, 184
Sprahan, Eliza, 180
St. Louis University, 178
Stafford, A., 79
Stafford, Anna, 176
Stamper, Sarah E., 155
Standard Oil, 129, 130
Stanely, Ruth, 34
Stanley, Justin, 193
Star and Journal, 200
Star Chemical Works, 134

State Board of Health, 184, 262
Steam Corner, 284
Stearman, Ora, 105
Steck, Fred, 46
Steele, George, 111, 126, 306
Steele, Jennie, 245
Steele, Joseph, 312
Steele, L.J., 312
Steele, Patsy, 308
Stephens Sr., Robert Ervin, 206
Stephens, Aaron, 182, 183, 186, 253
Stephens, Fannie, 207
Stephens, Harley, 44
Stephens, Jerry, 44, 243
Stephens, Patricia, 44
Stephens, Robert, 123, 207
Stephenson & Haire, 111
Stephenson, Beulah, 52
Stephenson, Clarence, 88
Stephenson, Dick, 101, 129
Stephenson, Eugene, 135
Stephenson, Inez, 135
Stephenson, John, 2
Stephenson, Mary, 20
Stephenson, Milford, 52
Stephenson, Mollie, 20
Stephenson, Richard, 129, 140
Stephenson, Will, 2
Steven's Fine Foods, 26
Stevenson, Jeremiah, 311
Stewart, Clara, 307
Stewart, Elizabeth, 307
Stewart, Georgia, 307
Stewart, James, 193, 285, 306, 337
Stewart, Nettie B., 179
Stine, Catherine, 10, 11
Stingley, Oscar, 66, 95
Stites, W.G., 153, 155
Stites, William, 306, 307, 308
Stockton, Willard, 34
Stoudt, F.M., 131
Stoudt, Foster, 132
Stout, Ira, 15, 16, 65, 66, 67, 68, 72, 73, 74, 76, 84, 88, 131, 199, 236, 244, 290, 323, 328, 336
Stover, Frank, 88
Strader, H.E., 48, 63
Straint, U.R. Fishel, 112
Strand Theatre, 304
Strawtown, 7, 71, 97, 229, 232, 323
Strawtown to Covington Road, 7, 71
Stribling, Maurice, 304, 355
Striley, Hattie, 265
Stuckey, Dennis, 159, 160
Stuckey, Ina, 160
Stucky, Dennis, 308
Stull's Auto Shop, 129
Sturm, Frances, 291
Sturm, Frank, 292
Sturm, William E., 292
Suffrage, 256
Sugar Bowl, 63
Sugar Creek Saga, 215
Sugar Grove, 71, 107, 145, 146, 147, 148, 149, 209, 252, 256, 264, 286, 287, 291, 340
Sugar Grove Ladies Aid Society, 287
Sugar Grove Methodist Episcopal Church, 264, 291
Suitors, Ed, 60

Summer, Alphonso C., 214
Sunger, Phillip, 253
Surplus Electric Equipment Company, 135
Sutton, Mrs. Ida D., 343
Swadley, Charles, 290
Swank & Clark, 54
Swank, Ben, 230
Swank, Benjamin, 275
Swank, Dan, 212
Swank, Doug, 129
Swank, Dr. W.G., 172
Swank, Effie, 275
Swank, Ellen (Cowan), 275
Swank, Floyd, 290
Swank, Grandpa, 211
Swank, Harold, 291
Swank, Harvey D., 343
Swank, J.B., 282
Swank, James, 213
Swank, John, 312
Swank, Julia, 219
Swank, Oscar, 173, 180
Swank, P.H., 219
Swank, Phillip, 211
Swank, Reuben, 7, 135, 140, 176, 180, 304
Swank, Susan C., 219
Swank, Thomas, 326
Swank, W. Winton, 343
Swank, William G., 168
Swank's Garage, 129
Swear, Charles, 167, 168, 311, 312
Swear, Malinda, 167, 168
Swearengen, James, 310
Sweeney, Z.T., 295
Swick, C.W., 130
Swick, Gladys, 55
Swick, John, 111
Swick, Monica, 291
Swick, William, 23, 129
Swier (Swear), Charles, 227
Switzer, Miss, 202
Switzer, Rev. George W., 145
Swope, 265
Sylvester's Restaurant, 64
Symmes, Samuel D., 171, 306

T

T.J. Oppy Hardware, 95
T.M. Layne Hardware, 93
T.N. Jones Hotel, 72
Tailhoit, 187, 188
Talbot, H.H., 313
Talbot, May Wood, 186
Talbot, William, 284
Tapp, Cynthia, 220
Tarpinning, Mr., 175
Tatlock, Fred E., 343
taxi service, 16, 24
Taylor, 11, 12, 60, 61, 63, 90, 91, 108, 118, 121, 128, 148, 164, 180, 181, 203, 204, 209, 227, 306, 343
Taylor Jr., Frederick, 203
Taylor,, 203
Taylor, Artemesa M., 354
Taylor, Bernice, 203
Taylor, Bessie, 203
Taylor, C.A., 48, 306
Taylor, C.O., 204
Taylor, Charles, 12, 60, 61, 108, 132, 203, 204, 235, 241, 251
Taylor, Dick, 108
Taylor, Don, 108
Taylor, Donald B., 343
Taylor, Fred, 12, 202, 203, 204
Taylor, Jim, 108
Taylor, Mary, 203
Taylor, Matilda, 180
Taylor, Thomas, 180, 219
Taylor, W.C., 61
Taylor, Winton, 12, 111, 203
Taylor's Restaurant, 63
Teague and Sons Hardware, 94
Teague, Harry F., 94
Teague, J.F., 94, 114
Teague, James F., 94, 354
Teague, Nellie, 94
Teague, Raymond B., 94
Tech, Ed, 133
Temperance, 66, 69, 70, 288
Temperance Saloon, 66
Templeton, 45, 282
Templeton, Nelle, 186
Templeton, S.P., 282
TerBush, Don E., 161
Terrell, Clelland, 307, 354
Terrill, Clelland, 75, 239, 244, 251
Territory School House, 219
Terry, Thomas Alton, 161
Tharp, Donald Monroe, 161
Tharp, William, 88
Thayer, Dick, 111
Thayer, Frances, 258, 292
Thayer, James R., 257
Thayer, Otis L., 257
Thayer, Robert, 130, 197, 198, 242, 253, 257, 258
Thayer's Standard Service, 130
The Eureka, 203
The Jungle, 42, 291
The Montgomery County Farmer, 200
Thomas, 1, 5, 8, 9, 10, 11, 12, 23, 31, 39, 41, 45, 54, 58, 64, 65, 73, 74, 81, 83, 88, 91, 92, 93, 95, 98, 99, 107, 111, 113, 115, 119, 120, 123, 127, 129, 130, 131, 135, 140, 145, 146, 147, 148, 152, 153, 155, 158, 159, 160, 161, 162, 168, 173, 175, 176, 177, 180, 181, 182, 183, 186, 187, 188, 191, 193, 195, 196, 206, 207, 209, 212, 216, 218, 219, 225, 227, 229, 231, 234, 235, 241, 242, 251, 253, 270, 281, 282, 283, 294, 298, 303, 305, 306, 307, 309, 312, 317, 324, 325, 326, 328, 332, 342, 343, 344, 349, 355
Thomas & Foley, 120
Thomas Patton's Hardware, 91
Thomas School, 186, 187
Thomas, Anson, 116, 253, 298, 343
Thomas, Clyde, 135, 176, 177, 241
Thomas, Conn & Conn, 135
Thomas, Flora, 11, 298
Thomas, George, 93, 193, 326
Thomas, Hay, 155
Thomas, J.D., 180, 285
Thomas, J.W., 111
Thomas, James, 67, 97, 177, 188, 193, 313, 343
Thomas, Jemima, 270
Thomas, John M., 11, 309
Thomas, Judith, 187
Thomas, Levi, 152, 160, 177, 240, 248, 251, 311
Thomas, Lud, 175, 186, 187, 188

Thomas, Luella, 180
Thomas, Mae, 64
Thomas, Martha, 187
Thomas, Mary E., 11, 12
Thomas, O.D., 323
Thomas, R.A., 67
Thomas, R.D., 251
Thomas, Richard, 76, 129, 130, 135, 239, 240, 251, 344
Thomas, Silas A., 187
Thomas, William, 22, 92, 93, 95, 96, 160
Thomas' Café, 64
Thompson, Lena, 186
Thompson, Mea, 56
Thompson, Rev., 146
Thompson, Walter, 92
Thomson, Charles, 162
Thurnblaser, Emil, 266
Tiddy Toppe Beauty Shoppe, 59
Tiffan, Edward, 1
Tiffany, W.W., 89, 214
Tiffany, Wiley, 173
Timmons, J.W., 110, 343
Timmons, Lynn, 240, 251, 253
tin pin alley, 73
tin shop, 16, 23, 24, 82, 83, 249
Tipmont REMC, 356
Tippecanoe, 4, 7, 9, 10, 30, 59, 82, 84, 85, 89, 90, 91, 97, 107, 121, 145, 147, 149, 152, 177, 178, 179, 182, 192, 208, 209, 210, 220, 227, 256, 263, 265, 268, 283, 284, 309, 311, 312, 313, 315, 316, 324, 327, 332, 347, 356
Tippecanoe Telephone Company, 356
Toat, Wm., 212
Toby's Garage, 128
Todd, Charlie, 136
Todd, Donald, 128
Todd, Ruth, 55
Todd, William M., 248
Toledo, St. Louis, & Kansas City Railroad Company, 333
Tom Cook's Saloon, 66
Tomlinson, 220
Tompson, John, 312
Toogood, Henry, 161
Tortorella, Alice Ebrite, 63
Tortorella, Joseph, 11, 126
Tortorella's Ice Cream Parlor and Lunch Counter, 63
Totten, Oliver, 93
Townsend, W.B., 295
Townsley, Andrew, 36, 249
Traction, 216, 345, 346, 347, 348
Tracy, Nancy, 186
Tracy, Vezey, 186
Traveler's Insurance Company, 188
Trembly, Clara, 56
Tretheway, Timothy, 162
Tribby, 5, 79, 80, 90, 104, 135, 148, 150, 170, 173, 177, 225, 282, 312, 343, 346
Tribby, Albert, 79
Tribby, Benjamin, 79
Tribby, Emory, 150
Tribby, Florence, 173
Tribby, Gaylord, 5, 16, 343
Tribby, George T., 79
Tribby, Harry, 23, 80, 90, 282
Tribby, Harvy, 79
Tribby, James, 80, 119, 147, 150, 151, 233, 274, 312, 346
Tribby, Jason, 79, 332
Tribby, Jessie, 150

Tribby, Jim, 1, 19, 20
Tribby, John, 90, 225
Tribby, Joseph, 145
Tribby, L.M., 20, 119, 120, 125, 193, 325
Tribby, Leander, 79, 325
Tribby, Maggie, 307
Tribby, Mahala, 79
Tribby, Mary Curnutt, 150
Tribby, Mildred, 16, 104
Tribby, Muriel, 148
Tribby, Nancy, 79
Tribby, Punk, 16
Tribby, Ruth, 150
Tribby, Samuel R., 79, 80, 82, 117, 131, 134, 145, 153, 170, 196, 282, 306
Tribby, Sarah A., 12
Tribby, William, 79, 150
Tri-County Telephone Company, 24, 25, 47, 125, 135, 136, 244, 251, 267, 271, 277
Tripp, A.A., 133
Trout, Dave, 110
Trout, Edith, 173
Trout, Sherman A., 313
Trustees, 14, 126, 139, 141, 144, 145, 147, 153, 157, 158, 160, 167, 168, 169, 171, 174, 177, 178, 179, 180, 181, 182, 186, 187, 188, 218, 219, 220, 221, 222, 224, 226, 237, 244, 245, 246, 247, 250, 251, 253, 274, 316, 354
Tuberculosis, 262
Turner, Ethel, 148
Turner, John, 291, 344
Turvey, Charles H., 168
Turvey, Mexie, 49, 55, 56, 57
Turvey, P.S., 236
Turvey, W.A., 250
Turvey, William R., 118, 354
Turvey, William S., 153, 230
Twiddy, James E., 93
Tydol On Products, 129

U

Ullman, Clifford, 290
Ulsar, William, 2
Union Elevator Company, 26, 90, 110, 118, 119, 120, 121, 126, 134
Utah, 215, 227, 335
Utterback Marketing Services, 25, 92, 143
Utterback, Elizabeth, 219
Utterback, J., 169
Utterback, James, 308, 343
Utterback, John, 23, 147, 171, 174, 184, 215, 229, 253, 282, 312
Utterback, Kezia, 219
Utterback, Lester, 307
Utterback, Sant, 84
Utterback, Thompson, 218
Utterback, Vincent, 214
Utterback, William, 176, 217, 218, 219
Utterback, Winton, 6

V

Vail, 219
Vail, Albert, 220
Vail, James H., 219
Vancleave, 169, 171, 175, 177, 180, 184, 185, 186, 212, 213
Vancleave, Clara, 186
Vancleave, George, 184

Vancleave, H.T., 184
Vancleave, Henry, 60, 171, 177, 253
Vancleave, John R., 213
VanCleave, Jonathan, 311
Vancleave, Margaret, 225
VanHook, Aaron, 86
VanHook, Bessie, 307
Vannatta, J.T., 337
Vanpelt, Mary, 8
Vanpelt, Phebe, 8, 10
Vanscoyoc, Eb, 215
Vaughan, J.S., 106
Vaughan, Walter S., 173
Vaughn, Richard, 243
Vaughn, W.S., 179
Verhey Erection, 100
Verhey, Richard, 243
Vess, Nellie, 307
Villa Grove Stock Farm, 110, 193
Vincent, 214, 225, 279
Vinegar Hill, 20, 28, 227
Volra, Nathan, 233

W

Wabash College, 158, 165, 178, 193, 215, 216, 266, 273, 294, 313
Wabash Prairie Telephone Corporation, 214
Wade, Artimesa, 72
Wade, Clyde, 76
Wagner, Orie, 159, 290
Wainscott, Armilda, 219
Wainscott, James, 218, 219, 312
Wainscott, Stephen, 343
Walker, Adam, 2
Wallace, Barney, 88, 106, 143, 170
Wallace, Bessie, 307
Wallace, J.T., 86, 88, 113
Wallace, Lew, 313
Walls, A., 120
Walls, W.B., 31
Walnut Grove, 10, 56, 84, 88, 165, 167, 168, 227, 270, 327, 328
Walnut Township, 5
Walts, Clyde, 201, 202, 203, 318, 351
Walts, Edgar, 19, 75, 109, 119, 160, 178, 201, 202, 204, 232, 239, 306, 316, 318, 351
Walts, Lawrence, 201
Walts, Rose, 202, 318
Walts, Samuel W., 201
Walts, Wallace S., 201
Walts, Wilbur A., 201
Waltz, Frank, 343
War of 1812, 208, 273
Warbington, William, 219
Warbinton, Ben, 31, 40
Warbitton, Cynthia, 168
Warbritton, Carrie, 181
Warbritton, Jno., 178
Ward Jr., Thomas, 227, 328
Ward, Gertrude G., 203
Ward, J.M., 307
Ward, James, 108, 340, 341
Ward, Mary (Patrick), 83
Ward, Sarah, 307
Ward, Thomas, 83, 88, 119, 227, 328
Ward, Walter Patrick, 83
Warren, Daryl, 122
Warren, Earl, 126, 197, 240, 241, 337
Warrick, William, 83
Washburn, 26, 31, 32, 34, 35, 36, 42, 43, 44, 53, 54, 61, 63, 64, 75, 77, 99, 110, 126, 148, 152, 153, 155, 160, 170, 192, 193, 197, 209, 256, 259, 260, 261, 263, 266, 268, 275, 276, 277, 282, 288, 291, 297, 298, 303, 308, 326, 335, 337
Washburn, Agnes Work, 245
Washburn, D. Manners, 37, 196, 249, 259, 260, 261, 267, 269, 275, 278, 354
Washburn, Ella, 192, 268
Washburn, George W., 23, 24, 32, 86, 89, 110, 111, 131, 139, 152, 153, 154, 155, 160, 170, 192, 193, 196, 234, 311, 312, 326, 332
Washburn, Jane, 192, 249
Washburn, Jessica L., 256
Washburn, Louise, 256, 268
Washburn, Manners, 49, 59, 170, 260, 276, 277
Washburn, Miss, 56
Washburn, Nicholas, 21, 24, 35, 53, 192, 199, 230, 250, 275, 291, 295, 296, 297, 308, 339
Washburn, Sarah, 354
Washburn, William Winter, 31, 36, 57, 110, 112, 193, 244, 306, 335, 339, 342
Wasson, Albert, 14
Water Superintendent, 243
Watkins, George W., 79, 111, 155, 161, 173, 230
Watkins, Maureen D., 155
Watts, Ruby, 291
Waugh, J.M., 356
Waye, Charles, 13, 81, 355
Waye, Clara, 135
Waye, Donald, 13, 82, 135, 140, 292
Waye, Earl, 32, 35, 72, 81, 155, 159, 290
Waye, Forrest, 5, 10, 13, 47, 50, 57, 71, 72, 81, 82, 87, 100, 113, 123, 124, 130, 135, 155, 159, 171, 176, 189, 242, 244, 247, 250, 257, 265, 267, 286, 290, 301, 316, 339, 349, 355, 356
Waye, Frances, 257, 291, 292
Waye, Gerald, 13, 81, 271
Waye, Jefferson, 2, 46, 123, 257, 355
Waye, Malcolm, 13, 82, 208, 210, 242, 243
Waye, Mary Grady, 265
Waye, Melvin, 13, 81, 140, 267
Waye, Phyllis, 13, 267
Waye, Ron, 81
Waye, Stephen, 225
Waye, Vera, 159, 267, 292
Waye, Virginia, 207
Wayne Township, 167, 175, 212, 229, 310
Waynetown, 14, 44, 46, 50, 109, 128, 132, 134, 192, 200, 204, 214, 217, 218, 266, 278, 282, 284, 289, 295, 301, 307, 310, 347, 351
Waynetown and Elmdale Telephone System, 214
Wea, 7, 53, 91
Webb, Harrison, 74
Webb, Sarah, 74
Webb, William, 74
Weekly Review, 175
Weesner, Margaret, 186
Wehner, Gene, 128
Weigand, Fred E., 175
Welby, George, 187
Welliver, J., 223, 225
Wells, Curtis E., 90
Welty, George B., 186
Wesley Church, 245
West, Gerald, 65
West, Jere, 68, 238
West, M.A., 282

Western Indiana Dairy Association, 126
Westfall, 42, 60, 98, 109, 113, 176, 252, 290, 295, 343
Westfall, Charles, 34
Westfall, Dayton, 110
Westfall, Elisha, 98, 113
Westfall, George, 81
Westfall, J.W., 60
Westfall, Job, 95, 289, 290
Westfall, John, 290, 343
Westfall, Lish, 149
Westfall, M.J., 141
Westfall, Marion, 176, 288, 294
Wethington, Grover, 122
Wetterhan, Steve, 162
Weyles, Evan (E.J.), 108
Weyles, Russell, 304
Weymer and Dudley, 34
Weymer, Edward R., 34, 42
Weymer's Department Store, 54
Wheeler, John, 103, 140
Wheeler, Milton, 60
Whelen, Lee J., 173, 176
Whetstone, Louise J., 153, 192
Whig, 229
Whipple, David, 343
Whipple, Elgie, 135
Whipple, Elsie, 135
Whiskey, 255, 263
White Eagle Packing Company, 133
White Plague, 262
White, Barbara G., 274
White, Charles, 208, 274
White, Daniel, 39, 206
White, Herbert, 129
White, M.D., 330
White, Mary (Leah), 274
White, Mike, 154
White, Park, 67, 107, 252
White, Wallace, 81, 116, 290
Whitehead, Royce, 81, 242
Whites, Park, 107
Whitlock, 117, 327, 332, 333, 334
Whittington, W.T., 67
whooping cough, 262
Widener, Clarence A., 213
Widener, G.W., 211, 212
Widener, John, 211
Widmer, Harold B., 243
Widner, A C., 175
Widner, Amelia, 177
Widner, E.M., 175
Widner, George, 107, 213
Widner, Guy O., 175
Widner, Minnie J., 175
Widner, Sarah, 168
Wight, John F., 93
Wilber, T.B., 147
Wild West Park, 108
Wilhite Band, 289
Wilhite, Henry T., 218
Wilhite, P., 218
Wilhite, Warner, 277
Wilking, J., 186
Wilkins, Clinton, 351
Wilkinson, Abram, 211
Wilkinson, William T., 343
Willhite, Voorhees W., 219

William Aulston's Saloon, 67
William Campbell's Saloon and Grocery, 65
William Hayworth's Saloon, 67
William Thomas' Hardware, 92
William's Pioneer Store, 22
Williams, Bazil, 308
Williams, E.E., 301
Williams, Maliah, 219
Williams, Rev. David H., 219
Wills, Joe, 252
Wills, Mary Murdock, 59
Wills, Perry, 86, 88
Willson, James, 219
Willson, Sarah, 226
Wilson, 37, 50, 84, 86, 95, 151, 152, 161, 163, 168, 172, 173, 177, 178, 179, 181, 225, 226, 317, 341, 343
Wilson, Albert, 177, 181, 223
Wilson, Belle, 202
Wilson, Charles, 116
Wilson, Ethel, 178
Wilson, Frances, 173
Wilson, Frank, 168
Wilson, Glen L., 253
Wilson, Harry, 50, 306
Wilson, Ira M., 193
Wilson, J.D., 172, 179, 224, 312
Wilson, James, 178, 179, 193, 223, 224, 253, 306, 341, 343
Wilson, John, 65, 93, 95, 113, 148
Wilson, Libby, 307
Wilson, Mary J., 178
Wilson, Mosses F., 311
Wilson, Oliver, 151, 160
Wilson, Ralph, 98, 178
Wilson, Samuel, 178, 221, 222, 225, 226
Wilson, Sarah, 219, 226
Wilson, Sophia (McGinnis), 178, 225
Wilson, Stella, 178
Wilson, W.H., 312
Wilson, William, 84, 152, 163, 178, 224, 225
Wilson-Killin, 225
Wilt, John A., 74
Wingate, 2, 15, 16, 49, 54, 57, 69, 74, 75, 86, 88, 93, 105, 108, 109, 110, 111, 116, 118, 142, 145, 146, 163, 165, 171, 172, 173, 176, 180, 183, 184, 185, 186, 187, 188, 189, 195, 199, 200, 203, 208, 213, 215, 216, 217, 218, 227, 230, 255, 259, 263, 264, 268, 271, 278, 279, 281, 285, 286, 287, 290, 292, 294, 296, 297, 301, 319, 324, 325, 327, 330, 331, 332, 333, 335, 337, 344, 345, 346, 347, 348, 351, 354, 355, 356
Wingate, John C., 296, 328, 330, 331, 332
Winnie, William H., 90
Winson, Richard D., 162
Winter, William, 36, 192, 244
Withrow, James, 120, 340
Withrow, Lewis, 176, 252, 340
Wolf, Jim, 162
Wolhever, Charles, 98
Woliver, Charley, 234
Women's Society for Christian Service, 148
Wood, Nick, 248
Woods, Michael, 312
Wooley, Sheb, 65
Work, Claude, 202, 245, 298, 300, 301
Work, Jennie (Steele), 273
Work, John, 111, 238, 239, 240, 245, 246, 247, 251, 253, 273, 295, 313, 325, 355
Work, Myrtle, 245, 273
Worland, Bob, 69, 96

Worth, Mr., 30
Wray, Curtis M., 259, 261, 277, 354
Wray, Doctor, 203
Wray, Henry, 114
Wright, Ed, 45
Wright, Harold, 68
Wright, J.P., 161
Wright, Jacob, 151, 152, 161
Wright, James, 242, 243
Wright, Mary, 12
Wright, Wilbur, 349, 351
Wright, William A., 214
Wumps, Mug, 170

Y

Y.M.C.A. Pool Room, 75
Yeagley, Donna, 207
Yencer, W.N., 310
Yoke, E.R., 93
Young Peoples Society of Christian Endeavor, 155
Young, Arthur, 217, 218
Young, David, 128
Young, Floyd W., 136
Young, J.M., 159
Young, Joseph, 238, 253, 354
Young, Leroy, 128
Young, Miss, 55
Young, Rose, 220
Young, William, 151, 161
Youngblood, Mattie, 55
Yount's Woolen Mills, 37
Yountsville Pike, 5

Z

Zachary, George, 98, 99
Zeke's Café, 64
Zerface, Jake, 105, 115
Zoo, 65, 73
Zook, 31
Zook, Charles, 67, 354
Zook, Edwin D., 199
Zook, Zebulon, 145, 312
Zoological Garden, 68

www.ingramcontent.com/pod-product-compliance
Lightning Source LLC
Chambersburg PA
CBHW080405300426
44113CB00015B/2407